Lecture Notes in Computer Science   8253

Commenced Publication in 1973
Founding and Former Series Editors:
Gerhard Goos, Juris Hartmanis, and Jan van Leeuwen

Editorial Board

T0180864

Dennis Reidsma   Haruhiro Katayose
Anton Nijholt (Eds.)

Advances in Computer Entertainment

10th International Conference, ACE 2013
Boekelo, The Netherlands, November 12-15, 2013
Proceedings

Springer

Volume Editors

Dennis Reidsma
University of Twente, Human Media Interaction/Creative Technology
Drienerlolaan 5, 7522 NB Enschede, The Netherlands
E-mail: d.reidsma@utwente.nl

Haruhiro Katayose
Kwansei Gakuin University, School of Science and Technology
Department of Human System Interaction
Gakuen Sanda 2-1, Sanda 669-1337, Japan
E-mail: katayose@kwansei.ac.jp

Anton Nijholt
University of Twente, Human Media Interaction
Drienerlolaan 5, 7522 NB Enschede, The Netherlands
E-mail: anijholt@cs.utwente.nl

ISSN 0302-9743   e-ISSN 1611-3349
ISBN 978-3-319-03160-6   e-ISBN 978-3-319-03161-3
DOI 10.1007/978-3-319-03161-3
Springer Cham Heidelberg New York Dordrecht London

Library of Congress Control Number: Applied for

CR Subject Classification (1998): I.2.1, H.5, H.3-4, I.4, F.1, I.5

LNCS Sublibrary: SL 3 – Information Systems and Application,
incl. Internet/Web and HCI

Typesetting: Camera-ready by author, data conversion by Scientific Publishing Services, Chennai, India

Printed on acid-free paper

Springer is part of Springer Science+Business Media (www.springer.com)

Preface

These are the proceedings of the 10th International Conference on Advances in Computer Entertainment (ACE 2013), hosted by the Human Media Interaction research group of the Centre for Telematics and Information Technology at the University of Twente, The Netherlands.

The ACE series of conferences, held yearly since 2004, has always been lively and interactive events. There are not just mainly paper presentations, but also many creative showcases, demonstrations, workshops, and often a game competition as well. For ten years now, ACE has shown itself to be a strong and vibrant community. Throughout the years, there has been a common element that ties together many of the different types of work presented at ACE. In their contributions, authors not only present solutions to known problems, or observe and describe aspects of the technological reality that is out there, but also actively explore what new things they can make, and why these new things might be important or interestingly different.

During ACE 2011, held in Lisbon (Portugal), Hiroshi Ishii challenged the ACE community by asking for the real value of entertainment computing, and especially the relevance of research in this field. At ACE 2012, held in Kathmandu (Nepal), this question was raised again during the panel session. We can try to address this question through some viewpoints on entertainment technologies. Clearly, entertainment can be a valuable goal in itself. People need to experience fun, engagement, social connectedness, and many other things achieved through entertainment. Entertainment can also be used as a powerful means for changing people's perceptions, ideas, and behavior. Entertainment with and through computers is a fact of daily life. It is there, and it has a huge economic impact that is not likely to decrease.

At ACE, we look at entertainment computing as the subject of our research. We look at changing perceptions and behaviors using serious games and other persuasive technologies. We try to analyze and understand various aspects of computer entertainment: besides "making new things", we "analyze the things that we find in the world of computer entertainment", how people use technology or play games. We explore the creative design space to find new forms of beauty, experience, and fun. Also, we attempt to re-create existing human experiences in an interestingly new way. New developments in multimodal interactive technology are used to re-create certain experiences as faithfully as possible; subsequently, we attempt to find out whether we can fundamentally enhance the experience, due to the technological innovation. What can we do better, differently, in a more interesting way, because we implemented technology for this particular experience?

The latter is also reflected in the theme of this anniversary edition, which was "Making New Knowledge". As already noted in last year's introduction to the proceedings of ACE 2012, creating has always been an important form of entertainment. People paint for a hobby, play music, build model airplanes, or write amateur poetry in their free time. Just for the fun of designing and creating their own entertainment; the final result may be less important than the process. Tinkering can also be a strong source of learning, something that has been known at least since the seminal work of Seymour Papert. In a video lecture on Carnegie Commons, John Seely Brown suggests that the role of a teacher partly shifts from imparting knowledge to building a learning community. Clearly, tools for programming and physical computing can serve as tinkering materials in such a community, and maybe there are further roles that computer entertainment technology can play in building and facilitating such a learning community.

These thoughts are not only reflected in a number of papers and extended abstracts in these proceedings, but also in several of the additional activities that were organized during this year's conference. There were panels, workshops in which the participants sit down together to actively make things or to discuss the role (and challenges!) of tinkering in scientific education, the Kids' Workshop Track featuring activities for children making stories, animations, and elements for games, and there were special efforts to include more students at various levels in their education in the conference. All this took place at the beautiful resort Bad Boekelo, situated in the pastoral countryside of Twente.

Of course, there cannot be a conference without the submission of many good papers. This year, 133 papers were submitted to the various tracks. With an acceptance rate of 22% for long regular presentations, and 54% for all contributions including extended abstracts for the poster presentations, these proceedings represent the very interesting and relevant work currently carried out by the ACE community.

Like every year, many people worked hard to make this 10th edition of ACE a success. To the Program Committee, reviewers, authors, track chairs, workshop organizers, delegates visiting the conference, and the sponsors supporting the conference in various ways: Thank you! We are proud to have served as this year's general and program chairs to bring everything together in the lovely countryside of Boekelo, The Netherlands!

November 2013   Dennis Reidsma
                                                  Haruhiro Katayose
                                                     Anton Nijholt

Organization

Steering Committee

Adrian David Cheok   Keio University, Japan and NUS, Singapore
Masahiko Inami   Keio University, Japan
Teresa Romão   CITI, FCT, Universidade Nova de Lisboa, Portugal

General Chair

Anton Nijholt   University of Twente, The Netherlands

Program Chairs

Haruhiro Katayose   Kwansei Gakuin University, Japan
Dennis Reidsma   University of Twente, The Netherlands

Creative Showcases and Interactive Art Chair

Itaru Kuramoto   Kyoto Institute of Technology, Japan
Edwin Dertien   University of Twente, The Netherlands

Children's Workshops Chairs

Yoram Chisik   University of Madeira, Portugal
Nanako Ishido   President of NPO Canvas in Japan
Betsy van Dijk   University of Twente, The Netherlands

Poster Chair

Günter Wallner   University of Applied Arts, Vienna, Austria

Game Competition Chair

Thomas de Groot   T-Xchange Serious Games, The Netherlands
Paul Coulton   Lancaster University, UK

Workshop Chair

Randy Klaassen   University of Twente, The Netherlands

Local Chair

Gijs Huisman   University of Twente, The Netherlands

Business Track Chair

Theo Huibers   University of Twente, The Netherlands
Iddo Bante   University of Twente, The Netherlands

Senior Program Committee

Elisabeth André   Augsburg University, Germany
Tetsuaki Baba   Tokyo Metropolitan University, Japan
Regina Bernhaupt   ICS-IRIT, Toulouse, France
Marc Cavazza   University of Teesside, UK
Luca Chittaro   HCI Lab, University of Udine, Italy
Nuno Correia   FCT, New University of Lisbon, Portugal
Chris Geiger   University of Applied Sciences Düsseldorf,
                                  Germany
Shoichi Hasegawa   Tokyo Institute of Technology, Japan
Itaru Kuramoto   Kyoto Institute of Technology, Japan
Angelika Mader   University of Twente, The Netherlands
Florian (Floyd) Mueller   RMIT University, Melbourne, Australia
Rui Prada   Instituto Superior Técnico-UTL and
                                  INESC-ID, Portugal
Beatriz Sousa-Santos   Universidade de Aveiro/IEETA, Portugal
Günter Wallner   University of Applied Arts, Vienna, Austria
Annika Waern   Mobile Life Center, Interactive Institute,
                                  Stockholm University, Sweden

Program Committee

A. Augusto Sousa   Angelika Mader
Aderito Marcos   Ann Morrison
Adrian Cheok   Annika Waern
Adrian Clark   Anton Nijholt
Akihiko Shirai   Antonio Coelho
Alan Chatham   Arjan Egges
Ana Veloso   Athanasios Vasilakos
Andrei Sherstyuk   Atsushi Hiyama

Beatriz Sousa-Santos
Ben Kirman
Betsy van Dijk
Cagdas Toprak
Carlos Duarte
Carlos Martinho
Cathy Ennis
Chek Yang Foo
Chris Geiger
Christian Sandor
Christina Hochleitner
Christopher Lindinger
Christos Gatzidis
Clemens Arth
Cristina Sylla
Daisuke Sakamoto
Daniel Rea
Dennis Reidsma
Dhaval Vyas
Eduardo Calvillo Gamez
Eduardo Dias
Edwin Dertien
Elisabeth Andre
Fernando Birra
Florian Floyd Mueller
Francesco Bellotti
Frank Dignum
Frank Nack
Fred Charles
Frutuoso Silva
Fusako Kusunoki
Guenter Wallner
Haakon Faste
Hartmut Seichter
Haruhiro Katayose
Hayrettin Gürkök
Helmut Munz
Henry Been-Lirn Duh
Hirokazu Kato
Hiroyuki Mitsuhara
Hitoshi Matsubara
Holger Reckter
Hongying Meng
Ichiroh Kanaya
Ido Aharon Iurgel

Igor Mayer
Iolanda Leite
Ionut Damian
Itaru Kuramoto
James Young
Jannicke Baalsrud Hauge
Jeffrey Tzu Kwan Valino Koh
Joaquim Madeira
Jongwon Kim
José Danado
Julian Togelius
Jussi Holopainen
Kai-Yin Cheng
Kaoru Sumi
Kaska Porayska-Pomsta
Kentaro Fukuchi
Kjetil Falkenberg Hansen
Kohei Matsumura
Kuramoto Itaru
Leonel Morgado
Licinio Roque
Lindsay Grace
Liselott Stenfeldt
Luca Chittaro
Luis Carriço
Luís Duarte
M. Carmen Juan
Mads Haahr
Maic Masuch
Maki Sugimoto
Manuel J. Fonseca
Marc Cavazza
Marco van Leeuwen
Mariet Theune
Mark Gajewski
Masahiko Inami
Masanori Sugimoto
Masataka Imura
Michael Lankes
Michiya Yamanoto
Mituru Minakuchi
Mónica Mendes
Nadia Berthouze
Nanako Ishido
Narisa Chu

Nicolas Gold
Nicolas Sabouret
Norbert Kikuchi
Nuno Correia
Óscar Mealha
Owen Noel Newton Fernando
Paul Coulton
Paulo Dias
Pedro A. Santos
Pedro Branco
Petri Lankoski
Philippe Palanque
Ramon Molla
Randy Klaassen
Regina Bernhaupt
Riccardo Berta
Robert Cercos
Rogério Bandeira
Roland Geraerts
Rui Jesus

Rui José
Rui Prada
Sandy Louchart
Sheng Liu
Shigeyuki Hirai
Shoichi Hasegawa
Simone Kriglstein
Sofia Tsekeridou
Staffan Björk
Stefan Bruckner
Sylvester Arnab
Takao Watanabe
Teresa Chambel
Teresa Romão
Tetsuaki Baba
Thomas de Groot
Veikko Ikonen
Wolfgang Huerst
Yoram Chisik
Yoshinari Takegawa

Additional Reviewers

Ana Tajadura
André Pereira
Andreas Hartl
Anton Eliens
Christian Pirchheim
Daniel Rea
Doros Polydorou
Jens Grubert
Katharina Emmerich
Kening Zhu
Marielle Stoelinga
Markus Steinberger

Philip Voglreiter
Philipp Grasmug
Raphael Grasset
Rui Craveirinha
Samuel Silva
Simon Hoermann
Stefan Hauswiesner
Stefan Liszio
Takao Watanabe
Tom Penney
Viridiana Silva-Rodriguez
Zsófia Ruttkay

Collaboration

ACE 2013 at the University of Twente, The Netherlands, was organized in partnership with the Centre for Telematics and Information Technology, The Netherlands Organisation for Scientific Research (NWO), the SIKS Graduate School, and Springer Publishing.

Netherlands Organisation for Scientific Research

CENTRE FOR TELEMATICS AND
INFORMATION TECHNOLOGY

 Springer

Keynote Talks

"Mindful or Mindless Entertainment?"

Yvonne Rogers

University College London

Abstract. We are increasingly living in our digital bubbles. Even when physically together – as families and friends in our living rooms, outdoors and public places – we have our eyes glued to our own phones, tablets and laptops. The new generation of 'all about me' health and fitness gadgets, wallpapered in gamification, is making it worse. Do we really need smart shoes that tell us when we are being lazy and glasses that tell us what we can and cannot eat? Is this what we want from technology – ever more forms of digital narcissism, virtual nagging and data addiction? In contrast, I argue for a radical rethink of our relationship with future digital technologies. One that inspires us, through shared devices, tools and data, to be more creative, playful and thoughtful of each other and our surrounding environments.

Yvonne Rogers is the director of the Interaction Centre at UCL and a professor of Interaction Design. She is internationally renowned for her work in HCI and ubiquitous computing. She has been awarded a prestigious EPSRC dream fellowship to rethink the relationship between ageing, computing and creativity. She is known for her visionary research agenda of user engagement in ubiquitous computing and has pioneered an approach to innovation and ubiquitous learning. She is a co-author of the definitive textbook on Interaction Design and HCI now in its 3rd edition that has sold over 150,000 copies worldwide.

Disney Research – "Haptics for Entertainment: Context without Content"

Ali Israr

Disney Research

Abstract. Haptics is an emerging field for enhancing interactivity and immersion. As a result, many new haptic technologies are developed and introduced in recent years for entertainment, education, communication, surgical, therapeutic and sensory substitution. In the last decade, there exists a buzz for haptics to be a 'game-changer' for gaming, mobile and VE applications, however, the main-stream consumers have yet to see compelling and popular haptic products. We have identified two main factors which must be addressed for success of haptics in gaming and entertainment markets. These are (1) novel haptic technologies and (2) new tools to create haptic content.

In this talk, I will present the background and vision for recent haptic technologies developed in the Disney Research labs (such as Tesla Touch, Surround Haptics, Aireal haptics devices) and our on-going efforts towards producing haptic products and content. I will highlight the challenges for us to generate interests and strategies for successful transfer of technology from research to product.

Ali Israr is a Haptic Researcher and Engineer working in Disney Research, The Walt Disney Company. He holds a doctoral degree in Mechanical Engineering and has been working in haptics research for the last 12 years. His research has been published in premium conferences and journals, presented in elite forums and has been successfully transferred in to consumer and amusement park product lines. Dr. Ali Israr obtained his Bachelors of Science from University of Engineering and Technology, Lahore Pakistan.

Introduction to the Special Session on Serious Game Technology

Arjan Egges * and Kaśka Porayska-Pomsta **

1 Session Overview

Over the last decade serious gaming has become a prominent and important field of research. Serious games are increasingly used to support learning of and training in diverse and traditionally unrelated domains. These domains range from formal learning of traditional subjects such as mathematics, vocational training for professions such as air pilots or dentists, coaching individuals in acquiring better job interview skills, to therapeutic applications which aim to support the development of skills associated with socio-emotional coping, e.g. in schizophrenia or autism. Serious games leverage both the intrinsic motivation associated with playing computer games as well as a serious intent to furnish their players with skills that are useful in the real world. As such, these games present their own set of challenges to game designers and developers. First, as most serious games will have some sort of educational goal, the design of a game should ensure that these educational goals are reached when someone plays the game. Second, a serious game should be able to measure the success of the player within the game itself. Although tracking a player's progress is something that any game should do, for serious games this is even more important to get right, since the quality of the training in part determines the performance of the trainee in the real world.

Serious games are also challenging from the technological and engineering point of view. In many cases, serious games use specific hardware such as 3D screens, plates that can measure exerted forces, motion trackers, or 3D sound generators. Incorporating all of these modalities into a coherent and seamless game environment is complex. Designing and developing serious games becomes even more challenging when one wants to incorporate capabilities such as tracking of individual players over different sessions, allowing for simultaneous participation of multiple players over a network connection. Furthermore, games often need to be adapted to different languages and cultures—this process is

---

* Virtual Human Technology Lab, Dept. of Information and Computing Sciences, Utrecht University, the Netherlands. Website: http://vhtlab.nl. Email: j.egges@uu.nl
** London Knowledge Lab, Institute of Education, United Kingdom. Website: http://http://www.lkl.ac.uk/. Email: K.Porayska-Pomsta@ioe.ac.uk

commonly referred to as *localization*. Finally, serious games increasingly require the availability of authoring tools for creating scenarios by users who are not game designers, which imposes the demand on the serious games technology to be robust and transparent in its design.

Much research is presently done on serious game technology in Europe. This special session will focus on a variety of current work related to serious game technologies, showcasing examples of research concerned with the challenges that are unique to serious games. The goal of the session is to bring serious gaming professionals together in an informal way, and to promote collaboration and exchange of experiences and future directions in this rapidly emerging field. Specifically, the session presents the ongoing work conducted within three European projects concerned with the development of serious games: TARDIS (EU-FP7), SHARE-IT (UK-EPSRC), and MASELTOV (EU-FP7). Each project has contributed a paper to the session.

The first paper is titled 'The TARDIS framework: intelligent virtual agents for social coaching in job interviews' and it describes the TARDIS serious game framework for building an intelligent training and coaching environment for young adults at risk of social exclusion from unemployment through which they can practice and improve their social interaction skills needed for conducting successful job interviews.

The second paper: 'Building Intelligent, Authorable Serious Game for Autistic Children and Their Carers' introduces the SHARE-IT project, which creates a serious game for children with Autism Spectrum Disorders through which they can learn and explore skills which are important to engaging in social communication with others. The paper focuses on the SHARE-IT game's architecture which enables the engineering of an intelligent game (in the AI sense) that is also authorable by parents and teachers.

The third paper is entitled: 'Advances in MASELTOV Serious Games in a Mobile Ecology of Services for Social Inclusion and Empowerment of Recent Immigrants'. As part of a comprehensive suite of services for immigrants, the MASELTOV game seeks to develop both practical tools and innovative learning services via mobile devices, providing recent immigrants across Europe with readily usable resource that would help in their integration within their adopted cultures and countries.

2   Program Committee

- Sylvester Arnab, Serious Games Institute, UK
- Jannicke Baalsrud Hauge, BIBA - Bremer Institut für Produktion und Logistik GmbH, Germany
- Francesco Bellotti, University of Genoa, Italy
- Ionut Damian, Augsburg University, Germany
- Cathy Ennis, Utrecht University, the Netherlands
- Igor Mayer, TU Delft, the Netherlands
- Nicolas Sabouret, LIMSI-CNRS, France

Table of Contents

Long Presentations

Short Presentations

Special Session on Serious Game Technology

Extended Abstracts

Web Analytics: The New Purpose towards Predictive Mobile Games

Mathew Burns and Martin Colbert

Kingston University, London, United Kingdom
m.r.burns@hotmail.co.uk, m.colbert@kingston.ac.uk

Abstract. Web Analytics have been confined to an iterative process of collecting online traffic data for the purpose of drawing conclusions. This research presents a concept where internet usage traffic can be predicted against through the means of a mobile game. Through investigating certain industries use and perceptions of playfulness certain aspects are identified for the design and development of the game. Using a usability based methodology for evaluative testing these features are questioned amongst two distinctive versions. From these, the feasibility of a mobile game and its playfulness for users is gauged. The research leaves the concept considering what other contexts web analytics can be used within.

Keywords: Web Analytics, mobile games, serious games, prediction, usability, prediction markets, spread betting, playfulness.

1 Introduction

Prediction is the simple designation to a possible outcome which can lead to one of two eventualities, right or wrong, win or lose [1]. Many businesses and theories exploit either possibility. In the instance of economics or gambling a prediction is supported on the supposed understanding of risk [2]. Placing a prediction in conjunction with a commodity is nothing new. However this concept has previously not been applied to the usage of internet traffic known as web analytics. Web analytics has remained confined to the repetitive accumulation and conclusion of online activity [3], where its predefined purpose has not yet been explored beyond.

The current wide acceptance and ever growing popularity of mobile technology over many cultural and social boundaries has witnessed a level of unity with a user's life [4]. Mobile technologies ability to allow access to games and applications beyond the geographical limitations of desktop computers presents a unique conduit to assess the effective entertainment of an analytic based prediction game. The domestication of users towards the technology has caused an "industrial revolution of data" [5]. The scale of this data explosion can be observed in a singular instance such as social media. Facebook in a single day alone generates sixty terabytes of data [6]. Potentially harnessing these scales of data in the form of a game presents an intriguing pursuit of research.

D. Reidsma, H. Katayose, and A. Nijholt (Eds.): ACE 2013, LNCS 8253, pp. 1–13, 2013.
© Springer International Publishing Switzerland 2013

Games can draw a player to be immersed in a number of ways. Gambling offers no difference in terms of its playfulness in order to encourage acceptance and extensive use. This addictive quality allows the prolonged success of placing a prediction [7]. Could the same be applied when making a prediction against web analytics in the form of a game?

2   The Aim and Objectives

The purpose of this paper is to explore how web analytics can be used beyond its previous connotations by employing prediction to develop a playful and entertaining mobile game for users. It specifically refers to the following objectives:

- Determine the feasibility of developing an analytics game.
- Identify how, why and what makes data playful.

3   Web Analytics

Web analytics is the process of collecting quantitative or qualitative data through measurement for the translation into an appropriate conclusion or action [8]. The conversion of factual data can be utilized to create an informed decision [9] which has accounted for the successful actions of businesses to improve upon their online presence [8].

3.1   Analytics Current Development of the Web

Google Analytics has developed the process into a cheap, easy and commonly used tool accounting for a significant 55.9 percent of all websites [10], which was once a grueling and drawn out task [11].

Google Analytics offers a three tier service using an iterative process of measure, analyze and change towards improving the online user experience. The fundamentals of the process are based upon the collection of behavioral metrics recorded when a user visits a web page. The simple measurement of a singular visitor can account for time duration spent and the path taken to and from the page [3]. Whilst a single visitor may appear insignificant, the accumulative collection of datasets can create an image towards the impression of a website. For example, three hundred visitors remain on a website for five seconds, which could indicate an inadequacy of content or design amongst issues. The measurement of metrics such as the total time spent can allow for deductions that can encourage change [11].

The iterative process remains a constant trend of use across the internet in many sectors. In particular with games, analytics have acted as a method to record player behavior. These studies have witnessed analytics repeat use to better measure and therefore understand player behavior for the development of in-game artificial intelligence [12] or assess a correct level of difficulty [13]. Overlooking the contexts for analytics, its use remains firmly within the focus towards measuring, analyzing and change. Analytics have remained exclusively to these main areas of use and therefore confined to this limited framework. This encourages new innovations to build upon what analytics is currently defined as, side step its original use by considering how it might be used in a previously unseen manner.

3.2   Analytics to Predict the Future

Tools for analytics reside heavily on the past for visitor behavior [14]. While the past measurement and analysis of data can influence an improved future user experience, analytics does not provide much of a future consideration. For instance, a result or value based upon a future outcome. Generally analytics is not concerned with the future behavior until collected in the present. Whilst analytics has remained rigid in this regard, businesses have made use of the future towards a prediction.

It is not uncommon for businesses to attempt to predict outcomes for its benefit. Google, Best Buy and P&G are known to analyze employee data in order to isolate those that are most likely to gain advantages for the business such as sales. The same can be gained for market segments with promotions and pricing strategies [15].

Both examples of analytic tools and businesses only focus on either the past or the future. Neither makes use of both past and future predictions. The proposed mobile game looks to meet this.

4   Gambling on Prediction

A prediction made by a single individual can provide a standing or belief on a topic. When predictions are applied collectively in a group on a large scale, the culmination of opinion can become a speculative market towards a likely probability [1]. Prediction markets are inherent of this, making use of a collective opinion of a question to become aggregative information. Its predictive ability has been repeatedly tested during the forecast of some of the most profound and controversial topics in recent time such as economic issues and the conclusion of foreign occupations [16]. As such, prediction markets have been seen as a success, which has lead to their wider use across businesses [17]. Specifically, examples of these can be witnessed with Google's Prediction Market (GPM). A question is put forth i.e. Product X will be a success, to employees where the prediction is represented in the form of any number of commodities such as shares [16]. GPM makes use of Goobles placed to determine the certainty that is held over a question. The placing of one hundred Goobles may demonstrate a level of certainty whilst only ten may represent reluctance to the question [1]. The ability to place a commodity for a prediction essentially represents a focal point of opinion, where the believed likelihood of an outcome is concluded with a simple value being placed.

Spread betting makes use of many of the same foundations as prediction markets. The significant difference is contained within the addition of a currency instead of artificial or a fabricated reward [1]. With the opportunity to win, there comes the risk to lose. This is an aspect that has reverberated through economic markets when a prediction is made [2]. Risk has been seen to have a profound effect on behavioral patterns. In particular, a recent win can provide a strong influence to take further risk [18]. The same can be true of losing causing a need to play [19]. It describes the imagery of an individual being drawn to place coins into a gambling machine but ultimately it shows the potential that risk has towards playfulness with a prediction game.

Clearly, the commodity placed against the prediction and the risk involved holds a certain level of playfulness to invoke continued use for industries such as gambling. The similarity that placing a prediction against online traffic has to gambling emphasizes the need to consider these points within the design of a mobile game. It points towards the consideration of how such a design might affect the user and specifically the question, when does playfulness end and addiction begin?

4.1   Addictions Takeover of Playfulness

Playfulness within a game can be associated to a joyful and fulfilling pursuit within a user's leisure time. This describes a positive association compared to addiction which generally indicates a certain need to carry out an action. With such opposing definitions, how could they intertwine where one takes over from the other?

In regards to technological addiction with game play, the repeated description of a level of compulsion and dependability exists [20]. While certain levels exist amongst the physical and digital, addiction appears to be higher online. Users of online gambling games such as roulette and poker are more likely to bet more online in terms of amount and risk compared to those offline [21]. It indicates an increased disregard for the value and risk simply because the game resides in a digital domain.

A further possible amplification of this can be caused by certain underlining psychological traits or predeterminations within users. Specifically, a concept known as the Favorite Long-Shot Bias (FLB) where a player demonstrates a reluctance to make a safer bet in favor of taking a larger risk. This type of behavior has been witnessed when identifying stocks within spread betting where an unpopular underdog is often preferred compared to those more dependable with a history of success [19]. The same has been observed within games when considering sports. For example, an online bookmaker provides a quote of +100 for a popular Team A compared to -120 for the unpopular Team B. When a player places £100 on the unpopular team and they win, the player is rewarded with £120. For a player to be rewarded with Team A they would require placing £100 which would only provide them with £100 assuming they win. The reward for winning on the unpopular Team B demonstrates a significant difference to Team A. The same applies to the risk with the likelihood of winning through the underdog however players continue to do so [22]. While it provides a concerning image of players being drawn to take risks when they are presumably aware of the odds [19], it demonstrates one possible explanation for addiction, psychology. Specific demographics of players such as male, single, young and educated have been found to be more prone to taking these steps towards addiction [21].

Many online games such as those mentioned make use of targeting these demographics with tactics that are likely to encourage players by isolating its appeal within their psychology. This appears to be the point at which playfulness within game play vanishes and addiction issues takeover. Clearly, addiction has a negative connotation associated with it, which is not in the interests of the user therefore it is noteworthy to emphasize the reluctance to employ such concepts within a game design.

5 Data-Driven Games

5.1 Discovery of Knowledge

Data is a powerful medium for all aspects within the digital and physical world. As such, the same applies to games. The usage of data to drive a game is not a new concept. With new and innovative forms of data, there has always been a purpose to capture it and utilize it for a previously unexplored purpose. Data was once used purely for the purpose of knowledge. Internet search engines have enabled this data to be accessed through a coherent and structured means [23]. Recent projects such as A Google A Day have investigated how data might be used further by making use of search data as a key aspect of a game. Specifically, A Google A Day provides a trivia question for the user to find through carrying out searches [24]. Each day a new question will require the user to engage their understanding of retrieving the correct topic to highlight an answer against a time limit [25].

Fig. 1. A Google A Day (Source: The New a Google a Day)

It makes use of a normal skill of searching for an answer into a playful activity. The pursuit of an answer encourages knowledge to be gained through discovery [27]. The development and change towards this new type of game has been as a result of recent findings. A significant effect in a user's ability to search effectively has been highlighted when appropriately engaged on an educational level [28]. Learning in an exploratory fashion can ensure that the search skills are retained far beyond the stage it was taught. This discoverable concept of enforcing a skill has begun to be seen amongst other business's products such as Bing, which demonstrates the popularity to engage with users in a playful manner [29]. While it has only recently begun to be integrated into games, other applications have made use of the same concept but through a different context.

Another project by Google known as the wonder wheel allowed users to visually identify possible words or phrases that may relate to those entered.

Fig. 2. The Wonder Wheel (Source: CSQI)

From the word entered, a visual link to possibly related phrases could be displayed. Users could follow a single word through a long list of corresponding meanings that may appear within a search. It enabled marketers to identify the most relevant keyword in order to gain the highest number of visitors. Essentially the user gained knowledge through a process of discovery [27]. The application has since been redesigned and launched as the Contextual Targeting Tool [30] after inspiring academic papers and success amongst users [27]. The new application has removed the visual representation used to find a word [25], which appears to have removed the core of discovering knowledge.

The commonality that the A Google A Day game and the Wonder Wheel applications shared was the obvious ability to allow the user to discover knowledge through their own means. Certain contradictions could be observed between the two, where a visual representation was a crucial feature whilst it was not relevant to the other as a result of its context. Ultimately, each instance demonstrated the power of using data and transforming it into an innovative product towards a certain context.

6   Design

In order to determine the feasibility of developing an analytics based prediction game and the success that it might have towards a user, two distinctive versions were created. Firstly, a web application consisting of the core functionality and features discussed. Secondly, a mobile game that would take into account the lessons learned from the first version.

Understandably, the technologies employed to make the versions possible were significantly different. The web application utilized ASP.NET C# with jQuery making it viewable to mobile devices. The mobile game made use of a JavaScript based native app as the front end to the user where results and data could be passed back and forth between an online web service via Ajax calls. Commonly, both versions made use of the Google Analytics Core Reporting API to channel data from a live analytics account to their users. The analytics account was linked to an online blog being supplied data by regular visitors.

The clear dependence on design and development required the repetitive approval of core aspects. A Rapid Application Development methodology was applied allowing for referral and demonstration to various users. As a result, the initial development became an evolutionary process moving from a web application to a game which was more enjoyable, usable and playful.

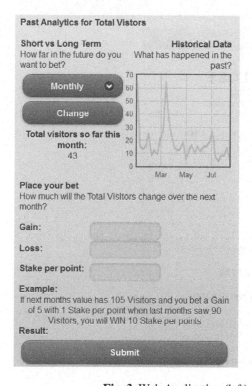
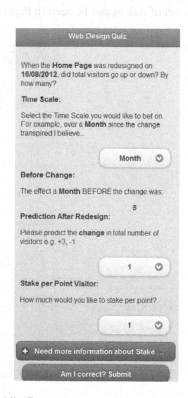

Fig. 3. Web Application (left) and Mobile Game (right)

As can be seen from Figure 1, there is a significant difference between the two versions. The web application provided the user with the necessary past data for the review and investigation of possible outcomes that could allow for a prediction to be made. The user could identify particular trends through the discovery of data. Depending upon the time scale selected, a user would be required to return to receive their success or failure of their prediction much like how spread betting might be used.

The mobile game made use of the web analytics in a different regard to time. Instead of waiting for occurrences to elapse in order to retrieve the verdict of a win or loss, questions would only be asked of the user when online events had already transpired therefore resembling a web design quiz.

6.1   Using Risk and Commodities

The traits regarding risk and commodities have been included within both versions. The fascinating psychological trait to continue to play in the face of risk when winning or losing [18] [19] was intertwined with a commodity known as Stakes per Point. This attempted to create the illusion of the potential to win/lose therefore presenting a level of risk as can be seen in Figure 2.

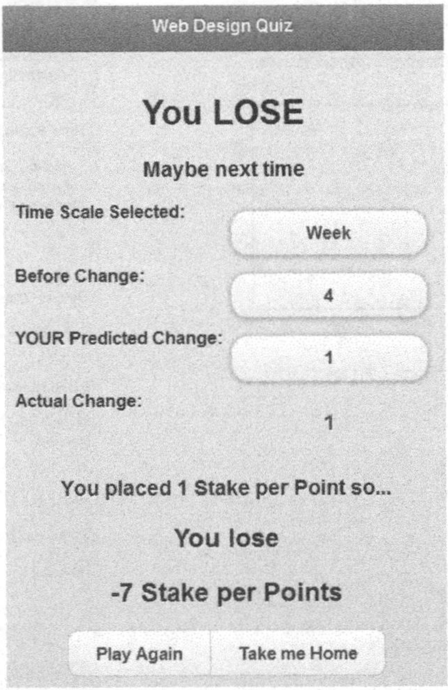

Fig. 4. Risk and Commodities used for a user's win or loss

When a prediction is submitted, a result is presented to the user. Through the form of a win or a loss, the user is rewarded or punished for their prediction. In order to gain the result a calculation was performed.

Simply, the calculation is represented by three key aspects in order to provide a result. As stated within (1) the overall outcome (a), the difference between the prediction and the actual outcome (b) and the commodity placed (c) is required to provide a result (d).

$$((a) - (b)) \times c = d \tag{1}$$

The calculation can be broken down further as stated within (2). An overall outcome is gained by subtracting from the value that occurred within the time frame prior to the prediction (b). For example, the user places a prediction within a certain week therefore the week before shall be used. This value is subtracted from the actual value (a) that transpired within the time frame selected.

As stated within (3) the prediction (c) is comprised of the actual value (a) in addition to the predicted change (f). The actual value (a) can then be subtracted from the prediction (b). The value of this process is then multiplied by the commodity (d) to provide the result (e) as shown below:

$$((a - b) - ((c) - a)) \times d = e \tag{2}$$

$$((a - b) - ((a + f) - a)) \times d = e \tag{3}$$

7   Methodology

The need to measure the success or failure of each version requires the collection of qualitative as well as quantitative data. A usability methodology was employed due to its inherent logical nature. Specifically, the Common Industry Format (CIF) to aid testing as a formal methodology making it applicable for testing with users and software [26].

At certain stages of the development process, formative feedback would be gained from certain users in order to refine the design through RAD. At the summative stage, a field based empirical evaluation allowed for the constant reporting of quantitative measurements to be gained. Building the necessary features into each version, certain metrics such as time spent, success and path of the user could be concluded. In conjunction, survey evaluation was utilized to cover the qualitative aspect of testing after a user's completion of tasks within an electronic format. This entire process began when a participant showed an interest to take part within the study; an electronic email was sent to them including the necessary instructions to carry out the tasks.

In the same way that a user will make use of a website, an application or game where the developer will not determine who necessarily uses it, random sampling was used. As conveyed by its name, it acted as an appropriate means to keep testing random and therefore unbiased.

The web application was tested against two random samples of five participants. In order to test the validity of risk in regards to winning and losing, the calculation mentioned was offset to cause five participants of each outcome. Whether this caused an effect to continue playing or not when winning or losing would be reflected within the summative feedback provided within the survey evaluation.

The mobile game was tested against a singular group of five participants in accordance to the previous versions methodology for consistency and reduced bias of results. As such, the main difference within testing was the design of each version.

8   Findings

8.1   The Web Application

Testing of the web application began to build an image of a possible user group or demographic to aim this type of concept towards. A preliminary examination of both winning (1) and losing (2) groups saw nine out of ten participants succeed at the tasks. The one participant that failed withdrew from testing expressing feelings of complication and an unlikely use for the web application. Follow-up interviews with the participant revealed comments of "it's not something that I would use regularly". When seeking an explanation for this feedback, another participant expressed similar issues where the duration to complete tasks were substantial with 687 seconds compared to the average 431.8. When comparing the participants, eight out the ten were between eighteen and twenty four years with a university education considering themselves to have a certain level of proficiency with technology. The two participants that opposed the web application were between the age range of forty six and fifty five years with a school education considering themselves to be novices in regards to technology. This preliminary examination of the results demonstrates a possible correlation towards an analytics game being accepted amongst younger age ranges that are more familiar with mobile technology.

When comparing both web application groups, initially it can be seen that the mean durations are very similar with the winning group (431.8 seconds) and losing group (490.2 seconds). When carrying out statistical analysis through an independent t-test, no significance can be found between winning (M = 431.8, S.D. = 209.17) and losing (M = 490.2, S.D. = 30.88), where the participants is predetermined to win (t(10) = 0.554; p > 0.05) or lose (t(10) = 0.569; p > 0.05). In regards to duration the participant is not affected or influenced by gaining a loss compared to a win. Essentially the participant does not take a more prolonged or shorter amount of time as a result of a certain verdict.

The subjective feedback gained from the survey evaluation indicated a negative picture for the web application. With fifteen questions allowing for an indication of feedback between one and five there is a potential of 525 points from each group. Each group received roughly one half of the total values available with the winning group accounting for 249 (47.4%) and the losing group providing 229 (43.6%). Whilst the overall values reveal very little, the individual identification and comparison of some questions demonstrate a possible consensus of opinion. In particular, questions relating to the addiction of playing were scored extremely low (Group 1 = 9 / 25.7%, Group 2 = 8 / 22.8 %). Similarly, the results from questions such as participants 'would happily use the application again' (Group 1 = 12 / 34.2%) (Group 2 = 10 / 28.5%) and the 'application being playful' (Group 1 = 15 / 42.8%) (Group 2 = 12 / 34.2%) indicated a lack of enjoyment. Alternatively, this could indicate a number of issues. When reviewing the qualitative data to identify an explanation, statements of "wasn't too sure on how to bet or what I was meant to do" and "a lot to look at, too much to take on" emphasized an overcomplicating of the web application. The intended functionality of user's being able to review data as a form of discovery clearly proved overwhelming and complicated. This reoccurring feedback of participants being unaware of what they were doing suggests the need to guide the user [27] through certain stages to make a prediction and gain results.

8.2 The Mobile Game

Learning from the issues of the web application, the mobile game was designed to include an intuitive guide to step the user through making a prediction. Differences applied like this and the alternate use of analytics in regard to time discussed previously, opens versions to be scrutinized comparatively.

Testing of the mobile game saw the five participant's progress through each task quicker than the last with individual means between 120 and 166 seconds whilst gaining an accumulative mean of 386.6 seconds. It indicated participants learning through repetition from the guided stages. It demonstrates that the mobile game was accepted once the initial workings were understood. A design that is hard to use may not exhibit this quality which may have been indicative of the web application.

When comparing the mobile game's participant group against that of the web application in order to identify participants taking a risk when winning (t(10 = 0.869; p > 0.05) or losing (t(10 = 1.131; p > 0.05), there is no significance for the tasks carried out. Within both accounts of each version, a significance cannot be found to prove a possibility that users are drawn to play a game due to their trend of winning or losing.

The survey evaluations overall total for the mobile game (257 / 56.4%) and the web application (Group 1 = 249 / 47.5%, Group 2 = 229 / 43.6%) provides the game with a lead of 10.9%. It generally highlighted a higher level of satisfaction with the mobile game compared to the web application. Additionally, an independent t-test between the winning group for the web application against the mobile game has found significances for certain questions regarding 'addiction' (t(10) = -2.530; p < 0.05) and the 'ability to find results' (t(10) = -3.939; p < 0.05). Both the 'addiction' (M = 2.60, S.D. = 0.548) and 'finding results' (M = 5.80, S.D. 1.304) for the mobile game were significantly higher than the web application (M = 2.80, S.D. = 1.095) (M = 1.80, S.D. = 0.447). It demonstrated a general preference to use the mobile game as well as finding it easier to find results and play when guided through a staged design.

9 Conclusion

The design and development of two distinctive versions making use of web analytics in a playful manner with prediction has identified:

- A potential demographic profile (18 – 24 and an expert user) has been formed of a user that is most likely to find this type of mobile game playful.
- Confusion was associated with the web application. A method of guiding the user through the stages as seen by the mobile game is required in order to simplify the design and therefore encourage use.

- The literature [19] based around a win or a loss having the potential to encourage further risks to be taken has been disproven.
- A mobile game making use of web analytics from events that have elapsed rather than having the user return to gain an answer appears to be the most suitable.

The findings have supported the feasibility of a web analytics mobile game. This research has demonstrated that web analytics can be broken out of its predefined purpose and used for more unique and creative means.

Whilst some of the features identified to encourage use such as risk were disproven for suitability, it was only tested against small participant groups. Carrying out additional tests could elaborate on aspects and potentials that placing predictions on web analytics can bring for the user.

The findings present a strong basis for future research. Already, testing has begun using an extensive dataset from Kingston University's live web analytics to provide questions and answers to drive predictions made from the mobile game. With a larger scale of participants across the mobile marketplace, this research leaves the question, what other contexts can web analytics be used for?

References

1. Danielson, M.: Prediction Markets. In: MAT, vol. 5900 (2010)
2. Hayden, B., Platt, M.: Gambling for Gatorade: Risk-sensitive Decision Making for Fluid Rewards in Humans. Anim. Cogn. 12, 201–207 (2009)
3. Ledford, K., Teixeira, J., Tyler, M.: Google Analytics. John Wiley & Sons
4. Rose, K.: The Long and Short of it, Herptile
5. Hellerstein, J.: Programming a Parallel Future. In: EECS, vol. 144 (2008)
6. Ashish, T., Suresh, A., Namit, J., Raghotham, M., Zheng, S., Dhruba, B., Joydeep, S., Hao, L.: Data Warehosuing and Analytics Infrastructure at Facebook. In: SIGMOD (2010)
7. Yechiam, E.: Risk Attitude in Decision Making: In Search of Trait Like Con-structs. Topic in Cognitive Science 3, 166–186 (2011)
8. Kaushik, A.: Web Analytics: An Hour a Day. John Wiley & Sons (2007)
9. Liberatore, M., Luo, W.: The Analytics Movement: Implications for Opera-tions Research. Informs., 1–12 (2010)
10. W3CTechs.: Usage of Traffic Analysis Tools for Websites (2012),
    http://w3techs.com/technologies/overview/
    traffic_analysis/all
11. Cutroni, J.: Google Analytics. O'Reilly Media (2010)
12. Lewis, C., Wardrip-Fruin, N.: Mining Game Statistics from Web Services: A World of Warcraft Armoury Case Study. In: Proceedings of the Fifth Internationsal Conference on the Foundations of Digital Games, pp. 100–107 (2010)
13. Kim, K., Gunn, D., Schuh, E., Phillips, B., Pagulayan, R., Wixon, D.: Tracking Real Time User Experience. In: Proceedings of the Twenty Sixth Annaul Conference on Human Factors in Computing Systems, pp. 443–351 (2008)
14. Sanfilippo, A., Cowell, A., Malone, C., Riensche, R., Thomas, J., Unwin, S., Whitney, P., Wong, P.: Technosocial Predictive Analytics in Support of Natu-ralistic Decision Making. In: Proceedings of NDM 2009 (2009)

15. Davenport, T., Harris, J., Shapiro, J.: Competing on Talent Analytics. In: The Big Idea. Hardvard Business Review
16. Wolfers, J., Zitzewitz, E.: Prediction Markets in Theory and Practice. National Bureau of Economic Research 12084, 1–16 (2006)
17. Nagar, Y., Malone, T.: Making Business Prediction By Combing Human and Machine Intelligence in Prediction markets. In: Thirty Second International Conference on Information Systems, pp. 1–16 (2011)
18. Hayden, B., Nair, A., McCoy, A., Platt, M.: Posterior Cingulate Cortex Me-diates Outcome-Contingent Allocation of Behaviour. PMC 60, 19–25 (2009)
19. Ottaviani, M., Sorensen, P.: Noise, Information and the Favorite-Longshot Bi-as in Parimutiel Prediction. American Economic Journal Microeconomics 2, 58–85 (2010)
20. Griffiths, M.: Technological Addictions. Clinical Psychology Forum 76, 14–19 (1995)
21. Kairouz, S., Paradis, C., Nadeau, L.: Are Online Gamblers More At Risk Than Offline Gamblers. Cyberpsychology, Behaviour and Social Networking 1, 1–6 (2011)
22. Stekler, H., Sendor, D., Verlander, R.: Issues in Sports Forecasting. International Journal of Forecasting 26, 606–621 (2010)
23. Jansen, B., Mullen, T.: Sponsored Search: An Overview of the Concept, History, and Technology. Electronic Business 6, 114–131 (2008)
24. Google: A Trivia Game Where Using Google is Allowed, http://googleblog.blogspot.co.uk/2011/04/trivia-game-where-using-google-is.html
25. Google: The New a Google a Day, http://agoogleaday.com/
26. CSQI Wonder Wheel, http://www.hmtweb.com/marketing-blog/
27. Mirizzi, R., Ragone, A., Di Noia, T., Di Sciascio, E.: Semantic Wonder Cloud: Exploratory Search in DBpedia. In: Daniel, F., Facca, F.M. (eds.) ICWE 2010. LNCS, vol. 6385, pp. 138–149. Springer, Heidelberg (2010)
28. Moraveji, N., Russel, D., Bien, J., Mease, D.: Measuring Improvement I User Search Performance Resulting from Optimal Search Tips. In: Proceedings of the 34th International Conference on Reaseage and Development in Information Retrieval, pp. 355–364 (2011)
29. Bateman, S., Teevan, J., White, R.: The Search Dashboard: How Reflection and Comparison Impact Search Behaviour. In: CHI, pp. 1–10 (2012)
30. Google Contextual Targeting Tool, http://www.google.com/ads/innovations/ctt.html
31. Bevan, N.: Extending Quality in Use to Provide a Framework for Usability Measurement. In: Kurosu, M. (ed.) HCD 2009. LNCS, vol. 5619, pp. 13–22. Springer, Heidelberg (2009)
32. Silva, E., Pires, L., Sinderen, M.: On the Design of User-Centric Supporting Service Composition Environments. In: ITNF, pp. 1–6 (2010)

An Author-Centric Approach to Procedural Content Generation

Rui Craveirinha[1], Lucas Santos[2], and Licínio Roque[1]

[1] Department of Informatics Engineering
Faculty of Sciences and Technology, University of Coimbra,
Coimbra, Portugal
[2] Universidade Estadual da Bahia,
Bahia, Brazil

Abstract. This paper describes an alternative approach for videogame procedural content generation focused on providing authors direct control on what gameplay ensues from the generated content. An architecture is proposed that allows designers to define, beforehand, target gameplay indicators, and then generates content for an existing base-design that achieves those same indicators in actual gameplay sessions with human players. Besides providing a description of this architecture, a trial intent on giving evidence of the approach's feasibility is presented. This experiment used an altered version of 'Infinite Mario Bros.' level generator, built to evolve design parameters so as to achieve 3 target gameplay indicators. Employing a Genetic Algorithm in generation of new parameter values, and using 25 players to test the end results, the platform was able to generate parameters that achieved, with precision, the values for those indicators. This result provides evidence of the approach's feasibility, hinting at its potential use for real-life design processes.

1 Introduction

Founding pillars of videogame theory come from different fields and are mostly general in nature, and while certainly useful for guidance in game design, they tend to lack a strong quantitative basis [Pedersen et al., 2010]. The past years have seen the rise of methods – such as Gameplay Metrics [Kim et al., 2008] – that can better inform creators during the videogame design process, by providing increasingly meaningful and objective data on how videogames are effectively played and experienced. Furthermore, procedural content generation aimed at improving user-experience (e.g. Experience-Driven Procedural Content Generation, EDPCG for short[Yannakakis and Togelius, 2011]) has become a reality, allowing designers access to tools that provide them active support through generation of game content. These advances deliver potential for creative processes that deliver more expressive designs. However, thus far, there are few examples of how these methods can be meaningfully incorporated in design contexts, as ways of facilitating or expanding production of videogame artifacts. What this paper describes then is an alternative procedural content generation approach,

D. Reidsma, H. Katayose, and A. Nijholt (Eds.): ACE 2013, LNCS 8253, pp. 14–28, 2013.

created to help creative game design and production processes. It seeks to utilize automatic generation and evaluation of artifacts to increase both the efficiency and effectiveness of the design process, whilst empowering authorial exploration of the design space and furthering designers' creative agendas for their artifacts.

The remaining paper is thus structured: section 2 gives a brief overview of the main EDPCG literature, and how it was framed in this research; section 3 details this research approach, its architectural details, and how it is intended to use these new technologies, while section 4 details a first trial to implement this solution. Finally, in the last section, results are discussed and future work for this project is described.

2   Literature Review

Experience-Driven Procedural Content Generation is a family of methods that can aid game design, with a growing body of research tackling directly how game experience can be improved through procedurally generated content [Yannakakis and Togelius, 2011]. The general concept is to use a data source to create a player experience model (product of the interaction of players with the game system), and then generate/evolve game content that improves player experience. Experience quality is then assessed based on player experience data, whether it be the result of gameplay metrics, questionnaires, or even AI simulated game-play sessions. Once quality has been assessed, content is represented in computational form, and new game content is generated. Procedurally generated content can encompass level design, art assets, etc. According to [Yannakakis and Togelius, 2011], the rationale of this approach takes into consideration the fact that videogame markets have become heterogeneous, catering to increasingly fragmented segments of the population, relying on different structural aspects to produce similar affective experiences.

As of now, several pioneering efforts have been made with this approach. For example, in [Yannakakis and Hallam, 2004], Yannakakis et al. studied how to measure game interest in predator/prey games (such as Pac-Man), based on the assumption that interest is mostly determined by qualities of computer characters' behavior as opposed to other features (such as the game's graphical properties). To this effect, they proposed and then implemented a neuro-evolution learning algorithm that maximized interest criteria based on gameplay metrics, validating the technique with pair-wise player questionnaires [Yannakakis and Hallam, 2004, 2005, 2007]. In [Pedersen et al., 2010], this methodology was expanded to classify and predict a greater number of experience variables, covering up to 6 emotional categories: fun, challenge, boredom, frustration, predictability, and anxiety. Metrics data from several gameplay sessions was used to track correlations with player experience reports and different Super Mario Bros. levels properties. Their model's accuracy for the six emotion types was very high. Finally, Super Mario Bros' levels were adapted in real time in order to optimize fun, both for human players and AI simulated agents [Shaker et al., 2010].

Several benefits have been studied and verified in relation to user-centered design philosophies, namely in terms of increased system quality thanks to more accurate requirements, heightened production efficiency, improved user acceptance, amongst others [Kujala, 2003]. But we share with other researchers [Steen et al., 2007] reasonable concerns over how extreme user-focused approaches can impair innovation and creativity. Even proponents are careful in how they frame a user-centered approach to design, maintaining a focus on designer's intervening in the process [Kujala, 2003]. Indeed, user-centered design presupposes designers to enter into meaningful dialogical debate with users, in such a way that knowledge is shared from both ends so that design decisions are rightfully informed in a collaborative manner [Steen et al., 2007], never dictated exclusively by users' preferences.

Game designers and producers, like other members of the design field, run the risk of *"reducing experience to the mere "pleasure due to the feel of the action"* [Hassenzahl, 2011], i.e., thinking of user satisfaction as opposed to user experience. For a number of reasons, players may not always like or feel something positive in their experience, despite designers' creative agenda being fulfilled. By focusing procedural tools on, for example, creating frictionless artifacts that can maximize 'fun', researchers seem to be establishing not only the means to an end, but the very end itself of the creative process. Consumers can be superficial, dismissive, indecisive and incapable of adequately expressing their thoughts and emotions [Gladwell, 2005] – and as such to put EDPCG quality measurements dependent only on their subjective evaluation may not be the best approach for creators.

As such, this paper proposes an Author-centric approach to Experience-Driven Procedural Content Generation for games, where the quality evaluation is measured in reference to designer's expectations of what gameplay behaviors should be elicited. Artistic expression has, for the most part, been sustained by authorial pursuit and vision, despite not always having been well accepted by audiences or critics [Gombrich, 2009]. So we propose to put the focus back on authors' formal considerations instead of users' own, while trying to maintain the usefulness of using procedural generation tools. This view seeks to empower designers and award them greater creative control, while permitting more effective ways of tailoring their artifact to mediate specific gameplay patterns according to their agenda.

3   An Author-Centric Approach to Procedural Content Genration

The goal for this alternative is to provide a procedural generation architecture that provides designers, irrespective of their agenda, a more efficient and effective way of getting their game-artifact to mediate an intended gameplay experience. The focus here is on enabling designer choice to lead the end-result for gameplay, as opposed to subjective experience aspects. As such, only the elicitation of gameplay behavior is meant to be improved by this approach, so that player experience becomes influenced by a dialogical relationship between designer and user, as is the case for other artistic media. In conforming to this view, the data source for the underlying experience model of the architecture is based on Gameplay Metrics, not utilizing any subject inquiries. Gameplay Metrics provide exactly the 'how' of gameplay, and have the advantage of being quantitative, objective, allowing also for large scale automatic data collection [Drachen and Canossa, 2009]. The analogy with other media is that, just as a set of brushes only allows painters to more accurately imprint forms and colors on a canvas, so should game-design tools only help better elicit intended gameplay behaviors to players. This view is in stark contrast with the notions of pre-selecting specific emotions, thoughts and valuations that audiences should take from the actual artifact, and preserves a strict interactionist view where the player, while being influenced by the artifact, retains voluntary translation of its meaning.

At this phase, this approach is only being considered to improve elements of an already existing game-prototype, namely, aspects such as the variables concerning physics or structural level components; though there is no apparent reason why this approach cannot be generalized to generate other aspects of a game's content. So, for designers to use this architecture, they would need to have a reasonably stable working prototype besides their design agenda for the gameplay. The proposed architecture can then support an approach for obtaining and validating improved variations of the original prototype, that elicit the gameplay agenda, as defined by the authors themselves.

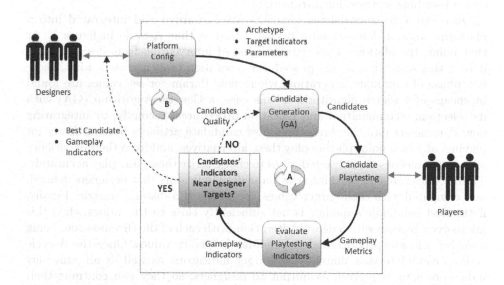

Fig. 1. Diagram of the Proposed Architecture for an Author-Centric approach to Content Generation for viedogames – see section 3 for further details

In terms of how this process is carried out, figure 1 shows the proposed architecture from a conceptual point of view. To start using the approach, the design team must provide 3 items: a game Archetype, a set of Target Indicators and respective target values, and a definition of Parameters that can be to generate new variations of the Archetype. These 3 elements are that which determines the overall specification of the problem they wish to solve in what regards to their game, and therefore the differentiating aspect of this approach. This is, in essence, the definition of the design domain in which the actual EDPCG optimization method will operate, and the notion of 'Quality' to be applied to the generated content.

Content quality is measured as the inverse of the difference between a set of Target Gameplay Indicator values chosen by Designers, and the values for those Gameplay Indicators that generated artifacts mediate to real players. Parameters are the set of design elements, implemented by designers, that they forfeit direct control of, and which a platform that implements this architecture will then use to generate new configurations. There is the assumption here that authors choose these in a sensible manner, so that they affect the desired target gameplay. The Archetype is the prototype they designed, deprived of the Parameter components, i.e. the base artifact of which all variations will evolve from. In continuing with the designer-centric stance, it is assumed that this Archetype is implemented by designers from the ground up. Naturally, all these elements involve a configuration process carried through a platform user-interface (determining, for example, the types of target indicators, their domain, etc.), and direct integration by means of computational interfaces (methods for publishing and subscribing metrics, for instance).

Once the 3 designer-defined elements are forwarded and integrated into a platform, its actual functioning begins – that is that A-cycle in figure 1. At that point, the platform runs without need of intervention from designers and it is at this stage that actual procedural generation tools are used. First, there is a phase of candidate generation, where new Parameter set values are found by means of a search algorithm; in this case, a Genetic Algorithm (GA) with its selection, recombination and mutation procedures. Secondly, by integrating new Parameters into the Archetype, new candidate artifacts become ready for playing, at which point players play these alternatives, and from their experience with them, metrics are extracted, so as to characterize their gameplay accurately. Thirdly, these are compiled into the Gameplay Indicators that designers defined, and compared with their target values, by means of a distance metric. Finally, if the best candidate's quality is not sufficiently close to the values, then this micro-cycle repeats with a new GA iteration, with each of the chromosomes being awarded a fitness proportional to candidate's quality values. Once the A-cycle ends, a candidate that matches the target indicators, as well as all gameplay indicators data, are given as output to designers, so they can continue their iterative design process, by choosing whether or not the end-result is satisfactory. If it is not, designers can fine-tune either of the elements provided, forwarding a new design specification to the platform, in a new iteration of the B-cycle.

GAs were selected for being a family of sub-optimal, stochastic, general search methods that can be easily adapted into a number of different problems [Haupt and Haupt, 2004], and that versatility suggested they can be fit into the proposed architecture. Note that the choice of the methods' generation algorithm and its technical specificities is not a major focus of this research, since, first and foremost, there is the aim to solve how to frame EDPCG-like methods for creative design use that maintains author choice. So it is implicitly accepted that this process can be carried out by more advanced search algorithms that can better fit the search landscape.

4 Experimental Trial

To put the approach into effect, a design case materialization was needed. The main goal for this research was to test the feasibility of this approach by implementing the architecture into a prototype software platform, and start to map its practical constraints. The idea of this first trial was to take the 'Infinite Mario Bros' level generator (also used in [Pedersen et al., 2009]) and impose a significant variation on the original 'Super Mario Bros.' design. Imagine a hypothetical author that wanted to make a hyped-up version of Mario, with high-speed and high-stakes gameplay, where player experience would be akin to that of doing a speed-run trial. So, this designer changed the core-physics of Mario accordingly: Mario jumps double the height, can shoot more fireballs, and his default state is Super Mario (though he is still turned to normal as he is hurt, as in the original game). Now, these subtle changes in the game's design affect the experience – the game becomes a caricature of the original, both more frantic, exaggerated and difficult to play. The core gameplay system is completed, even though the experience is far from polished; the altered 'Infinite Mario Bros.' base game thus serves as this trial's Archetype. The designer wants users to play as he envisioned: very fast, with a high rhythm of actions, all whilst maintaining it playable enough so that players can conquer levels without much trying.

Now he must define target indicator values for gameplay metrics: Number Tries for conquering a level, as a measure for player difficulty and challenge; number of player triggered Actions per Second, as a measure of the experience's rhythm; and level play-through Time, as a measure of play-speed. He establishes a target mean value for each of these metrics, as well as suitable maximum range value that defines acceptable variation for these metrics; see table 1 for the tested values. That is his experience ideal, materialized into target indicators for gameplay behavior. As a measure of success for this first research trial, it was established beforehand that the system would be deemed feasible if it was shown to be capable of generating a best candidate that, at least, could statistically guarantee indicator values between the target and a maximum of a quarter of the accepted range for a population of players (see table 1).

Eight Parameters with a varied range of design objectives were chosen to be permitted to be altered by the platform: game speed (24–48 cycles per second), number of cannons (0–5), number of goomba enemies (0–30), number of koopa

Table 1. The three gameplay indicators that the algorithm meant to optimize, their target value, and the maximum variation that was considered. Also, the minimum condition for success for this trial – to have the best candidate's indicator values nested in the success range.

Indicator	T. Value	Max. Var.	Sucess Range
Actions	2	±4	1–3
Tries	1	±4	0–2
Time	40	±80	20–60

enemies (0–30), number of holes (0–7), number of item-blocks (0–15), number of coins (0-100) and number of hills (0–5). Apart from speed, all parameters were given a range from 0 to as high a number as possible, keeping in mind that these values had to produce levels that could not break the constraint of the level size of 480 tiles. This is why the number of holes and cannons, structural level properties that occupied several tiles, had to be kept relatively short. This Parameter set encompasses one physics parameter – Game Speed – which radically alters game experience, as well as impacting game difficulty (as a faster game becomes harder to play). This parameter was allowed to fluctuate between the games' normal speed of 24 cycles per second (which resembles Super Mario's original speed) to double that, 48 cycles, which is so fast it borders th nigh unplayable. The speed variable is bound to affect all 3 of the chosen target indicators, as it makes both faster and more difficult to play. Four parameters were chosen that determine adversarial forces to hinder player progress (cannons, goombas, koopas and holes). These are expected to affect all three indicators, as more enemies and holes impact difficulty, as well as delay player traversal of the level, while increasing opportunities for actions (jump, stomp and shoot). Two parameters were chosen that allow explorative rewards, coins and item power-ups. Coins only affect rhythm and traversal time, as collecting them increases the number of actions, while taking time. Coins do not have impact on difficulty, as they do not improve chances of conquering a level, and because in this prototype the player is given 999 lives to play the game, there is no tangible benefit to collecting 100 of them so as to gain lives. Item-power ups should provide the reverse set of indicator impact: mushrooms and flowers ease player difficulty in clearing a level, while only marginally affecting action rhythm and traversal speed (as they are few and disperse in a level). Finally, the number of hills parameter was expected to be quasi-neutral to all indicators, as it is a structural feat that provides a mostly cosmetic effect (hills are just platforms where player and enemies can go to). It is possible that it could slight increase the number of actions (as it provides a jump affordance) or that it could hinder progress (as it could present a slightly more complex level structure for players to overcome).

4.1   Genetic Algorithm Implementation

Parameter set candidates are evolved by means of a simple Genetic Algorithm with the following configuration. Each individual is represented by a chromosome that is a vector of real values, each a gene corresponding to a given game design parameter which can be varied. For each generation, the population size was of 12 individuals, plus one extra slot reserved for elitist maintenance of the best individual. Uniform crossover was used as a recombination method, with a rate of 90%. Mutation operated by replacing a gene to a new random value, and had a starting probability of 5%, and that was increased 0.5% in each generation (these seem large values, but one must consider that for this test, there were only 8 genes and 12 individuals, so lower values would practically exclude mutation from ocurring). Selection was made by tournament for pairs of chromosome. Evaluation of each candidate's fitness is as follows: in each evaluation phase, all the chromosome population is converted into full sets of design specifications that are stored in the server. Players use a client application which automatically downloads the next available set, which users then play and experience, after which the metrics data from their play session is uploaded to the server. It is from the metrics data that fitness is directly calculated, using the formula 1:

$$fitness = \sum_{i}^{N} \frac{1}{N} q(i) \qquad (1)$$

$$q(i) = \begin{cases} (1 - \frac{|tgt(i) - avg(i)|}{max(i)}), & |tgt(i) - avg(i)| \leq max(i) \\ 0, & |tgt(i) - avg(i)| > max(i) \end{cases} \qquad (2)$$

where N is the total number of indicators, $tgt(i)$ the target value for a given indicator i, $avg(i)$ the average value for indicator i measured from the available sample of gameplay sessions, and $max(i)$ is a value determined by designers on what the maximum variation they are accepting in terms of the end sample, before the usefulness of the candidate becomes 0.

The evaluation phase goes on until every population member has had at least 5 evaluations, i.e. 5 different play-throughs of the same level. Once this condition is fulfilled, the GA will run its evolutionary mechanisms, and a new generation will be evaluated. In between, if at any moment the best chromosome produces a candidate whose fitness is above 0.9, an external validation phase is carried out, where it is played at least 30 times, to validate its fitness level with greater levels of credibility. Only after this process does the GA resume. Candidates in the form of game parameter sets are forwarded to client-applications sequentially, which means that once a player plays, he will likely experience a given generations' entire population in sequence. However, the system is connected asynchronously, with no control over who, how and when experiments a given set, so play-testers were free to access the game at their own leisure, throughout the one week span of the test.

4.2 Population Sample

The playtester group was comprised of 25 Informatics Engineering and Multi-media and Design Master students, 21 male, 4 female, ages 22–26. They were

Table 2. The table shows the total number gameplay sessions evaluated per generation. Note that generation 7 was incomplete, and as such its data will not be further contemplated (with the exception of new evaluations of the best individual that happened in that final stage).

Generation	0	1	2	3	4	5	6	7*
Sessions	76	176	138	107	105	106	184	26*

asked to play the game as means of collecting data for research purposes. No incentives were given, and no questionnaires were collected from the population. There were a total of 696 gameplay sessions played on subjects' own time and convenience, giving 27.84 gameplay sessions per player on average. Data from these sessions was used for 6 GA generations, plus a few more evaluations that occurred afterwards that were not enough to complete a generation's cycle. In total, 68 different procedurally generated candidates were tested until the sixth generation, in an equal number of fitness calculations. This means an average of 9.85 gameplay sessions played per generated candidate ($stdev = 5.52$), distributed unevenly throughout generations and playtesters (see table 2).

4.3   Results

As can be seen from figure 2, the GA was able to improve solutions relatively steadily until the final generation, assuring us of its overall convergence. Both the population's average fitness, as well as the best individual's fitness increased

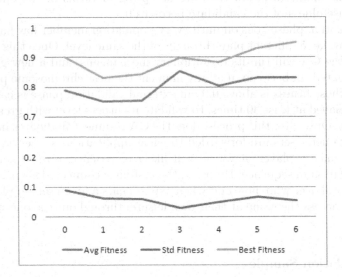

Fig. 2. Evolution of average population fitness, its standard deviation and the fitness of the best individual in the population. Note there is folding in the y-axis.

moderately until the final generation. Fitness variance in the population shows a tendency for decreasing, though it increases slightly from 4th generation onwards (presumably from the increase in mutation rate, designed precisely to avoid stagnation). While the best results seemed close to ideal, several things are in need of improvement. For one, in this test, the initial setup seems overly positive, with average fitness levels already in 0.8 levels (on a 0–1 scale). To a certain extent this is to be expected, given that the platform's aim is to iterate on existing designs, and not necessarily to generate an entirely new design from a completely broken one. That being said, the improvement that was measured, while substantial in terms of player experience, did not allow a strong validation of this method's power to achieve the desired target indicators.

Also to take into account, when interpreting the graph, is that the fitness landscape is, in essence, dynamic, as it depends on players behavioral patterns during game sessions. This happens, for instance, when a chromosome passes from one generation to another, and is then evaluated again, which can cause significant fluctuations to its fitness level. One particular instance of this dynamic component affecting fitness levels, is easily perceived in the second generation, where a higher number of gameplay sessions seems to have led to a drift in values for all individuals, with a significant decrease in both average and best fitness (see chart 2 and table 2 side by side). This means that part of that initially excessive positive assessment of the population was likely to be due to statistical misrepresentation of the sample. Even so, overall, the test presented a good trend for improvement of solutions, though from these results, it seems it presented a low difficulty problem.

Figure 3 shows how parameters varied, on average, across generations. Given the tendency for GA to improve the average fitness of the population (and therefore converge with target metrics), the major tendencies for parameters variation mirror an improvement of the candidates. The seemingly more meaningful trends in these parameter variations are: a steady value for the number of hills, a slow decrease in cannons, holes, goombas and game speed, a subtle increase in item blocks, and an initial sharp decrease in number of coins followed by sharp increase. The lack of variation in number of hills is unsurprising, given how little they impact gameplay other then providing players with a few extra platforms for jumping. These could have improved the number of actions, but in this test the effect proved negligible. The decrease in cannons, holes, goombas and game speed, hand in hand with the small increment to item blocks, can be seen as the algorithm seeking to decrease the game's difficulty and its action rhythm, both of which were initially higher than target levels (this trend is visible when comparing this graph with figure 4 and target gameplay indicators absolute values). The initial decrease of coins followed by increase around generation 3, are probably the result of trying to adjust the number of actions, as these are above target average before generation 3, and below afterwards.

Looking at each of the quality vectors in the fitness variable in figure 4, one can discriminate how the algorithm fared at improving each of them. While 'Actions' and 'Tries' seem to follow a somewhat stable convergence curve, tentatively

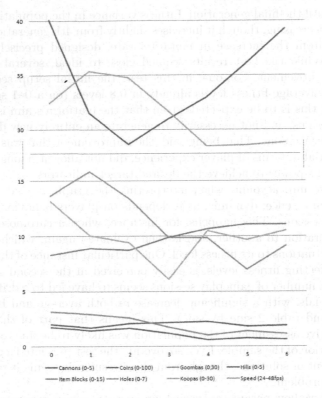

Fig. 3. Evolution of game parameters throughout generations. Note that there is a folding of the y-axis, between 15–30, for ease of visualization.

improving on average, 'Traversal Time' seems to oscillate with no clear tendency to improve on a population basis. The reason for this result only becomes clear once the relationship between parameters and indicators is analyzed further, per table 3.

The correlation table establishes clearly why the "Time to Traverse Level" indicator could not be radically improved across generations – none of the chosen game parameters seem to have a statistically significant relation with its variation. This indicates that the parameter set was insufficient for an adequate optimization of that particular indicator. This failure of one of the indicators to converge in terms of the overall population, hints at the dangers of a poor choice of 'Parameters' in finding an adequate solution, as well as the need for subsequent iterations of the cycle, by means of designer intervention (as introduced in the architecture). As to the other two indicators, it is clear that the set of 'Parameters' was sufficiently capable of producing some degree of optimization. All parameters with exception of number of 'Koopas' impacted the 'Actions Per Second' in a statistically significant manner, though only three could explain more than 0.3 of its variability: Goombas, Coins and Game Speed, three parameters

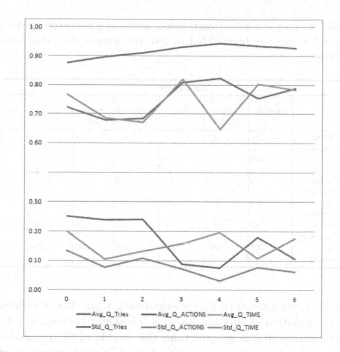

Fig. 4. Evolution of the three quality components, each for one of the indicators ('Tries', 'Actions' and 'Time') used to calculate the fitness function. There is folding in the y-axis between 0.3 and 0.6.

that we previously saw were probably varied by the GA to improve the number of actions. Number of 'Holes' and 'Cannons' affect negatively the action rhythm, though this is most likely only due to the increase in difficulty – more challenge means a more cautious gameplay style which then means slower actions' rhythm. As for the 'Tries' indicator, difficulty seems to have been mostly dictated by number of Holes, and on a smaller level, by Game Speed and number of Cannons, and as expected, counter-weighed by number of item-blocks. Unexpectedly, there is a weak, barely significant relationship between more coins and less 'Tries', though it eludes us how more coins could improve survivability in a play-through.

4.4   Best Solution

The best Individual found by the GA had a final fitness value of 0.96, calculated out of a total of 15 evaluations. Level retries: $m = 1.13, std = 1.85$; actions per second: $m = 2.14, std = 0.63$; time to complete level: $m = 45.26, std = 15.83$. Its parameter set was: 0 Cannons, 30 Coins, 15 Goombas, 1 Hill, 4 item blocks, 2 Holes, 9 Koopas and speed of 28 cycles per second. However, despite the closeness of indicator results to their intended values, the distributions are uneven, thus failing to provide a strong validation for the parameter set being able to generalize this behavioral pattern. To study the extent of the generalization possibilities

Table 3. Table showing statistical correlation between parameters and target indicators. Significant values are highlighted in red and greater font size means greater variance prediction.

		Correlations						
		Cannons (0-5)	Coins (0-100)	Hills (0-5)	ItemBlocks (0-15)	Holes (0-7)	Koopas (0-30)	Speed (24-48fps)
Actions per Second	Pearson Correlation	-.191	.319	-.164		-.172	.059	.333
	Sig. (2-tailed)	.000	.000	.000	.001	.000	.117	.000
Time Traverse Level	Pearson Correlation	-.015	-.019	-.001	-.015	.049	-.016	-.077
	Sig. (2-tailed)	.694	.613	.988	.693	.195	.675	.042
Tries	Pearson Correlation	.257	-.102	-.071	-.199	.420	.043	.197
	Sig. (2-tailed)	.000	.007	.058	.000	.000	.254	.000

for this candidate, one must turn to statistical indicators. The standard error for skewness in a population of this small size is 0.580 and kurtosis is 1.121, so any skewness and kurtosis that is greater than the double of these values is indicative of a non-normal distribution. The 'Number of Tries' distribution of the best candidate has skewness +1.739 and kurtosis 2.431, therefore being both skewed and leptokurtic, i.e. significantly non-normal. Skewness and kurtosis values for Actions Per Second were -0.679 and -0.844, and for Time To Traverse Level were -0.697 and 1.791 respectively, therefore not significantly non-normal in both these aspects. Consequently, now it is possible to use the Shapiro-Wilk test of normality for both distributions, verifying that it is not possible to reject their normality ($sig = 0.203$ and $sig = 0.478$ respectively). Given these facts, it can be asserted to be somewhat likely that these two indicators are samples of a normal distribution. With this in mind, and assuming the playtester sample to be representative, it is possible to calculate how close this game was to achieving the target metrics for the population at large. The confidence interval, at 95% confidence levels, for the "Actions Per Second" distribution is $[1.79, 2.48]$; for "Time To Traverse Level", $[36.50, 54.03]$, at 14 degrees of freedom. Both these ranges are well within the conditions of success for this trial, and while it is not possible to extend this calculation for the 'Tries' distribution, at least its average did not veer off course (see table 1 for success ranges). Admittedly, the pre-established values for success turned out to be underwhelming considering the results, in line with the higher than expected fitness levels for candidates. To conclude, of the three target indicators, the best candidate achieved appropriate mean levels for all, though only 2 of these produced sound distributions that hint at generalization of this success. Only these 2 can, with an adequate confidence level, be seen as statistically trust-worthy representatives of the candidate's indicators imprint. So, this method was a success for the two indicators that the Parameters were capable of provoking variations (as statistical correlations attested to).

5   Conclusions and Future Work

Given the obtained results, it is with confidence one can conclude that in this instance, it was possible to develop and implement a platform that subscribes to the proposed Author-centric approach to EDPCG. It proved capable of achieving sub-optimal values for gameplay indicators, though only as long as the design space was well defined (meaning, when Parameters were shown to be capable of significantly affecting said indicators). This entails that the experimental trial achieved its goal: to find sufficient evidence to sustain the feasibility of this approach. Moreover, this points towards the relevance of the approach herein proposed, and specifically, towards the importance of incorporating forms of design-space specification by designers in EDPCG methods.

In terms of the implementation details, results showed that some elements are in need of revising. The simple GA that was used for generation purposes did achieve moderate improvement to the game instances, though the fact remained that convergence was achieved from an exceedingly positive starting point. Further, both the high variability and dynamic nature of the fitness landscape impacted significantly its optimization process. To solve this issue, in the future the minimum number of gameplay sessions to evaluate candidates will need to increase (therefore decreasing the likelihood of more drastic fitness variations), and the selection process will be adapted to account for the varying nature of the landscape. Coming trials must also see an improvement to the definition of target gameplay indicators that provides designers with some form of control over how much variability they intend to have in their candidates, as a measure of quality introduced in the algorithm.

If future trials repeatedly show the approach's capacity to find parameter sets that can mediate specific gameplay metrics imprints to a playtester population, it is our opinion that this will be a huge advantage for the videogame production process. This test however, only showed the method's plausibility. Coming experiments shall study how to better interface this approach with designers while also providing further evidence of the method's capability to generate good candidates, and the constraints in which such is possible. Only once its efficacy, specifications and interface are fully studied can this approach be considered validated.

Acknowledgements. This work was financed under PhD Scholarship number SFRH/BD/75196/2010, awarded by the Portuguese FCT - Fundacao de Ciencias e Tecnologia and Project ICIS with reference CENTRO-07-0224-FEDER-002003.

References

Drachen, A., Canossap, A.: Towards gameplay analysis via gameplay metrics. In: Proceedings of the 13th International MindTrek Conference: Everyday Life in the Ubiquitous Era, MindTrek 2009, pp. 202–209. ACM, New York (2009) ISBN 978-1-60558-633-5, doi:http://doi.acm.org/10.1145/1621841.1621878

Gladwell, M.: Blink: The Power of Thinking Without Thinking. Little, Brown and Company (2005)

Gombrich, E.H.: The story of art. Phaidon (2009)

Hassenzahl, M.: User experience and experience design. In: Soegaard, M., Dam, R.F. (eds.) Encyclopedia of Human-Computer Interaction. Interaction-Design.org (2011)

Haupt, R.L., Haupt, S.E.: Practical genetic algorithms, 2nd edn. John Wiley & Sons, Inc. (2004)

Kim, J.H., Gunn, D.V., Schuh, E., Phillips, B., Pagulayan, R.J., Wixon, D.R.: Tracking real-time user experience (true): A comprehensive instrumentation solution for complex systems. In: Computer Human Interaction, pp. 443–452 (2008), doi:10.1145/1357054.1357126

Kujala, S.: User involvement: A review of the benefits and challenges. Behaviour & Information Technology 22(1), 1–16 (2003), http://dx.doi.org/10.1080/01449290301782

Pedersen, C., Togelius, J., Yannakakis, G.N.: Modeling player experience for content creation. IEEE Transactions on Computational Intelligence and AI in Games 2(1), 54–67 (2010) ISSN 1943-068X, doi:10.1109/TCIAIG.2010.2043950

Pedersen, C., Togelius, J., Yannakakis, G.N.: Modeling player experience in super mario bros. In: Proceedings of the 5th International Conference on Computational Intelligence and Games, CIG 2009, pp. 132–139. IEEE Press, Piscataway (2009) ISBN 978-1-4244-4814-2, http://portal.acm.org/citation.cfm?id=1719293.1719323

Shaker, N., Yannakakis, G.N., Togelius, J.: Towards Automatic Personalized Content Generation for Platform Games. In: Proceedings of the AAAI Conference on Artificial Intelligence and Interactive Digital Entertainment, AIIDE. AAAI Press (October 2010)

Steen, M., Kuijt-Evers, L., Klok, J.: Early user involvement in research and design projects – A review of methods and practices. In: 23rd EGOS Colloquium (European Group for Organizational Studies) (2007)

Yannakakis, G., Hallam, J.: A generic approach for generating interesting interactive pac-man opponents. In: Proceedings of the IEEE Symposium on Computational Intelligence and Games, pp. 94–101 (2005)

Yannakakis, G.N., Hallam, J.: Evolving opponents for interesting interactive computer games. In: Simulation of Adaptive Behavior (2004)

Yannakakis, G.N., Hallam, J.: Towards optimizing entertainment in computer games. Appl. Artif. Intell. 21, 933–971 (2007) ISSN 0883-9514, http://portal.acm.org/citation.cfm?id=1392651.1392653, doi:10.1080/08839510701527580

Yannakakis, G.N., Togelius, J.: Experience-driven procedural content generation. IEEE Transactions on Affective Computing 99(PrePrints) (2011) ISSN 1949-3045, http://doi.ieeecomputersociety.org/10.1109/T-AFFC.2011.6

Providing Adaptive Visual Interface Feedback in Massively Multiplayer Online Games

Chris Deaker, Masood Masoodian, and Bill Rogers

Department of Computer Science
The University of Waikato
Hamilton, New Zealand
{cjd27,masood,coms0108}@cs.waikato.ac.nz

Abstract. Massively multiplayer online role-playing games typically feature rich and complex game environments to provide more engaging game-play experiences. The complexity of the underlying system in such games can however result in increased complexity of their interfaces, which may diminish player enjoyment—a major element of players' game experience. Players may customise their in-game interfaces to deal with this type of complexity and hence improve their performance, but the challenges associated with manual interface customisation may prevent some players from effectively personalising their own game interface. In this paper we present an adaptive feedback system with a visual interface component, which dynamically provides the player with a list of predicted actions they are likely to take, in order to simplify the game interface and improve players' game experience. We also report on the outcomes of a user evaluation of this system which demonstrate the potential value of adaptive user interfaces in game design.

Keywords: Adaptive game interfaces, visual interface feedback, feedback visualisation, massively multiplayer online games, user evaluation.

1 Introduction

Massively multiplayer online role-playing games (MMORPGs), such as World of Warcraft[1] (WoW), are providing increasing complex feature-rich game environments to enhance their players' experience. As this underlying complexity of games continues to grow, there is the potential for that complexity to be exposed to the player, especially when attempting to provide the player with important information through the game interface.

Many games attempt to manage player exposure to complexity by limiting the level of system detail which is shown to the player at early stages in the game, and then gradually introducing the player to other concepts as they continue to play the game. A common implementation of this approach, which is typically seen in MMORPGs (e.g. RIFT[2], Age of Conan[3]), is to limit the number of

---

[1] http://us.battle.net/wow/en/
[2] http://www.riftgame.come/en/
[3] http://www.ageofconan.com

D. Reidsma, H. Katayose, and A. Nijholt (Eds.): ACE 2013, LNCS 8253, pp. 29–44, 2013.
© Springer International Publishing Switzerland 2013

possible actions players can perform at early stages in the game, and as they progress "reward" them by giving them access to larger number of actions.

Another method of managing interface-specific game complexity is to allow players to customise their in-game interfaces. This allows individual players to determine which information is displayed, and how it is displayed to them. Interface customisation can be achieved by installing packages or plug-ins which alter the game interface in some way. A number of popular MMORPGs, including WoW, provide support for such plug-ins. These plug-ins allow customisation of game interface by modifying its visual aspects (e.g. colour, texture, position of items), on-screen information (e.g. detailed game statistics), game-play assistance (e.g. hints and alerts), etc. However, plug-ins often require advanced configuration manually in order to provide significant benefits to the player.

An alternative, or perhaps complimentary, method of assisting players is for the game interface to dynamically change and adapt to individual players based on their in-game behaviour and past actions. In this paper we present one such system, called *WatchAndLearn*, which includes a visual interface feedback mechanism for dynamically providing players with a list of predicted actions they are likely to take, in order to simplify the game interface and improve players' game experience. We also describe a user study of *WatchAndLearn* that we have carried out to evaluate its potential for improving player experience.

2   Adaptive Computer Games

Development of any game system which aims to assist players by dynamically adapting to their behaviour, needs to take into account factors relating to player motivation, so that the complexity of the game interface is managed without negatively impacting the game flow.

Several studies of motivational factors relating to MMORPG players have been conducted in recent years. For instance, a survey of WoW players has shown that players consider interface customisation to have varying levels of importance for different motivational components [6]. For example, interface customisation is considered to be more important for achievement-related motivational components than others. This study was based on an earlier study of MMORPG players by Yee [10] which revealed 10 motivational subcomponents, that could be grouped into 3 over-arching components of achievement, social, and immersion based motivations. However, Yee's analysis suggested that different motivational components in MMORPGs did not necessarily exclude each other, as previously posited by Bartle [1].

Games clearly need to manage and increase player motivation, often by improving game flow. Flow describes a balanced mental state, where a player's ability allows them to perform an activity successfully, while the level of challenge of the activity remains high enough so that the player does not become bored [5]. The result is a sensation of complete focus and absorption in a task. By recognising the elements required in order to support and encourage a sensation of flow in players, games can be designed to provide players with more immersive and enjoyable experiences.

While a theoretical understanding of what impacts player enjoyment is valuable, in order to apply this information dynamically, a game must develop an understanding of the current player. Player modelling allows player interaction to be captured and described in such a way that the characteristics of the player can be identified. Cowley et al. [4] discuss the need to understand and describe "the player as well as the game and the experience" in order to analyse how games can enable a state of flow for the player.

Charles et al. [3] suggest a factorial approach to player modelling, where designers "manually partition data space to attach different meanings to various aspects of the data". Players are profiled by measuring the strength of their tendencies towards particular factors, with a complete player model being comprised of a series of numerical values—one for each pre-determined factor. This approach allows for application of the model wherever the recorded factors are relevant, with the major drawback being that factors must be pre-determined in order to track data for later inspection and usage.

Van Hoorn et al. [9] discuss another modelling technique, which is intended to support "the creation of controllers for computer game agents which are able to play a game in a manner similar to a particular human player". This represents a departure from typical approaches to artificially intelligent non-player game characters, where the goal is to learn to play the game as well as possible, rather than learning to play the game "realistically", in the same way as a typical human player would. This is described by Bryant and Miikkulainen [2] as "visible intelligence", where the goal of developing visibly intelligent autonomous agents is to "devise agent behaviours that display the visible attributes of intelligence, rather than simply performing optimally".

Visible intelligence has been demonstrated in a strategy game by monitoring player decisions, and using these decisions to train the controller of the game agent, thus creating a game agent which is visibly more intelligent [2]. This concept has been extended and applied to car racing games, by dividing the racing track into a number of individual, distinct segments, and observing the actions taken by the player within each of those segments [8, 9].

Similarly, the popular *Forza*[4] racing game, provides players with a selection of optional driver-assist features, which simplify driving for inexperienced players and eases the transition from novice to expert. These options include features such as braking and steering assist, and stability and traction control. Rather than taking control away from the player, the game reacts to situations where the player is struggling, by engaging any activated assist controls only when they are needed. This adaptive approach to difficulty tuning allows novice players to experience the game with minimal frustration, encouraging them to continue playing and enhancing their skills, until they may be able to drive effectively with the automatic assistance disabled.

A more visually focused assistance feature is the suggested line driver assist, which renders a series of colour-coded arrows on the track, providing the player with a suggestion of an optimal racing line for the upcoming corner, based upon

---

[4] http://forzamotorsport.net

the player's current position and speed. This approach to adaptive suggestion does not require robust player modelling, since suggestions are based upon immediately available factors (e.g. player position, direction, and speed) and an optimal approach which can be calculated using the same approach used by the game to calculate routes for AI drivers.

Having an understanding of the individual player and of their gameplay experience is insufficient if the goal is to improve the player's game experience. In order to impact the experience of different players, games must utilise this understanding and adapt the game accordingly. While previous research has explored the benefits of the adaptation of general-purpose user interfaces, examples of applications of adaptive interfaces in computer games are lacking. In particular, there has been little research or commercial development that has focused on applying adaptive interfaces for the purpose of improving player experience.

3   WatchAndLearn Plug-in for World of Warcraft

We have developed a demonstrative prototype, called *WatchAndLearn*, to better investigate the potential of providing adaptive feedback through a visual interface component for improving player experience in MMORPGs. *WatchAndLearn* generates a game play model based on player's past actions (or those of other players' if selected), and uses this model to predict what actions the player is likely to take next. These predicted actions are then presented to the player in a visual list, which simplifies the game interface. The aim of *WatchAndLearn*, however, is not to teach the player what actions to take, and thus change the actual game play, but rather to provide easy access to actions they are likely to take, and by doing so simplify the game interface.

WatchAndLearn was designed as a plug-in for World of Warcraft, because WoW, as the world's most-subscribed MMORPG, provides a number of features which have become standard within the genre. In particular, the general layout of the WoW interface has become a commonly used template for other modern MMORPGs. Therefore, it was envisaged that interface improvements developed and tested within WoW would be applicable to a wider range of other MMORPGs. Figure 1 provides an overview of the data flow of the *WatchAndLearn* plug-in and its various components, which are discussed in the following sections.

3.1   Monitoring Player Behaviour

The WoW interface is driven entirely by *events*[5], which are created by the game client and sent to registered interface frames. These events are generated in response to changes within the in-game world, or within the user interface itself.

Upon initial loading, the *WatchAndLearn* plug-in registers an event handler for each relevant event type. These handlers capture events as they occur, and

---

[5] The WoW API is documented at http://www.wowwiki.com/Event_API

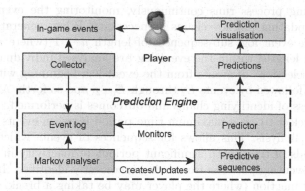

Fig. 1. Overview of the data flow of the *WatchAndLearn* plug-in and its components

add them to a time-stamped player event log. This log persists between play sessions, allowing for collection of data over an extended period of time, which is useful for generating more robust behavioural models. Additionally, events are added to a buffer and used for player modelling, as will be discussed below.

3.2 Player Modelling

Player ability usage[6] is modelled by generating Markov chains [7] of observed event history. The process is automated, allowing for chains to be updated regularly without requiring any additional player action. The key data source for this process is the event buffer, which contains the $n + 1$ most recent relevant events, where n is the pre-defined length of Markov chain pre-sequences. Players can configure the Markov chain pre-sequence length, as well as a variety of other settings affecting prediction using the configuration interface of *WatchAndLearn*.

On every interface update cycle, *WatchAndLearn* checks whether the contents of the event buffer have changed. If a change is observed, the most recent event is taken as the "outcome", with all n preceding events in the buffer being taken as the pre-sequence chain resulting in that outcome.

With a pre-sequence chain now identified, the model dictionary is queried to determine whether that chain has been previously observed. The queried dictionary contains a collection of pre-sequences as keys, and lists of outcome-count pairs as values (where the count is the number of times this outcome has been observed following the key pre-sequence).

If the key chain is not present in the dictionary, it is inserted, with an initial value containing only the observed outcome, with a count of 1. If the key is found, the value list is checked to see whether the outcome has been previously observed. If a matching value is found, the count for that outcome is incremented. If no matching value is found, the outcome is inserted into the outcome list, with the count initialised to 1.

---

[6] In WoW and similar games, players have a discrete set of actions available for use by their character. This paper refers to these actions as *abilities*.

The modelling process runs continuously, monitoring the event buffer for changes and updating Markov chains as necessary. When generating a model using the entire event log, sub-sequences of length $n + 1$ (where n is the pre-sequence chain length) within the event log are analysed individually, by making a "sliding selection" of events from the event log, beginning with events E_1 through E_{n+1}, followed by events E_2 through E_{n+2}, and so forth. After this, the standard process of identifying chains and outcomes is performed.

Players can elect to set a maximum time period between events that will be considered for analysis. This allows for sequences of events which occur over extended periods of time (with significant periods of inactivity in between) to be ignored, preventing patterns from being incorrectly identified. In particular, long periods of inaction (where the player may be taking a break, or otherwise occupied) will also result in a break in terms of model generation. Where the event buffer is found to contain two consecutive events with timestamps which differ by a value exceeding the specified period, all events which occurred prior to the latter event are flushed from the buffer. The result is that no chain pre-sequences will ever be created where there is a delay of more than the allowed time period between two consecutive events.

As more events are observed, the robustness of any generated model increases as uncommon outliers are suppressed by more commonly occurring outcomes. Because of this, models that are generated based upon a small number of actions will generally be less accurate than models generated using a more substantial event history. At early stages in model generation (with few source events), it is impossible to establish which outcomes are potential outliers. Events which occur rarely within limited event logs may in fact be common outcomes. Because of this, total number of event observations should be taken into consideration when estimating the potential accuracy of a generated model.

As chain pre-sequence length increases, the total number of unique pre-sequence chains will increase, and the total number of predicted outcomes for each of those chains will, in general, decrease. Because of this, it is expected that longer pre-sequence chains will result in fewer but more accurate predictions. While increased accuracy is desirable, for shorter event logs increasing the pre-sequence length may reduce the number of predictions to the point that the model fails to predict any outcome at all.

The trade-off in this case is between fewer but more accurate predictions (with the risk of having no predictions made at all), and more but less accurate predictions. In cases where a large number of events have been observed, longer pre-sequence chains may be used to generate more accurate predictions without running the risk of failing to predict any outcome. The ideal chain pre-sequence length will ultimately be determined by the size of the source event log.

3.3 Prediction Generation

With a player's game-play habits observed and recorded, the player model can then be used to generate predictions of future behaviour. The prediction generation process is automatically triggered whenever the contents of the event buffer have changed (indicating that the player has recently performed a relevant action). The contents of the event buffer are inspected, with the most recent n events (where n is the Markov chain pre-sequence length) are selected. These events are used to form a chain pre-sequence, which is then used as the key for a look-up in the model dictionary, as described earlier. The retrieved value is a list of all abilities that have been previously observed following the key chain sequence, along with their observation counts.

In order to calculate the estimated likelihood for each prediction, the number of observed occurrences (for all outcomes) is summed. The estimated likelihood of each outcome is then calculated as the observation count for that outcome, as a proportion of the sum of all observation counts. The result is a set of predicted outcomes with predicted likelihoods ranging between 0.0 and 1.0, with the sum of all likelihood estimations being 1.0. With predicted likelihood values calculated, outcomes can also be ranked according to the order of estimated likelihood.

While Markov chains are used to identify likely outcomes and base-line estimations for the likelihood of those outcomes, these estimations can be augmented by considering characteristics of other collected data, such as currently active buffs[7] and state information. The goal is to utilise this additional information in order to improve the accuracy of estimations of predicted likelihood. Historically observed buff and state data are applied to likelihood estimations in a similar manner.

- **Estimation using buff history:** using the name of the predicted ability as a key, the buff history dictionary is queried in order to retrieve a record containing all buffs that had been previously observed (and their observation counts) when the key ability was used. This list is compared with the currently active player buffs, with the total observation counts for all buffs which are also currently active being summed up. The number of observed occurrences for all buffs is also summed. The raw outcome estimation is then calculated as the sum of observation counts for currently active buffs as a proportion of the sum of observation counts for all buffs.
- **Estimation using state history:** the name of an ability predicted according to event history is used to query the state history dictionary, retrieving a record which contains occurrence counts for pre-determined state factors. The similarity between this retrieved record and the current player and target state is calculated, resulting in a value between 0.0 and 1.0, where 0.0 indicates no similarity between the current state and any historically observed states for the key ability, and 1.0 indicates complete parity between the current state and all historically observed states for the key ability.

WatchAndLearn allows the player to configure the relative weightings of event history, active buff history, and state history for prediction likelihood estimations. As buff and state-based histories are used to modify likelihood estimations only

---

[7] In WoW, player characters may be affected by *buffs*—temporary spells or effects which positively impact attributes and characteristics of the character.

(and not predict outcomes), the minimum weighting for event history is greater than zero.

The following equation shows the process of calculating a predicted likelihood P for an outcome O, where E is the initial estimation based upon event history, B is estimation based upon buff history, S is estimation based upon state history, and W is the weighting for each factor:

$$P_O = \frac{E_O \times W_E + B_O \times W_B + S_O \times W_S}{W_E + W_B + W_S}$$

3.4   Prediction Visualisation

WatchAndLearn provides visual feedback of the predicted abilities using a *prediction visualisation* panel, as shown in Figure 2, which allows the player to more easily locate abilities which they are likely to use within their game interface. Predictions are displayed as a ranked list of abilities, with the ability icon, ability name, and predicted likelihood listed. The predicted abilities are ranked in descending order of estimated likelihood. Since it is possible that a large number of different abilities may be predicted at any time, the total number of predictions shown to the player at a given time is capped, with the default cap value being set to 5 predicted abilities. This value can be adjusted in the in-game settings configuration interface.

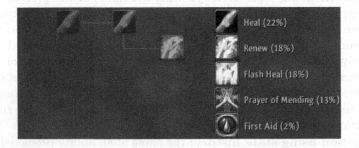

Fig. 2. Prediction visualisation of *WatchAndLearn*, showing an ordered list of predicted abilities on the right, and the sequences of used abilities on the left

The prediction list is populated and updated as predictions occur. As a result, by default the prediction list will be empty, with the list only being populated once a number of actions have been observed (as determined by the pre-configured length of Markov chain pre-sequences). Once enough events have occurred, the list will be populated with any predicted abilities.

In addition to showing ability predictions, the visualisation aims to illustrate to the player what ability pattern resulted in the current set of predictions. Once the player selects a displayed ability, the icon for that ability begins to slowly "float" leftward across the screen. As the player continues to use abilities, the visualisation continues to move the appropriate icon across the screen, creating a short history visualisation, and allowing for identification of the patterns recognised by the plug-in. As the icons of abilities used previously continue to float further away from the visualisation, their opacity is gradually reduced until they are eventually removed from the interface. In the case that the player uses an ability which is not contained in the predicted list, all predictions temporarily disappear (until familiar sequences begin to be recognised again).

While all historically used abilities (that were previously shown in the prediction list) are shown for a short amount of time, only the most recent abilities are used for prediction. The actual number of abilities used depends on the pre-configured Markov chain pre-sequence size. Sequences of abilities which were used as pre-sequences for Markov chain prediction are shown with lines drawn between those abilities (see the left side of Figure 2).

3.5   Model Subscriptions

WatchAndLearn also provides a model subscription component, allowing players to generate predictive models based upon other players' behaviour. As well as supporting single-model prediction based upon an external source, models can be generated from a combination of an arbitrary number of sources, including external sources as well as the player's own historical data. This allows the player to augment their own predictive data in different ways, by applying different model combinations, or by completely replacing predictions with those based upon other players' behaviour.

Model subscriptions can be used as a training tool, providing novice players with suggestions based upon expert player behaviour. Similarly, more advanced players that are inexperienced with specific play-styles, or are curious about other advanced players' approaches to game-play may benefit from being able to practice ability rotations while using predictions based upon model subscriptions for suggestions.

Subscriptions are managed and maintained using the add-on communication channels of WoW, which allow for communication between different game clients running the same game plug-in. Messages are sent directly, and privately, between the subscriber and the subscription source.

Prediction with multiple active subscriptions is handled very similarly to standard prediction using a single player event log (see Section 3.3). When the player's event buffer is updated, the prediction cycle is triggered, resulting in the creation or update of Markov chains based upon event log data. However, in the case of multiple source prediction, the event log used is a composite log containing events from all currently active sources. Depending upon the configuration, this could be a single external source, multiple external sources, or a combination of external sources and the player's own event log. With this composite event log created, analysis for prediction generation is identical to the standard single-source prediction process.

3.6 Model Accuracy

The accuracy of the generated predictive model can be calculated retrospectively by comparing predicted outcomes with actual observed outcomes (i.e. actions taken by the player). This provides a means of evaluating the appropriateness of the applied model, and possibly identifying potential improvements to the modelling approach. At least two types of accuracy can be calculated:

– **Ranking accuracy** describes the accuracy of the ordering of predicted outcomes. This can be determined using a simple calculation where a set number n is divided by the summed ranked predicted likelihood for the previous n abilities used. The result of this calculation is a number between 0.0 and 1.0, with 0.0 indicating total inaccuracy, and 1.0 indicating total accuracy for the last n predictions. This metric is simplistic in that it does not take into account the actual predicted likelihood of any event—rather, it simply measures the accuracy of the ranked ordering.
– **Accuracy of predicted likelihood** provides an indication of the reliability of specific likelihood predictions. Every predicted event has an associated likelihood, which is proportional to the number of times that this event has occurred previously given the pre-sequence, relative to the number of times any other event has occurred given the same pre-sequence. This is presented to the player as a percentage, where the summed likelihood of all predicted events always equals 100%. In order to evaluate the accuracy of predictions for the last n events, the likelihood of all events is summed, with the total result divided by n, resulting in a value between 0 and 100, with 0 indicating total inaccuracy and 100 indicating complete accuracy.

4 User Evaluation of WatchAndLearn

An evaluation of *WatchAndLearn* was conducted with WoW players in order to determine the effectiveness of the techniques we have developed. In this section we discuss this user evaluation and its findings.

4.1 Methodology

Requests for participation in the evaluation were posted on a number of WoW-related internet discussion forums. Upon agreeing to take part in the evaluation, participants were directed to a link where they could download an adapted version of the *WatchAndLearn* plug-in[8], which was augmented to automatically run a series of trials with different configuration settings, as well as administering an in-game questionnaire with the participants to collect demographic data and feedback. After completing the survey, participants were asked to upload a log file which included all collected predictive data, the predictive sequences

---

[8] Available for download at http://bit.ly/WZtp8b

used, accuracy measurements for all predictions, and the feedback and answers provided by the participants.

The evaluation itself consisted of a "warm-up" period, during which the system was trained as players generated predictive sequences through play. Following the warm-up, three trials were conducted. The only differing factor between the three trials was the pre-sequence length of Markov chains used to generate predictions, with this variable set at 2, 3, and 4 for trials 1, 2, and 3 respectively. Each trial continued until the participant had performed 50 actions, with the exception of the warm-up trial which consisted of 100 actions (more actions were required during training in order to generate a more robust predictive model). While the predictive model continued to develop during each trial as actions were observed, it was reset at the end of each trial to the state that was recorded at the end of the warm-up period. This was intended to ensure that later trials were not favoured by more robust predictive models than earlier trials.

Participants were asked to play in their normal (typical) manner while performing the evaluation.

4.2   Study Participants

Twenty participants took part in the evaluation, 3 were female (15%) and 17 male (85%). On average, the participants reported having played WoW for 5.4 years ($SD = 2.2$), with an average weekly play-time of 31.9 hours ($SD = 16.8$). On a 7-point Likert scale, the average self-rating for mechanical knowledge was 6 ($SD = 1.2$). These statistics suggest that the participants were, in general, expert players with a high level of understanding of the game.

4.3   Questionnaires

After logging into the game with the *WatchAndLearn* plug-in activated, using an in-game dialogue box the participants were asked to answer a number of questions providing basic demographic information, as well as some information regarding their game-play habits in WoW.

After each trial (excluding the warm-up trial), participants were asked to rate how accurate they felt the predictions were, on a 7-point Likert scale with the anchors 1 being *Not accurate* and 7 being *Very accurate*.

After the three trials were completed, the participants were asked a series of follow-up questions, all of which were rated on a 7-point Likert scale:

1. Overall, how accurate did you feel the predictions were (for all trials)?
2. Do you feel that the system correctly identified patterns of ability usage?
3. How clear was the visualisation in terms of communicating which abilities were predicted to occur next (regardless of the accuracy of the prediction)?
4. Did you select your abilities based upon the predictions provided?
5. Did you check all predicted abilities before selecting an ability to use?
6. Did you feel that you had enough time to inspect all predicted abilities before selecting an ability to use?

4.4   Data Collection

A number of data elements describing the evaluation session were captured, including the complete predictive model (which included both predictive sequences and historical data used to generate those sequences), player ability usage (time-stamped), and a list of abilities predicted by the plug-in each time the participant used any ability. The "actual" accuracy of predictions was also measured, where the likelihood estimations (ranging from 0 to 100) and the ranked ordering (from 1 to 5, where 1 indicates the ability with the highest predicted likelihood) of whichever ability the player selected was recorded. In cases where the selected ability was not predicted at all (including when no predictions were made), the accuracy and rank was recorded as 0.

4.5   Results

Prediction Accuracy. The accuracy of the applied model was analysed in three different ways: accuracy as perceived by the participants, accuracy of the likelihood estimations, and accuracy of the ranked ordering of the predicted abilities.

Perceived Accuracy: Table 1 shows the participant ratings (on a 7-point Likert scale) of perceived accuracy for each of the three trials, as well as the perceived overall accuracy. A one-way repeated measures analysis of variance was carried out to test for differences between participant ratings of perceived accuracy for each trial. No significant difference between trial ratings was found ($F_{2,57} = 1.53$, $p = 0.23$).

Table 1. Rating counts of perceived accuracy for each trial, and overall

	Rating 1: not accurate, 7: very accurate							
	1	2	3	4	5	6	7	Average (*SD*)
Trial 1	0	2	5	5	5	3	0	4.1 (1.3)
Trial 2	0	1	3	4	5	6	1	4.8 (1.3)
Trial 3	0	1	4	2	7	5	1	4.7 (1.3)
Overall	0	3	1	5	6	4	1	4.5 (1.4)

Accuracy of Likelihood Estimation: The accuracy of likelihood predictions (see Section 3.6) was also measured, where the predicted likelihood (ranging from 0 to 100) of whichever ability the player selected was recorded. This measure of accuracy was intended to primarily serve as a means of comparing estimated likelihood accuracy between trials. Table 2 shows the average prediction accuracies for each of the three trials, and overall. A one-way repeated measures analysis of variance was carried out to test for differences between the measured prediction accuracy for each trial. No significant difference between accuracy for each trial was found ($F_{2,57} = 1.51$, $p = 0.23$).

Table 2. Average measured accuracy for all trials

	Average Accuracy % (*SD*)
Trial 1	31.18 (13.40)
Trial 2	36.46 (15.09)
Trial 3	40.26 (20.49)
Overall	35.97 (16.33)

Figure 3 shows the perceived and measured accuracy across all three trials. There was a moderate correlation between the ratings for perceived accuracy and the measured accuracy over the three trials ($r^2 = 0.77$).

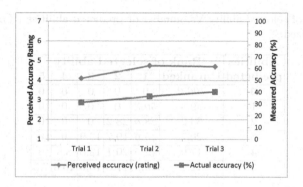

Fig. 3. Perceived accuracy ratings compared to measured accuracy

It was expected that as Markov chain pre-sequence length is increased, fewer and more accurate predictions would be made. Collected data supports this expectation. Figure 4 shows a strong inverse correlation between the number of predictions made per trial and the average accuracy of those predictions ($r^2 = 1.0$), with accuracy increasing and the total number of predictions made decreasing as the pre-sequence length increased between trials.

Ranking Accuracy: In addition to explicit percentage values expressing estimated predicted likelihood, predicted abilities were displayed as a ranked list, ordered from the most likely to the least likely. The intention of this was to more clearly express which abilities were estimated to be more likely, allowing players to recognise this without needing to parse more specific estimation values.

The rank of selected abilities was recorded, as was the list of predicted abilities. Table 3 shows a breakdown of the number of predicted abilities against the actual rank of the selected ability, expressed as a percentage of observations. This data shows that in all cases where one or more predictions were made, the first ranked ability was most likely to be chosen. Further, as more abilities are predicted, the chances of an unranked (unpredicted) ability being selected reduce substantially.

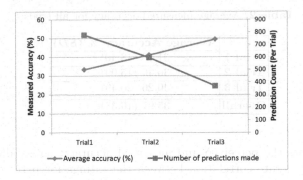

Fig. 4. Measured accuracy compared to the number of predictions made for each trial

Table 3. Rank of selected ability Vs. number of predicted abilities (%). Highest proportion emphasized.

Abilities predicted	Rank of selected ability					
	Unranked	1	2	3	4	5
0	*100.0*	0	0	0	0	0
1	49.8	*50.2*	0	0	0	0
2	33.2	*38.6*	28.2	0	0	0
3	20.7	*45.6*	19.7	13.9	0	0
4	17.0	*42.5*	20.1	12.0	8.5	0
5	12.1	*36.8*	17.8	15.5	10.3	7.5

Final Questionnaire Ratings. Following the completion of all three trials, participants were asked a number of follow-up questions, intended to gauge their general reaction to various aspects of *WatchAndLearn*. The 7-point Likert scale ratings provided by participants for these questions are shown in Table 4. Participants' ratings were generally very positive, particularly the ratings for the visualisation used to display predictions, indicating that regardless of the prediction accuracy, the visualisation was effective at conveying which abilities were predicted to occur next (Question 5: average rating = 5.8, $SD = 1.3$).

Participant Feedback. In addition to accuracy ratings, participants were asked to provide any additional comments they had regarding *WatchAndLearn*. Participants' comments were mixed, but generally positive. Most of the feedback received was in regard to the overall accuracy of the system. While accuracy levels were not high, the overall level of accuracy was high enough that most participants were satisfied with the ability of *WatchAndLearn* to model their behaviour to some degree. Participant comments included the following:

"[...] for the most part it recognized a pattern and displayed pretty accurate results."

Table 4. Average ratings for the questions of the final questionnaire

#	Question	Average Rating (SD)
1	Did you select your abilities based upon the predictions provided?	3.2 (1.7)
2	Do you feel that the system correctly identified patterns of ability usage?	4.8 (1.7)
3	Did you check all predicted abilities before selecting an ability to use?	3.3 (1.8)
4	Did you feel that you had enough time to inspect all predicted abilities before selecting an ability to use?	4.1 (1.8)
5	How clear was the visualisation in communicating which abilities were predicted to occur next (regardless of the accuracy of the prediction)?	5.8 (1.3)

"Really neat, it actually helped me concentrate and try to focus on my rotation[9] more."

Most negative feedback was in regard to the model's inability to provide accurate predictions for abilities which were used rarely.

"Its good, but unless it takes cool-downs into account [...] it won't be that accurate."

4.6   Conclusions

In this paper we have presented *WatchAndLearn*, an adaptive feedback system with a visual interface component, which aims to provide players with relevant information in order to improve their game experience. We have also discussed a user evaluation of this system.

Overall, the approach taken by *WatchAndLearn* is successful in modelling and predicting player behaviour. While the accuracy of likelihood estimations is not always very high, ordered ranking is generally accurate, with accuracy levels increasing as more abilities are predicted. Given the short model training period required, this indicates that the model is able to accurately predict which abilities will be used (though the exact likelihood values are lacking in accuracy). Higher levels of accuracy are possible given a longer training period.

The user study participants of *WatchAndLearn* responded positively to the model visualisation, which allowed them to easily recognise abilities that they were likely to use. However, their feedback also highlighted apparent issues with the inability of *WatchAndLearn* to accurately predict those abilities which are rarely used. While observed ability usage patterns can provide a basis for predicting actions, taking other factors into account may allow for the generation of more robust and accurate predictions.

---

[9] *Rotations* are short sequences of abilities which players may execute repeatedly.

There are a number of areas of potential future research that need to be investigated. These include: augmenting the player model with additional information to improve its prediction accuracy, exploring alternate applications of model predictions (e.g. to create more visibly intelligent game agents), and applying this approach to other massively multiplayer online games.

Acknowledgements. The user evaluation discussed in this paper was approved by the Ethics Committee of the Faculty of Computing and Mathematical Sciences of the University of Waikato. We would like to thank all our study participants.

References

1. Bartle, R.: Hearts, clubs, diamonds, spades: Players who suit muds. The Journal of Virtual Environments 1(1) (1996)
2. Bryant, B.D., Miikkulainen, R.: Acquiring visibly intelligent behavior with example-guided neuroevolution. In: Proceedings of the National Conference on Artificial Intelligence, vol. 1, pp. 801–808. AAAI Press (2007)
3. Charles, D., Kerr, A., McNeill, M., McAlister, M., Black, M., Kcklich, J., Moore, A., Stringer, K.: Player-centred game design: Player modelling and adaptive digital games. In: Proceedings of the Digital Games Research Conference, pp. 285–298 (2005)
4. Cowley, B., Charles, D., Black, M., Hickey, R.: Toward an understanding of flow in video games. Computers in Entertainment (CIE) 6(2), Article No. 20 (2008)
5. Csikszentmihalyi, M., Csikszentmihalyi, I.: Optimal experience: Psychological studies of flow in consciousness. Cambridge University Press (1992)
6. Deaker, C., Masoodian, M., Rogers, B.: A survey of players' opinions on interface customization in world of warcraft. In: Nijholt, A., Romão, T., Reidsma, D. (eds.) ACE 2012. LNCS, vol. 7624, pp. 198–213. Springer, Heidelberg (2012)
7. Markov, A.: Extension of the limit theorems of probability theory to a sum of variables connected in a chain. John Wiley & Sons, Inc. (1971)
8. Togelius, J., Nardi, R.D., Lucas, S.M.: Towards automatic personalised content creation for racing games. In: IEEE Symposium on Computational Intelligence and Games, pp. 252–259. IEEE (2007)
9. Hoorn, N.V., Togelius, J., Wierstra, D., Schmidhuber, J.: Robust player imitation using multiobjective evolution. In: IEEE Congress on Evolutionary Computation, pp. 652–659. IEEE (2009)
10. Yee, N.: Motivations of play in online games. Journal of CyberPsychology and Behavior 9(6), 772–775 (2006)

Persuasive Elements in Videogames: Effects on Player Performance and Physiological State

Luís Duarte and Luís Carriço

LaSIGE & Department of Informatics, University of Lisbon,
FCUL, Edifício C6, Campo-Grande, 1749-016 Lisboa, Portugal
lduarte@lasige.di.fc.ul.pt, lmc@di.fc.ul.pt

Abstract. This paper presents an exploration into the effects of specific types of persuasive technology in videogames according to a performance and a physiological perspective. Persuasive mechanisms are often employed to change the behavior of a determined person during a known time frame. In videogames, these approaches are expected to produce results in a more limited time window especially concerning the player's performance. Literature regarding how this type of persuasive mechanisms affects a user during a game is scarce. We conducted a set of experiments with different games, on distinct platforms and with thirty individuals per experimental period. Results suggest that different persuasive techniques can effectively be used to improve or decrease player performance as well as to regulate physiological state. We provide a detailed analysis of these results along with a thorough discussion regarding the design implications and opportunities of these findings and how they are related with existing literature in the area.

Keywords: Persuasive Interfaces, Deception, Videogames.

1 Introduction

Videogames are currently one of the most important segments within the entertainment industry. Annual ESA reports shows a growth tendency from 2007 to 2010, where revenues have gone up from US$9.5 billion to US$25.1 billion, respectively. As of 2011, the videogame industry was valued at US$65 billion [9]. In recent years, we witnessed a focus into using videogames as a driving force for behavior changes [2], promoting a less sedentary life [29] and improving personal well-being [17][25]. Regardless of the game's purpose and area of application (e.g. pure entertainment, rehabilitation [11], therapy or sports [15]), players typically desire to achieve the best performance possible according to their skill set. Different mechanics are often employed to motivate users into achieving better performances [1] such as providing rewards, attempting to gather the attention of the user by exploring emotionally engaging gameplay sequences, etc. While some of these provide a positive experience to users [3], others may detract them from having an enjoyable time [12], ultimately leading them to forfeit playing the game. Independently of how they are delivered to players, these mechanisms are, in their nature, persuasive technology (henceforth PT)

D. Reidsma, H. Katayose, and A. Nijholt (Eds.): ACE 2013, LNCS 8253, pp. 45–60, 2013.
© Springer International Publishing Switzerland 2013 2013

[19] – they are employed to effectively motivate the player within the game, promote better performance displays and, in particular cases, attempt at changing the player's behavior or improving their well-being [2][22][27].

Persuasive technology gained momentum in recent years, particularly through the interdisciplinary commitment to create applications which are augmented with videogame-related features (via a technique called gamification [6][7][14]). The aforementioned temporary rewards, scoreboards and motivational messages are some of the approaches used to accomplish the desired results. Among these techniques emerged what some researchers address as nudge interfaces – a strategy which capitalized on subtle persuasive and motivational cues to drive end-users into improving their performance in an application / game [1][8][16] or effectively changing their behavior [18][21]. Nudge interfaces typically recur to well-known persuasive approaches (e.g. motivating through natural language or through the employment of persistent / temporary reinforcements such as achievements). Unfortunately, information concerning what kind of immediate effect these mechanisms have on end-users is virtually non-existent [4][20][28], leaving more questions unanswered. Furthermore, existing research often relies on long persuasive intervention processes [25][29], failing to address the disruptive effect of persuasive interfaces. Recent research trends in HCI also explore the possibility of capitalizing on deceptive designs to motivate and drive users to change their behavior [1]. However, empirical evidence on these effects is scarce.

We seek to research the effects of specific types of PT (which are not related with task completeness or long motivational processes) in videogames and how a player reacts from both a physiological and performance perspective. We also want to drive the existing literature about PT forward, by providing empirical evidence whether the knowledge about presence of persuasive rewards [13] is sufficient regardless of that reward being delivered or not [1]. This article presents the main results of this research, focusing on the physiological and performance shifts presented by players. Testing was carried out with a total of 60 users in two different games. Results show quite different effects and open the way to the definition of a set of PT design guidelines according to the categorization of the empirical evidence hereby presented.

2   Related Work

Our review of existing literature tackles a few themes: PT and related models, how these are applied in videogames and game studies regarding the influence of such mechanisms on player experience.

3   Persuasive Technology

PT typically relies on identifying a behavior which should be modified by presenting the target user with adequate information, steering him / her towards a desired chain of events. This approach has been conceptualized in the Persuasive System Design (PSD henceforth) model [24]. The model is composed by three primary elements – the intent, the event and the strategy. In sum, these three elements stipulate what is the expected behavioral change, the environmental context (e.g. technology involved, user characteristics) of the subject of intervention and the way the persuasive cues are delivered to the subject, respectively. This model comprises the typical approach adopted to convey a behavior changing chain of events, profiling a user and choosing an appropriate medium to deliver the persuasive content.

The number of applications which recur to PT has been increasing in recent years. This momentum might be, in part, justified due to the proliferation of low cost modern smart-phones [25][27]. Cheap downloadable applications which promote healthier lifestyles [2][22] and are able to effectively change an individual's habits [27] are part of the driving force behind this momentum. Nevertheless, PT was rooted way before the popularization of these devices. Fogg [10] provides a thorough overview of the application of such technology in everyday life situations and scenarios. Two approaches stand out from the rest in what concerns our research: influencing users through language and persuasion through praise. The first relies on presenting written content in a language understandable by the recipient. For instance, informative cues ("Are you sure you want to proceed?") and teasing messages (e.g. "You have 29 new mails. Why don't you check them?") fall into this category. More sophisticated approaches rely on practically human-like persuasive messages to convey information to a target user or even induce him / her to pursue determined goals. Commerce sites such as Amazon[1] or gaming / lottery sites such as Iwin[2] typically recur to such techniques. Persuasion through praise slightly capitalizes on psychology and seduction to motivate the target person: by emphasizing the positive aspects of a performance (e.g. messages such as "good job!", "congratulations!"), the user is able to feel more confident in him / herself. Fogg supports this approach by presenting a study in which users were confronted with this type of messages. The results show that they felt empowered, had more confidence in their capabilities and generally felt better about themselves. King [19] discusses yet another persuasive approach named "the environment of discovery", which effectively empowers users by giving them rewards [13] according to their performance, behavior or as a mere stimulant for the persuasive process. This approach is relevant to our research, since videogames are known to sport different types of rewards (persistent or temporary) to entice players to perform better or explore the game using different strategies.

3.1 Persuasion in Videogames

Persuasive technology has not been thoroughly explored and researched in commercially available videogames. The lack of a clear physical or cognitive improvement driving force behind this type of entertainment may be a decisive factor for this scarcity. Nevertheless, there are still many opportunities and challenges which may influence the design of such mechanisms for this and other areas. In fact, games have historically recurred to PT to motivate players. Scoreboards (e.g. Dead Nation[3]),

---

[1] http://www.amazon.com
[2] http://www.iwin.com
[3] http://uk.playstation.com/psn/games/detail/item228392/
Dead-Nation™/

presentation of informative messages (e.g. Guitar Hero[4]), conveyance of praise messages (e.g. Unreal Tournament[5]), use of achievement lists (e.g. World of Warcraft[6]) or the inclusion of temporary reward mechanics (e.g. Super Mario[7]) are but a few of the mechanisms used in modern videogames. If we analyze these approaches closely we can identify a parallel between these mechanics and the PT strategies proposed by both Fogg [10] and King [19]. However, what are the effects of these disruptive PT mechanisms on a player from both a physiological standpoint and a performance perspective? Is there a relation between player performance, his / her physiological state and the employed PT mechanism? Unfortunately, research regarding this issue is practically non-existent. Following these questions, Adar [1] also suggests deception may have an important role to play in application design, effectively helping users to achieve better results. This line of thought was not, unfortunately, supported by appropriate empirical evidence, leaving a research opportunity to assess whether deceptive persuasive mechanisms are able to boost a player's performance within a game.

Persuasive technology has not only been paired with commercially available videogames. Serious games – ludic applications which aim at raising awareness for particular issues, and are often related with well-being promotion, healthy habits or exercising – are a popular way to achieve this goal. These applications typically adopt the Persuasive Systems Design (PSD) model, ensuring designers are conscious about the idiosyncrasies of both target domain and target demographic. Examples such as MoviPill [25], Molarcropolis [27] and Playful Bottle [2] testify the importance of applications for improving medicice in-take compliance, oral hygiene and water saving, respectively. These examples, while successful in their own way, rely on long intervention periods, attempting to alter the target user's behavior over that time frame. This type of games rarely combines continuous and disruptive persuasion, thus covering research regarding the first type of persuasion (continuous) but leaving any existing opportunities and challenges concerning the latter open.

4   Research Questions

With this research we seek to enrich the HCI, persuasive and videogame research communities, broadening existing knowledge and empirical evidence about the effects of PT on players. Particularly we want to address if any changes are produced on the player physiological state and on the performance within the game. To drive current literature even further we question whether players are able to feel motivated through reinforcements whether the latter is effectively delivered to them or not. The following are the research questions for this work:

- **RQ1:** can different types of PT effectively regulate (e.g. increase or decrease) a player's physiological signals while playing a videogame?

---

[4] http://hub.guitarhero.com/
[5] http://www.unrealtournament.com/
[6] http://eu.battle.net/wow
[7] http://mario.nintendo.com/

- **RQ2:** are different types of PT able to induce a player to improve or decrease their performance within a videogame?
- **RQ3:** do players react in the same way (physiological and performance perspective) to the existence of rewards regardless of these being delivered to them or not (deceptive persuasive elements)?

5 Experimental Games

Two games were developed to support our research: a casual game capitalizing on "Whack-a-Mole" gameplay mechanics called Ctrl-Mole-Del and an arcade racing game entitled Wrong Lane Chase.

5.1 Ctrl-Mole-Del

The first game developed within the context of this work was Ctrl-Mole-Del (Fig. 1) for Windows Mobile platforms. This is a simplistic game which has Whack-a-Mole (Aaron Fechter, Creating Engineering, Inc. 1971) as its main inspiration.

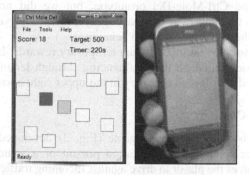

Fig. 1. Ctrl-Mole-Del's interface

The goal of the game is to interrupt an invasion of moles in an open field – the gaming area is typically populated by various holes from which the moles emerge for a brief period of time. The players need to hit them using a plastic tool (arcade version) or clicking / tapping over the mole (in recent versions).

Rules. Players are rewarded for hitting active moles and are penalized for missing to hit the moles or idling (i.e. not taking any action for several seconds). The intent of these design options is to keep the users interested in the game. Table 1 contains a summary of the scoring rules for the game. Moles appear at random intervals, with a 1.5 to 3 seconds interval between each other. Once they spawn, the player has approximately 1 second to hit them before they disappear. Each game lasts until the player earns 500 points or for a maximum of 4 minutes. To interact with the game players are able to tap the screen to hit the targets. Each time the game is executed, the locations of the targets is randomly chosen, in order to avoid training bias.

Table 1. Ctrl-Mole-Del's actions and score modifiers

Action	Score Modifier
Successfully hit a target	2 points
Failing to hit a target	-1 point
Idling	-1 point per second after 3 seconds without taking any action

Experimental Prototypes and Persuasive Mechanisms. In order to assess the different types of reinforcements we detailed in the previous sections we developed four different Ctrl-Mole-Del prototypes:

- **First prototype** – consists in the basic version of the game, stripped of any PT mechanics. Targets are highlighted using a yellow tint and the player must hit them while the target is lit.
- **Second prototype** – comprises a reinforcement mechanic which consisted in extending the time available to earn 500 points in 7 seconds. The reinforcement appears at random time intervals and is represented by a teal colored target.
- **Third prototype** – the third prototype was created with the intent of assessing the deceitful reward mechanic. We mimicked all features present in the second Ctrl-Mole-Del prototype, but we did not award any time extension to the player. In summary, players still observe the rewards, they can collect them, but they have no behaviour.
- **Fourth prototype** – stripped of any temporary rewards. Instead, we adhered to an approach based on the "influencing through language" PT paradigm and displayed the player's accuracy in the upper right corner of the screen.

5.2 Wrong Lane Chase

Wrong Lane Chase is an arcade racing game (Fig. 2) developed for Windows PC platforms. The player controls a police car in pursuit of a vehicle driven by bank robbers. The chase forces the player to drive against incoming traffic on a busy highway with 4 lanes. While doing so, the player must also retrieve gold coins being dropped by the robbers. After collecting enough coins, the player enters a final confrontation

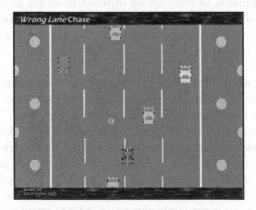

Fig. 2. Wrong Lane Chase's interface

to stop the robbers, having to shoot their vehicle until they pull over while dodging spike strips spawned by the fugitives.

Rules. Wrong Lane Chase is a two phase game: during the first, the player needs to avoid incoming traffic and collect gold coins; during the second phase, the player is required to pull over the robbers' vehicle by shooting it, while avoiding spike strips spawned by the enemy. Table 2 presents the score policies for phase 1 and phase 2.

Table 2. Wrong Lane Chase's scoring policy

Action	Score Modifier
Collect gold coin	200 points
Hit incoming obstacle	-40 points
Avoid an incoming obstacle	2 points
Bullet hit	10 points
Avoid 40 obstacles in a row	100 points

On both phases, obstacles are generated at random positions within the highway and at random intervals. Players control their police vehicle with the keyboard's arrow keys during both phase 1 and phase 2. A new command is introduced in phase 2 – shooting a bullet – which is triggered by pressing the Z key. The full list of controls is available in Table 3.

Table 3. Wrong Lane Chase control scheme

Command	Action
Press ↑ key	Moves police car up
Press ↓ key	Moves police car down
Press ← key	Moves police car to the left
Press → key	Moves police car to the right
Press 'Z' key	Shoots a bullet (phase 2 only)

Experimental Prototypes and Persuasive Mechanisms. Four Wrong-Lane-Chase prototypes were developed to test the different types of reinforcements:

- **First prototype** – contains a basic version of the game deprived of any PT.
- **Second prototype** – encompasses a real reinforcement which temporarily decreases the speed of incoming obstacles. The reinforcement appears on the game as a green bubble containing the letter 'B'. Note that for the sake of realism, both the obstacles and the background scenery are slowed down.
- **Third prototype** – contemplates a deceitful reinforcement mechanic. Upon picking this reinforcement, only the background scenery slows down, while the obstacles maintain their normal speed. In sum, again, no reward is provided for the player in the third prototype.
- **Fourth prototype** – employs a set of feedback messages which are displayed when the player attains a certain achievement (e.g. "You avoided 40 obstacles in a row", "You earned 2000 points", etc.), reminiscent of the persuasion through praise approach.

6   Experiment

We designed two experimental periods which aimed at testing the PT features present in both games. Each experimental period encompassed 30 subjects.

6.1   Users

A total of 60 individuals (50 male, 10 female; M=27.5; SD = 8.3) participated on both experimental periods. 30 subjects were recruited for our first experimental period with Ctrl-Mole-Del, while the remaining 30 participants were recruited for Wrong Lane Chase's experiment. No significant age differences were found between the two groups. A quick profiling interview revealed that over 95% of the subjects played videogames with some regularity and all of them were proficient and daily users of computers and modern smart-phones.

6.2   Metrics

We chose the following metrics for both experimental periods:

- **Average Heartbeat Rate (HBR)** – this metric is capable of quickly reflecting changes due to stress or anxiety [23][26].
- **Score** – score policies are described in the previous section. They are relevant to include as a game performance metric in both experimental periods.
- **Average Obstacle Avoidance Streak** – an obstacle pass streak corresponds to the number of obstacles a player is able to avoid in a row without colliding with them. This metric represents the average obstacle pass streak for a given player. This only pertains to Wrong Lane Chase.

6.3   Procedure

Both experimental periods were comprised by a pre-task and a set of tasks pertaining to each one of Ctrl-Mole-Del and Wrong Lane Chase prototypes. Each task lasted for roughly 4 to 5 minutes. The following tasks are coincident for both experiments, allowing users to interact with the basic version of each game and improved versions encompassing the addition of the reinforcements described in previous sections:

- **Pre-Task** – during this period, players had a one minute trial to get acquainted with either Ctrl-Mole-Del's or Wrong Lane Chase's controls (using each game's first prototype). We also took this opportunity to obtain a quick profile about the subject's proficiency with technology and videogames.
- **Task 1** – participants interacted with the first prototype of either Ctrl-Mole-Del or Wrong Lane Chase. We used this task to establish the baseline for the users' physiological signals.
- **Task 2** – for this task, participants were confronted with the second prototype of the game they were assigned to. As a reminder, the second

prototype encompassed a time extension reinforcement mechanic for Ctrl-Mole-Del and a temporary obstacle slow-down mechanism for Wrong Lane Chase.

- **Task 3** – here, participants had to interact with the third prototype of the game assigned to them (the deceitful version of the reward). For Ctrl-Mole-Del, players were informed about a time extension of 3 seconds if they successfully hit the bonus, while in reality no added time was given to them. In Wrong Lane Chase, the game simulated the obstacle delay by employing a visual technique which decreased the speed of the background scenery (akin to what happens in the real version of the incentive). In any variant, participants were not informed about the existence of a deceitful mechanic.

- **Task 4** – in this task participants played the fourth prototype of either Ctrl-Mole-Del or Wrong Lane Chase. This prototype presented some sort of feedback to users during gameplay period: the player's accuracy in Ctrl-Mole-Del and praise messages for certain feats in Wrong Lane Chase.

- **Post-Task** – during this debriefing period, we disclosed all of the experiment's details to the subjects, while simultaneously asking them to comment on any play-style options they assumed during each task.

Task order was randomly assigned to each subject. In our experimental design we assured there was a balanced distribution in the task order to eliminate any task order related bias. Participants were in stationary settings sitting in a chair on a well-lit room interacting with the different games (even though Ctrl-Mole-Del was played on a mobile device). Scoring policies were disclosed to players with one exception: in Wrong Lane Chase they were not informed that avoiding a certain number of obstacles in a row awarded more points. Subjects were only informed about the purpose of the experiment at the end. For Ctrl-Mole-Del's experimental period, subjects were handed a Windows Mobile phone (HTC HD2), previously loaded with the 4 prototypes for that game. For Wrong Lane Chase's experiment, participants had access to a Sony VAIO VPCS13S9E laptop model connected to a Dell 27'' 2709W monitor. In both settings, an AliveTec Heart Monitor[8] sensor, previously prepared with electro-gel for better signal acquisition was used to retrieve heartbeat rate data. Sensors were placed approximately 5cm apart over the heart's location on the subject's chest.

6.4 Results

In our result analysis we employed a set of Friedman tests (data was not normally distributed) accompanied by signed-rank Wilcoxon post-hoc tests to identify which tasks yielded statistically significant results. The presented results account for a Bonferroni correction to eliminate type-I errors.

Ctrl-Mole-Del. Table 4 and Fig. 3 present the results for Ctrl-Mole-Del's trial. We found statistically significant differences between tasks for the HBR metric ($\chi2 = 26.46$; $p < 0.001$) and for the score metric ($\chi2 = 52.41$; $p < 0.001$), leading us to assess which ones yielded those results.

---

[8] AliveTec: http://www.alivetec.com/products.htm

Table 4. Ctrl-Mole-Del's results

		Task 1	Task 2	Task 3	Task 4
HBR	M	99.92	85.02	86.88	93.3
	SD	20.23	15.08	14.18	20.3
Score	M	299	350.12	339.53	297.63
	SD	57.26	32.41	46.88	48.98

In what concerns the average HBR, players presented a significantly lower HBR when comparing Task 2 (Z = -4.14; p < 0.001), Task 3 (Z = -4.23; p < 0.001) and Task 4 (Z = -3.54; p < 0.001) to Task 1. No statistically significant differences were found when comparing Task 2 to Task 3 (Z = -1.73; p = 0.082).

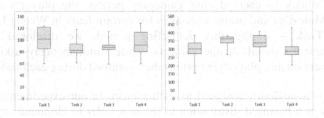

Fig. 3. Ctrl-Mole-Del's box plots for HBR (left) and score (right)

Score results show that the only statistically significant results emerged from the comparison between Task 1 and Task 2 (Z = -4.55; p < 0.001) and Task 1 and Task 3 (Z = -3.04; p = 0.002). The tasks which involved PT based on a real reward (Task 2) and on a deceitful reward (Task 3) did not present any statistically significant differences between them (Z = -1.36; p = 0.171).

Wrong Lane Chase. Table 5 and Fig. 4 present the results for the participants' average HBR, score and obstacle avoidance streak for the 4 tasks of Wrong Lane Chase, respectively. The Friedman test for the HBR metric indicated there were statistically significant differences across tasks (χ^2 = 36.92; p < 0.001). The same happened to the score metric (χ^2 = 50.04; p < 0.001) and the average number of obstacles avoided in a row (χ^2 = 42.19; p < 0.001).

Table 5. Wrong Lane Chase's results

		Task 1	Task 2	Task 3	Task 4
HBR	M	83.98	80.17	79.2	79.38
	SD	11.33	10.6	11.13	10.54
Score	M	4262.86	4628.6	4535.9	5259.33
	SD	827.21	728.6	774.48	1333.31
Obstacle Avoidance Streak	M	68.53	81.93	82.9	134.86
	SD	22.44	26.39	25.6	24.1

A deeper analysis showed that the differences between Task 1 and Task 2 (Z = - 4.78; p < 0.001), Task 1 and Task 3 (Z = -4-43; p < 0.001) and Task 1 and Task 4 (Z = -3.78; p < 0.001) yielded statistically significant differences. No statistically significant differences were found between Task 2 and Task 3 (Z = -0.89; p = 0.371).

We also found statistical significance when addressing the score metric (χ^2 = 50.04; p < 0.001). Players displayed significantly better performances when confronted with a real reward when compared to Task 1 (Z = -4.20; p < 0.001); similarly, they also reacted positively in terms of performance when confronted with the deceitful reward mechanic (Z = -3.15; p = 0.002). Here we need to emphasize the lack of statistical significance when comparing Task 2 to Task 3 (Z = -0.83; p = 0.405).

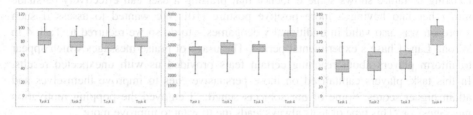

Fig. 4. Wrong Lane Chase's box plots for HBR (left), score (middle) and average obstacle avoidance streak (right)

The results for the average obstacle avoidance streak (χ^2 = 42.19; p < 0.001) again forced us to carry out a full comparative analysis between all tasks. Players presented significantly higher avoidance streaks when comparing Task 2 (Z = -1.99; p = 0.046), Task 3 (Z = -2.55; p = 0.011) or Task 4 to Task 1 (Z = -4.72; p < 0.001). Task 4 also presented significantly higher streaks than any other task.

7   Discussion

The discussion of the obtained results tackles a few fronts: how different types of PT affect players, the potential of deception as a persuasive mechanism and the challenges behind this strategy.

7.1   Persistent Persuasive Messages

In Ctrl-Mole-Del's experiment we assessed whether the display of informative data regarding the player performance (respecting Fogg's influence through language approach) was able to produce any significant changes in a player's physiological traits and / or performance. Our experiment is not entirely conclusive regarding this particular type of PT applied to videogames. While players did present significantly lower average HBR values when confronted with this PT, there were no significant differences concerning their score performance. Are we able to state that influencing through language may not be a valid PT approach? We disagree. In fact, we believe there are two justifications for our results: our feedback design approach was not the most adequate and was ignored by most users; or the game genre was too fast paced for them to momentarily peek at the feedback area. Judging by some of the user feedback we obtained from the debriefing period, we have to abide that it was a mix of the two which caused the players to completely ignore the language based PT used for Ctrl-Mole-Del: "I was so focused on hitting the targets, I completely forgot about my accuracy"; "I noticed how much time I had left in the beginning, but then I just wanted to play the game and score the highest possible". Can we already answer any of our research questions? Not entirely, but these results partially support RQ1.

7.2   Praise the Player

Existing literature shows some evidence that praising a user can effectively persuade him / her into having a more positive posture [10]. We wanted to assess if such approach was also valid in traditional videogames – to do so we recurred to Task 4 in Wrong Lane Chase's experimental period. The usage of praise messages which appear to inform players about reaching certain feats provided us with unexpected results. In this task, players capitalized on those persuasive cues to improve themselves and attain higher scores. Some of our subjects stated: "I enjoyed the popping motivation messages" or "This type of feats always leads me to want to improve more".

Results for Task 4 are straightforward: not only players had a lower average heartbeat rate throughout the test, they also had a significantly higher score and, more importantly, presented longer obstacle avoidance streaks. The first remark can be linked with a tenuous relaxation due to the praise effect. Taking into account existing literature on flow in videogames and that "players should be warned about the outcome of their actions" [5][28], it is natural that showing this type of information relieves the players of some stress. The higher score, on the other hand, is a direct consequence of a behaviour shift and compliance with the PT in play. Like previously mentioned, players were not informed that avoiding a certain number of obstacles in a row awarded them with extra points. As such, they did not feel the obligation to pursue this feat in other tasks due to the lack of an obvious reward. However, we witnessed that players often preferred to skip a gold coin to avoid an incoming obstacle than collecting all coins as fast as possible. Such behavioural change resulted in them attaining multiple avoidance streaks which ultimately awarded them with even more points. In summary, displaying these praise messages was a catalyst to the creation of a sub-game or a secondary objective which, in a vast number of cases, replaced the main goal of Wrong Lane Chase. Based on these results, we argue that the display of praise sentences regarding feats is able to not only prompt users to pursue different ways of playing the same game, but also to excel and overcome their own limits as players. In light of these results and on the previous ones (regarding persistent persuasive messages) we can point that RQ1 and RQ2 have been answered positively.

7.3   Temporary Reinforcements as Motivators

Existing literature on rewards in videogames summarize the utilization of reinforcements in the following fashion: "players should be rewarded when they achieve a certain milestone" [28]. Although we agree with this sentence and it holds true for a diversity of games, there are numerous cases in which players are able to benefit from temporary reinforcement mechanics which are not related with any accomplishment at all. Developers populate games with multiple ephemeral rewards which, although not game-breaking, can alter the player's abilities in order to introduce brief changes in gameplay. Compared to the stripped versions of Ctrl-Mole-Del and Wrong Lane Chase, the addition of reinforcements produced less physiological strain on our subjects. Furthermore, their scores were higher on both games. Although this performance assessment may seem minimalistic, having into account we are merely analysing one metric, we stay true to our arguments and experimental design, which both capitalize on the usage of two different games, in distinct genres. Also, the analyzed rewards are completely different from each other, reinforcing the importance of the empirical evidence here discussed. Overall, we are able to confirm King's view on rewards as PT and conclude that their usage is capable of providing players with a sense of reinforcement, actively aiding them in performing better than with the absence of these mechanisms.

Deceitful Persuasion Technology. The most interesting contribution of this work concerns the analysis of whether reinforcement's persuasive nature was strong enough for players to perform better, despite no actual change taking place in the game. Results indicate that our subjects, indeed, had a significant higher performance in the presence of such persuasive mechanisms. Their average HBR decreased, hinting at a possible relaxation effect. To conclude, we have to emphasize the importance of not having statistically significant differences between the tasks in which real reinforcements were offered (Task 2 for both experiments) and the tasks where deceitful reinforcements were provided (Task 3) – this means that the physiological and performance effects of these incentives can be independent of whether a real reward is offered or not. We also found a negative correlation (Spearman's Rank Order ($\rho s=-0.49$; $p=0.006$) between the players' average heartbeat rate and average number of obstacles avoided in Wrong Lane Chase's Task 2 (presence of a real reward) and a positive correlation between the players' heart rate variance (the standard variation of their heartbeat rate over time) and the average number of obstacles they avoided in Task 3 ($\rho s=0.53$; $p=0.003$). These correlations support and answer RQ3 as we found two relations between physiological and performance metrics supporting both the real and deceitful rewards we addressed. Furthermore, they are in line with Adar's [1] theoretical essay on benevolent deception.

Ethics. A final question can be asked regarding deceitful PT: is it ethically acceptable? We defend that these are acceptable mechanics for games. Provided the deceitful rewards are carefully designed to avoid easily identifying them, our results show that these have a similar persuasive / motivational effect as real rewards. Of course, the identification of a deceitful persuasive element by a player might alienate him / her and provoke a feeling of distrust towards the game or the developer. However, this is a design exercise which falls outside the scope of our research and competence.

8   Conclusion and Future Work

Our main conclusions point that PT can act as a physiological regulator, allowing players to present more relaxed states depending on the type of PT employed, answering our first research question. User performance can also be significantly affected by the PT approach used in a videogame, thus providing the support to answer our second research question. In this case, praise messages and reward provision displayed different impacts on how they changed a player's performance. Nevertheless, this experiment's breakthrough was the analysis of whether the knowledge of the existence of rewards was a strong enough persuasive cue to influence players regardless of that reward actually changing anything within the game. Results showed no statistically significant differences regarding the players' physiological reactions as well as their performance shifts. This introduces a new type of PT which can be applied to videogames and this provides enough evidence to answer our final research question.

In the future we want to explore scenarios of application for deceitful persuasive mechanics. In particular, we want to address some of the questions we left unanswered in this article such as whether the deceitful persuasive element derived changes decay with experience and what is the best design strategy to seamlessly transit from a deceitful reward mechanic towards a real one.

Acknowledgements. This work was funded by FCT, through Individual Scholarship SFRH / BD / 39496 / 2007, through project PTDC/EIA-EIA/117058/2010 and the Multiannual Funding Programme.

References

1. Adar, E., Tan, D.S., Teevan, J.: Benevolent deception in human computer interaction. In: Proceedings of the 2013 ACM Annual Conference on Human Factors in Computing systems (CHI 2013), pp. 1863–1872. ACM, New York (2013)
2. Chiu, M.-C., Chang, S.-P., Chang, Y.-C., Chu, H.-H., Chen, C.C.-H., Hsiao, F.-H., Ko, J.-C.: Playful bottle: A mobile social persuasion system to motivate healthy water intake. In: Proceedings of the 11th International Conference on Ubiquitous Computing (Ubicomp 2009), pp. 185–194. ACM, New York (2009)
3. Chumbley, J., et al.: Affect and the computer game player: the effect of gender, personality, and game reinforcement structure on affective responses to computer game-play. CyberPsychology & Behavior 9(3), 308–316 (2006)
4. Cowley, B., Charles, D., Black, M., Hickey, R.: Toward an understanding of flow in video games. Comput. Entertain. 6(2), Article 20, 27 pages (2008)
5. Csíkszentmihályi, M.: Flow: The Psychology of Optimal Experience. Harper & Row (1990)
6. Deterding, S., Dixon, D., Khaled, R., Nacke, L.: From game design elements to gamefulness: Defining "gamification". In: Proceedings of the 15th International Academic MindTrek Conference: Envisioning Future Media Environments (MindTrek 2011), pp. 9–15. ACM, New York (2011)

7. Deterding, S., Sicart, M., Nacke, L., O'Hara, K., Dixon, D.: Gamification. Using game-design elements in non-gaming contexts. In: CHI 2011 Extended Abstracts on Human Factors in Computing Systems, pp. 2425–2428. ACM, New York (2011)
8. Eslambolchilar, P., Wilson, M.L., Komninos, A.: Nudge & influence through mobile devices. In: Proceedings of the 12th International Conference on Human Computer Interaction with Mobile Devices and Services, pp. 527–530. ACM, New York (2010)
9. Factbox: A look at the $65 billion video games industry. Reuters (June 6, 2011) (July 17, 2011) (retrieved)
10. Fogg, B.J.: Persuasive technology: Using computers to change what we think and do. Ubiquity (December 2002)
11. Gouaïch, A., Hocine, N., Dokkum, L.V., Mottetp, D.: Digital-pheromone based difficulty adaptation in post-stroke therapeutic games. In: Proceedings of the 2nd ACM SIGHIT International Health Informatics Symposium (IHI 2012), pp. 5–12. ACM, New York (2012)
12. Hackbarth, G., et al.: Computer playfulness and anxiety: Positive and negative mediators of the system experience effect on perceived ease of use. Information & Management 40, 221–232 (2003)
13. Hopson, J.: Behavioral Game Design. GamaSutra Featured Articles, http://www.gamasutra.com/view/feature/3085/behavioral_game_design.php
14. Huotari, K., Hamari, J.: Defining gamification: A service marketing perspective. In: Proceeding of the 16th International Academic MindTrek Conference (MindTrek 2012), pp. 17–22. ACM, New York (2012)
15. Jensen, K.L., Krishnasamy, R., Selvadurai, V.: Studying PH. A. N. T. O. M. in the wild: A pervasive persuasive game for daily physical activity. In: Proceedings of the 22nd Conference of the Computer-Human Interaction Special Interest Group of Australia on Computer-Human Interaction (OZCHI 2010), pp. 17–20. ACM, New York (2010)
16. Jianu, R., Laidlaw, D.: An evaluation of how small user interface changes can improve scientists' analytic strategies. In: Proceedings of the 2012 ACM Annual Conference on Human Factors in Computing Systems (CHI 2012), pp. 2953–2962. ACM, NY (2012)
17. Jung, Y., Li, K.J., Janissa, N.S., Gladys, W.L.C., Lee, K.M.: Games for a better life: Effects of playing Wii games on the well-being of seniors in a long-term care facility. In: Proceedings of the Sixth Australasian Conference on Interactive Entertainment (IE 2009). ACM, New York (2009)
18. Kalnikaite, V., Rogers, Y., Bird, J., Villar, N., Bachour, K., Payne, S., Todd, P.M., Schöning, J., Krüger, A., Kreitmayer, S.: How to nudge in Situ: Designing lambent devices to deliver salient information in supermarkets. In: Proceedings of the 13th International Conference on Ubiquitous Computing (UbiComp 2011), pp. 11–20. ACM, New York (2011)
19. King, P., Tester, J.: The landscape of persuasive technologies. Communications of ACM 42(5), 31–38 (1999)
20. Kultima, A., Stenros, J.: Designing games for everyone: The expanded game experience model. In: Proceedings of the International Academic Conference on the Future of Game Design and Technology (Futureplay 2010), pp. 66–73 (2010)
21. Loumidi, A.K., Mittag, S., Lathrop, W.B., Althoff, F.: Eco-driving incentives in the North American market. In: Kranz, M., Weinberg, G., Meschtscherjakov, A., Murer, M., Wilfinger, D. (eds.) Proceedings of the 3rd International Conference on Automotive User Interfaces and Interactive Vehicular Applications (AutomotiveUI 2011), pp. 185–192. ACM, New York (2011)

22. Mahmud, A.A., Mubin, O., Shahid, S., Juola, J.F., de Ruyter, B.: EZ phone: Persuading mobile users to conserve energy. In: Proceedings of the 22nd British HCI Group Annual Conference on People and Computers: Culture, Creativity, Interaction (BCS-HCI 2008), vol. 2, pp. 7–10. British Computer Society, Swinton (2008)

23. Nacke, L.E., Kalyn, M., Lough, C., Mandryk, R.L.: Biofeedback game design: Using direct and indirect physiological control to enhance game interaction. In: Proceedings of the SIGCHI Conference on Human Factors in Computing Systems (CHI 2011), pp. 103–112 (2011)

24. Oinas-Kukkonen, H., Harjumaa, M.: Persuasive Systems Design: Key Issues, Process Model, and System Features. The Communications of the Association for Information Systems (2009)

25. de Oliveira, R., Cherubini, M., Oliver, N.: MoviPill: Improving medication compliance for elders using a mobile persuasive social game. In: Proceedings of the 12th ACM International Conference on Ubiquitous Computing (Ubicomp 2010), pp. 251–260. ACM, New York (2010)

26. Rowe, D., et al.: Heart Rate Variability: Indicator of user state as an aid to human-computer interaction. In: Procs. of CHI 1998, pp. 480–487 (1998)

27. Soler, C., Zacarías, A., Lucero, A.: Molarcropolis: A mobile persuasive game to raise oral health and dental hygiene awareness. In: Proceedings of the International Conference on Advances in Computer Enterntainment Technology (ACE 2009), pp. 388–391. ACM, New York (2009)

28. Sweetser, P., Johnson, D., Wyeth, P., Ozdowska, A.: GameFlow heuristics for designing and evaluating real-time strategy games. In: Proceedings of the 8th Australasian Conference on Interactive Entertainment: Playing the System (IE 2012), Article 1, 10 pages. ACM, New York (2012)

29. Yim, J., Nicholas Graham, T.C.: Using games to increase exercise motivation. In: Proceedings of the 2007 Conference on Future Play (Future Play 2007), pp. 166–173 (2007)

Evaluating Human-like Behaviors of Video-Game Agents Autonomously Acquired with Biological Constraints

Nobuto Fujii, Yuichi Sato, Hironori Wakama, Koji Kazai,
and Haruhiro Katayose

Graduate School of Science and Technology, Kwansei Gakuin University
2-1 Gakuen, Sanda, Hyogo, Japan
Research Fellow of Japan Society for the Promotion of Science
{nobuto,kazai,katayose}@kwansei.ac.jp

Abstract. Designing the behavioral patterns of video game agents
(Non-player character: NPC) is a crucial aspect in developing video games.
While various systems that have aimed at automatically acquiring behavioral patterns have been proposed and some have successfully obtained
stronger patterns than human players, those patterns have looked mechanical. When human players play video games together with NPCs as
their opponents/supporters, NPCs' behavioral patterns have not only to
be strong but also to be human-like. We propose the autonomous acquisition of NPCs' behaviors, which emulate the behaviors of human players. Instead of implementing straightforward heuristics, the behaviors are
acquired using techniques of reinforcement learning with Q-Learning and
pathfinding through an A* algorithm, where *biological constraints* are imposed. Human-like behaviors that imply human cognitive processes were
obtained by imposing *sensory error, perceptual and motion delay, physical fatigue*, and *balancing between repetition and novelty* as the biological constraints in computational simulations using "Infinite Mario Bros.".
We evaluated human-like behavioral patterns through subjective assessments, and discuss the possibility of implementing the proposed system.

Keywords: Autonomously strategy acquisition, Machine learning,
Biological constraints, Video game agent, Infinite Mario Bros.

1 Introduction

Video games, from the human players' partners/opponents perspective, are divided into two types: those where another human player controls the partner/opponent, and where the *video game agent (NPC)* does so. For the latter,
game programmers have elaborately programmed the NPCs' "behavior" and
"strategy" using the cut-and-trial approach, as those simulate human players'
approaches. Because of designing good degree of difficulty into video games,
programmers are obliged to engage in extremely complicated and difficult tasks.
Therefore, an automated method called "procedural technology" has received

D. Reidsma, H. Katayose, and A. Nijholt (Eds.): ACE 2013, LNCS 8253, pp. 61–76, 2013.

attention as a method to lower the programmers' burden. Introducing machine learning techniques and pathfinding techniques is a promising and rational way to automate designing the NPCs' behavior and strategy[13,4] .

The "Mario AI Competition" [6] and "world computer-*shogi* championship" have been held every year to incubate new computer algorithms to attain "behaviors" and "strategies," where first prize is awarded to the best (strongest) automatic computer algorithm. The highly ranked champion [13] of the "Mario AI Competition" is an extremely strong algorithm. The strongest computer-*shogi* engine [4] first defeated top-level professional *shogi* players in April 2013. Probably, all human players will not be able to win these games within the next ten years. However the behaviors of the best algorithms look extraordinarily mechanical. It is thus crucial to design NPCs that make players feel like they are playing with a human player. More importance is being attached to develop human-like NPCs that make human players enjoy. It is more difficult to make human-like NPCs than strong ones, because subjective criteria should be accessed to attain this goal. We must determine other tactics, i.e., achieving human-like "behaviors," with as few required exhaustive heuristics as possible.

This study proposed a system that autonomously acquires NPCs' "behaviors" and "strategies," thus making players feel like they are playing with a human player, instead of implementing straightforward heuristics. We framed a hypothesis that "biological constraints" were the origins of "behaviors" that give the impression of being human in their appearance [5]. Here, we describe how human-like behaviors emerge based on machine learning techniques and pathfinding techniques, where "biological constraints" are imposed, i.e., *sensory error, perceptual and motion delay, physical fatigue,* and *balancing between repetition and novelty.* In our previous study, we confirmed that our system could acquire human-like behaviors by Q-learning techniques with biological constraints[1]. In this paper, we introduce biological constraints to path finding techniques in addition to Q-learning techniques. Furthermore, we carried out a subjective assessment to examine human-like behavioral patterns that the agents obtained.

The remainder of this paper is organized as follows. Section 2 introduces previous work related to our study and Section 3 defines "biological constraints". Section 4 presents a system overview and Section 5 examines human-like behavioral patterns through subjective assessments. Finally, we discuss the potential of our system in Section 6.

2   Related Work

We introduce previous work related to our study on the automatic acquisition of "behaviors" and "strategies." Development of strong algorithms have involved two approaches. The first has involved case-based (supervised) techniques, and the second has involved non-case-based (unsupervised) techniques. Supervised learning techniques are categorized into the former [3] and pathfinding [13] and reinforcement learning techniques [2] are categorized into the latter.

Supervised learning techniques are methods of inferring functions from supervised training data. The training data contain input data and the required output data from training examples. Supervised learning techniques extract useful rules by analyzing massive numbers of training data sets including play-logs and scores. Hoki proposed "Bonanza" for Computer-*shogi* [3] as a typical approach using supervised learning based on human play-logs. Hoki's Bonanza is a well-known computer-*shogi* algorithm, whose inference engine was based on the analysis of human play-logs. Many later computer-*shogi* engines [12,4] have applied the Bonanza method. Supervised learning techniques can effectively acquire behavioral patterns when we prepare enormous numbers of play-logs obtained from expert human players.

Pathfinding techniques find a least-cost path from a given initial node to one goal node on a game tree. Baumgarten implemented a video game agent based on the A* algorithm at the Mario AI Competition in 2009 as the typical approach using pathfinding technique and won the championship [13]. The Mario AI Competition [6] is a contest where algorithms compete for scores in "Infinite Mario Bros. ". "Infinite Mario Bros." is an action video game like traditional "Mario Bros.," whose goal is to obtain a high score during a time limit. (The specifications for "Infinite Mario Bros." are detailed in Section 4.3.) This system analyzes the information from Mario and his enemies, and Mario's actions are determined according to the optimum route calculated by pathfinding based on the A* algorithm. The video game agent implemented by the A* algorithm acquires optimum behavioral patterns. As these behavioral patterns are extraordinarily "mechanical," human players do not feel like they are playing with other human players.

Reinforcement learning techniques repeat trial and error processes using their own behaviors and obtain optimum behavioral patterns. Fujita and Ishii presented a strategy-acquisition system as the typical approach using reinforcement learning for the card game "Hearts" that could acquire a strategy using Q-learning in a multi-player game [2]. They encountered three difficulties in strategy-acquisition: 1) it required a large-scale state space because the game needed 52 cards, 2) it involved a partially observable situation because players could not see their opponent's cards, and 3) it was a multi-agent game designed for four players. They suggested four techniques of alleviating these difficulties: 1) a sampling method with a particle filter, 2) an action predictor to forecast their opponents' actions, 3) a value function to estimate the value of the current state, and 4) a feature extraction technique based on game features. They successfully acquired a stronger strategy than that by expert humans.

Human players of these games will not be able to win in the near future. Developing human-like NPCs are gaining importance in the field of game AI research [11,10]. We aimed at obtaining the behavioral patterns of NPCs as if a human player were playing a video game.

Schrum et al. examined autonomously acquiring human-like NPCs[10] at the 2K BotPrize and won the prize. In this competition, computer-controlled NPCs (bots) and human players played the FPS (First-person shooter) video game

"Unreal Tournament 2004", and the judges tried to guess which opponents are human. To win the prize, an NPC was required to be indistinguishable from human players. Schrum et al. heuristically determined the human-like behavioral patterns based on the database which stores the collected human players' play-logs, and they imposed these patterns as constraints to neural networks. Their NPC's behavioral patterns were judged more human-like than human players' ones in October 2012.

The above approach can acquire human-like behavioral patterns using programmer's heuristics, however the problem that programmers need to engage in extremely complicated tasks has not been resolved.

3   Biological Constraints

We framed a hypothesis that "biological constraints" were the origins of "behaviors" that give the impression of being human in their appearance. In this section, we explain the conception that we introduce "biological constraints" into our system, and we define the biological constraints based on it.

3.1   Importance to Impose Biological Constraints

Zajonc proposed the mere-exposure effect (familiarity principle) that is psychological phenomenon by which people tend to develop a preference for things merely because they are familiar with them. His experiments demonstrated that simply exposing subjects to a familiar stimulus led them to rate it more positively than other, similar stimuli which had not been presented[15]. This effect has been demonstrated with many kinds of things, paintings, pictures of faces, sounds, and so on. According to Zajonc, this effect is capable of taking place without conscious cognition, and that preferences need no inferences.

The mere-exposure effect must occurs to human players who play the video game. Human players tend to develop a preference for human-like behaviors because they expose own behaviors to themselves whenever they play the video game. Human-like NPCs should be introduced humans' physical limitations and the innate curiosity as biological constraints. Instead of implementing straightforward heuristics, we propose imposing "biological constraints" on the pathfinding technique (i.e. Baumgarten's A* algorithm [13]) and the reinforcement learning technique (i.e., Q-learning) in this study.

Strong NPCs' behaviors make human players feel uncomfortable because their mechanical behaviors have looked unfamiliar, e.g., their reactions are too fast, they are controlled by too precise key input and they always repeatedly perform same actions. In addition, NPCs' behaviors lack consistency when game programmers try to design good degree of difficulty, e.g., they become weak suddenly from the middle and they make unnatural mistakes. While human players play a video game with these NPCs, they suspect that the NPC intentionally fail to win. The unnaturalness of NPCs' behaviors becomes the factor that makes human players lose their motivation. NPCs with biological constraints may obtain consistent and irrational actions, e.g., hesitating to jump over an enemy, unsteady key input and deliberating the most optimum action.

Cabrera et al. conducted an psychological experimentation which subjects balance a vertical stick on a fingertip [5]. humans' physical limitations occur in this task, i.e., sensory error should occurs while they look at the tip of a vertical stick with a fixed gaze, response time for moving their arm and finger should be delayed and they should be tired from this task. Cabrera et al. verified that subjects will be able to consider these physical limitations consciously or unconsciously by training this task many times. Subjects will be able to handle own arm and finger by imposing some noises on them. They eventually cope with this task more safely and more efficiently.

Maslow proposed a theory in psychology "Maslow's hierarchy of needs[7]" based on his observations of humans' innate curiosity. Maslow used the terms "Physiological", "Safety", "Belongingness and Love", "Esteem" and "Self-Actualization" needs to describe the pattern that human motivations generally move through. These needs should satisfy humans' innate curiosity while human players play a video game, e.g., a training to acquire knowledge and a challenge to reduce tiresomeness.

3.2   Definition of Biological Constraints

Given the Cabrera's study and Maslow's hierarchy of needs we define the biological constraints as follows:

1. **"Sensory error"**
   As it is difficult for a human player to precisely recognize the position (coordinates) of an object, a sensory error is imposed on the observable objects' position. The video game agent can observe the position by applying Gaussian noise to the correct coordinates of the object.

2. **"Perceptual and motion delay"**
   "Perceptual and motion delay" means the time-lag between when a human player observes and recognizes the game situation and when he/she inputs keys. When the human player inputs keys, the observable game information becomes the situation in a past game. The video game agent can observe a game situation in several frames before the current frame.

3. **"Physical fatigue"**
   Inputting keys successively within a long time, as well as inputting keys repeatedly within a short time, makes human players tired. Therefore, the video game agent should obtain better scores with fewer key controls.

4. **"Balancing between repetition and novelty"**
   Human players often repeatedly train themselves with the same actions to habituate themselves, and eventually they become skillful players. When human players repeat failure with actions, they challenge themselves with novel actions to fend off boredom and failure. The video game agent should balance training and challenges like those engaged in by human players.

The three main advantages of our system for game programmers are that they can reduce development costs because they do not have to do extremely complicated and difficult tasks, they can provide these concepts intuitively in various game genres, and they can easily introduce these concepts to various techniques of strategy acquisition.

4   Framework under "Biological Constraints"

In this section, we explain how "biological constraints" are handled in Q-learning and A* algorithm. We adopted the action game "Infinite Mario Bros." as a target game, and our system acquires Mario's behavioral patterns in a learning framework on which "biological constraints" are imposed.

4.1   Imposing "Biological Constraints" on Q-Learning

Although training data sets on learning phases are necessary to implement our system, there were no supervisors in the video games, e.g., play-logs of human players. We thus adopted Q-learning and A* algorithm as techniques of acquiring strategies, because supervisors are unnecessary with these techniques.

Q-learning[14] works by learning an action-value function. The highest Q-value means that the agent's action is effective in this game:

$$argmax_{a_t} Q(s_t, a_t) \qquad (1)$$

where t means the number of frames, s_t means the game state at frame t, and a_t means the agent's action at frame t. Here, $Q(s_t, a_t)$ means the evaluation value (i.e., Q-value) for an s_t and a_t pair. The action-value function updates the Q-value whenever an agent decides its own action in a game state:

$$Q(s_t, a_t) = (1 - \alpha)Q(s_t, a_t) + \alpha((r + \gamma max_p Q(s_{t+1}, p)) \qquad (2)$$

where, α is called the "learning rate," γ is called the "discount factor," and these parameters are constant between 0 and 1. Here, r means the acquired reward when the video game agent takes action a_t in game state s_t. The technique to select an action of the video game agent is an epsilon-greedy strategy. The best action is selected for probability $1 - \epsilon$ of the trials, and another action is randomly selected with uniform probability for probability ϵ. Game state s_t and action a_t are dimensions reduced by feature extractions in our system.

Our system imposes four "Biological constraints" on Q-learning. As "Sensory error," s_t is given Mario's and enemies' positions with Gaussian noise generated by various standard deviations when our system calculates $Q(s_t, a_t)$. As "Perceptual and motion delay," s_t is given the game state several frames before the current frame. As "Physical fatigue," r is given a negative reward which is calculated based on the number of key inputs. The details on reward r are described below. As "Balancing between repetition and novelty," if the agent repeatedly fails in certain game state s_t, our system sets higher random selection probability ϵ and the agent frequently starts challenge with novel actions. In contrast, if the agent never fails in certain game state s_t, our system sets lower probability ϵ and the agent repeatedly starts to train the same actions.

4.2   Imposing "Biological Constraints" on A* Algorithm

The A* algorithm is a well-known algorithm to find shortest paths.

$$f^*(n) = g^*(n) + h^*(n) \tag{3}$$

where, $f^*(n)$ denotes the estimated cost function of node n to determine the order in which the search algorithm visits nodes in the game tree, $f^*(n)$ is the sum of two functions: the estimated past path-cost function, $g^*(n)$, which is the known distance from the starting node to the current node, n, and the estimated future path-cost function, $h^*(n)$, which is a heuristic estimate of the distance from n to the goal.

Our system imposes "Biological constraints" on the A* algorithm as well as the Q-Learning. "Balancing between repetition and novelty" cannot be implemented on the A* algorithm because there are no learning phases in pathfinding techniques. As "Sensory error," it is given character's coordinates with Gaussian noise generated by various standard deviations when our system defines the starting node. As "Perceptual and motion delay," it is given character's coordinates several frames before the current frame. As "Physical fatigue," the video game agent imposes restrictions on the number of key inputs per second because it is impossible for a human player to press the key many times within a short period.

4.3   Specifications for Infinite Mario Bros.

A game with three factors is required for a target game: 1) the human player must control a character in real time in an environment in which "sensory error," "perceptual and motion delay," and "physical fatigue" occur, 2) the game situation can regenerate many times, and 3) programmers can set specific learning goals to acquire behavioral patterns.

We adopted the action game "Infinite Mario Bros." [6] as a target game in our study. Figure 1 has a screen capture of "Infinite Mario Bros." This game is based on Nintendo's well-known action game "Super Mario Bros.". The five specifications for "Infinite Mario Bros." are described below.

- **Level generator**
  Levels are generated infinitely to obey a given seed parameter.
- **Mario (agent control)**
  The video game agent can control Mario with key input (LEFT, RIGHT, DOWN, SPEED, and JUMP). Mario performs action depending on the key input every frame (24 fps).
- **Enemy characters**
  Several enemy characters appear on the screen, and they move individually. The video game agent must decide either to avoid or defeat them.
- **Game score**
  The video game agent obtains a score when Mario is dead or the play time reaches its time limit. An established evaluation function calculates the score using the arrival distance. Video game agents with higher scores are considered excellent.

- **Observable information for video game agent**

  The video game agent can observe game information, i.e., Mario's position, whether he is a "Small Mario" or a "Super Mario," the enemies' positions, and ground positions in the level. Ground positions consist of block positions located on the screen (there are 22 times 22 blocks). The video game agent can observe the situation in the game, and it can input the keys to control Mario's actions in every frame.

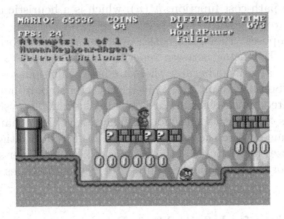

Fig. 1. Screen capture of "Infinite Mario Bros." This game emulates the well-known action game "Super Mario Bros" in a JAVA environment. Its game parameters are public.

4.4   Acquiring Behaviors for Infinite Mario Bros.

The video game agent must avoid as many enemies as possible and obtain higher scores by more quickly finishing longer levels.

Our Q-learning agent gives positive rewards for finishing levels and negative rewards for factors that prevent states from finishing, including damage and dying. The reward function is:

$$reward = distance + damaged + death + keyPress \qquad (4)$$

where, $distance$ indicates positive rewards calculated by the horizontal length where Mario advances with an action, $damaged$ denotes negative rewards where Mario is damaged by clashing with enemies in an action, and $death$ means negative rewards where Mario is dead after an action. Here, $keyPress$ means negative rewards when the agent has changed key control from a previous frame. The parameters used here are those adjusted based on preliminary experiments executed before this experiment, i.e., $damaged$ equals -50, $death$ equals -100, and $keyPress$ equals -5.0 in our system.

Our A* algorithm agent generates game tree and calculate path-cost by cost function. In Baumgarten's A* algorithm agent[13], $g^*(n)$ is given by the total time from the starting node to the current node n, and $h^*(n)$ is given by simulating the time required to reach the right border of the screen. For further details, refer to Baumgarten's study [13].

5   Subjective Assessments

In this section, we carried out a subjective assessment to examine human-like behavioral patterns that our system obtained. We must confirm that NPCs' behaviors make human players feel human-like and familiar by introducing humans' physical limitations and the innate curiosity as biological constraints.

5.1   Agents' Behavioral Patterns in Q-Learning and A* Algorithm

We compared an agent without "biological constraints" (i.e., delay was 0 frame, standard deviation was 0, and there was no physical fatigue) to an agent with them (i.e., delay was 3 frames, standard deviation was 4, and there was physical fatigue), and we evaluated differences in the behavioral patterns that the agents obtained. Each agent learned the behavioral patterns on a fixed level generated by the same seed parameter. Each learning trial was 50,000 games, and we sampled a trial when an agent could obtain the highest score in a learning phase. Learning rate α was 0.2, the discount factor γ was 0.9, and random selection probability ϵ for the epsilon-greedy strategy was 0.05 as the parameter settings for Q-learning.

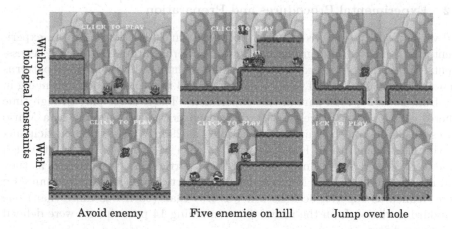

Avoid enemy   Five enemies on hill   Jump over hole

Fig. 2. Comparison of agent without biological constraints (top) and agent with them (bottom): when agent avoids untouchable enemy (left), when there are five enemies on hill (middle), and when agent jumps over a hole (right)

We carried out a preliminary experiment to evaluate the behavioral patterns that the agents obtained. Ten participants, i.e., eight men and two women, ranging in age from 20 to 26, took part in it. The results, in Figure 2 indicate differences in the tendencies of behavioral patterns.

When Mario avoids an untouchable enemy(Figure 2, left column)
- Mario without biological constraints (top) goes forward nonstop with a minimal jump.
- Mario with biological constraints (bottom) goes forward with a big jump and stops for a while.

When there are five enemies on hill(Figure 2, center column)
- Mario without biological constraints (top) finishes with precise action control because of reliable observable information.
- Mario with biological constraints (bottom) stops in front of a hill until he is safe.

When Mario jumps over hole(Figure 2, right column)
- Mario without biological constraints (top) jumps from the edge with a minimal jump.
- Mario with biological constraints (bottom) jumps short of a hole safely with a big jump.

An agent without biological constraints acquires behavioral patterns that only take performance into consideration, but an agent with them can acquire these by taking performance and safety into consideration. This computational simulation revealed that behavioral patterns were varied by imposing "biological constraints" in the reinforcement learning and the pathfinding techniques.

5.2   Experimental Procedures and Preparation

We verified our hypotheses that were proposed in Subsection 5.1 in an experiment. We evaluated human-like behavioral patterns through subjective assessments. We carried out an experiment to evaluate human-like behavioral patterns that the agents obtained. Twenty participants, 13 men and 7 women, ranging in age from 20 to 24, took part in this experiment. The average playthrough time where participants had previously experienced horizontal scrolling in a Mario series was 34 h, and the standard deviation was 29 h. We classified participants by the playthrough time. Four participants with less than 5 h of playthrough time were defined as beginners (three of these participants were novices as they had never experienced the Mario series.), two participants with more than 63 h were defined as experts, because 5 h was less than (63 h was more than) one standard deviation from the mean. The remaining 14 participants were defined as intermediates.

The experimental procedures in this subjective assessment were as follows. First, participants were instructed to play "Super Mario Bros." in 10 trials of 25 sec. They were also instructed to play safely, and to ignore coins, blocks, and items. Second, participants compared two videos played by a human or NPC, and answered questions in a seven-scale relative evaluation: "which Mario was human-like?" and "which Mario was skillful?". Finally, participants replied to questionnaires on one video played by a human or NPC: "What behavior made the Mario human-like?", "What behavior do you feel made Mario skillful?", and "Human or NPC, which controlled Mario in this video?".

Table 1 summarizes the eight videos we prepared. We prepared five videos in which Mario was controlled by NPC, and three videos in which Mario was controlled by a human. The sections recorded in the game level were fixed in all videos, i.e., the play time was not fixed, because the number of objects (i.e., enemies, pipes, and holes) may have affected the assessments. In addition, we omitted a scene in which Mario was injured by his enemies from these videos. After this, the labels in Table 1 indicate the videos in this experiment.

Table 1. Prepared videos. Beginner's playthrough time was 5 h, intermediate's was 50 h, and expert's was 200 h.

Label	Human or NPC	Biological constraints	Play time	Score
[Q, None]	Q-learning	None	10.62 sec	5448
[Q, Imp, Balance]	Q-learning	Imposed(balance training with challenge)	14.25 sec	4069
[Q, Imp, Challenge]	Q-learning	Imposed(not training, challenge only)	15.57 sec	3458
[A*, None]	A* algorithm	None	7.29 sec	7926
[A*, Imp]	A* algorithm	Imposed	9.34 sec	3118
[INT]	Intermediate	-	10.08 sec	6031
[BEG]	Beginner	-	14.25 sec	3644
[EXP]	Expert	-	7.68 sec	7371

5.3 Method of Analysis and Results

Participants compared two videos that were randomly displayed and answered questions on a seven-scale relative evaluation. We analyzed the answers statistically by using Scheffe's method of paired comparisons[9]; first, we found the significant differences in the analysis of variance, second, we plotted "relative preferences" on the horizontal axis, and finally, we verified the confidence interval for "relative preferences" of each video.

As shown in Figure 3 (a), the top line indicates the relative preferences for human-like behaviors when comparing the Q-learning and a human, and the bottom line indicates them when comparing the A* algorithm and a human.

First, we will present the results obtained by comparing NPCs. We demonstrated in this experiment where [Q, Imp, Balance] and [A*, Imp] with the biological constraints were more human-like than [Q, None] and [A*, None] without them. There were significant differences between [A*, Imp] (0.48) and [A*, None] (−0.87): The difference in relative preferences of 1.35 (0.48 − (−0.87)) was wider than the 99 percent confidence interval, 0.72. (After this, we will describe this

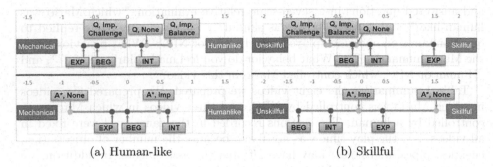

(a) Human-like   (b) Skillful

Fig. 3. Relative preferences for human-like and skillful behaviors plotted by comparing Q-learning and Human (top) and comparing A* algorithm and Human (bottom)

as "1.35 > 0.72: 99%"). However, there were no significant differences between [Q, Imp, Balance] and [Q, None] (0.37 < 0.48: 95%).

Next, we will present the results obtained by comparing NPCs and Humans. We demonstrated that [Q, Imp, Balance] was more human-like than the humans: [BEG], [INT], and [EXP]. Similarly, [A*, Imp] was more human-like than the humans: [BEG] and [EXP]. There were significant differences between [Q, Imp, Balance] and [BEG] (1.12 > 0.58: 99%), [Q, Imp, Balance] and [EXP] (1.33 > 0.58: 99%), and [A*, Imp] and [EXP] (0.71 > 0.59: 95%), but there were no significant differences between [Q, Imp, Balance] and [INT] (0.44 < 0.48: 95%) and [A*, Imp] and [BEG] (0.48 < 0.59: 95%).

As shown in Figure 3 (b), the top line indicates the relative preferences for skillful behaviors when comparing the Q-learning and humans, and the bottom line indicates them when comparing the A* algorithm and humans. The results correspond to the order of video play times as expected (see Table 1 for video play times), because the video play time was shorter if Mario was faster. The agents with biological constraints, i.e., [Q, Imp, Balance], [Q, Imp, Challenge], and [A*, Imp] were less skillful than agents without biological constraints, i.e., [Q, None] and [A*, None]. There were significant differences between all combinations in the 99% confidence interval ([Q, Imp, Balance]-[Q, None]: 0.54 > 0.46, [Q, Imp, Challenge]-[Q, None]: 0.62 > 0.46, and [A*, Imp]-[A*, None]: 1.59 > 0.52).

5.4 Discussion Based on Experimental Results

The experimental results in Figure 3 (a) indicate that introducing biological constraints made the agents more human-like. The participants' answers about agents with biological constraints were "Mario hesitated in jumping over his enemies," "Mario sometimes jumped unnecessarily." Conversely, participants tended to sense mechanical behavior when Mario was controlled very smoothly as in [A*, None] and [EXP].

Here, we discuss two issues in Figure 3 (a). First, [Q, Imp, Challenge] was not human-like despite the introduction of biological constraints; the participants' answers to this video were "Mario jumped over steps and pipes after he had collided with them." The reasons for this might be that this agent was like a novice player who had never previously played a Mario series. Participants who had more advanced skills than beginners, tended to sense [Q, Imp, Challenge] behaved mechanically. Three participants who had never played a Mario series actually judged that "this Mario was controlled by a human." Second, although [BEG] was controlled by a human player, it was not as human-like as the others. The reasons for this might be that the beginner was going to control Mario slowly and safely by reducing the number of key inputs. The beginner continued pushing the RIGHT key throughout and sometimes pushed the JUMP key. The participants' answers for this video were "Mario jumped constantly and smoothly."

The experimental results in Figure 3 (b) indicate that introducing biological constraints contributed to the design of a good degree of difficulty in video games. There was a correlation between Mario's speed (play time) in each video and these results. It is remarkable that [BEG] was considered to be more skillful than [Q, Imp, Balance] (0.47 > 0.46: 99%), although the play time for [BEG] was the same as that for [Q, Imp, Balance]. The participants' answers about this video were that "although Mario did not dash, he jumped constantly and smoothly."

Next, We investigated reasons into why there were no significant differences between [Q, Imp, Balance]-[Q, None] and [Q, Imp, Balance]-[INT] in Figure 3 (a). We adopted a working hypothesis that the evaluation criteria to determine human-like behaviors were shifted by some kind of bias. We calculated the correlation coefficients between video play times and evaluations of human-like behaviors by participants, and we classified the 20 participants into three groups.

Speedy Group: Human-like assessments were correlated with speedy Mario Correlation coefficients r were less than -0.4 for five participants. Their average playthrough time was 46 h.

Slow Group: Human-like assessments were correlated with slow Mario Correlation coefficients r were greater than 0.4 for nine participants. Their average playthrough time was 25 h.

No correlation between human-like assessments and Mario's speed Correlation coefficients r were between -0.4 and 0.4 for six participants. Their average playthrough time was 36 h.

Participants for whom the assessment was correlated with a speedy Mario felt [Q, None], [A*, None], [A*, Imp], [INT], and [EXP] were more human-like than the other group. Conversely, participants for whom the assessment was correlated with a slow Mario felt [Q, Imp, Balance], [Q, Imp, Challenge], and [BEG] were more human-like than the other group. We called the former group the Speedy Group, and the latter group the Slow Group.

Figure 4 indicates the relative preferences for human-like assessment by the 15 participants except for 5 in the Speedy Group. The top line indicates the assessments for the Q-learning and humans, and the bottom line indicates the assessments for the A* algorithm and humans. There were significant differences between [Q, Imp, Balance]-[Q, None] (0.62 > 0.57: 95%) and [Q, Imp,

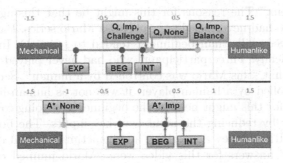

Fig. 4. Relative preferences for human-like behaviors plotted by comparing Q-learning and humans (top) and comparing A* algorithm and humans (bottom) for 15 participants except for 5 in Speedy Group

Balance]-[INT] $(0.74 > 0.67: 99\%)$. We demonstrated that agents with biological constraints were more human-like than humans and agents without them in analyzing these 15 particular participants. One plausible reason there were no significant differences when we included the remaining five participants was that the agents with biological constraints controlled Mario too slowly and safely. The agents generated by the higher parameters of biological constraints obtained slower and safer actions for Mario. If we had prepared the agents generated by the intermediate parameters of biological constraints, the participants in the Speedy Group could have assessed agents with biological constraints as being more human-like.

We found that the evaluation criteria to determine human-like behaviors were correlated with Mario's speed in these experimental results where there were significant differences for 15 participants except for 5 in the Speedy Group. Mario's speed that made participants feel he was human-like differed for the participants. The higher the deviation from their own evaluation criteria, the more participants could not feel Mario's behavior to be human-like in the videos. Because the average playthrough time for the Speedy Group was longer than it was for the Slow Group, we expected that there was the possibility that the evaluation criteria depended on the participants' efficiency in the video game.

6   Discussion

We discuss the possibility of applying our framework to various techniques of strategy acquisition and game genres. "Biological constraints" always occur when humans play video games. Our framework only introduced "biological constraints" into techniques of strategy acquisition. It is unnecessary to introduce them because game programmers analyze the most effective factors to make NPCs human-like and they need to engage in extremely complicated and difficult tasks to implement straightforward heuristics. Most video game titles include rules that video game agents can observe in game situations and then output the most effective actions. Therefore, our framework was neither oriented toward techniques of strategy acquisition nor game genres.

We discuss that whether our agents will become alternatives to human players or not from the viewpoint of psychology. Feeling characters are "human-like" has not been established as explicit knowledge. We assume that humans acquire this posteriori feeling by inferring it from physical laws and common knowledge. Minsky proposed a scheme in which human emotions were organized into six different levels of processes [8] so that they could be handled by machine. Beginning with simple instinctive reactions, each layer was built on the previous one, until they extended to processes that involved our highest ideals. This scheme consisted of 1) instinctive reactions, 2) learned reactions, 3) deliberative thinking, 4) reflective thinking, 5) self-reflective thinking, and 6) self-conscious reflection. The strongest NPCs generated by reinforcement learning techniques and pathfinding techniques consisted of only Nos. 2) and 3). Number 2) denotes learning about advantages or disadvantages of game situations, and No. 3) denotes thinking about the most effective action. Because No. 1) are not introduced to these NPCs, their behavioral patterns are extraordinarily "mechanical." However, as our human-like NPCs introduce No. 1) as "biological constraints," their behavioral patterns are "human-like." When participants assess NPCs as "human-like" in subjective assessments, they should access higher levels of processes, i.e., Nos. 4), 5), and 6) acquired by inferring from their own past experiences. We aim to achieve human-like NPCs in future work that can interpret what it is to be "human-like" by implementing all six levels of Minsky's scheme.

7   Conclusion

We proposed an autonomous system of behavior-acquisition to obtain the "behaviors" and "strategies" of video game agents that played video games like human players. Our study led us to conclude that we could obtain human-like behaviors by introducing only "biological constraints" into techniques of strategy acquisition. The computational simulations revealed that introducing biological constraints effectively improved both reinforcement learning and pathfinding techniques. The subjective assessments indicated that agents with biological constraints could acquire more human-like behavioral patterns than humans and agents without them. The validity of the biological constraints was confirmed by examining the evaluation criteria for human-like behaviors. Our concepts of *sensory error*, *perceptual and motion delay*, *physical fatigue*, and *balancing between repetition and novelty* proved to be effective in NPCs acquiring human-like behavioral patterns. If game programmers use our framework, it is possible for them to design good degree of difficulty into video games without ruining their human-like features.

Additional experiments with grouping participants into several strategy types are required in future work to confirm the evaluation criteria to make NPCs feel human-like. It is also meaningful to apply our framework to various game genres other than action games.

References

1. Fujii, N., Sato, Y., Wakama, H., Katayose, H.: Autonomously acquiring a video game agent's behavior: Letting players feel like playing with a human player. In: Nijholt, A., Romão, T., Reidsma, D. (eds.) ACE 2012. LNCS, vol. 7624, pp. 490–493. Springer, Heidelberg (2012)
2. Fujita, H., Ishii, S.: Model-based reinforcement learning for partially observable games with sampling-based state estimation. Neural Computation 19, 3051–3087 (2007)
3. Hoki, K.: Optimal control of minimax search results to learn positional evaluation. In: Game Programming Workshop 2006, pp. 78–83 (2006)
4. Hoki, K., Kaneko, T.: The global landscape of objective functions for the optimization of shogi piece values with a game-tree search. In: van den Herik, H.J., Plaat, A. (eds.) ACG 2011. LNCS, vol. 7168, pp. 184–195. Springer, Heidelberg (2012)
5. Cabrera, J.L., Milton, J.G.: On-off intermittency in a human balancing task. Physical Review Letters 89(15) (September 2002)
6. Karakovskiy, S., Togelius, J.: The mario ai benchmark and competitions. IEEE Transactions on Computational Intelligence and AI in Games 4, 55–67 (2012)
7. Maslow, A.H.: A theory of human motivation. Psychological Review 50, 370–396 (1943)
8. Minsky, M.: The Emotion Machine: Commonsense Thinking, Artificial Intelligence, and the Future of the Human Mind, reprint edition. Simon and Schuster (2007)
9. Scheffe, H.: An analysis of variance for paired comparisons. Journal of the American Statistical Association 47(259), 381–400 (1952)
10. Schrum, J., Karpov, I.V., Miikkulainen, R.: Human-like behavior via neuroevolution of combat behavior and replay of human traces. In: 2011 IEEE Conference, CIG 2011, pp. 329–336 (2011)
11. Soni, B., Hingston, P.: Bots trained to play like a human are more fun. In: 2008 IEEE International Joint Conference on Neural Networks, pp. 363–369 (2008)
12. Sugiyama, T., Obata, T., Hoki, K., Ito, T.: Optimistic selection rule better than majority voting system. In: van den Herik, H.J., Iida, H., Plaat, A. (eds.) CG 2010. LNCS, vol. 6515, pp. 166–175. Springer, Heidelberg (2011)
13. Togelius, J., Karakovskiy, S., Baumgarten, R.: The 2009 mario AI competition. In: 2010 IEEE Evolutionary Computation (CEC), pp. 1–8 (2010)
14. Watkins, C.: Learning from delayed rewards. PhD thesis, Cambridge University, Cambridge, England (1989)
15. Zajonc, R.B.: Attitudinal effects of mere exposure. Journal of Personality and Social Psychology 9, 1–27 (1968)

Comparing Game User Research Methodologies for the Improvement of Level Design in a 2-D Platformer

Marcello Andres Gómez Maureira, Dirk P. Janssen, Stefano Gualeni, Michelle Westerlaken, and Licia Calvi

NHTV University of Applied Sciences,
Monseigneur Hopmansstraat 1, 4817 JT Breda, The Netherlands
http://www.nhtv.nl

Abstract. In this paper we compare the effects of using three game user research methodologies to assist in shaping levels for a 2-D platformer game, and illustrate how the use of such methodologies can help level designers to make more informed decisions in an otherwise qualitative oriented design process. Game user interviews, game metrics and psychophysiology (biometrics) were combined in pairs to gauge usefulness in small-scale commercial game development scenarios such as the casual game industry. Based on the recommendations made by the methods, three sample levels of a Super Mario clone were improved and the opinions of a second sample of users indicated the success of these changes. We conclude that user interviews provide the clearest indications for improvement among the considered methodologies while metrics and biometrics add different types of information that cannot be obtained otherwise.

Keywords: Games, Games User Research, Quality Assurance, User Testing, Level Design, Platformer, Game Industry, Casual Games, Combined Methodologies, Biometrics, Physiological Measures.

1 Introduction

In the late 1970s and early 1980s, when video games were still in their infancy, developers and programmers produced very personal and sometimes low-quality games as fast as they could [1]. This led to the North American video game crash of 1983, which demonstrated what it means if low quality products saturate a market [2]. In 1985 Nintendo started a strategy of far reaching quality testing and became the most successful console system [3]. Since then, quality assurance (QA) has become an essential phase of commercial video game releases. QA is almost always part of an iterative production process, with test results being reported back to the designers for evaluation. The objective of this process is to ensure that the intentions and goals of the underlying game design are successfully conveyed to the player, that the players understand the metaphors and new

D. Reidsma, H. Katayose, and A. Nijholt (Eds.): ACE 2013, LNCS 8253, pp. 77–92, 2013.
© Springer International Publishing Switzerland 2013

concepts that the game introduces, and finally that the positive and negative feedback is successful in motivating the player.

In this paper, we will concern ourselves with one particular type of QA which is also called Game User Research (GUR). The term GUR is mainly used in academic research, but industry practice also distinguishes between for example fault-testing (*"Is the product bug free?"*) and user testing (*"Do players like it?"*) and the usage of methods to provide feedback directly on the design [4].

Within GUR, there are three major types of information available: Data from interviews (the user's opinion); data from player metrics (the in-game behavior), and data from psychophysiology (the bodily responses caused by the game).

There has been some previous work on the value of the different types of information relative to each other. It has been suggested that biometric testing is useful for adjusting level design and difficulty [5]. Comparing interviews and psychophysiological data, it was found that both data sources made the game experience more pleasant and satisfactory for the target audience. On a few other dimensions, implementing the suggestions from psychophysiological data increased the quality of the game by a small but significant amount, while implementing the changes suggested by interview data did not raise the game above a non-GUR method [6]. Mirza-Babaei and colleagues conclude that a study into the combined effects of data sources would be prudent.

In this paper we look at three methodologies, using three different sources of information, and compare which combinations are most productive in terms of the quality of the changes and the user evaluation of these changes. Through this comparison we want to illustrate how designers can gather and use GUR data to make informed decisions in their games. To simplify matters, we focus on 2-D level design: This is modular, fast and relatively easy to produce and iterate, and provides a clear basis for comparison among level-sets. The choice for a clone of a well-known 2-D platformer *Super Mario Bros.* meant that almost all players know the objectives, mechanics and metaphors used in this type of game, so we can look at the effect of level design while excluding other variables.

The methodologies tested were:

1. Participant *interviews* with player observation by researchers.
2. Data collection through *metrics*; The game was modified to log data about user behavior and user-game interaction [7]. We logged a large number of events such as movements, attacks, collection of bonus items and key presses.
3. Data collection through psychophysiology (also called *biometrics*); This data was gathered from the play tester by using sensors to monitor heart rate, skin conductivity and the activity of the facial muscles [8].

In our game improvement phase, data from two methodologies were combined to create a new version of the levels. This was done three times to cover all possible combinations.

The first phase of the research involved evaluation of the initial three levels by a team of level designers. In the second phase we gathered GUR data on these three levels. The third phase is the evaluation and the processing of the gathered data by means of various (statistical) methods. The result of phase 2 and 3 was a clear set of problems and recommendations that should be dealt with. Each methodology rendered its own results. The fourth phase involved the qualitative implementation of these recommendations in changes to the levels by a level designer. There were three implementations, corresponding to the three possible combinations of GUR methods (we did not make changes based on all three recommendations combined). The fifth phase compared the different level-sets created by the three combinations.

Why include metrics and psychophysiology in this comparison? The collection of metrics data has gained an enormous popularity with the advent of web-based games, mobile gaming and consoles that are connected to the internet permanently [9]. In its wake, psychophysiological (biometric) testing has become available to companies within the game industry and several development studios have added the methodology to their QA efforts [10,11]. So far, there is little actual research into just how useful biometrics can really be, what other parts of game design it can be used for and how it compares to traditional testing methods such as interviewing or observing players.

2 Related Work

Game user research (GUR) is a relatively recent field of research, which draws upon theories and methodologies from Human Computer Interaction and Experimental Psychology to study digital games [12]. Research in this field may also be called 'player experience research' or research into 'user-centered game design'. It involves studying the interaction between users and games with the aim of understanding, and ultimately improving, the user experience. While the body of research grows, there is currently no universally accepted methodology. Many questions remain about validity and procedure, about data collection and analysis methods [12].

Recent GUR studies have highlighted the need for research into a better understanding of the value of the different testing methodologies relative to each other. A 2011 study [13] compared the data obtained from traditional observation-based methods with that of biometric methods only (using input from galvanic skin response (GSR) as a data collection measurement). The results showed that different types of issues are revealed by the two approaches: Observation-based methods mainly exposed issues related to usability and game mechanics, while biometric research analysis was more suited to discovering issues related to game-play and emotional immersion. Both methods uncovered unique issues that the other method did not reveal. The study concludes that using a mixed-methods approach allows for greater confidence and validation of issues. The approach has received positive feedback from game developers and producers that the researchers have collaborated with [13].

Mirza-Babaei et al. [6] performed another study in the same direction, which is strongly in line with the aims of our research. Their experiment aimed to "identify the strengths, weaknesses and qualitative differences between the findings of a biometrics-based, event logging approach and the results of a full, observation-based user test study". The authors compared a game modified with the help of 'Classic User Testing' (Classic UT) to one modified through 'Biometric Storyboards User Testing' (BioSt UT). They found that "BioSt can help designers deliver significantly better visuals, more fun, and higher gameplay quality than designing without UTs and that classic UTs do not provide this significant advantage". From the point of view of the players, however, BioSt UT and Classic UT did not differ from each other in terms of the ratings given to the resulting games. It is important to highlight that the two approaches compared are already mixed method approaches: the Classic UT consisted of interview and observation, while the 'Biometric Storyboards' included a blend of interview, metric, and biometric data.

The paper points out that "the usefulness of **user tests** for game designers has not been studied sufficiently" [6, p. 1]. The authors attempt to remedy this by evaluating how the game designers in their study approached and used the data from the user tests, and how the generated design recommendations differed qualitatively. Their results show that designers working with BioSt UT generated the largest number of game changes, and had the highest confidence ratings about changes compared to the designers working with Classic UT or no UT.

Where this previous paper provides valuable insights and findings in the use of BioSt UT to provide more nuanced game design improvement, our study attempts to separately pair the three introduced GUR methodologies to find out which combination leads to improved player satisfaction. In our experiment we look at participants with a casual player profile rather than experienced PC gamers.

3 The Game

As basis for our game research we chose *SuperTux*, a side-scrolling 2-D platforming game developed by the open source community (see Figure 1). The game follows the design mechanics of the early Super Mario franchise on the Nintendo Entertainment System. As is the case in Super Mario, the player has to maneuver an avatar through a two-dimensional game environment (a level) by means of running and jumping until the end is reached. In the course of the game, the player has to avoid obstacles such as pits or enemies. The level typically features not only ground surfaces to jump to and from, but also platforms in mid-air that can be traversed. It is the occurrence of such platforms that give the genre its name. Platform games that largely imitate the game mechanics of Super Mario are often referred to as 'Super Mario Clones'. SuperTux is one of such clones.

We chose SuperTux specifically since it is freely available and can be modified by anyone due to its open source nature. Since we logged game states as part of the metric and biometric data collection (described in later chapters), this was a necessity in absence of a collaborating game development team. The game comes with a tile-based level editor, allowing for easy and modular modification of levels.

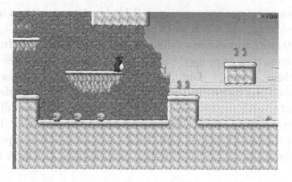

Fig. 1. A screenshot of SuperTux showing Tux - the protagonist - in its upgraded form (with red helmet), three enemies, several bonus coins, and four platforms

4   Experiment

The comparative design of this study consisted out of 5 different phases and entailed a comparison between levels that have been modified with a different combination of GUR methodologies. The levels were part of a sequence (level-set), which consisted of a tutorial (which was not changed) and three levels of increasing difficulty.

A flowchart of the approach is shown in Figure 2.

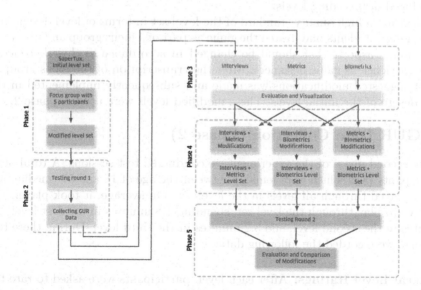

Fig. 2. Flowchart illustrating the five phases of the experiment

In phase 1 a focus group of designers evaluated the initial benchmark level-set which incorporated the first three levels of the game SuperTux and suggested modifications as a basic quality assurance. This level-set was then tested in phase 2, where the first round of GUR data was collected. In phase 3, the collected data of the first testing round was evaluated and visualized according to the three GUR methodologies that were used in this study. Phase 4 involves implementing changes using three different combinations of GUR methodologies (including modifications based on results derived from interviews + metrics data, interviews + biometrics data, and metrics + biometrics data). This resulted into three different level-set versions. These level-sets formed the basis for Testing Round 2 in phase 5 and the modifications were then evaluated and compared with each other. Each of these phases will be further described in the next section of this paper.

5   Preparation of the Benchmark Levels (Phase 1)

The first phase of the experiment focused on providing an initial quality assurance of the level-set. By evaluating the quality of the original first three levels in the game before conducting further experiments, we intended to emulate a point during level development at which professional designers would release their work to internal quality assurance. The decision to base this on the original first three levels of the game was taken under the assumption that the creators of the game intended these levels to be playable without requiring prior knowledge or advanced skills while still providing a progression in difficulty. The individual levels are unique and require the player to understand game mechanics that were introduced in preceding levels.

To ensure a high quality standard of the level-set in terms of level design, five game design students play-tested the game as part of a focus group and discussed problematic aspects that should be changed in accordance to their knowledge and experience as game designers. After the transcription of the focus group, a list of suggested modifications was made and subsequently implemented in the level design of the initial levels. These modified levels were used in phase 2.

6   GUR Data Collection (Phase 2)

In the second phase of the experiment we conducted test sessions. A total of 20 participants (8 of which were female) between the age of 18 and 57 (median age of 25) played through all levels in the level-set. On average, it took players 7.2 minutes to play through the level-set, spending 1.8 minutes in the first level, 2.2 minutes in the second level, and 3.2 minutes in the third level. During these test sessions, we recorded the following data:

General Level Ratings. After each level, participants were asked to rate the level regarding fun, length, and difficulty. Ratings were given based on a 5-point Likert scale with fun ranging from 'Not at All' to 'Very Fun', length ranging from 'Too Short' to 'Too Long', and difficulty ranging from 'Easy' to 'Difficult'. The ratings of a level were used in all three GUR methodology combinations as a basic reference point.

Interview Data. During the test sessions, the researchers monitored participants with two video cameras and a microphone through which they recorded both the participant and the game screen. Observations were noted down and peculiar situations were brought up during open-ended interviews.

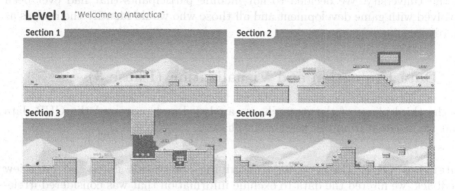

Fig. 3. Example of a level sheet used to aid participants in recalling details about their play experience. Levels are divided into four uniformly sized sections and are numbered chronologically.

The interviews took place after each level and asked participants to answer a set of semi-structured questions, which inquired about confusing, frustrating, enjoyable, and surprising parts in the level. While answering these questions, the participants could refer to a visual aid that divided each level into four equally sized and numbered sections (see Figure 3) to allow locating the source of the remark. Participants were asked to give any remaining comments or feedback after all questions.

Game Metric Data. Due to the open source nature of SuperTux, the researchers were able to add logging functionality to the game, which periodically tracked the position of the player character as well as relevant game events, such as defeating enemies, jumps, collecting of bonus items, etc. Game metrics were stored in clear text and time-stamped to be in sync with audio and video recordings.

Biometric GUR Data. All participants were monitored with several biometric sensors during the test sessions. Based on prior research in this field, we used facial Electromyography (EMG) sensors to detect activity in the *Corrugator Supercilii* muscle group (associated with frowning), and the *Zygomaticus Major* muscle group (associated with smiling). Both muscles are commonly used to measure emotional valence [14]. Finger sensors were used to measure blood volume pressure (BVP) and galvanic skin response (GSR), which have been correlated to excitement, fear, engagement and arousal [14]. Due to technical difficulties, we had to exclude the skin conductivity data.

Test sessions ended with a demographic questionnaire that also asked how frequent participants played video games. Participants in this research phase were selected by using convenience sampling [15] in the immediate surroundings of the University. We decided to not include participants that had ever been involved with game development and all those who would identify themselves as 'hardcore gamers'.

7 Data Evaluation and Visualization (Phase 3)

In the third phase of the research, we analyzed and processed the GUR data that we acquired from test sessions in phase 2.

Interview GUR Data. After transcribing observation notes and interview feedback, we filtered the data to exclude information that was considered irrelevant for the goals of this research, such as requests for additional game mechanics. The filtered data was then divided into different general themes in correlation to the topics of the interview questions ('Confusing Instances', 'Frustrating Instances', 'Enjoyable Instances' and 'Surprising Instances'). By visualizing the

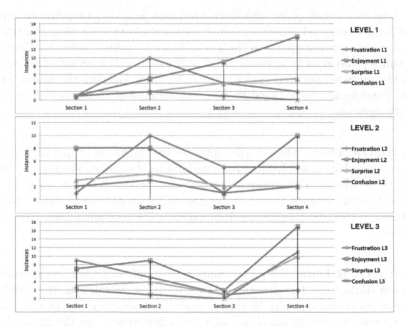

Fig. 4. The graphs show aggregated counts of instances in each of the three levels that during interviews have been described as frustrating, enjoyful, surprising or confusing. Note that the graphs are not in the same scale (specifically level 2)

frequency of themed instances (see Figure 4) for each level, data from the interviews could be used to highlight the need for improvements within the four sections of a level.

In order to determine which improvements to conduct, the filtered data was divided into actionable changes and sorted based on demand for change. Here we encountered situations that were mentioned positively by some participants and negatively by others. In general, uncontested changes were prioritized when looking for potential modifications.

Metrics Data. For the evaluation of metric GUR data we developed scripts that analyzed logs from the test sessions to derive aggregated measures of play statistics, such as amount of collected pick-ups, defeated enemies, etc. Where necessary, measurements were normalized in terms of time that was spent in the level, since the play duration had a direct affect on many play statistics. In addition to deriving information from the individual measurements, we calculated correlations of the acquired metric data. While these correlations could have been useful to uncover possibilities for the improvement of a level, we did not find actionable correlations. Apart from acquiring play statistics for each participant, the logs were used to create heatmaps (see Figure 5), which tied the position of the player as well as jumps, enemy kills, player deaths, and changes in direction to locations in the level.

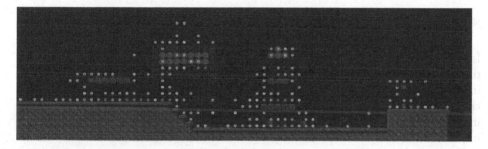

Fig. 5. Heatmap example showing part of a level overlayed with colored markers that indicate where in the level players switched their movement direction. Marker colors range from green (indicating a single event) to red (indicating the maximum amount of events in a level). As the level geometry is tile-based, events were logged and illustrated as heatmap marker per tile.

Biometrics Data. For the evaluation of biometric GUR data, each level was divided into 12 sections of equal size in terms of quantity of horizontal modules. Since biometric data works with averages, we chose this number to keep a balance between getting useful as well as localized data. We programmed scripts to analyze the data and remove noise. For the visualization of biometric data, the individual biometric measures were expressed in graphs and presented next to the corresponding level sections as shown in Figure 6. Similar to [6], we analyze biometrics data by investigating the signals and their relation to game events. Usually, we investigate relative changes in biometrics signals compared to the participant average. Although an initial classification of user mental states from combined biometric signals has been shown in the research literature [16] we do not think that this method is applicable to small samples of widely different games that we analyze.

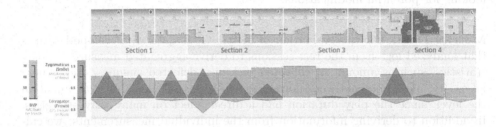

Fig. 6. Biometric data superimposed over map sections of level 3. The top row shows the level graphics split into the four sections used during interviews and 12 sections used for biometric GUR data. The red bars show the mean BVP of all participants in each section. The height of the green triangles pointing upwards shows the mean of all smiles for each section while the purple triangles pointing downwards show the mean of all frowns for each section.

8   Modifications (Phase 4)

In this phase we used the evaluated data and their visualizations to facilitate improvements in the level design. The first author, who has an industry background in game and level design, made all the level changes based on his perception on the shortcomings and the sub-optimal level design choices made for the game in relation to the target audience. This allowed for a consistent skill in terms of implementing modifications in the level. Furthermore, all modifications had to be connected to data that supports a change.

We looked at the three possible combinations of two GUR methodologies: (1) Interviews and Metrics; (2) Interviews and Biometrics; and (3) Metrics and Biometrics.

General level ratings (fun, length and difficulty of a level rated by participants) were added to each of the three combinations to contextualize the gathered data. For each of the three combinations we then decided to make the six most important changes across the three levels. Where we made the changes depended on where the data would support change.

We discuss the recommendations from the methodologies and the choice of implementation in detail elsewhere [17]. In this paper we explain the process of implementing the changes by one representative example. This particular change was made in the first level and was based on the combination of interview and biometric data:

For each change to a level, we started by inspecting the results of one of the two methodologies for issues that attracted comments from or were causing unwanted effects on the players. In this case biometric data showed very little player response throughout the level, especially in the beginning, as illustrated by low and steady BVP and lack of discernible facial emotion. We then checked this with the data from the other methodology to see if there was a common basis for a change. Interview data showed that the start of the level was rated consistently low across all measures (frustration, enjoyment, surprise and confusion). With the data from both methodologies, the designer (first author) concluded change in this area was desirable to induce higher player excitement and changed the level in a way that would solve the perceived problem without impacting the rest of the level: We decided to add more platforms and visual elements to give the section a more interesting look. The changes also encourage more action from the player if they want to collect all collectables, yet there is no increased risk of death, which would not be desirable at the beginning of the first level. An illustration of the changes can be seen in Figure 7.

The decision of how modifications should be implemented in terms of level design were taken based on the professional experience, sensibility, and best efforts of the level designer. All level changes are therefore of qualitative nature yet based on data from GUR methodologies that has been evaluated in a quantitative approach.

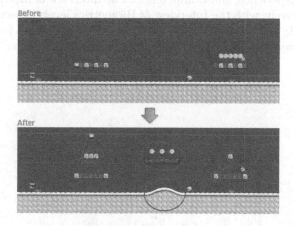

Fig. 7. Example of changes in a level segment that have been performed in response to interviews and biometric GUR data

9   Evaluation of the Modifications (Phase 5)

In the final phase of the experiment, new participants, chosen through convenience sampling in the environment of our University, were recruited to playtest one of the three modified level-sets that had been created in previous phase. A total of 40 participants (22 of which were female) in ages ranging from 15 to 27 years (median age of 23 years) took part in this concluding test session.

Since some modifications in the level design tended to be subtle, we decided that participants should only play one of the level-sets with randomizing which of the level-set would be played. To compare the player experience between level-sets we used the Game Experience Questionnaire (GEQ, [18]), which has been developed to classify player experience in multiple fields. The questionnaire has been used in several publications within the academic field [19,5]. In our research we used two of the five GEQ modules: The 'Core' module and the 'Postgame' module, both of which were administered after having played through the levels. The GEQ contains a large number of questions, which are reduced to 11 dimensions through averaging. This procedure removes the noise that is associated with every single question and produces more reliable results. With the conclusion of the final test session, the results of the GEQ were calculated. We discuss these results in the next section.

10 Results

The graph shown in Figure 8 illustrates the results of the GEQ. On the whole, the differences between the combined methodologies were much smaller than we expected. A consistent pattern can be seen across the variables Positive Affect, Flow, Positive Experience, and Competence: The Interview & Metrics levels were rated most positively, with the Interview & Biometrics levels in second place and the Biometrics & Metrics levels last. This pattern is replicated for some of the negative dimensions Tension/Annoyance, Challenge and Negative Affect.

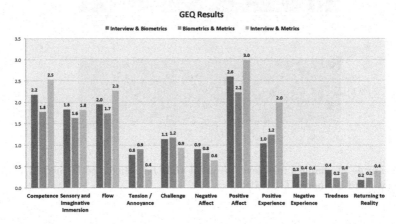

Fig. 8. Graph showing the GEQ scores of the individual methodology testing groups divided by the aspects that are scored by the GEQ

From the point of view of a level designer, each pair of GUR methodologies was able to provide action-able indications regarding locations or situations that should be modified to improve player satisfaction. With few exceptions, each pair of methodologies offered a unique change recommendation for the designer to act on. As a result none of the combined methodologies could fully substitute another.

11   Discussion

Given the insight gained in the five phases of the research and the GEQ results of the individual methodologies, we feel that player interviews are essential to the success of improving level design and should therefore always be involved.

The combination of interviews and metric methodologies puts both subjective and objective information into context. While interviews are great to uncover problems in a level, we found that metric data provides useful information regarding how to solve these problems, for example on the basis of heatmaps. We feel that the biggest challenge for the use of metric data is the complexity (and consequent time consumption) of its evaluation. Furthermore, it ideally requires designers to establish rough goals that can be expressed in metric parameters.

The addition of biometric methodologies into QA processes remains a promising possibility, especially for the exploration of qualitative aspects in design that are hard to evaluate through other means. As of the time of writing however, we believe that further efforts need to go into making the addition of this methodology less intrusive, less time intensive and therefore less costly. Only then can biometric methodologies be a viable addition to the QA processes of commercial game development.

Whether the Interview & Biometric combination will be ranked second to Interview & Metrics outside of the domain of level design for a 2-D platformer is an open question. From our own experience, the strongest limitation of the biometrics data was its lack of spatial precision. Because most participants completed a level in about 2 to 3 minutes, the amount of biometric data per game tile is minimal. When aggregating over many tiles, the data becomes insightful, however it is difficult to derive specific level design recommendations from this.

While it would have been interesting to add a control group to the second testing round in form of a unmodified level-set, our research focused on the comparison of methodologies. In our study the assumption was taken that the implementation of GUR methodologies will raise player satisfaction. For future comparisons of methodologies we do however advise to include such a control group in order to better evaluate the magnitude of improvement.

As a final point of discussion, we would like to address the possibility of replicating the processes of this study in 3-D games, which are arguably the majority of game titles nowadays. While the addition of a third spatial dimension raises the complexity in terms of visualizing data, there is no reason why the approaches we have taken would not work in 3-D space. Heatmaps in 3-D games are already part of metric evaluations and usually take an aerial perspective for the visualization of level geometry. Likewise we can imagine the use of such depictions of a level as visual aids during player interviews. In other words, while implementing GUR methodologies in 3-D games certainly raise the complexity compared to their use in 2-D games, we believe that such challenges can be overcome.

11.1 Limitations

Lead Researcher As Level Designer and Participant Observer. The author of this document was the lead researcher of this study as well as acting game designer and was therefore involved in all steps of the research. In being so, it becomes a challenge to remain objective over the course of the research. Also, while prior experiences as game and level designer have given the researcher insights into common design practices, it is ultimately difficult to prove a qualification in terms of level design. We have been aware of these limitations from the beginning of the study and attempted to mitigate these potential influences, for instance by providing the research with external input in form of a focus group and by requiring every level change to be based on research findings.

Level Designers Provide Subjective Influences. While there are many aspects of level design that follow certain logics and rules, the design of a level is highly dependent on the designer in terms of personal sensitivity, experience and interpretation of the development objectives for that particular product. Consequently it is inherently difficult to compare the quality and the merits of a design decision objectively. It should however be noted that a certain subjectivity of the designer is found in real world scenarios and is therefore always a factor in dealing with modifications due to GUR methodologies [6].

Combining Methodologies. Combining all methodologies or testing them separately could have yielded different results.While we argue that the combination of GUR methodologies is a common practice and partly necessary depending on the methodology, it is likely that a combination of all methodologies would have given slightly different results. At the same time, it would have been interesting to see the individual influences of each methodology. However, it was beyond the scope of this study to compare seven versions of the same game.

12 Conclusion

In sum, we can conclude that QA efforts regarding improvements in level design benefit strongly from the involvement of player interviews and direct player observations. It stands to reason that having access to all three of the methodologies discussed in this paper has strongest benefit for designers, as each methodology offers unique insights that can often not be accessed by other means. However, given the constraints of time and resources, studios may well be looking to add only one additional method. From our research, in-game metrics seem to be the most useful addition. This should be qualified by the observations that psychophysiological data may be less applicable to (2-D platformer) level design than to game design at large because of its relatively low spatial resolution. We think that the most important take-away point is that we found complementary benefits when combining methodologies: each methodology offers unique insights that can often not be accessed by other means. It is for this reason that the addition of biometric GUR as design evaluation method remains promising, despite the challenges in the evaluation and implementation.

Acknowledgments. The authors wish to thank Isabelle Kniestedt, Meggy Pepelanova, the game design students participating in the focus group and all the testers who took part in our experiments; the RAAK International Funding body, NHTV Breda University of Applied Sciences, and the SuperTux development community for their support in this research.

References

1. Ernkvist, M.: Down many times, but still playing the game: Creative destruction and industry crashes in the early video game industry 1971-1986. History of Insolvency and Bankruptcy, 161 (2008)
2. Wesley, D., Barczak, G.: Innovation and Marketing in the Video Game Industry: Avoiding the Performance Trap. Gower Publishing, Ltd. (2012)
3. Sheff, D.: Game Over: How Nintendo Zapped an American Industry, Captured Your Dollars, and Enslaved Your Children. Diane Publishing Company (1993)
4. Seif El-Nasr, M., Drachen, A., Canossa, A.: Introduction. In: Seif El-Nasr, M., Drachen, A., Canossa, A. (eds.) Game Analytics, pp. 3–13. Springer, London (2013)
5. Gualeni, S., Janssen, D., Calvi, L.: How psychophysiology can aid the design process of casual games: A tale of stress, facial muscles, and paper beasts. In: Proceedings of the International Conference on the Foundations of Digital Games, pp. 149–155. ACM (2012)
6. Mirza-Babaei, P., Nacke, L.E., Gregory, J., Collins, N., Fitzpatrick, G.: How does it play better? exploring user testing and biometric storyboards in games user research (2013)
7. Drachen, A., Canossa, A.: Analyzing user behavior via gameplay metrics. In: Proceedings of the 2009 Conference on Future Play on GDC Canada, pp. 19–20. ACM (2009)
8. Nacke, L.E.: An introduction to physiological player metrics for evaluating games. In: Seif El-Nasr, M., Drachen, A., Canossa, A. (eds.) Game Analytics, pp. 585–621. Springer, London (2013)
9. Canossa, A.: Interview with nicholas francis and thomas hagen from unity technologies. In: Seif El-Nasr, M., Drachen, A., Canossa, A. (eds.) Game Analytics, pp. 137–143. Springer, London (2013)
10. Ambinder, M.: Valves approach to playtesting: The application of empiricism. In: Game Developer's Conference (2009)
11. Zammitto, V., Seif El-Nasr, M.: User experience research for sports games. Presented at GDC Summit on Games User Research
12. Seif El-Nasr, M., Desurvire, H., Nacke, L., Drachen, A., Calvi, L., Isbister, K., Bernhaupt, R.: Game user research. In: Proceedings of the 2012 ACM Annual Conference Extended Abstracts on Human Factors in Computing Systems Extended Abstracts, pp. 2679–2682. ACM (2012)

13. Mirza-Babaei, P., Long, S., Foley, E., McAllister, G.: Understanding the contribution of biometrics to games user research. In: Proc. DIGRA (2011)
14. Cacioppo, J.T., Tassinary, L.G., Berntson, G. (eds.): Handbook of Psychophysiology, 3rd edn. Cambridge University Press (2007)
15. Singleton, R.A., Straits, B.C.: Approaches to Social Research, vol. 4. Oxford University Press, New York (2005)
16. Mandryk, R.L., Atkins, M.S.: A fuzzy physiological approach for continuously modeling emotion during interaction with play technologies. International Journal of Human-Computer Studies 65(4), 329–347 (2007)
17. Maureira, M.G.: Supertux a song of ice and metrics: Comparing metrics, biometrics and classic methodologies for improving level design. Master's thesis, NHTV University of Applied Sciences, Breda, the Netherlands (February 2013)
18. IJsselsteijn, W., de Kort, Y., Poels, K., Jurgelionis, A., Bellotti, F.: Characterising and measuring user experiences in digital games. In: International Conference on Advances in Computer Entertainment Technology, vol. 2, p. 27 (2007)
19. Nacke, L.: Affective ludology: Scientific measurement of user experience in interactive entertainment (2009)

Touch Me, Tilt Me – Comparing Interaction Modalities for Navigation in 2D and 3D Worlds on Mobiles

Wolfgang Hürst and Hector Cunat Nunez

Information and Computing Sciences, Utrecht University, The Netherlands
huerst@uu.nl, h.cunatnunez@students.uu.nl

Abstract. Different modalities, such as tilting or touch screen gestures, can be used to navigate 2D and 3D virtual worlds on handheld mobile devices. There are however few studies so far investigating the characteristics of these interaction modes, although it is important to be aware of individual advantages and disadvantages when creating real immersive interaction experiences. We present an experiment comparing different ways to navigate 2D and 3D virtual worlds on handheld mobile devices. In a comparative study, a total of 48 test subjects solve navigation tasks in 2D and 3D environments using different interaction modalities, in particular: touch gestures, an on-screen joypad implementation, and tilting gestures. Our results reveal important characteristics of the individual interaction modes and provide insight that is relevant for better interface design for virtual reality interaction on mobiles.

Keywords: Mobile interaction, mobile user interfaces, mobile virtual reality, mobile 3D, navigation in virtual reality.

1   Introduction

Interaction has always been a critical issue with mobile phones due to the small form factor of these handheld devices. Since the introduction of the iPhone in 2007, touch screens have become the predominant interaction mode on high-end smartphones. The establishment of touch-based interaction as de facto standard for such devices can be explained by two reasons. First, they enable designers to flexibly create interfaces that are most suitable for the task at hand given a particular situation and context. Icons can be made large enough to be easy to click. They can be arranged flexibly and change in size, order, and location depending on the task. Swipe, flick, and multi touch gestures can be used, if appropriate, to scroll various kinds of data, and so on. Second, in a lot of situations, direct touch interaction is very intuitive. Clicking an icon directly is normally considered more natural than using remote buttons. Most users are able to handle touch gestures such as dragging and flicking or pinch and zoom without any need for training when browsing lists of data and interacting with maps, respectively. Yet, these arguments do not necessarily hold for navigation of 2D and 3D environments on mobiles. For example, is it intuitive to "grab" a virtual character and move it to another place, or is it better to control its movements remotely,

D. Reidsma, H. Katayose, and A. Nijholt (Eds.): ACE 2013, LNCS 8253, pp. 93–108, 2013.
© Springer International Publishing Switzerland 2013

for example via an on-screen joystick? Likewise, when you have a virtual environment, such as in a 3D game, an educational application, or the visualization of scientific data, interface design is not as flexible but partly dependent on the actual content. For example, large buttons might block too much of the environment and the actual content might restrict their placement to some dedicated areas of the screen. Not surprisingly, there is no real dominant interaction mode for such situations yet. Different applications use different options or sometimes offer multiple ones and let users decide which one to chose. The most common ones used right now are:

- **Touch gestures**, which have become popular especially for navigating 2D worlds, where gestures such as swipe left or right can cause a virtual character to walk in that direction.
- **On-screen controllers**, which are often used for 3D games, which in turn is not surprising, since they usually resemble a software implementation of the actual controllers used on game consoles.
- **Tilting gestures**, which are also common but are mostly used in games where characters are controlled from a third person view via steering actions (e.g. car racing games) or for balancing tasks (e.g. marbles rolling through a 3D maze).

The goal of the work presented in this paper is to further investigate these three different interaction modalities for navigation of 2D and 3D virtual worlds on handheld mobile devices such as smartphones in order to answer questions such as: What are general characteristics for each individual modality? Are some better suited in certain contexts than others? What are the differences between 2D and 3D environments? We start by reviewing related work in section 2. Section 3 presents the setup of a comparative study of these three interaction types for navigation in 2D and 3D virtual environments and introduces our implementation. Results are analyzed and discussed in section 4. Section 5 concludes the paper with a summary of the major contributions and an outlook on potential future research.

2   Related Work

2D and 3D virtual environments are gaining increasing popularity on mobile devices especially in the domain of mobile gaming. Yet, related work with respect to interaction with and navigation in such mobile 2D and 3D virtual worlds is rather limited so far. Duh et al. [3] present an interesting study on gameplay on mobile phones, but focus more on different game types rather then interaction modes. Ponnada and Kannan [9] analyze games with respect to certain playability heuristics but focus more on overall gameplay experience rather than interaction issues. Lubitz and Krause [8] present an interesting study on user inputs for mobile games but their work is limited to a single jump and run game.

With respect to individual interaction modalities, hardly any scientific work can be found about on-screen controller and joystick design. Related comments about implementation options and related characteristics can mostly be found in related developer sites (see [4] for a good example) and are often restricted to important but rather simple rules of thumb (see [11] for example).

The same goes for touch gestures which have been extensively studied with respect to traditional interface design, evaluating for example optimum icon sizes, characteristics of different touch gestures for 1D and 2D data scrolling, etc., but have not gained similar attention from the scientific community with respect to 2D and 3D virtual world navigation yet. Hürst and Helder [7] evaluate touchscreen interaction in relation to virtual reality on smartphones and tablets, but focus on object interaction and different implementations of the 3D visualization rather than navigation and exploration of 2D and 3D worlds.

Using device tilting as a means to navigate and scroll text and other static data has been studied extensively in the past – see [10] for an example of one of the earlier works. Newer research applies this technique to other media types such as video [6]. In fact, controlling video playback via tilting was already proposed in the earliest work on handheld virtual reality [2]. Baillie et al. [1] use tilt to access additional information in a geographic information system scenario. Most relevant for the research presented in this paper are the works done by Gilbertson et al. [5] who study the usability of tilt for control of a first person racing game ("tunnel run"). While all of these related works demonstrate certain advantages of tilt for navigation of 3D data, none of them provides a comparative evaluation of the basic characteristics with respect to different interaction types.

3   Experimental Design

In order to investigate the characteristics and usability of the previously discussed three major interaction modalities – touch gestures, on-screen controllers, and tilting gestures – we set up two comparative studies – one for navigation in 2D environments and one to investigate navigation in 3D worlds. In the following, we describe the setup of the experiment and used implementations for each of these two scenarios.

3.1   2D Experiment: Implementation

To compare the different interaction modes with each other, we implemented the 2D environment shown in Figure 1 on a state of the art smartphone. It contains the

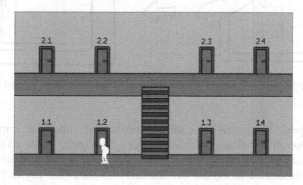

Fig. 1. Map illustrating the whole 2D environment

simplified illustration of a two-story building, with each of the two floors featuring four doors. Users can move left and right on each floor, and switch between them by using the staircase in the center. On the mobile phone, users only see parts of the whole environment as illustrated in Figure 2. In the experiments, participants were asked to go to certain dedicated doors and enter the rooms using the three interaction modes described below. Entering a room is depicted by changing the texture of a door.

Fig. 2. Example for the excerpt visible to a user on the device used in the experiments (left) and visualization of the event "character has entered a room" (right)

Touch Gestures. There are many different ways to use gestures in order to control the navigation of a virtual character on the screen. After reviewing common implementations in typical state of the art mobile apps, we decided to choose a rather simple, yet powerful and flexible one for this experiment. As illustrated in Figure 3, navigation is done by simply clicking on the dedicated target location, i.e. the character automatically walks along the floor or up and down the stairs towards the latest location in the virtual 2D world tapped by the user. Clicking on a door makes the character enter the related room.

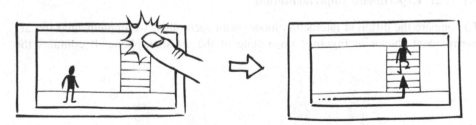

Fig. 3. 2D touch gesture-based navigation: the virtual character walks to the last screen location tapped by the user.

On-screen Joypad. Motivated by common on-screen controller implementations, which in turn resemble similar controller devices of popular game consoles, we implemented a virtual joypad that is visualized as a widget in the bottom left corner of the screen (cf. illustration in Figure 4). Similarly to hardware joysticks, "dragging" this virtual joystick to the left or right evokes a related movement of the character along the floor. Up and down movements are used to climb or descend stairs and exit or enter a room, depending if the character stands in front of a staircase or door, respectively.

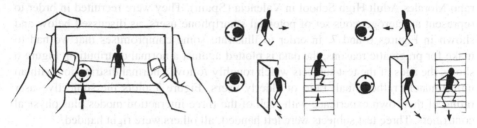

Fig. 4. 2D on-screen joypad: left/right drags of the virtual joystick evoke left/right movements of the virtual character, up/down drags are used to climb/descend stairs and enter/exit rooms

Tilting Gestures. Using the accelerometer integrated in almost all modern smartphones we can map horizontal and vertical rotations of the device to related movements of the virtual character. Naturally, we map horizontal rotations to left/right movements and use vertical rotations to climb and descend stairs or enter and exit rooms depending on the context, as illustrated in Figure 5. It should be noticed that "natural" in this case depends on the context. For example, in flight simulations, up/down movements might be interpreted reversely due to what kind of steering wheel they aim to resemble.

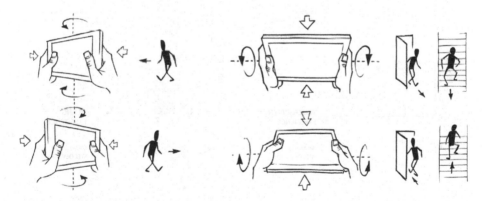

Fig. 5. 2D tilting-based navigation: horizontal device rotations evoke left/right movements of the virtual character, vertical rotations are used to climb/descend stairs and enter/exit rooms

Implementation. The virtual 2D environment and interaction styles discussed above have been implemented with Microsoft Visual Studio 2010 using C# and the XNA libraries on a Nokia Lumia 800 smartphone with 3.7 inch screen, 800x480 resolution, and a 1.4 GHz single core CPU, running the Windows Phone 7.5 operating system, that was used for all evaluations reported in this paper. In order to objectively compare the different interaction modes, all parameters such as the velocity of the character have been set to the same values for each of the three navigation options.

3.2   2D Experiment: Setup and Methodology

Participants. The 24 test subjects (10 male, 14 female, ages 18 to 60) participating in the 2D experiment were volunteers of evening classes for adult education at the Serrano Morales Adult High School in Valencia (Spain). They were recruited in order to represent a heterogeneous set of potential smartphone users, as discussed below and shown in Figures 6 and 7. In order to illustrate some compromises that we had to make for pragmatic reasons, the data is plotted against a normal distribution. Figure 6 shows the ages of the test subjects which roughly follow a normal distribution with an unfortunately rather small ratio of elderly users. Figure 7 plots the subjective user rating of their own experience with each of the three interaction modes plus physical controllers. Three test subjects were left handed, all others were right handed.

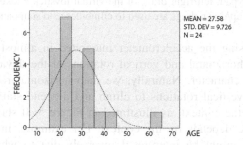

Fig. 6. Histogram of the age distribution of the test subject sample used

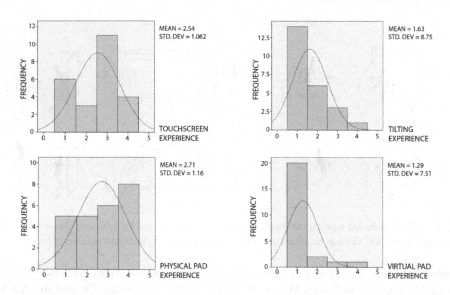

Fig. 7. Histograms illustrating the subjects' experience with (left to right) touch screens, tilting virtual, and physical joypads, according to their own judgment about their usage, i.e. "1" for "never", 2 for "barely", "3" for "often", and "4" for "everyday" (= labels on x-axis)

We will discuss the results of our experiment with respect to these characteristics in the following section. A statistical analysis of the presented data using a Chi-square test revealed only one significant correlation: male subjects had much more experience with physical controllers than females. It is further worth noticing that experience with on-screen joypads was almost nonexistent among the test subjects.

Study Design and Tasks. Our study used a within-subjects design with the only independent variable being the interaction method. The order of interaction modality was counterbalanced across the participants to avoid related influences on the results. For each of these modes, users had to visit as many rooms as possible in a given order within a three minutes time limit. In particular, users were provided with the image in Figure 1 and asked to visit rooms 2.4, 1.3, 1.1, 2.1, 1.4, 2.2, 2.3, and 1.2 in exactly this order. As dependent variable, we recorded the number of rooms visited within the given time limit. In addition, the total distance travelled by the virtual character during the test phase was recorded.

Procedure. All experiments were conducted individually with each subject in a classroom of the school. Questionnaires were used to gather personal statistics (cf. Fig. 6 and 7), user feedback and ratings after the test (to be discussed in the next section), and notes of the neutral observer. After a short introduction into the problem, the otherwise neutral observer gave a short demonstration of each interaction mode. Before the actual tests, subjects were asked to perform a single subtask (visiting one room) to familiarize them with the interaction metaphor. A whole session lasted approximately 15 minutes per participant with about five minutes of evaluation time per interaction mode (training plus three minutes evaluation). Between the tests for each interaction type, users took a short break to relax and concentrate on the next task.

3.3   3D Experiment: Implementation

For the test of navigation in 3D, we implemented the simple 3D model of the interior of a house that is depicted in Figure 8. The number of floors and doors are comparable to

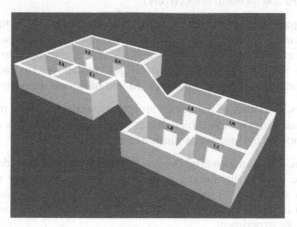

Fig. 8. Model illustrating the whole 3D environment

the 2D case (cf. Fig. 1), but the actual implementation depicted a first person view of the related 3D world as shown in Figure 9. Again users could freely roam along the floors, enter rooms, and change between floors using one of the interaction modes described below. Because we are now exploring a 3D world, motions are not just simple up/down and left/right movements like in the 2D case, but can be described by a virtual camera that represents the first person view of the virtual character. In the following, we describe how the different interaction modes are mapped to related modifications of the virtual camera.

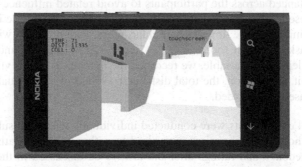

Fig. 9. Example for the view of the 3D environment on the device used in the experiments

Touch Gestures. An informal analysis revealed a surprisingly low number of usages of touch screen gestures for navigation in currently available 3D games on mobiles. Most implementations are rather restrictive insofar as they limit the amount of space that a user can explore and the locations one can visit. In order to achieve comparability with the preceding 2D experiment but most importantly the other two interaction modes of this evaluation, we implemented the gestures illustrated in Figure 10: Dragging the finger left or right on the screen results in a rotation of the virtual camera in the same direction (creating a visual feedback resembling "looking around"). Backward motion is achieved by a horizontal flick. Repeated taps on the screen evoke a forward movement of the virtual camera (creating the visual feedback resembling walking backward and forward, respectively).

On-screen Joypad. Figure 11 shows how movements of the virtual joypad are mapped to the virtual camera, which in turn defines the field of view shown on the mobile device. Left and right movements of the joypad are mapped to a related rotation similarly to the left and right drag touch gestures above. Up and down movements evoke a virtual character to walk forward and backward, respectively.

Tilting Gestures. Rotations of the device around its vertical axis are mapped to rotations of the virtual camera, device rotations around its horizontal axis are mapped on backward and forward movements as illustrated in Figure 12.

Implementation. The same smartphone as in the 2D experiments described above was used for the implementation and in the experiments. Again, we made sure that parameters such as velocity of the character when moving are comparable across all three interaction modes in order to guarantee that the latter one are the only independent variable in our experiment.

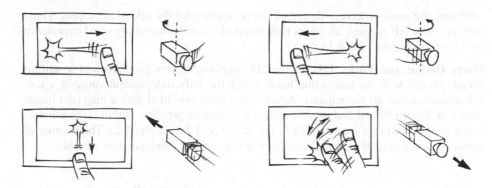

Fig. 10. 3D touch gesture-based navigation: horizontal drags result in corresponding rotations of the virtual camera, flicking and tapping evokes backward and forward motion, respectively

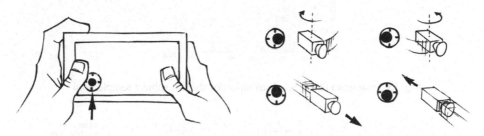

Fig. 11. 3D on-screen joypad: horizontal drags of the joypad result in corresponding rotations of the virtual camera, up/down movements evokes forward and backward motion, respectively

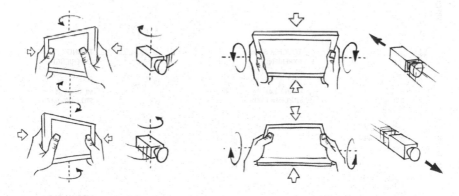

Fig. 12. 3D tilting-based navigation: horizontal rotations of the device evoke corresponding rotations of the virtual camera, vertical rotations are used to move forward and backward

3.4   3D Experiment: Setup and Methodology

Participants. Again, 24 subjects were recruited for the test (12 male, 12 female, ages 18 to 59). They have not been involved in any way in the 2D experiment at all, but otherwise the same criteria as described above applied for the selection process. Three subjects were left-handed, all others right-handed. Distribution of ages and experience are plotted in Figure 13 and 14.

Study Design and Tasks. Like in the 2D experiment, this test followed a within-subject design with the interaction mode being the only independent variable, counterbalanced across all participants. Again, users were provided with a map (the image shown in Figure 8) and had to visit as many rooms as possible within three minutes based on a given order (room 2.4, 1.3, 1.1, 2.1, 1.4, 2.2, 2.3, and 1.2). The number of rooms visited and total distance travelled were recorded as independent variable.

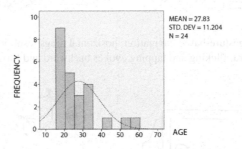

Fig. 13. Histogram of the age distribution of the test subject sample used

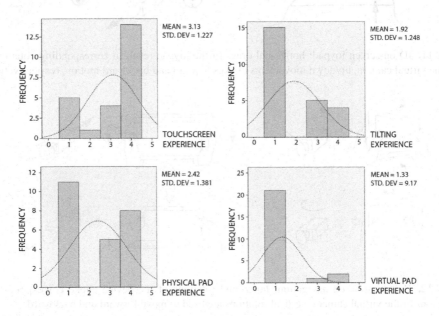

Fig. 14. Histograms illustrating the experience of the test subjects in the 3D experiment with touch screens, virtual joypads, physical joypads, and tilting (from left to right) according to their own judgment on a scale representing their usage, i.e. "1" for "never", 2 for "barely", "3" for "often", and "4" for "everyday" (labels on the x-axis)

Procedure. Experiments were done individually on later dates, but under otherwise similar conditions as the 2D experiment, with a short explanation and demonstration of each interaction style at the beginning, followed by a training task for each mode and the actual test. Sessions again took about 15 minutes with short breaks between the three tests. Aside from a small modification of the questionnaire, which we will describe when discussing the results, data was gathered in a similar way as in the 2D case.

4   Results

In the statistic analysis of the following data, we measured correlations using Chi-square tests (when dealing with categorical data), and Pearson Correlation tests (when dealing with numerical data only). Statistical significance of the differences between groups was tested using ANOVA, additionally performing Tukey's post-hoc test in order to cluster groups according to the significance of their differences. Tests were carried out at a 95% significance level (p value < 0.05).

4.1   2D Experiment: Results

Statistical Analysis of Performance Indicators. First, we evaluate performance of each interaction mode with respect to efficiency, which in turn can be measured in different ways (Table 1).

Table 1. Efficiency indicators (2D experiment; averages and standard deviation over all users)

	Number of rooms visited	Distance travelled per room visited	Navigation mistakes made
Touch gestures	9.750 (SD: 2.707)	14300 (SD: 3655)	0.167 (SD: 0.482)
On-screen joypad	9.542 (SD: 3.647)	16228 (SD: 3494)	0.9858 (SD: 1.268)
Tilting	10.375 (SD: 2.428)	16870 (SD: 3960)	3.583 (SD: 3.006)

If measured as number of rooms visited within the time limit, we cannot observe any significant differences ($p > 0.05$ with ANOVA test; left column in Table 1). Performance strongly varies across participants. Some subjects did very well with some method whereas others performed very poorly with it.

If measured as distance travelled by the virtual character per number of rooms visited, touch gestures were significantly more efficient than the on-screen joypad ($p < 0.05$ with ANOVA test; center column in Table 1). A statistically significant difference between tilting and the other two approaches could not be observed however. Looking at the implementation (cf. Section 3.2) this seems reasonable because for touch interaction, people could click directly on a target position, thus avoiding situations in which a character misses a target and has to go back. The reason why this significant difference is not reflected in the number of rooms visited is simply that the distance between two rooms was too large to create a difference in absolute room numbers.

If efficiency is measured as experiencing a lower amount of navigation mistakes (such as missing a door, accidentally entering a wrong one, loosing control of the virtual character, etc.), tilting proved to be significantly less efficient than the other two interaction modes (p< 0.05 with ANOVA test; right column in Table 1).

User Feedback and Qualitative Data. In the closing questionnaire, users were asked about efficiency and how much they enjoyed the interaction modes. In particular, they were asked to rank them with respect to "efficiency" and "enjoyability".

Although the analysis of the related performance indicators above did not reveal any significant difference, subjects perceived touch screen as more efficient than tilting (significance verified with ANOVA test, p< 0.05). Yet, a significant difference regarding the preference of the on-screen joypad could not be observed – neither compared to touch nor to tilt.

Relating the background data provided at the beginning of Section 3.2 (cf. text and Figures 6 and 7) only revealed one significant difference (Chi-Square, p< 0.05): Female participants considered touch gestures significantly more enjoyable than the on-screen joypad, whereas for male subjects, it was just the other way around. This is however most likely due to the larger level of experience of the males with physical controllers which we already commented on. This is also reflected in the qualitative user statements where typical comments by male subjects included: "The virtual joystick was nice because it was kind of similar to the X-Box controller." "With the virtual joystick I felt like playing on the PSP." And: "I guess (virtual joypad) was more similar to how I am used to play games." Females, on the other hand, commented more positive about the touch gestures, with typical remarks being: "With touch screen I felt way more in control of the character." "I think I was faster using touch screen." And: "With touch screen you just got to tell the character where to go ... and he goes there ... that's nice." Comments for the tilting approach had no clear relation to a subject's gender and included positive remarks such as "it's innovative a challenging ... I like it!" but also negative comments such as "I didn't feel like I was in control of the virtual character."

4.2   3D Experiment: Results

Statistical Analysis of Performance Indicators. Again, we look at the performance with respect to efficiency from different perspectives (Table 2). Like in the 2D case, there is no significant difference with the total number of rooms visited using either of the three interaction modes (ANOVA, p> 0.05). Likewise, statistical significance cannot be proven based on the observed data considering the distance travelled by the virtual character per number of rooms visited (ANOVA, p> 0.05). Only when looking at the amount of navigation mistakes, we see that tilting appears to be significantly less efficient than the other two approaches (ANOVA, p< 0.05). Most of these mistakes were due to situations where a user's virtual character collided with a wall.

Unlike in the 2D case, the Pearson correlation test showed that age highly correlated with the efficiencies mentioned above. In particular, the older the subject, the lower their performance (correlation coefficient: -0.740). Chi-Square tests could not reveal a correlation between any of the other background factors and the efficiency factors, except for gender and physical controller experience which again was significantly higher for male subjects (Chi-Square test, p< 0.05).

Table 2. Efficiency indicators (3D experiment; averages and standard deviation over all users)

	Number of rooms visited	Distance travelled per room visited	Navigation mistakes made
Touch gestures	9.417 (SD: 3.020)	174422 (SD: 38329)	5.750 (SD: 5.682)
On-screen joypad	9.250 (SD: 3.859)	185874 (SD: 33009)	6.042 (SD: 5.820)
Tilting	8.875 (SD: 3.301)	224470 (SD: 14841)	13.417 (SD: 13.56)

User Feedback and Qualitative Data. In the 2D experiment, most users rated the most efficient system also as their most preferred one. In order to get a clearer idea of their qualitative ratings, we therefore changed the questionnaire from asking for a ranking to asking for a rating on a scale from -2 (worst) to 2 (best). Yet, again, no statistically significant difference among the three interaction styles could be observed. A Chi-Square test still showed a high correlation between the method users perceived as more efficient and the one they considered more enjoyable. Similarly, a preference for touch gestures among female subjects was observed again (Chi-Square test, p< 0.05).

In order to gain more qualitative statements, we asked users to describe each of the methods with one positive and one negative statement. Unfortunately, they had problems coming up with good words of their own, but most of them used one of the examples provided for each category. Touch gestures were positively described as "easy" and "precise" by 33% and 50% of the subjects, respectively, and negatively characterized as "boring" (33%). The most used words to describe positive aspects of the on-screen joypad were "easy" (45%) and "precise" (41%). The mostly used negative words included "unstable" (45%), "prone-to-errors" (25%), and "difficult" (16%). Tilting was described as "challenging" (in a positive, entertaining way, 75%) and "innovative" (25%), yet negatively characterized as "unstable" (58%) "prone-to-errors" (25%), and "difficult" (16%).

4.3   Discussion and 2D-3D Comparison

The major goal of our experiments was to study the characteristics of different interaction modalities for navigation in 2D and 3D environments with the ultimate aim of gaining information that enables us to create better interaction experiences. We expected to observe clear trends with respect to which modularity is more suited for either of the two cases, 2D or 3D. Surprisingly, our results did not reveal such a trend, but give a clear indication that both pure performance measures as well as personal preference seem to be rather based on very individual aspects with no clear characteristics or user profiles that would prioritize one approach over another.

In the 2D case, we expected tilt to be the least favorable of the three options because it is also hardly used for this kind of data in current applications but mostly applied in 3D environments. Apparently, many test subjects shared our view, because we could observe a slight related trend in the qualitative user statements. Yet, our analysis revealed no clear evidence that speaks against this interaction mode. In fact, some users even enjoyed that it appeared to be more "challenging" and thus more entertaining for them. We expected touch gestures to perform best because users could directly select a target position instead of having to direct the virtual character to it. Again, our intuitive assumptions were confirmed by some of the qualitative user statements, but could not be verified with any of the data. Instead, personal preference and individual performance again seems to dominate the outcome. What further surprised us was the apparent influence of experience with comparable physical controllers on the preference of male users for the virtual joypad implementation. Yet, given that there were no performance differences, and the fact that positive statements about all three interaction types were equally distributed among subjects of both genders we cannot conclude with a clear recommendation, i.e. we can neither suggest that experienced users should be trained to use other modes of interaction nor should inexperienced ones be forced to adapt to traditional modes, because none of the methods proved to be superior.

In the 3D case, we actually expected tilt to perform better, not only because it is often used in current games and 3D apps, but also because the related interactions appeared more natural for us in this case. Although the virtual character moves in 3D now, the actual interactions on the virtual joypad are still in 2D – resulting in the situation that users have to move their fingers up and down in order to evoke forward and backward movements of the virtual character. In case of tilting, the device is rotated forward or backward in accordance to the resulting movement of the character, thus suggesting a more intuitive and natural interaction. Yet, the results could not confirm these assumptions. Neither performance nor the subjective user ratings could show any significant difference between interaction modes. In fact, even the personal preference did not reveal any significant trend in the 3D case, although subjects still remarked that touch interaction appears to be more accurate and easier to control than tilting actions. Again, the overall conclusion is that picking the best interaction mode is less a question of dedicated user characteristics but more a matter of personal preference and individual habits.

5   Conclusion and Future Work

Our experiments did not identify any best interaction mode, neither for 2D nor for 3D virtual environment navigation. This came surprising to us and initially even seemed disappointing. Yet, the fact that no clear trend could be identified – despite the detailed evaluation and related data analysis – is an unexpected and thus important statement that highlights the relevance of our work. While experience seems to play a role in user preference, there is no clear indication for either of the modalities. Even people who expressed preference for one of the interaction types did not necessarily perform well with it. In addition, experience depends on the past, and related user preferences might change over time. In the 3D case, there was a trend that performance correlates negatively with increasing age. Yet, the ratio of elderly within the sample set was too small to draw a strong conclusion, but suggests interesting alleys for future research. The concluding observation that personal preference and individual habits and abilities seem to be the major reasons for differences in the measured quantitative and qualitative data, leads to the recommendation that developers should not aim at providing one "best" interaction style, but rather offer a set of different ones and let users decide which one to use. In fact, some of the current 3D games that we used in the informal analysis when setting up our experiments are already doing this. Yet, the different options are often hidden in the settings menus and therefore frequently overlooked by users who then feel forced to use the default interaction method, which might not be the most appropriate one for them.

Given the apparently strong influence of experience on user preference, we already suggested that further, long term studies investigating how, for example, those preferences change over time might reveal interesting observations. Based on our experimental results, we assume that such a study would require users to utilize the interaction mode several weeks, and thus is beyond the scope of this paper. Yet, it provides an interesting area for further exploration in future works. Likewise, the influence of age that was identified in an initial trend should be studied further, as already suggested above. Considering other options for future work, we like to quote one test subject who noted on the tilting interaction: "It was way too unstable. I couldn't center the character in front of the doors easily." On the one hand, this statement suggests that individual interaction modes might not be suitable for all kind of tasks. For example, with tilting it is indeed harder to put a virtual character at a fixed location due to the constant change in the accelerometer data because of minor movements of the device – even if appropriate filtering techniques are applied to the sensor data. Yet, in situations where this is not required, for example because the virtual character is in constant motion, tilting might be favored by most users – a speculation that seems to be confirmed by dominant usage of this modality for racing and balancing games on mobile devices. On the other hand, this statement also indicates room for optimization of the concrete implementation of the interaction modes. For our initial study, we took particular care to set the parameters in a comparable way in order to guarantee that interaction modality is the only independent variable in our tests. Yet, individual optimizations, for example of the virtual character's speed when tilting a device might have an effect on user preference and performance and is therefore worth further investigation. Likewise, there are different ways to implement an on-screen controller, suggesting comparative studies of different designs.

References

1. Baillie, L., Kunczier, H., Anegg, H.: Rolling, rotating and imagining in a virtual mobile world. In: MobileHCI 2005: Proceedings of the 7th International Conference on Human Computer Interaction with Mobile Devices & Services, pp. 283–286. ACM, New York (2005)

2. Buxton, B., Fitzmaurice, G.W.: HMDs, caves & chameleon: A human-centric analysis of interaction in virtual space. SIGGRAPH Comput. Graph. 32(4), 69–74 (1998)
3. Duh, H.B.-L., Chen, V.H.H., Tan, C.B.: Playing different games on different phones: An empirical study on mobile gaming. In: Proceedings of the 10th International Conference on Human Computer Interaction with Mobile Devices and Services (MobileHCI 2008), pp. 391–394. ACM, New York (2008)
4. Gamasutra.com: A Guide to iOS Twin Stick Shooter, cf,
   http://www.gamasutra.com/view/feature/6323/
   a_guide_to_ios_twin_stick_shooter_.php?print=1
5. Gilbertson, P., Coulton, P., Chehimi, F., Vajk, T.: Using "tilt" as an interface to control "no-button" 3-d mobile games. Comput. Entertain. 6, 38:1–38:13 (2008)
6. Huber, J., Steimle, J., Mühlhäuser, M.: Toward more efficient user interfaces for mobile video browsing: An in-depth exploration of the design space. In: Proceedings of the International Conference on Multimedia (MM 2010), pp. 341–350. ACM, New York (2010)
7. Hürst, W., Helder, M.: Mobile 3D graphics and virtual reality interaction. In: Romão, T., Correia, N., Inami, M., Kato, H., Prada, R., Terada, T., Dias, E., Chambel, T. (eds.) Proceedings of the 8th International Conference on Advances in Computer Entertainment Technology (ACE 2011), Article 28, 8 pages. ACM, New York (2011)
8. Lubitz, K., Krause, M.: Exploring user input metaphors for jump and run games on mobile devices. In: Herrlich, M., Malaka, R., Masuch, M. (eds.) ICEC 2012. LNCS, vol. 7522, pp. 473–475. Springer, Heidelberg (2012)
9. Ponnada, A., Kannan, A.: Evaluation of mobile games using playability heuristics. In: Proceedings of the International Conference on Advances in Computing, Communications and Informatics (ICACCI 2012), pp. 244–247. ACM, New York (2012)
10. Rekimoto, J.: Tilting operations for small screen interfaces. In: Proceedings of the 9th Annual ACM Symposium on User Interface Software and Technology (UIST 1996), pp. 167–168. ACM, New York (1996)
11. SimpleUsability.com: Mobile Gaming – A usability study, cf,
    http://www.simpleusability.com/our-news/2012/01/
    mobile-gaming-usability/

Virtual Robotization of the Human Body via Data-Driven Vibrotactile Feedback

Yosuke Kurihara[1,2], Taku Hachisu[1,3],
Katherine J. Kuchenbecker[2], and Hiroyuki Kajimoto[1,4]

[1] The University of Electro-Communications, Tokyo, Japan
[2] University of Pennsylvania, Philadelphia, PA, USA
[3] JSPS Research Fellow
[4] Japan Science and Technology Agency
{kurihara,hachisu,kajimoto}@kaji-lab.jp,
kuchenbe@seas.upenn.edu

Abstract. Worlds of science fiction frequently involve robotic heroes composed of metallic parts. Although these characters exist only in the realm of fantasy, many of us would be interested in becoming them, or becoming like them. Therefore, we developed a virtual robotization system that provides a robot-like feeling to the human body not only by using a visual display and sound effects, but also by rendering a robot's haptic vibration to the user's arm. The vibrotactile stimulus was recorded using real robot actuation and modeled using linear predictive coding (LPC). We experimentally confirmed that the subjective robot-like feeling was significantly increased by combining the robot-vibration feedback with a robot-joint animation and creaking sound effects.

Keywords: Body Sense, Material, Robotization, Vibrotactile Feedback.

1 Introduction

While there are a number of industrial robots that support our daily lives, there are also numerous fictional robots that have appeared in movies, comics and video games. Many of us would be interested in understanding the experience of having a tough iron body, hoping to become like these robotic heroes, if only for a short time. The question naturally arises: what would it feel to be a robot? While we are seldom conscious of the activities of our biological muscles or tendons, a robotic body would have a definite robotic body sense that is different from that of humans.

In this paper, we focus on the body sense of robots and simulate robot-like feelings on the human arm (Fig. 1). To create a realistic robot-like body sense, we provide vibrotactile feedback based on vibration recording, modeling, and rendering of a real robot's actuation. Combined with conventional visual animation and sound effects, our system allows the user to virtually robotize his or her body visually, aurally, and haptically.

This paper mainly contributes to the field of computer entertainment technology by presenting a new alternative for achieving an immersive experience in video games.

D. Reidsma, H. Katayose, and A. Nijholt (Eds.): ACE 2013, LNCS 8253, pp. 109–122, 2013.
© Springer International Publishing Switzerland 2013

Gesture input devices, sometimes referred to as natural user interfaces (e.g., the Kinect sensor from Microsoft, the Wii remote from Nintendo, and the Omni from Virtuix) increase the player's feeling of oneness with the game character by synchronizing the character's motion with the player's body motion, resulting in an immersive game experience. Also, some previous tactile entertainment systems have enhanced the immersive experience by displaying vibrotactile feedback to the player's body, synchronized with characters being shot [1] or getting slashed [2].

However, playable characters in video games are not always human – sometimes they are, for example, metallic robots. By creating a robot-like body sense and simulating a situation in which the player becomes the robot, experiencing the game with a robotic body could be made more immersive. Therefore, we envision that the technique of virtual robotization of the human body could enrich immersive video games by offering the experience of being a fictional robotic hero.

Fig. 1. Concept image of virtual robotization of human arms

2   Related Work

2.1   Vibration of Robot Actuation

A robot's own internal motors and gears inevitably generate high-frequency vibrations, which are termed as ego-vibrations. These ego-vibrations cause a crucial problem in that they deteriorate acceleration and sound signals, so much research has dealt with noise subtraction to improve the sensing skill of robots [3-4].

In terms of robotization, we believe that the ego-vibrations are essential in the induction of a robot-like feeling. We propose to apply the annoying robot acceleration and noisy operating sounds to the human body and thus help to create a robotic body sense.

2.2   Haptic Alteration by Vibration Recording and Rendering

Recording vibrations resulting from object interaction and rendering the modeled vibrations is often used to alter haptic perception. For instance, the feeling of walking on gravel or snow [5], plunging a hand into a volume of fluid [6], tapping on rubber, wood, or aluminum [7-8], and scraping various surface textures [9] can be realistically simulated by vibrotactile feedback. Some studies have developed haptic recording and rendering systems with simple setups that allow the sharing of haptic experience [10-11]. These systems allow the user to touch a variety of objects in the environment. However, to the best of our knowledge, none of these studies has focused on the changed presentation of the haptic properties of the human body.

We previously implemented a system that virtually alters the feeling of a material on the body using periodic vibrotactile feedback [12]. We employed a decaying sinusoidal vibration model, which simulates the haptic properties of materials when they collide [7], [13]. The periodic ticking vibrotactile feedback we created could simulate rubber, wood, and aluminum collisions, but these were not robotic sensations.

On the other hand, this paper focuses on a robot-like "creaking" sensation. The present system involves continuous vibrations captured from real robot actuation, instead of the discrete collision-based vibrations from the prior study. Furthermore, we combine the vibrotactile feedback with visual and auditory feedback to improve the robotizing effect.

2.3   Illusion of Human Body Sense

The alteration of human proprioception has also been studied. One method of altering the sense of the body in space is called the kinesthetic illusion, which creates an illusory arm motion [14-16]. The illusion can be produced by using a vibration of about 100 Hz to activate the muscle spindles. It can be extended to the elongation of parts of the human body, which is known as the Pinocchio illusion [17].

An illusion of body-ownership called the rubber hand illusion [18-20] is provoked by simultaneously tapping on a person's hidden real hand and a visible rubber hand placed next to the real hand. The person feels as if the rubber hand has become their real hand. This illusion can also be induced by the synchronous movement of the person's real hand and a virtual hand on a screen [20]. Additionally, the visual realism of the virtual hand does not seem to contribute much to the enhancement of the body-ownership illusion. In this study, we use this phenomenon to create the feeling of ownership of a virtual robot arm using synchronous movements of the user's real arm and the virtual robot arm.

3   Virtual Robotization of the Human Arm

Our hypothesis is that presenting robot ego-vibrations to the user's body in accordance with his or her motion will make users believe that their body has become robotic. Thus, we employed a data-driven approach using vibration recording, modeling, and rendering, which has been reported to be a promising method in the creation of realistic virtual textures [9], [21-22].

3.1   Haptic Recording

We recorded the vibrations of the elbow joint of a robot arm (Unimate PUMA 260) that is used in general assembly lines, as shown in Fig. 2. After testing some other robots, we chose the PUMA because its simple servomotor and gear mechanism generates a strong vibration that humans can clearly recognize. A three-axis digital accelerometer (BMA180, Bosch Sensortec, ±16 g, 14 bit) was rigidly attached to the elbow joint with hot glue. The elbow joint was actuated at 0, 10, 20, 30 … 80 °/s in each direction. Note that actuation at 0 °/s means that the robot was actually stationary, but it still had some background vibration from its other components. We did not record the vibration at more than 80 °/s because the maximum angular velocity of the elbow joint was around 85 °/s. During each operation, the accelerometer recorded the three-axis acceleration data at a sampling rate of 2.5 kHz to capture what the robot felt as it moved at the specified angular velocity. The captured data were stored in the PC through a microcontroller (mbed NXP LPC1768, NXP semiconductors). In this vibration recording, we applied a 1.2 kHz low-pass filter to avoid an aliasing effect using a filter integrated in the accelerometer. This bandwidth covers the whole human haptic perceptual domain.

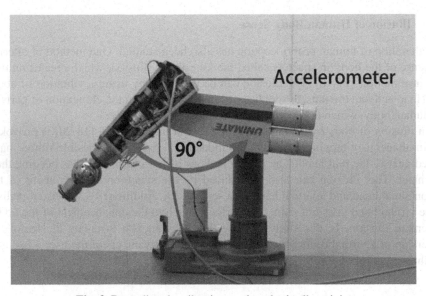

Fig. 2. Recording the vibration on the robot's elbow joint

3.2   Acceleration Data Modeling

We performed off-line processing steps to create a vibration model from each set of recorded raw data. First, we applied a 20 Hz high-pass filter to remove low-frequency components attributed to the change of orientation of the robot's forearm. Next, the three acceleration channels were summed to a single wave. We normalized the duration of acceleration data captured at the various angular velocities by selecting clipping one second of data around 45°, which is the center of the range of motion.

We employed Linear Predictive Cording (LPC) to approximate the spectral density of the raw acceleration data (Fig. 3). LPC is known as one of the most powerful speech processing techniques, and it is also used in haptic data modeling [9][22]. To make a model that approximates the spectral density of the raw data, we applied a tenth-order finite impulse response (FIR) filter to the acceleration data, and we calculated the coefficient vectors $\vec{a}(k)$ (k=1, 2 ... 10) of the LPC as a function of angular velocity, by minimizing the prediction error in the least squares sense. This calculation was performed using the `lpc` function in MATLAB (The MathWorks, Inc.).

The purpose of this modeling was to predict the next vibration value from a series of past data samples. The predicted value $\hat{x}(n)$ can be written as:

$$\hat{x}(n) = w - \sum_{k=1}^{10} a(k)\,x(n-k) \tag{1}$$

where n is the number of steps (n=0 is substituted), $x(n-k)$ is the value at the past k steps, $a(k)$ are the LPC coefficients, w is a sample of white Gaussian noise. While the model contains a similar spectral density to the raw data, the model in the time domain is not a representation of the same waves, because of the randomness of the white Gaussian noise. Therefore, users can feel natural continuous vibration.

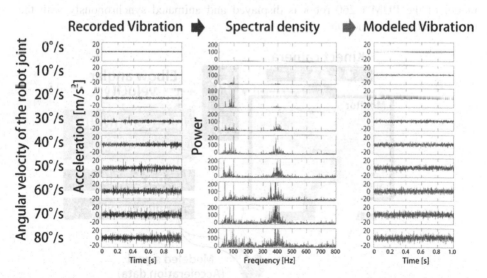

Fig. 3. Recorded vibration (left), example of LPC-modeled vibration (right), and overlaid spectral density (center)

3.3   Rendering the Robot-Like Feeling

Fig. 4 illustrates the configuration of the virtual robotization system. First, a motion tracking camera (Kinect sensor, Microsoft Corp.) captures the three-dimensional positions of the user's right shoulder, elbow, and hand at a sampling rate of 30 Hz. Next, the PC calculates the angular velocity of the user's right elbow joint from the three sets of position data and sends this value to the mbed microcontroller. The LPC coefficients for each angular velocity (0, 10, 20...80°/s), which were calculated in advance, are stored in the microcontroller. The microcontroller perform the real-time rendering based on Eq. 1 using a sample of white Gaussian noise and the LPC coefficients related to the closest elbow angular velocity. For example, when the user moves his or her elbow at angular velocity within the 35-44 °/s range, the system performs the rendering with the coefficients for 40 °/s. While the LPC coefficients for the rendering switch at the specific angular velocity (i.e., 34-35 or 44-45 °/s), none of the participants (see Section 4) noticed the transition. Then, the microcontroller outputs the modeled signal through a D/A converter (LTC1660, Linear Technology Corp., 10 bit) at a refresh rate of 2.5 kHz. The output is amplified by an audio amplifier (RSDA202, Rasteme Systems Co., Ltd.), and finally it is used to actuate the vibrotactile transducer (Force Reactor, Alps Electronic Co., Ltd.) mounted under an armband. The armband is attached to the right forearm close to the elbow joint so that the transducer makes contact with the lateral side of the elbow joint.

The armband also includes a small speaker that is actuated by the same signal as the transducer to emit an operating sound. However, we used headphones instead of the speaker in the experiment (see Section 4) to control the conditions. The visual model of the PUMA 260 robot is displayed and animated synchronously with the user's right forearm motion.

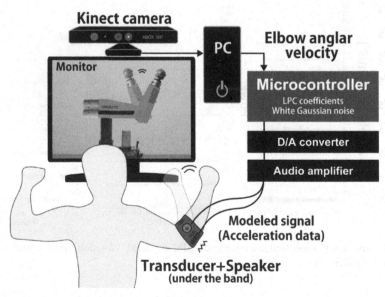

Fig. 4. The prototype of virtual robotization system

3.4   Latency Evaluation

We measured the latency from the movement of the user's real arm to animation of virtual robot arm. When the real arm movement was about 90 °/s angular speed, the latency was approximately 50 ms. Most of the latency was due to the camera. Because the gap was less than the latency (100-200ms) allowable between human motion and graphical responses [23], we considered it to be sufficiently small.

We demonstrated a preliminary version of the system to laboratory members who had never experienced the system (Fig. 5). None of the participants noticed the latency. The reactions of the participants appeared to be positive, including comments such as "My arm became the robot's arm" or "I have motors and gears in my elbow".

Fig. 5. User reactions at the demonstration

4   Verification of Robot-Like Feeling

The purpose of this psychophysical experiment was to verify the contribution of vibrotactile feedback to the subjective robot-like feeling. Using our virtual robotization system, we compared four sensory feedback conditions: visual only (V), visual + auditory (V+A), visual + haptic (V+H), and visual + auditory + haptic (V+A+H) by means of questionnaires.

4.1   Experimental Environment

We recruited six males and one female (aged 21-23, right-handed) who had never experienced the system. As shown in Fig. 6, all participants stood in front of the Kinect camera and wore the armband on their right elbow. The participants also wore noise-canceling headphones (QuietComfort 15, BOSE Corp.) to cancel out any sound generated by the actuation of the transducer. The operating sound of the robot was emitted from the right channel only because the position of the auditory and vibrotactile feedback should be the same for a more realistic robot-like feeling. The experimenter confirmed with the participants that they could feel the vibrotactile stimuli clearly.

The participants were asked to flex and extend their right elbow at various velocities, looking at the robot arm animation in the monitor. Each trial was 15 seconds long. After each trial, the participants were asked to answer the following two questions:

How Much Did You Feel the Robot-Like Feeling in Your Arm? The participants evaluated their confidence about whether their right arm felt like the robot in the monitor, on a visual analog scale (0: not robot at all, 100: totally robot). Note that we defined the central point (50) as the robot-like feeling in the V+A condition, since the participants had never before experienced a robot-like body sense and the reference point of the evaluation would be different between participants. In other conditions, the participants evaluated the robot-like feeling by comparing with the V+A condition.

How Much Did You Feel a Reaction Force? The typical expectation of a robotic body would be a friction-like force opposing the direction of body movement. Therefore, if the participants felt a resistance force when the there was none, as in this system, it might be a good quantitative measure of the perceived robot-like feeling. The participants answered the amount of the perceived reaction force with the visual-analog scale (0: completely smooth, 50: the same as usual, 100: felt strong force). Scores less than 50 points meant that the arm movement felt smoother than usual.

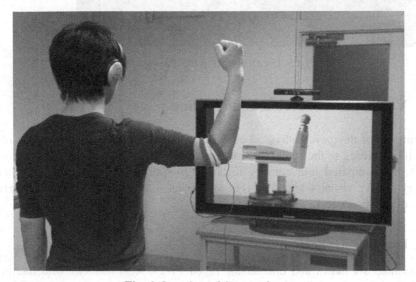

Fig. 6. Overview of the experiment

4.2   Experimental Procedure

First, the participants preliminarily experienced all four conditions once to ensure they understood the experimental procedures. The participants did not answer the two questions in this preliminary sequence, but the experimenter asked them to evaluate them in their mind. All participants started in the V+A condition, which corresponds to the reference point (50 points) of the robot-like feeling evaluation, and then they experienced the other three conditions in a random order.

In the main sequence, the participant first experienced the V+A condition to remember the reference point for the robot-like feeling evaluation. After that, all four conditions including V+A were conducted in a random order, and the participants answered the two questions. This sequence was repeated three times for each participant.

4.3   Results

Fig. 7 shows the perceived amount of robot-like feeling and reaction force. Whiskers indicate the standard deviation. The robot-like feeling was highest in the V+A+H condition, followed by the V+A, V+H, and V conditions. We performed a one-way analysis of variance (ANOVA) and found significant differences between the feedback conditions (F(3,24) = 3.35, p < 0.001). A post-hoc comparison using Tukey's HSD method between the feedback conditions showed a significant difference (p < 0.05) in all the pairs except V+A vs. V+H. The comparison between V+A and V+H showed a marginally significant difference (p = 0.07 < 0.10).

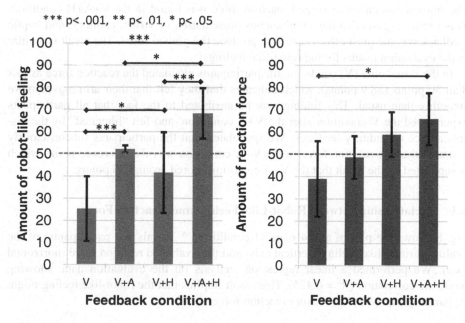

Fig. 7. Mean values of the evaluation of robot-like feeling (left) and reaction force (right)

Participants felt that the reaction force was highest in the V+A+H condition, followed by the V+H, V+A, and V conditions. A one-way ANOVA between feedback conditions showed significant differences ($F(3,24) = 3.34$, $p < 0.05$). A post-hoc test revealed significant differences only between the V and V+A+H conditions ($p < 0.05$).

5   Discussion

5.1   Robot-Like Feeling

Robot-like feeling was perceived most strongly in the V+A+H condition. This result suggests that the combination of the visual, auditory, and haptic feedback was the most effective in enhancing the robot-like feeling. Simultaneous feedback of auditory and haptic feedback particularly contributed to robot-like feeling, which was supported by the fact that the evaluation of the V+A+H condition was significantly higher than the V+A and V+H conditions, as well as the more traditional V condition.

The evaluation of robot-like feeling in the V+A condition (52.1 points), which we defined as the reference, was close to the actual reference (50 points) and the standard deviation was particularly small. These results imply that the participants could understand the reference position and were able to compare the robot-like feelings between the conditions.

5.2   Reaction Force

The highest amount of evaluated reaction force was found in the V+A+H condition. This result suggests that the simultaneous presentation of visual, auditory, and haptic feedback was the most effective way to produce the pseudo force. The result is similar to the evaluation results for the robot-like feeling.

In the visual only (V) condition, the participants evaluated the reaction force as less than 50 points (38.9 points), which indicates that they felt that their arm moved more smoothly than usual. This finding may be attributed to the fact that all participants experienced the V condition after the V+A condition, and felt "liberated" by the disappearance of auditory feedback. We speculated that the participants subconsciously assumed that the reaction force in the V+A condition was the reference point, which is supported by the result that the V+A condition scored around 50 points.

5.3   Relationship between Robot-Like Feeling and Reaction Force

Fig. 8 shows the plot of all 84 pairs (4 conditions * 3 trials * 7 participants) of the evaluated robot-like feeling (vertical axis) and the evaluated reaction force (horizontal axis). We performed a linear regression analysis on the evaluation data, showing moderate correlation ($R^2 = 0.425$). This result implies that the robot-like feeling might be partially caused by the illusory reaction force.

However, as shown in Fig. 7, there was a different tendency between the V+A and V+H condition; the robot-like feeling in V+H condition was lower, while the reaction force was higher. This inconsistency might be attributed to a higher contribution of the auditory cue to the robot-like feeling, and a higher contribution of the vibrotactile cue to the resultant illusory force cues, another haptic sensation.

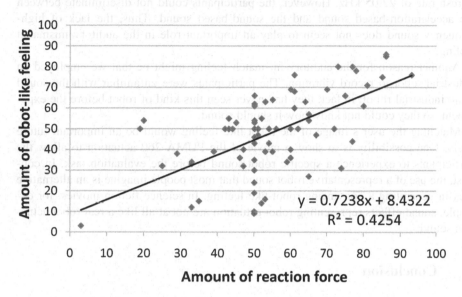

Fig. 8. Relationship between the robot-like feeling and the reaction force

Realism of Robot-Like Body Sense. Three participants commented that they felt creaking in the conditions using haptic feedback (i.e., V+H and V+A+H). This comment implies that the haptic feedback of robot vibration could produce a feeling of creaking friction to some participants. Also, two participants reported that they felt as if the robot arm model on the monitor became their right arm, because the robot model was synchronized with the movement of their real arm. As reported in [20], synchronous movement of the virtual arm and the real arm can facilitate the body-ownership illusion. However, we intend to improve the level of the body-ownership illusion in the future studies. Completely hiding the participant's real arm and over-laying the virtual robot arm would be one promising approach in the facilitation of this illusion.

According to these comments and the evaluation of the robot-like feeling and reaction force, it was confirmed that the integration of robot vibration, creaking sound effects, and the visual robot model synchronized with the user's motion could cause the participant to feel that their body had become robotic.

Realism of Auditory Feedback. A negative comment, stated by three participants, was that the presented sound was mismatched with the participant's expectation of a robot's sound. In this experiment, the auditory feedback was computed using acceleration data, to which a 1.2 kHz low-pass filter was applied. The lack of high-frequency components might cause an auditory mismatch between the generated sound and the original noise.

To verify this effect, we performed an experiment that recorded robot sound using a microphone (Gigaware 60139B, RadioShack Corp.) and the sound feedback at a refresh rate of 22.05 kHz. However, the participants could not discriminate between the acceleration-based sound and the sound-based sound. Thus, the lack of high-frequency sound does not seem to play an important role in the auditory mismatch feeling.

Another reason for the auditory mismatch feeling might be that we employed an industrial robot to record vibration. The participants were unfamiliar with the sound of an industrial robot; in fact, they had never seen this kind of robot before the experiment, so they could not know how it should sound.

Matching the user's image of the robot-like feeling would be an important future study. One possibility is to show a movie of the PUMA 260 actuation to allow the participants to experience a specific robot sound before the evaluation task. In contrast, the use of a representative robot sound that most people imagine is an alternative idea in generating a convincing robot-like feeling. In science fiction movies, for example, sound effects representing robot actuation are not at all like a real robot actuation sound.

6   Conclusion

This paper presented a method to create a robot-like body sense, aiming for a new entertainment experience as if the human user had actually become a robot. We proposed the vibration recording of real robot actuation, data-driven modeling based on spectral approximation, and vibrotactile rendering to the user's elbow as a function of the elbow angular velocity. We also developed a system that virtually robotized the human arm visually, aurally and haptically by means of integrating a visual robot model that tracks the user's arm motion and produces a creaking sound and vibrotactile feedback. Using this system, we compared four sensory conditions to evaluate the participants' subjective robot-like feeling and perceived reaction force. This experiment revealed that the combination of visual, auditory, and haptic feedback was the most effective in inducing a robot-like feeling. The pseudo reaction force, which might also reflect a robot-like feeling, was generated most strongly with this combination. Additionally, some comments from the participants suggested that our approach can simulate friction of the robot joint.

We intend to upgrade our system to an augmented reality (AR) system using a video see-though head mounted display (HMD) so that the users can see their own body visually changed into that of a robot (Fig. 9). A camera mounted on the HMD captures the user's subjective view and tracks markers attached on the arms. The HMD then superimposes virtual robot arms on the user's arms. The AR system will provide an even more immersive experience of the robotized body.

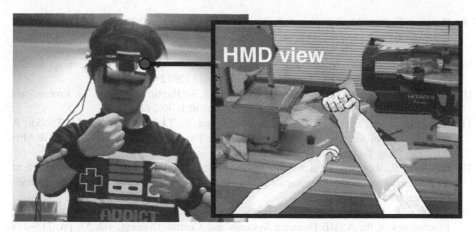

Fig. 9. AR system for virtual robotization of human arms

We can alter the user's body to feel like various other objects with a similar setup. We have tested a clicking multimeter dial, a water-spurting garden hose, a groaning vacuum cleaner, and peeling Velcro tape. We have anecdotally observed that vibrotactile stimuli of these materials provides an entertainingly weird body sense, like ticking-dial elbow, water-spurting or air-breathing palm, and Velcro arm.

Acknowledgements. This work was supported by the JSPS Institutional Program for Young Researcher Overseas Visits.

References

1. TN Games, FPS Gaming Vest, http://tngames.com/products (last access: August 18, 2013)
2. Ooshima, S., Hashimoto, Y., Ando, H., Watanabe, J., Kajimoto, H.: Simultaneous Presentation of Tactile and Auditory Motion to the Abdomen to Present the Feeling of Being Slashed. In: Proceedings of the SICE Annual Conference, pp. 467–471 (2008)
3. McMahan, W., Kuchenbecker, K.J.: Spectral subtraction of robot motion noise for improved event detection in tactile acceleration signals. In: Isokoski, P., Springare, J. (eds.) EuroHaptics 2012, Part I. LNCS, vol. 7282, pp. 326–337. Springer, Heidelberg (2012)
4. Ince, G., Nakadai, K., Rodemann, T., Hasegawa, Y., Tsujino, H., Imura, J.I.: Ego noise suppression of a robot using template subtraction. In: Proceedings of the IEEE/RSJ International Conference on Intelligent Robots and Systems (IROS), pp. 199–204 (2009)
5. Visell, Y., Law, A., Cooperstock, J.R.: Touch is everywhere: Floor surfaces as ambient haptic interfaces. IEEE Transactions on Haptics 2, 148–159 (2009)
6. Cirio, G., Marchal, M., L'ecuyer, A., Cooperstock, J.R.: Vibrotactile rendering of splashing fluids. IEEE Transactions on Haptics 6, 117–122 (2012)
7. Okamura, A.M., Cutkosky, M.R., Dennerlein, J.T.: Reality-based models for vibration feedback in virtual environments. IEEE/ASME Transactions on Mechatronics 6, 245–252 (2001)

8. Hachisu, T., Sato, M., Fukushima, S., Kajimoto, H.: Augmentation of material property by modulating vibration resulting from tapping. In: Isokoski, P., Springare, J. (eds.) EuroHaptics 2012, Part I. LNCS, vol. 7282, pp. 173–180. Springer, Heidelberg (2012)

9. Romano, J.M., Kuchenbecker, K.J.: Creating realistic virtual textures from contact acceleration data. IEEE Transactions on Haptics 5, 109–119 (2012)

10. Takeuchi, Y., Kamuro, S., Minamizawa, K., Tachi, S.: Haptic Duplicator. In: Proceedings of the Virtual Reality International Conference, pp. 30:1–30:2 (2012)

11. Minamizawa, K., Kakehi, Y., Nakatani, M., Mihara, S., Tachi, S.: TECHTILE Toolkit: A prototyping tool for designing haptic media. In: Proceedings of the ACM SIGGRAPH 2012 Emerging Technologies, p. 22 (2012)

12. Kurihara, Y., Hachisu, T., Sato, M., Fukushima, S., Kajimoto, H.: Virtual alteration of body material by periodic vibrotactile feedback. In: Proceedings of the IEEE Virtual Reality Conference (2013)

13. Wellman, P., Howe, R.D.: Towards realistic vibrotactile display in virtual environments. In: Proceedings of the ASME Dynamic Systems and Control Division, vol. 57, pp. 713–718 (1995)

14. Goodwin, G.M., McCloskey, D.I., Matthews, P.B.C.: The contribution of muscle afferents to kinaesthesia shown by vibration induced illusions of movement and by the effects of paralysing joint afferents. Brain 95, 705–748 (1972)

15. Burke, D., Hagbarth, K.E., Löfstedt, L., Wallin, G.: The responses of human muscle spindle endings to vibration of non-contracting muscles. J. Physiol. (Lond.) 261, 673–693 (1976)

16. Naito, E.: Sensing limb movements in the motor cortex: How humans sense limb movement. Neuroscientist 10, 73–82 (2004)

17. Lackner, J.R.: Some proprioceptive influences on the perceptual representation of body shape and orientation. Brain 111, 281–297 (1988)

18. Botvinick, M., Cohen, J.: Rubber hands "feel" touch that eyes see. Nature 391, 756 (1998)

19. Tsakiris, M.: My body in the brain: A neurocognitive model of body-ownership. Neuropsychologica 48, 703–712 (2010)

20. Slater, M., Perez-Marcos, D., Ehrsson, H.H., Sanchez-Vives, M.V.: Inducing illusory ownership of virtual body. Frontiers in Neuroscience 3, 214–220 (2009)

21. Okamura, A.M., Webster, R.J., Nolin, J., Johnson, K.W., Jafry, H.: The haptic scissors: Cutting in virtual environments. In: Proceedings of the IEEE International Conference on Robotics and Automation (ICRA), pp. 828–833 (2003)

22. Romano, J.M., Yoshioka, T., Kuchenbecker, K.J.: Automatic filter design for synthesis of haptic textures from recorded acceleration data. In: Proceedings of the IEEE International Conference on Robotics and Automation (ICRA), pp. 1815–1821 (2010)

23. Dabrowski, J.R., Munsone, V.: Is 100 milliseconds too fast? In: Proceedings of the ACM Human Factors in Computing Systems (CHI), pp. 317–318 (2001)

BOLLOCKS!! Designing Pervasive Games That Play with the Social Rules of Built Environments

Conor Linehan, Nick Bull, and Ben Kirman

Lincoln Social Computing Research Centre, University of Lincoln, LN6 7TS, UK
clinehan@lincoln.ac.uk

Abstract. We propose that pervasive games designed with mechanics that are specifically in opposition with, or disruptive of, social rules of the environment in which they are played, have unique potential to provide interesting, provocative experiences for players. We explore this concept through the design and evaluation of an experimental game prototype, *Shhh!*, inspired by the juvenile game *Bollocks,* and implemented on Android mobile devices, which challenges players to make loud noises in libraries. Six participants played the game before engaging in semi-structured interviews, explored through inductive thematic analysis. Results suggest that the game provoked in players a heightened awareness of social rules, as well as a complex social dilemma of whether or not to act. We conclude by presenting a model for designing games that play with the social, as well as physical, rules of the environments in which they are set.

Keywords: Pervasive Games, Social rules, Social Context, Unwritten rules, Non-players, Critical Games.

1 Introduction

Pervasive games [22,24], location-based games [5], and mixed reality games [7,9] are all terms that describe entertainment computing applications in which the geography of the real world functions as an essential component of game play. These games typically use mobile computing technologies such as GSM [30], Bluetooth [8,27], WiFi [4] GPS, or augmented reality [8] in order to incorporate the movement of players through the real world as part of the fantasy narrative of the game. The assumption is that game tasks can make real world locations and activities more interesting or meaningful [28]. However, there is a surprising lack of variety in the design of these games and in the types of experiences they are designed to provoke. The majority take the form of treasure hunts, where players must visit real-world locations in order to tick off game-world tasks. Rarely do these games acknowledge or encourage players to engage with interesting physical or social features of the environments in which they are played. It appears that the motivation behind developing these games is often to explore the capabilities of the enabling technologies, rather than to provide interesting experiences for players.

D. Reidsma, H. Katayose, and A. Nijholt (Eds.): ACE 2013, LNCS 8253, pp. 123–137, 2013.
© Springer International Publishing Switzerland 2013

Researchers have recently argued [20,21] that pervasive games have relatively unexplored potential to provide engaging experiences through provoking players to interact meaningfully with already interesting real-world environments. For example, the game *Blowtooth* [20,21] is designed to explore the unique affordances of international airports (see [16]). The game narrative requires players to smuggle virtual goods through real airport security by planting them on fellow passengers, before later tracking those passengers down and retrieving their goods. Blowtooth is extremely simple both technologically and in terms of game design. Kirman, Linehan and Lawson [20] argue that, despite its simplicity, the game provokes interesting experiences for players, because, through the game mechanics, the player is confronted with aspects of the environment that already cause anxiety and exhilaration; in this case the unparalleled security and surveillance of the airport environment. Conversely, the game is not interesting or fun, or even a coherent game, if played anywhere other than an airport.

The Blowtooth game provides an interesting starting point for the current paper. Specifically, we were interested in exploring further the concept of designing simple pervasive games that interact provocatively with the implicit features of *built environments* (i.e., the human-made surroundings that provide the setting for human activity [26]). It must be noted that Blowtooth gained much of its engaging power from the extraordinary nature of the airport environment. Here, we aim to investigate whether similarly interesting experiences can be designed for more commonly experienced environments. Specifically, we propose that these experiences can be achieved through the design of game mechanics that are in opposition with, or disruptive of, social rules that exist in everyday built environments. Indeed, the mischievous breaking of social rules is a type of play that many find engaging [19]. Of course, all games are social experiences that take place in social spaces, as discussed at length in the literature (i.e., [18,29]). Here we investigate specifically how pervasive games can create engaging experiences through encouraging people to consider, explore, and play with, existing social rules of their environment.

The following sections of the paper will explore the rationale for designing pervasive games that ask the player to engage in the mischievous breaking of social rules. We first discuss how social rules effect the expression of behaviour, and identify the built environment as a particular type of behavioural cue. We then discuss mischief and naughtiness as a game play aesthetic, and consider the effects of mischievous play on non-players. Subsequently, we present the design and evaluation of a game, *Shhh!*, which challenges players to make loud noises in libraries.

2   Background

2.1   Social Rule Following and the Built Environment

Human behaviour is highly sensitive to social influence. The expression of our desires, goals, intentions and impulses is mediated at all times by expectations, spoken or unspoken, of what is appropriate in the particular context in which we find ourselves [3]. The definition of what is appropriate behaviour is often complex, and changes depending on a seemingly endless variety of variables, such as whether you are inside or outside, how many other people are present, what those people are wearing, your relationship with those people, the time of day, and so on. For example, there are very different expectations on behaviour when attending a football match in comparison with attending a lecture, despite these being topographically similar behaviours (i.e., both feature large audiences passively focused on the activities of central actors). Humans show remarkable ability to adapt appropriately to these subtle changes in expectations [2]. Researchers have suggested that *social acceptance* is one of the most powerful unconditioned reinforcers for humans [1]. We work hard to gain acceptance and to avoid disapproval.

The specific expectations of any given context are both signalled and enforced by the behaviour of others. We observe others and infer appropriate social norms based on those observations [1]. For example, a busy dance floor invites participation, and while around children, an adult may soften their tone of voice and vocabulary. In situations where we have misinterpreted the norms, people are often quick to intervene directly and make sure that we understand. This is often an embarrassing and memorable experience for both parties.

Interestingly, buildings function as particularly strong contextual cues for behaviour. Indeed, there is a field of academic study that examines specifically how the 'built environment' (human-made environments) affects our experience and supports and encourages particular patterns of behaviour (see [26]). Thus, there seems great potential in designing games that are located in specific types of buildings. Such games could take advantage of the fact that certain types of buildings evoke certain types of behaviour, regardless of where in the world they are found.

2.2   Mischief as a Gameplay Aesthetic

Social rules are essential to all game playing. For example, the 'Magic Circle' [15,29] is a term that describes the unspoken agreement about acceptable behaviour in the social context of game playing. The game-playing context provides players with cues for, and gives permission for, many types of behaviour that would be unacceptable or confusing in other contexts. Similarly, there are certain behaviours, such as cheating, which are unacceptable in the game-playing context. Thus, games inherently function as powerful social cues for appropriate behaviour and, indeed, all games are inherently social experiences [18,29].

Mischievous play is a type of behaviour that serves to explore and test the boundaries of social acceptability in game playing contexts [19]. Mischievous players enjoy subverting and appropriating game rules and social expectations of the game-playing context in order to produce surprising and entertaining experiences for themselves and other players. For example, in farming games, players create elaborate pictures using variety of crops [17], and in Spore [23], players used design tools to make humorous creatures modelled after various parts of human anatomy [19].

Importantly, there is a distinction between mischievous play and genuinely anti-social behaviour. The key to mischief is the apparent attitude of playfulness. The mischievous player knows there are limits to their behaviour, and the *intent* is to do no harm [13]. This is in stark contrast to the intent of griefing or trolling, which is purposefully disruptive, often with negative and anti-social intentions. Researchers have argued that mischievous play is a valid, interesting and valuable form of game play behaviour, which designers should acknowledge and facilitate [19].

Kirman, Linehan and Lawson [19] primarily discuss mischievous play in terms of playing with the social environment that surrounds game playing. However, there are games that encourage players to mischievously explore and test the boundaries of social acceptability in other environments (i.e., beyond the safety of the magic circle of a game). For example, consider the game played by school children where a (typically obscene) word is chosen and players must take turns to speak the word in class (generally called "Bollocks" in the UK and Ireland). Each successive player must say the word louder than the previous, until somebody is caught by the teacher, or gives in. The attraction of the game lies in the tension between the rules of the environment (stay silent) and the rules of the game (make a noise), creating an exhilarating social experience. Another example is that of juvenile "kissing" games (e.g. "Spin the Bottle"), which give players permission to explore the social boundaries of intimacy.

We propose an extension to the conclusions of Kirman, Linehan and Lawson [19], who insist that mischievous play in game playing contexts should be acknowledged and supported. We suggest that mischievous playing with social rules can form the basis of exhilarating, memorable experiences beyond traditional game playing contexts. We call for the design of games that specifically encourage players to engage in behaviour that is in opposition with, or disruptive of, the social rules of built environments. We suggest that this approach may be particularly beneficial to the design of pervasive games. Since buildings function as powerful signals for controlling the expression of behaviour, and games do similarly, the playing of games in the built environment may present complex, challenging social experiences for players, particularly in situations where the rules of the game are in competition with the rules of the environment for control over player behaviour. This could be seen as an example of a 'dark gameplay pattern' that intentionally causes emotional dilemmas for players [31].

2.3   Considering Non-players

The experimental game prototype described and evaluated in this paper, *Shhh,* asks players to make noise in a library. It is envisioned that, due to the convention for quiet working in the library environment, players will experience exhilaration at the challenge to break that rule, since that the consequence of being noticed involves harsh disapproval by peers. However, in designing such a game, some consideration must be given to the effects that game play may have on other library users. Indeed, such considerations are a necessary step in the design of all pervasive games [14,25].

Niemi, Sawano and Waern [25] suggest that *anonymity* and *accountability* are the most important factors when considering non-players in pervasive game design. *Anonymity* refers to whether the game intrudes on non-players privacy, or reveals information about non-players to the players through the technology employed in the game. Shhh! makes no attempt to record anything about the environment other than the loudness of sounds produced by the player. It doesn't even record the sound itself, just a measure of loudness. Thus, the game does not infringe upon non-player privacy, according to the definition provided by Niemi et al. It could be argued, however, that encouraging noise in a quiet environment is in some way an infringement on privacy. We must remind the reader that the intention is not to provoke players into making lots of noise, rather, to encourage in players a heightened awareness of how well defined and understood the social rules are, as well as the implications of breaking those social rules. We envision that few, if any, players will cause any serious disruption to fellow library users. Further, any noise that players do create will be rare, brief and more than likely contextually appropriate. This is something that we will investigate in the user study.

Accountability refers to whether actions are traceable to the source, who can be held accountable for any adverse effects caused [14,25]. In the current game, the potentially invasive behaviour (the making of noise) is inseparably and observably linked with the player (i.e., the person who makes the noise). Not only is the player easily held accountable for their actions by non-players, but that accountability is actually a core component that drives fun of the game. Indeed, if players do not feel any compulsion to remain quiet, the game will not provide an interesting experience.

The experience that the game is designed to provoke is the complex dilemma of whether or not to act. This dilemma serves as an analogue for some of the most challenging situations that we commonly experience, which often involve the strong urge to act but reluctance to do so because of social norms; such as whether to intervene in arguments between spouses, or the need to tolerate the extreme political beliefs of a relative at a family gathering. We believe that pervasive games can provide fascinating, memorable experiences through allowing players to explore exactly these types of complex social dilemmas.

3   Game Design

The experimental game prototype, called *Shhh!*, was inspired by the children's playground game, mentioned above, which dares players to make loud noises in inappropriate situations (usually the classroom). This game provides an interesting basis for our exploration of social rules of built environments as game mechanics, due to the combination of simple mechanics and the genuine excitement it encourages in players. We decided to set the game in libraries, as these are buildings that have obvious and easily understood rules that are (primarily) enforced by social convention (i.e., disapproval by other library users is a much more likely consequence of play than formal action by the library staff). Moreover, since we had a great deal of experience with observing the social rules of the library, were confident that players would feel compelled to engage in socially acceptable behaviour, thus creating for players the desired social dilemma of whether or not to act.

The original playground game was altered through the development of an application that runs on Android mobile devices. Specifically, the application uses the phones' audio input to measure sound levels. This allows players, upon making a noise, to see a score that corresponds to the sound that they made. It also allows for that score to be saved to a leader board, facilitating asynchronous play.

Upon reaching a library in which they wish to play, the player launches the game application on their mobile device. The application initially verifies whether the player is genuinely in a library (this feature was not implemented in the prototype evaluated), before presenting the main input screen (figure 1). This screen is composed primarily of one large button, which, when pressed, activates the device's microphone. The player is expected to make a noise at this point. The application identifies the volume of sound in the environment at that moment (using an algorithm that averages values returned by the 'getMaxAmplitude' function of the 'Media Recorder' utility within the Android OS). When they have finished making noise, the player clicks the button again to stop recording. The application returns a score to the player; louder noises produce higher scores. This score is then added to both the overall league table for the game, plus a league table for the specific library in which they played. The local league table facilitates people to compete with their friends, colleagues and classmates in an uncomplicated manner.

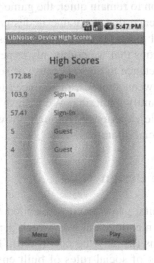

Fig. 1. Screenshots of prototype application. Left panel shows the input screen. Right panel shows the leader board.

4   Plan for Evaluation

The intention of the study was to understand participants' experience of engaging with the experimental game. Since no model already exists for explaining the type of task the game asks players to undertake, it was important to explore participant experiences in an open-ended, qualitative manner. Six participants were recruited through a combination of advertisements and personal contacts. Each participant engaged with the study separately. The study took place in the main library of a UK University. Participants initially met the researcher outside the library, where a brief explanation of the game was presented. A smart phone, on which the game had been installed, was then given to the participant and they were asked to carry out three simple tasks using the application to ensure that they understood how it worked; view the local high scores, view the global high scores, sign in. Participants were then asked to enter the library, to try to "get a high score," and to return when they were finished. Subsequently, participants were taken to a more relaxed environment, where a semi-structured interview took place to understand the player's experience of playing the game. The researcher began by asking participants how they felt generally about the experience, before asking specifically about the library environment, how they felt about making noise and playing games in that environment, and whether other library users reacted in any way to their behaviour. Participant responses were audio recorded and later transcribed. These transcripts form the basis of the analysis presented below.

Interview transcripts were analysed through inductive thematic analysis [6], a form of qualitative analysis particularly useful for investigating novel subjects in little-understood domains. Data was first read carefully multiple times by the first author. The structure of the data was then broken down to allow for analysis. Specifically, each separate concept (often, but not necessarily corresponding to a sentence) expressed by a participant was assigned a separate row in a spreadsheet. A total of 24 relevant conceptual labels, formed of short sentences and quotes, were derived from the corpus of interview data by the second author. These, together with a description and examples of each code, were given to the first author, who analysed the data independently and examined the fit of the codes to the data. Results of both analyses were compared and consensus reached on a code list of 13 categories.

5   Results and Discussion

Six first-order themes were identified, which formed two second-order themes; *considerations of the library environment*, and *considerations of game play*. The coding scheme is illustrated in (Figure 2). While the themes identified appear to represent distinct concepts, it must be noted that they all discuss aspects of the tension between playing the game and behaving appropriately in the library. Hence, participant's utterances could often be classified under a number of these codes. However, we are

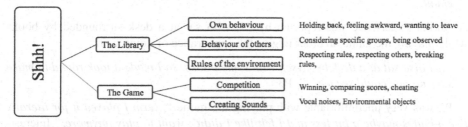

Fig. 2. Illustration of the coding scheme used to describe qualitative data

confident that this coding structure aids the reader in understanding the subjective experience of participants. The identified themes are expanded upon in detail below. All quotes are presented unedited.

5.1   Considerations of the Library Environment

Understandably, a lot of discussion focused on the nature of the library as an environment in which to play. These discussions can be described under three first order themes; players' awareness of their *own behaviour,* the *consideration of others* and the *rules of the environment.*

Own Behaviour. This theme refers to instances when participants expressed acute awareness of their own behaviour while playing the game. This is interesting as it provides some insight into their willingness (or reluctance) to engage with the game task, as well as the impact of the social environment on their behaviour. Participants often regretted making sounds and drawing attention to themselves;

> *"....I was stood in a stairwell where it was quite busy and I just yelled 'mic check' as if I was checking the microphone to get the levels right and I realised it was quite loud.....I sort of looked at it and went ' I'm in a library I need to be quiet'"* (P6).

The majority of the participants reported feeling out of place and out of their comfort zone by playing the game in the environment chosen. P1 suggested, *"it was a bit weird to be honest and very strange.* The word most commonly used by participants when describing how they felt when playing the game was *"awkward".* They reported feeling awkward while walking around the library devising strategies for making sounds that wouldn't draw attention to them. Another participant mentioned that they spent a lot of the time sitting at a desk, speaking random words into the phone, which led to them feeling *"rather odd."*

Many participants tried to blend into the environment while playing the game, so that non-participants wouldn't think they were acting strangely or inappropriate. For example, P5 reported,

> *"...the librarian walked passed me while I was sat at a desk and I turned the phone off and just sort of opened up an email from my tutor and pretended to compose an email..."*

A similar experience was reported by P3, who sat at a desk surrounded by books while playing the game, in order to give the appearance of doing work;

> *"...I also sat at a desk by myself with some books, so I made a look round to make sure no one could see me..."*- P3.

P2 was very uncomfortable with playing the game; *"...erm I played it for literally five minutes maybe a bit less and I felt like I didn't want to play anymore."* Interestingly, despite only staying in the library for a few minutes, the above participant reported one instance of shouting directly into the microphone at the top of their voice.

"I was like, I cannot get any louder than what they have done ..." In fact, it was after making this very loud sound that the participant refused to play anymore due to people staring at them.

The finding that the majority of participants felt very aware of their own behaviour, often to the point of awkwardness, suggests that they were very aware of the social environment while playing. However, it must be noted that only one participant (P1) failed to engage enthusiastically with the task. This participant reported discomfort at the task that the game asked them to carry out, *"it had a whole stigma over the noise levels."* Thus, despite their awkwardness and reluctance, most players did seem to engage (cautiously) with the game, taking steps to minimise social disapproval.

Consideration of Others. This theme refers to instances when participants specifically expressed consideration of other library users (i.e., non-participants) in their discussion of game play experience. This provides further insight into their awareness of the social environment. One participant reported that, when in a part of the library where it wasn't frowned upon to talk, they still felt a bit uncomfortable making loud noises. This was due to the fact that some of the nearby library users were mature students (the UK term for older students in higher education), *"there were more older people in the library at that time as well. Yeah I thought about that a bit more as I didn't want to disturb them"* (P1).

Due to the fact that the prototype application was installed on a specific device, which was given to participants at the beginning of the session, participants often had two phones with them in the library. Participants reported awareness that people looked at them strangely for having two phones on them. *"No-one came up to me, just the funny looks I had from holding two phones at one point...."* (P4). Indeed, participants reported noticing that sometimes non-participants sat and stared at them in an intimidating manner. Interestingly, none of the non-participants actually came up to the participants to find out what they were doing or why they were acting so strangely. P6 suggested, *"Most people are shy when you see someone doing something.*

A number of participants reported paying more attention than normal to the behaviour and conversations of others in the library. For instance, P3 noticed how much non-participants discussed nights out and other social events rather than their work: *"It has people who annoy you as they speak about their night out, but I suppose that's it really, people have different attitudes towards the library."* This was very interesting, as it is some indication that the game led participants to not only notice others more than normal, but also pay attention to their conversations and actions. Interestingly, the above participant mentioned that if they were talking so much they would, *" feel quite embarrassed by doing that. Just how it is really."* Ironically, they were also playing the game at the time, making sounds and breaking the rules of the environment. Overall, it seems that the game provoked participants into deeper contemplation of social features of the library environment.

Rules of the Environment. This theme examines how players' awareness of the social rules of the library environment affected their experience of playing the game. Most participants reported initially respecting the rules of the environment, *"When I* *was first in there I was quite reserved 'cus I didn't want to make too much noise in the library"* (P1). Interestingly, while most participants felt like this initially, none of them refused to engage with the game entirely.

In the particular library where this research was carried out, there are numerous floors, only one of which has a strict rule on absolute silence. It seems that, out of respect for the rules, participants largely avoided playing games on that floor, *"...you see I was on the first floor, you're allowed to speak and do what you want, if I was on the third floor the yes, obviously."* That participant was then asked if they had been on the third floor would they have played the game or been too afraid to. They responded with *"I would have felt to embarrassed and scared to do it."* Thus, even while playing an intentionally disruptive game, participants carefully adapted their behaviour to subtle differences in social rules in different parts of the same building. This finding is fascinating, as it illustrates the dilemma that players of *Shhh!* felt they were faced with; the complex calculations involved in balancing the competitive, goal directed behaviour of game playing versus the social rules of the environment in which it was played. Players wanted to win, but they didn't want to be embarrassed or to get caught.

Since the third floor of the library in which we held the study has uniquely strict rules on noise levels, we assumed that absolutely none of the players would attempt to play there. However, this was not the case. Two participants saw the strict rules of this floor as a challenge. Fascinatingly, players adapted the sounds they made due to the less forgiving environment to something more *"subtle and something you could get away with"* (P5). These participants felt the need to make sounds that seemed natural in that context, for example, dropping books on the floor. P6 tried blowing into the microphone as a way of making noise. However, instead of simply picking the phone up blowing into the microphone the participant reported, *"I'll pick up the phone and look a bit confused into the phone and blow into the mic."* (P6). The participant felt the need to put on an act in order to avoid disapproval.

The playing of the game on this floor by a minority of players is interesting, but not unproblematic, since it is not clear whether it crosses the line between mischief and genuinely antisocial behaviour.

"...you could almost argue that competition in this game almost encourages extreme behaviour or cheating because you can't beat them without extreme behaviour." (P5).

However, these players did not simply go into the quiet area and shout into their phones, they attempted creative ways of gaining high scores that had less likelihood of bringing about undesirable consequences, and thus were interacting thoughtfully within subtle social rules of the social environment. In social terms, playing in this location had a higher likelihood to cause embarrassment for the player, to cause disruption to non-players, and, indeed, to bring about disciplinary action for the player. In gaming terms, these players saw this floor as having a higher level of difficulty and were intrigued and challenged to produce a high score in this less forgiving environment.

5.2   Considerations of Game Play

While the majority of discussion focused on the library environment, there was also significant discussion regarding the playing of the game. These topics of discussion can be described under two first order themes; *competition*, and *strategies for gaining high scores.*

Competition. Competition was facilitated through a simple leader board in the application. Discussions of competition are interesting, as they demonstrate that the game design, while incredibly simple, was engaging enough to present participants with the dilemma of whether or not to break the social rules of the library environment.

Most participants reported competition as a motivator for their continued play, *"It said the world high score was 112. So I aimed for to beat that and I did beat that. I didn't smash that record but I beat it! Will you acknowledge that I beat your score?"* (P3). Other participants found that they just wanted to get on to the leader board and not worry about being the best, *"...I mean I saw the scores and I wasn't aiming for the top I was aiming to go mid table and I ended up score quite high on my first few tries...."* (P6). When participants saw that their scores were close to the record, it made them want to play more, *"...that's when I thought, you know what if I'm going to make my mark on the game, you got to set the bar for someone so I just raised the bar an extra bit higher."* (P6).

It became apparent through analysis of the data that what was happening in the game was being discussed amongst friends. For example, a number of participants reported that, before they participated, they discussed the game with people who had already played it. Rather than being upset at the apparent corruption of the naivety of our participant pool, we saw this as evidence of the engaging nature of the game and the inherent competition that if provoked. *"...I heard from a previous person ... that he coughed also and I thought I would just try and beat him"* (P1); *"Well yeah, I wanted to beat my house mate."* (P2); *"it is more fun in a group"* (P1). Participants mentioned that their discussions of the game pushed them to get higher scores, as they dared other players to beat their scores, *"I mean I could twang a bass string or hit a drum and be like 'yeah go on, try and beat my score, I dare you"* (P6); *it is bragging rights really......So you know it is good fun to see that I had taken over all the leader board, absolutely"* (P6).

Strategies for Gaining High Scores. The only action available in the game was to make and record a noise. However, this action was in direct contradiction of the social rules of the library environment. Thus, it is interesting to understand the strategies adopted by players in making those noises, as they give some indication of the dilemmas faced in playing this game. It seems that generally the strategy was to use sounds that are naturally loud, but also not uncommon in library environments. Figure 3 presents a summary of the different strategies reported by players. As seen in figure 3 many participants chose to play by coughing into the microphone. This strategy was chosen in an effort to not draw attention to themselves. When asked whether they tried anything else, many replied in the negative. Participant 1's response was this: *"No, as I didn't want people looking at me in a funny way".*

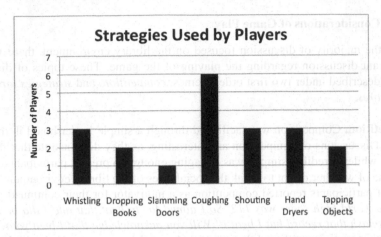

Fig. 3. Number of players who reported using each of a number of strategies for generating sounds. Note: some players used multiple strategies.

A number of participants did have creative ideas to make sounds, often choosing to stage 'accidents' in order to create loud noises without incurring the disapproval of fellow library users,

> "...as you know they have those little step stool kind of things to get to the top shelves. I sort of considered walking down the aisle with a book and not notice and just kick it by "mistake" and maybe try and pretend I sort of fell over. But yeah I didn't do that in the end" (P5).

This combination of creativity and reluctance demonstrates the tension between the social rules and game rules, and the complex dilemma experienced by game players. As shown in figure 3 the most popular 'accident' was the dropping of books on the floor. Indeed, this strategy often led to high scores for the participants. Other players slammed doors, and tapped the device on objects such as desks. Participants preference to be seen as clumsy rather than intentionally loud demonstrates the powerful need for social acceptance in this environment.

Many of the participants felt that they couldn't achieve a high score by simply using their own voice or by making noises with books and door. This led to them to, in their own words, cheating, through using the hand dryer in the toilets to gain a score. Specifically, participants walked in to the toilets and put their hands under the dryer to set it off, put the phone underneath and pressed 'Go!' This produced a very high score. In discussion, these participants mentioned they did this because they couldn't find any other way of achieving the high score without shouting "...I was kind of coughing really loudly....to beat him, but I didn't so I thought I will cheat because I want that score!" (P5). Participants were apparently more willing to break the rules of the game than the rules of the environment.

In summary, due to the competing demands of the game rules and the social environment, players demonstrated great creativity in adapting their behaviour to social expectations. This emphasises the social dilemma presented by the game as well as the power of the social environment over player behaviour. Players were reluctant to ever cause significant disruption to non-players.

6   Conclusions

This paper proposes the harnessing of existing social rules in built environments as a basis for designing provocative and engaging pervasive games. An experimental game, *Shhh!*, was designed, which challenged players to make noise in an environment (a library) where that is acknowledged as inappropriate behaviour. Six participants played the game before engaging in semi-structured interviews. Participants reported a keen awareness of the rules of the social environment in which they played. While they demonstrated a willingness to play the game, and enjoyment at doing so, they also demonstrated a commitment to cause as little disruption as possible to non-players, taking steps to minimise social disapproval. Players showed remarkable sensitivity and creativity in adapting their behaviour to social expectations, and indeed, demonstrated great complexity of behaviour in playing with the rules of the social environment. These findings suggest that pervasive games that play with social rules of built environments have great potential to provide interesting, challenging and fun experiences for players.

Since participants in this study found their playing with social rules a challenging and engaging activity, it may be worth exploring this design strategy further. Specifically, few pervasive games have explored how the social rules inherent in the built environment can function as part of pervasive game play mechanics. We propose a model for designing pervasive games that acknowledges the engaging potential of the social, as well as physical, characteristics of a built environment (see Table 1). This model describes how, when designing the mechanics of a pervasive game, we should consider devices and mobility as means for players to navigate the physical environment, and the subjective experience and behaviour of the player as means to navigate the social environment.

Table 1. Description of the features that must be considered in the design of pervasive games

Opportunities for Design	Environment	Players
Physical	Geography	Devices, Mobility
Social	Social Rules	Behaviour, Experience

In designing games that play with existing social rules it is important to consider the line between mischievous and antisocial behaviour. Mischievous behaviour is playful and serves to explore and test the boundaries of social acceptability [19]. This is contrast to the intent of griefing or trolling, which is purposefully disruptive, often with negative and anti-social intentions. As pervasive game designers, we must consider our own behaviour in these terms, ensuring that while our games allow for an exploration and questioning of social rules, they don't simply give permission for players to behave in an antisocial manner (for example, 'dark play' [31]). We do not want to lower the barriers to behaviour that could cause real harm to the experienced quality of life of non-players. In this respect, we were guided by Niemi, Sawano and Waern [25], in understanding gameplay in terms of anonymity and accountability. In the design of the current game we speculated, based on a great deal of experience with the environment in question, that players were unlikely to ever cause significant disruption to the library. However, we could not be certain of this without carrying out a user study. Findings suggested that players were extremely reluctant to engage in any majorly disruptive behaviour, and indeed, went to great lengths to only generate context-appropriate noises. We suggest that an observational user study is particularly important, for ethical reasons, when designing a game that plays with social expectations in order to ensure that the game does not unintentionally provoke or facilitate genuinely antisocial behaviour.

The approach to pervasive game design outlined here may serve useful for the design of games for purposes other than entertainment (see [11]). Indeed, the approach seems ideal for provoking in players critical reflection on the values underlying the design of built environments, the social rules inherent in those environments, and the ways in which our behaviour is controlled by those rules. This seems to align well with the goals of critical design [10], which *"provides a critique of the prevailing situation through designs that embody social, cultural or technical values"* (p.58). Indeed, the approach outlined here may represent a uniquely powerful type of critical design, since it allows the designer to provoke users to reflection in the very environment the artefact is intended to criticise.

References

1. Bandura, A., McClelland, D.C.: Social learning theory. Prentice Hall, NJ (1977)
2. Bandura, A.: Social cognitive theory: An agentic perspective. Annual Review of Psychology 52, 1–26 (2001)
3. Baron, R.A., Byrne, D.E., Branscombe, N.R.: Social psychology, 9th edn. Holt, Rinehart and Winston (1999)
4. Bell, M., Chalmers, M., Barkhuus, L., Hall, M., Sherwood, S., et al.: Interweaving mobile games with everyday life. In: Proceedings of ACM CHI, pp. 417–426. ACM (2006)
5. Benford, S., Anastasi, R., Flintham, M., Greenhalgh, C., Tandavanitj, N., et al.: Coping with uncertainty in a location-based game. Pervasive Computing 2, 34–41 (2003)
6. Braun, V., Clarke, V.: Using thematic analysis in psychology. Qualitative Research in Psychology 3, 77–101 (2006)
7. Cheok, A.D., Yang, X., Ying, Z.Z., Billinghurst, M., Kato, H.: Touch-space: Mixed reality game space based on ubiquitous, tangible, and social computing. Personal and Ubiquitous Computing 6, 430–442 (2002)
8. Cheok, A.D., Goh, K.H., Liu, W., Farbiz, F., Fong, S.W., Teo, S.L., et al.: Human pacman: A mobile, wide-area entertainment system based on physical, social, and ubiquitous computing. Personal Ubiquitous Computing 8, 71–81 (2004)
9. Crabtree, A., Benford, S., Rodden, T., Greenhalgh, C., Flintham, M., et al.: Orchestrating a mixed reality game'on the ground'. In: Proc. ACM CHI, pp. 391–398. ACM (2004)
10. Dunne, A., Raby, F.: Design noir: The secret life of electronic objects. Springer (2001)
11. Flanagan, M.: Critical Play: Radical Game Design. MIT press (2009)
12. Gentile, A.P.: Reinventing Airspace: Spectatorship, fluidity, intimacy at PEK T3. J of Architecture, City & Environment 4, 9–19 (2009)
13. Foo, C.Y., Koivisto, E.M.I.: Defining grief play in MMORPGs: Player and developer perceptions. In: Proc. of ACE 2004, pp. 245–250. ACM (2004)

14. Friedman, B., Kahn Jr., P.H., Borning, A.: Value sensitive design and information systems. In: Human-Computer Interaction in Management Information Systems: Foundations, vol. 4 (2006)
15. Huizinga, J.: Homo ludens. Rowohlt, Hamburg (1956)
16. Kellerman, A.: International airports: Passengers in an environment of 'authorities'. Mobilities 3, 161–178 (2008)
17. Kirman, B.: Emergence and playfulness in social games. In: Proceedings of Mindtrek, pp. 71–77. ACM (2010)
18. Kirman, B.: Playful networks: Measuring, Analysing and Understanding the Social Effects of Game Design. PhD Thesis, University of Lincoln (2011)
19. Kirman, B., Linehan, C., Lawson, S.: Exploring mischief and mayhem in social computing or: How we learned to stop worrying and love the trolls. In: Proceedings of ACM CHI, pp. 121–130. ACM (2012)
20. Kirman, B., Linehan, C., Lawson, S.: Blowtooth: A Provocative Pervasive Game for Smuggling Virtual Drugs through Real Airport Security. Personal and Ubiquitous Computing 16, 767–775 (2012)
21. Linehan, C., Kirman, B., Lawson, S., Doughty, M.: Blowtooth: Pervasive gaming in unique and challenging environments. In: Proc. ACM CHI Extended Abstracts, pp. 2695–2704. ACM (2010)
22. Magerkurth, C., Cheok, A.D., Mandryk, R.L., Nilsen, T.: Pervasive games: Bringing computer entertainment back to the real world. Computers in Entertainment 3, 4 (2005)
23. Maxis. Spore. PC: Electronic Arts (2008)
24. Montola, M., Stenros, J., Waern, A.: Pervasive Games: Theory and Design. Morgan Kaufmann (2009)
25. Niemi, J., Sawano, S., Waern, A.: Involving non-players in pervasive games. In: Proc. 4th Conference on Critical Computing (2005)
26. Rapoport, A.: The meaning of the built environment: A nonverbal communication approach. University of Arizona Press (1982)
27. Rashid, O., Mullins, I., Coulton, P., Edwards, R.: Extending cyberspace: Location based games using cellular phones. Computers in Entertainment 4, 4 (2006)
28. Reid, J.: Design for Coincidence: Incorporating real world artifacts in location based games. In: Proceedings of the 3rd International Conference on Digital Inter-Active Media in Entertainment and Arts, pp. 18–25. ACM (September 2008)
29. Salen, K., Zimmerman, E.: Rules of Play: Game Design Fundamentals. MIT Press (2003)
30. Sotamaa, O.: All the World's a Botfighter Stage: Notes on Location-Based Multi-User Gaming. In: CGDC Conference Proceedings, pp. 35–45 (2002)
31. Zagal, J.P., Björk, S., Lewis, C.: Dark Patterns in the Design of Games. In: Proceedings of Foundations of Digital Games (2013)

Cuddly: Enchant Your Soft Objects with a Mobile Phone

Suzanne Low, Yuta Sugiura, Kevin Fan, and Masahiko Inami

Graduate School of Media Design, Keio University
4-1-1 Hiyoshi, Kohoku-ku, Yokohama 223-8526, Japan
{suzannedbel,y-sugiura,inami}@kmd.keio.ac.jp,
kevin0228ca@gmail.com

Abstract. Cuddly is a mobile phone application that will enchant soft objects to enhance human's interaction with the objects. Cuddly utilizes the mobile phone's camera and flash light (LED) to detect the surrounding brightness value captured by the camera. When one integrate Cuddly with a soft object and compresses the object, the brightness level captured by the camera will decrease. Utilizing the measurement change in brightness values, we can implement diverse entertainment applications using the different functions a mobile phone is embedded with, such as animation, sound, Bluetooth communication etc. For example, we created a boxing game by connecting two devices through Bluetooth; with one device inserted into a soft object and the other acting as a screen.

Keywords: Soft objects, mobile phone based computing, camera-based measurement, flash light.

1   Introduction

We are surrounded by soft objects such as plush toys, cushions, mattress, sofas and others in our daily lives. Soft objects act as a buffer between people and hard objects such as the floor or furniture. People often hug soft objects when they are feeling emotional such as while watching movies, or they tend to punch or throw soft objects when they are feeling frustrated. These actions show that there is a close emotional, physical interaction between soft objects and oneself. From the psychological point of view, soft objects can highly influence people's lives and behavior [1]. Research shows that it can help reduce stress as well as increase effectiveness [18]. Because of that, soft objects are often used in different fields such as medical therapy [25], communication [12], gaming purposes [19] etc. Our research group has also created FuwaFuwa, a sensing module that uses soft object as an interface in the past.

However, in order to develop and commercialize these soft interfaces and robots to the society, developers require users to purchase the device. When choosing a pet from a wide variety of animals or just choosing, for example, a pet dog based on its breed, people make their choices based on their own likes and dislikes. Similarly, when choosing soft objects, the same rules apply. Taking this into account, it can be seen that for the creations of a well-accepted and loved soft object, one needs to

D. Reidsma, H. Katayose, and A. Nijholt (Eds.): ACE 2013, LNCS 8253, pp. 138–151, 2013.
© Springer International Publishing Switzerland 2013

provide either many varieties, as with the case of 'Furby'[6], or re-design repeatedly until universally accepted, as with the case of 'Paro'[25]. This shows what huge leap there would be between the initial development stage and final manufacture for sales.

Currently, majority of our society is not aware of the usefulness of soft interfaces. Therefore, by providing a system which users can easily obtain and experience at low cost, we can spread the benefits of soft interfaces. We believe that this is important to discover new ways and playing methods to fulfill human needs. Based upon which, this research, entitle Cuddly, aims to utilize a device, which a majority of us are equipped with, to create interaction with soft objects which we already have in our home.

This research utilizes a smart mobile phone, which has had very high sales in the recent years, to create an application to enhance user's interaction with their soft objects (Fig. 1). This is done by embedding the mobile phone into a soft object. Cuddly then utilizes the mobile phone's camera and flashlight (LED) to detect the surrounding brightness values captured by the camera. When user inserts the mobile phone into a soft object and presses the object, the density of the material surrounding the mobile phone increases. This increase in density decreases the brightness of the material surrounding the camera. The camera captures its surroundings in the form of average RGB values and converts these values into brightness values. With this data of brightness change, Cuddly can return feedback by utilizing functions a mobile phone has, such as sounds, lights, or even the animation on the display. In addition, as a mobile phone is a tool for communication, we can connect two or more mobile phones together to create a multi-user interaction.

Fig. 1. Mobile phone can be placed in many soft objects to convert them to soft interfaces

2   Related Work

2.1   Soft User Interface

As soft interfaces stimulate emotional affection in people, there is much research created to incorporate soft interfaces to enhance the interaction between people and their devices. Marti et al. developed a user interface consisting of a small wireless animatronic device in an animal form to promote an interactive call handling agent by imitating animal behavior when a call is received [12]. Ueki et al. proposed Tabby, an alteration of a lamp by embedding sensors and covering it with soft fur, which shows to improve the interaction between people and their furniture [23].

Soft interfaces are also commonly used for entertainment or gaming purposes. Hiramatsu et al. created Puyocon, a throw-able, soft, ball-shaped controller consisting of sensors surrounded by sponges, which reacts when it is shaken, thrown or squeezed [9]. Anne created a pillow fighting game by inserting Wii remote controllers into 6 pillows and connecting them to a Macbook [19].

However, many of these devices require either sensors already embedded in their soft objects or they required getting a new object. As compare to that, Cuddly is a phone application and thus, users can utilize their own phone.

2.2   Soft Interface Detection

There are many attempts to create tactile sensors to be used on flexible or soft interfaces. Kadowaki et al. embedded LED and phototransistors into soft urethane foam; sensing different deformation gestures such as push, stroke, pinch etc., due to pressure applied [11]. Rossiter et al. created a novel tactile sensor by using a matrix of LED covered by a pliable foam surface – these LEDs act as photodetectors depending on its operation mode [16]. However, most of the sensors are to be attached on the surface of the devices, making it hard to be implemented with many soft objects.

Besides that, much research integrates soft surface with the use of a camera to detect the changes on the surface. Sato et al proposed PhotoElasticTouch; a novel tabletop system comprising of an LCD and an overhead camera, which detect deformed regions of the elastic materials [17]. Harrison et al. describe a technique for creating dynamic physical buttons using pneumatic actuation while accommodating a visual display and multitouch sensing [8]. Bianchi et al. proposed a bi-elastic fabric-based display for rendering softness when the fingertips interact with the display [2].

In addition, there are also studies that focus on inserting sensors into pillows or other soft devices to detect the behavior change. Yagi et al. developed a pillow inserted with an arduino, and 3 sensors -- which can control one's living environment depending on human's natural behavior [26]. Sugiura et al. proposed a method to detect density changes in the cotton material using photo reflective sensors [21]. Our concept is very similar to these research projects, but differs in that we use the mobile phone's in-built sensors, while these researches require separate sensors. These related researches show how important and advanced researches are heading in terms of soft-based interface.

2.3   Mobile Phone Based Computing

New interactions in mobile phones tend to leverage the device's built-in sensors or attached external sensors. Miyaki et al. proposed "GraspZoom", an input model using pressure sensing, sensed by a force sensitive resistor attached to the backside of a mobile phone [14]. Similarly, Goel et al. introduced GripSense, to detect hand postures by sensing the pressure exerted by the user, through observing gyroscope readings, and using it to facilitate interactions [7]. Iwasaki et al developed AffectPhone, a system that detects the user's emotional state using galvanic skin response electrode attached to the side of the handset and covert the data into warmth or coolness in a Peltier module attached the back panel of another device [10]. Our proposal leverages the device in-built proximity sensor, camera and flash light for interaction. Other sensors can be taken into account as well.

Many gadgets in the market can enhance the ability of a smart phone or protect the phone. For example, Fisher Price introduced Apptivity Case for iPhone and iPod devices, a sturdy case accommodated for babies, protecting the iPhone from dribbles, drool and unwanted call making. These allow babies to play and experience advance devices from a young age [5]. Cube-works released CocoloBear, an interactive teddy bear whereby users place their iPhone on the bear's stomach and the bear's mouth will move according to the frequency received [4]. This shows that innovations leveraging soft interfaces for mobile devices are gradually expanding in the market. This enhances the motivation to create soft user interface to increase hands-on experiences for younger generations with computing devices.

2.4   Computing Daily Objects

We are surrounded by objects that we use on a daily basis. Our gestures towards these objects are quite similar to our interaction with smart devices. Therefore, there is much research in enhancing the functions of existing daily objects by combining them with smart devices.

Cheng explored the approach of utilizing everyday objects as tabletop controllers, taking into account common computer gestures such as rotate, drag, click etc. [3]. Masui et al. proposed MouseField, a device that allows user to control various information appliances. This device consists of an ID recognizer and motion sensors, which sense the movement of objects placed onto it, and interprets it as a command to control the flow of information [13]. Sugiura et al. developed a skin-like user interface consisting of an elastic fabric, photoreflectors and phototransistors, to measure tangential force by pinching and dragging interactions on the interface [20]. His development can be used in daily wearable such as stockings. Sugiura et al. also developed a ring-like device that can be attached to any plush toys to animate the plush toys, converting it into a soft robot [22].

Seeing how important daily objects are to our lives, we are more attached to them than other random objects. Therefore, our proposal is to use our plush toys or pillow, an item that we have hold for a long time or have stronger memory, as the interface for the interaction.

3   Principle

Soft objects are usually encapsulated with soft, fluffy materials such as cotton, wool, feather etc. as their padding. These materials have many spaces in between the atoms allowing a flow of light to spread out.

Previously, our research group has created FuwaFuwa [21], a sensor module that uses photoreflectors sensors to detect the changes in brightness when integrated with soft objects. These sensors consist of an infrared emitter and a transistor side-by-side whereby the transistor detects the infrared light reflected back to it. From this concept, we discover that this measurement is possible even when the two components are at varied distance apart, until a maximum distance. As a note, the measurement method is the opposite of FuwaFuwa: the brightness sensed increases with compression for FuwaFuwa, while when the two components are apart for Cuddly, the brightness sensed decreases with compression.

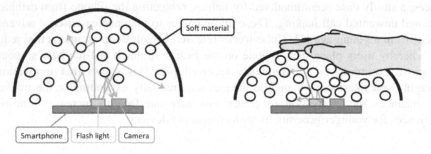

Fig. 2. Surrounding detected by camera is brighter at low density (left) than at high density (right)

We then implemented our test with a mobile phone by making use of its camera and flashlight. We integrate the mobile phone into soft objects and utilize the camera as a sensor to detect the brightness of the surrounding area; thereby distinguishing the change in density of the padding. In order to do so, the flashlight will act as the source of light and the camera will detect its reflection. In a mobile phone, the flashlight and camera are at a distance apart. When there is no pressure applied to the soft material, the surrounding is bright and numerous external light sources can enter the camera (Fig. 2 left). However, when the soft object is compressed, the density of the material surrounding the light source increases, reducing the light reflection – thus, reducing the surrounding brightness (Fig. 2 right).

The camera will capture the video of the surroundings and convert the pixels into average RGB values. These values will then be converted into brightness value using the equation below:-

$$Brightness = 0.3R + 0.59G + 0.11B$$

$$[R = red; G = green; B = blue]$$

(1)

There are quite a number of equations for brightness that can be found. We chose to use the equation which best corresponds to the human perception [15]. The data of this brightness value is used to create different feedbacks such as sounds, lights, animation etc.

4   Experimentation

We conducted an experiment to investigate the relationship between the change in density of soft material and the brightness of the surrounding detected by a mobile phone. A mobile phone (nexus) was positioned at the bottom of a clear acrylic box (104 x 104 x 146 mm) covered by a cover that could be set at different heights (Fig. 3). This accommodates the calculation of the density of soft material. The box was filled with soft material, the cover height varied from 12 to 5.2 cm in intervals of 2 mm. The brightness detected by the camera was measured at each height. This experiment was repeated for four soft materials with different densities (Fig. 4): polyester cotton, natural cotton, sponge and feather.

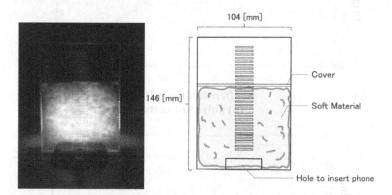

Fig. 3. Experiment Apparatus

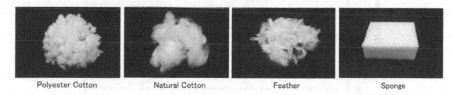

Polyester Cotton   Natural Cotton   Feather   Sponge

Fig. 4. Different materials tested

4.1   Experiment Result

Fig. 5 shows plots of the changes in surrounding brightness measured by the mobile phone's camera depending on the changes in density of the different materials used. Each graph represents an average of about 3 trials. The brightness detected decreases when density increases by pushing, and increases when density decreases by pulling. However, there is a certain level of hysteresis observed. Most soft materials have many holes in between their atoms. After undergoing push-pull activity, some does not return to its original state. Instead, they still remain in their compressed form. Therefore, the camera detects less brightness when it undergoes pulling activity than pushing activity. This is what causes the hysteresis. However, all the graphs show a significant decrease in brightness value when compressed. This proves that our proposal is capable to detect the change in brightness values.

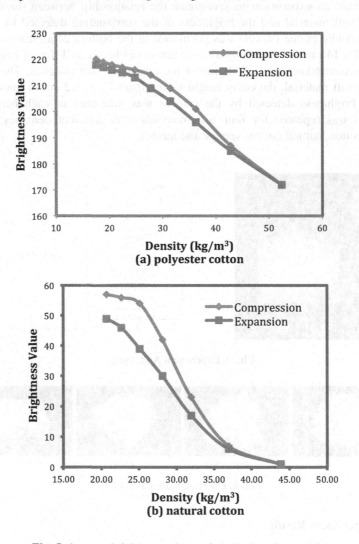

Fig. 5. Average brightness value against density of materials

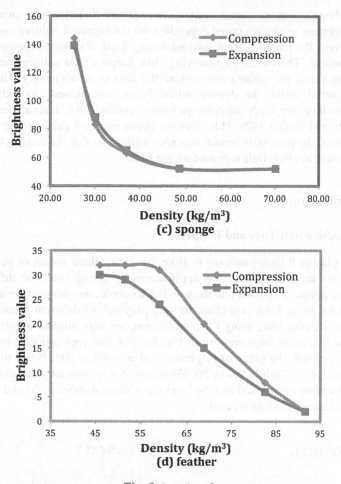

Fig. 5. (*continued*)

4.2   Experiment Discussion

The RGB value changes according to the material color: with Black's RGB value [0,0,0] and White's RGB value [255,255,255]. This illustrates that brightness value reduce as brightness reduces. From our experiment, the values for three other colors are involved as well; natural polyester: brown and sponge: pink (back side) and blue (front side). The graphs also illustrates that all three RGB values also reduce when the material was being compressed. This shows that, the material color do not have a strong effect on the brightness level.

4.3   Implementation

For this proposal, we tested the application on Galaxy Nexus (API 4.1.1), HTC J (API 4.0) and Galaxy S SC-02b (API 2.3.6); making use of Android SDK and Eclipse.

Mobile phone's camera comes with auto-exposure function that automatically adjusts the aperture or shutter speed depending on the captured lighting condition. In order to prevent the readings from auto-adjusting itself, this auto-exposure function has to be locked. Therefore, by removing this function and setting the exposure compensation value, the camera can capture the data more accurately. However, as different material differs in density when being compressed, we adjusted the compensation level for each material: polyester cotton (-50), natural cotton (-10), sponge (-30), and feather (40). This allows a better range of values to be taken. For the applications, the proximity sensor was also utilized so that the feedback will only occur when there are materials surrounding the phone.

5   Application

5.1   Interactive Soft Toys and Puppets

Kids like to play as if their plush toy is alive, by giving them voices or moving their limbs [18]. We have designed a few applications by giving voices to different soft toys when the phone is inserted into the toy. For example, dog barking sound for a toy dog, a character voice for a cute character and playback of different recorded voices for a puppet. Besides that, using this application, we can animate a soft object by creating visual faces on the screen itself (Fig. 6). For this application, when the soft object is not pressed, the range of brightness value is about 100. When the object is pressed, it reduces to slightly below 50. Therefore, the brightness value chosen is 50. When the soft object is pressed and the brightness value reduces to 50 and below, the animated character will close its eyes.

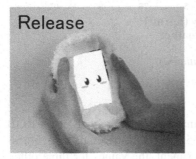
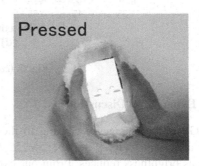

Fig. 6. Character

5.2   Game

We have also designed a gaming application that utilizes the screen while integrating part of the phone with a soft object. For example, depending on the brightness value, the character on the screen will jump at a different height (Fig. 7). For this game, as the brightness value decreases, the height increases and vice versa.

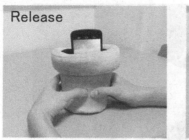
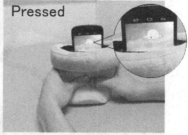

Fig. 7. Game

5.3   Music and Lighting

We have designed an application whereby when user insert the phone into a pillow and presses the pillow, music will flow according to the compression strength. At the same time, the screen color changes with the music. When this application is used in the dark with the pillow, it resembles the display of colorful lights (Fig. 8). The typical musical instrument notes were chosen. At the certain range of brightness value, it will play one note. And at another range, it will play another note and so on.

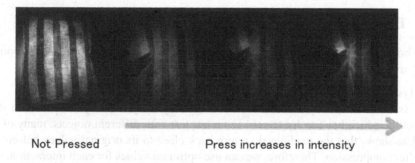

Fig. 8. Musical pillow

5.4   Alarm Clock

We have designed an alarm clock system whereby the user will set the time as a typical alarm clock and insert into the pillow. User will then lie on the pillow. At the designated time, the alarm will ring and vibrate. When user lifts his head up, the alarm will stop. However, when user lies back down, it will ring again.

5.5   Multiple Device Interaction through Bluetooth Communication

As mentioned in the introduction, as a mobile phone has a connectivity function to connect to other devices through Bluetooth, we can create a soft toy interaction with multiple devices. An example application as shown in Fig. 9, is a connection of a phone with a tablet. The phone is inserted into the pillow. When user applies pressure to the pillow, the character on the tablet will receive the punch. Through this, we can create soft controllers just by utilizing a mobile phone.

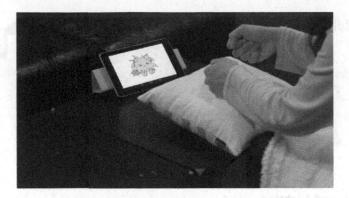

Fig. 9. Bluetooth connection with other device

Another interesting way of using Bluetooth is for storytelling. An example would be for multiple users to play together, such as creating a joint conversation between devices. When two people insert their mobile phones into their individual soft toy and one presses one's toy, both toys will play recorded script similar to telling a story. With this, users can create connecting stories with their soft objects.

6   Discussion

From both the experiment and test for application creation, a few points were brought up regarding its influence on the accuracy of the application.

- **Hysteresis:**
  Hysteresis differs by materials. However, many daily soft objects are filled with cotton, which has low hysteresis. From our test with different objects, many of the data shows that the readings do return back close to its original values before and after compression. Therefore, we can use optimum values for each interaction.
- **Ambient light from the surroundings:**
  We conducted the experiment in both a dark and bright environment. From observations, the results were similar as the light's reflection was too bright, that the ambient light does not highly affect its performance.
- **Movement of the phone in the object:**
  The phone is constraint by material in the object and thus, small movement may cause some glitches, but will not highly affect the application. However, Cuddly can detect harsh movements as the pressure does change and can generate versatile interactions. For example, when one pulls the soft object at both ends, there would be pressure change in the center of the object. Through this, other interactions such as pulling a part of the soft object can also trigger interactions.
- **Color of material:**
  In the experiment, we have tested with three different colored materials as well as each application presented uses a different colored soft objects. As the brightness value taken is an average, the colors of the material do not highly effect the application.

7   Limitation and Future Works

In this section, we will explain some of the limitations and possible future works to reduce these limitations. One of the limitations is the size of the mobile phone. Currently most mobile phones are rather long in size. Therefore, Cuddly can only be used in soft objects that are bigger than the size of the mobile phone. In addition, the hardness of the phone may be a challenge if the soft object does not have much stuffing in it. In this case, users may detect the phone when they press the soft object.

The compensation level and hysteresis are also some of the limitations as different materials have different compensation level and hysteresis level. As a future work, it may be possible to calibrate both accordingly using different algorithms.

Currently, Cuddly is only programmed to take an average value of the all the pixels captured by the camera – taking only readings in one dimension. However, by sing better image processing techniques, it may be possible to detect the areas of pressure – allowing to obtain readings in two dimension. Besides that, for an extra large interface, one may insert multiple phones and communicate the phone's data with each other to detect the brightness value at different spots. Besides that, another suggestion is to insert a few mobile devices into a big soft object (e.g. a bean bag) to detect the position where the interaction is taken place. This allows the object to act like a controller for different functions such as for gaming purposes. Currently, only the proximity sensor is being utilized – other sensors will be utilize as well in the future to create a more sensitive detection.

8   Conclusion

Cuddly is a phone application that allows users to integrate their mobile phone with soft objects found in the surrounding environment. This application works like a light sensor; making use of the mobile phone's camera and flash light. When the mobile phone is inserted into a soft object, the light from the flashlight will be reflected into the camera. This camera will capture RGB values of the surroundings and convert it into brightness value. When a soft object is compressed, the material's density surrounding the mobile phone will increase and reduces the light reflection. This causes the brightness value detected to decrease; thus, causing a range of value changes. Using these values, Cuddly can create feedback interactions with the soft objects. For example, sound feedback, light feedback, making a call, etc. Our experiment shows that Cuddly is capable of detecting the change in brightness.

In conclusion, this allows users to make use of their most common device, a mobile phone with soft objects from their surrounding environment. This may enhance their user experience with their objects.

Acknowledgment. This work was supported by the Strategic Information and Communication R&D Promotion Programme (SCOPE) of the Ministry of Internal Affairs and Communications, Japan.

References

1. Ackerman, J.M., Nocera, C.C., Bargh, J.A.: Incidental haptic sensations influence social judgments and decisions. Science 328(5986), 1712–1715 (2010)
2. Bianchi, M., Serio, A., Bicchi, A., Scilingo, E.P.: A new fabric-based softness display. In: Proc. Haptics Symposium 2010, pp. 105–112. IEEE (2010)
3. Cheng, K.Y., Liang, R.H., Chen, B.Y., Liang, R.H., Kuoy, S.Y.: iCon: Utilizing Everyday Objects as Additional, Auxiliary and Instant Tabletop Controllers. In: Proc. CHI 2010, pp. 1155–1164. ACM (2010)
4. Cube Works official website, http://www.cube-works.co.jp/works/index_sub.html?/works/cocolobear/index.html
5. Fisher Price official website, http://www.fisher-price.com/en_US/products/64176
6. Furby official website, http://www.furby.com
7. Goel, M., Wobbrock, J.O., Patel, S.N.: GripSense: Using Built-In Sensors to Detect Hand Posture and Pressure on Commodity Mobile Phones. In: Proc. UIST 2012, pp. 545–554. ACM (2012)
8. Harrison, C., Hudson, S.E.: Providing Dynamically Changeable Physical Buttons on a Visual Display. In: Proc. CHI 2009, pp. 299–308. ACM (2009)
9. Hiramatsu, R.: Puyo-con. In: ACM SIGGRAPH ASIA 2009 Art Gallery & Emerging Technologies, p. 81. ACM (2009)
10. Iwasaki, K., Miyaki, T., Rekimoto, J.: AffectPhone: A Handset Device to Present User's Emotional State with Warmth/Coolness. In: BIOSTEC 2010, Workshop on B-Interface (2010)
11. Kadowaki, A., Yoshikai, T., Hayashi, M., Inaba, M.: Development of Soft Sensor Exterior Embedded with Multiaxis Deformable Tactile Sensor System. In: Proc. Ro-Man 2009, pp. 1093–1098. IEEE (2009)
12. Marti, S., Schmandt, C.: Physical Embodiments for Mobile Communication Agents. In: Proc. UIST 2005, pp. 231–240. ACM (2005)
13. Masui, T., Tsukada, K., Siio, I.: MouseField: A Simple and Versatile Input Device for Ubiquitous Computing. In: Mynatt, E.D., Siio, I. (eds.) UbiComp 2004. LNCS, vol. 3205, pp. 319–328. Springer, Heidelberg (2004)
14. Miyaki, T., Rekimoto, J.: GraspZoom: zooming and scrolling control model for single-handed mobile interaction. In: Proc. MobileHCI, Article No. 11 (2009)
15. Relating HSV to RGB, http://www.dig.cs.gc.cuny.edu/manuals/Gimp2/Grokking-the-GIMP-v1.0/node52.html
16. Rossiter, J., Mukai, T.: A Novel Tactile Sensor Using a Matrix of LEDs Operating in Both Photoemitter and Photodetector Modes. In: Proc. Sensors. IEEE (2005)
17. Sato, T., Mamiya, H., Koike, H., Fukuchi, K.: PhotoelasticTouch: Transparent Rubbery Tangible Interface using an LCD and Photoelasticity. In: Proc. UIST 2009, pp. 43–50 (2009)
18. Strommen, E., Alexander, K.: Emotional Interfaces for Interactive Aardvarks: Designing affect into social interfaces for children. In: Proceedings of ACM CHI 1999, pp. 528–535 (1999)
19. Juul Sørensen, A.S.: Pillow Fight 2.0: A Creative Use of Technology for Physical Interaction. In: Nijholt, A., Romão, T., Reidsma, D. (eds.) ACE 2012. LNCS, vol. 7624, pp. 506–512. Springer, Heidelberg (2012)
20. Sugiura, Y., Inami, M., Igarashi, T.: A Thin Stretchable Interface for Tangential Force Measurement. In: Proc. UIST 2012, pp. 529–536. ACM (2012)

21. Sugiura, Y., Kakehi, G., Withana, A., Lee, C., Sakamoto, D., Sugimoto, M., Inami, M., Igarashi, T.: Detecting Shape Deformation of Soft Objects Using Directional Photoreflectivity Measurement. In: Proc. UIST 2011, pp. 509–516. ACM (2011)
22. Sugiura, Y., Lee, C., Ogata, M., Withana, A., Makino, Y., Sakamoto, D., Inami, M., Igarashi, T.: PINOKY: A Ring That Animates Your Plush Toys. In: Proc. CHI 2012, pp. 725–734. ACM (2012)
23. Ueki, A., Kamata, M., Inakage, M.: Tabby: Designing of Coexisting Entertainment Content in Everyday Life by Expanding the Design of Furniture. In: Proc. ACE 2007, pp. 72–78. ACM (2007)
24. Väänänen-Vainio-Mattila, K., Haustola, T., Häkkilä, J., Karukka, M., Kytökorpi, K.: Exploring Non-verbal Communication of Presence between Young Childrenand Their Parents through the Embodied Teddy Bear. In: Paternò, F., de Ruyter, B., Markopoulos, P., Santoro, C., van Loenen, E., Luyten, K. (eds.) AmI 2012. LNCS, vol. 7683, pp. 81–96. Springer, Heidelberg (2012)
25. Wada, K., Shibata, T., Saito, T., Sakamoto, K., Tanie, K.: Psychological and Social Effects of One YearRobotAssisted Activity on Elderly Peopleat a Health Service Facility for the Aged. In: Proc. International Conference on Robotics and Automation 2005, pp. 2785–2790. IEEE (2005)
26. Yagi, I., Kobayashi, S., Kashiwagi, R., Uriu, D., Okude, N.: Media cushion: soft interface to control living environment using human natural behavior. In: ACM SIGGRAPH 2011 Posters, Article 46, 1 page. ACM (2011)

GuideMe: A Mobile Augmented Reality System to Display User Manuals for Home Appliances

Lars Müller[1], Ilhan Aslan[2], and Lucas Krüßen[1]

[1] FZI Research Center for Information Technology, Karlsruhe, Germany
[2] ICT&S Center, University of Salzburg, Salzburg, Austria

Abstract. In this paper we present GuideMe, a mobile augmented reality application that provides assistance in using appliances. In order to explore how users perceive GuideMe, as a design of an interactive and digital manual, we conducted two user studies. We compared GuideMe first with paper-based manuals and then with video-based manuals. Our results indicate that the paper-based manuals were superior regarding typical usability measures (i.e. error rates and completion times). However, participants reported a significantly higher perceived task load when using paper-based manuals. Due to a better user experience, GuideMe was preferred by 9 of 10 participants over paper-based manuals. We present our design in detail and discuss broader implications of designing digital manuals. Furthermore, we introduce a custom format to define manual structures for mobile augmented reality enabled manuals.

1 Introduction

Many of today's challenges in designing interfaces relate to the spread of technology to our homes and everyday lives with a shift from a rather narrow task-orientation to qualities of everyday experiences [3,2]. For example, ten years ago a baking oven would be operated by choosing temperature and mode. Today, an oven can be programmed to start at a predefined time with a predefined temperature and several operation modes. Interfaces of everyday products in our homes have gained in complexity. Getting familiar with all the features that such a product provides is challenging. In order to assist users, to handle their appliances and consumer electronics, manuals are created by technical writers and illustrators, who carefully describe the operation of the product. However, very few people enjoy interacting with a manual; i.e., going through a book consisting of technical writings and illustrations to find out how to operate a system or to solve an existing problem. Off the shelf mobile devices could be used as digital manuals and thereby performance and the user experience of interacting with manuals could be improved. However, designing a digital manual based on inspirations taken from physical manuals can be a cumbersome task.

In this paper we present GuideMe, a design that aims at exploring alternatives to traditional paper-based manuals. GuideMe is an interactive "digital"

D. Reidsma, H. Katayose, and A. Nijholt (Eds.): ACE 2013, LNCS 8253, pp. 152–167, 2013.
© Springer International Publishing Switzerland 2013

manual informed by properties of mobile devices and augmented reality technology. Hereby, our intention was to make use of people's familiarity with mobile devices and create a design that would be timelier and exciting to use.

This paper is structured as follows. In the next section we provide the background on mobile augmented reality and current practices for user manuals. Then we discuss in more general how GuideMe fits into current concepts and notions in interaction design. Building on these fundamentals we present details of the technical implementation of the prototype. Hereby, we introduce a custom format to define manual structures, which we refer to as User Manual Markup Language (UMML): an XML based format to define user manuals and especially technical illustrations. The GuideMe prototype is evaluated using manuals for two ovens and compared to a video tutorial and excerpts from the original printed manual. The results are summarized and discussed.

2   Background

The development of GuideMe builds on knowledge from traditional user manual design and the technical progress in the field of augmented reality (AR).

2.1   User Manuals

User manuals are a part of the technical documentation of a product. The Secure-Doc guideline [18] states, "Products are not complete without documentation." The guideline interprets, an important standard in technical documentation, the IEC 62079:2001 on "Preparation of instructions. Structuring, content and presentation" [10] and helps designing the technical documentation of a product. It outlines the requirements that are induced by European law, such as to enable customers to use all features of a product and to protect customers of potential hazards. The guideline relates to factors that are often ignored when a product is accompanied by a user manual of poor quality. For instance, "High quality documentation helps reduce customer support costs," because with the right information at hand it enables customers to solve many problems without further assistance. Furthermore, "High quality documentation enhances customer satisfaction," because a poorly designed user manual can prevent customers from exploring the full potential of a product. Another factor is that customers relate the quality of the product to the quality of its documentation. Therefore, the need for high quality user manuals is given and the exploration of emerging technologies, such as augmented reality, to improve their usability is worthwhile.

Although other formats are available, the standard format for user manuals is still the printed handbook. Typically it offers an index that lists all functionalities or use cases of a product. Each one of them is then described in a step-by-step manner. Technical illustrations improve understandability by "expressive images that effectively convey certain information via the visual channel to the human observer" [20]. Mainly for cost reasons comprehensive user manuals are often included as digital PDF documents on CD or for download. Although the content is normally taken one-to-one from the printed version, it improves the aspects of information retrieval concerning finding the user manual itself (if available for download) and finding the relevant information in it by searching the document.

2.2 Augmented Reality

Initially research in AR-based user manuals has been conducted using head-mounted displays (HMD) to provide information while having two free hands. The KARMA project uses such an HMD to convey step-by-step instructions and superimposed instructions to specialized mechanics [4]. Henderson et al. [9] built an advanced HMD-based AR interface and showed that their system improves the current documentation of mechanics. However, AR research currently explores new platforms. An increasing number of AR applications uses the mobile phone to display virtual objects [7,5,13]. Furthermore, mobile projectors provide new means to augmented objects with information by projecting the interface directly on the surface of the object [11].

As early as 2001, the AR-PDA prototype [5] mentioned mobile AR manuals as one possible application domain. Since this time, researchers have explored different technical implementations and hardware platforms. Hakkarainen et al. [7] actually applied mobile AR to user manuals to showcase their developed system that still relied on a server infrastructure to calculate the positioning of superimposed instructions. Liu et al. [13] evaluated a new mobile AR approach in the domain of user manuals. They show that "real-time AR feedback on physical actions in the real world" is beneficial regarding usability and task load of users. The test was based on an adapted MIDI station that could provide such a feedback channel.

The technology to build AR-based manuals is developing rapidly. First applications are already available, e.g. an app to explain a new car model[1] or a prototype of Aurasma that uses augmented reality to explain how to connect cables of a router[2]. These approaches cannot be generalized to other home appliances. They are impressive technology demonstrations, and showcase state of the art marker-less object recognition of 3D objects. However, they require highly textured user interfaces and are tied to a specific car or appliance.

The research focus shifts from the technological feasibility to the design of such applications. Several companies offer mobile AR SDKs that support the development of AR applications for example Qualcomm[3] and Metaio[4].

3 Designing Digital Manuals for and with Mobile Devices

From the beginning mobile devices have been recognized as personal digital assistants, which help to manage personal information. Later mobile devices

---

[1] Audi A1 user manual
   http://itunes.apple.com/de/app/audi-a1-ekurzinfo/id436341817?mt=8
[2] Aurasma Visual Browser http://www.aurasma.com/
[3] Vuforia SDK http://www.qualcomm.com/solutions/augmented-reality
[4] Metaio http://www.metaio.com/

were also perceived as a tool that can manage contextual information. They have pervaded our everyday life, and the number of mobile applications is growing.

> As computational things become everyday things, what we design for can not be restricted to how to enable people to become more productive. Thus, there is a need for complementary design philosophies. [14]

Redström herby, refers to how HCI researchers used to focus on performance and supporting people in accomplishing tasks. In the last decade many researchers started to focus on creating new experiences enabled by mobile devices. De Sa and Churchill [16] argue that the new affordances offered by mobile augmented reality have potential to enhance users' experiences. More specifically they discuss how this can be achieved through the provision of digital information which is relevant for the user context. With mobile devices information that is digitally stored can be processed anywhere anytime. Consequently, more and more information is presented in digital form as and through mobile media.

> One experiences the world through the technology, and the technology inevitably becomes part of the way one relates to the world. While many technologies appear in between the user and the world, not all are embodied. For a technology to hold an embodiment relation it must be technically transparent, it must allow its user to "see through" it. [3]

Based on philosopher Don Ihde's non-neutrality of technology-mediated experience, Fallman hereby points out that for technology to be embodied it needs to recede into the background of experience. One could argue that this is true for mobile devices and mobile augmented reality applications. Similar to how one does not feel the weight of glasses after carrying them for a while, a mobile device, although heavier, recedes into the background of experience during interaction with the real world. However, this real world becomes augmented with digital information.

Different lines of research within HCI have recognized the increasing blur between the digital and the physical in today's designs. Efforts to improve the understanding of those kinds of designs exist. For example, Vallgårda et al. discuss how knowledge of materials has been essential to design practice and how computers share important characteristics with other materials that are used in, for example, industrial design or architecture. They introduced computational composites as a new type of composite material [19]. They argued that computational properties of a computer are difficult to exploit, but through combining it with other material can come to use.

In mobile augmented reality applications, mobile devices are used to augment real-world objects and materials. One could regard mobile augmented reality as a computational property of a mobile device. Through augmenting a specific real world object (e.g. an oven); i.e. combining a mobile device with the real world object, augmented reality as a computational property comes to use.

While printed manuals are still the standard media for manuals, there is a need for digital manuals and interaction that is more timely and uses features of mobile devices that people have already become familiar with.

However the mobile device itself is a medium that supports through its properties (e.g. being mobile, lightweight, having a camera, having a screen etc.) interaction that is fundamentally different from paper. Finding out how to best interact with new media is in general a difficult task and requires exploration. This is particularly true for digital counter parts of physical designs. For example, Grasset et al. [6] try to answer the question if a mixed-reality book is still a book and explore the design and development process of visually augmented books. They argue that exploring design issues becomes more important as technology gets more mature; and that the development of prototypes requires time and very specialized experts.

The intention of this section was to reflect on what it means to exploit mobile devices for interaction in a broader sense and to remind the reader of current design notions and problems. A mobile device is a new medium and mobile augmented reality can provide rich sensory effects. The key challenge for AR-based user manuals lies in building on the aforementioned technological advances in AR and to connect the device and the required information in a manner that is intuitive to the user and if possible even fun to use. It is unclear how much of the knowledge on user manual design can be applied to mobile phones and which new challenges arise when user manuals are adapted to the mobile device.

In order to provide some insights we now move to a concrete implementation of a digital manual that is inspired by properties of a mobile device.

4   GuideMe Prototype

The GuideMe system identifies home appliances by using the camera and retrieves an interactive manual from a server. The interactive manual is specified in the User Manual Markup Language (UMML). The following sections outline the method used to recognize the device, the UMML specification and the resulting user interface.

4.1   Connect to the Physical User Interface

To use a mobile device to interact with an appliance a connection between those has to be established. Both components should become a single user interface to display the required information.

For this purpose, a marker-based object recognition similar to [15] was chosen because the preferred marker-less recognition of an appliance requires textured surfaces [17] and therefore cannot be applied properly to home appliances which often have monochromatic or reflecting user interfaces. Marker-less approaches struggle to distinguish two devices of similar color and form. If marker-less recognition is applied the reflective user interfaces, the reflections will become part of the calculated feature, thus making it difficult to recognize the same device with different reflections. In a marker-based recognition the marker becomes part of the user interface.

4.2   Definition of the Digital User Manual

Appliances differ in size, form and functionality. In result each user manual has to be customized. GuideMe aims at providing the best possible user manual for a specific appliance and a specific mobile device. Therefore, we decided to put the design of the user interface into the hands of the experts by providing them a simple format to author user manuals. In consequence designers can adapt existing manuals to a specific device and experiment with different layouts and structures. We developed a new format to define manuals and refer to it as User Manual Markup Language (UMML). UMML defines the layout of the recognized user interface. In comparison to existing formats like APRIL [12], UMML benefits from a clear focus on user manuals. APRIL aims at structuring narrative content and defines cast, interactions and behavior. This flexibility leads to complex definitions that require advanced knowledge.

The resulting schema builds on a smaller set of XML statements to define the user manual. The user interface was split into the basic elements like text, arrows or any other graphical element. Custom elements can be defined and used as well. The grouping of these elements and the final structure of UMML was inspired by the design of current printed user manuals.

An UMML file consists of two parts: the menu description and the list of functionalities. Each functionality definition has a unique ID. The menu description organizes the available functionalities into a hierarchical structure of menus that can contain functionalities or submenus. Functionalities can be linked into a menu several times at several levels, if desired. Functionalities contain a title tag and consist of a number of steps. The steps are identified and linked by a unique ID. Each step definition contains a list of virtual objects and their position in relation to the frame marker, e.g. an arrow pointing to a button. Furthermore, images, videos and audio files can be linked into the manual.

4.3   Magic Lens User Interface

The GuideMe application is an UMML interpreter that builds on the Vuforia SDK to implement a so called "magic lens" interface [1]. The fixed components of the user interface are minimal to leave the screen to the manual designer. Only a small tool bar at the top supports the navigation and shows the current progress. The remaining part of the screen can be used to display the augmented camera image. This design aims at providing a maximum of possibilities to the manual designer and restricts the design considerations to providing the appropriate components to use the available space in an easy and intuitive manner.

Figure 1 shows how the camera image of the physical user interface (figure a) is combined with instructions (figure b and c). Two hand icons point at the available buttons. A frame is used to highlight the part of the display that will change by pressing the buttons. The user sees a live image of the real oven. Therefore, the user does not need to compare a depicted oven in a manual with the real oven. Furthermore, if the participant moves the hand to press a button, the camera will display this action on the screen as well. The virtual

(a) Oven with Vuforia frame marker and enclosed QR code
(b) GuideMe highlights the corresponding operating elements
(c) GuideMe screenshot with highlighted operating elements

Fig. 1. GuideMe prototype in action

objects defined in the UMML file can be classified by their positioning on the screen. The user has to hold the tablet in front of the user interface to recognize the marker. GuideMe uses the size and position of the marker to adapt the coordinate plane. Texture components, symbols, arrows, frames and user defined graphics are placed relative to the recognized marker position. In general these components are placed in the same plane as the marker but a 3-dimensional placement is possible as well.

In some cases superimposed objects might not be sufficient to indicate the correct action. For example, if one button has to be held while pressing other buttons, an image of two arrows pointing to both buttons will not be enough. The instructions that are printed in a manual have to be conveyed to the user as well. Using UMML and GuideMe, they can be printed on the screen or played as an audio or video clip. All three methods are possible with the existing UMML elements. Videos, audio clips, Android webviews, buttons and option menus are placed at fixed positions on the screen. Android webviews can load HTML context into the Android application from a file or the Internet. Video and audio clips start automatically when the corresponding step is rendered. Textual descriptions are placed at the top of the screen. All components can be freely combined, although a full screen video overlaps other components.

Navigation between user manual steps is possible by pressing buttons or by selecting from an options menu. Options menus and buttons can be defined in the UMML file. Users can always return to the last step using the Android back button or return to the menu by using the navigation bar at the top.

5   Evaluation

We conducted two subsequent studies to obtain first insights on the user experience and task performance using GuideMe. The first study compared GuideMe based manuals against excerpts from the original printed user manual and the second against video tutorials.

We selected two state-of-the-art ovens, the *Stoves SEB900MFSe* and the *Bosch HBL78B7.1.* Both provide sufficient complexity to require a manual for first usage of advanced functionality and provide several user interface elements, such as knobs, buttons and displays that could be augmented. They are similar enough to allow a comparison but have different user interfaces to mitigate learning effects during the study.

5.1 User Manual Design

One simple and one complex task were selected from the original printed user manual. In a pre-test the two tasks were completed on both ovens with similar effort. However, the complexity of the selected task was reduced by one step after the pre-test. Participants needed more than 10 minutes to set the start of the cooking period using the original manual. Hence, the complex task in the study consisted of only four steps.

For the first study the relevant pages of the original manual were used as is. All unrelated pages were removed to limit the scope of the evaluation to the presentation of instruction. The original manual served as a basis for all other manuals. For the second study, video tutorials were needed. The authoring of the video tutorials was inspired by existing video tutorials. Each video tutorial was implemented as one continuous video. The video contained the text as spoken comment and as superimposed text on top of the screen. Furthermore, additional annotations in the video highlighted important user interface elements of the oven. Users can navigate the video by using the standard Android controls, e.g. jumping to any point of the video sequence by selecting it from the progress bar.

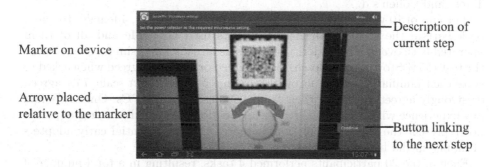

Fig. 2. GuideMe example manual: explaining a microwave oven

The GuideMe manual was structured according to the numbered steps in the manual. For each step, the corresponding explanation is shown at the top of the screen and the step is visualized on the screen as shown in figure 2. Arrows images and further markers are superimposed on the camera image to indicate relevant buttons and displays. Navigation between steps was realized by buttons.

5.2 Study Design

The first conducted study compares (a) the original printed version and (b) a manual based on GuideMe on a tablet. GuideMe ran on a Samsung Galaxy Tab

10.1 tablet with Android 3.1. We measured task completion times and used the NASA TLX [8] to measure the subjective task load of participants. Participants were asked to think aloud while completing the given tasks. Observers noted down their statements, the perceived body language and the operation of the appliance. A concluding questionnaire captured the subjective preferences of the user. The subsequent second study replicates the design of the first study, but compares (a) a video-based tutorial on a tablet and (b) GuideMe on a tablet. The participants in the second study did not overlap with participants from the first study.

During the user study, each participant performed overall 4 measured tasks, two on each oven: (a) 1 simple and 1 complex task using GuideMe for one oven and (b) 1 simple and 1 complex task using the printed original manual for the other oven. Switching between devices and reversing the order of technologies and devices aimed at mitigating learning effects of the oven's user interface. Participants could use as much time as necessary and should mention when they deemed the task to be completed or if they want to give up on it. There was no additional help offered except the manual to be tested. After each task participants completed the NASA TLX questionnaire. The concluding questionnaire collected overall feedback on both used technologies and the perceived complexity of the used ovens.

This data was evaluated in a within subjects design to mitigate the individual differences in performance and NASA TLX usage. The significance of quantitative data (NASA TLX and task completion times) was analyzed using a paired T-test and Cohen's d.

2 groups of 10 young technology-savvy participants (22-31, 4 female, 16 male) took part in the studies. All 20 participants used GuideMe and all of them operated both ovens. The majority of the users already knew similar ovens before the test (55 % Stoves, 70 % Bosch). 53 % agreed or strongly agreed when asked to state their familiarity with Android device on a 5 point Likert scale. 74% agreed or strongly agreed regarding their familiarity using tablet PCs. Only 10% had any experience with augmented reality applications. Albeit this user group does not represent the overall population, it represents the potential early adopters of mobile media based user manuals.

Each of the 20 participants performed 4 tasks, resulting in a total number of 80 measurements. 5 of these measurements were classified as outliers, because participants required exceptionally long to complete a given task. Participants were stuck because they entered unforeseen menus and got lost in the mismatch between instructions and available options. As we use a pairwise T-test the corresponding measurement using the second device was excluded from the analysis as well.

6   Results

All participants in both studies reported that the two provided user manuals were useful to complete the given tasks. Nevertheless, when asked if the oven was difficult to use the majority of users disagreed or strongly disagreed (65% Stoves, 85% Bosch). According to this question, the Stoves oven was experienced as more difficult.

6.1   GuideMe vs. Printed Manual

A first group of 10 participants completed a simple and a complex task using GuideMe on one oven and a similar task using the original paper manual on another oven. 90% of them stated in the concluding questionnaire that they preferred GuideMe over printed manuals. As shown in figure 3(a), they needed significantly more time ($p < 0.0003, d = 1.46$) to complete both tasks using GuideMe than by using the printed manual. Although all 10 participants deemed each task completed, the final result of the complex task included errors for the majority of participants. One specific error stood out. Users of the Stoves oven ignored the icon indicating the selected mode and ended up setting a timer instead of setting the cooking time. In many of the observed cases this was due to the timeout of the user interface after 5 seconds. After changing from main menu to the timer menu, participants looked at the manual. They did not notice when the oven display changed and subsequently showed the main menu again. Pressing the next button, as advised in the manual, switched again from the main menu to the time menu instead of from the timer menu to the cooking time menu. The error was very common for GuideMe users (70%), while none of the users of the paper manual made this mistake. A similar problem with a timeout of menu occurred at the Bosch oven. However, the changes in the display of the Bosch are more apparent so users recognized the problem and could avoid a mistake.

In the original manual all steps of the desired functionality were printed on the same page. Participants could scan all steps at once and quickly jump between the different steps. Therefore, they could often perform several steps at once. Afterwards they had to look at the device to synchronize their expectations with the current behavior of the device in front of them. GuideMe users could only see one step at a time. If users wanted to look at another step they had to

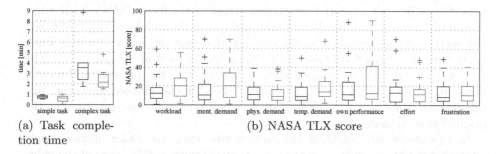

(a) Task completion time

(b) NASA TLX score

Fig. 3. GuideMe (black, left columns) compared to the original printed manual (blue, right columns)

press the forward/back button or return to the manual overview. It appeared to be counterintuitive for participants to go one step back in the manual because of the timeout in user interface.

Nevertheless, the NASA TLX scores depicted in figure 3(b), are significantly lower ($p < 0.046, d = 1.4$) for GuideMe. The NASA TLX subscales show the reasons. Participants felt that printed manuals induced an increased mental and temporal demand as well as higher concerns about performance compared to GuideMe. Participants stated in the concluding questionnaire that GuideMe makes it easier to associate instruction symbols with user interface elements. Using GuideMe, it was easier to follow the defined steps, e.g. *"It shows an easier way to act"* or *"You get only the relevant information"*. The main drawback of GuideMe was seen in the weight of the tablet (565 g) that had to be held with the camera pointed at the marker. The detailed analysis of the NASA TLX dimensions in figure 3 shows how users of the printed user manual underestimated their performance. Although, the observed results show a flawless and swift operation of the device, they did not feel as confident in their performance using the original manual. p No matter which technology was used, there was always a disruption between gathering information from the manual and applying the new knowledge by operating the oven. Participants using GuideMe did rarely manipulate the oven controls while looking at the camera image on the tablet screen. On the one hand, this behavior was induced by marker recognition problems, e.g. when the marker was no longer in the cameras field of view because of the attempt to operate the oven. On the other hand, participants had problems to operate a control in 3-dimensional space, e.g. pressing a button, while looking at a 2-dimensional image of their hand movement. Furthermore, one user said, *"The tablet blocked operation of the oven because it had to be pointed at the marker."*.

6.2   GuideMe vs. Mobile Video Tutorial

The remaining 10 participants used GuideMe in comparison to the video tutorial. There was not a clear preference of one technology as 6 out of 10 preferred the video tutorial over GuideMe. The task completion time depicted in 4 was significantly faster ($p < 0.0056, d = 1.26$) using the video than using GuideMe. The video tutorial received a significantly lower NASA TLX score ($p < 0.0108, d = 0.9$). Participants said again that the weight of the tablet and the need to point the tablet at the user interface are the main obstacles when using GuideMe *"You don't have to hold the tablet in front of the QR Code."* The NASA TLX subscales in figure 4 show a difference in the physical and mental demand, because users had to point the tablet at the marker. However, this difference did not occur in the first study when GuideMe was compared to the original printed manual.

In this study 50% of GuideMe users made again the same mistake while operating the Stoves oven as in the first study. Moreover, 60% users of the video tutorial made the same mistake. The mobile video tutorial does not provide a visible separation into steps. Users had to use the standard video navigation

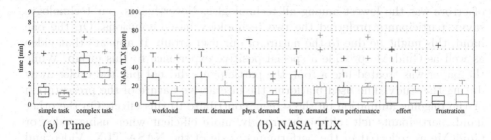

(a) Time   (b) NASA TLX

Fig. 4. GuideMe (black, left columns) compared to a video tutorial on a tablet (red, right columns)

to go forward and backward. However, it was difficult for participants to scan through the video, and go to one specific step. When GuideMe manuals were read and applied in a step-by-step manner, the video tutorials were watched as a whole, before operating the oven. Participants rarely stopped the video. They rather watched the whole video again and aimed at memorizing the whole procedure to perform it afterwards. The users that preferred video said *"It's faster"* or *"Description is more detailed and easier to watch"*. 4 user preferred GuideMe because they felt that the video induced *"time pressure"* and they like the *"step-by-step"* approach of GuideMe because the *"steps are better separated"*.

The body language in this study differed from the participants using the paper manual in the first study. In the first study participants held the paper manual only while reading and put it aside while operating the oven. Some users put the manual on top of the oven while reading from it. Body language suggested that participant were focused scanning the printed manual to extract relevant information. In the second study, participants using the video tutorial or GuideMe were looking expectantly at the tablet screen. They kept on holding the tablet in their hands. For instance, even when operating the oven, one hand was still holding the tablet. In the first study this behavior was attributed to the need to point the camera at the oven, but the same behavior was now observed for users of the mobile video tutorial.

7 Discussion

The two studies and the design of the GuideMe prototype provide insights into the usage of different user manual formats, the developed prototype and the design challenges when creating user manuals for and with mobile devices that combine physical user interface elements and digital information.

7.1 User Manual Formats

Three different formats of user manuals were used in the two studies. The average task completion time for the printed user manuals is the fastest and the number of errors was the lowest among all technologies. Nevertheless, our technology-savvy participants preferred the two technology based solutions. On the one hand, this might be due to the nature of our user group. It appears that video as well as GuideMe provide a special positive experience to this group. While the paper was treated like a tool, the participants did not put the tablet away during the study. The used platform, the interactive nature of the presentation or the ongoing animation on the screen, contribute to this effect. On the other hand, participants felt, although wrongly, more efficient when using video or GuideMe as reflected in the performance scale of the NASA TLX. Video and GuideMe allow users to simply imitate actions or follow detailed advice. The paper manual had to be understood and mapped to the ovens' user interface. The participants have to decide more in the mapping process and each small decision adds to their uncertainty.

Although GuideMe learned from the printed manual, some design aspects became only clear by comparing both media in the study. For instance, the step structure of GuideMe was copied from the original manual but not the arrangement of steps on a single page. Each augmented image requires the whole screen of the mobile device. Hence, content that is printed on one page in the manual is split into a sequence of screens. This split is a critical point as users can no longer scan through all steps on a page to recognize the current state of the device. Future implementations should aim at supporting this type of scanning, e.g. by employing similar methods as in mobile image browsing. Furthermore, GuideMe could combine benefits of printed paper and digital augmented objects by combining both media as explored by Grasset et al. [6].

A user manual does not only contain a series of steps, but aims at teaching the user interface of the device. Hence, task descriptions contain additional information such as warnings on possible errors, the impact on other functionality and a method to revert or abort the current task. Video tutorials often select a simple subset of steps and neglect this additional information for the sake of a shorter and clearer presentation. However, this background information is essential to actually create an understanding of a new device. Albeit we included all this information in the video, the video was praised for the clarity of the explained steps. However, participants criticized the perceived "time pressure". Participants did not use the available controls to stop the video. Splitting the instructions into a linked set of small videos may eliminate this behavior. Such manuals can be realized using the current functionality of GuideMe.

Both studies were influenced by the weight and size of the used tablet. The weight increased the physical demand. The size of the tablet was perceived as a barrier between user and the oven. Further evaluations using smaller devices can research the resulting trade-off between screen size and weight for this application domain.

7.2   GuideMe Prototype

The marker-based object recognition did highlight the challenges induced by the properties of the appliance and the employed tablet. The camera on the tablet is located on the top of the tablet thus creating a shift of the image that can be confusing. The camera is expected to be in the middle of the tablet. Completely different devices like wearable displays[5] or personal projection devices [11] would better align movements of the device and the created image.

The ovens' user interface in our study was too wide for the used tablet camera. Ovens were identified by a single marker in the middle of the user interface that had to be within the cameras' field of sight all the time. On the Stoves oven for example, the knob to change the temperature is more than 20 cm away from the marker. Participants often held the tablet too close to the user interface to see marker and knob in the magic lens. Multiple markers or a new kind of distributed markers could provide a solution. Another option would be to decorate the user interface in a manner to enable marker-less object recognition. The participants themselves came up with a third simple solution. They missed a button to freeze the current state of the screen. This approach would combine augmented reality and image based user manuals.

UMML enables GuideMe to be flexible and abstracts from the required programming. Technical documentation experts can design augmented reality user manuals by writing UMML. However, we did not evaluate the modeling capabilities of UMML in this paper.

7.3 Digital Manuals for Mobile Devices

Future user manuals should emphasize the playful exploration of the functionality provided by mobile devices. The two conducted studies have provided first evidence that video and AR-based manuals can support this change. Users felt more secure using these manuals. Moreover, their body language indicated a positive attitude towards this new medium. This preference was confirmed in the concluding questionnaire.

However, the initial positive attitude may change, if the design of such user manuals does not account for the specific properties of the mobile devices, e.g. the position of the camera. Designers and technical documentation experts are needed to facilitate this change. Until now technology has dominated the development. UMML is a first approach to simplify development and include the experts. The notion of computational composites as suggested by Vallgårda [19] can help to bridge the gap between designers and technology driven developers.

In AR-based manuals the appliance becomes part of the user interface. For instance, the color of superimposed graphics has to to blend into the camera picture of the device. The design of the appliance is linked to the design of the manual. Properties of both components influence each other and create the final design. Therefore, GuideMe aims at a maximizing the flexibility of the design.

A further integration on the technical level was proposed by Liu et al. [13]. They compared AR manual implementations and concluded that "the conventional AR approach performs almost as well as pictures" but feedback from the device would "significantly improve task performance and user experience". A

---

[5] Project Glass http://plus.google.com/+projectglass/

direct feedback from the home appliance to GuideMe would prevent possible discrepancies between the actual state of a device and the state that GuideMe is assuming and thus significantly lowering error rates and frustration. Although standardized methods for device feedback would be beneficial to applications like GuideMe such a standardization of feedback mechanisms across appliances and manufacturers is not foreseeable.

8   Conclusion

We described GuideMe a mobile design for AR-based user manuals, discussed the underlying combination of mobile media and physical user interfaces and presented the results of two small scale studies. Both studies compared GuideMe manuals to current alternatives, the printed manual and mobile video tutorials, with young users and real home appliances. The printed manual resulted in the fastest task completion times and the lowest error rates. However, these classic usability metrics were not decisive arguments for the participants; they preferred video tutorials and GuideMe on the tablet. Both are interactive formats that allow users to imitate actions. In result participants enjoyed using these manuals on the tablet.

Augmented Reality and video provide starting points to new user manuals that are fun to use. Both manual types can be designed, combined and tested using UMML and GuideMe. A mobile application for consumers to adapt and create simple UMML manuals by drag and drop is currently in development. Applications like GuideMe and a simple editor would open the explored design space for a broader audience. The current progress in mobile media has the potential to transform the user manual but requires more research on the manual design.

Acknowledgments. This work has been co-funded by the German Federal Ministry of Education and Research in the CHICO project under grant number 16SV6186.

References

1. Bier, E., Stone, M., Pier, K., Buxton, W., DeRose, T.: Toolglass and magic lenses: the see-through interface. In: SIGGRAPH 1993, pp. 73–80. ACM (1993)
2. Bødker, S.: When second wave hci meets third wave challenges. In: Proceedings of the 4th Nordic Conference on Human-computer Interaction: Changing Roles, pp. 1–8. ACM (2006)
3. Fallman, D.: The new good: exploring the potential of philosophy of technology to contribute to human-computer interaction. In: Proceedings of the 2011 Annual Conference on Human Factors in Computing Systems, pp. 1051–1060. ACM (2011)
4. Feiner, S., Macintyre, B., Seligmann, D.: Knowledge-based augmented reality. Communications of the ACM 36(7), 53–62 (1993)
5. Geiger, C., Kleinnjohann, B., Reimann, C., Stichling, D.: Mobile AR4ALL. In: ISAR 2001, pp. 181–182. IEEE Comput. Soc. (2001)

6. Grasset, R., Dunser, A., Billinghurst, M.: The design of a mixed-reality book: Is it still a real book? In: 7th IEEE/ACM International Symposium on Mixed and Augmented Reality, ISMAR 2008, pp. 99–102. IEEE (2008)
7. Hakkarainen, M., Woodward, C., Billinghurst, M.: Augmented assembly using a mobile phone. In: Proceedings of the 7th IEEE/ACM International Symposium on Mixed and Augmented Reality, ISMAR 2008, pp. 167–168. IEEE Computer Society, Washington, DC (2008)
8. Hart, S., Staveland, L.: Development of nasa-tlx (task load index): Results of empirical and theoretical research. In: Hancock, P.A., Meshkati, N. (eds.) Human Mental Workload, pp. 139–183. Elsevier, Amsterdam (1988)
9. Henderson, S., Feiner, S.: Exploring the benefits of augmented reality documentation for maintenance and repair. IEEE Transactions on Visualization and Computer Graphics 17(10), 1355–1368 (2011)
10. IEC International Electrotechnical Commission: IEC 62079:2001 - Preparation of instructions. Structuring, content and presentation (July 2001)
11. Kawsar, F., Rukzio, E., Kortuem, G.: An explorative comparison of magic lens and personal projection for interacting with smart objects. In: Mobile HCI 2010, pp. 157–160. ACM (2010)
12. Ledermann, F., Schmalstieg, D.: April: a high-level framework for creating augmented reality presentations. In: Proceedings of the Virtual Reality, VR 2005, pp. 187–194. IEEE (March 2005)
13. Liu, C., Huot, S., Diehl, J., Mackay, W.E., Beaudouin-lafon, M.: Evaluating the Benefits of Real-time Feedback in Mobile Augmented Reality with Hand-held Devices. In: CHI 2012, vol. 2012, pp. 2973–2976 (2012)
14. Redström, J.: Designing Everyday Computational Things. Ph.D. thesis, Göteborg (2001)
15. Rohs, M.: Marker-based embodied interaction for handheld augmented reality games. Journal of Virtual Reality and Broadcasting 4(5) (2007)
16. de Sa, M., Churchill, E., Isbister, K.: Mobile augmented reality: design issues and opportunities. In: Proceedings of the 13th International Conference on Human Computer Interaction with Mobile Devices and Services, pp. 749–752. ACM (2011)
17. Takacs, G., Chandrasekhar, V., Gelfand, N., Xiong, Y., Chen, W.C., Bismpigiannis, T., Grzeszczuk, R., Pulli, K., Girod, B.: Outdoors augmented reality on mobile phone using loxel-based visual feature organization. In: Proceedings of the 1st ACM International Conference on Multimedia Information Retrieval, MIR 2008, pp. 427–434. ACM, New York (2008)
18. TCeurope (Organisation) and European Commission: SecureDoc Guideline for Usable and Safe Operating Manuals for Consumer Goods: Fourth Brussels Colloquium for User-friendly Product Information. TCeurope (March 29, 2004)
19. Vallgårda, A., Redström, J.: Computational composites. In: Proceedings of the SIGCHI Conference on Human Factors in Computing Systems, CHI 2007, pp. 513–522. ACM, New York (2007)
20. Viola, I., Meister, E.G.: Smart visibility in visualization. In: Computational Aesthetics in Graphics, Visualization, pp. 209–216 (2005)

Petanko Roller:
A VR System with a Rolling-Pin Haptic Interface for Entertainment

Ken Nakagaki[1], Keina Konno[2], Shuntaro Tashiro[1], Ayaka Ikezawa[3],
Yusaku Kimura[3], Masaru Jingi[3], and Yasuaki Kakehi[3]

[1] Graduate School of Media and Governance, Keio University
[2] Keio Research Institute at SFC, Keio University
[3] Faculty of Environment and Information Studies, Keio University
[4] 5322 Endo, Fujisawa-shi, Kanagawa, 252-0882 Japan
{nakagaki,ykakehi}@sfc.keio.ac.jp
http://www.xlab.sfc.keio.ac.jp

Abstract. Most people will have experienced squishing clay and making it flat. The action of changing the shapes of real objects induces pleasant feelings or excitement. In this research, we propose a system, named Petanko Roller, which enables users to experience the sensation of rolling out any object in the real world with a rolling pin virtually. This system, by detecting the shapes of physical objects with a range camera, can represent haptic sensations of unevenness or friction of the objects, using modules for clunk mechanisms and brakes of a rolling-pin-based interface. Furthermore, by projecting images of the objects being squished on a tabletop display, it can also give optical feedback to users. In this paper, we discuss the system design, implementation, and behavior of users in exhibitions.

Keywords: Rolling Pin, VR Entertainment, Haptic Interface, Tangible Interface.

1 Introduction

When playing with clay, mixing cookie dough, or crushing cans, most people will have experienced squishing something and making it flat. Changing the shapes of real objects induces pleasant feelings or excitement. In cartoons or comics, we are often shown characters or physical objects being flattened by large objects. In contrast, in the real world, there are many objects that cannot be flattened because of their hardness, costliness, or uniqueness.

Under such backgrounds, we propose an entertainment system that can provide a virtual experience of flattening any physical objects including human's body by giving haptic and visual feedbacks. In this research, to realize such system, we mainly aimed to develop a novel interface that can represent textures and shapes of digital objects.

D. Reidsma, H. Katayose, and A. Nijholt (Eds.): ACE 2013, LNCS 8253, pp. 168–181, 2013.

In concrete, we propose an entertainment system which can represent both shape and texture of digital objects intuitively, named "Petanko Roller" (Fig. 1). To increase user's intuitiveness of interface, a technique to use daily tools as a metaphor for inducing specific action is often introduced in the field of human computer interface(HCI). As adapting this point of view for designing haptic interface, we used the metaphor of "rolling pin" which is a tool for rolling out cookie dough or clay. By moving a rolling-pin-based interface on a visual image on a tabletop display, the user can feel the unevenness and friction of the object according to the position of the device. Putting pressure on the digital object through the device stretches the object so that user feel the sensation of rolling out the object. It is also able to represent variety of haptic sensation such as hardness or texture of digital objects by adjusting the algorithm. Actuators for representing haptic sensations are all installed in the device, thus users are free from wearing particular device or other limitations.

In this paper, we describe the related work, the system design, and the feedbacks through exhibitions.

Fig. 1. Overview of Petanko Roller

2   Related Work

In resent years, in the field of HCI or VR, many systems have been proposed to provide rich and realistic experience to users by giving multi modal feedbacks other than visual or audio. Especially, interfaces which provide haptic sensation have been popular these days[10][12][5]. Such interfaces can dynamically represent shapes or textures of digital objects.

Among such researches, there are approaches that encourage intuitive interaction by using common tools or objects as metaphors. As for a major example of such interface in HCI, the metaDESK[11] utilizes physical objects as a computer interface under the concept of Tangible Bits[4][3]. There are also haptic interfaces proposed under such approaches. Virtual Chanbara[6] is a VR system that uses the inertial force of a spinning weight to enable users to feel Chanbara feedback. It can represent the reaction force when a player's sword hits virtual enemies. Funbrella[13] can record and replay rain with an umbrella-like interface that is composed of a vibration-giving mechanism based on a speaker and a microphone. Ikegami et al. proposed handy haptic feedback devices imitating daily tools such as a tweezer or a syringe named Tool Device[2]. Using the metaphor of everyday tools, they enable users to manipulate informations intuitively. The advantages of taking such approaches are that users can figure out how to use the device easily and also that it is easy to install various actuators or sensors in devices because they can have a certain size according to the tools used as metaphors. As basing on such approaches and focusing on a "rolling pin", we aim to develop an interface which represents the shape and resistance of digital objects with haptic and visual feedbacks.

One of the major feature of Petanko Roller is that it can represent the three dimensional shape of objects. Pin-displays [1][8] are similar purposed system for representing shapes. They physically represents the shape information by actuating arrayed pins up and down. Although pins are arrayed on tabletop device in such system, in our research it is the interface that includes linear actuated modules. It is able to represent the haptic sensation of rolling over objects with rolling pin by regulating the modules up and down according to the motion of the device. In the pin-display system, the size of the object which can be represented depends on the size of the display, but in our system, the size of the interface doesn't limit it, because of its unique system design.

Also there are related work on expressing hardness or texture of virtual objects. Claytric Surface[9] is a tangible display which can change the hardness of its surface by regulating internal particle density. The Haptic Touch Toolkit[7] can express the height and friction of virtual objects at single point, with a device which has an actuating rod and a brake. In contrast with these system, we propose a handheld sized interface which can represent 3D physical shape with clunk and brake modules placed in parallel.

3   Petanko Roller

3.1   Concept

As focusing on the pleasant feelings or excitement induced when changing the shapes of physical objects, we propose an entertainment system that user can virtually squish any object in real world as if they were clay. We developed a VR haptic system, named Petanko Roller, which user can experience flattening any physical object in the real world.

We describe the process of the user's experience in the system of Petanko Roller below (Fig. 2).

First, a user chooses an object in the real world that he/she wants to make flat. The system then captures the 3D shape of the object.

Secondly, by moving a rolling-pin-based device on the visual image on a tabletop display, the user can feel the unevenness and friction of the object. Putting pressure on the virtual object through the device stretches the object according to the force of the pressure and the motion of the device. With time, the object will be flat.

Thirdly, at the end, the user can keep a printout of the flat object that he/she rolled out as a souvenir.

Fig. 2. Process of user experience

3.2   System Overview

The system of Petanko Roller consists of a rolling-pin-based haptic interface, a tabletop display, PC, Microsoft Kinect and a printer (Fig. 3). The system first detect the shape of an object using Kinect. The rolling-pin-based interface detects the pressure of users and provides haptic sensations of unevenness and friction of virtual objects. To provide the unevenness and the friction, servomotors and brakes are attached on tires. With a micro controller, the rolling-pin-based interface can communicate input and output data with PC. The tabletop display is composed with a projector to provide visual sensations and an infrared camera to recognize the motion of the rolling-pin-based interface by detecting the IR LED in it. Both of them are connected to PC to process input and output data, so that the system can provide both haptic and visual feedbacks according to detected users' action in real time. The printer is used for printing a flattened object as a piece of paper.

We describe the details of system design for each process and how they interact.

4   System Design

4.1   Detection of the Object

We implemented Kinect which is an infrared depth sensor for measuring the physical object's shape. Kinect is fixed approximately 100 cm above the tabletop display, in a downward direction (Fig. 4). On the basis of the range data acquired

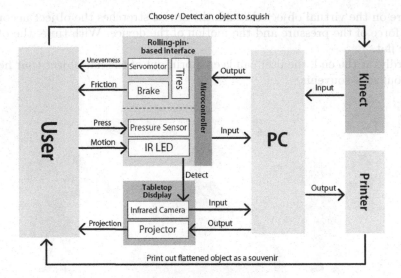

Fig. 3. Configuration of the system

from Kinect, shape data are generated and saved for PC processing. In the shape data, Each pixel's height datum is allocated from 0 to 255 by setting 0 as the top of the tabletop display and 255 as the highest part of the object. Kinect is preliminarily calibrated.

In addition, color image data clipped according to the height data are also saved at the same time(Fig. 5).

4.2   Rolling-Pin-Based Haptic Interface

We describe the rolling-pin-based interface that represents haptic sensations. As noted above, the rolling-pin-based interface represents the unevenness of the virtual objects and the frictional forces acting on them.

Fig. 6 shows the appearance and configuration of the device. In this device, tires and brakes are installed in parallel at the bottom, and clunk modules are connected to servomotors at the top. A pressure sensor is installed in each handle to detect the force of the pressure as Fig. 7 shows, and two IR LED modules are installed at the bottom for detecting the motion of the device.

When an actual rolling pin is rolled, each part of it bumps, according to the shape of the object. To represent such unevenness of virtual objects, in this system, each clunk module is actuated up and down, according to the relation between the digital object data and the position of the device(Fig. 8). Thus, users can perceive the overall shape of the objects by moving the interface.

When rolling a real rolling pin over an object, frictional forces act between the object and the rolling pin. To represent this, brakes are applied to the tires using servo motors. This mechanism is composed of a servo motor, a gear cut

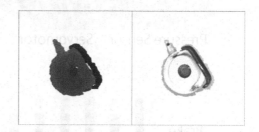

Fig. 4. Kinect detecting a physical object

Fig. 5. Generated image data and shape data using Kinect

on the cross, a brake plate, and two tires (Fig. 9). A gear cut is attached to the servo motor, so that it pushes the plate when the servo motor actuates. With this mechanism, users feel the friction between the tires and the plate as the friction of the virtual object. Also, as the tension of brake is adjustable, it can represent various kinds of material texture or changes in resistance according to the shape.

We implemented the device, which is 580 mm in length and 1.7 kg in weight, and has a handle of length 90 mm at each end (Fig. 6). Clunk modules are installed every 35 mm on the device. The device diameter, excluding the clunk modules, is 104 mm, and it can represent a maximum thickness range of 30 mm. We used servomotors as following: S11H/2BBMC/JR manufactured by GWS for the clunk module, and ZS-F135 by ZEBRA for the brakes. Each motor has torques of 7.6 [kgcm] and 1.6 [kgcm]. We used FSR402 by Interlink Electronics Inc. for the pressure sensors. The interface is connected to PC by wired from one end of the interface.

4.3   Tabletop Display

Next, we describe the tabletop display on which the rolling-pin-based device is used. In this system, the display gives visual feedback as projected images, and detects the position of the device on the display. Fig. 10 shows its overview. It consists of a projector, an infrared camera, a mirror, and a screen at the top. The projector is used to show images of the virtual objects on the screen. As the object becomes flatter, the projected image of the object also stretches with the software running on PC, so that users get feedback as both haptic and visual sensations.

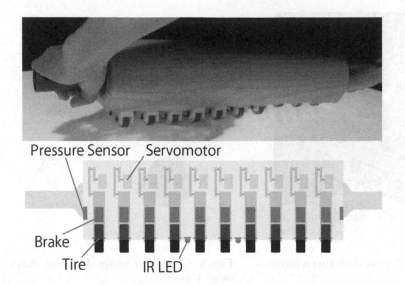

Fig. 6. The appearance and the internal composition of the interface

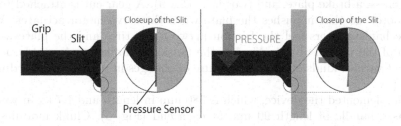

Fig. 7. Structure for pressure sensing

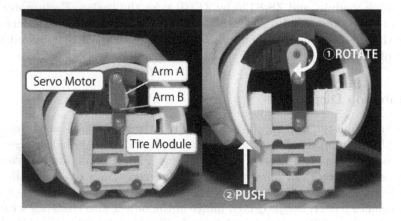

Fig. 8. Sectional view of Actuating the clunk module

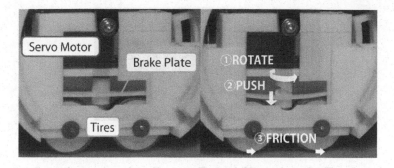

Fig. 9. Sectional view of Actuating the brake

Also, the infrared camera detects two IR LED modules installed at the bottom of the device, so it is able to regulate the clunk modules according to the position and the rotation of the device in real-time. Fig. 11 shows an example of the detected data and the calculated position of each module.

The tabletop display is 75 cm wide by 75 cm deep by 90 cm high.

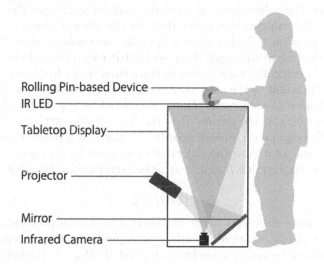

Fig. 10. Structure of the tabletop display

4.4 Software

We describe the software for representing the sensation of squishing doughy objects. This time, we developed simple original algorithms which do not use advanced physical simulations. There are 2 general phases for the software processing; one is processing for deforming object data and another is processing for providing haptic sensations. We describe each phase below.

Fig. 11. Detected image of device using infrared camera

Processing for Deforming Object Data. For the processing of deforming object data, we converted the shape and image data generated using Kinect according to input data. As for the shape data, each pixel's height datum is allocated from 0 to 255 by setting 0 as the lowest part and 255 as the highest part of the object. Hence, we use a grayscale data for the shape data. The image data which is an overhead image of the object is saved in RGB image data.

As input data for processing changes in an objects shape, we used the position of the device, shape data, and the values from the pressure sensors in the handles.

For processing, the image and shape data are first divided into 60 x 60 grids (Fig. 12). When the values from the pressure sensors are higher than a specific threshold and the value of the height data of the virtual object with respect to the device position is higher than a specific threshold, each grid vertex is translated, according to the input data, so that it can represent the object being stretched. Specifically, each vertex is translated away from the device in a direction perpendicular to the axis connecting the end points of the device. The translation distance of each vertex D is represented by Eq. 1: L is the distance between the vertex and the device, P is the force value extracted by pressure sensor, H is the height data on each coordinate, and a is a positive constant. By adjusting the value of a, how the object stretches can be changed. The smaller value L is or the larger value P and H are, the larger translation distance D will be.

$$D = (aPH)/L \tag{1}$$

In the processing of objects being flattened, the system processes the shape data from 0 to 255 in real-time according to input data. Eq. 2 represents the concrete processing for height value for each pixel H: H_{prev} is the height value in last frame, H_{th} is a threshold that represents the the minimum value of height, D is the translation distance of the nearest vertex to each pixel, b is a positive constant. Regulating b changes the degree of the object being flat. The right side of the Fig. 12 shows the deforming process of shape data.

$$H = \begin{cases} H_{prev} - bD \ (H_{prev} > H_{th}) \\ H_{prev} \qquad (otherwise) \end{cases} \tag{2}$$

With these processing, when a user put force to the interface, the object data gradually stretches and flattens until it cannot stretch any further. Thus, the visual images of the flattened objects can be displayed with the projector.

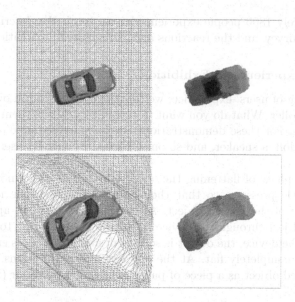

Fig. 12. Processing of the object data (Left: image data, Right: shape data)

Processing for Providing Haptic Sensations. Next, we describe the software processing for providing haptic sensations. As previously noted, the rolling-pin-based interface can represent 2 sensations; the unevenness and the friction. As for the unevenness each clunk modules in the interface actuates to express unevenness according to the coordinate height datum in the shape data. In concrete, the height data written in 0 to 255 are mapped into 0 to 3 cm for the clunk modules.

As for the friction, we used the change in shape data to represent the frictional force acting when the unevenness changes. For example, when a rolling pin moves up on a slope, user would feel the stronger frictional force. To represent such changes in friction, friction value F is represented by Eq. 3: H is the height value on the position of each clunk module, H_{ave} is the average height value in previous 10 frames. c represents the basis frictional force of virtual object and d is a coefficient of friction according to height data. By adjusting these positive constant values c and d, it can provide various textures of digital objects. We used these algorithms to represent haptic and visual sensations with a rolling-pin-based device and tabletop display in real-time.

$$F = \begin{cases} 0 & (H = 0) \\ c + (H - H_{ave})d & (H > 0) \end{cases} \tag{3}$$

5   Exhibitions and User Feedbacks

We demonstrated this system at exhibitions 8 times for general users both in Japan and overseas. In the exhibitions, we exhibited the entertainment system and approximately 1800 people experienced it in total. We describe the users' experiences, a survey, and the reactions and comments in exhibitions below.

5.1   Users' Experience in Exhibitions

At the beginning of users' experience, we tell them You can roll out any object with Petanko Roller. What do you want to roll out?, and ask them to choose an object to squish. For these demonstrations, we prepared sample objects: a toy car, a kettle, a doll, a sneaker, and so on. Objects brought by users can also be chosen.

In the initial phase of flattening the object, we tell users to move the device slowly, with little pressure, so that they can better check the reality of the haptic sensation of the virtual object. After that, we let them apply pressure to the virtual object through the device to flatten it. According to the pressure and motion of the device, the object is squished, and the process ends when the object becomes completely flat. At the end, at some exhibitions, we gave the user the flattened object as a piece of paper (card) as a souvenir (Fig. 13).

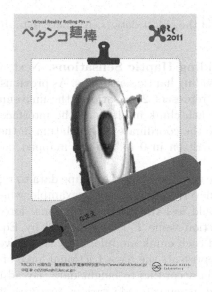

Fig. 13. An example of a printed card as a flattened object

5.2   Reactions and Comments in Exhibitions

Next, we describe the reactions and concrete comments of users at the exhibitions. Objects that are too hard to deform in the real world, such as the toy car or the kettle, were quite often chosen as the object to roll out. Users' personal objects, not only bags or cameras but also body parts of themselves or an accompanying person, were often chosen. When human's body were chosen, we let users to lay their upper body on the table top display in the detecting phase.

At the stage of checking the reality of haptic sensations, many users were surprised when the device actuated at the moment it was placed over the image. Moreover, many users commented, The sensation of rolling out objects was pleasant. In particular, when body parts such as faces were chosen, we could see users enjoying the visual changes, as if their facial expressions were changing as they squashed them. Also, some people commented that they felt special sensation or emotion when squishing themselves or accompanying person.

However, some users commented, "It was hard to feel the haptic sensations," when the detected objects were too small, or when the object was not very uneven. One reason for this could be that the system is unable to detect small unevennesses with the distance resolution of Kinect. In addition, there were some cases of poor object measurement because the infrared rays emitted from Kinect were reflected by, or went through, objects with a reflecting surface or some degree of transparency. Also, there were difficulties for children such as less power to squish or short arms to reach at the back of tabletop display, especially seen at some exhibitions which has many children for visitors. However, we could see many children enjoying squishing object together with the help of their parents (Fig. 14).

Fig. 14. A child and a parent enjoying Petanko Roller together

We also conducted a survey in the form of a questionnaire to collect users' comments in an exhibition named "Ishikawa Dream Future Festival 2011." There were 99 questionees answered. Each participant was asked to answer their impression through the experience as below.

- *Q*1 How much did you felt squishing objects in this system? (1=Not at all, 2=Little, 3=N/A, 4=Somewhat well, 5=Well.)
- *Q*2 What did cause you to feel the sensation of squishing objects? (Visual Feedback, Haptic Feedback, Unknown, Others) [multiple answers allowed]

– $Q3$ How fun was it to experience squishing objects in this system? (1=Not at all, 2=Little, 3=N/A, 4=Somewhat well, 5=Well.)

As for the result, toward $Q1$, our result came out to an average of 4.51 and variance of 1.06 (Fig. 15 (a)). This indicates that most participants understood the intention of the work and they actually felt it.

In addition, as asking 93 participants, who answered more than 4 in $Q1$, to answer the reason in $Q2$, we got the result of 44% chose visual feedbacks, 86% chose haptic feedbacks, 1% chose unknown, and no one chose others (Fig. 15 (b)). This result prove that haptic sensation using the interface was primary factor to express squishing objects. The visual feedbacks provided by projector also had effects in some extent for representing it.

Besides, for the result of $Q3$ which asked participants for the satisfaction of the experience, the an average was 4.7 and the variance was 0.34 (Fig. 15 (c)). From this outcome, it can be said that the experience provided in the system have high entertainment rate.

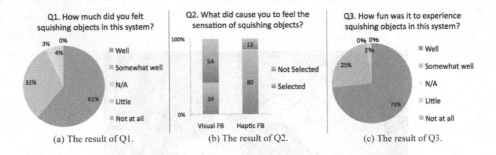

(a) The result of Q1.   (b) The result of Q2.   (c) The result of Q3.

Fig. 15. The result of the questionnaire

6   Conclusions

In this paper, we proposed an entertainment system for flattening any physical object in real world using rolling-pin-based interface. The interface we developed can represent both shapes and textures of digital objects by clunk modules and brake for the tires. Through exhibiting the system, we found that the experience of squishing objects provided by this system is realistic and enjoyable to some extent.

Future research could consider using advanced physical simulations in the algorithm, to obtain greater realism. Representing various kinds of materials other than clay, by adjusting the algorithm and device design could be another subject. To enhance the haptic sensations, several ways of upgrading the device design could be considered: installing vibration speakers, increasing the maximum value of the thickness range for the clunk mechanism, or downsizing the device.

In addition, the previously noted problem of errors in object measurement using Kinect need to be solved. We are thinking of increasing the precision by introducing a high-resolution camera with Kinect, or upgrading the image-processing algorithm.

In future work, we will propose other applications using this interface. Examples are applications for representing information that is difficult to interpret visually, such as the representation of altitudes on maps, or applications that include game elements as entertainment content. We will also propose to apply this interface for computer aided design (CAD) softwares, which enable users to manipulate shape of digital objects intuitively and provide the shape and texture of the object as haptic feedbacks interactively at the same time.

Acknowledgement. This research is supported by CREST, JST.

References

1. Blackshaw, M., Lkatos, D., Devincenzi, A., Leithinger, D., Ishii, H.: Recompose: Direct and Gestural Interaction With an Actuated Surface. In: Proceedings of ACM SIGGRAPH 2011, Emerging Technologies (2011)
2. Ikeda, Y., Sato, K., Kimura, A.: Tool Device: handy haptic feedback devices imitating every day tools. In: Proceedings of HCI Int. 2003 (2003)
3. Ishii, H.: Tangible Bits: Tangible bits: beyond pixels. In: Second International Conference on Tangible, Embedded, and Embodied Interaction, TEI 2008 (2008)
4. Ishii, H., Ullmer, B.: Tangible Bits: Towards Seamless Interfaces between People, Bits, and Atoms. In: Proceedings of ACM CHI 1997 (1997)
5. Iwamoto, T., Takezono, M., Hoshi, T., Shinoda, H.: Airborne ultrasound tactile display. In: Proceedings of ACM SIGGRAPH 2008 New Tech Demos (2008)
6. Koga, D., Itagaki, T.: Virtual Chanbara. In: Proceedings of ACM SIGGRAPH 2002, Emerging Technologies (2002)
7. Ledo, D., Nacenta, M., Marquardt, N., Boring, S., Greenberg, S.: The Haptic Touch Toolkit Enabling Exploration of Haptic Interactions. In: Sixth International Conference on Tangible, Embedded, and Embodied Interaction, TEI 2012 (2012)
8. Leithinger, D., Ishii, H.: Relief: a scalable actuated shape display. In: Fourth International Conference on Tangible, Embedded, and Embodied Interaction, TEI 2010 (2010)
9. Matoba, Y., Sato, T., Takahashi, N., Koike, H.: ClaytrcSufrace: an interactive surface with dynamic softness control capability. In: Proceedings of ACM SIGGRAPH 2012, Emerging Technologies (2012)
10. Sato, M.: Development of String-based Force Display: SPIDAR. In: Proceedings of VSMM 2002 (The Eighth International Conference on Virtual Systems and Multi Media) (2002)
11. Ullmer, B., Ishii, H.: The metaDESK: Models and Prototypes for Tangible User Interfaces. In: Proceedings of the 10th Annual ACM Symposium on User Interface Software and Technology, UIST 1997 (1997)
12. Minamizawa, K., Fukamachi, S., Kajimoto, H., Kawakami, N., Tachi, S.: GravityGrabber: Wearable Haptic Display to present Virtual Mass Sensation. In: Proceedings of ACM SIGGRAPH 2007 Emerging Technologies (2007)
13. Yoshida, A., Itoh, Y., Fujita, K., Ozaki, M., Kikukawa, T., Fukazawa, R., Kitamura, Y., Kishino, F.: Funbrella: making rain fun. In: Proceedings of ACM SIGGRAPH 2009, Emerging Technologies (2009)

Emoballoon

A Balloon-Shaped Interface Recognizing Social Touch Interactions

Kosuke Nakajima, Yuichi Itoh, Yusuke Hayashi,
Kazuaki Ikeda, Kazuyuki Fujita, and Takao Onoye

1-5 Yamadaoka, Suita, Osaka, 565-0871, Japan
balloon@hi-mail.ise.eng.osaka-u.ac.jp

Abstract. People often communicate with others using social touch interactions including hugging, rubbing, and punching. We propose a soft social-touchable interface called "Emoballoon" that can recognize the types of social touch interactions. The proposed interface consists of a balloon and some sensors including a barometric pressure sensor inside of a balloon, and has a soft surface and ability to detect the force of the touch input. We construct the prototype of Emoballoon using a simple configuration based on the features of a balloon, and evaluate the implemented prototype. The evaluation indicates that our implementation can distinguish seven types of touch interactions with 83.5% accuracy. Finally, we discuss possibilities and future applications of the balloon-made interface.

Keywords: Soft interface, social touch interaction, gesture recognition.

1   Introduction

When people communicate with others, they often make various forms of physical contact. For example, they shake hands or hug in amiable greeting, and also punch or slap to express anger. Since these physical expressions called "social touch interactions" can be used as natural interactions with surroundings, many studies attempt to detect these physical expressions to expand human-computer interaction [1, 19]. Using these social touch interactions, users can input their intentions and emotions. For example, in human-robot interaction, some robots recognize rubbing and hitting as communication with users [14]. Previously, for therapy applications, stuffed toys with

Fig. 1. Conceptual image of Emoballoon

D. Reidsma, H. Katayose, and A. Nijholt (Eds.): ACE 2013, LNCS 8253, pp. 182–197, 2013.
© Springer International Publishing Switzerland 2013

touch sensors that can distinguish some types of social touch interactions have been developed [19]. Haptic telecommunication [1] is one of the novel applications that expand the channels of social touch interactions. The usage of social touch interaction is an intuitive and natural way to express intention.

Interfaces ready for social touch interactions require two features. The first is a surface soft enough to accept hard contact like hugging, grasping, and slapping. The other is the ability to detect the force of the touch. Soft surfaces are more appropriate than conventional rigid ones regarding safety. In addition, soft interfaces have another advantage in that they can provide passive haptic feedback in response to user's touch interactions. Some soft interfaces have been proposed to accept such strong actions as hugging and grasping [10, 19]. They employ many sensors inside their components to detect the force of touch interactions.

To satisfy these conditions to implement an interactive surface for recognizing social touch interaction, we use such a well-sealed container as a balloon. The balloon is soft enough to accept hard contact. As well, barometric pressure inside such a well-sealed container as a balloon reflects the force of a user's touch. This feature of a balloon means that a barometric pressure sensor inside can detect the force of the touch. Since the force is one of the important factors for recognizing kinds of social touch interactions, sealed containers are suitable materials for constructing devices to recognize social touch interactions. Furthermore, these features of a balloon would not be lost when changing the size or the shape of a balloon, which means the balloon-shaped interface could have many possibilities of device-design and its application. Naturally, equipment other than pressure sensors is necessary to detect the touched area. However, the sealed containers and the barometric pressure sensor are still effective for distinguishing the types of social touch interactions.

In this paper, we propose a soft social-touchable interface called "Emoballoon". Figure 1 shows the conceptual image of Emoballoon. It can recognize various social touch interactions such as rubbing, hugging, and so on with a balloon. The soft interactive surface accepts social touch interaction from users with no harm to them. The Emoballoon has a handheld elastic sphere and simple configuration that contains sensors to recognize social touch interactions. A balloon is one of the soft objects and has such large space inside that we could enclose some electronic devices. The Emoballoon can present some visual feedback on its surface as well using an internal LED or external display device. Emoballoon employs a thin elastic skin as a soft material. The elastic skin is convenient material not only to receive strong actions but also to project some visual feedback through its thin surface [5, 18]. We implement Emoballoon using a balloon, and evaluate recognition accuracy for various actions acquired with the investigation of people's interaction with it.

We try to recognize basic touch interactions with a balloon. This attempt should contribute to solving more complex recognition issues such as mixed actions. Our challenge expands the input technique with inflatable soft interfaces. Our balloon-shaped interface provides users with a wider range of social touch interactions in a simpler configuration using a barometric pressure sensor than with existing handheld soft interfaces. The proposed interface can contribute to creating not only handheld interfaces detecting social touch interactions but also a large interactive surface by arraying them. Thus, Emoballoon has a possibility to change and extend the interactions between human and surfaces.

2   Related Work

2.1   Gestural Input Technique

The social touch interaction can be considered as a sort of gesture. Thus far, a lot of research has tried to utilize gestural input techniques to achieve intuitive control for graphical user interfaces [11]. Recently, such gestural input techniques have become more prevalent in video games due to development of inexpensive depth camera sensors. Though these hands-free gestures are effective for inputting direction information and several commands, it is basically difficult for users to express social touch interactions using gestural input systems because users have to pantomime them. To recognize the social touch interactions, it is more natural to use tangible interfaces.

On the other hand, in human-robot interaction, social touch interactions have been considered important. Some social robots can recognize social interactions from users [14, 19]. They have a human-like shape or animal-like skin, and have sensors including QTC sensors, temperature sensors, and accelerometers in each part of their bodies. In this paper, we propose a soft surface recognizing more types of social touch interactions in an elegant configuration using a barometric pressure sensor and elastic objects.

2.2   Graspable Interfaces

Many researchers have developed recognition techniques for physical contacts. Physical and handheld interfaces called Graspable User Interfaces have been proposed to recognize various types of touch interactions [3, 4, 15]. In the field of Graspable User Interfaces, recognizing how users grasp a mobile device is a major concern because grasp recognition is available to automatically change the function of mobile devices. Kim et al. have proposed a grip recognition technique on handheld mobile devices using 64 capacitive sensors and a 3-axis accelerometer [9]. This technique can distinguish eight different grips with approximately 90% accuracy between participants. Similarly, Handsense [23] is a mobile device that tackles how to recognize in which hand the device is held, and how, using capacitive sensors. Both of these grasp recognition techniques expand interaction with mobile devices based on static grasp recognition. The Graspables projects [21] have tried to recognize some dynamic gestures on handheld mobile devices as well as static grip posture. These projects have implemented the Bar of Soap as a prototype of grasp recognition systems using 72 capacitive sensors and a 3-axis accelerometer. This prototype can recognize five static grips with approximately 80% accuracy between 13 participants and with approximately 95% on average within each participant.

While these grasp recognition techniques recognize static touch interactions and gentle gestures to improve manipulation of handheld devices, it is not evaluated whether these approaches accept rougher touch interactions including punching and hugging tightly. We consider these rougher interactions as important touch interaction to enhance a user's input technique.

Thus far, some handheld huggable soft interfaces have been proposed. FuwaFuwa [20] is a sensor module to make huggable soft interfaces. The modules arrayed in the cotton measure the position and depth of a user's pressing onto the cotton surface. Since FuwaFuwa uses cotton as soft material, it can work well even when strong touch interactions are performed. Knight et al. have proposed a cotton-made sensate robot that recognizes social touch [12]. They have implemented five gestures including tickle, poke, pet, hold, and no touch with capacitive sensors. Formerly, they had implemented another social touch recognition using QTC sensors, temperature sensors, and electric field sensors [19]. Their evaluation with the heavily equipped version reveals that the recognition accuracy is 54.3% on average among eight gestures including tickle, poke, scratch, pet, pat, rub, squeeze, and contact. We achieve an effective recognition technique for various touch interactions in a simple and convenient configuration using an inflatable object and a barometric pressure sensor.

2.3   Elastic Surface and Balloon-Shaped Interfaces

In this paper, we employ a balloon as a soft inflatable material. Previously, soft interfaces provided the users with novel interaction techniques [5, 18]. Some interfaces utilizing thin elastic can present visual feedback on their surfaces with projectors or a sort of light source. Some soft interfaces have utilized elastic to detect the force of the touch [8, 17]. These silicon-made physical widgets detect direction and strength of the force of a user's touch based on the deformation of widgets. While the soft physical widgets have no electronic equipment to detect touch interactions, the system can detect them accurately and robustly in the special environment containing a camera and some optics.

On the other hand, some elastic interfaces detect the force of touch based on the changes of barometric pressure. Harrison et al. have developed a shape-changing touch screen for fusion of flexibility of a touch screen and physical cues of a physical button [5]. The surface of the shape-changing touch screen consists of an elastic sheet. Since this elastic sheet seals a space under the surface, barometric pressure under the sheet reflects the shape changing caused by touch interactions. The system can present uneven shapes on the surface by controlling the barometric pressure, and detect the force of a user's pressing by detecting it. Stevenson et al. also have proposed an elastic interactive surface [18]. In these soft surfaces, inflatable materials play an important role in novel input and output techniques.

Inflatable materials have also been used for handheld devices. Volflex [7] is one of the volumetric displays using an array of small balloons. The display shows various shapes and elasticity by controlling barometric pressure inside each balloon. Interactive Balloon [16] can record and play a sound using a piezo film on a balloon. The vision for this balloon-shaped interface is geared towards sensing and actuation in everyday objects. The implementation is more focused on acoustic interaction rather than social touch interactions. Balloon Messenger[1] is a balloon-shaped voice recorder whose volume changes to indicate the length of the recorded signal. The playback speed can be adjusted by squeezing the balloon. Although the speed control by squeezing is a kind of touch interaction with a balloon, the operation scenario seems a command input because the strong relation between squeezing and speed control function constrains the user to a fixed number of actions. Inflatable Mouse [10] has enhanced interaction with a mouse by applying a handheld-sized balloon to the body of the mouse. It achieves a pressure-sensitive input technique on the WIMP-based graphical user interface. This research considers how the inflatable objects improve interactions with WIMP-based graphical user interfaces.

Our challenge expands the social touch interaction using inflatable soft interfaces. Our balloon-shaped interface provides users with a wider range of social touch interactions in a simpler and more elegant configuration than with existing handheld soft interfaces. The proposed interface can contribute to creating not only handheld interfaces detecting social touch interactions but also a large interactive surface by arraying them.

3 Emoballoon

3.1 Preliminary Measurement 1: Force Sensing Using a Balloon

Sealed objects like a balloon containing a pressure sensor have the potential to be utilized as a soft and low-cost force sensor module. The force sensing would be helpful for recognizing social touch interactions like hugging, grasping, and so on. We measure the change of the pressure in a balloon pressed with various force intensities. In this measurement, we used a balloon (Qualatex 16 inch, white, Pioneer Balloon Company), and BMP085 (Bosch Sensortec) as a barometric pressure sensor. The sensor was inserted in a balloon, and the hole of the balloon was sealed with a clay-made cylinder. We inflated the balloon until its longest diameter was 1.5 times the size of the non-inflated one. The size was determined by a preliminary study that indicated that the size made the balloon spherical and its surface thick enough to guard against the balloon popping. Figure 2 shows the result of the measurement. The result indicates that the pressure inside the balloon clearly reflects the force of pressing on its surface. From the result, we can find that the force of pressing or touching can be detected by the barometric pressure of a soft-sealed container like a balloon.

3.2 Preliminary Measurement 2: Suitability of Balloon as Social Touch Device

A balloon has appropriate physical properties for a body of social touch device because it has softness and ability to sense the force of the touch. In addition to these physical properties, we investigate how natural a balloon is as a form of an input device for users to input social touch interactions. We observed what actions participants perform with a balloon. If the participants perform the same touch interactions

---

[1] Balloon Messenger, http://projects.kumpf.cc/

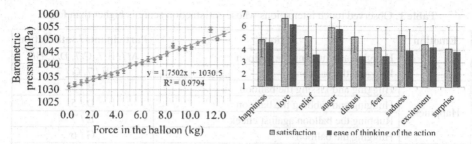

Fig. 2. Barometric pressure vs. force in the balloon

Fig. 3. Average scores of satisfaction with and ease of thinking of performed actions

on a balloon as they do with other people, the balloon can be considered a natural object for social touch interactions. While the shape of the balloon is an important factor for the naturalness, we used a simple spherical shape to evaluate the primitive property of a balloon. In this observation, we also focused on the variation of participants' actions to construct the list of natural touch interactions with a balloon.

In the observation, we asked participants to perform actions with an ordinary balloon as if they experiencing certain emotions (happiness, love, relief, anger, sadness, disgust, excitement, and surprise). These emotions contain Ekman's list of basic emotions (anger, disgust, fear, happiness, sadness, surprise) and some additional emotions (relief, love, excitement) to balance the number of positive emotions and negative ones. Participants could try to express instructed emotion in one minute per emotion. In this trial period, the participants were left alone in a room so as not to be ashamed to perform various actions. After the one-minute trial, we asked them to select the most appropriate actions to express the instructed emotion, and perform it again. Finally, they answered two following questionnaires on a seven-point scale.

- How satisfied are you with your selected actions as an expression of the instructed emotion? (1: not at all – 7: very well)
- How easily did you think of the appropriate actions? (1: not at all – 7: very well)

The experiment from trial to questionnaire was repeated for each emotion. The longest diameter of the balloon was approximately 25 cm. A female and seven males (average age 23.0, from 21 to 26) participated in this study. The whole of the experiments including the one-minute trial were recorded on video. We observed their performance by watching the video, and picked up touch interactions with the balloon.

Figure 3 shows results of the questionnaires. The actions performed by participants have much diversity, and participants responded to the questionnaires referring to their own performance. The satisfaction scores of "anger" and "love" are quite high. These high scores indicate these emotions have a strong relationship to performed actions, and the participants smoothly think of physical expression of these emotions. Seven of eight participants performed a "hug" as an expression for "love", and most of them performed "punch" as "anger". These results indicate that "hug" and "punch" are natural interactions with a balloon. On the other hand, there is great diversity in actions of the other emotions. In the emotions other than "love" and "anger", we

Table 1. Observed touch interactions whose satisfaction score is higher than four

Emotion	Actions	Participants / satisfaction
Love	Hugging and rubbing the balloon	A/7, B/7, C/7, D/7, H/7
	Hugging the balloon	E / 7, G / 7
Happiness	Hugging and kissing the balloon	B / 5
	Hugging and rubbing the balloon	D / 5
	Rubbing the balloon against cheek	E / 7
	Hugging the balloon	G / 6
Relief	Slapping the balloon gently	A / 5
	Hugging the balloon	C / 5, G / 7
	Pressing the head on the balloon	E / 7
	Hugging and slapping the balloon gently	H / 5
Anger	Punching the balloon	A / 7, B / 7, C / 7, D / 7
	Grasping the balloon hard with all fingers	E / 6, H / 5
	Slapping the balloon hard	F / 5, G / 5
Disgust	Grasping the balloon hard with five fingers	C / 5
	Slapping the balloon hard	E / 7
	Punching the balloon	H / 7
Sadness	Hugging the balloon and pressing the head on it	B / 5
	Hugging the balloon	C / 7, E / 6
	Pressing the head on the balloon	D / 5
Excitement	Slapping the balloon	A / 7, F / 6

could not find common actions among all participants. Table 1 shows the list of actions that acquired a 5 or higher satisfaction score. While these actions were not commonly found among participants, the actions acquired a high satisfaction score and included slapping or rubbing. In expressing some emotions, participants accepted and felt it natural to interact with a balloon using touch interactions.

From the observational result, participants seemed to think of the same touch interactions as they did in human-human communication even when the shape of the balloon was just spherical. They performed hugging and rubbing as if they considered the balloon as a representation of a human. The result indicates that participants did not really hesitate to interact with a balloon using social touch interactions, and a balloon is one of the convenient objects with which to construct a physical interface to input social touch interactions.

Next, from the observational study, we extracted touch interactions to be recognized. We also consider the performances listed in Table 1 as natural interactions with a balloon. While the list includes minor actions not to be found among most participants, we selected all listed actions because even minor actions might be performed commonly with many people in other contexts. To construct a set of actions to be recognized, we extract basic touch interactions with a balloon from the listed actions as follows: "hug", "punch", "kiss", "rub", "slap", "grasp", and "press".

From this observational study, we define six basic interactions with the exception of "kiss" as target interactions to be recognized by a balloon-shaped interface. We eliminated "kiss" from the targets due to hygienic issues.

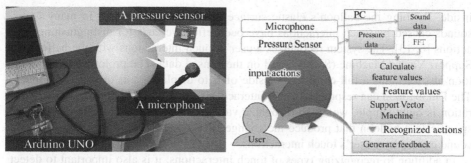

Fig. 4. Implementation of Emoballoon using a balloon

Fig. 5. System configuration

Actually, participants performed these basic actions with various force intensities and some did multiple actions at the same time. For example, one of participants rubbed a balloon while hugging it for expressing "love". Another participant performed a "hug" action both for "love" and "relief" with different force. These observed behaviors indicate that it is necessary not only to recognize basic interactions but also to detect the force of touch and to understand mixed actions. In this paper, we try to recognize basic interactions with a balloon. This challenge should contribute to solving more complex recognition problems such as mixed interactions.

3.3   System Configuration

Figure 4 shows our implementation of "Emoballoon". The balloon-made interface recognizes a wide range of social touch interactions and provides users with a reasonable input technique to express their intent or emotions. It greatly extends a user's input technique, and is useful for various applications including telecommunication and entertainment. We have already found natural basic interactions with a balloon from the observational study. Based on the result of this observation, in order to distinguish the six basic interactions, we have to sense two kinds of measurements. One is the shape-change of the balloon, and the other is the gentle touch to the surface of the balloon.

For these requirements, we utilize a barometric pressure sensor and a microphone inside its elastic surface. Figure 5 shows the system configuration. The elastic soft surface of this interface accepts strong and rough actions including slapping or tight hugging, and presents passive force feedback depending on changes of the shape, unlike conventional rigid interfaces. Since the inside barometric pressure reflects the changing shape of the balloon, the pressure sensor is effective at recognizing strong actions like tight "hug" and "press". The barometric pressure depends on the force of the user's touch regardless of the touched area. The change of barometric pressure is one of the unique features about inflatable objects. It is easy to detect the force of the touch interactions by measuring the pressure. We employ the barometric pressure as one of the important cues in recognizing touch interactions with the balloon-shaped interface. For detecting more gentle actions like "rub", we also attach a microphone inside. Rubbing the balloon's elastic surface produces loud sounds. In many cases, sounds caused by touch interactions have been effective cues for distinguishing user actions [6, 13]. The system recognizes a user's touch interactions with the balloon by Support Vector Machine (SVM) based on the sensed data. The prototype of Emoballoon also contains a full-color LED inside of it to display a sort of visual feedback. The Emoballoon can respond to touch interactions itself. Though the current configuration is quite simple, we try to recognize various interactions based on the features specific to a balloon that produce the change of barometric pressure and the unique sound caused by a user's touch interactions.

In addition to recognizing types of touch interactions, it is also important to detect touched areas. Thus far, some interactive surfaces using elastic material have utilized a basic touch detection technique based on infrared light and an infrared camera put behind the elastic surface [5, 18]. On the other hand, a flexible capacitive sensor is becoming more familiar in the research field to detect a touched area. In the future, flexible sensors should be available for such soft elastic interfaces as mentioned above. Naturally, they will also be applied to elastic handheld interfaces including our Emoballoon, and should enable a remarkable input recognition technique in combination with the other sensors. We believe that, in the future, force sensing will be considered as a more important touch input technique in combination with detecting the touched areas, and inflatable objects with a barometric pressure sensor will be reasonable equipment for sensing the force of touch. Our challenge contributes to expanding possibilities of input recognition using the force of touch.

3.4   Implementation

Emoballoon includes a barometric pressure sensor and a microphone to recognize touch interactions. We use BMP085 (Bosch Sensortec) as a pressure sensor, and AT810F (Audio-Technica Corporation) as a microphone. The pressure sensor is connected to Arduino UNO, and the Arduino sends pressure values to a PC. The microphone is connected to the PC directly. The pressure sensor captures barometric pressure inside the balloon at approximately 25 Hz, and the microphone captures the audio signal at 44,100 Hz. Based on the captured audio signals, the system calculates the average signal from 3 chunks of 1,024 audio samples (or 23.2 msec of audio at 44,100 Hz). Then Discrete Fourier Transformation calculates frequency spectrum from the averaged signal. We use LIBSVM [2] for SVM.

For now, all connections are wired. To seal the hole of the balloon, we insert a clay cylinder into the hole. All wires connecting sensors and PC are buried in the clay cylinder. While the wired connections may constrain a user's actions in our prototype, using wireless communication in the future should improve handling of this interface.

We put a full-color LED inside, which is controlled by the Arduino, in order to display visual feedbacks with users' interactions. We use a white balloon for Emoballoon so that the system can display various colors using the LED. We could utilize a small projector to display some visual feedbacks like Floating Avatar [22]. For Emoballoon, we choose a relatively thick balloon whose shrinking force is stronger than a thinner one. The stronger force makes the pressure change more sensitive. Furthermore, thicker

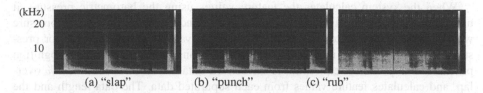

Fig. 6. Frequency spectrums of audio signals in touch interactions with loud sound. The spectrum is calculated per 1024 samples (or 23.2 msec).

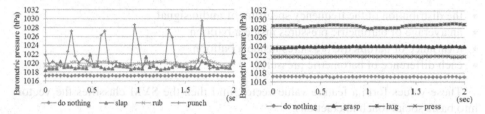

(a) Pressures in touch interactions with loud sound (b) Pressures in silent touch interactions.

Fig. 7. Barometric pressures in basic touch interactions

elastic is more resistant to bursting. The diameter of the selected white balloon when fully inflated is approximately 40 cm. In consideration of the safety of the following user study, we inflate the white balloon 2.0 times from the initial one in diameter, and the diameter is approximately 20 cm, which is not fully inflated but quite safe against hard physical contact like punching and slapping.

3.5   Recognition Process

Figure 6 shows the frequency spectrum of audio signal, and Figure 7 shows the barometric pressure when one participant performed basic touch interactions. We eliminate the spectrum of "grasp", "press", and "hug" from Figure 6 since in these three interactions the hands have been kept at the same posture without producing any sound. The "punch" and "slap" actions cause sharp sounds. Additionally, the sound in "punch" is distributed in a wide frequency range. On the other hand, "rub" causes low sound. We found the difference in distribution of frequency of the sound among touch interactions. Figure 7 (a) shows pressure inside a balloon when one participant repeatedly did four interactions including "do nothing" and three actions with a loud sound such as "punch", "rub" and "slap". There is a clear difference between "punch" and the others. "Punch" causes a sharp rise in pressure. The difference of pressure is available to distinguish touch interactions. Figure 7 (b) shows the pressure when the same participant did three silent actions such as "grasp", "hug", and "press". The pressure rises in "hug" and "grasp" according to deformation of the balloon. Although these static actions do not make loud sounds, the level of the pressure can be effective cues in distinguishing them.

When the system calculates the feature values using the barometric pressure, it uses difference values between measured pressure and the initial one (or the pressure when doing nothing) instead of measured pressure values. This preprocess for pressure values prevents the initial pressure of a balloon from affecting the recognition process. Finally, the system separates the sensed data in 150 msec with 33.3% overlap, and calculates feature values from each separated data. The data length and the overlap rate for separation are decided by a preliminary evaluation. According to these differences in sounds and pressures, we apply the following values to feature values for the recognition process:

- the distribution of the frequency spectrum of audio signal
- an average of barometric pressures inside a balloon
- a variance of barometric pressures inside a balloon
- each difference of barometric pressures.

These values form a feature value vector, and then the SVM classifies the vector into basic social touch interactions.

4   Evaluation

We evaluated the performance of our implemented system by calculating recognition rates for basic touch interactions with it. For evaluation, we asked nine participants to perform each of six basic touch interactions and "do nothing" continuously in 7 seconds. Nine participants were a female and eight males, and their average age was 23.6 (from 21 to 26). We instructed the participants that they could change the strength of their actions at any time. While they performed the instructed actions, the system collected the sensed data and we did not show the participants the measurement result. They repeated each action 5 times. We calculated feature value vectors from the sensed data, and we extracted the vectors of equal size among participants and actions as a validation dataset. In this evaluation, we extracted 50 feature value vectors per participant and action; in total, we used 15,750 vectors (= 50 vectors x 9 participants x 7 actions x 5 times). Then, we calculated recognition rate by 10-fold cross validation. The kernel for the SVM is radial basis function (RBF). From the preliminary 5-fold cross validation, we decided to set 2^{15} for complexity parameter (C) and 2^{-5} for the width in RBF (γ). The preliminary validation tried $2^{-5}, 2^{-3}, \ldots, 2^{15}$ for parameter C, and $2^{-5}, 2^{-3}, \ldots, 2^{7}$ for parameter γ, and indicated the above settings were the best.

Table 2 shows results of average recognition rates within participants. The recognition rate is approximately 74.7% among all participants. In the same setting of the SVM, the recognition accuracy within the participants is 83.5% on average. The result indicates that the system can recognize various types of touch interactions based on the change of barometric pressure and sound inside a balloon.

Table 2. Average recognition rates within participants (green color density of cells means degree of recognition rate)

		Recognition rates (%)						
		nothing	grasp	hug	punch	press	rub	slap
In-put	nothing	94	0	1	0	3	1	0
	grasp	0	85	1	0	13	0	0
	hug	1	1	97	0	1	0	0
	punch	0	0	0	74	0	8	18
	press	3	12	0	0	83	1	0
	rub	2	0	1	9	1	83	4
	slap	0	0	0	21	0	6	72

5   Discussion

5.1   Possibility to Recognize Social Touch Interaction

Our implementation can distinguish seven basic actions with 83.5% accuracy on average even though it has a quite simple configuration with a microphone and a barometric pressure sensor. From the result shown in Table 2, there are many incorrect recognitions between "grasp" and "press", and between "punch" and "slap". It is still difficult to distinguish exactly these pairs of touch interactions. However, additional evaluation indicates the system can recognize five actions with the exception of "press" and "slap" with 88.1% accuracy among all participants, and with approximately 93.7% within participants on average. The system can recognize five actions including "do nothing", "hug", "grasp", "punch", "rub" with high accuracy. To improve the accuracy in the future, it would be useful to consider the duration of each interaction. The "punch" and "slap" are finished in a short time while some actions including "hug" and "rub" can be continued for a relatively long time. Thus, the difference in duration among touch interactions would be a good cue to distinguish users' touch input.

In our current implementation, the barometric pressure is utilized to recognize touch interactions with a balloon. Furthermore, it is also useful to detect the force of touch as well. The balloon-shaped interfaces with a barometric pressure sensor potentially can recognize both the types and the force of the touch simultaneously. If it is possible to detect both, for example, the system can distinguish a tight hug from a gentle hug, and a soft punch from a hard punch. Thus far, Huggable [19] has tried to distinguish between hard and gentle touch interactions by using QTC sensors, temperature sensors, and accelerometers, and it did not work well. However, employing inflatable objects with a barometric pressure sensor will be a simple but effective way to sense the force of touch interactions. One of our future steps is recognizing both the types and the force of touch interactions simultaneously.

As far as we observed people in various ages interacted with our implementation, the system does not tend to make more false recognition to the elderly than the other. The age seems not to be a serious error factor. However, since the difference of muscular strength might have a bigger impact to recognition accuracy, the evaluation with more diverse participants has to be conducted in the future.

5.2   Force Sensing Based on Barometric Pressure in Sealed Objects

Barometric pressure of sealed objects reflects the force of a user's touch independently from the touched area, and contributes to input recognition. The combination of a well-sealed container and a barometric pressure sensor can act as a flexible force sensor. By changing the shape of sealed objects, we can design the shape and size of the force sensors. For example, we can obtain the distribution of the force applied to a soft surface by arraying many small balloons with pressure sensors under the surface, and we can also obtain the force applied to a large area by just using a single pressure sensor and a large sealed container. The soft sensor modules can respond to the applied force independently of the direction of the force. The independence from direction of the force means that a few sensor modules can detect the total amount of force of the touch even when the modules are applied to handheld devices, large surfaces, and non-flat surfaces. Such a convenient force-sensing technique brings novel input techniques including pressing and hard touch to mobile devices, wall-sized interactive displays, and interactive floors at a low cost.

5.3   Softness and Durability

Another important aspect of our recognition technique is softness of the sensor module itself. The balloon-shaped interfaces can make surrounding soft objects interactive by being inserted into them. In this case, the balloon-shaped one would work well while maintaining the original softness. We received such comments from the participant of the evaluation as "It is comfortable for me to input strong contact like punching and slapping because of the softness of the balloon". The comment also indicates that the softness of the module is an important factor for social touch input technique.

To construct the soft interface recognizing touch interactions, we used a general balloon as a sealed container. The balloon has a risk of popping. Actually, some participants sometimes seemed to be afraid of the risk when they were asked to punch or slap the balloon. (Naturally, for risk avoidance, we used a thick balloon not fully inflated in all experiments. There was no popping in the entire observational study and evaluation). However, the proposed recognition technique can be applied to other sealed objects. The soft plastic-made balls used as kids' toys are appropriate sealed objects that have enough durability to input hard touch interactions. Such durable objects are also useful when inserting the sensor modules into soft artifacts.

6   Future Application

Our current implementation can be applied for an emotive game controller even while it only shows ambiguous feedback such as changing its color. Using this controller, the users can communicate with the avatar in video games by social touch interactions and determine the internal state of the avatar by the color emission from the controller. Such a soft game controller enables more emotive and intuitive interactions with the avatar than a touch pen by which user pokes the avatar on touch screen or gesture input in the air like pantomime.

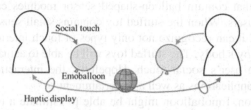 

(a) Conceptual image of haptic telecommunication system using social touch recognition techniques

(b) Conceptual image of an interactive stuffed toy containing sensor modules using balloons

Fig. 8. Future applications

In the future, the social touch recognition could allow computers to understand users' emotional expression. When the input device is connected to a computer, it enables the users to easily tell the computer about their satisfaction with the output or the performance of the computer not by computer language but by such physical contacts as rubbing, hugging, and slapping. For simplified example, hugging or rubbing the device would mean user's very satisfaction, and punching or slapping would do user's dissatisfaction. The measured user's satisfaction is useful to make the computer smarter since the measured satisfaction could supervise the computer's various calculations including the autocomplete function in text input, the recommendations in shopping websites, and so on.

The inflatable interfaces can also enrich telecommunication by providing users with a technique to input various physical interactions. While InTouch [1] has achieved one of the most fundamental haptic communications using rollers as a force input device and a haptic display, the social touch recognition is necessary to realize more complex haptic communication. The proposed inflatable interfaces would enable the users to communicate with others using such physical expressions as hugging, shaking hands, and slapping. These physical expressions reflect a user's emotions including familiarity, anger, and so on. Figure 8 (a) shows a conceptual image of haptic telecommunication using inflatable interfaces. In this application, when the user performs the social touch with the balloon, the type and strength of touch are transmitted to the other user in a remote location over a network, and she or he receives haptic feedback by a sort of haptic displays. The proposed recognition technique for an inflatable object can enrich communication between the users in remote location.

We believe that a balloon is a familiar and appropriate object as an avatar. Floating Avatar [22] is one of the representative examples of applications using inflatable interfaces. The floating balloon of the avatar's body provides the avatar with tangible existence. We can regard our balloon-shaped interface as a physical avatar that can accept such user touch interaction as rubbing and slapping. In the distant future, the users and the operator of the avatar will be able to communicate their haptic sensation over the balloon-made avatar.

The balloon-shaped interfaces are also useful to construct interactive stuffed toys. Figure 8 (b) shows a conceptual image of a stuffed toy capable of responding to social touch interactions. The stuffed toys that contain balloon-shaped sensor modules can detect social touch interactions from users. When the stuffed toy contains small sensor modules in some parts of their bodies, it can recognize not only types of touch interactions, but also the touched area of the toy's body. The stuffed toys will be able to actuate their arms and legs in response to a user's social touch. Hopefully, the interactive stuffed toys will contribute to therapy applications as well as entertainment.

In addition to haptic communication, Emoballoon might be able to estimate a user's emotion. In the observational study, we found that almost all participants performed the same actions to express some of the instructed emotions. For example, they performed "punch" for anger, and they did "hug" for love. These common behaviors imply a strong relationship between emotions and physical expressions with a balloon. To estimate a user's emotions, it will be necessary not only to greatly improve the recognition process for touch interaction with a balloon, but also to further study the relationships between users' emotions and behaviors.

7   Conclusion and Future Work

We propose a balloon-shaped interface called "Emoballoon" that can recognize various social touch interactions with a simple configuration. We investigated the variation of social touch interactions with a balloon based on observational study, and found basic ones. The Emoballoon, which has an elegant configuration with a microphone and a pressure sensor inside a balloon, can recognize 7 actions with 83.5% accuracy within nine people on average. Since the proposed recognition technique can be applied to the other inflatable material, future work will implement it using safer and more durable materials as well as a balloon. It also remains as future work to improve the recognition process, and achieve such application as a haptic telecommunication. We also plan to construct a large interactive surface as an array of the soft modules made of balloons, and explore new possibilities of touch interaction with a soft surface sensitive to the force of touch.

References

1. Brave, S., Dahley, A.: inTouch: a medium for haptic interpersonal communication. Extended abstracts on CHI 1997, pp. 363–364 (1997)
2. Chang, C., Lin, C.: LIBSVM: a library for support vector machines. ACM Transactions on Intelligent Systems and Technology 2, 27:1–27:27 (2011)
3. Fitzmaurice, G.W., Buxton, W.: An empirical evaluation of graspable user interfaces: towards specialized, space-multiplexed input. In: Proc. CHI 1997, pp. 43–50 (1997)
4. Fitzmaurice, G.W., Ishii, H., Buxton, W.A.S.: Bricks: laying the foundations for graspable user interfaces. In: Proc. CHI 1995, pp. 442–449 (1995)
5. Harrison, C., Hudson, S.E.: Providing dynamically changeable physical buttons on a visual display. In: Proc. CHI 2009, pp. 299–308 (2009)
6. Harrison, C., Hudson, S.E.: Scratch input: creating large, inexpensive, unpowered and mobile finger input surfaces. In: Proc. of UIST 2008, pp. 205–208 (2008)

7. Iwata, H., Yano, H., Ono, N.: Volflex. In: ACM SIGGRAPH 2005 Emerging Technologies, Article No. 31 (2005)

8. Kakehi, Y., Jo, K., Sato, K., Minamizawa, K., Nii, H., Kawakami, N., Naemura, T., Tachi, S.: ForceTile: tabletop tangible interface with vision-based force distribution sensing. ACM SIGGRAPH 2008 New Tech. Demos, 17:1–17:1 (2008)

9. Kim, K.-E., Chang, W., Cho, S.-J., Shim, J., Lee, H., Park, J., Lee, Y., Kim, S.: Hand grip pattern recognition for mobile user interfaces. In: Proc. IAAI 2006, vol. 2, pp. 1789–1794 (2006)

10. Kim, S., Kim, H., Lee, B., Nam, T.-J., Lee, W.: Inflatable mouse: volume-adjustable mouse with air-pressure-sensitive input and haptic feedback. In: Proc. CHI 2008, pp. 211–224 (2008)

11. Kitamura, Y., Sakurai, S., Yamaguchi, T., Fukazawa, R., Itoh, Y., Kishino, F.: Multimodal Interface in Multi-Display Environment for Multi-users. In: Jacko, J.A. (ed.) Human-Computer Interaction, Part II, HCII 2009. LNCS, vol. 5611, pp. 66–74. Springer, Heidelberg (2009)

12. Knight, H., Toscano, R., Stiehl, W.D., Chang, A., Wang, Y., Breazeal, C.: Real-time social touch gesture recognition for sensate robots. In: Proc. IROS 2009, pp. 3715–3720 (2009)

13. Lopes, P., Jota, R., Jorge, J.A.: Augmenting touch interaction through acoustic sensing. In: Proc. ITS 2011, pp. 53–56 (2011)

14. Mitsunaga, N., Miyashita, T., Yoshikawa, Y., Ishiguro, H., Kogure, K., Hagita, N.: Robovie-IV: a robot enhances co-experience. In: Proc. the Workshop on Ubiquitous Experience Media at ISWC 2005, pp. 17–23 (2005)

15. Pai, D., VanDerLoo, E., Sadhukhan, S., Kry, P.: The Tango: a tangible tangoreceptive whole-hand human interface. In: Proc. World Haptics (Joint Eurohaptics Conference and IEEE Symposium on Haptic Interfaces for Virtual Environment and Teleoperator Systems), pp. 141–147 (2005)

16. Paradiso, J.A.: The interactive balloon: Sensing, actuation and behavior in a common object. IBM Systems Journal 4, 473–487 (1996)

17. Sato, T., Mamiya, H., Koike, H., Fukuchi, K.: PhotoelasticTouch: transparent rubbery tangible interface using an LCD and photoelasticity. In: Proc. UIST 2009, pp. 43–50 (2009)

18. Stevenson, A., Perez, C., Vertegaal, R.: An inflatable hemispherical multi-touch display. In: Proc. TEI 2011, pp. 289–292 (2011)

19. Stiehl, W.D., Breazeal, C.: Affective Touch for Robotic Companions. In: Tao, J., Tan, T., Picard, R.W. (eds.) ACII 2005. LNCS, vol. 3784, pp. 747–754. Springer, Heidelberg (2005)

20. Sugiura, Y., Kakehi, G., Withana, A., Lee, C., Sakamoto, D., Sugimoto, M., Inami, M., Igarashi, T.: Detecting shape deformation of soft objects using directional photoreflectivity measurement. In: Proc. UIST 2011, pp. 509–516 (2011)

21. Taylor, B.T., Bove Jr., V.M.: Graspables: grasp-recognition as a user interface. In: Proc. CHI 2009, pp. 917–926 (2009)

22. Tobita, H., Maruyama, S., Kuji, T.: Floating avatar: blimp-based telepresence system for communication and entertainment. ACM SIGGRAPH 2011 Emerging Technologies, 4:1–4:1 (2011)

23. Wimmer, R., Boring, S.: HandSense: discriminating different ways of grasping and holding a tangible user interface. In: Proc. TEI 2009, pp. 359–362 (2009)

Theory and Application of the Colloidal Display: Programmable Bubble Screen for Computer Entertainment

Yoichi Ochiai[1,2], Alexis Oyama[3], Takayuki Hoshi[4], and Jun Rekimoto[1,5]

[1] The University of Tokyo
Graduate School of Interdisciplinary Information Studies
7-3-1 Hongo, Bunkyo-ku, Tokyo, 113-0033 Japan
ochyai@me.com, rekimoto@acm.org
[2] Japan Society for the Promotion of Science
6 Ichiban-cho, Chiyoda-ku, Tokyo, 102-8471 Japan
[3] jiseCHI Interactive Lab
1-4-9 Azabudai, Minato-ku, Tokyo, 106-0041 Japan
alexis@betadreamer.com
[4] Nagoya Institute of Technology, Nagoya, Japan
Gokisocho, Showa-ku,Nagoyashi, Aichi, 466-855 Japan
star@nitech.ac.jp
[5] Sony CSL, Tokyo, Japan
3-14-13 Higashigotanda, Shinagawa-ku Tokyo 141-0022 Japan

Abstract. It is difficult to dynamically change the optical properties of ordinary screens. In conventional projection systems, the choice of screens is limited; and the brightness of projected images and the viewing angle are unalterable once a screen is fixed, even though demand for altering the viewing angle according to the locations and the requirements of installations exists.

The results of a study conducted by us indicate that a colloidal membrane can be used as a screen by vibrating it at a high frequency using ultrasonic waves. On the basis of those results, in this paper we discuss the implementation of a screen that allows us to dynamically change its brightness and view angle. We also discuss our investigation of its optical characteristics.

Our investigations reveal that the screen can be deformed by stronger ultrasonic waves, frames of various shapes can be used to create it, and that we can interact with it by inserting our fingers because it is made of colloidal solution.

Keywords: Colloidal Display, Entertainment Computing, Virtual Reality, HCI.

1 Introduction

All over the world, screens are used to display various digital contents, such as movies, presentations, and shows, and are essential in the field of entertainment. The fundamental process utilized to display content on a screen is as follows: digital content is created, the content is rendered, and the content is shown on a screen via a

D. Reidsma, H. Katayose, and A. Nijholt (Eds.): ACE 2013, LNCS 8253, pp. 198–214, 2013.
© Springer International Publishing Switzerland 2013

projector. A significant amount of information is lost when the content is shown on a static surface because ordinary screens are rigid and static and the texture of the screen cannot change dynamically. However, in the digital world, we can dynamically specify an object's texture by modifying its light and bump maps. Consequently, in our research, we are attempting to take the first step in bringing digital to physical by applying this computer graphics concept to screens in the real world.

We propose to control the optical characteristics of screens in order to reproduce the realistic appearance of contents, and thereby provide a new entertainment systems option. To realize this concept, we choose a colloidal film and excite it with an ultrasonic wave (Figure 1). The ultrasonic wave induces a minute wave (known as a "capillary wave") on the colloidal film that leads to an expansion of the viewing angle. To the best of our knowledge, ours is the first approach to utilize this phenomenon to control the optical characteristics of a screen. We can control the vibration of the screen at high frequency. In addition to expanding the viewing angle, we can induce an optical illusion to reproduce glitter by means of time division control.

The main application of colloidal screen [1] is control of reflection and texture. In addition, colloidal film is a unique material, which imbues a screen made from it with flexible characteristics such as screen deformation, physical popping, and actual screen reconstruction. The possibility exists for these features to be applied in entertainment computing.

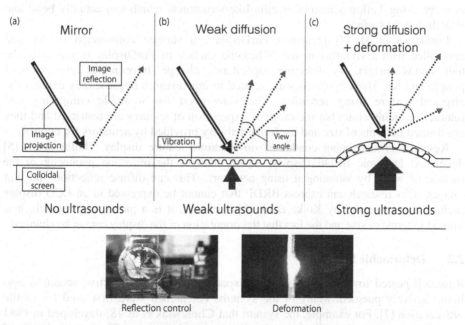

Fig. 1. The image is projected (black arrow with line) from the top. The ultrasonic waves (black arrow) hit the membrane to reflect the image (light dotted arrow). Note that there are two types of effects related to the intensity of ultrasound: A weak ultrasound mainly changes the viewing angle while a stronger ultrasound additionally changes the shape of the screen.

The remainder of this paper is organized as follows. In Section 2, we cite related research and discuss the reason why our research is relevant. In Section 3, we explain the theory underpinning our work. In Section 4, we give an overview of our system, including system requirements. In Section 5, we discuss an evaluation conducted by means of a laser experiment, and discuss prototype applications developed in Section 6. Finally, we discuss the limitations of our proposed system, Section 7, and conclude by looking at possible future work, Section 8.

2   Related Work

In our study, we dynamically change the shape and texture of the screen (Figure 1). Therefore, in this section, we cite researches that are relevant to active screens, and which either change the spatial position or the texture of an object. We then look at how our research relates to these relevant research efforts.

2.1   Texture Displays

In this subsection, we look at research done to control the surface textures of an active screen.

In [2], Raffle et al. proposed Super Cilia Skin, a conceptual interactive surface comprising thousands of cilia-sized actuators, and actually developed 128 magnetic cilia. Coelho and Maes [3] subsequently presented Sprout I/O, which expanded on the concept using Teflon actuators as cilia-like structures, which can actually bend and stretch, for the surface.

Furukawa et al. [4] presented FurDisplay, a surface constructed of fur and controlled with a vibrating motor. When the surface of FurDisplay is activated, the hair stands upright. By detecting capacitance change, it promotes interaction of people and fur. These researches are related to our research because they express the physical texture using actuation. They are good for wearable computing and interactive architecture, but the range of expression of textures are restricted and they are limited in terms of size and the limited ability provided by actuators for control.

Research is also being conducted on dynamic texture display. Hullin et al. [5] developed Dynamic BRDF Display, which changes the reflection parameter of the surface of water by vibrating it using actuators. This can diffuse reflection and blur images. This research can express BRDF that cannot be expressed in an LCD display such as that presented by Koike et al. [6]. Although it is a pioneering research, it is limited in terms of size and the fact that the orientation of the display cannot be changed.

2.2   Deformable Screens

Research geared towards controlling the spatial position of an active screen is also being actively pursued. Many of the systems researched were first used for tactile presentation [7]. For example, the system that Cholewiak et al. [8] developed in 1981 was used as a tactile skin display and utilized several actuators. The system displayed the vibratory stimulation using several cylindrical actuators that moved up and down. There are also other systems with similar mechanisms to that used by Cholewiak et al. [8]; for example, the deformable actuated screen "Project FEELEX" [9], which constructs 3D forms on the surface of the screen using an actuator array set under the screen. In addition, LUMEN, proposed by Poupyrev et al. [10], comprised actuated dot matrix LEDs—physical pixels shown in RGB and H (height). Leithinger et al. [11] also proposed an interactive deformable screen called Recompose.

Other researches dealing with control of the spatial positions of displays also exist. There are image projection technologies that use fog as a screen, such as the systems proposed by Rakkolainen et al. [12] and Lee et al. [13]. These technologies display images in the air using a fog screen and a camera. This is projected in the air as a result of fog's diffusibility characteristics.

Research on displays using water is also being conducted. Sugihara et al. [14] used fountain as a deformable water screen. Barnum et al. [15] developed a screen that uses the water drops in the air. Water drops have lens-like characteristics. By using these characteristics, they were able to project an image onto the water drops. They made a water drop sequence in the air and projected the image corresponding to the spatial position by synchronizing the projector with the water bulbs, and applied their technology to create a multilayer screen. Other interesting artworks include those presented by Suzuki et al. [16], which uses underwater air bubbles, and Kodama et al. [17], which uses magnetic liquid.

Displays have also been made using soap bubbles. Bubble Cosmos [18] is a technology that constructs a screen in the air by confining fog in a bubble; and Shaboned Display [19] turns a bubble into a pixel. Bubbles have also been used as a musical instrument [20].

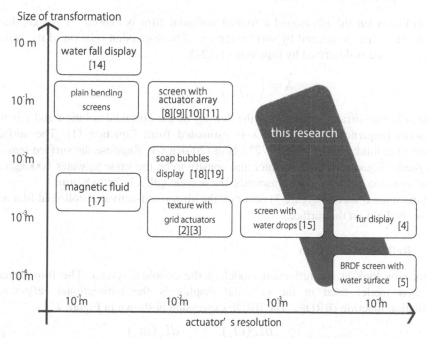

Fig. 2. Position of our research corresponding to other relevant researches. Vertical axis represents the amount of transformation dealt to the object while the horizontal axis represents the actuator's resolution. Notice how our research (red) covers the areas that have not been explored yet.

2.3   Position of This Study

Our research is positioned as shown in Figure 2. The size of the changes on the vertical and horizontal axes represents the resolution of actuation. For example, since a dynamic BRDF [5] changes the surface texture by detailed vibration, the resolution of actuation is high and the size of change is small. Researches on dynamic textures with small actuators are not high-resolution and the size of spatial change is limited.

Using this rationale, we positioned our research in the area colored in red. The actuator resolution of our research is high when the spatial change is small and low when the spatial change is large. No research equivalent to this domain exists. Our research contribution is high because we use the same hardware settings to accomplish many of the features achieved in related research.

3   Theory

In this section, we describe the theory underpinning the colloidal screen technology. First, we describe the capillary waves that are induced on the soap film, then introduce the reflection model of the colloidal display, and finally, describe the ultrasounds.

3.1   Capillary Waves on Soap Film

The diffusion on the ultrasound-activated colloidal film is caused by the capillary waves, which are dominated by surface tension. The dispersion relation of the waves on the interface is described by Equation (1) [21].

$$\lambda = \left(\frac{8\pi\sigma}{\rho f^2}\right)^{\frac{1}{3}} \tag{1}$$

where σ is the surface tension, ρ is the density of the colloidal solution and f is the excitation frequency. Wavelength λ is estimated from Equation (1). The surface tension of colloidal liquid σ is 0.07275 N/m (20 deg C). Suppose the surface tension of colloidal liquid to be 1/2 of water and density to be the same as water 1000kg/m^3. In this situation, with 40kHz ultrasounds, the wavelength λ is $2\pi/k=83\mu m$.

These minute waves (Figure 3) occur on the ultrasound-activated colloidal film and diffuse the light on the surface.

3.2   Reflection of Screen

Let us now look at the reflection model of the colloidal screen. The film surface reflection model used in the colloidal display is the bidirectional reflectance distribution function (BRDF). The BRDF expression is shown in Figure 4.

$$f_r(\omega_i, \omega_o) = \frac{dL_r(\omega_o)}{dE_i(\omega_i)} = \frac{dL_r(\omega_o)}{L_i(\omega_i)\cos\theta_i d\omega_i} \tag{2}$$

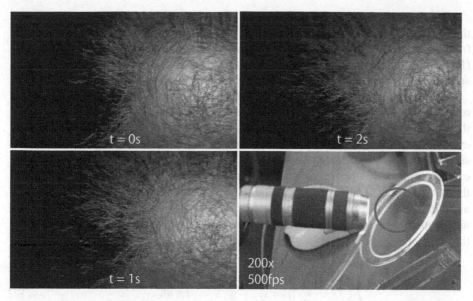

Fig. 3. Capillary waves on the colloidal film. (200x, 500 fps high speed camera capture image).

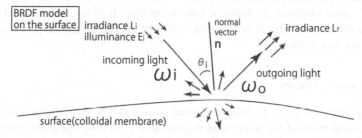

Fig. 4. BRDF model on the screen

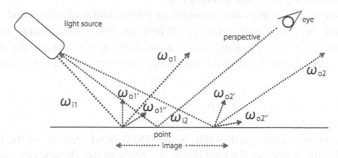

Fig. 5. View angle of the image

This expression is intended to represent the relationship between the direction of the reflected light (ω_o) and the direction of the incident light (ω_i) on the surface by E (radiance) and L (irradiance). Bidirectional transmittance distribution function (BTDF) also exists, but it is possible to ignore BTDF by specifying the state of the surface to only speculate BRDF, resulting in only front projection.

A uniform thin film surface that does not have the characteristics of diffuse reflection is close to being a mirror. We cannot project the image onto a mirror. For these reasons, the light emitted from the light source shown in the figure reaches the eyes via a dotted line in perspective, resulting in only a dot or a light source being seen on the mirror surface. However, it is possible to project images onto it by expanding the scope or the view angle of the reflected light in the presence of ω_o in the BRDF model. The expansion of the existing range of reflection is shown as ω_{ol}'' and ω_{ol}' for ω_{ol} in Figure 5. The perspective light source covering a certain range makes the image appear on the film. We project the image on the colloidal screen in this manner.

$$dE(\omega_i) = L_i(\omega_i)\, d\sigma^\perp(\omega_i) \tag{3}$$

$$\int_{\mathcal{H}_o^2} f_r(\omega_i \rightarrow \omega_o)\, d\sigma^\perp(\omega_o) \leq 1 \qquad \text{for all } \omega_i \in \mathcal{H}_i^2 \tag{4}$$

In our research, we can control the reflectance distribution to some extent, but we cannot control the radiation and absorption of the material. The relationship between radiance L_r and radiance L_i follows two formulas. It does not depend on the distribution ratio of ω_o. This indicates that a very bright image can be presented when ω_o is a narrow distribution.

3.3   Ultrasonic Waves

The phased array focusing technique is used to achieve a high-intensity ultrasound wave. The focal point of the ultrasound is generated by setting adequate phase delays of multiple transducers. In addition, the focal point can be moved to an arbitrary position by controlling the phase delays [22].

The acoustic radiation pressure, a nonlinear phenomenon of ultrasound, acts when the ultrasound becomes high-intensity. When an ultrasound beam is reflected vertically at the soap film, it is subjected to a constant vertical force in the direction of the incident beam. Assuming a plane wave, the acoustic radiation pressure P [Pa] is described as

$$P = \alpha E = \alpha \frac{p^2}{\rho c^2} \tag{5}$$

where c [m/s] is the sound speed, p [Pa] is the RMS sound pressure of the ultrasound, and ρ [kg/m³] is the density of the medium. α is a constant that depends on the reflection coefficient of the soap film. In a case where there is total reflection, its value is two.

The phased array focusing technique is used to deform the screen within a localized area and activate the screen with more intensity.

The focal point of the ultrasound is generated by setting adequate phase delays in the multiple transducers. In addition, the focal point can be moved to an arbitrary position by controlling the phase delays. A trade-off exists between the spatial resolution and the array size. Theoretically, the spatial distribution of ultrasound generated from a rectangular transducer array approximates the shape of a sinc function [23]. The width of the main lobe (w [m]) is parallel to the side of the rectangular and is written as

$$w = \frac{2\lambda R}{D} \tag{6}$$

where λ [m] is the wavelength, R [m] is the focal length, and D [m] is the side length of the rectangular array (Figure 8). Our system can control the spatial position of focus and it contributes to activate the films partially.

4   Design

In this section, we look at the design requirements for the colloidal display and give an overview of the system.

4.1   System Requirements

The concept underlying our system is changing the appearances of images by switching the screen's reflectance at high frequency. Therefore, the system has to satisfy the following requirements:

- The film must be light and soft enough for its optical properties to be changed using vibration.
- The ultrasonic systems must be operated at high frequency.
- Colloidal frames must continuously supply the colloidal solution to the colloidal membrane, resulting in an extension of the membrane's life with high stability against the powerful ultrasonic waves.

To satisfy these requirements, we use a strong ultrasonic actuator power speaker to vibrate the screen remotely and use colloid film that, although it is made from light material that is weak and fragile, has a high surface tension and is flexible.

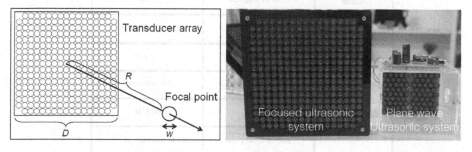

Fig. 6. Equipment for ultrasonic vibration

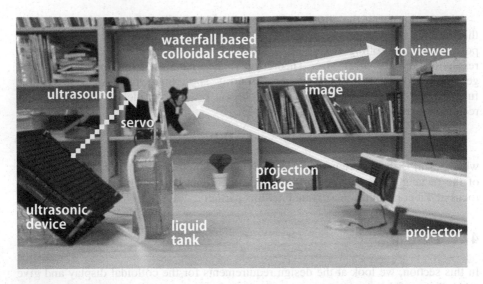

Fig. 7. Colloidal display system components: focused ultrasonic devise set on the opposite side of projector. The image on the screen can only be seen from the projector side.

Ultrasonic waves directly affect the reflection of the film, so if we switch the ultrasonic waves on/off, to human eyes, it appears as if a switch is being made from transparent to opaque.

4.2   System Overview

- LCD or DLP projector, such as a video equipment, which emits light.
- Colloidal film
- Film's frame with waterfall system and the mechanism to replace the film
- Equipments for ultrasonic vibration.

Table 1. Specifications of components

Projector	LCD or DLP	
Screen	Colloid solution	Soap
	Size of membrane	8 cm in diameter
Ultrasound	Transducers	285 pics
	Focus control	Phased array
	Frequency	40 kHz
	Size of focal point	2 cm at distance of 20 cm

Figure 7 shows one of the configuration that uses these components. Projector's light goes to the film and film's frame. Ultrasound waves are produced from the speaker simultaneously and hit the film, vibrating it. When the film is broken, it is replaced by servo-motors. The specifications of each part are described in table 1.

5   Evaluation

5.1   Laser Experiment

The colloidal screen's view angle varies when the intensity of the ultrasonic wave is changed or modulated. Figure 8 displays experimental results obtained using different ultrasonic waves. However, the same effect can be seen when the intensity and the focus length are changed. The more intense the wave is, the more view angle it creates. Looking at the BRDF equation, Equation (2) (Section 3.2), it is obvious that this means that it is changing parameter ω_o. We are able to control this parameter from zero to 90 degrees. Because the screen is vibrated intensely, the laser's reflection is not consistent. This is shown in Figure 8 (right), where t is time. There are slight differences in each image but the shape of the laser reflection is similar.

The graph of the brightness on each angle is shown in Figure 9. It shows that the narrow reflection angle (with low ultrasonic intensity) is bright in the center of the reflection and the brightness diminishes in the neighborhood of the center of the reflection. In contrast, the wide reflection angle (with high ultrasonic intensity) results in a gentle decrease in brightness.

This result shows that we can control the view angle and distribution of the brightness by changing the intensity of the ultrasonic wave. It indicates that the colloidal screen solves the problem of screen selection and enlarges the application of the projector screen.

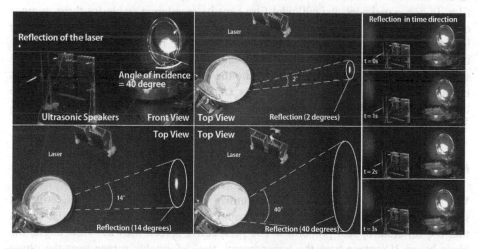

Fig. 8. Laser experiment example of wave form modulation. Different types of waves create different view angles. White noises create 40 degrees, sine waves create 14 degrees, and square waves create 2 degrees.

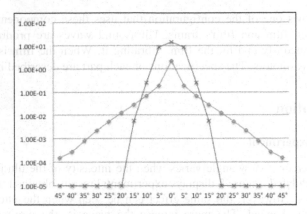

Fig. 9. This graph shows how view angle affects brightness. The red line has a small viewing angle but it is brighter than the blue line, while the blue line has a wider viewing angle but brightness is low.

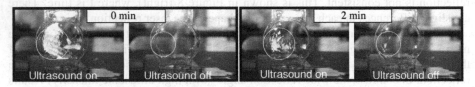

Fig. 10. From left to right the image quality decreases in relation to time due to water evaporation

5.2   Stability

In this subsection, we describe the retention time along with the stability of the colloid film. In our experiment, the colloidal film kept its membrane stable for three minutes on average when the ultrasonic waves were applied. The key component is water; the less water there is in the membrane, the more noisy the image. Figure 10 shows how the image quality changes with time. Observing the circle on the four images, it can be seen that the images on the left devolve into the images on the right over time. This is because as time passes the water evaporates, causing the transmission characteristics to be reduced, which results in the image being disturbed. The main reason for this disturbance of the display is failure to control the reflection characteristic.

6   Applications

We developed several prototypes that utilize the characteristics of the colloidal screen. In this section, we describe four sample applications of the colloidal screen that use different optical properties. The perspective screen uses the view angle, the plane-based 3D screen uses the transparency, the deformable screen uses the phase array to change the shape, and the bump mapped screen uses deformation with specifications.

6.1   Perspective Screen

We developed a display to show multiple images from multiple angles using the characteristics of the colloidal screen. The principle of operation depends on the characteristics of reflectance distribution of ωo for multiple light sources, as shown in Figure 11. Different projection sources provide several different images for each angle. The images are being multiplexed at the same time but one image can only be seen in one direction.

In this application, five components are needed: different directional light source, colloidal solution, frame for the membrane, film replacement mechanism, and ultrasonic oscillation. The installation position is shown in Figure 11.

We projected the image from above and decomposed a single image into three images by angling the three mirrors in different directions. We also set an ultrasonic oscillator behind the screen to operate it. The result is shown in Figure 11. There are three images: one from the left, one from the center, and one from the right. We set the left edge at r = 0 degrees and the mirrors at positions r = 45, 90, and 135 degrees. We adjusted the colloidal screen so that the reflection angle was 40 degrees (by ultrasonic modulation). The actual transition of the images is shown on the right side of Figure 11. The transition is smooth and there are no image overlaps.

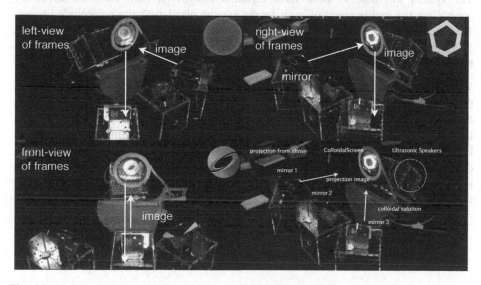

Fig. 11. (Perspective Screen) Three different images from different perspectives are shown. The top image viewed from the left, the middle from the center, and the bottom from the right.

6.2   Plane-Based 3D Screen

In this subsection, we describe the development of a 3D display using multiple planes (Figure 12). LCD displays have a problem when it comes to viewing multiple layers; because of polarization, it is not possible to display multiple planes at the same time. In this respect, the colloidal display has several advantages. This colloidal screen can display more than one plane at the same time, and the image is very bright.

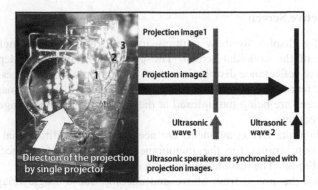

Fig. 12. (Plane based 3D screen) The transparency alternates within the 3 screens

We set up multiple sets of colloidal screen and ultrasonic speakers with ultrasonic oscillations synchronized with the projector. The installation position is shown in Figure 12. Each colloidal screen had an ultrasonic speaker that set its transparency. Toggling the transparency of each screen was achieved by simply turning the speakers on and off. The system was able to show three different images on each colloidal screen by controlling the transparency of each screen synchronized with the projector's images. This is effectively a 20 Hz time division plane-based 3D screen with a single projector.

6.3   Material Display

We also implemented a display that reproduces the appearances of various materials along the concept (Figure 13) in which different reflective states overlap in the time division. In the mirror reflection state, the light can be seen at a different area on the screen according to the viewpoint. No additional calculation is needed to render the images for projection because the reflection control is done on the screen. Moreover, reflection parameters are determined by two factors: the degree of mix in the time division and the power of the ultrasonic waves. This display has a simple structure but wide application range.

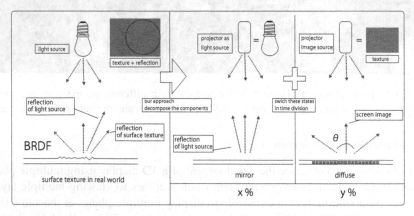

Fig. 13. Shows how we can mimic a texture in real world controlling the percentage between mirror (x%) and diffuse (y %) in time division

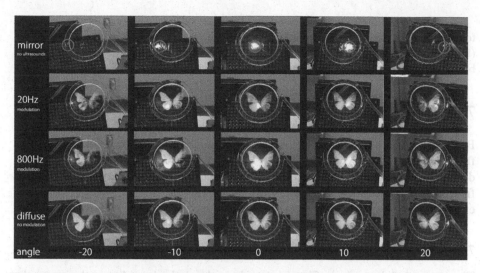

Fig. 14. Sample results for four reflective states from five different view angle. Note that red circle shows the reflective spot from the mirror and it is consistent with the bottom images.

Colloidal film is a unique material whose reflection range can be controlled. This characteristic, coupled with high frequency control of ultrasounds, facilitates this application. The results depicted in Figure 14 shows that our system successfully operated as a reflective display. It follows the reflection of the viewing point.

6.4   Deformable Screen

We also developed a deformable screen using the colloidal membrane. In this implementation, we used the ultrasonic speakers in two ways. One purpose was to change the reflection of the screen and the other was to create a deformation using the radiation pressure. The five components used are shown in Figure 7. The objective was to use the phased array to make a force field. The force field was generated by focusing the ultrasound in the range 25 cm and 15 cm. When the force field was created, it pushed the membrane, allowing it to deform.

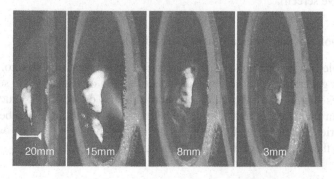

Fig. 15. Screen deformed from 2 mm to 20 mm

By controlling the focus and the spatial position of the force field, it was possible to change the size of the deformation point on the membrane from 2 mm to 20 mm (Figure 15). In addition, when two phased arrays were used we were able to control both the projection and the deformation.

7   Discussions

By turning soap film into a projector screen, we gained controllable properties such as flexibility, transparency, and durability. However, we acknowledge that a soap film does not last forever and there are limitations on the view angles. In this section, we first look at the limitations, then discuss the possibilities of our system for use in entertainment computing.

7.1   Soap Films Limitation

The amount of time a soap film can last depends on the humidity in the room, the power of the ultrasonic speaker, disturbance factors like wind, and the soap product. In our experiment, a soap film lasted an average of three minutes. We found an ingredient that can enable a soap bubble to last over a day by using a glue-like substance. However, this kind of material cannot create interactions such as popping. which regular soap film supports. In addition, soap film is flexible but has shape limitations. The shape has to be concave and cannot replicate complex shapes. This can be solved by using a polygon-like frame with multiple soap films.

7.2   Limitation on View Angles

The maximum view angle is 180 deg because this display is based on reflection. We achieved a maximum view angle of 40 deg. The view angle changes according to the intensity, the waveform of amplitude modulation, and the frequency of the ultrasound. If the view angle is too small, only the light is shown and not the content of the projected image because it is too acute for human eyes. However, we used this to our advantage and displayed three different images from different angles (we applied it to the perspective screen).

7.3   Outlook for the Entertainment Computing

A soap bubble is a unique material that users can insert their fingers into. Moreover, soap bubbles generate a lot of joy by their beauty and in our making and seeing them. Soap bubbles are used in the entertainment industry on occasions such as party events, and in theme parks and science museums. This technology can be applied in these industries to enable video projections on the bubbles. In this way, it can contribute to the expansion of the entertainment computing field.

8   Conclusion and Future Work

In this paper, we proposed an innovative first step to dynamically altering the brightness, shape, and view angle of screens by using soap film and ultrasonic speakers.

Many future potential projects are envisioned. One potential project is a dynamic 3D model with a minimal view angle and various images projected from different angles. This would be more cost effective than other methods such as holographic viewers. Furthermore, it would be interesting to see a 3D model made out of soap film on a polygon shaped frame (Figure 18) with several ultrasonic speakers. Many 3D models, such as those in games, tend to use the same models with different textures to create new enemies. The same concept can be applied to this display. Another usage for this display is to utilize its interesting interactive properties such as inserting and popping. For example, a game in which the player has to cut the screen to kill an enemy can be facilitated. In general, if we are able carry this concept to a bigger scale; it would open up many possibilities for the future of the entertainment computing industry.

References

1. Ochiai, Y., Oyama, A., Toyoshima, K.: A colloidal display: Membrane screen that combines transparency, BRDF and 3D volume. In: ACM SIGGRAPH 2012 Emerging Technologies (SIGGRAPH 2012), Article 2, 1 page. ACM, New York (2012)
2. Raffle, H., Joachim, W.M., Tichenor, J.: Super cilia skin: An interactive membrane. In: CHI 2003 Extended Abstracts on Human Factors in Computing Systems (CHI EA 2003), pp. 808–809 (2003)
3. Coelho, M., Maes, P.: Sprout I/O: A texturally rich interface. In: Proceedings of the 2nd International Conference on Tangible and Embedded Interaction (TEI 2008), pp. 221–222 (2008)
4. Furukawa, M., Uema, Y., Sugimoto, M., Inami, M.: Fur interface with bristling effect induced by vibration. In: Proceedings of the 1st Augmented Human International Conference (AH 2010), Article 17, 6 page (2010)
5. Hullin, B.M., Hendrik, P., Lensch, A., Rasker, R., Seidel, H., Ihrke, I.: A dynamic BRDF display. In: ACM SIGGRAPH 2011 Emerging Technologies (SIGGRAPH 2011), Article 1, 1 page (2011)
6. Koike, T., Naemura, T.: BRDF display. In: ACM SIGGRAPH 2007 Posters, SIGGRAPH 2007, Article 116 (2007)
7. Poupyrev, I., Nashida, T., Okabe, M.: Actuation and tangible user interfaces: The Vaucanson duck, robots, and shape displays. In: Proceedings of the 1st International Conference on Tangible and Embedded Interaction (TEI 2007), pp. 205–212 (2007)
8. Cholewiak, R., Sherrick, C.: A computer-controlled matrix system for presentation to skin of complex spatiotemporal pattern. Behavior Research Methods and Instrumentation 13(5), 667–673 (1981)
9. Iwata, H., Yano, H., Nakaizumi, F., Kawamura, R.: Project FEELEX: Adding haptic surface to graphics. In: Proceedings of the 28th Annual Conference on Computer Graphics and Interactive Techniques, pp. 469–476 (2001)

10. Poupyrev, I., Nashida, T., Maruyama, S., Rekimoto, J., Yamaji, Y.: Lumen: Interactive visual and shape display for calm computing. ACM SIGGRAPH 2004 Emerging Technologies (2004)
11. Leithinger, D., Lakatos, D., Devincezi, A., Blackshaw, M., Ishii, H.: Direct and gestural interaction with relief: A 2.5D shape display. In: Proceedings of the 24th Annual ACM Symposium on User Interface Software and Technology (UIST 2011), pp. 541–548 (2011)
12. Rakkolainen, I., Diverdi, S., Olwal, A., Candussi, N., Hoellerer, T., Laitinen, M., Piirto, M., Palovouri, K.: The Interactive FogScreen. ACM SIGGRAPH 2005, Emerging Technologies (2005)
13. Lee, C., Diverdi, S., Hoellerer, T.: Depth-fused 3D imagery on an immaterial display. IEEE Transactions on Visualization and Computer Graphics 15(1), 20–33 (2009)
14. Sugihara, Y., Hashimoto, H., Yamamoto, K.: A proposal of water display. In: Proceedings of the Seventh International Conference on Artificial Reality and Tele-Existence, pp. 63–70 (1997)
15. Barnum, P.C., Narasimhan, S.G., Kanade, T.: A multi-layered display with water drops. ACM Trans. Graph. 29(4), Article 76, 7 page (2010)
16. Suzuki, T.: Water Canvas 2004-2013
17. Kodama, S., Takeno, M.: Protrude, Flow. In: SIGGRAPH 2001 Electronic Arts and Animation Catalogue, p. 138 (2001)
18. Nakamura, M., Inaba, G., Tamaoki, J., Shiratori, K., Hoshino, J.: Bubble cosmos. In: ACM SIGGRAPH 2006 Emerging Technologies, SIGGRAPH 2006, Article 3 (2006)
19. Hirayama, S., Kakehi, Y.: Shaboned display: An interactive substantial display using soap bubbles. In: ACM SIGGRAPH 2010 Emerging Technologies (SIGGRAPH 2010), Article 21, 1 page (2010)
20. Suzuki, R., Suzuki, T., Ariga, S., Iida, M., Arakawa, C.: "Ephemeral melody": Music played with wind and bubbles. In: ACM SIGGRAPH 2008 Posters (SIGGRAPH 2008), Article 80, 1 page (2008)
21. Lamb, H.: Hydrodynamics, 6th edn. Cambridge University Press (1994) ISBN 978-0-521-45868-9
22. Hoshi, T.: Compact ultrasound device for noncontact interaction. In: Nijholt, A., Romão, T., Reidsma, D. (eds.) ACE 2012. LNCS, vol. 7624, pp. 502–505. Springer, Heidelberg (2012)
23. Hoshi, T., Takahashi, M., Iwamoto, T., Shinoda, H.: Noncontact tactile display based on radiation pressure of airborne ultrasound. IEEE Transactions on Haptics 3(3), 155–165 (2010)

Return of the Man-Machine Interface: Violent Interactions

Duncan Rowland[1], Conor Linehan[1],
Kwamena Appiah-Kubi[1], and Maureen Schoonheyt[2]

[1] University of Lincoln, Brayford Pool, LN67TS, UK
{drowland,clinehan,kappiahkubi}@lincoln.ac.uk
[2] Hague University of Applied Sciences, Johanna Westerdijkplein 75, The Hague, Netherlands
maureenschoonheyt@hhs.nl

Abstract. This paper presents the design and evaluation of "the man-machine interface" a punchable interface designed to criticise and react against the values inherent in modern systems that tacitly favour one type of user (linguistically and technically gifted) and alienate another (physically gifted). We report a user study, where participants used the device to express their opinions before engaging in a group discussion about the implications of strength-based interactions. We draw connections between our own work and that of evolutionary biologists whose recent findings indicate the shape of the human hand is likely to have been partly evolved for the purpose of punching, and conclude by examining violent force as an appropriate means for expressing thoughts and feelings.

Keywords: Man-machine interface, punch interface, critical design, values-sensitive design.

1   Introduction

This paper presents a project designed to explore, criticise and provoke consideration of values and biases inherent in modern interface design. We propose that communication technologies have become increasingly advantageous to linguistically talented people, to the detriment of those whose strengths lie more in gross motor movements and physical prowess. Further, due to the increasing technological mediation of many aspects of modern life such as work, education, health care, play, socializing, and governance, we are concerned over the potential wide scale disenfranchisement and disillusionment of people whose talents are primarily physical. As a case study, we examine inherent biases in contemporary methods for expressing preferences and opinions. We challenge these biases through the design of a provocative artefact, the "man-machine interface," which intentionally privileges physically gifted people at the expense of those who are less physically talented. The approach is inspired by the methods of feminism, which are designed to identify and criticise systematic inequalities.

Below, we first make the argument that contemporary technology, designed by 'nerds', serves the interests of nerds far better than their traditional enemy, the 'jock' [1]. We introduce critical design as a methodology for both understanding and

D. Reidsma, H. Katayose, and A. Nijholt (Eds.): ACE 2013, LNCS 8253, pp. 215–229, 2013.

protesting against such perceived inequality. We briefly discuss contemporary methods for expressing preferences, opinions and strength of feeling, before describing the design and implementation of "the man machine interface," a system designed to allow the expression of preference through physical violence. Subsequently, we discuss the findings of a user study that was carried out to explore the subjective experience of interacting with this device.

1.1   Background

Since the first proto-human picked up a bone club to cave in the skull of his oppressor [2], tools have often been used by the physically weak to subjugate the strong. Just as David slew Goliath through his covert use of technology, modern technology disempowers honest strength in favour of (wordy) obscurantism. Further, it is apparent that today's systems of symbolic manipulation have allowed a disconnect to develop between work and value, allowing the subjugation of the most physically able. Staggering sums of money (c.f. work) can be manipulated by a few clicks or the effortless swipe over a tablet's surface. There is no feedback that relates to the physical consequences of such casual gesture.

"Written words destroy memory and weaken the mind, relieving it of work that makes it strong... They are an inhuman thing." Socrates (in Plato's *Phaedrus*)

In general, a system develops to benefit those who develop the system [3]. Modern society functions through mechanisms put in place by successive generations of bureaucrats whose chief skills are in the manipulation of symbolic information. Those best able to engage with these semiotic mechanisms will naturally flourish and be promoted to positions whereby they can strengthen the same system by which they were valued in the first place. A runaway process of natural selection has occurred with systems of governance becoming ever more bloated and the majority of populace ever more distant from the policy makers [4].

Computing technology is an essential component of the systems through which the modern world is governed. There is fundamental digital mediation in almost all aspects of our experience, from work, to education, health care, play, socializing, and government. Indeed, much discussion has taken place recently on the consequences, both intended and unintended, and both potential and already realised, of delegating decisions and responsibility to technology [5]. It is beyond question that computing technology serves to perpetuate and promote societal inequalities. However, the idea of technological determinism; that a society is solely a product of its enabling technology [6], is a fallacy. Digital computers have the capacity to deploy any number of systems, and have no requirement to benefit any particular group. So, the values designed into computing technology - either deliberately, or by default - do not necessarily need to conform to any present set of agreed upon social norms. Instead, technology can, and should, react against the status quo and provoke the development of new values and morals.

As feminism has provided a lens on the gender inequalities in society, and the often tacit discrimination that occurs through the unquestioning implementation of systems within a specific set of norms [7]; we draw inspiration from these ideas to develop work which can benefit those currently disenfranchised by the disempowerment of strength [8,9,10].

1.2   Critical Design

This project should be considered an instance of critical design; a theoretical approach to design that is intended to provoke deeper thought about the values inherent, but not necessarily obvious, in the design of products. Dunne and Raby [11], in introducing the concept of critical design, suggest that all design is ideological and that the design process is informed by values consistent with a specific worldview. Critical design "rejects how things are now as being the only possibility, it provides a critique of the prevailing situation through designs that embody social, cultural, technical and economic values." (p.58). It is, "a way of looking at design and imagining its possibilities beyond the narrow definitions of what is presented through media and in the shops".

Critical design has recently been discussed in HCI research as a means for exploring and criticizing the values inherent in the design of interactive technology [12,13]. Examples of critical HCI include the work of Linsay Grace [14], whose critical gameplay project aims to subvert the dominant assumptions in contemporary video game experiences.

The project presented in the current paper should be understood as a feminist-inspired critique. Our goals in this work mirror that of feminism, in that we are critically examining the status quo of interface design in order to provoke deeper thought about inequalities in how advantageous that technology is to different groups of people, based on their physical or socially constructed characteristics. The use of the phrase man-machine interface is therefore intended to be humorous, provocative and confrontational, in the true spirit of critical design.

The work reported here could also be considered as a form of 'values-sensitive design' [15,16], which is a theoretically grounded approach to design that takes account of human values as a specific part of the design process. The concept was introduced by Friedman to illustrate how human values, whether intentional or not, are inherent in the design process and the outputs of that process. Indeed, the role of human values in the design of technology has recently been discussed at length [17].

1.3   Strength, Society and Interaction Design

We believe that it is important for society to recognise, accept and learn to deal with, the inherently aggressive and violent nature of the human species. Indeed, recent work in evolutionary biology emphasises that fighting, specifically the use of the hand as a fist, has markedly shaped its evolution [18]. Prof David Carrier discusses this in a recent interview,

> "I think there is a lot of resistance - maybe more so among academics than people in general - resistance to the idea that, at some level humans are by nature aggressive animals. I actually think that attitude, and the people who have tried to make the case that we don't have a nature - those people have not served us well..... I think we would be better off if we faced the reality that we have these strong emotions and sometimes they prime us to behave in violent ways. I think if we acknowledged that we'd be better able to prevent violence in future." [19].

Fig. 1. Amusement Machine

If humans are inherently aggressive and violent in nature, the design of interactive technology that allows for the expression of that aggression seems interesting and useful. However, there are few existing interfaces to computer systems based on brute physicality [20, 21]. The traditional 'Test Your Strength' fun fair attraction is the most commonly experienced exception (see Figure 1). Interestingly, Test Your Strength devices provide an opportunity for males to publicly display physical prowess in the context of a vanishing landscape of opportunities for such sexual display. Even though practical reasons for strength are increasingly rare, exaggerated muscle mass is still seen as desirable, though now more likely grown for show, e.g. the 'ripped six-pack' or 'arm guns' commonly on display in nightclubs (i.e. for the purpose of attracting a mate through exaggerated secondary sexual characteristics).

Other notable exceptions, where physical effort have been incorporated into design requirements, include medicine containers which are made deliberately difficult to open (to prevent children from obtaining the contents), and 'fitness' machines where physical exertion is their sole purpose, and although there is much excellent work on exertion based interfaces [22, 23], this is specifically not the topic of this paper (which focuses on systemic value bias in interface design).

1.4 Expression of Internal Values

There are many methods used in the social sciences that allow participants to express internal values; opinions, thoughts and feelings (e.g. questionnaires, interviews, forms with Likert scales and so on). These methods are all inherently verbal; they require the participant to undertake complex linguistic, or relational, reasoning in order to produce a response that can be used by others when making decisions. The response produced by a participant is typically accepted as a valid measure of that person's opinions, thoughts and feelings, regardless of their relative ease or difficulty in formulating that response. Crucially, those who have greater skill at matching their internal experience with the specific response produced, have greater chance of being understood, and of having their interests acknowledged and represented. It seems interesting to investigate methods through which physically talented people can express opinions with similar finesse.

1.5 Measuring Strength of Feeling

The prototype interface described in this paper, the *man-machine interface,* provides a novel means for people to express not only their opinions and feelings, but also the strength of those opinions and feelings. The measurement of how strongly people feel (often referred to as valence and arousal measurements) towards a product, service, experience, or concept has a long history where many different approaches have been investigated [24]. As stated above, a commonly used measurement technique is the Likert scale type of questionnaire that allows for an expression of peoples opinion or feelings verbally on a scale between "strongly disagree" and "strongly agree." The man machine interface is presented as an alternative to this linguistic form of measurement, and offers an interesting measure by tapping into base motor responses.

2   Design

2.1   Conceptual Design

In addition to affording a novel and physically active method of soliciting feedback that may reveal baser truths about a participants' internal state, the design of the system highlights the inherent inequalities in existing methods of feedback and decision-making. The system *deliberately* allows individuals who are able to punch more strongly to have a greater impact on results. This is in contrast to traditional systems of voting in which each individual's vote is valued the same; however, the ability to engage in verbal debate is not equitable and the feelings of the rhetorically weak are often left underrepresented. The interface is designed to facilitate public display of physical prowess (with some targets able to be punched powerfully merely for show). This contrasts with the 'secret-ballot' in which individuals are forced to cloak their representations in the plebiscite veil of the voting booth.

The design of the man machine interface is conceptually simple. A martial arts training aid is used as input for a computer application that allows participants to express opinions. A screen presents participants with questions. Paddles to the left and right of the device (see Figure 5) are used to answer yes/no (or agree/disagree etc.) questions. The paddle at the top is used for expressing strength of feeling. All three paddles measure the strength with which participants punched it.

There are some pragmatic considerations in relation to the design. Some people are left-handed some are right-handed. An interface based on punching power therefore needs to be symmetric so as to favour neither. Hence, while binary left/no triggers are suitable for asymmetric distribution (ignoring any cognitive bias), a power measurement is not. Thus the central head target was used to detect power; with the left/right targets used for selection. The character used to ask questions was a bland, non-threatening automated character (see Figure 6) that would generate little response in and of itself (and early prototypes showed this to be the case). Practically, the automated creation of the animation (based on a text script) allowed the interface dialog to be altered very quickly, which allowed rapid iteration of the design.

2.2   Technology

The system has been adapted from a standard martial arts training aid (a Body Opponent Bag, or BOB). The device selected was the MATT (the Mixed Martial Arts Target Trainer)[1] and this was selected as it was advertised as being the only home based fitness product capable of simulating the feeling "punching a man's head" (although there are now more products offering this feature of debatable benefit).

---

[1] http://www.bayls.co.uk/products/fitness/
mmatt-mixed-martial-arts-target-trainer/

Three of the four targets were used (the left and right 'hands' and the 'head'), with the central ('body') target being replaced with a flat screen monitor to provide instruction and feedback to the participants.

Fig. 2. Main System Components (USB Mic)

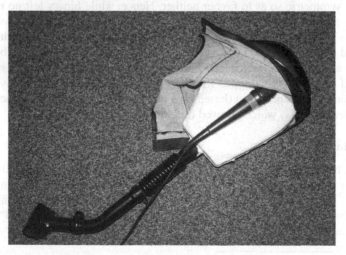

Fig. 3. Main System Components (USB Mic)

Fig. 4. Main System Component (Raspberry Pi)

Fig. 5. User's View of the Punchable Interface

USB (Singstar^tm) microphones were loosely embedded on the back of each target and these were connected to a Raspberry Pi computer for processing.

The Raspberry Pi ran a standard Raspbian version of the Linux operating system. A Python script was developed to detect punches (via the RMS of the microphone responses). Punches were recorded to a text file (with volume deemed to approximate the strength of each punch) and used to trigger sound effects (via an external USB speaker) and to start and pause a full screen HD video rendering (oxplayer) of a cute character reading the following instructions.

2.3   Instruction Script

"◼️◼️⬛️😊Hi! Welcome to Lincoln University's experimental student feedback system. To begin, please enter your ID. ⏸️Thanks. Please stand in front of the device and only hit the targets when asked to. OK! Question One. Do you consider this to have been a good module? Please ↩️hit either ↩️the: "yes" or "no" target now. ⏸️Next please indicate the strength of your feelings 👊about this by punching the central head target now. 😊⏸️Thanks. Question Two. Do you think that punching things 👊is a good way to express your feelings? Please hit the appropriate yes or no target now. ⏸️OK! Please indicate the strength 👊of your feelings about this by punching the head.😊⏸️Thank you and have a nice day. 😊⏸️"

⏸️ - Pause and await punch/input
😊 - Joy facial expression (Smile)
↩️ - Character points to left or right target
👊 - Character punches towards the central target

Fig. 7. Punchable Interface Trial

3   Evaluation

Thirty potential participants - the entire (all male) undergraduate game design class - were asked at the end of the semesters final practical session if they would consider participating in a study relating to interface design. Nine participants, aged 20-23, were recruited and were fully informed as to the purpose of the study and what was required from them. All those who volunteered initially gave written consent to participate and were then asked to fill in a paper-based module evaluation form. This form allows students to anonymously express opinions regarding the quality of that module and is a task routinely undertaken at the end of each module studied. Next, participants were asked to use the interface situated in the Games Computing Lab, one at a time, following the instructions outlined above. Afterwards, two focus groups were conducted in a semi-structured manner, led by the authors. Discussion initially focused on the subjective experience of users engaging with the device, before exploring the concept of expressing "strength of feeling" through "physical strength" and the effects that such a means of expression may have on users, and use, of technology.

3.1   Evaluation Plan

Before reporting the results of focus group discussions, it is important, due to the narrative of the paper, to acknowledge the particular characteristics of the participant sample from which data was gathered. All participants were young males. We may expect such a group to engage readily with competitive activities and opportunities to display physical prowess. Thus, we might expect to find their responses more positive and enthusiastic than other groups that we could have sampled. However, participants were also third- and fourth-year computer science students. As such, they are people who have already benefitted from the shift in cultural values away from physical towards linguistic and technological skills, and may expect to continue to do so in future. Due to these potentially conflicting opinions, we believe that they are a particularly interesting group with which to discuss the concept of strength-based interfaces.

Two separate focus groups were convened to discuss the man-machine interface. Group one consisted of five participants and group two consisted of four. Both sessions were audio recorded and those recordings were transcribed for analysis. Group one discussion lasted for approximately one hour; group two lasted for 30 minutes.

3.2   Thematic Analysis

A thematic analysis was conducted on the data recorded from focus groups. Both transcripts were initially read closely by one researcher, who defined a set of eighteen codes. Two researchers then independently applied this coding scheme to the transcripts, before meeting to discuss the fit of the codes to the data. It was agreed that fourteen separate codes were necessary to explain the data gathered. These were collapsed into five overarching themes; expressing strength of feeling via punching, performance, unfairness, politics and punching as an interaction technique. Participants also demonstrated great interest in the novelty of the experience, but this was not deemed sufficiently interesting to discuss below. In addition, we have chosen to omit analysis of the discussion of politics due to space constraints, as there was a huge amount of discussion on this topic.

Punching as an Interaction Technique. Participants were prompted to discuss whether a punch-based interface would be interesting or useful as a means of controlling computing devices more generally. All participants expressed some interest in this concept, particularly in relation to the frustration commonly experienced by users of interactive technology.

"I mean everyone wants to punch on the computer sometime when it freezes over."
"it would de-stress people. Because if they're getting real stressed at it, [...] maybe if they hit a couple of hits that's it. And then, like a pretty picture of a dog just comes up and just goes,
"Relax." "It's a stress reducing program. Basically, you're taking out on the system."

There were also suggestions for what types of functions the punch interface might be most suitable for controlling, the most common of which was to force quit programs that had crashed. However, there were also other suggestions,

"A super like on facebook,"
"It will fake smash the window, the desktop. If it's basically not working, you can beat the crap out of something until your like really, really relaxed again, and then you start to see more clear with it,"
"It's going to have to have just one outcome when you punch it in per program,"
"to open up a set program, you can assign it a set program like if you're on Skype,

someone is following you, you could just punch something over ten, it would either turn on or turn off,"

"Definitely off."

Expressing Strength of Feeling through Punching. Quite a lot of discussion focused on the opportunity that the device offered people to express the strength of their opinions or feelings via their physical strength. This was seen as novel, and participants expressed both positive and negative reactions to the concept:

Positive. As described in the background section, this project proposes that expressing opinions and feelings via gross physical strength is an activity that may appeal to some people, and for those people may represent a valid means of expression. Participants largely agreed with this concept;

"there's definitely some sort of emotional attachment to something that you punch,"

"there was a lot of emotion behind the punch, so depending on like if you're really strongly for something, and then you punch definitely more power [...] behind it than if you're not for it,"

"If you're angry, you might try and use more force that you [...] normally would."
Indeed, one participant bemoaned the lack of existing opportunities to express them self physically;

"I wouldn't like physically hit a person, but if like I was given the action [...] I'd sort of punch something to show how strong I'd feel about something. That was pretty interesting,"

"Having that ability to express how strongly you feel about something is a good way of showing how you're thinking and feeling."

Negative. Participants also expressed some reservations and concerns. Interestingly, most of these focused around the expectations placed on people by a culture that disapproves of aggression;

"Um, I just thought it was just a bit weird. Like, um, like, as a kid, you was taught not to hit anyone or anything. And like constantly, you're getting told that"

"It was like, uh, going against the grain of what I would imagine what most people were told growing up. Like: "Show your emotions by hitting something" isn't usually our primal guidance sort of thing,"

"You could say having young kids punching something could send the wrong message as well as a moral thing, that it's okay to punch things to express yourselves, which isn't really what people go for nowadays?"

Two participants were very negative towards the concept;

"No, I don't like answering with punches,"

"I haven't really got really like a motivation to hit things. So it's like I'd rather just sulk, or something."

There was clearly a good deal of cognitive dissonance provoked through the request to act in a 'violent' way within the confines of a computing laboratory. Even though the actions were against martial arts training aids specifically designed for this purpose, this particular group seemed unusually averse to acts of physical expression. This is perhaps to be expected given those activities that would have likely received positive reinforcement through the participants' formative development and training, and, a different group of participants in a different context may well not exhibit such extremes.

Performance. As the session wherein participants interacted with the device took place in public, and classmates were allowed to watch if they wished, there was an element of performance to the behaviour of participants. Participants discussed how they were very conscious of being watched while punching the device;

> *"It was a little bit weird getting in front of everybody while they was looking at you, punching something,"*

and how being watched affected their subjective experience and their actions;

> *"I mean, you don't want to like, hit really slightly if everyone else is like, smacking it,"*
> *"you don't want to be like the worst person,"*
> *"How am I supposed to react to this properly ... ?... in a way that won't make me look like an idiot," "You didn't want it to look like we were weak."*

These comments are fascinating in the context of this paper as they underline the disruptive influence of the device. Specifically, this group of people rarely if ever interact with each other in a way that values physical strength. Rather, being an undergraduate computer science cohort, the social hierarchy of most influential or valued members of that group is determined more by their technical skills. The device provided a disruptive influence on the established pecking order and provided the opportunity for physicality-based sexual display.

Reliability. The majority of participants expressed concerns over the reliability of measurements taken by the interface;

> *"each person is built differently, skill wise. One person might be able to, uh, strongly agree more than another,"*
> *"Yeah, because if it was: "How strongly do you feel about this?" You circle "Seven" and someone else circles "Seven." If they both punch it [.....] thinking about "Seven" [...] the forces will be different," "The body type of everybody is completely different,"*
> *"It's completely inaccurate."*

These comments are interesting, since the interface was designed intentionally to advantage stronger people. Participants identified this inequality, but it did not provoke them, as intended, to think more critically about similar inequalities inherent in other types of input device.

Some participants pointed out problems with reliability of measurement by identifying factors that could affect the strength of punch recorded, but which are not related to strength of emotion or opinion. These include punching technique, *"a lot of people would do like a typical movie punch and just swing from the side, [...] where as I do [...] a straight sort of punch, which generally gets more power. So, [...] I think from that I might feel strongly about something more so than someone else,"*

or confidence,

"Not even the physical size, just like more confident in yourself. You get up and don't care if those people watch you, then you're going to do what you're going to do," "if you get people that aren't confident standing in front of other people, [...] even if they are very strong, they're still going to be really, really reserved."

Participants also suggested means for remedying the unreliability of the interface. Specifically, they suggested taking baseline readings for every user,

"You'd have to look at baseline," "You have like a frame of reference. Everyone's working then on the same kind of relevant level," "Unless, of course, like, the second part was like I saw, a mini-baseline hits, because people are bound to hit either "Yes," and punch it really hard," "Or hit "X" amount of between zero and ten times."

Indeed, the researchers had to repeatedly steer discussion away from implementation of baselines and how they could be implemented. This insistence on fairness across participants is very interesting.

Unfairness of the Interface. Most participants expressed some concerns over general "unfairness" inherent in a device that uses physical strength as an input technique. These concerns came in two forms; the first addressed reliability of measurement across individuals, the second focused on the potentially discriminatory effects of this type of input mechanism on those people who use it. Disappointingly none of the groups seemed willing to accept that these biases were a ***deliberate*** aspect of the design, and were largely blind to the inherent inequalities in existing systems of societal operation. It seems that participants had difficulty considering the meaning of the design. Given time and opportunity for greater reflection and discussion it is possible that deeper insights may have emerged (though again, results from this idiosyncratic participant pool may not generalise well).

Discrimination. Participants were asked to consider a situation where decisions would be made, whether at university, in national elections, or in government, based on the data gathered from a strength-based interface. They were asked to consider the consequences that this would have on the people that those decisions affected. Participants almost unanimously expressed outrage and sympathy on the part of less physically gifted people.

"It would put everybody else completely out. Everyone that's above a certain age that can't punch as hard as you is then completely cast aside,"
"You could ostracize everyone apart from a small portion of people,"
"If you're, for example, an elderly person, you might not be able to hit it as hard,"
"being rather short myself, it was ... I had to kind of reach a bit further than I would have really liked to."

Again, while participants identified and discussed the inherent discrimination in the punch interface system, there was little evidence of further thought around existing inequalities perpetuated by other types of systems, whether technological, political or social.

4   Conclusion

The expression of physical force is a natural aspect of human behaviour. This study provides an initial exploration of violent force as an input mechanic to interactive technology (tapping into emotions and providing an outlet for pent up aggression). It seems that punching is an interesting interaction technique, enabling responses to be collected based on momentary expression of explosive power. The system reliably detected punches of various strengths, and although more sophisticated measuring devices could make the measurement of force more accurate, in terms of this initial enquiry the correlation with volume proved to be accurate enough.

Participants in the current study demonstrated an ability to effectively control the strength of their punches. They also demonstrated, and reported, significant individual differences in base level of strength, skill in punching, and reaction to the public test situation. The design of the system sought to make use of these differences to provoke discussion relating to the inequalities in other systems. There was clearly a good deal of cognitive dissonance in the group caused by this request and the activity of behaving in a 'violent' manner in a computer lab, there are several aspects to this.

Firstly, we found indications that social conditioning undermines tendencies towards violence in social situations. Participants reported being taught by parents from a young age that violence is not appropriate, particularly as a means of expression. Secondly, the group was highly sensitive to disturbances of the status quo. This included threats to their position within the group hierarchy (through embarrassment or lack of ability). Thirdly, participants were concerned with notions of fairness. Many of the objections to the interface sought to rectify, or reinstate existing bias (e.g. by calculating power relative to a base line). The findings that participants naturally (and unknowingly) wish to reinstate bias that benefits themselves is broadly as predicted, and is coherent in terms of the initial assertions regarding the development of societal structures.

In summary, this study constitutes an initial exploration of violent force as an interaction style for interactive technology. It also examines violent force as a means for expressing thoughts and feelings. While participants reported enjoyment at interacting with the device, they also expressed reservations about the social acceptability of behaving in violent ways. In addition, while participants recognised that the interface was not fairly designed, there was very little evidence that it provoked critical insight on the inherent inequalities in existing systems of societal operation. We intend, in future studies, to explore further the critical potential of violent interaction.

References

1. Gilsdorf, E.: Geek Pride: Jocks vs. Nerds, Brawn vs. Brain, Hunks vs. Dweebs. Psychology Today (September 25, 2010), http://www.psychologytoday.com/blog/geek-pride/201009/jocks-vs-nerds-brawn-vs-brain-hunks-vs-dweebs (retrieved January 7, 2013)

2. Kubrick, S., Clarke, A.C.: 2001: A Space Odyssey, Screenplay (1968)
3. Wallerstein, I.: The Capitalist World-Economy. Cambridge University Press, Cambridge (1979)
4. Garry, P.: The meaning of big government. Renew America (2011), http://www.renewamerica.com/analysis/garry/110614 (retrieved January 7, 2013)
5. Rushkoff, D.: Present Shock: When Everything Happens Now. Current Hardcover (2013) ISBN-13: 978-1591844761
6. Levy, S.: Hackers: Heros of the Computer Revolution. Penguin (2002) ISBN-13: 978-0141000510
7. Hooks, B.: Feminist Theory: From Margin to Center, 2nd edn. Pluto Press (2000)
8. Harrington, G.S., Farias, S.T.: Sex differences in language processing: functional MRI methodological considerations. J. Magn. Reson. Imaging 27(6), 1221–1228 (2008), doi:10.1002/jmri.21374
9. Fine, C.: Delusions of Gender: How Our Minds, Society, and Neurosexism Create Difference, 1st edn. W. W. Norton & Company (2010) ISBN 978-0-393-06838-2
10. Jordan-Young, R.: Brain Storm: The Flaws in the Science of Sex Differences, 2nd edn. Harvard University Press (2010) ISBN 978-0-674-05730-2
11. Dunne, A., Raby, F.: Design Noir: The secret life of electronic objects. Berkhauser, Berlin (2001)
12. Bardzell, J.: Interaction Criticism and Aesthetics. In: Proceedings of ACM CHI, pp. 2357–2366 (2009)
13. Blythe, M.A.: The digital music box: using cultural and critical theory to inform design. In: Proceedings of ACM CHI Extended Abstracts, pp. 2297–2302 (2007)
14. Grace, L.: Creating Critical Gameplay Design. In: Proceedings of ACE (2010)
15. Cockton, G.: A development framework for value-centred design. In: CHI 2005 Extended Abstracts on Human Factors in Computing Systems (CHI EA 2005), pp. 1292–1295. ACM, New York (2005)
16. Friedman, B.: Value-sensitive design. Interactions 3(6), 16–23 (1996)
17. Sellen, A., Rogers, Y., Harper, R., Rodden, T.: Reflecting human values in the digital age. Commun. ACM 52(3), 58–66 (2009)
18. Morgan, M.H., Carrier, D.R.: Protective buttressing of the human fist and the evolution of hominin hands. J. Exp. Biol. 216, 236–244 (2013), doi:10.1242/jeb.075713
19. BBC News, Fighting may have shaped evolution of human hand (December 2012), http://www.bbc.co.uk/news/science-environment-20790294 (retrieved January 7, 2013)
20. Gross, S., Boess, S.: Love Hate Punch (2010), http://v2.nl/archive/works/love-hate-punch (retrieved January 7, 2013)
21. Nexersys (2012), http://nexersys.com/ (retrieved January 7, 2013)
22. Mueller, F.: Academic Publications about Exertion Interfaces, http://exertioninterfaces.com/cms/academic-publications.html (retrieved January 7, 2013)
23. Mueller, F., Agamanolis, S., Gibbs, M., Vetere, F.: Remote Impact: Shadow-boxing over a Distance. In: CHI 2009: Extended Abstracts, Boston, MA, USA, pp. 3531–3532. ACM, New York (2009)
24. Hazlett, R.L.: Measuring emotional valence during interactive experiences: boys at video game play. In: Proceedings of ACM CHI, pp. 1023–1026 (2006)

Non-branching Interactive Comics

Edirlei Soares de Lima[1], Bruno Feijó[1], Antonio L. Furtado[1],
Simone Diniz Junqueira Barbosa[1], Cesar T. Pozzer[2], and Angelo E.M. Ciarlini[3]

[1] PUC-Rio – Department of Informatics, Rio de Janeiro, RJ, Brazil
{elima,bfeijo,furtado,simone}@inf.puc-rio.br
[2] UFSM – Department of Applied Computing, Santa Maria, RS, Brazil
pozzer@inf.ufsm.br
[3] UNIRIO – Department of Applied Informatics, Rio de Janeiro, RJ, Brazil
angelo.ciarlini@uniriotec.br

Abstract. Comics are a unique and classical form of storytelling. The advent of interactive narratives brings the possibility of interaction to the traditional comic books. In this paper we present a non-branching interactive comics system capable of generating dynamic interactive narratives in the format of comic books. The system allows users to interact with certain objects, and then observe the consequences of their actions in the unfolding story. We validate the proposed system with a user study conducted with 18 participants. The results indicate that such systems may indeed provide an attractive form of entertainment.

Keywords: Interactive Comics, Interactive Storytelling, Comic Book.

1 Introduction

Comics are a popular form of visual storytelling, wherein juxtaposed still images are combined with text. Modern comic books emerged at the turn of the 19th century and evolved in different ways in Europe, America and Japan. In the early 19th century, the Swiss artist Rodolphe Töpffer published the book *Histoire de M. Vieux Bois*, which some consider the first "comic book" [17]. In America, the genre of superheroes has dominated the mainstream for decades, and its popularity has varied widely since the first period of popularity in the 1940s, known as the American Golden Age of comic books. The appreciation for the storytelling abilities of comics, however, was even more remarkable in Japan, where *manga* (Japanese term for comics) gained reputation both for profitable sales and diversity of genres. Nowadays, classical printed books are sharing space with digital forms of comics, such as *Marvel's The Avengers: Iron Man – Mark VII* [34]. The developers of *Webcomics*, which are comics published on a website [31], are now exploring new forms of comics, such as narrative branching structures (also known as *hypercomics*) and animated panels with sounds (also known as *motion comics*). An example of hypercomic is *Meanwhile* [30], which is a branching interactive comics where one navigates making choices and solving puzzles. Through the last ten years, many researchers have attempted to transform the classical form of comics into a new form of digital interactive content. The applications

D. Reidsma, H. Katayose, and A. Nijholt (Eds.): ACE 2013, LNCS 8253, pp. 230–245, 2013.

include the automatic generation of non-interactive comics [5][6][8], interactive experiences for web and mobile devices [22][30], and some interactive narratives [19][20]. However, most of the applications that include some form of interactivity are based on the concept of branching narrative structures [26], which are known in the area of interactive storytelling as having several limitations, such as the authoring complexity and the lack of story diversity. Research on interactive storytelling has been exploring the generation of interactive narratives since the 1970s and may provide the proper foundation for the creation of a new form of interactive content based on comics.

The most robust forms of interactive narratives rely on artificial intelligence techniques, such as planning [15], to dynamically generate the sequence of narrative events rather than following predefined branching points. The techniques that support the dynamic generation of stories are also useful to maintain the coherence of the entire narrative. Moreover, they support the propagation of changes introduced by the users, allowing them to effectively interact and change the unfolding stories.

Although artificial intelligence techniques can help improve the diversity of stories, they face the challenge of generating comics in real-time from a story that is not known beforehand. In branching narratives, all the possible storylines are predefined by the author, and the system is prepared to represent them in the best possible way. On the other hand, in systems based on planning techniques, stories are created by the planning algorithm, guided to some extent by the user interactions, and it is not easy to predict all the possible storylines that can emerge. These unpredictable outcomes require intelligent systems capable of adapting themselves to represent emergent narratives correctly. In the case of comics, the intelligent system must also know how to use comic language to generate, in real-time, each panel representing the narrative events. In other words, the system should also generate part of the comic art.

In this paper we explore the use of artificial intelligence techniques to blend narrative generation and interactive comics. We present and evaluate a non-branching interactive comic system capable of generating dynamic interactive narratives in the format of comic books. The system allows users to freely intervene in the stories by interacting with the scene objects, and then observe the consequences of their actions in the unfolding story. As far as we are aware, there is no other work proposing a system for non-branching interactive comics in the literature.

2   Related Work

The automatic generation of comics has been an active topic of research since Kurlander et al. proposed their famous Comic Chat system [1] in the nineties. Comic Chat is a system capable of automatically generating comics from chat sessions. It determines the correct poses for each character and situation through a semantic analysis of the participants' messages. Following a similar approach, Sumi et al. present ComicDiary [2], a system that automatically creates personal diaries in a comic style.

In the gaming context, Shamir et al. [3] and Shuda and Thawonmas [4] propose a system to automatically generate comics from game sessions summarizing the game events. Chan et al. [5] adopt a similar approach and present a system that automatically summarizes players' actions and interactions in the game World of Warcraft through comics. Pizzi *et al.* [6] use comic-like storyboards to represent game level solutions as a game design tool. Their system generates all possible solutions to a given game level using the player character as the main agent. Then, they attach elements of storyboards to the planning operators so that a complete solution generates a comic strip representing the storyboard.

Alves *et al.* [7] describe an XML-based language that semantically describes comics. They also present Comics2D, a system able to interpret the XML language and generate comic strips. In a more recent work, Alves *et al.* [8] present another system able to create comic-like summaries of agent-based stories generated by the interactive storytelling system FearNot! [9]. The system analyses the story logs, characters' emotional information to understand their actions and their importance in the story, and then selects the most important events to create comic strips.

There are some interactive experiences based on comics designed for mobile devices, like Nawlz [22], which is an adventure comic book designed for iPad that combines animation, interactivity, music, and text in a panoramic comic format. However, the story is entirely linear and user interactions don't have any effect in the story outcome. Some major comic publishers have tried to create interactive comic books. A recent example is the already cited Marvel's The Avengers: Iron Man - Mark VII [34], which is an interactive comic book designed for mobile devices that allow users to play with some interactive elements of the scenarios, but without affecting the story.

The possibility of choosing between different story paths is explored by Goodbrey [19][20]. The author presents several web applications that combine the concept of branching narratives with the idea of "infinite canvas" proposed by McCloud [21]. The commercial product Meanwhile for iPad and iPhone [30] is another example of branching technique. Taking a different approach, Andrews *et al.* [23] explore the application of interactive comics in a projected multi-touch interface. Their system projects on a sheet of paper predefined lower-level narrative elements, such as characters and dialogues, allowing users to enrich the story by adding "top level" objects.

Our system differs from the aforementioned works because we integrate three important features: plot generation; interaction affecting the plot generation; and automatic layout generation based on the plot. Furthermore, the story unfolds from a logical framework rather than from a predefined branching structure. Such an integrated and flexible approach is possible because the system is supported by the following components: (1) a planning module that automatically generates coherent and diversified stories according to the user interventions; (2) intelligent algorithms capable of generating comics in real-time. To the best of our knowledge, this is the first work on non-branching interactive comics in the literature.

3   Comics

Comics are a narrative form that uses a sequence of panels containing signs and images combined with texts, where the reader perceives time spatially. The texts are in the form of speech balloons, captions, and onomatopoeic words for sound effects

(SFX). Our treatment of comics relies on the understanding that comics consist of: "sequential art", as pointed by Eisner [18]; semiotic entities, as claimed by O'Neil [29]; and juxtaposed images in deliberate sequences, where time and space are one and the same, as observed by McCloud [17]. The question of time is clearly explained by McCloud using a comparison with movies in his book. He points out that each successive movie frame is projected on exactly the same space, while each comic frame occupies a different space – and concludes that space does for comics what time does for film.

An easy way to understand the language of comics is by looking at the structure of a comic book. A comic book usually comprises one or more pages, each page consisting of panels, whose varying size and location influence the reader's progress. These panels convey space and time and behave as picture planes through which the reader views the action of the story. Inside the panels, story events are represented through three types of visual elements: figurative, iconic, and textual [16]. Figurative elements are the characters themselves, their actions, facial expressions, and gestures, representing what they are doing and what they are feeling. Iconic elements include speech balloons, thought balloons, SFX balloons, and narration boxes. These icons inform the reader which words are being thought, said, or narrated. In addition, the shapes of these icons can be altered to add nuance to the words found within them. Finally, the textual elements represent the text found within the speech balloons, thought balloons and narration boxes. Figure 1 indicates the basic elements of comic books. A more complete and detailed analysis of the visual language of comics is presented by McCloud [17] and Eisner [18].

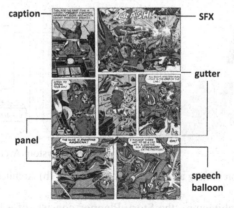

Fig. 1. Elements of comic books (panel, gutter, caption, speech balloon, SFX). Copyright material under "fair use" policy.

Although comics are sometimes seen as a childish form of storytelling, with images that are often deliberately simplified, they are still capable of evoking strong emotional reactions from readers, creating identification, and effectively conveying a story in an very appealing manner [3].

4   Interactive Comics

Our method to create a new form of interactive content for comics has three main tasks: (1) the automatic generation of interactive narratives using a story planner; (2) the definition and compositing of panels in the format of comic books; (3) the interaction with the user. The proposed system is embedded in a tablet computer, where users are able to visualize narratives through comic panels and interact with certain objects that can affect the unfolding stories (Figure 2a).

Initially, the system generates an entire story plot and users can read it as a traditional comic book. Additionally, some scenarios include interactive objects that can be activated by users by tapping on the tablet. When this happens, the logical context of the story is modified at that specific point of the narrative according to the effects of the activated object. The intervention propagates to the next story events, and the comic panels are updated to represent the new storyline. Users thus have a way to interact with the story and observe the consequences of their actions in real time.

Tablet computers are the most suitable platform to support the visualization of comics in a digital format, because they come closer to real comic books than desktop computers. However, the limited processing power of tablets may not be capable of running a complex planning algorithm in real time. Consequently, the proposed system is based on a client-server architecture (Figure 2b), where the server hosts the planner responsible for generating the stories, and the client contains the visualization interface that presents the narrative in the format of comics.

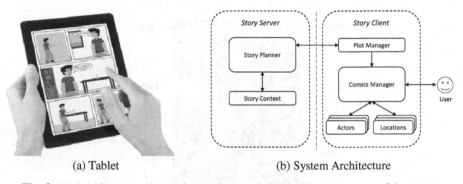

(a) Tablet   (b) System Architecture

Fig. 2. (a) A tablet presenting an interactive comic book. (b) Architecture of the system.

In the proposed architecture, the Story Planner consists of a heuristic search planner that performs a forward search in the space of world states to find a path from a given state to a goal state based on the Story Context. The Story Context defines the characters, locations, a set of authorial goals, and a set of planning operators using the STRIPS formalism [24]. On the client side, the Plot Manager is responsible for requesting new plans for the remote Story Planner through a TCP/IP connection. The Plot Manager sends the current state of the story to the Story Planner, and receives back the sequence of story events to achieve an authorial goal. Then the Plot Manager sends the story events to the Comics Manager, which uses its graphical resources (Actors and Locations) to generate comic panels to represent the events in the format of a comic book and interacts with the user.

5   Story Planner

Interactive storytelling systems can follow three basic approaches: plot-based [10], character-based [11], or a hybrid approach [12]. In our system we adopted a plot-based approach, where the story plot is automatically built and updated in real time by a planning algorithm. The Story Planner is based on a standard Heuristic Search Planning (HSP) [13] algorithm that performs a forward search in the space of world states using a weighted A* algorithm [14] with inadmissible heuristic values. The planner solves STRIPS-like planning problems with ground operators. The Story Context contains the definition of the planning problem, which includes a set of propositions P used to describe the states and operators, a set of planning operators O, the initial state $I \subseteq P$, and a hierarchy of authorial goals $G \subseteq P$. Each operator $o \in O$ has a list of preconditions and a list of effects.

The initial state is represented by a set of propositions describing the starting point of the story. It includes the definition of the characters, their current situation, and a description of the world. Examples of propositions for the initial state could be: *character(emma)* for "Emma is a character"; *at(emma, house)* for "Emma is at House"; *healthy(emma)* for "Emma is healthy"; and *path(house, hospital)* for "There is a path connecting the House to the Hospital".

Goal states are also represented by sets of propositions, and are used by the comic writer to guide the development of the story towards an admissible outcome. The planner adopts a hierarchy of authorial goals, in the sense that if a higher goal cannot be achieved, the planner tries its successor. The planner can fail to achieve a desired goal either if there is no valid sequence of actions that leads from the initial state to the goal state; or if the prescribed time limit for searching for a solution is exceeded. In both cases, the planner tries to achieve the next successor goal from the authorial goal hierarchy.

The planning operators correspond to the events that may occur in narratives. They are represented using a STRIPS-like formalism. Each operator has: (1) a list of arguments, indicating the roles played by the characters involved in the event, and other features of the corresponding actions; (2) a list of preconditions, specifying facts that must hold prior to the execution of the event; and (3) a list of effects, specifying facts that hold immediately after the execution of the event. An example of event is "*a zombie attacking a victim*" (where ∧ means AND and ¬ means NOT):

operator: attack(CH1, CH2, PL)
preconditions: zombie(CH1) ∧ ¬zombie(CH2) ∧ at(CH1, PL) ∧ at(CH2, PL)
effects: ¬healthy(CH2) ∧ infected(CH2)

In this case, the operator has 3 arguments: two characters (CH_1 and CH_2) and a place PL. The preconditions for the execution of this event indicate that CH_1 must be a zombie, CH_2 cannot be a zombie, and both CH_1 and CH_2 must be at the place PL. The effects of this event indicate that CH_2 is not healthy and is infected.

Each planning operator is also associated with an action template that describes the story event in terms of actions. For example, if $Get(Emma, Toy, House)$ is an instance of the planning operator $Get(CH, OB, PL)$, the event will be decomposed into 5 actions: (1) Emma looks at the object; (2) Emma says "Wow! It's a Toy!"; (3) Emma is happy; (4) Emma crouches; and (5) Emma gets the Toy. The use of the action templates allows the planner to produce more detailed stories without sacrificing its performance. However, it requires an addition authorial effort, since it is up to the author to specify a detailed vision of how the event occurs.

The client-server architecture of the system allows several clients to be connected with the planning server simultaneously. However, a large number of clients requesting new story plots and the server having to run several instances of the planning algorithm may compromise the real-time performance of the system. To remedy this problem, the story planner stores all computed story plots in a database of plans indexed by the initial state and the goal state. When a client requests a new story plot, the server checks the database of plans. If the requested initial state and goal state are found, the server returns the corresponding precomputed plan; only if they are not found, the server runs a new instance of the planning algorithm.

6   Panel Definition and Compositing

The proposed process for the visualization of interactive comics is divided in two phases. The panel definition phase comprises the process of assigning the story events to their corresponding panels, computing the size required for each panel, and defining the layout of each page. The panel compositing phase includes the process of rendering the content of the panels (background, characters, objects, and word balloons).

6.1   Panel Definition

Panels are used to present a single moment frozen in time. Letting i refer to time, a panel P_i represents a discrete instant t_i (Figure 3). Besides the association with time, the specification of panel P_i comprises a specific location L_i and a set of events E_i: $P_i = \{L_i, E_i\}, E_i = \{e_{i,1}, e_{i,2}, \cdots, e_{i,j}, \cdots, e_{i,NE}\}$. An event e is an instance of a planning operator (e.g. $Get(Emma, Toy, House)$) or of a simple action (e.g. $Talk(Emma, $ "Wow! It's a Toy")$, which corresponds to a speech balloon. Events are always sequential in time (i.e. the story planner does not generate parallel events), but this sequence is compressed in the discrete instant of time t_i represented by the panel P_i. The story planner generates a long sequence of events to be assigned to panels. Furthermore, the nature and emotional intensity of the events attributed to a panel determine its size and shape.

We establish the following rules to decide whether or not a new event e_n can be grouped with its preceding event e_p in a panel P, without breaking the continuity of time and space:

1. If e_n and e_p are both speeches of the same character, or different characters that are at the same place, and the number of speeches already added to the panel P is smaller than α (maximum number of speeches supported by a single panel), then the event e_n can be assigned to the panel P.
2. If e_n is a speech and e_p contains an action performed by the speaking character, then the event e_n can be assigned to the panel P.
3. If e_p and e_n are the same event (which is not a speech) performed by two different characters at the same place, then the event e_n can be assigned to the panel P.
4. Otherwise, e_n is assigned to a new panel.

The next step is the process of creating the pages that will support the panels. A page is composed of a sequence of panels with varying size and location, which present the story events to the reader. The size of a panel is generally proportional to the amount of narrative content presented, and its position is relative to the chronological order of the events. In order to dynamically calculate the size of the panels, we propose a method to estimate the importance of a panel based on weights associated with the events and the location where the events take place.

Firstly, each class of event (*e.g. Go, Talk, LookAt*) and the locations where the events can happen are associated with a weight based on their importance to the narrative. For example, a *Go* event (where a character goes from one place to another) may have less importance to the narrative than an *Attack* event (where a character is attacked and infected by a zombie). The same idea is valid to the locations where the events happen, some places are more important than others. The story author assigns weights to the events and locations. These assignments can be done by a single numerical value or a conditional expression (*e.g.* a *Go* event may have its weight increased if certain specific events occur at time t_i represented by panel P_i). Therefore the weights are calculated by a function that depends on P_i. Weights are also calculated for each row and, finally, for the whole page. We propose the following equations to calculate the weights of a panel P_i, a row R_k, and a page F_j:

$$P_i^{weight} = L_i^{weight}(P_i) + \sum_{j=1}^{NE} e_{i,j}^{weight}(P_i)$$

$$R_k^{weight} = \sum_{j=1}^{NK} P_j^{weight} , P_j \subseteq R_k$$

$$R_k^{weight} \leq \beta$$

$$F_j^{weight} = \sum_{k=1}^{NR} R_k^{weight} , NR \leq \gamma$$

where $L_i^{weight}(P_i)$ is a function that returns the weight of the location $L_i \subset P_i$; $e_{i,j}^{weight}(P_i)$ is a function that returns the weight of the event $e_{i,j} \in E_i, E_i \subset P_i$; NE is the number of events in the panel P_i; NK is the number of panels in a row R_k; NR is the number of rows in a page; β is the maximum value allowed for a row; and γ is the maximum number of rows allowed in a page.

The algorithm that calculates the size of the panels and the layout of the pages starts by iterating through the panels and assigning them to a page and a row according to their chronological order. When the weight of a row (sum of the row panels' weights) reaches β (maximum weight allowed to a row), the panels begin to be assigned to next row. When the number of rows reaches the maximum number of rows per page (γ), the panels begin to be assigned to the first row of the next page. The algorithm ends when all panels are assigned to a page and a row. We must notice that the parameters β and γ determine the general aspect of the comic book page. In our prototype we assume $\beta=6$, and $\gamma=3$.

In the next step, the actual size of each panel is calculated according to its weight and position in the page. The width d_i of a panel P_i in a row R_k and the height h_i of a row R_k in a page are given by:

$$d_i(P_i, R_k) = \left(\frac{P_i^{weight}}{R_k^{weight}} \right) \times D - gutter, \ P_i \subseteq R_k$$

$$h_k(R_k, F_j) = \left(\frac{R_k^{weight}}{F_j^{weight}} \right) \times H - gutter$$

where D is the horizontal size of the page and H is the vertical size of the page in pixels, and *gutter* is the space between panels (Figure 3a). Figure 3b illustrates the process of the panel definition phase. First, the story events {A,B,C,G,I,J,M,N,Q} are grouped in panels {P_1, P_2, ..., P_6} and their respective weights are calculated. Then, the panels are chronologically assigned to their corresponding rows {R_1, R_2, R_3} and pages {F_1}, considering the maximum weight supported by a row $\beta=6$. The weights of the rows and pages are also calculated. Finally, the actual size of the panels is calculated and the layout of the page is defined. In this example, the page size is D = 800 and H = 1000 pixels, the width of the panel P_1 is $d_1(P_1, R_1) = 800 \times 3/5 = 480$ and its height is $h_1(R_1, F_1) = 1000 \times 5/16 = 312$ without discounting the gutters.,

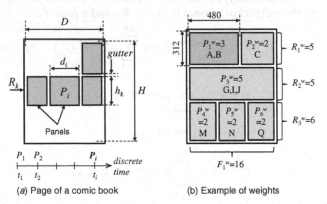

(a) Page of a comic book   (b) Example of weights

Fig. 3. (a) Elements of a comic book page of size $D \times H$, where the panel P_i is within row R_k and has a size of $d_i \times h_k$. (b) Example where the story events {A,B,C,G,I,J,M,N,Q} are grouped in panels {P1,...,P6} and row weights R_k^w are calculated. The subscript w stands for *weight*.

6.2   Panel Compositing

Panels can be composed of four types of objects: background layers, characters, interactive objects, and word balloons.

Background layers are a representation of the environment where the events occur. Every available location of the story context is associated with a set of static or dynamic image layers used to create the scenarios of the story. Each scenario has a set of waypoints indicating the available positions where characters and other objects can be placed during the panel compositing process. Each waypoint includes additional information about the size and angle of the character occupying that position.

Panels are composed according to the story events that must be represented on each panel. Characters participating in the events are placed on the available waypoints of the scenario using the spatial information provided by those waypoints. The characters are composed of a set of behaviors representing the actions that they can perform during the story. Each behavior comprises a set of static images representing the action from 6 different angles. During the compositing process, the behavior is selected according to the action performed by the character, and the angle is defined by its current waypoint and action.

Interactive objects allow users to interact with the narrative by changing the content of the panels, and consequently, altering the logical context of the story. Such interventions may force the characters to take other actions and change the course of the narrative. The story author defines the interactive objects and associates them with the scenarios. Each object is composed of two images: one representing the object before user interaction, and other representing the object after its activation. During the compositing process, the objects are added to the panels as part of the scenarios.

Word balloons are the last objects to be incorporated into some panels. The correct placement of each word balloon is crucial to convey the story events without breaking the temporal continuity of the narrative. Comic writers have developed through the years some general rules on how to place word balloons in comic panels and keep the narrative content easily understandable. Based on the comic literature, we establish the following rules to adequately place a balloon B_i in its corresponding panel:

1. $B_i \cap B_n = \emptyset$: Balloons should not overlap each other.
2. $B_i \cap C_n = \emptyset$: Every balloon B_i should not overlap any of the characters C_n.
3. $B_i \cap O_n = \emptyset$: Every balloon B_i should not overlap any of the interactive objects O_n.
4. B_i must be placed according to its chronological and reading order.

In order to comply with these rules, we adopted a method for balloon placement based on the procedure presented by Chun et al. [25]. We divided our method in three steps: (1) region selection and occlusion detection; (2) reading order arrangement; and (3) balloon generation and placement. Figure 4 illustrates the proposed method for word balloon placement. First, for each speaking character (C_1 and C_2), four candidate regions (C_iR_1, C_iR_2, C_iR_3, and C_iR_4) are generated around the character's face for the placement of word balloons. The region of each word balloon is selected according to weights associated with the available candidate regions based on their importance for the layout of the panel. We consider, for example, a balloon placed in front of a speaking character to be better than one placed on its back, so candidate regions in front of the speaking character have a higher weight associated with them. If a region overlaps an occupied candidate region of another character that speaks first, the region is marked as unavailable (C_2R_1). The same happens when the candidate region overlaps another character or interactive object. In the second step, the selected regions are expanded (EC_1R_2, EC_2R_3) to allow the arrangement of the word balloons according to the reading order of comics, where word balloons must be placed in a left-right and top-down order. Finally, in step 3, the word balloons are generated and placed in their corresponding regions.

(Step 1) Region Selection and Occlusion Detection

(Step 2) Reading Order Arrangement   **(Step 3)** Balloon Generation and Placement

Fig. 4. Balloon placement process

After placing the characters, interactive objects and word balloons, the size of the image frame being generated is adjusted to match the actual size of its respective panel. Panels that don't include changes of the emotional state of the characters are framed so that all the characters, interactive objects and word balloons stay visible and centered in the panel. Panels that include modification of the emotional state of the characters are framed starting from the character's hips, which emphasizes the emotional expressions of the character's face.

7   User Interaction

The proposed method for user interaction is based on interactive objects. Through this device users are allowed to interact with the narrative by changing the content of the panels, and, consequently, altering the logical context of the story. Such interventions may force the characters to take other actions and change the course of the narrative.

Each interactive object includes a list of effects consisting of facts to be added or removed from the current state of the world when the object is activated. The story events generated by the planner are associated with a description of the current state of the world when the event occurred during the planning process. When an interactive object is activated by the user, the state of the world at that specific point of the narrative is modified according to the predefined effects of the activated object (*i.e.* facts are added or removed from the state).

To complement the world state modification operated by the user interaction, the system requests a new plot for the story planner, so as to create an alternative story that is consistent with the changes caused by the activation of the object. In this case, the modified state is sent to the planner as the initial state of the story. In the new plan, the previous events remain unaffected, whereas the effects of the user intervention are propagated to the next story events. Consequently, the comic panels are updated to reflect the new storyline.

In order to exemplify the user interaction process, let us consider the example illustrated in Figure 5. In this example, an antidote bottle is an interactive object that has the effect: ¬*at(antidote, hospital_room_1)*, where the negation symbol (¬) indicates a fact to be removed from the world state when the object is activated. In this case, the effect removes the fact that the antidote exists in hospital room number 1. The current state of the world during the event where the antidote bottle is visible (panel 3 on Figure 5a) is described by the following facts: {*healthy(anne)*, *healthy(john)*, *healthy(jimmy)*, *wasinfected(emma)*, **at(antidote, hospital_room_1)**, *at(jimmy, house)*, *at(emma, house)*, *at(anne, house)*, *at(john, hospital_room_1)*}. If the user touches the antidote bottle (Figure 5b), the antidote will be dropped on the table, and the effects of the interactive object will be applied. In particular, the fact *at(antidote, hospital_room_1)* is removed from the world state of the event where the interaction occurred. A new story plot is then requested to the story planner, where, as explained before, the modified world state is now the initial state for the plan. As a result, a new plot describing what happened next is generated and the comic panels are updated according to the new storyline (Figure 5c).

(a)   (b)   (c)

Fig. 5. User interaction

8   Application and Evaluation

The prototype application developed to test our system pertains to a zombie survival genre. It tells the story of a family that lives in a world dominated by a zombie plague. The main characters of the narrative are: the brave husband, Mr. John; his beautiful wife, Anne; and their children, Emma and Jimmy, who are always getting in trouble.

In the main storyline, one of the characters is attacked and infected by a zombie and the family tries to get an antidote to save the victim's life. The story takes place in three main locations: the family house, a dangerous park, and a hospital. Users can interact with the story through the following interactive objects: (1) house door - opening the door of the family house allows a zombie to enter in the house and possibly attack someone; (2) old trunk - opening an old trunk in the family house reveals a toy that can entertain the children; (3) zombie at the park - pushing a zombie in the park makes the zombie fall and die; (4) hospital main door - closing the main door of the hospital prevents the entrance/exit of the characters in/from the hospital through the main door, while opening the door allows their entrance/exit; (5) hospital back door - closing the main back door of the hospital prevents the entrance/exit of the characters in/from the hospital through the back door, while opening the door allows the entrance/exit; and (6) antidote bottle - pushing the antidote bottle makes it fall and spill the antidote. The interactive objects can have different effects in the story depending on which part of the narrative is occurring when they are activated.

The prototype application is able to generate a considerable number of diversified stories. In the more conventional stories, Emma is attacked by a zombie in the park and then saved by her father who finds an antidote in the hospital; in stories with a not so happy ending, John does not find the antidote and decides to kill his daughter in order to protect the others; and in stories with an even darker outcome, John gets stuck in the hospital and cannot return home with the antidote, the daughter turns into a zombie, kills the rest of the family, and John commits suicide in the hospital.

8.1   User Evaluation

In order to evaluate our system, we have conducted a user evaluation with 18 high school students, 15 male and 3 female, aged 16-17. Six of them had previous experiences with interactive storytelling systems. Twelve of them play video games at least weekly. Sixteen of them like comic books, of which four read comics at least weekly.

We asked participants to use both our interactive storytelling system (S) and the mobile interactive comic book *The Avengers: Iron Man - Mark VII* [34] (M) for Android (Figure 6). We aimed to compare the proposed system with the "state of the art" of interactivity in comics. In order to avoid the focus on the appealing art quality of Marvel's system, we asked participants to concentrate their attention mainly on the application flow, user interaction, and the way the story is presented. And to reduce learning effects, half of the participants used S first, and the other half used M first. On average, each session of S lasted 12.3 minutes ($\sigma=2.4$) and included 5.8 interactions ($\sigma=2.2$). In M, each session lasted 7.5 minutes ($\sigma=1.1$).

After using each version, the participants filled out a questionnaire with 25 questions derived from the IRIS Evaluation Toolkit [27][28]. We evaluated the system usability, the correspondence of system capabilities with user expectations (user satisfaction), the interaction effectiveness and the users' experience (curiosity, flow and enjoyment). Each statement was followed by a seven-point Likert scale ranging from "strongly disagree" (-3) through "neutral" (0) to "strongly agree" (+3). After having interacted with both systems, the participants were interviewed about their experience.

(a) Our Interactive Comics System   (b) The Avengers: Iron Man - Mark VII

Fig. 6. Visual comparison of the evaluated systems. Our system presents several panels on the screen (a), while Marvel's system presents only one panel per screen (b).

Figure 7 summarizes the results of the questionnaires. Our interactive comics system clearly obtained better results in the evaluated topics (system usability, interaction effectiveness, user satisfaction, and user experience). *Marvel's The Avengers: Iron Man - Mark VII* obtained very low interaction effectiveness, mainly because it has a linear storyline and user interactions don't have any real effect in the story plot. As far as the interviews are concerned, sixteen of the participants stated that they preferred our interactive comics system. They declared that the layout of our system is more similar to real comic books, and the possibility of changing the story is very attractive and innovative. According to them, Marvel's system is more similar to a game than to a comic book. Following are some quotes from users regarding their experience while using our system:

"The experience was amazing! It was really cool to see the panels and the story changing according to my actions." (P1)
"The ability to interfere in the story was very exciting. I felt very curious and interested in finding out everything that my actions could do, and what else might happen in the story." (P2)
"I really enjoyed the possibility of changing the story by touching the objects in the panels." (P3)

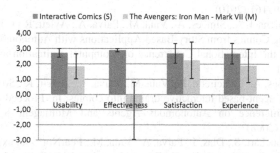

Fig. 7. Average and standard deviation of questionnaire topics for our *Interactive Comics* system and Marvel's *The Avengers: Iron Man - Mark VII* system

9 Conclusion

In this paper we presented a comics-based interactive storytelling system capable of generating dynamic interactive narratives in the format of comic books. The system combines planning techniques for the dynamic creation of interactive plots with intelligent algorithms for the automatic generation of comics. We believe that non-branching interactive comics can expand the boundaries of the classical style of comic books towards a new form of digital storytelling.

Although the preliminary results of the user study are still inconclusive due to the small number of participants, their positive feedback suggests the effectiveness of the proposed approach and indicates a promising direction for future research.

For the sake of conciseness, in this paper we decided to leave out details covered in our previous works on how to automatically define the type of shot, type of panel transitions, and scene illumination depending on the characters' emotions and the comic artist's style [32][33]. Those adaptations would substantially improve the capacity of the system in dealing with other artistic aspects of the generated comics, while keeping the signature of the human artist.

References

1. Kurlander, D., Skelly, T., Salesin, D.: Comic Chat. In: Proceedings of the 23rd Annual Conference on Computer Graphics and Interactive Techniques, pp. 225–236 (1996)
2. Sumi, Y., Sakamoto, R., Nakao, K., Mase, K.: ComicDiary: Representing individual experiences in a comics style. In: Borriello, G., Holmquist, L.E. (eds.) UbiComp 2002. LNCS, vol. 2498, pp. 16–32. Springer, Heidelberg (2002)
3. Shamir, A., Rubinstein, M., Levinboim, T.: Generating Comics from 3D Interactive Computer Graphics. IEEE Computer Graphics and Applications 26(3), 53–61 (2006)
4. Shuda, T., Thawonmas, R.: Frame Selection for Automatic Comic Generation from Game Log. In: Stevens, S.M., Saldamarco, S.J. (eds.) ICEC 2008. LNCS, vol. 5309, pp. 179–184. Springer, Heidelberg (2008)
5. Chan, C.J., Thawonmas, R., Chen, K.T.: Automatic Storytelling in Comics: A Case Study on World of Warcraft. In: Proceedings of the 27th International Conference on Human factors in Computing Systems (CHI 2009), pp. 3589–3594 (2009)
6. Pizzi, D., Lugrin, J., Whittaker, A., Cavazza, M.: Automatic Generation of Game Level Solutions as Storyboards. IEEE Transactions on Computational Intelligence and AI in Games 2(3), 149–161 (2010)
7. Alves, T., Mcmichael, A., Simões, A., Vala, M., Paiva, A., Aylett, R.: Comics2D: Describing and Creating Comics from Story-Based Applications with Autonomous Characters. In: Proceedings of the International Conference on Computer Animation and Social Agents, Belgium (2007)
8. Alves, T., Simões, A., Figueiredo, R., Vala, M., Paiva, A., Aylett, R.: So tell me what happened: Turning agent-based interactive drama into comics. In: Proceedings of the 7th International Conference on Autonomous Agents and Multiagent Systems, Portugal, pp. 1269–1272 (2008)
9. Aylett, R.S., Louchart, S., Dias, J., Paiva, A., Vala, M.: FearNot! - an experiment in emergent narrative. In: Panayiotopoulos, T., Gratch, J., Aylett, R.S., Ballin, D., Olivier, P., Rist, T. (eds.) IVA 2005. LNCS (LNAI), vol. 3661, pp. 305–316. Springer, Heidelberg (2005)

10. Spierling, U., Braun, N., Iurgel, I., Grasbon, D.: Setting the scene: playing digital director in interactive storytelling and creation. Computers & Graphics 26(1), 31–44 (2002)
11. Cavazza, M., Charles, F., Mead, S.: Character-based interactive storytelling. IEEE Intelligent Systems, Special issue AI in Interactive Entertainment 17(4), 17–24 (2002)
12. Mateas, M.: Interactive Drama, Art, and Artificial Intelligence. Ph.D. Thesis. School of Computer Science, Carnegie Mellon University, Pittsburgh, USA (2002)
13. Bonet, B., Geffner, H.: Planning as Heuristic Search. Artificial Intelligence Special Issue on Heuristic Search 129(1), 5–33 (2001)
14. Pearl, J.: Heuristics: Intelligent Search Strategies for Computer Problem Solving. Addison-Wesley (1985)
15. Ghallab, M., Nau, D., Traverso, P.: Automated Planning: Theory and Practice, 1st edn. Morgan Kaufmann Publishers, Amsterdam (2004)
16. Witty, S.: Illustrative Text: Transformed Words and the Language of Comics. In: International Conference of Arts and Humanities, Honolulu, Hawaii (2007)
17. McCloud, S.: Understanding Comics. Kitchen Sink Press, Northampton (1993)
18. Eisner, W.: Comics & Sequential Art. Poorhouse Press, Tamarac (1985)
19. Goodbrey, D.M.: PoCom-UK-001 (2003), http://e-merl.com/pocom.htm
20. Goodbrey, D. M.: The Archivist. Available at: http://e-merl.com/archivist/, 2010
21. McCloud, S.: Reinventing Comics: How Imagination and Technology are Revolutionizing an Art Form. William Morrow Paperbacks (2000)
22. Campbell, S.: Nawlz – Interactive Comic, http://www.nawlz.com/hq/about/
23. Andrews, D., Baber, C., Efremov, S., Komarov, M.: Creating and Using Interactive Narratives: Reading and Writing Branching Comics. In: Proceedings of the SIGCHI Conference on Human Factors in Computing Systems (CHI 2012), pp. 1703–1712 (2012)
24. Fikes, R., Nilsson, N.: STRIPS: A new approach to the application of theorem proving to problem solving. Artificial Intellligence 2, 189–208 (1971)
25. Chun, B.-K., Ryu, D.-S., Hwang, W.-I., Cho, H.-G.: An Automated Procedure for Word Balloon Placement in Cinema Comics. In: Bebis, G., et al. (eds.) ISVC 2006. LNCS, vol. 4292, pp. 576–585. Springer, Heidelberg (2006)
26. Riedl, M.O., Young, R.M.: From Linear Story Generation to Branching Story Graphs. IEEE Computer Graphics and Applications 26(3) (2006)
27. Klimmt, C., Roth, C., Vermeulen, I., Vorderer, P.: The Empirical Assessment of The User Experienc. In: Interactive Storytelling: Construct Validation Of Candidate Evaluation Measures. Technical Report, Integrating Research in Interactive Storytelling - IRIS (2010)
28. Roth, C., Vorderer, P., Klimmt, C.: The Motivational Appeal of Interactive Storytelling: Towards a Dimensional Model of the User Experience. In: Iurgel, I.A., Zagalo, N., Petta, P. (eds.) ICIDS 2009. LNCS, vol. 5915, pp. 38–43. Springer, Heidelberg (2009)
29. O'Neil, D.: The DC Comics Guide to Writing Comics, 1st edn. Watson-Guptill (2001)
30. Shiga, J., Plotkin, A.: Meanwhile, http://zarfhome.com/meanwhile
31. Fenty, S., Houp, T., Taylor, L.: Webcomics: The Influence and Continuation of the Comix Revolution. ImageTexT: Interdisciplinary Comics Studies, vol. 1. Univ. of Florida (2004)
32. Lima, E.S., Pozzer, C.T., Feijo, B., Ciarlini, A.E.M., Furtado, A.L.: Director of Photography and Music Director for Interactive Storytelling. In: IX Brazilian Symposium on Games and Digital Entertainment - SBGames 2010, Brazil, pp. 122–131 (2010)
33. Lima, E.S., Feijo, B., Furtado, A.L., Pozzer, C.T., Ciarlini, A.E.M.: Automatic Video Editing For Video-Based Interactive Storytelling. In: Proceedings of the 2012 IEEE International Conference on Multimedia and Expo (ICME 2012), Melbourne, pp. 806–811 (2012)
34. Loudcrow Interactive. Marvel's The Avengers: Iron Man – Mark VII, http://loudcrow.com/marvels-the-avengers-iron-man-mark-vii

The Art of Tug of War: Investigating the Influence of Remote Touch on Social Presence in a Distributed Rope Pulling Game

Thomas Beelen[1], Robert Blaauboer[1], Noraly Bovenmars[1], Bob Loos[1],
Lukas Zielonka[1], Robby van Delden[2], Gijs Huisman[2], and Dennis Reidsma[2]

[1] Creative Technology Bachelor, University of Twente
{t.h.j.beelen,r.j.blaauboer,n.m.bovenmars,
b.loos,l.zielonka}@student.utwente.nl
[2] Human Media Interaction Group, University of Twente
{r.w.vandelden,gijs.huisman,d.reidsma}@.utwente.nl

Abstract. In this paper we investigate whether remote touch in the form of force feedback from another player's actions can enhance feelings of social presence and enjoyment of a collaborative, spatially distributed rope pulling game. Dyads of players situated in different rooms were either given an 'elastic band' type force feedback, or were given force feedback of the other player's actions (i.e. remote touch). Results showed that feedback from another player's actions enhanced feelings of social presence but not enjoyment of the game.

Keywords: Remote touch, Social presence, Distributed play, Haptic feedback.

1 Introduction

The well-known game of tug of war, where two teams, each holding one end of a rope, attempt to pull the other team over a predesignated point, is a prime example of a game where players are physically engaged with their whole body. What is more, force feedback plays a crucial role. Here, the rope serves as a medium that delivers the force feedback generated by each of the teams over a short distance. In essence, we can speak of a spatially distributed game, where players are in physical contact with each other through the shared medium of the rope. Though the spatial distribution of a classic rope pulling game is limited by the length of the rope, efforts have been made to enlarge the spatial distribution of the rope pulling game through the use of Internet communication [1][2]. Harfield et al. [1] describe a distributed rope pulling system that was designed to enable children in distant locations to play a game of tug of war over the Internet. Similarly Christian et al. [2] present a tug of war game in which the player plays against a virtual character. The strength of the virtual character's pull is determined by the player's own strength.

In distributed rope pulling systems, remote touch [3], in the form of active force feedback about the actions of the other player, could play an important

D. Reidsma, H. Katayose, and A. Nijholt (Eds.): ACE 2013, LNCS 8253, pp. 246–257, 2013.

role in providing a sense of presence of the other player. Indeed, in presence research remote touch has been found to enhance task performance [4][5], and enhance feelings of presence [4][5][6][7]. However, empirical investigations into such effects of remote touch in entertainment systems are more scarce. In this paper, we investigate whether remote touch, rather than general haptic feedback, can enhance feelings of social presence and enjoyment in a collaborative game. To this end we developed a desktop-sized rope pulling installation that allows two players to play a collaborative game over the Internet. To investigate the effect of remote touch in this distributed rope pulling setup, we designed a study where dyads of players played a collaborative game in which they either received general elastic band type force feedback, or force feedback from the other player's actions (i.e. remote touch).

2 Related Work

2.1 Distributed Exertion Interfaces

In distributed entertainment, players play with each other at a distance with the use of interactive technologies, giving the feeling as if the players are co-located. These entertainment technologies can vary in their goal, style of play, and the used technology [8]. Work by Mueller et al. [9] [10][11] provides a number of examples of systems that enable players to engage in physically demanding exertion games with other players at a distance. Mueller et al. [9] created a competitive break-out-style game where players had to kick or throw a ball against a wall with a video projection of another player. Compared to an alternative played with a standard computer keyboard, the physical game showed an increase in social bonding and a perceived increase in quality of the sound and video. An example of a similar game is Mueller et al.'s [10] "Airhockey over a distance". Here, players play on an augmented airhockey table that incorporates a projection screen of a player in another location, and "puck-launchers" that can launch physical pucks, creating the illusion that the physical object crossed the space between the players. An informal evaluation indicated the potential for enhancing players' feelings of connectedness. In Mueller et al.'s [11] shadow boxing, two physically separated players each stand in front of a screen showing a projection of the other player's silhouette. Players can punch, kick or use their whole body to hit the projection of the other player and score points. The aim of the system was to demonstrate the possibilities of creating sports-like social games that can be played at a distance. In a similar fashion, Harfield et al. [1] developed a tug-of-war exertion game that can be played by physically separated players. The system is capable of measuring forces of up to 250 kg. Two teams of physically separated players are tasked with generating as much force as possible. The position of the rope is visualized on a screen and adjusted in accordance with the amount of force generated by each team. Though no formal evaluation was conducted the authors conjectured that the system helped young students collaborate with students from another continent. Finally, Yao et al. [12] describe a number of rope-based exertion games. For example, Multi-jump is a distributed rope jumping system where one player twirls a real rope. The motion of the rope is measured, and is displayed on a projection screen in front of another player in a distant location, who has to time his/her jumps in accordance with the visualization. Other games include a collaborative kite flying game, a competitive horse riding game, and a wood cutting game. In informal evaluations, the authors found that the rope-based games show the potential to stimulate social experiences, by providing users with the feeling of being engaged in a co-located activity.

Each of the systems described above incorporate some tangible element which allows players to physically interact with each other at a distance. However, none of these systems incorporate any haptic feedback technology. Research into haptics and telepresence shows benefits of using haptic feedback in interactions between users at a distance. The next section provides a brief overview of literature on haptics and remote touch.

2.2 Haptics and Remote Touch

Researchers have constructed numerous devices that allow users to touch each other at a distance. Such remote touch, or mediated social touch [3] devices are generally built with the idea that haptic feedback can be used for affective communication, and to enhance feelings of presence. Devices are for example used to communicate different types of touch through vibration patterns [13], or to provide intimate contact at a distance [14]. Another approach is to have users interact through a shared object [15]. This approach bears close resemblance to a distributed rope pulling system where active force feedback would provide users with the feeling that they are manipulating separate ends of the same rope.

Though effects of remote touch have been understudied compared to the number of devices that have been created [3], remote touch has been found to be experienced similar to real touch [16], to have effects on compliance to requests that are comparable to real touch [17], and to enable people to haptically communicate emotions at a distance [18][19].

In telepresence research the addition of remote touch in collaborative virtual environments has been found to have a number of beneficial effects on task performance and feelings of presence. For example Chellali et al. [4] demonstrated that in a collaborative biopsy simulator for medical students, a combination of visual and force feedback improved collaborative performance between students, and increased feelings of copresence. Sallnäs et al. [5] present a study in which two participants collaborated, using two force feedback joysticks, to manipulate an object in a virtual environment. Results showed that, compared to the condition where no haptic feedback about the other participant's actions was provided, force feedback improved task performance, perceived task performance, and perceived virtual presence in the collaborative virtual environment. Giannopoulos et al. [6] had two participants in different locations collaborate to complete a jigsaw puzzle. In one condition, turn-taking between participants occurred by 'nudging' the other participant using a force feedback joystick. In the other condition participants only had visual feedback of the other participant. Force feedback was found to increase feelings of social presence in the virtual environment. Finally, Sallnäs [7] conducted a study in which participants passed objects to each other in a virtual environment, using two force feedback joysticks. Compared to the condition where no force feedback was provided, force feedback improved perceived virtual presence, perceived social presence and perceived performance.

It is worthwhile to note here that in the studies described above, all of the tasks are collaborative. Research into social touch between co-located individuals suggests that this may be a very important contextual factor. Camps et al. [20] found that touch in competitive settings reduces helping behavior, whereas touch in collaborative settings enhances helping behavior. Therefore, beneficial effects of remote touch in a rope pulling game are most likely to occur in collaborative settings. This was considered in the design of our distributed rope pulling system described in the next section.

3   Rope Pulling System Design

3.1   First Prototype

The first prototype consists of two small rope pulling devices, with which users can manipulate a single paddle in a brick-breaker game. By pulling their respective ropes, one player can pull the paddle to the left and the other player can pull the paddle to the right. When one player pulls the rope, the other player will feel a resistance in their rope, equal to the amount of force exerted by the first player.

In this setup, a video call is running in the background of the brick-breaker game. The physical setup of the device contains a servo motor (Modelcraft rs-2), a load cell and an Arduino micro-controller. A rope, in this version a thin plastic wire, is connected to a wheel on the servo motor. The load cells measure the pulling force of each player and the servos move the ropes according to the force difference. The units are connected to different computers and communicate via the Internet in a server-client manner.

This test setup was used to compare the user experience of playing the brick-breaker game with the rope pulling system, to the user experience of playing the same game with a regular computer keyboard. In an informal evaluation with eight student participants playing with both versions, all indicated their preference for the rope pulling system. Although this prototype showed it is possible to play such a game over the Internet, the implemented server-client connection caused noticeable lag that lead to somewhat unstable gameplay. As the boxes were not yet attached to anything the user had to hold the box with one hand while pulling with the other, which did not represent a natural rope-pulling experience. Furthermore, the feeling of the plastic wire did not represent the actual tactile sense of a real rope. These issues were addressed in the design of the final prototype.

Fig. 1. The final pro-   **Fig. 2.** The test condition in use
totype

3.2 Final Prototype

Hardware. Based on the results of the informal evaluation, the final prototype contains two boxes that are fastened to a table. The plastic wire used in the first prototype was replaced with an actual rope. To rule out any potential lag issues, the Internet connection was removed, and instead, a direct serial connection on a single computer was used in the final prototype. To further enhance the experience, the servos were replaced with faster models (Blue Bird BMS-661DMG+HS) that also allowed for a higher maximum pull-force. Figure 1 depicts the final prototype.

Game. We designed a game in which players have to catch eggs falling from the top of the screen with a basket. The game was intentionally designed to be very minimalistic and only shows the basket, falling eggs and score. The basket also slants slightly when it is pulled to one side as to provide players with additional visual feedback about the movement of the basket.

4 User Studies

The final prototype was used in two studies. First, a pilot study that served to assess the level of enjoyment of the egg-catching game played with the rope pulling system. Second, the main study was conducted to investigate the effect of remote touch on feelings of social presence and enjoyment within the collaborative egg-catching game.

4.1 Pilot Study

During development of the final prototype, the rope pulling system was tested with a group of 16 children in the age range 7-11. We pilot tested the setup with children because we considered them to be a viable target group for a potential large scale distributed rope pulling installation (see also [1]). All children played the game once. Two rope pulling devices were placed next to each other on a table, and a computer monitor displayed the game.

After playing the game we ask each individual child three questions: 1) *"What did you like about the installation?"*, 2) *"What did you not like about the installation?"* and based on the again-again table method [21]: 3) *"If there was more time, would you like to play this game again?"* with three possible answers: *yes*, *maybe* or *no*. The children were also asked whether they had any comments on the game and system in general.

From this informal evaluation we gathered that the children generally liked the rope pulling system and egg-catching game. Eleven children had no negative comments, and all except one child liked at least one aspect of the game. The most frequent positive comment was the aspect of working together (mentioned 5 times). The social aspect of trust in the other player and arguing with the other player were also mentioned as positive. The act of physically pulling the rope was mentioned as a positive aspect of the system (4 times). Finally, the majority of children stated that they would have liked to play the game again (14 yes, 1 maybe, 1 not). Other observations included that some children tried to take the rope from the other player and play the game by themselves. Others tested the limits of the system and most were very curious about how the system worked.

The pilot study indicated that the system definitely has the potential to be a fun and interesting way for children to interact with each other in a physical game environment. After observing the children playing with the rope pulling system and hearing their comments we were confident that the system would be suitable for use in the main study.

4.2 Main Study

The main study was conducted in order to study the effect of remote touch, in the form of active force feedback about another player's actions, on feelings of social presence and enjoyment of a collaborative game. To this end we formulated two hypotheses, namely:

H1: Remote touch in the form of active force feedback about another player's actions will increase feelings of social presence in a collaborative game;

H2: Remote touch in the form of active force feedback about another player's actions will increase enjoyment of a collaborative game.

These hypotheses were tested in a study where dyads of players, situated in different rooms, played a variant of the collaborative egg-catching game using the rope pulling system. Players either received general force feedback or remote touch force feedback.

Participants. The participants were all voluntarily participating students or employees of a Dutch university. A total of 40 participants (20 dyads, 10 dyads in each condition) participated in the study. In total, 25 participants were male and 15 were female. The participants' age ranged from 18-62 years old (M = 22.9, SD = 8.54). We used adults for the main study because it was easier to get a larger sample size this way, and use more robust measures. As part of the demographics, we asked participants to indicate how well they knew each other on a 5-point Likert scale (1 = not at all, 5 = very well). Results showed that the majority of participants did not know each other (M = 1.13, SD = .52).

Materials. Each participant used a rope pulling device as depicted in Figure 1. Depending on the experimental condition, participants played a slightly different version of the egg-catching game, and received either general force feedback or remote touch force feedback. Both versions of the game were collaborative in nature. The control group played a version of the game in which the feedback was similar to an elastic band, pulling the basket to one side of the screen. We chose this type of feedback because it fit the game, providing natural feedback from the rope itself (i.e. stretching), and would provide force feedback similar to the remote touch condition. The side to which the basket was pulled was different for both players (i.e. one player's basket was automatically pulled to the left, and the other player's basket was automatically pulled to the right). Both players had a separate basket of a different color. To underline the collaborative nature of the game, the score in the top left corner of the screen was a cumulative score representing the total number of eggs caught by both players. The test group played a version of the game in which they received remote touch force feedback depending on the way the other player manipulated their rope. A single basket was visible on the screen. When one player would pull their rope, the basket would move to the left and when the other player pulled their rope the basket would move to the right. This created the illusion that both players manipulated one end of a continuous rope to which the basket would appear to be attached. The score represented the total amount of eggs caught in the basket. Figure 3 shows two screenshots comparing each version of the game. Participants could communicate with each other using a headset and through a video call displayed on a separate screen. Figure 2 depicts the setup used in the main study. As a measure of social presence we used the validated social presence questionnaire by Harms and Biocca [22]. We asked participants seven additional questions (Table 2).

Procedures. The study was conducted with dyads of participants. Participants were guided to two adjacent rooms. The first participant arrived a few minutes before the second so that participants could not meet prior to the study. Each room was equipped with an identical rope pulling setup (Figure 2). Participants signed an informed consent form, and were given a written explanation of the experimental procedures, an explanation of the rope pulling system, and an explanation of the egg-catching game. It was explained that the goal of the game was to collaborate with the other player in a distant location and catch as many eggs as possible, as indicated by the score (Figure 3). Players were

Fig. 3. Screenshot of the two different conditions of the game. The test condition is shown on the left, the control condition is shown on the right.

free to communicate as they liked using the headset and video call. Next, participants were asked to play the game for two minutes. After the play session, participants completed the social presence questionnaire, additional questions, and demographic questions on the computer that previously displayed the video call. Finally, participants were debriefed about the goals of the study.

Results. After correcting for the reversed questions, the items on the social presence scale showed acceptable to good internal-consistency (Cronbach's α), as can be seen in Table 1. Note, that two items were removed from the Perceived Emotional Interdependence scale.

To test the hypotheses, we used a one-tailed independent samples t-test. Scores on the six social presence items and the scores on the additional questions were compared between the control group and the test group. The results for the social presence items are shown in Table 1. As can be observed from Table 1 four of the six items of the social presence questionnaire showed a significant difference ($p < .05$) between the control group and the test group, and two items showed a marginally significant difference. The test group showed significantly higher scores than the control group for co-presence, perceived affective understanding, perceived emotional interdependence and perceived behavioral interdependence (all at $p < .05$). In addition, the test group showed higher scores for perceived message understanding and attention allocation, although the difference was only marginally significant (at $.05 < p < .1$). These findings support H1.

Table 1. Social presence questionnaire items. 5-point Likert scale, 1 = strongly disagree, 5 = strongly agree.

Item dimension	α	$M_{control}$	M_{test}	$t(38)$
Co-Presence	.68	3.88	4.18	-1.80[1]
Attentional Allocation	.78	3.10	3.46	-1.56[2]
Perceived Message Understanding	.79	3.73	4.00	-1.43[2]
Perceived Affective Understanding	.93	2.95	3.39	-1.76[1]
Perceived Emotional Interdependence	.84	2.70	3.23	-1.83[1]
Perceived Behavioral Interdependence	.79	3.34	3.75	-2.00[1]

[1] $p < .05$; [2] $.05 < p < .1$

Table 2. Results of additional questions (5-point Likert scale, 1 = strongly disagree, 5 = strongly agree)

Questions	$M_{control}$	M_{test}	$t(38)$
1) I enjoyed playing this game	4.25	4.55	-1.64^3
2) I thought playing this game was boring	1.85	1.55	1.21^3
3) While playing this game with this specific installation I felt more connected to the other player than when I'm playing with a traditional setup (keyboard, controller)	3.35	4.50	-4.83^1
4) I enjoyed playing this game with this specific installation more than when I'm playing with a traditional setup (keyboard, controller)	2.95	3.39	-1.76^2
5) While playing the game it felt like the feedback the system gave came from my opponent	3.95	4.60	-2.41^1
6) Playing the game felt similar to playing rope pulling in real life	1.95	2.70	-2.18^2
7) If there would be more time available, I would play this game again	3.60	3.75	$-.48^3$

^{1} $p < .001$; ^{2} $p < .05$; ^{3} *not significant*

Table 2 shows the seven additional questions about game experience. Four of the questions show a significant difference between the groups. For questions 3, 5 and 6 the test group showed significantly higher scores than the control group. Again, these findings support H1. Question 4, which was about enjoyment, showed a significant difference between the groups. Participants in the test group indicated more strongly than participants in the control group, that they enjoyed playing the game with the rope pulling interface more than they would have enjoyed playing the game with a more traditional controller. For the other three questions (questions 1, 2, and 7) about enjoyment, scores in the test group were higher than in the control group, but the difference was not significant. With this H2 is not supported.

5   Discussion and Future Work

The findings from the main study support H1. Indeed, results from the social presence questionnaire showed that the test group who received remote touch force feedback, had stronger feelings of social presence towards their game partner than participants in the control group who received the elastic band force feedback. This shows that the social aspect of the remote touch force feedback added to the feelings of social presence, more than did the general type of haptic feedback. This statement is supported by the additional questions in which participants in the test group indicated feeling a stronger connection to their game partner than did participants in the control group. In addition, participants in the test group indicated strongly that they had the feeling that the force feedback was generated by their partner. This indicates that the remote touch force feedback was indeed perceived as a form of physical contact between the two players. Furthermore, participants in the test group found the game to be more like real life rope pulling than participants in the control group. However, it is possible that the slight difference between both versions of the egg-catching game (i.e. participants in the test group actually pulled 'against' each other), explains this difference. This can be considered a limitation of the approach of our study. In our current approach we can not infer a difference between the role and effect of the remote touch force feedback and the effect of sharing control over a single entity in the game (i.e. the basket) versus only sharing an overall goal but with each player controlling an individual entity in the game (i.e. separate baskets, but a cumulative score). However, research into telepresence [4][5][6][7] shows clear effects of remote touch force feedback on feelings of social presence in different contexts with and without manipulation of a common object. Therefore it seems most likely that the effects found in this study are due to the differences in haptic feedback.

Overall the rope pulling system was considered to be very enjoyable by players in both groups. However, no significant differences were found for any of the additional questions dealing with player enjoyment. These findings do not support H2. Though for all the enjoyment questions (see Table 2 questions 1, 2, 4, and 7) the test group did have higher mean scores. A potential explanation is that, although the remote touch did make the game more enjoyable, the base level of enjoyability was already high for both variations of the game, reducing potential differences on the 5-point Likert scale. It also has to be noted here that this is only a first time use measure. It would be interesting for future research to look at long term effects and different types of games.

The findings from our study have a number of implications for research, as well as the entertainment industry. Our findings support the notion that adding remote touch haptic feedback, in our case force feedback, can add to a player's feelings of social presence of another player more so than general haptic feedback. The inclusion of remote touch haptic feedback into games and game controllers might be a fruitful direction for providing entertaining, social experiences. Exertion type games, played at a distance, might benefit from remote touch in that it could provide additional realism (i.e. the physical aspect of playing sports together). Moreover, a full-scale installation, that would ideally feature high torque motors that could handle multiple children pulling at a larger rope, would seem a viable approach to connecting children with their peers across cities, countries and continents.

6   Conclusions

In this paper we investigated whether remote touch in the form of force feedback from another player's actions could enhance feelings of social presence and enjoyment of a collaborative distributed rope pulling game. To this end, in an iterative fashion, we designed, created and tested a desktop-sized distributed rope pulling game. We created two variations of a collaborative egg-catching game where players had to catch eggs falling from the top of the screen to increase their cumulative score. In one version of the game players each had an individual basket to catch eggs and received elastic band force feedback, while in the other version players controlled a shared basket and received remote touch force feedback of the other player's actions. The main study with 40 participants playing the game in dyads showed that players in the remote touch condition, had significantly stronger feelings of social presence towards the other player, than did players in the control condition. Players in both groups found the game to be very entertaining, but this was slightly more so the case for players in the remote touch group. However, ratings for enjoyment did not differ significantly between the remote touch and control groups.

Overall, our results point to the importance of remote touch haptic feedback for enhancing feelings of social presence in collaborative games.

Acknowledgements. This publication was supported by the Dutch national program COMMIT.

References

1. Harfield, A., Jormanainen, I., Shujau, H.: First steps in distributed tangible technologies: a virtual tug of war. In: Proceedings of the 8th International Conference on Interaction Design and Children, IDC 2009, pp. 178–181. ACM (2009)
2. Christian, V., Smetschka, J., Pötzelberger, W., Lindinger, C., Praxmarer, R., Stadler, W.: Ars Electronica Futurelab Tug of War,
   http://www.aec.at/futurelab/en/referenzen/alle-jahre/2000/tug-of-war/
   (June 6, 2013) (retrieved)
3. Haans, A., IJsselsteijn, W.: Mediated social touch: a review of current research and future directions. Virtual Reality 9(2-3), 149–159 (2006)
4. Chellali, A., Dumas, C., Milleville-Pennel, I.: Influences of haptic communication on a shared manual task. Interacting with Computers 23(4), 317–328 (2011)
5. Sallnäs, E.L., Rassmus-Gröhn, K., Sjöström, C.: Supporting presence in collaborative environments by haptic force feedback. ACM Trans. Comput.-Hum. Interact. 7(4), 461–476 (2000)
6. Giannopoulos, E., Eslava, V., Oyarzabal, M., Hierro, T., González, L., Ferre, M., Slater, M.: The effect of haptic feedback on basic social interaction within shared virtual environments. In: Ferre, M. (ed.) EuroHaptics 2008. LNCS, vol. 5024, pp. 301–307. Springer, Heidelberg (2008)
7. Sallnäs, E.-L.: Haptic feedback increases perceived social presence. In: Kappers, A.M.L., van Erp, J.B.F., Bergmann Tiest, W.M., van der Helm, F.C.T. (eds.) EuroHaptics 2010, Part II. LNCS, vol. 6192, pp. 178–185. Springer, Heidelberg (2010)
8. Moreno, A., van Delden, R., Poppe, R., Reidsma, D.: Socially Aware Interactive Playgrounds. IEEE Pervasive Computing 12(3), 40–47 (2013)
9. Mueller, F.F., Agamanolis, S., Picard, R.: Exertion interfaces: sports over a distance for social bonding and fun. In: Proceedings of the SIGCHI Conference on Human Factors in Computing Systems, CHI 2003, pp. 561–568. ACM (2003)

10. Mueller, F.F., Cole, L., O'Brien, S., Walmink, W.: Airhockey over a distance: a networked physical game to support social interactions. In: Proceedings of the 2006 ACM SIGCHI International Conference on Advances in Computer Entertainment Technology, ACE 2006. ACM (2006)

11. Mueller, F.F., Agamanolis, S., Gibbs, M.R., Vetere, F.: Remote impact: shadowboxing over a distance. In: CHI 2008 Extended Abstracts on Human Factors in Computing Systems, CHI EA 2008, pp. 2291–2296. ACM (2008)

12. Yao, L., Dasgupta, S., Cheng, N., Spingarn-Koff, J., Rudakevych, O., Ishii, H.: Rope revolution: tangible and gestural rope interface for collaborative play. In: Proceedings of the 8th International Conference on Advances in Computer Entertainment Technology, ACE 2011, pp. 11:1–11:8. ACM (2011)

13. Huisman, G., Darriba Frederiks, A., Van Dijk, E., Heylen, D., Kröse, B.: The TaSST: Tactile Sleeve for Social Touch. In: Proceedings of the IEEE World Haptics Conference 2013, WHC 2013, pp. 211–216. IEEE (2013)

14. Park, Y.W., Nam, T.J.: Poke: a new way of sharing emotional touches during phone conversations. In: CHI 2013 Extended Abstracts on Human Factors in Computing Systems, CHI EA 2013, pp. 2859–2860. ACM (2013)

15. Brave, S., Dahley, A.: intouch: a medium for haptic interpersonal communication. In: CHI 1997 Extended Abstracts on Human Factors in Computing Systems , CHI EA 1997, pp. 363–364. ACM (1997)

16. Haans, A., de Nood, C., IJsselsteijn, W.A.: Investigating response similarities between real and mediated social touch: a first test. In: CHI 2007 Extended Abstracts on Human Factors in Computing Systems , EA 2007, pp. 2405–2410. ACM (2007)

17. Haans, A., IJsselsteijn, W.A.: The Virtual Midas Touch: Helping Behavior After a Mediated Social Touch. IEEE Transactions on Haptics 2(3), 136–140 (2009)

18. Bailenson, J., Yee, N., Brave, S., Merget, D., Koslow, D.: Virtual interpersonal touch: Expressing and recognizing emotions through haptic devices. Human-Computer Interaction 22(3), 325–353 (2007)

19. Huisman, G., Darriba Frederiks, A.: Towards tactile expressions of emotion through mediated touch. In: CHI 2013 Extended Abstracts on Human Factors in Computing Systems , CHI EA 2013, pp. 1575–1580. ACM (2013)

20. Camps, J., Tuteleers, C., Stouten, J., Nelissen, J.: A situational touch: How touch affects people's decision behavior. Social Influence 8(4), 237–250 (2013)

21. Read, J.C., MacFarlane, S.: Using the fun toolkit and other survey methods to gather opinions in child computer interaction. In: Proceedings of the 2006 Conference on Interaction Design and Children, IDC 2006, pp. 81–88. ACM (2006)

22. Harms, C., Biocca, F.: Internal consistency and reliability of the networked minds measure of social presence. In: Alcaniz, M., Rey, B. (eds.) Proceedings of the 7th Annual International Workshop on Presence (2004)

Singing Like a Tenor without a Real Voice

Jochen Feitsch, Marco Strobel, and Christian Geiger

University of Applied Sciences Düsseldorf, Department of Media, Germany
{jochen.feitsch,marco.strobel,geiger}@fh-duesseldorf.de

Abstract. We describe a multimedia installation that provides users with the experience to sing like a tenor from the early 20th century. The user defines vowels with her mouth but does not produce sound. The mouth shape is recognized and tracked by a depth-sensing camera and synthesized using a dedicated sound analysis using formants. Arm gestures are recognized and used to determine pitch and volume of an artificially generated voice. This synthesized voice is additionally modified by acoustic filters to sound like a singing voice from an old gramophone. The installation allows to scan the user's face and to create an individual 3D model of a tenor character that is used to visualize the user performance.

1 Introduction

The purpose of this project is to develop a system that allows users to act like a tenor by moving their arms and lips but without real singing. Shaping vowels with her mouth and getting corresponding multimodal feedback creates a believable user experience. It is difficult to synthesize the human voice based on purely visual analysis of the mouth's shape. A possible solution is to restrict the recognition and synthesis to trackable vowels and use additional cues like arm gestures for other vowels and to generate pitch and volume of the singing voice.

The origin of music, and thus singing as part of it, has been researched for a long time. Charles Darwin advanced the theory that the human antecessors learned musical notes and rhythms to charm the other sex. According to evolutionary biologist Geoffrey Miller, music and dancing emerged from rituals symbolizing combat and hunting [6]. A different approach arose from the observation that every human culture has lullabies used by mothers to calm their children. Due to anthropologist Dean Falk singing provided sort of a remote maintenance for the helpless baby, as long as the mother stayed within hearing distance [3]. Singing apparently had an important impact in human evolution and cultural development. Nevertheless, nowadays there is a strong tendency towards consumption of externally generated music and few people are able to really experience the positive feeling of their own successful singing voice production. This is the motivation of the project presented in this paper: to provide users with a believable user experience of performing an aria. Although we know that it is not possible to exactly simulate the performance of a professional opera singer we aim to create an entertaining user experience with our work.

D. Reidsma, H. Katayose, and A. Nijholt (Eds.): ACE 2013, LNCS 8253, pp. 258–269, 2013.
© Springer International Publishing Switzerland 2013

Fig. 1. System prototype

2   Related Work

Several projects studied the synthesis of sound with the mouth or with gestures.
De Silva et al present a face tracking mouth controller [11]. The application
example focused on a bioacoustics model of an avian syrinx that is simulated
by a computer and controlled with this interface. The image-based recognition
tracks the user's nostrils and mouth shape and maps this to parameters of a
syrinx's model. This model is used to generate sound. At NIME 2003 Lyons
et al presented a vision-based mouth interface that used facial action to control
musical sound. A head-worn camera tracks mouth height, width and aspect ratio.
These parameters are processed and used to control guitar effects, a keyboard
and look sequences [5]. Closely related to our approach is the "Artificial Singing"
project, a device that controls a singing synthesizer with mouth movements
that are tracked by a web camera. The user's mouth is tracked and recognized
mouth parameters like width, height, opening, rounding, etc. are mapped to a
synthesizers parameters like pitch, loudness, vibrato, etc [4]. Recently, Cheng
and Huang published an advanced mouth tracking approach that combines real-
time mouth tracking and 3D reconstruction [2]. The synthesis of singing is an

ambitious area of research with a long tradition and the human singing voice is a most complex instrument to be synthesized. A good overview is presented in [10], [12]. The creation and control of a 3D avatar has also been discussed in a number of projects. FaceGen (www.facegen.com) is a prominent base technology used in many AAA game productions. Many musical interfaces apply RGB-D cameras like Kinect for controlling sound synthesis (e.g., [7]) and we also chose this device for our purposes. While most projects focus on either body tracking or facial tracking, we combine both tracking methods to give the user a better overall experience. The body tracking used to control the movement of a virtual tenor character and aims at giving the user the impression of "being" that character. Thus, body movement is an essential part of our performance and also used for sound synthesis by controlling pitch and volume. Mouth gestures are used to control the sound synthesis by simply shaping the desired vowel with the user's mouth.

3   System Overview

The installation consists of a 3x3 video wall with 46" monitors, one Microsoft Kinect for full body skeleton tracking and a Primesense Carmine (or another Kinect) sensor for facial tracking. Figure 2 provides an overview of the system. The processing is done by two computers connected via Ethernet. One is responsible for operating the hardware system for facial tracking and the synthesizer modules while the other runs the main application with a software-based skeleton tracking system and the hardware sensors. The sensor for skeleton tracking is placed in about two to three meters distance to the user. The facial sensor is positioned and fixed hanging in the air in front of and above the user, looking at the user in about a 20°C angle. This minimizes the interference of the two depth cameras by reducing the overlapping region of both cameras. One computer processes all tracking data and uses this data also to fully animate a virtual 3D character on a theater stage. The character's head can be adapted towards the user's face by optionally using an integrated face generation module. To use this feature the user takes a picture of him/herself and the system creates a corresponding textured 3D face model. The user can also choose to modify several face model parameters to modify the final look of the 3D character. After this face generation step the user starts the performance mode and positions him/herself in front go the two depth cams (see fig 2). By moving the arms und shaping vowels with the mouth, the user can not only control the tenor's arms and facial expression, but also produce a singing voice and thus feel as being in an opera performance. The user's goal during the performance is to reproduce the original singing voice of an aria for a given background music as accurately as possible. This is similar to the well-known Karaoke music game but in our installation the user does not really sing with her own voice. With an increasing positive rating of the user's performance the 3D character's face morphs from the user's face to a virtual Enrico Caruso, a famous tenor from the 20th century.

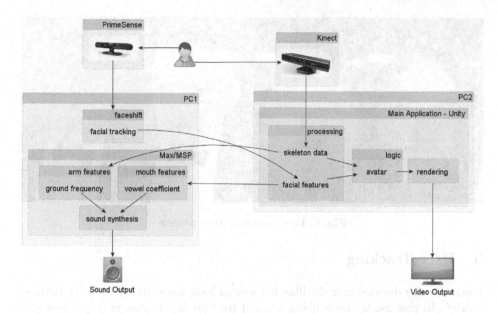

Fig. 2. System overview

4   Avatars Generation and Customization

To provide users with an individual performance experience one of the features of this project is to create a user-defined 3D avatar with the user's face. This was realized by integrating the FaceGen SDK (www.facegen.com) for the Unity3D Engine. To use this feature the application switches to "avatar customization" mode (3). The user takes a two-dimensional picture of his/her face using an HD camera. In a sequent step this image is mapped as texture on the user is represented with her image and asked to place eleven fiducial markers on the photograph to identify the facial structure. Attempts to automate this last step have failed to provide an acceptable result compared to manually set the markers (see fig 3, pic 2). After the last marker is set manually and the user finishes the manual mapping step the system will calculate a corresponding 3D mesh representation of the user's face in texture and shape. This model is used to create the user-defined tenor character (see fig 3, pic 3).

Once this process is completed the user has a number of options to further modify the avatar using a simple user interface with virtual sliders to adjust different facial parameters. These options include to make the avatar look older or younger, more male or female or to mix up racial features making the avatar look more afro-american, eastern asian, southern asian or european (see fig 3, pic 4). It may also be possible to modify the facial structure towards a more (or lesser) asymmetric face model or to modify characteristic face features from a "generic look"-level to a "caricature"-level.

Fig. 3. Face customization process

5   User Tracking

Once the user decided that she likes her avatar look she switches to "performance mode". In this mode she is being tracked by two depth sensors (e.g. Microsoft Kinect) for full body skeleton tracking for facial motion tracking. The tracking quality of two sensors decreases significantly if the sensors are positioned with a larger the overlap of the camera's structured infra-red pattern. This problem was solved by shielding the field of view of both sensors from each other as well as possible by having the facial tracker hang in the air and only aim at the face while the full body tracker is further away capturing the full picture. In addition to solve the last bit of interference the "Shake'n'Sense" [1] approach was applied. We attached a small vibrating servo motor to one Kinect sensor and introduces artificial motion blur through vibration and eliminates crosstalk.

5.1   Full Body Tracking

The full body skeleton tracking takes all the provided joint data from the Kinect and maps it to the avatar's skeleton, either with full body tracking enabled or only upper body tracking. In addition to this hand, elbow and shoulder joints are processed to control the volume and pitch parameters of the generated singing voice. The joints' position values are used to calculate the arm stretch by dividing the shoulder-to-hand length (current stretch) to the sum of shoulder-to-elbow and elbow-to-hand length (maximum stretch), providing a normalized volume range from approximately 0 (no stretch) to 1 (full stretch). Furthermore, the height value of the shoulder's position (y-axis) is subtracted from the height value of the hand's position and this sum is divided by the maximum arm stretch to get a normalized range of approximately -1 (lowest height value of the hand) to 1 (highest possible height) for the pitch value. These calculations are done separately for each side of the body and the largest value is selected.

5.2   Facial Tracking

The current prototype of our facial motion tracking system utilizes faceshift (http://www.faceshift.com), a software originally used for marker-less facial motion capturing and 3D character face animation. Previous prototypes used a 2D face tracking using OpenCV and the face tracking provided by the Microsofts Kinect SDK 1.5+ but were too inaccurate for our purposes. The integration of faceshift resulted in a much better performance. To get reliable data from the faceshift tracking module the user has to create a profile that is efficiently used during the performance. This profile has to be created in the software's training mode by capturing a few default facial expressions in order to create a suitable 3D representation of the user's facial structure. Although an existing profile can be used for new user's the tracking performance may be less accurate without an individual profile.

Fig. 4. Training of a user-specific profile for face tracking using face shift

After the calibration step is completed the user proceeds to "performance mode". If the user's face is recognized in this mode the camera image, the corresponding 3D representation and all the facial parameters are captured and tracked. During this mode a network server provides a streaming service for clients that can connect via the network. The sound synthesis module described in section 6 connects to this service, streams the tracking data from a custom protocol consisting of head pose information, blend shapes (also called coefficients), eye gaze and additional manually set virtual markers. The coefficients and marker positions are sent directly to the audio synthesizer where they are processed for sound generation. Furthermore the head pose, blend shapes and eye gaze are used to animate the avatar's facial features in real time. The head pose is used to rotate the neck bone and the eye gaze to rotate the specific eyes while the blend shapes are used to change the look of the avatar's face using the morph capabilities of the FaceGen SDK. To make this work correctly with our avatar customization we adjusted our tenor model to work well with both the facial tracking data from faceshift and the fitting and morphing system of FaceGen. This was done by adjusting the basic face shape to the base model used by FaceGen, creating custom blend shapes that mimic the blend shapes of faceshift and finally converting this into a suitable model base. To give the user feedback

Fig. 5. Facial animation shots of vowel synthesis

on the quality of her performance we've also created functionality to morph between the user's customized 3D head and a 3D head created from a real opera
singer's photograph (e.g. Enrico Caruso). The better she performs singing an
pre-selected song like "Ave Maria" the more she will turn into a virtual tenor
character like Caruso. This is done using the same base structure for both heads
and simply interpolating between the 3D mesh data of the two models.

Fig. 6. Morphing between custom user head and Caruso

To make it easier to calibrate the user's body and face gestures we developed a
small Android app that functions as a control panel for the different calibration
modules. This makes it possible to send networked commands to start or stop
tracking, calibrate the neutral position and angle and whether to treat the head
position relative or absolute simply from or nearby the user's place on the stage
and not directly in front of the laptops.

6 Sound Synthesis

The sound synthesis of this work is based on formants which we introduce in this section.

6.1 Preface

The analysis technique used for transforming signals from the time domain to the frequency domain to generate the illustrations for this paper is somewhat inaccurate. This is due to the fact, that most illustrations are snapshots taken while performing with the installation, and thus the transformations had to be operated in real time. A sample is shown in Fig. 7 b): only the peaks of the "hills" represent contained sine waves, the remainder is to be seen as "overshoot". In Fig. 7 a) the corresponding correct analysis is shown schematically. Only contained frequencies display a bar in the graph. Both figures represent an analysis of the same signal and are to been seen equal in this paper.

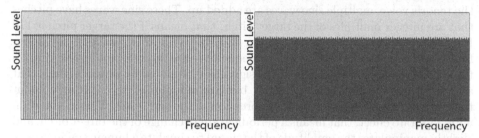

Fig. 7. Fundamental frequency 110Hz a) schematic, b) perfomance snapshot

6.2 Formants

A formant is a concentration of acoustical energy in a specific frequency range, that means these frequency ranges are emphasized in relation to other frequency ranges. The middle of this frequency range contains the most energy, the frequencies to both sides have gradually decreasing energy levels. Talking about a formant at 730 Hz refers to the formant with the mid-frequency of 730 Hz. Fig. 8 displays a signal in the frequency domain that features three formants, 8 a) serves for better understanding of the allocation of the frequencies. The middle of these formants is marked with the blue arrows (in this case at 730 Hz, 1090 Hz and 2440 Hz). The signal is based on the signal shown in Fig. 7. The relevant filters used to generate the formants are outlined by the colored curves.

Formants are an essential part of the characteristic sound of an instrument (there are other factors as well). Even though two sounds might have the same fundamental frequency, they can sound differently. If a piano and a guitar play the same note, they are still clearly distinguishable. In this sense, the human voice is an instrument as well, and its different vowels can be distinguished because of their different formants.

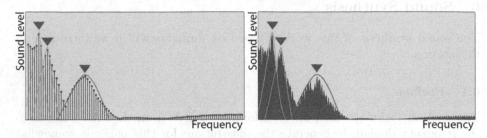

Fig. 8. Vowel "A" formants at 110Hz a) schematic, b) perfomance snapshot

6.3   Synthesis

The tenor's voice is synthesized by using a vowel synthesis via formants. Max/MSP is used for audio processing and calculations, while data is sent as OSC packages from one program to another. The user determines the target fundamental pitch of the singing with her arms (see chapter Mapping). Based on the target pitch of the tenor's voice, multiple sine waves are added up. These sine waves have pitches that are integer multiples of the target pitch, that means if the target pitch is 110 Hz, the added sine waves are at 220 Hz, 330 Hz etc. In this synthesis, the upper limit was defined at 12 kHz, as higher frequencies are not relevant for the characteristics of the human voice. Next, the signal is modulated by several signals that also depend on the fundamental pitch, but are randomized to a certain amount to create a preferably non-artificial impression of the end result. This modulation adds a vibrato effect, that means a periodical small change of the target pitch, and slightly manipulates the amplitude of the signal to simulate a human singing voice, assuming that a singer can't produce a perfectly constant tone. Three band pass filters are used to create the target vowel's characteristic formants. These formants have the property of being more or less independent of the generated fundamental pitch. Fig. 7 shows the unfiltered signal with a fundamental frequency of 110 Hz and it's harmonic frequencies at 220 Hz, 330 Hz etc. In Fig. 8 this signal was filtered by three bandpass filters (outlined by the colored curves) to "cut out" the characteristic formants and thus create the apparent envelope curve with three summits (in this example at 730 Hz, 1090 Hz and 2440 Hz marked by the blue arrows to form the vowel "A"). The example in Fig. 10 a) shows the result of the same process with a fundamental frequency of 220 Hz and it's harmonic frequencies at 440 Hz, 660 Hz etc. The resulting formants are the same as the one at a fundamental frequency of 110 Hz, so the resulting vowel is still "A". This shows that formants are more or less independent from the fundamental frequency. As an evaluation of our synthesized voice, we separated the vowel "A" from a recorded aria in Fig. 10 b). The real singing has three apparent formants at the beginning of the frequency spectrum that have similar middle frequencies to those that are created in our system. The difference in sound level and the other amplified regions form the singer's personal timbre. The selected formant frequencies were taken from [8]. Most other sources give only two formants, as two of them are sufficient for the perception of a vowel. However, a third formant turned out to be useful to make the result more human. The synthesis actually uses an additional fourth formant at 2,7 kHz. That formant is both independent of the fundamental frequency and the target vowel. It's called "singers' formant" and is only visible in the frequency spectrum of trained singers. This formant is essential when singing with an orchestra and allows professional singers to be heard without further amplification, as the peak frequency range of an orchestra is much lower than 2,7 kHz. After the formant filtering process, several additional filters are used to achieve a 20th century gramophone like sound. In a final step, vowel-dependent amplitude variations are reduced by normalizing and compressing the signal. Additionally, an optional reverb effect can be added to simulate the acoustic of an opera.

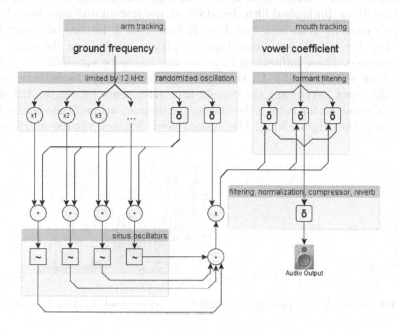

Fig. 9. Sound synthesis using Max/MSP

7 Mapping

The user controls pitch and volume of the synthesized singing voice with her arms. The volume is determined by the user's arm stretch and is directly mapped to the system's gain control. The arm-height is used to calculate the target pitch by using the change of arm-height over time. This method was selected to make it easier and more enjoyable to use the system (previous methods used fixed positions for determining the pitch). The simplest implementation uses only three commands: "no change", "change upwards" and "change downwards" (finer steps can be chosen to make playing more precisely, for example "big change upwards", "small change upwards" etc). If the melody's next note is above the current pitch, the user has to move her arms upward, if the next note is below, she has to move her arms downwards. The system then automatically chooses the right note to play the correct melody. If the user makes a "wrong" move, the system either stays at the currently sung pitch ("no change"), or uses a mapping-table to determine the next higher respectively next lower pitch. There are a total of 25 MIDI-pitches that can be sung, from MIDI-pitch 41 (≈ 87 Hz) to MIDI-pitch 65 (≈ 349 Hz). The actual singable pitches are limited by the song's current key (all keys need to be predefined for the whole song). The program triggers events in accordance to the song's beat to change the currently used mapping table. The basis of these mapping tables has always the keynote "C", that is transposed later, with a variety of scales: C-Major, C-Minor, C diminished and C augmented, as well with optionally added seventh, major seventh, sixth or diminished fifth. In addition, the system distinguishes whether the song's measure is in beat 1 or 4, or in beat 2 or 3. In case one, only pitch values from the current key's chord can be played, in case two the whole scale can be selected. These limitations help the user to create a melody that sounds always more or less suitable for the currently chosen song's background music, even if she is not performing the correct arm movements for singing the song's melody. This allows for more or less harmonic improvisation if the user does not want to sing the original song. The desired vowel is given via the user's mouth

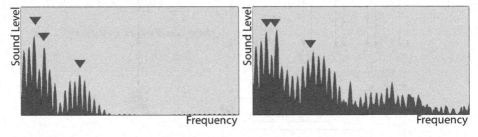

Fig. 10. Vowel "A" at approximately 220Hz a) synthesized, b) sung by real tenor

shape. 23 of the 46 parameters provided by the face tracking module are relevant for the area around the user's mouth. Therefore they are used as input nodes for a neural network trained to identify vowels by a given mouth shape. The neural network uses resilient back-propagation. This is a fast back-propagation algorithm that allows to train new data to the network in a matter of seconds [9]. The output of the neural network consists of 4 probability parameters, "Closed Mouth", "A" [aː], "E" [eː] and "O" [oː]. These four values are monitored, and the highest determines the current vowel, sending the frequency values to the representing formant filters. To give the user the opportunity of choosing another set of vowels "Ä [ɛː]", "I" [iː] and "U" [uː], the option to switch between the two sets is activated by moving the eyebrows up and down or by means of a dedicated hand / finger gesture.

8   Conclusion

The current prototype is functional, i.e., the individual components work but are still a bit limited concerning the tracking quality and the range of expressively synthesized vocals. The integration into a final system prototype is complete but we are still working on an expressive performance mode. Currently we use an old gramophone induced by an exciter to produce an enjoyable auditive experience for both the user and the audience. We also evaluate the combination of vibrational feedback and bone conduction headphones to enhance the user experience and support the immersion of the user during the performance. This should further increase the intended believability and enjoyment of being an opera tenor during a performance.

References

1. Butler, A., Izadi, S., Hilliges, O., Molyneaux, D., Hodges, S., Kim, D.: Shake'n'Sense: Reducing Interference for Overlapping Structured Light Depth Cameras. In: ACM SIGCHI Conference on Human Factors in Computing Systems (2012)
2. Cheng, J., Huang, P.: Real-Time Mouth Tracking and 3D reconstruction. In: Int. Conf. on Image and Signal Processing (2010)
3. Falk, D.: Finding our Tongues: Mothers, Infants, and the Origins of Language. Basic Books (2009)
4. Hapipis, A., Miranda, E.R.: Artificial Singing with a webcam mouth-controller. In: Int Conf. on Sound and Music Computing (2005)
5. Lyons, M., Haehnel, M., Tetsutani, N.: Designing, Playing, and Performing with a Vision-based Mouth Interface. In: Proc. of NIME 2003 (2003)
6. Miller, G.: The mating mind, how sexual choice shaped the evolution of human nature. Anchor (2001)
7. Odowichuk, G., Trail, S., Driessen, P., Nie, W., Page, W.: Sensor fusion: Towards a fully expressive 3D music control interface. In: Pacific Rim Conference on Communications, Computers and Signal Processing (2011)
8. Peterson, G.E., Barney, H.L.: Control methods used in a study of the vowels. J. of the Acoustical Society of America 24, 183 (1952)
9. Riedmiller, M., Braun, H.: Rprop - A Fast Adaptive Learning Algorithm. In: Proc. of the International Symposium on Computer and Information Science VII (1992)
10. Rodet, X.: Synthesis and Processing of the Singing Voice. In: 1st IEEE Workshop on Model Based Processing and Coding of Audio (2002)
11. de Silva, C., Smyth, T., Lyons, M.J.: A novel face-tracking mouth controller and its application to interacting with bioacoustic models. In: Proc. of NIME (2004)
12. Sundberg, J.: The KTH Synthesis of Singing. J. on Advances in Cognitive Psychology 2(2-3) (2006)

An Experimental Approach to Identifying Prominent Factors in Video Game Difficulty

James Fraser, Michael Katchabaw, and Robert E. Mercer

The University of Western Ontario, London, Ontario, Canada
{jfraser,katchab,mercer}@csd.uwo.ca

Abstract. This paper explores a full factorial analysis methodology to identify game factors with practical significance on the level of difficulty of a game. To evaluate this methodology, we designed an experimental testbed game, based on the classic game Pac-Man. Our experiment decomposes the evaluation of the level of difficulty of the game into a set of response variables, such as the score. Our offline experiment simulates the behaviour of Pac-Man and the ghosts to evaluate each game factor's impact on a set of response variables. Our analysis highlights factors that significantly contribute to the game play of individual players as well as to general player strategies. This offline evaluation provides a benefit to commercial games as a useful tool for performing tasks such as game balancing, level tuning and identifying playability and usability issues.

Keywords: Dynamic Difficulty, Game Balancing, Adaptive Game System.

1 Introduction

One of the keys to the recent and continued success of the game industry has been the ability to expand to new demographics of game players outside the normal user groups [2]. A large portion of the recent success can be attributed to a developmental shift in the way players interact with gaming systems, such as Nintendo Wii, PlayStation Move and Microsoft Kinect. As the demographics of game players expands, so too will the range of players abilities and entertainment needs. Players have varying skill levels in terms of characteristics such as reaction times, hand eye coordination, and tolerance for failure. The variation in players' abilities will increase the difficulty for game designers to sort players into the usual static and preset difficulty settings of easy, medium and hard. When the game's difficulty is not correctly matched to the player's ability, the player could become bored or frustrated with the game [2], which results in reduced play time or abandonment of the game. To overcome these problems, there is a growing need to more thoroughly understand game difficulty, especially the impact of various factors and design decisions on difficulty and outcomes.

To form this understanding, experimental methods are required to collect and analyze the necessary data in a rigorous fashion. This, unfortunately, is a daunting task for any game of reasonable size and complexity. Consequently,

D. Reidsma, H. Katayose, and A. Nijholt (Eds.): ACE 2013, LNCS 8253, pp. 270–283, 2013.
© Springer International Publishing Switzerland 2013

the goal of our current work is to formalize an approach to studying game difficulty, in particular identifying prominent factors and determining their impact on player experience. This approach has applications to offline analysis during production to support game balancing, level tuning, and issues with playability and usability. Online applications for adjusting adaptive game systems include determining suitable factors and the granularity of the adjustment to optimize the player's experience. In this paper, we present our approach, based on a full factorial analysis methodology, and demonstrate its usefulness through applying an experimental assessment to a variant of the classic game Pac-Man.

2   Related Work

Current research on adaptive gaming systems focused on performing dynamic difficulty via three broad areas of gameplay. The first method of adjustment alters characteristics of the player's avatar. Performing adjustments to the player's character can be the most intrusive method if incorrectly performed. As the player has a high level of involvement and an increasing emotional attachment to their character, they can be sensitive to modifications and less willing to accept changes [2]. If a player identifies that an adaptive difficulty system is controlling the pace of their game play, their sense of achievement for completing difficult tasks can be diminished or extinguished [5]. If the player begins to attribute the result of their game play to external factors, they can become extremely frustrated and can completely lose interest in participation [2].

Dynamically modifying the level layout or the placement of game items or level objectives is another method of performing adaptive difficulty. Researchers have dynamically created entire levels in [11,12] or dynamically repositioned items within the world [4]. One interesting criticism is that although the adaptive system can provide that desperately needed change that comes just in time to save the player, it reduces the player's ability to formulate a consistent strategy for a level. The dynamic aspect of item value and placement reduces the player's ability to accurately assess the risk to reward ratio in accomplishing a task.

The third and most prevalent method of adaptive games is to modify the attributes and behaviours of non-playable characters (NPC). NPCs are characters outside the player's control. The advantages of adapting the NPC is that NPC's attribute information is rarely visible and players expect the opponents to increase in difficulty throughout the game. Thus, the player is less likely to notice modifications to the difficulty of the game or feel cheated by the adaptive game system when changes occur. Modifying the decision process of the NPCs provides additional variation to the game play, which can be exciting and challenging in addition to providing a range of difficulty. Research for adapting NPCs' behaviour uses a variety of approaches from machine learning for interest heuristics and balanced games [1,14], to other methods of dynamic scripting behaviours [8,9].

Current research has treated these three methods in adaptive gaming as independent in identifying difficulty and adapting the game. As areas for adaptation are intertwined, it is important to understand their relationship to avoid unexpected emergent effects in the level of difficulty. Understanding the relationship between each of these adaptable areas, provides a greater flexibility in approaching the adaptive process. It allows the adaptive process to prioritize types of adjustments to avoid drawing attention to the adaptive system and minimize the risk in breaking the player's immersive state and level of believability in the game. The adaptive game system could avoid drawing attention to itself by making subtle adjustments to alter the NPC's behaviour during level play. Then, between levels, larger structural changes can be made to the level design that substitutes an equal level of challenge, so that the difficulty of individual NPCs can be reduced to their original values. It can also be beneficial to have multiple methods of adapting the game to add variety to the type of adjustment. Our experimental methodology allows the simultaneous evaluation of the three types of adjustments previously mentioned for adaptive gaming. It provides a consistent, rigorous method of comparing the effects of the modifications to game factors in each of these areas. Collecting data from a large number of games provides the potential to generalize how the changes impact specific strategies or particular player types.

Adaptive game research has focused on controlling a single response variable such as score or health to balance gameplay. However, a game with a balanced score or health might not produce an engaging or an immersive player state and such an adaptive system has no alternative avenues for adaptive adjustments. A single response variable might help balance the end result of the game, but it does not address the pace or progression of the game. Our research will evaluate a larger number of response variables, which provides greater expressive power in the methods of adapting the game and can provide a finer level of granularity in the selection of adjustments. By improving granularity, quantity and variety in the types of adjustments, our approach provides the adaptive system greater control over the pace and progression of the game.

3   Methodology for Game Difficulty Assessment

Our experimental methodology is designed with the objective of identifying significant game factors relating to the level of difficulty of the game. The design should be flexible and modular allowing game designers to quickly integrate this methodology in the early stages of the development process to reinforce design decisions or into the later stages as a tool for game balancing. To determine the full effect of a game factor and its significance on the response variables, we must view the effects in isolation, and in relation to other factors to discover emergent interactions. Different players will be affected by the game factors in different ways, thus we must explore each game factor's effect on a variety of player strategies. Using a variety of different player strategies increases the potential of representing a wider range of players types.

Our methodology for evaluating the significance of game factors on a set of response variables is as follows:

- Identify game factors to be modified during the experiment.
- Select a set of factor levels for each game factor.
- Identify metrics of performance goals.
- Simulate gameplay in an experimental testbed with factors at each factor level.
- Repeat the simulation to identify error rates.
- Collect the response variables related to performance goals.
- Perform the full factorial analysis, which calculates effect sizes and statistically significant terms
- Evaluate the quality of player models via the R-Sq values.
- Identify and evaluate results of significant factors on player strategies.

Our evaluation method for identifying factors with statistical significance effects on the response variables involves the use of a full 2^k factorial design. A full 2^k factorial analysis, contains k factors, each with 2 values or levels. A full factorial analysis calculates the effect sizes and statistical significance of each factor and for all possible combinations of the set of factors for each response variable. This information provides the magnitude and direction of the effect on a particular response variable. Although, this creates a large volume of terms and data to evaluate, in practice the game significance of many of these terms will be minimal and thus the amount of information stored in the adaptive game system can be greatly reduced.

4 Application of Our Approach

Pac Man is a classic 2D game, the object of the game is to navigate through a fully visible maze and collect all of the tokens. Ghosts attempt to eat Pac-Man when in predator mode, except for a short period of time after Pac-Man has collected a power-pellet. Pac-Man is awarded points during game play for collecting tokens, power-pellets, bonus fruit, eating ghosts or completing levels. To progress past a level, Pac-Man must collect all the tokens and power-pellets in the level. At regular intervals during game play, bonus fruit items will appear on screen.

Pac-Man is a common testbed in video gaming research and is an ideal context for our research objectives because the entire game is composed of a relatively small number of game elements. However, the small number of factors will not limit the players level of engagement, as Pac-Man can provide a unique game experience due to the emergent behaviour of the opponents.

4.1 Factor Selection

In the initial stage of the experiment, we refined the list of factors to be included for definition modeling by performing a 2^k exploratory analysis. The 2^k analysis, requires a high and low value for each factor.

4.1.1   Agent Factors

Agent factors directly relate to the attributes of Pac-Man or the ghosts' behavior. Each agent has 3 active states; fleeing when the agent is escaping predators, chasing when the agent is a predator and can see the prey, and wandering when an agent is unable to view any predators or prey. Ghosts can be in a fourth state of inactivity, which occurs when they have been killed and are returning to their spawn position on the board. The selected factors and their factor levels are: the number of steps in the flee and death state time (10, 20) and Manhattan distance of the vision range (5 or 10 squares)

4.1.2   Bonus Factors

The bonus fruit will be generated at regular intervals and placed in a random empty square. The three selected bonus fruit factors and their low and high factor level respectively are: the number of steps the bonus item is available for (10,20), the perceived value of the bonus item (75, 200) and the frequency in steps at which the bonus will be generated (50, 100). By increasing or decreasing the frequency of the fruit, we alter the highest possible score that a player can achieve during a single session. Thus, we controlled for this variable by separating results into two categories for each factor level. The bonus factors provide possible insight into the perceived level of difficulty by the player, since the choice to participate in bonus tasks could indicate that the player is ready for an adjustment in the level of challenge.

4.1.3   Pac-Man SSS-AB* Algorithm

The SSS-AB* is a special case of the minimax algorithm [6]. This algorithm represents a near-optimal player capable of surviving and obtaining higher scores. Our SSS-AB* algorithm will simulate paths associated with the current intersection point to the next intersection point. This restriction improves the computation time and has limited effect on the outcome because the search depth is partially controlled by the vision factor. Pac-Man's vision range may not allow the SSS-AB* algorithm to fully simulate all the results over the set of possible successor paths, in which case the score Pac-Man can achieve given a limited view will be returned.

4.1.4   Pac-Man Weight Heuristics (PW) Algorithm

The PW algorithm sums weighted heuristics calculated using information about Pac-Man's visible world and produces a score for each possible moves; the move with the highest score is selected. For each Pac-Man heuristic, the selected weight factor levels are 0.5 or 1.0. Pac-Man's heuristics are organized into to three categories: edible goals, avoiding ghosts and global positioning. All distance based heuristics use the Manhattan distance to the objective; objectives include the collection of objects such as: tokens, power-pellets, fruits and any edible ghosts. Pac-Man must avoid ghosts while playing the game, thus a distance and direction function are used for avoiding the ghosts. The two final heuristics are: one which keeps Pac-Man away from the centroid of the ghosts, and another which moves Pac-Man towards the centroid of the remaining items. These heuristics are modified versions of heuristics shown to be successful for improving Pac-Man's score in the work of other researchers [10,13].

4.1.5   Ghost Flocking Algorithm

The flocking algorithm is an emergent behavior algorithm, in which each member of the flock follows a set of simple rules based on the position of other visible flock members[7]. A flocking algorithm normalizes and sums the results of each of the governing rules, to decided on the best direction to move. The rules that govern our flocking algorithm are: separation, cohesion, alignment and hunger. The first three parameters place emphasis on an individual separating, moving toward and aligning direction with other members of the flock. The hunger rule places emphasis on the aggressiveness in chasing Pac-Man. For each of flocking rules, the factor levels are 0.5 or 1.0 for the weights of each rule.

4.1.6   Ghost Weight Heuristics (GW) Algorithm

The GW algorithm implements a strategy of weighted heuristics similar to the PW algorithm section. The heuristics selected are similar to those selected in the Pac-Man case; which include distance functions to objectives for protecting: tokens, power-pellets and bonus fruit. In addition, ghosts have heuristics objectives for moving towards Pac-Man, the end of Pac-Man's current path and toward and away from other ghosts. The factor levels values are 0.5 or 1.0 for the weights for each heuristic.

4.2   Performance Measures

The response variables selected for this experiment are the: 1: score (Sc), 2: number of steps (STP), 3: number of close calls (CC), 4: number of repeated steps (RSq), 5: number of fruits collected (FC), 5: number of tokens collected (TOK), 7: number of power-pellets collected (PP), 8: number of ghosts eaten (GE) and 9: the number of levels completed (LVL). Close calls occurs if a ghost comes within 2-squares of Pac-Man. Repeated step indicate Pac-Man returned to a square with no point value.

5   Conducting Experimentation

In each simulated game, Pac-Man has 3 lives and is unable to gain additional lives via points or bonus items. Due to the fact that our experiment continuously runs using the same level, if the player exceeded 350 steps, that particular life would be halted. This restriction helped normalize situations where Pac-Man was significantly better than the opponents or where Pac-Man is unable to complete the level but remains alive. Our experiment consists of four cases; one for the simulation of each of the algorithm pairs: SSS-AB* and flocking (SSS_FLOCK), SSS-AB* and GW (SSS_GW), PW and flocking (PW_FLOCK) and PW and GW algorithms (PW_GW). In our largest case, the PW_GW algorithm pair has

20 factors. The 2^k factor analysis of this case results in over a million simulations, which is then multiplied by 3 repetitions for over 3 million simulations. One of the key benefits of the full factorial analysis is that it is orthogonal, meaning the analysis can be divided and performed in a distributed method. Thus, we further separated the cases for the algorithm pairs into groups containing 10 factors, thus 1024 minimal runs. The decision to review groups of 10 factors was partially made because of the total number of factors for each algorithm, but it also minimized the intermediate file sizes and was computationally efficient. Furthermore, if cases in the analysis use the same number of factors, index information for the factorial analysis only needs to be calculated once.

6   Experimental Results

Presenting the massive volume of data collected and organized from the simulations would be verbose and would detract from the experiment goals of evaluating the application of our methodology to the domain of gaming and dynamic difficulty. Instead, we focus the discussion of our results on the main effects of selected cases from the experiments; in-depth results can be reviewed in [3]. For SSS_FLOCK, we selected the fruit frequency at a low level, as the two cases have nearly identical results. For the SSS_GW algorithm, we selected the fruit time at a high level value. For the PW_FLOCK and PW_GW algorithm, we selected the factor for avoiding the ghosts at a high level value, as it had the most positive influence on the response variables for PW algorithm.

6.1   Model Evaluation

The model evaluation indicates the percent of variation that our model was capable of explaining with the 127 highest sum of square terms. The 127 terms limitation comes from the commercial software Minitab; this evaluation method could indicate whether additional terms are required to improve the model's performance. Calculating the R-Squared (R-Sq) values provides two useful pieces of the information: it indicates the percentage of variance that our model explains and the model's accuracy in predicting other data points. This information can be used in adaptive systems to distinguish between response variables that are potentially less predictable or difficult to adapt for a particular player. The second part of the model evaluation investigates the consequences of the commercial term limitation, as not all 1024 terms could be included in the model; we calculated the lack-of-fit values for the 897 terms not included and whether their exclusion played a significant role in the results of the experiment.

The results in Table 1 identified that the most difficult and inconsistent response variables to predict and adapt for are collecting the fruit and the number of levels completed. The models for the number of close calls, steps and score showed higher levels of predictability among the response variable models and are potentially good candidates for the adjustment process. The lack-of-fit F-values ranges for the models are: SSS_FLOCK (0.16 - 0.38), PW_FLOCK (

Table 1. Model evaluation using the R-Sq (Adj) for each algorithm and all response variables

Response Variables	SSS_FLOCK R-Sq%	PW_FLOCK R-Sq%	SSS_GW R-Sq%	PW_GW R-Sq%
CC	83.1	70.6	63.7	69.5
FC	69.6	70.0	58.2	61.0
GE	80.4	71.0	69.3	72.8
LVL	79.5	65.1	60.4	58.1
PP	80.3	66.0	64.4	65.7
RSq	78.5	74.0	67.0	76.5
Sc	80.2	68.4	59.3	67.17
STP	79.7	74.0	67.2	77.62
TOK	80.52	67.4	65.0	68.8

0.29 - 0.39), SSS_GW (0.34 - 0.47) and PW_GW (0.33 - 0.41). The lack-of-fit testing proved the commercial limit of 127 terms did not play a significant role in limiting the results of our separated case models, although the term limit did force splitting the models into separate cases due to the large number of factors included in the design phase. The lack-of-fit results indicate that many terms were not statistically significant to the game. This highlights one of the benefits of this methodology; we identified a large number of factors game designers would have experimented with but had no impact on the results of game play.

6.2 Statistical and Game Significance

The statistically significant terms play an important role in the selection of game elements to adjust by identifying consistent terms. Statistically significant factors whose influence exceeds a minimal threshold that actually impact the player's strategy will be referred to as game significant factors. The game significant factors will have the largest effect on the response variables, as they have the greatest potential to impact the gameplay experience.

6.2.1 SSS_FLOCK Statistical and Game Significance
The results for the flocking algorithm suggest that Pac-Man is capable of avoiding the ghosts if they become overly aggressive or separated and has no difficulty in tracking and eating the ghosts. A less aggressive tactic proved effective at limiting Pac-Man's progression, by increasing the cohesion and alignment of the flock. The ghosts' vision is the most prominent statistical and game significant factor causing large decreases in all response variables, which suggests a vast improvement in the efficiency and performance of the ghosts. The flee and death state time contributes significantly to nearly all response variables, the exception is the number of fruit eaten; this supports the idea this player is not using the additional flee time to perform bonus tasks. The length of time the fruit results indicates that the player is unable to consistently improve their score via the

additional time the bonus items are available. The perceived value of the fruit not being a statistically significant main effect for more response variables could be due to the bonus item always being worth more than tokens or power-pellets. As such, it represents a goal the SSS-AB* algorithm will always attempt to complete, while minimizing uncertainty and unnecessary risks.

Table 2. SSS_FLOCK statistically significant main effects are listed with: P for positive or N for negative effect. Non-statistically significant main effects are indicated by the - symbol.

	CC	Sc	STP	TOK	GE	PP	RSq	FE	LVL
Flee State	N	P	P	P	P	P	P	-	P
Death Time	-	P	P	P	-	P	P	P	P
Fruit Time	-	-	-	-	-	-	-	P	-
Perceived Value of Fruit	-	-	N	-	-	-	-	P	-
Flock Separation	N	-	-	-	P	-	P	P	-
Flock Cohesion	N	-	-	-	N	-	N	-	-
Flock Alignment	N	-	-	-	N	-	N	-	-
Flock Hunger	P	P	P	P	-	P	P	-	P
Pac-Man Vision	P	P	-	P	P	P	P	P	P
Ghost Vision	N	N	N	N	N	N	N	N	N

6.2.2   SSS_GW Statistical and Game Significance

The GW ghosts protecting the tokens significantly decreases several of the response variables, despite the decrease in performance, there is no statistically significant decrease in the number of steps which suggests the player is capable of staying alive but is unable to complete additional points based tasks. The ghosts protecting the power-pellets or the bonus fruit item proves to be an ineffective strategy, having either no statistical significant or improving Pac-Man's performance. The remaining GW ghost factors all have a negative impact on the response variables. The results indicate that chasing Pac-Man's position does not limit Pac-Man's ability to stay alive but does minimize the ability to collect items. Chasing the end of Pac-Man's path proves slightly more effective in diminishing the number of items collected. Interestingly, while chasing Pac-Man's position increases the number of the close calls and levels completed, it reduces the score and the number of ghosts eaten. Chasing the end position of Pac-Man's current path results in a higher number of close calls while decreasing the score and the number of ghosts, fruit and power-pellets eaten. Thus, chasing Pac-Man's end position proves slightly more effective in terms of limiting a wider range of response variables. Similar, to the previous case the flee and death state time factors produce nearly all positive effects, while the ghost's vision range has produces nearly all negative effects.

6.2.3   PW_FLOCK Statistical and Game Significance

The three PW̄ algorithm factors chasing edible ghosts, avoiding the centroid of the ghosts, and moving toward the centroid of the remaining items prove to

Table 3. SSS_GW statistically significant main effects are listed with: P for positive or N for negative effect. Non-statistically significant main effects are indicated by the - symbol..

	CC	Sc	STP	TOK	GE	PP	RSq	FE	LVL
Protect Tokens	N	N	-	N	N	N	P	-	N
Protect PP	N	P	P	P	N	N	P	-	P
Protected Fruit	-	-	-	-	-	-	-	-	-
Toward Ghosts	N	N	N	N	N	N	N	N	N
Away Ghosts	N	N	N	N	N	N	N	N	N
Pac-Man Pos	P	N	-	-	N	-	-	-	P
Pac-Man Direction	P	N	-	-	N	N	-	N	-
Flee Time	N	P	P	P	P	P	P	P	P
Death Time	P	P	P	P	N	P	P	P	P
Ghost Vision	P	N	N	N	P	N	N	N	N

have a statistically significant effect for only a few response variables. For these three cases, we observe a similar pattern in which Pac-Man successfully collects additional points from fruits and ghosts, at the expense of a shorter lifetime. So while these factors had minimal impact on the statistical significance of the response variables, these factors seemed to have altered the risk and reward ratio tempting the player to gain more points at the risk of a shorter life span. The PW algorithm takes a greater number of chances to collect the fruit. This behaviour is unlike the SSS-AB* algorithm, which uses the extra flee and death time to complete level tasks. The PW_FLOCK session results indicate that nearly all factors had a statistically significant impact on the fruit collected. The flock struggled to capture Pac-Man, especially when becoming overly aggressive, however, they were effective in stopping Pac-Man from engaging in too many bonus tasks. This suggests small modifications to the flock's behaviour focusing on cohesion and hunger would provide a more balanced challenge.

6.2.4 PW_GW Statistical and Game Significance

The GW algorithm factors for protecting tokens or the fruit are not statistically significant for any of the response variables. Protecting the power-pellets also proves to be an ineffective strategy, as nearly every collectable response variables has a statistically significant increase. The GW algorithm factors to pursue either Pac-Man's current position or the end of current path produce overall similar results. The two factors differed in that chasing Pac-Man's path end point is explicitly less direct and may appear less aggressive, which is supported by the decrease in the ghosts eaten. The GW algorithm proved less effective when the ghosts hunted as a cohesive unit, then when becomes more aggressive and separating to chase Pac-Man. Unlike the other cases we reviewed, increasing the vision range actually increased the number of close calls the number of ghosts eaten, which indicates Pac-Man is more effective at evading the GW ghosts and the more aggressive ghosts are frequently being eaten by Pac-Man. The GW ghosts demonstrate slightly improved performance when chasing the end point

Table 4. PW_FLOCK statistically significant main effects are listed with: P for positive or N for negative effect. Non-statistically significant main effects are indicated by the - symbol..

	CC	Sc	STP	TOK	GE	PP	RSq	FE	LVL
Edible Ghost	-	-	-	-	-	-	-	P	-
Ghost Center	-	-	-	-	P	-	-	N	-
Item Center	N	-	-	-	-	-	-	P	-
Flee Time	-	P	P	P	P	P	P	P	P
Death Time	-	P	P	P	P	P	P	P	P
Flock Hunger	-	P	P	P	P	P	P	P	P
Flock Separation	N	-	-	-	-	-	-	P	-
Flock Alignment	P	P	P	-	P	-	P	-	-
Flock Cohesion	-	-	-	-	-	-	-	P	-
Ghost Vision	N	N	N	N	N	N	N	N	N

Table 5. PW_GW statistically significant main effects are listed with: P for positive or N for negative effect. Non-statistically significant main effects are indicated by the - symbol..

	CC	Sc	STP	TOK	GE	PP	RSq	FE	LVL
Protect Tokens	-	-	-	-	-	-	-	-	-
Protect Fruit	-	-	-	-	-	-	-	-	-
Protecting PP	N	P	P	-	P	-	P	P	-
Pac-Man Position	P	-	-	P	-	P	-	N	-
Pac-Man Direction	P	-	-	P	N	P	-	N	-
Ghosts Toward	-	-	-	-	-	P	-	-	-
Ghosts Away	N	N	N	N	N	N	N	-	N
Flee Time	N	P	P	P	P	-	P	P	-
Death Time	P	P	P	P	-	P	P	P	P
Ghost Vision	P	N	N	N	P	N	N	N	N

of Pac-Man's path. Interestingly, chasing the end point of Pac-Man's path produced less direct challenge but ultimately produced comparable overall results to chasing Pac-Man's current position. The overall result of these cases is nearly identical for most response variables, but gameplay would provide less conflict and likely a less stressful game session to the players.

6.3 Limitations

One of the largest caveats to examining game difficulty using a full factorial analysis methodology is the exponential growth of calculations that occurs for the inclusion of each additional factor. Fortunately, one of the strengths of the full factorial analysis is that it is orthogonal, which allows the calculations to be separated and calculated independently, reducing some of the strain of the data size issues. The complexity of the full factorial statistical analysis scales well and remains quite simple in theory, in practical non-distributed calculations exceeding 7-8 factors cause the memory and computational requirements to exceed even the capabilities of current statistical software programs, such as SPSS, R and Minitab and evaluation might best be accomplished using a "Big Data" approach. Our experiment illustrates that even in the analysis of a smaller video games such as Pac-Man, careful consideration must be used in the methods of calculating results and managing the volume of data.

Within our experiment, the player's behaviour and development remained constant, meaning that the goals or strategies of the player never changed. Within this context, it was easier to develop player models and accurately identify statistically and game significant factors to the response variables. However, real player models are adaptive and progress as players become more experienced and begin to explore new strategies and techniques. Thus, a full player model would require progression from one player state to another; as such, it is more accurate to view the models in our results as snapshots of factors which affect a player's performance and not as complete player models. A player's type will be more accurately described via a collection of models, as they progress throughout the game, and the current player model will continually need to be re-evaluated and set to the closest matching player model. Identifying, which player model accurately describes the player's current state is not addressed nor required in our experiment but is a complex task which requires consideration in an adaptive gaming system.

7   Conclusions and Future Work

Our research investigated a methodology to identify game factors which altered the simulated player's performance on a set of response variables and the difficulty of the game. Understanding the relationship between game factors and their impact on level of difficulty and thus the player's performance is the first step toward customizing gameplay to improve the player's emotional investment and experience. The methodology used in this experiment examines factors from the three main types of adaptive adjustments relating to the player's avatar, the level layout and item placement and the behaviour of non-playable characters. Our research demonstrates the ability to quantify each factor's impact on the player's performance on a set of response variables. A small consistent set of factors played prominent roles in altering the performance of the player for all response variables. Although, intuitively, a number of these factors could be predicted as being prominent factors, it is important to identify and quantify impact, granularity and predictability.

The results of our analysis provided interesting insight into the interaction of game factors and algorithms which produced emergent behavior. This type of information can be difficult to discover during testing and can be valuable for game designers in understanding unintended changes in difficulty. The analysis highlighted interesting properties relating to the perceived level of challenge; when the player engages in bonus tasks, it often resulted in a diminished overall performance rather than additional points scored by the player. Given this result, game designers could strategically place bonus items or tasks in areas with lower levels of interest or challenge. The placement of bonus items could be gradually adjusted into more challenging areas, which could be used to gauge the level of risk the player is comfortable competing against.

Commercially, this methodology has the potential to be effective for testing new features and tuning final factor settings for release. An advantage of this methodology is that the factorial analysis is completely independent of the factor level values or game values selected, so integration of this subsystem requires only identifying response variables to collect information about and thus this subsystem can easily be injected into a wide variety of games. It can be easily integrated into commercial products during the testing phase and due to the independence and modularity of these methodologies as a sub-system, it can be easily removed before the product is released. The ability of the analysis to evaluate any modifications to the player attributes, NPCs or level factors offers the advantage of a wider variety of adaptive decisions.

7.1 Future Work

Continuing with the design goals of this research, future research will focus the structure of our adaptive system on being a viable to the progression of both commercial and academic game development. Our future work will utilize the results of statistical methodology presented in this paper, in an adaptive game prototype. The adaptive prototype will adjust game factors during gameplay in an attempt to control the overall outcome on a selection of response variables representing difficulty. The goal of future research will be to successfully adjust game factors for multiple player sessions and to control the results for a single or multiple response variables. Our adaptive game prototype will further investigate the goals of an adaptive system and issues relating to game progression and conflicting difficulty adjustment goals.

References

1. Andrade, G., Ramalho, G., Santana, H., Corruble, V.: Challenge-sensitive action selection: An application to game balancing. Intelligent Agent Technology, 194–200 (2005)
2. Bateman, C., Boon, R.: 21st Century Game Design. Charles River Media (2006)
3. Fraser, I.J.: Game challenge: A factorial analysis approach. Master's thesis, University Of Western Ontario (2012), http://ir.lib.uwo.ca/etd/563/
4. Hunicke, R., Chapman, V.: Ai for dynamic difficulty adjustment in games. In: Challenges in Game Artificial Intelligence AAAI Workshop, pp. 91–96 (2004)
5. Miller, S.: Auto-Dynamic Difficulty. Published in Scott Miller Game Matters Blog (2004), http://dukenukem.typepad.com/game-matters/2004/01/autoadjusting.html
6. Plaat, A., Schaeffer, J., Pijls, W., Bruin, A.: SSS*= AB+ TT (1995)
7. Reynolds, C.: Flocks, Herds and Schools: A Distributed Behavioral Model. ACM SIGGRAPH Computer Graphics, 25–34 (1987)

8. Spronck, P., Sprinkhuizen-Kuyper, I., Postma, E.: Difficulty scaling of game ai. Intelligent Games and Simulation, 33–37 (2004)
9. Spronck, P.H.M.: Adaptive game ai. Ph.D. thesis (2005)
10. Szita, I., Lorincz, A.: Learning to Play Using Low-Complexity Rule-Based Policies: Illustrations through Ms. Pac-Man. Artificial Intelligence Research pp. 659–684 (2007)
11. Togelius, J., De Nardi, R., Lucas, S.: Towards automatic personalised content creation for racing games. Computational Intelligence and Games, 252–259 (2007)
12. Togelius, J., Lucas, S.: Evolving controllers for simulated car racing. Evolutionary Computation, 1906–1913 (2005)
13. Yannakakis, G., Hallam, J.: Evolving opponents for interesting interactive computer games. In: From Animals to Animats, pp. 499–508 (2004)
14. Yannakakis, G., Hallam, J.: A Generic Approach for Generating Interesting Interactive Pac-Man Opponents. In: IEEE Symposium on Computational Intelligence and Games, pp. 94–101 (2005)

Goin' Goblins - Iterative Design
of an Entertaining Archery Experience

Christian Geiger[1], Simon Thiele[1], Laurid Meyer[1], Stefan Meyer[1], Lutz Hören[1],
and Daniel Drochtert[1]

University of Applied Sciences Duesseldorf, Duesseldorf, Germany

Abstract. We present the iterative development of a 3D simulator for traditional archery and the design of a gaming level that should attract visitors at trade fairs and exhibitions. We want to provide users with a believable archery experience and support novel users in practicing the motion sequence of traditional archery using a virtual 3D environment. To provide a realistic haptic feedback we used a real bow interaction device and wind output in our simulation. We extended a bow damping system by electronic sensors to detect draw and release of the bow, aiming at a virtual target and user movement in front of a large projection screen. To entertain visitors at trade fairs and exhibitions we designed a two-player mode and a small 3D adventure with different tasks.

1 Introduction

Traditional field archers aim without a conscious sight picture or additional means like peep holes, releases or stabilisers. Good shooting results require an excellent arm/body-eye coordination that allows users to perform identical movements during the shot. To hit targets at unmarked distances the archer relies on his experience to subconsciously measure the distance and move the bow correctly. In opposite to target archers this intuitive action allows to shoot moving targets at unknown distances. For novice archers these movements can only be practiced with the advice of an experienced trainer who continuously controls and corrects the archer's movements. Therefore the goal of our project is a VR simulator that allows novices to experience the basic movements and experience the positive feelings usually associated with this activity. Of course it should be entertaining as well.

An archery simulation that provides a believable and enjoyable user experience should fulfill a number of requirements: a set of easy-to-use interaction techniques with appropriate user feedback, a believable behavior simulation and an attractive 3D visualization. Users should be entertained when using the system and it should be easy to learn how to use it without a long and complex introduction. Based on these requirements we built a 3D simulator with an entertaining gaming level for traditional archery.

Our work aims to simulate traditional archery by means of a novel user interface and provide an adventure-like content. Previous work included the hardware

D. Reidsma, H. Katayose, and A. Nijholt (Eds.): ACE 2013, LNCS 8253, pp. 284–295, 2013.

design of a appropriate archery user interface, using a real bow that is extended with electronics and a damping system [1]. This allowed realistic and safe indoor practicing of the archery sport in reality-based virtual outdoor scenes. Based on positive feedback from this work we extended the interaction methods and the previous realistic content of the virtual environment for entertaining show-cases at a large public fairs. With the goal of making the archery experience most entertaining for every type of visitor in mind, an adventure game called "Goin' Goblins" (GG) was developed in a design process that extends techniques from user centered design, software engineering and digital media production. In addition to the interaction with the real bow, a set of advanced interaction techniques extends the regular way of using the archery simulator towards a more fun-oriented application. This includes choosing different projectiles, switching to an rookie mode or cooperation of multiple users, by featuring a wizard that helps the main player through the game. However, we learnt during the design and evaluation of this project that not every technique that is technically feasible and looks like an exciting idea on its own is also suitable to be used in a fair scenario where users usually have only a limited time frame and attention span.

2   Related Work

Apart from archery simulation, the design of interfaces and simulations of sport activities has been proposed in several works in the past. One example for this are exertion interfaces by Floyd Mueller et al. [2]. Their projects, like Table Tennis for Three, Jogging over a Distance or Shadow Boxing over distance, aim at creating social bonding through physical activity between user that are spatially separated. The proposed conceptional design framework consists of a design vocabulary that is suitable for usage in the design process of exertion games. Most of the exertion interfaces, however, focus the design on the spatial separation and social bonding aspects and thereby neglect simulating a real-life activity and providing entertaining experiences. Other sports interfaces focus on being beneficial for training purposes. Examples for these interfaces, focussing of realism, are proposed by Multon et al. [3], who created a training system for gymnasts or Zhang and Liu [4] for training in ball sports.

Archery simulations with focus on entertaining experiences are available with the commercial games on the PlayStation and Nintendo Wii, using the move controller, as well as the Wiimote. Both games feature a virtual environment that resembles a real archery range, with varying visual realism, where the players' goal is to achieve highscores by shooting at static and moving targets in various distances from a static position. While the archery game on the PlayStation offers a more realistic simulation than the Wii, by adapting the posture of the bow to the players' movements, the realism of both games however, comes short because of the lack of haptic feedback, the triggering of the shot through pressing a button and the accuracy constraints of the hardware of the controllers. The archery simulator by TechnoHunt [5], aimed at expert archers, features the realistic feeling of handling a real bow, however, the visual simulation is achieved through playing video sequences that lack an immersive feeling.

The work described in this paper is based on the development of the bow as the user interface and the design process of the archery simulation that has begun with previous prototypes that first used infrared tracking for all movements of the bow [6], serving as a proof of concept, and that was subsequently further developed by enhancing the bow with various sensors [1] that greatly increased the accuracy of the tracking and shot detection and thereby creating a realistic experience of the activity. The content of the virtual environment described in [1] is based on a realistic simulation of an outdoor archery setting. This paper describes the adaption of the realistic sensation of shooting with a bow to an entertaining game environment with further advanced user interaction methods to make the experience attractive to a broad audience.

3   A Design Process for Advanced User Interfaces

Advanced user interfaces (AUI) include natural user interfaces and reality-based interaction that try to mimic the users' everyday experience and provide a easy-to-use and expressive way to interact with digital content. These interfaces are useful for short-time use of applications and a large, heterogenous user base as it is the case when developing attractive interactive installations for trade / science fairs or exhibitions. The target group is able to instantly interact and attain their goals with only a very short learning curve. The development of these advanced UIs is rather complex as the field of expertise is more demanding in relation to traditional computer and GUI based applications. Few design experience exists and there is no structured design approach available of design guidelines that guide designers how to create a compelling AUI. We provide a pragmatic approach that uses state of the art concepts in user centered design (UCD) and specified a structured workflow that combines an extended Scrum model with techniques from UCD, SE and Usability Engineering (UE). The approach is based on Paelke's and Nebe's work [7] and additionally applies methods and techniques from UCD and digital media production (see fig 1). A detailed description of this process is beyond the scope of this work and we will focus only on selected methods we used to design of our archery experience.

The process described in figure 1 only suggests suitable methods in different iteration cycles. It depends on the project and the design team which methods should be applied and to what extent. For our project we applied:

Creativity techniques We applied Forced Analogy, Speed Inventing and 3-12-3 Brainstorming in this project. Suitable techniques could be found in [8].
Persona Personas are well known in HCI and help to identify user types based on interviews and other means to gather user relevant data, see [9].
Task/Goals and Scenarios Goals of a persona are accomplished by more technical tasks. This activity is described narratively in a scenario, see [9].
Scribble and Storyboard Scenarios could be visualized using sketches and storyboards. This approach is borrowed from film making and animation.

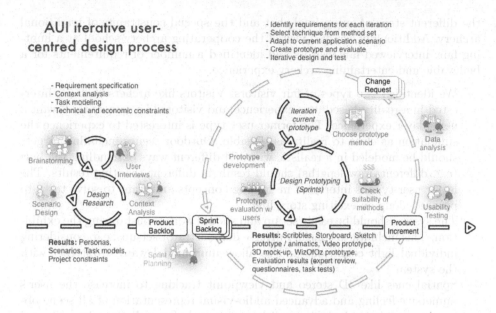

Fig. 1. Iterative User-Centred Design Process

Animatics or Video Prototype Timing static images and illustration helps to get a first impression of the future user interface. A suitable way of communicating this is to create a full video prototype that describes relevant UI functionality that has not yet been realized in a small video production [10].

WizardOfOz Prototyping and 3D MockUp More interactive prototypes could be realized using the "Wizard of Oz" technique. The design team simulates a non-existent system while a prospective user is interacting with the interface [11].

Expert Reviews and Questionnaires Evaluation is a fundamental part of our iterative design approach. In early phases we conduct internal reviews, e.g. using the Disney method [8] or mental walkthroughs but in later steps we talked to experienced archers and asked users at fairs to fill out different questionnaires to measure game experience [12], hedonic / pragmatic qualities [13] or presence [14].

System tests Due to the complex system architecture consisting of hardware, 3D software, tracking system and a custom input device we tested individual components independently first and intreated them in subsequent iterations.

4   Requirement Specification

Before the design process was initiated, a number of professional archers were interviewed to identify the most important factors for a believable user experience. Furthermore, we participated in a 2-day archery course to understand the different steps of an optimal shot and the special constraints of traditional archery. Additionally, we also visited the cooperating archery school at a hunting fair, interviewed fair visitors and identified a number of requirements for a believable and entertaining archery experience.

- We identified two types of fair visitors. Visitors like archers that are interested in a reality-based user experience and visitors like gamers that want a new player experience. The former user type is interested to experience the simulation as close to reality as possible. Outdoor scenes including targets should be modeled in a realistic way and different ways of handling the bow (e.g. different draw lengths) should result in different shooting results. The latter user type is interested in gaming concepts and want to solve tasks to proceed along an exciting story line.
- The system should be easily set up and should work robust during the exhibition. This includes to consider diverse demonstrator set-ups, e.g. considering individual light conditions and to allow multimodal ways to interact with the system
- Spatial cues like 3D stereo and viewpoint tracking to increase the user's immersive feeling and advanced audio-visual representation of all scene objects to maximize hedonic qualities. This includes realistic animation and expressive sound design.

Based on these requirements and the client's primary goal to attract novice users at trade fairs to start archery courses we decided to focus on providing a believable and entertaining archery experience. Virtual reality techniques like spatial user tracking, stereo viewing, haptic feedback, user adaptive viewpoint control on a large projection screen and advanced 3D graphics should be implemented to create a semi-realistic application scenario of traditional archery. Based on the user interviews we first created personas with task/goals and a small scenario [9]. The following description is a brief summary of the results.

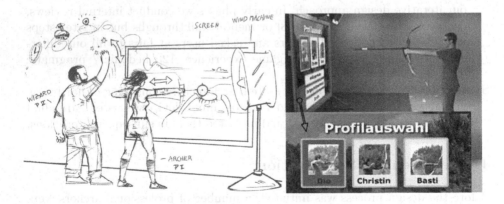

Fig. 2. Scribbled scenario and video prototype

Fred B. and his daughter Sophie visit a science fair and want to experience the archery simulator featuring the "Goin' Goblins" level. The demonstrator's goal its to provide an entertaining archery experience for two people. Fred is a passionated traditional archer practicing his hobby 2-3 times a month. Sophie is interested in sporting games with full-body interaction. She has practiced archery in Wii Sports Resort and PS3 Sports Champion Archery. They both are interested in fantasy films and like adventure games which they play together sometimes. An assistant introduces them on how to handle the bow and the application. A number of quests have to be solved in cooperation to proceed through the storyline. The first player acts as an archer and the second player acts as a magician that assists to solve the quests.

Design Experience: In this phase we successfully used the design methods user interviews, Personas, task / goals and scenarios. For illustration we also created scribbles and a story board. Figure 2 shows a scribble of the described scenario that was also used as part of a story board.

5   Design of Advanced Interaction Techniques

The main goals of this project is to create a believable and enjoyable user experience that motivates visitors at trade fairs and exhibitions to pick up the virtual archery. Realistic haptic feedback thus was a necessary requirement. A central concept was to use a real bow for all user interaction of the player. In opposite to game controllers or bows equipped with low-cost sensors like the Wiimote we want to exactly track bow position / orientation, draw length and release. The user should feel the draw weight of a bow during the simulation and the realistic behavior of a bow during the shot.

We applied this concept not only to the application scenarios but also for menu selection and the adjustment of parameters when interacting with a 2D graphical user interface. Moving a cursor is controlled by rotating the bow and selection is realized through a short pull of the bow string (see fig 2). Realistic feedback was also considered for windy outdoor environments. If virtual wind affects the simulation this should also be felt by using a wind machine that was interfaced with the simulation (see fig. 5). We also created a user-generated 3D character acting as archer. The player could generate a 3D face of herself using our Unity3D plug-in for Facegen (www.facegen.com) that is used to generate a 3D archer character. After successful shots, the shooting sequence is replayed showing the user avatar in action (see fig. 3).

Furthermore, we provided three arrow types with different scoring behavior: regular arrow, fire works arrow and cartoon arrow. This was realized attaching miniature models of an arrow, a small pyrotechnic article and a boxing glove equipped with RFID tags to the bow. Another fun interaction is the "Merida" mode that was used for entertainment purposes. If the user wears a red-haired wig the system detects an attached RFID tag and every shot hits a target. We also provide an alternative shooting method, called "Help Daddy" for small

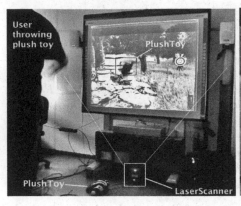

Fig. 3. Selected interaction techniques: Help Daddy and user-generated 3D character

children that are not able to handle the heavy bow. By using a dedicated laser tracking system, touches on large vertical planar surfaces in front of the projection can be detected. If a plush toy hits the projection screen and thus the invisible tracking plane, the center of the touch area is used as the target point for the arrow simulation (see fig. 3).

The two-player mode requires interaction of the archer player using the bow and the wizard player using two gestures for healing and magic. We selected a wipe gesture with the right hand to heal from damage and a wand to create magic. The healing spells are casted with the sliding left hand gestures that is detected by the Kinect sensor. The magic spell is casted using a magic wand with an integrated Wiimote controller. Due to connection problems with the Wiimote during a 8-hour presentation day at fairs, we also provided an alternate wave gesture with the other (right) hand. See the video for further explanations or visit www.virtual-arrow.net.

Design Experience: To illustrate and discuss the interaction techniques we created a video prototype of the system before we implemented a first system prototype. This helped us to discuss the interaction design with experts. Video prototypes are a powerful means to quickly create first impressions of intended systems [10]. It served also a very valuable communication tools to discuss design ideas and prototypes.

6   System Design

The user handling the bow can move freely inside the interaction area in front of the projection screen. The tracking itself is accomplished by two camera systems facing in opposite directions. One, installed underneath the projection screen, facing the interaction area, is used for providing data on the movements and gestures of the users inside the interaction area and the other one, facing the projection screen, for tracking the shot direction of the bow into the virtual scene. The visualization is then calculated based on the data of the sensors of

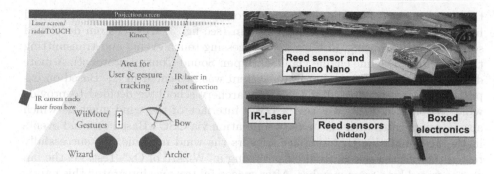

Fig. 4. System Architecture and Hardware Prototype

the bow and the two camera systems and rendered in full HD quality on a large screen.

The bow is equipped with a custom damping system based on a archery shot trainer (see fig. 4), that allows to dry-fire a real bow without damaging it. It uses a pneumatical approach similar to an air pump to safely release and stop an arrow shaft. The correct draw length, aim and the release is measured using magnetic switches, also know as reed sensors. These sensors are cheap, light-weighted, and rugged and have very little interference liability. If a magnetic field appears close to the sensor then a pair of ferrous metal reeds of an electronic switch connect and the switch closes. If the attractive force of the magnetic field is not strong enough anymore the reeds are disconnected and the electronic switch is opened.

We attached a strong neodymium magnet to the compression ring of the arrow damper and attached a dozen of reed sensors outside of the tube (see fig. 4). This way we can measure the movement of the arrow. These sensors are connected to an Arduino Nano, which calculates the position, speed and acceleration of the arrow shaft and transmits them to the host computer via Bluetooth or USB. To detect the position in the virtual scene that the real bow is aiming at we attached an infrared (IR) laser to the bow (see fig. 4). The laser invisibly points to the screen position the user is aiming at. The system uses an IR sensitive camera and can thereby easily detect the IR spot and calculate the orientation and position of a virtual arrow in the 3D environment. Tracking of the user/bow is only used for viewpoint animation. We selected a pragmatic and inexpensive solution with a Kinect that detects the nearest person in front of the camera. The viewpoint (the virtual camera in the 3D world) is moved accordingly to provide an immersive depth cue.

Different shooting modes can be switched using RFID objects that are detected using a RFID sensor at the Arduino Nano board. The physical objects used for mode triggering are equipped with corresponding RFID tags. If an object is attached to the bow, the RFID reader detects the tag of the object and the corresponding mode is triggered until another object is detected. Although this feature worked quite well, we decided not to use it in the Goin' Goblins level described in this paper because the switching of arrows slowed down the game flow as we experienced during some walk-through sessions. For smaller children that are not able to handle the bow we provide an alternative shooting method by using a dedicated laser tracking system (see fig. 3) with custom developed software for recognising, filtering and processing touch events and transmitting the data to a 3D game engine via OSC (Open Sound Control protocol). A more detailed description of the hardware system was presented in [1]. Based on expert reviews we conducted at the client archery school we decided to provide wind feedback in 2013. We used a DMX interface of the wind machine which also communicates with our archery simulation via OSC . Based on wind events in the 3D simulation this interface triggers the wind machine. We successfully tested the effectiveness of wind output using a "Wizard of Oz"-Test, i.e. the fan was operated by a team member. After successful tests we integrated this haptic feedback into the game level at selected places.

Design Experience: The design of the project's hardware parts was not trivial because we had to test a number of alternative ways to track the draw length and release of the bow damper, the orientation of the bow and the position of the players. For selected interaction techniques the "Wizard of Oz" served useful to rule-out unsuitable interaction techniques and get first impressions without investing too many resources. Detailed hardware test in the lab and in "real-life" scenarios were necessary to find the best available option.

7 Content Design and Application

We designed the small 3D adventure called "Goin' Goblins" to provide an entertaining archery experience. It features a more complex game level than the other scene we developed in [1]. In this gaming level the player has to rescue a kidnapped leprechaun from the castle of the evil goblins. A number of quests have to be solved to proceed through the storyline and the user needs help of another player. The second player acts as a magician that can help to solve the quests with magic and healing / protecting spells.

Figure 5 illustrates scenes from selected events where players have to cooperate to proceed. We decided a total gameplay time of 7-8 minutes depending how well users shoot with the bow. A first walkthrough was performed using a "Wizard of Oz" prototype. We created a number of screenshots in a presentation program and simulated a complete walkthrough during several internal test in our design team. While we were satisfied with a playtime of eight minutes for two cooperating users we learnt at a science fair that we did not designed the player's roles equally, i.e. the wizard is only a side-kick for the player with the bow and visitors playing the wizard complaint after a game that they also wanted to shoot. To provide an equal experience for both players and not to double the playtime we decided to switch roles in the middle of the game.

Special attention was given to a believable sound design for this level. It features self-created background music and sounds in order to create the desired atmosphere for the different quests. The necessary 3D models were imported

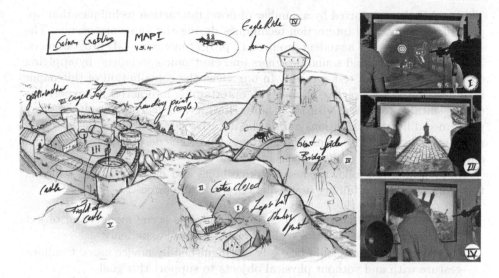

Fig. 5. Level Design and corresponding 3D scenes of the final game level

from the Unity 3D asset store and adapted to the design of the scenario. Shooting targets were imported or modeled, rigged, animated and integrated into the application logic. We reused most of the content from other projects due to the limited time frame (6 weeks) we had to create this game level.

Design Experience: Due to timing constraints our design approach was to design the game level after(!) the assets have been selected. This proved to be rather useful for the given short project period for the game development. We managed to create the level from scratch within the given time frame, but heavily reused 3D assets from other projects and the Unity asset store. Due to the large variety of users we needed to easily configure the system on-the-fly (e.g changing the virtual draw weight, recalibrating the system and interactively adjusting offsets for precise tracking). To easily help unexperienced players that could not easily hit the targets to proceed in the story we developed key shortcuts that were mapped to a Ring Mouse that one of our team members wears. S/he could "solve" the current quest if it took too long for the users to complete the task.

8   Conclusion and Design Rules

This paper presented the technical and design-oriented aspects of a 3D archery simulator. Goal of the project was to provide visitors of exhibitions and trade fairs with a believable and enjoyable user experience similar to a real archery experience. We developed an indoor system that allows safe interaction with a real bow in a virtual 3D world. We implemented a set of different scenarios that support a believable user experience using realistic haptic and audio-visual feedback. A game-based level called "Goin' Goblins" allows for an entertaining interaction.

This goal is also supported by a number of novel interaction techniques that apply different advanced interaction techniques during the game experience. The system was created by a student group of 12 project members (3D programmers, 3D artists, graphics and sound designers and electronic specialists) by applying an iterative 'design & test' process. In our view, the contribution of this paper is to describe a best practice to create an entertaining interactive 3D experience that is suitable to attract visitors at fairs. However, we learnt that although we performed different evaluations during the iterative design process and we could rule out many wrong decisions at early stages that some design approaches could only be validated in a real life setting.

We identified the following best-practice hints and design guidelines during this work for an entertaining user experience at trade fairs:

- Immersion techniques, realistic and/or believable scene models and object behavior are necessary for a reality-based [archery] experience
- Provide gesture that could be easily distinguished by novice users. Combine gesture with and without physical objects to support this goal
- Provide similar experience for all users and reduce maximum play time to 3-5 minutes per person. Avoid a lengthy set-up procedure for users even if this provides an additional benefit for visitors.
- Be prepared for failure and provide multiple ways to operate your system, e.g. provide multiple ways for tracking if the environment conditions are not suitable for your preferred method. Provide different ways to control the game and short-cuts to solve a level for unexperienced users.
- If there is not much time for development then design the story based on existing assets
- Evaluate your ideas as early as possible and use simulation techniques like cognitive walk-throughs, video prototyping and "Wizard of Oz" simulations to evaluate ideas without realizing them
- A structured design approach with a set of suitable methods helps to speed up the iterative design process.

Fig. 6. Goin' Goblins at the science fair "Ideenpark"

After successful tests at a number of exhibitions and trade fairs we currently work on a mobile version of this project. Moreover, we continue our work to create a light-weight hardware solution for the damping mechanism and even more easy-to-use set-up procedure for our client. The client has presented this prototype at over 10 fairs in Europe and is still happy with the user feedback. He is frequently asked if he is able to sell the system on a regular base.

References

1. Geiger, C., Thiele, S., Meyer, L., Drochtert, D., Stöcklein, J., Wöldecke, B.: Virtual archery with tangible interaction. In: IEEE 3DUI (2013)
2. Mueller, F.F., Edge, D., Vetere, F., Gibbs, M.R., Agamanolis, S., Bongers, B., Sheridan, J.G.: Designing sports: a framework for exertion games. In: Proceedings of the SIGCHI Conference on Human Factors in Computing Systems, CHI 2011, pp. 2651–2660. ACM, New York (2011)
3. Multon, F., Hoyet, L., Komura, T., Kulpa, R.: Interactive control of physically-valid aerial motion: application to vr training system for gymnasts. In: Proceedings of the 2007 ACM Symposium on Virtual Reality Software and Technology, VRST 2007, pp. 77–80. ACM, New York (2007)
4. Zhang, L., Liu, Q.: Application of simulation and virtual reality to physical education and athletic training. In: Pan, Z., Cheok, A.D., Müller, W., Chang, M., Zhang, M. (eds.) Transactions on Edutainment VII. LNCS, vol. 7145, pp. 24–33. Springer, Heidelberg (2012)
5. ArcheryInteractive: Technohunt bow simulator, http://www.technohunt.com
6. Geiger, C., Herder, J., Göbel, S., Heinze, C., Marinos, D.: Design and virtual studio presentation of a traditional archery simulator. In: Entertainment Interfaces Track 2010 at Interaktive Kulturen (2010)
7. Paelke, V., Nebe, K.: Integrating agile methods for mixed reality design space exploration. In: Proceedings of the 7th ACM Conference on Designing Interactive Systems, pp. 240–249. ACM (2008)
8. Gray, D., Brown, S., Macanufo, J.: Gamestorming - A Playbook for Innovators, Rulebreakers and CHangemakers. O'Reilly (2010)
9. Cooper, A.: About Face 3 - The Essentials of Interaction Design. Wiley (2007)
10. Zimmermann, J.: Video sketches: Exploring pervasive computing video sketches: Exploring pervasive computing interaction designs. Pervasive Computing 4(4), 91–94 (2005)
11. Höysniemi, J., Hämäläinen, P., Turkki, L.: Wizard of oz prototyping of computer vision based action games for children. In: Proceedings of the 2004 Conference on Interaction Design and Children: Building a Community, IDC 2004, pp. 27–34. ACM, New York (2004)
12. Ijsselsteijn, W.A., Poels, K., de Kort, Y.A.W.: Game experience questionnaire (fuga the fun of gaming: Measuring the human experience of media enjoyment. Technical report Deliverable 3.3 (2008)
13. Hassenzahl, M., Platz, A., Burmester, M., Lerner, K.: Hedonic and ergonomic quality aspects determine a software's appeal. CHI Letters 2(1), 201–208 (2000)
14. Schubert, T.W.: The sense of presence in virtual environments: A three-component scale measuring spatial presence, involvement, and realness. Zeitschrift für Medienpsychologie 15(2), 69–71 (2003)

Engaging Users in Audio Labelling as a Movie Browsing Game with a Purpose

Jorge M. A. Gomes, Teresa Chambel, and Thibault Langlois

LaSIGE, Faculty of Sciences, University of Lisbon
1749-016 Lisboa, Portugal
jgomes@lasige.di.fc.ul.pt, {tc,tl}@di.fc.ul.pt

Abstract. Nowadays, movies, video, audio and games have a strong presence in human life, being a massive source of entertainment. Increasingly, movies and videos are becoming accessible as enormous collections over the Internet, in social media and interactive TV, demanding for more powerful ways to search, browse and view them, that benefit from video content-based analysis and classification techniques. From the point of view of the content-based analysis methods, a challenging aspect is the constitution of collections of labelled data. Inspired by the Game With A Purpose approach we propose SoundsLike, a game that pursues two goals: 1) entertaining the user in movie browsing; 2) use this interaction to collect data and improve our content-based sound analysis techniques. SoundsLike is integrated in MovieClouds, an interactive web application designed to access, explore and visualize movies based on the information conveyed in the different tracks or perspectives of its content.

Keywords: Interactive Browsing, Audio, Music, Soundtrack, Video, Movies, Tagging, Labelling, Human Computation, Game With A Purpose, Gamification, Entertainment, Engagement, User Experience.

1   Introduction

Movies and video are amongst the biggest sources of entertainment, in individual and social contexts. The evolution of technology has enabled the fast expansion of media and social networks over the internet, giving rise to huge and increasing collections of videos and movies accessible over the internet and through video on demand services on iTV. These multimedia collections are tremendously vast and demand for new and more powerful search mechanisms that may benefit from video and audio content based analysis and classification techniques. Some researchers [2,6] pointed the importance for the development of methods to extract interesting and meaningful features in video to effectively summarize and index them at the level of subtitles, audio and video image. The approach described in this paper was designed for the VIRUS[1] project [9] to help towards

---

[1] Video Information Retrieval Using Subtitles.

D. Reidsma, H. Katayose, and A. Nijholt (Eds.): ACE 2013, LNCS 8253, pp. 296–307, 2013.

the resolution of a cold-start problem in data acquisition for content classification. This project aims to provide users the access to a database of movies and TV series, through a rich graphical interface. MovieClouds [9], an interactive web application was developed, adopting a tagcloud paradigm for search, overview, and exploratory browsing of movies in different tracks or perspectives of their content (subtitles, emotions in subtitles, audio events, audio mood, and felt emotions). The back-end is based on the analysis of: video image, and especially audio and subtitles, where most of the semantics is expressed. In the present paper, we focus on the analysis and classification of the audio track for the inherent challenge and potential benefit if addressed from a game perspective to involve the users.

In this context, our objective is to provide overviews or summaries of the audio and indexing mechanisms to access the video moments containing audio events (e.g. gun shots, telephone ringing, animal noises, shouting, etc.) and moods to users. To this end, we build statistical models for such events that rely on labelled data. Unfortunately these kinds of databases are rare. The building of our own dataset is a huge task requiring many hours of listening and manual classification - often coined the "Cold Start" problem. With models that perform relatively well, we could use the models to collect data similar to the audio events we want to detect, and human operators would be asked to label (or simply verify the classification assigned automatically from) a reduced amount of data. This idea of bringing the human into the processing loop became popular with the rise of applications referred to as Games With A Purpose (GWAP), using Gamification and a Human Computation approach. These games have a goal which is collecting data from the interaction with users.

Gamification can be defined as the use of game design elements in non-game contexts [3]. These elements can be designed to augment and complement the entertaining qualities of movies, motivating and supporting users to contribute to the content classification, combining utility and usability aspects [3,7]. Main properties to aim for include: Persuasion and Motivation, to induce and facilitate mass-collaboration, or crowd sourcing, in the audio labeling; Engagement, possibly leading to increased time on the task; Joy, Fun and improved user experience; Reward and Reputation inspired in incentive design. Here, attention must be paid to the cultural contexts and values [7], involving balanced intrinsic and extrinsic motivations and rewards.

This paper describes an application that innovates upon previous Human Computation applications both in terms of entertainment aspects and in terms of the definition of the game in order to stimulate the interest of the user in labelling audio in movies, allowing us to collect data that will help solve the cold start problem. In the scope of this paper, the terms "tag" and "label" represent non-hierarchical keywords or terms assigned to a piece of information with the purpose of describing its contents and help finding it through browsing and searching mechanisms.

2 Related Work

The approach to create entertainment applications to collect data from the user is not a novelty, being currently identified with the terms "Game With A Purpose" (GWAP) and "Human Computation".

One of the first applications to apply such ideas was the ESP application [13] where players label the same image in pairs without any kind of communication between them, and are rewarded when the labels used are the same. This approach is named "output-agreement" because a reward is received when the output used by the players matches, being used also by other games such as Peekaboom [14], ListenGame [12], TagaTune [10], MajorMiner [11], and Herdit [1].

Herdit [1] is a GWAP dedicated to the gathering of audio data (from music) and provides a multi-player experience (more than the common two player games) over a social network. Another GWAP for music is TagaTune [10], proposing a different approach. This two player game is based on *input-agreement*. The two players, that cannot communicate, listen to the same sound clip and propose labels that describe it. Each player sees the labels proposed by the other player and the round finishes when players indicate if they are listening to the same piece of music. The agreement is therefore on the input and not on the output as in the previous ones. The ListenGame [12] is also a game for labelling music. In this game, players choose among a predefined list of labels those that fit best and worse to a given music piece. Based on the answers of several players, a confidence level is associated to each tag.

Concerning the aspect of user-interfaces, the authors of the games previously mentioned opted for minimalistic features. Several aspects can be identified: 1) the item (music clip) has often no graphical representation (HerdIt, ListenGame, MajorMiner, MoodSwing), in this case the music clip is automatically played and the users cannot interfere (stop/pause/continue) nor can they see the progress of the listening. In the case of TagATune, more traditional media player controls are presented. 2) Labels are represented by simple words (no decoration) in MajorMiner and TagATune or by buttons (ListenGame) or in the case of HerdIt, by floating bubbles. When labels are chosen by the user, they are entered using a text box and buttons (or bubbles) are used in case of predefined labels. 3) The use of colours differ between interfaces. In TagATune only two colours are used (purple and white) with gradients in order to produce an aesthetic effect. The bubbles in HerdIt are coloured but the colouring scheme seems to be random. In the ListenGame, the colours are used to identify the choices made (labels) by the two players. Finally, the MajorMiner game uses very few colours, for differentiating levels of confidence of each label (italicised font is also used for this purpose). 4) Scores are represented either by a numerical value (ListenGame, MajorMiner, and TagATune) or using a thermometer metaphor (HerdIt and ESP game).

3 Our Aproach

This section summarizes our approach, exposing the differentiating aspects to the related work. Now we present our approach, exposing the differentiating aspects to the related work.

We have the mission of providing a joyful experience to the user and not only focus on the data collecting task. We opted for a much richer interface compared with the previous applications, which provides a lot of contextual information about the audio excerpt that users are asked to label. The context given to the user is composed by: 1) a temporal context through three timelines with different time scales; 2) a video representing the "real" visual context as a scene from where the excerpts were extracted; 3) a dynamic force-directed graph where nodes correspond to similar excerpts the user can listen to, before deciding on the labels.

Our application is oriented to the classification of small pieces of audio of any kind of sound, not being limited to just music. The audio samples presented to the user are four seconds long, compared with the thirty seconds or more for other games, which gives us the following benefits: shorter samples are easier to classify due to the highly sounds' heterogeneous nature and the unlikeness in having a larger number of different sound events. And if we were able to identify reliably sounds in these excerpts, it would be easier to extend to longer samples by combining the output of four seconds chunks.

People will play asynchronously over the Internet, not needing for users to be online at the same time to initiate a game session. This approach is similar to MajorMiner game and have the benefits of increasing the complexity required for cheating due to the fact of eliminating most of the communication issues (e.g. communication through labels, a similar issue observed in the TagATune Game), and users can be rewarded while offline when labels proposed by the user are reused by others, thus working as a incentive to return to the game.

4 SoundsLike Interaction Design

SoundsLike is integrated as a part of MovieClouds [9] and is dedicated to soundtrack interactive browsing and labelling. Along with a movie navigation, game elements are used to engage users into the labelling of audio elements. The user interface not only is designed with the objective to persuade the chance of playing and contribute, but also by supporting users in this task, allowing and simplifying listening to the audio in the context of the movie, by presenting similar audio excerpts, and suggesting labels. The main design options for SoundsLike are presented as labelling simple scenario starting in the context of a movie navigation from MovieClouds.

In Figure 1, the user is in the Movies Space View, where movies can be searched, overviewed and browsed, before one is selected to be explored in more detail, and watched along time, in the Movie View (Fig.1a-1b and [9]).Tag clouds were adopted in both views to represent summaries or overviews of the content

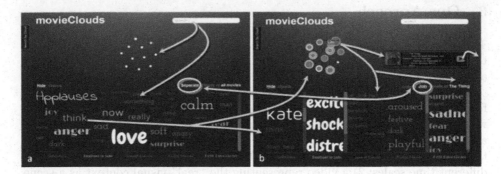

Fig. 1. MovieClouds Movie View navigation[9]: a) unique tagcloud for 5 content tracks; b) 5 separated tag clouds for each track. Some tags selected and highlighted in the movies where they appear (top).

in five tracks (subtitles, emotions in subtitles, audio events, audio mood (based on music), and felt emotions), for the power, flexibility, engagement and fun usually associated with them.

4.1   The Challenge

After selecting the Back to the Future movie in Figure 1b) (top right), it plays in the Movie View in Figure 2a), with five timelines for the content tracks showed below the movie, and a selected overview tag cloud of the content presented on the right (audio events in the example), synchronized with the movie that is playing and thus with the video timeline, to emphasize when the events occur along the movie. Users may choose to see, on the right, any of the five content tracks, and compare in the timelines where the selected tags occur along time (e.g. what is happening in the other tracks when the audio has a gunshot event?). From the timelines, users may select which time to watch in the video. If the user is registered, a small head-up display is always displayed in the top-right corner with the name, accumulated points and rank level (based on points: "rookie" in the example) to the left of the SoundsLike star logo, reminding the user to access it.

4.2   Playing with SoundsLike

After pressing the SoundsLike logo (Fig.2a-b), a challenge appears: an audio excerpt is highlighted in three audio timelines with different zoom levels below the video, and represented, to the right, in the center of a force-directed graph displaying similar excerpts, with a field for selection of suggested or insertion of new tags below, to classify the current audio excerpt, and hopefully earn more points. By allowing to present the current excerpt and surrounding neighbours, to inspect details of the audio signals, and to navigate and listen to entire audio

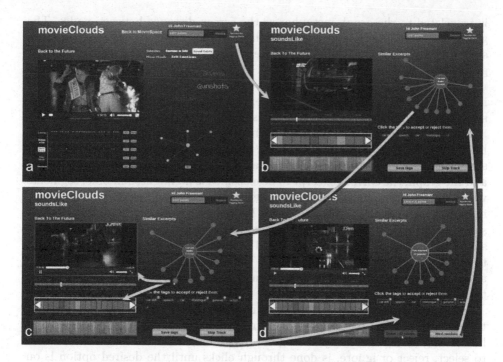

Fig. 2. SoundsLike interaction: a) audio events track in MovieClouds Movie View; b) selection (click) of a neighbour excerpt; c) to be played as video, providing more context to identify the audio (excerpt highlighted with brownish red frame on the graph, timelines and video; d) saving labels, winning from labeling, and choosing to play again and label one more.

excerpts and possibly watch them in the context of the movie, SoundsLike was designed to support the identification of the current audio excerpts to be labelled.

Three timelines are presented below the video: the top timeline represents an overview of the entire video soundtrack; the middle one presents a zoomed-in timeline view with the level of detail chosen by the user, by dragging a marker on the soundtrack timeline. Here, audio excerpts are smaller fragments from the movie's soundtrack represented as coloured rectangles; the bottom timeline displays a close-up on a chosen excerpt as an audio spectrogram. We designed the audio timelines to be similar to the timelines already used in Movieclouds for content tracks (figure 2a)). The relation between each of the timelines is reinforced by colour matching of selection and frames.

The audio similarity graph is provided as a helping tool for the classification of audio excerpts by displaying similar sounds to the current excerpt. The visualization is achieved through a dynamic force-directed graph representing the similarity relations to most similar audio excerpts in the movie (the shorter connection, the similar). The similarity value is the Euclidean distance between audio histograms computed from extracted features (more details in [4]), and it is translated to the graph metaphor as the screen distance between nodes. The graph defines minimum and maximum distances for its edges and normalizes all similarity values between those distances. The nodes repel each other and the graph may be dragged around with an elastic behaviour. This is particularly useful, if the users identify this audio better than the one they were trying to identify, and had not classified it before, allowing to earn points faster; and to select similar audios after they have finished the current classification.

Similar to MovieClouds' navigation, the views are synchronized in SoundsLike besides the synchronization between the timelines. This is adopted by using the same colours mappings and similar behaviours in all views. In all the timelines and the graph, the current excerpt to be classified is highlighted in blue, segments which are yet to be classified are grey, excerpts classified before or skipped are marked with green and yellow colours. In a similar way, all representations of sound excerpts have the same interaction: hovering over an excerpt will play the sound associated and display a bright red coloured frame to temporarily highlight the location of the excerpts everywhere, while selecting for play (simple click an audio excerpt) will display the same frame in a brownish tone of red, also around the video.

Below the graph lies the labelling area. Here users will choose one or more textual labels (tags) to describe the current sound segment by choosing from a list of suggested labels or by adding new custom labels. Choosing a label either to select, reject or ignore, is done through clicks until the desired option is on (green v marker to accept, red x marker to reject, and no marker to ignore). In addition, labels that were introduced by the users have an additional frame in the same colour of the marker (green, red) or grey to ignore. The choices are saved when the save button is pressed. At any time, the user can skip an excerpt and choose another one, or simply leave the game. The score will remain registered. When choices are submitted, the current excerpt changes colour to green in the similarity graph and the timelines, displaying the earned score at the central node of the graph that is also enlarged. Now, the user may use the Next Sound button to randomly navigate to another segment in the same movie, or may choose a specific excerpt from the similarity graph or from the timeline. Excerpts already labelled (green) cannot be labelled again.

5   SoundsLike Gaming Elements

In this section, we present the main design options to persuade users to contribute for the labelling task of movies soundtracks through a gamification approach.

Before users are allowed to freely label audio pieces, we need to assess the user level of expertise to assign a confidence level to their labelling. When users play for the first time, the system will present audio excerpts for which the confidence level by the model is very high (i.e. Audio excerpts labelled by experts or with a considerable amount of aggregated labels and users consensus). These excerpts are introduced seamlessly in the game flow, being chosen frequently in the beginning and fading over time. This approach provide us with information that can be used to better step up or down the difficulty of the queries presented to the user and the consequent rewards. Our models give us a confidence level for each label, indicating how "difficult" the query is; and an estimate of the similarity between two audio excerpts (independently of labels).

Gamification typically involves a kind of reward to the users. Points are earned by the users as consequence of the following achievements: 1) When their corresponds to a consensus by partial or entire textual matching, taking into account their confidence level; 2) When the consensual answer corresponds to a difficult query. An audio excerpt is considered difficult when we observe a high level of disagreement in the users' labels; and 3) When a label proposed by a user gets confirmed by others, the former is rewarded. This way, users can see their score increase even when off-line, through in-game and email notifications that can act as an incentive to return to the game later.

6   User Evaluation

We performed an evaluation to assess SoundsLike and detect usability problems and obtain feedback directly from the users about future improvements in the application. 10 users participated in the assessment of the application interface and features, with ages ranging from 21 to 44 years (24 mean value), computer experience and frequent use of internet. The evaluation focused into the user perceived usefulness, satisfaction and ease of use.

On an interview fashion evaluation, a task-oriented approach was conducted to guide the user interactions with the different features, while the evaluator was observing and taking notes of every relevant reaction or commentary. Every task involved a set of features and its evaluation was focused on the user experience, emphasising perceived Usefulness, Satisfaction and Ease of Use (based on the USE questionnaire [8] and using a 1-5 Lickert scale).

In the end, users were asked to rate the application globally, refer to the aspects or features they liked the most and the least, and classify it with a group of terms from a table representing the perceived ergonomic, hedonic and appeal quality aspects [5].

6.1   Assessing SoundsLike Features

Results from the USE based evaluation are presented in table 1, by mean and standard deviation values for each feature, performed in the context of the 8 tasks, described next, followed by a global evaluation of SoundsLike.

In task 1, users had the first visual interaction, where the interface was challenging them to label a random (non tagged) audio excerpt. Here users were asked to identify every element that would represent the current audio excerpt in the interface, i.e. in the timelines (T1.1), and in the similarity graph (T1.2). Most users were able to quickly identify all the components from the interface, even though some users had difficulties pointing to the current audio segment in the similarity graph, in the first contact.

In the second task we asked the users to play the sound (T2.1) and video (T2.2) of some excerpts from the timeline and graph. Most users identified a relationship between the graph nodes and the timeline elements and appreciated the interaction between every component during the video playback.

The third task is similar to the previous, but focused on the timeline features, such as the overview of the film provided by the video timeline, scrolling and manipulation of the dynamic zoom. Users were told to play the video audio excerpts in the zoom timeline in a fashion that would require them to manipulate the timeline to attain the task's objectives (T3.1). All users used the scroll buttons without problems, and the majority quickly perceived the zoom manipulation in the video timeline (T3.2). But most users did not find utility about the audio spectrogram (T3.3), which they reported was due to a lack of knowledge in the area of sound analysis, but recognized its importance to users that would have that knowledge.

The fourth task was meant to introduce the user to the similarity graph and navigation by changing (selecting) the current audio excerpt. We simply asked the user to listen to the 3 most similar sounds, select one of them and observe the transition to become the current excerpt (T4.1). We observed that most users got the distance metaphor correctly, but they did not move the graph to verify ambiguous cases (when every node stands almost at the same distance), until they got instructed to do so (T4.2) and since the distances did not differ that much, in this case the usefulness was 3.5. We also evaluated the user's perception about each audio element and their colouring (T4.3).

In the fifth task, we introduced labelling (tagging) to the users, where they could accept suggested tags (T5.1) and add some labels (T5.2) to audio excerpts and submit the changes to the database. We prepared three cases: one audio excerpt without any kind of labels associated, and two with suggested labels: one case where labels were presented related with the current audio excerpt, the other one with unrelated labels. We observed that the users were able to introduce and accept suggestions without significant problems, but some failed to perceive the label rejection feature (T5.3) without a proper explanation from the evaluator. Despite the usefulness of the fast labelling feature (comma separated text), without a proper tooltip, users were unable to find and use it without help (T5.4 - U:5,S:4.4,E:2.4), but it is a typical feature for more experienced users as a shortcut, and we observed that it was very appreciated as soon as they became aware of it.

With every user interface section covered, tasks 6, 7 and 8 were meant to immerse the user inside the labelling experience in the application by labelling a considerable amount of excerpts. Users were asked about the utility of audio (T6.1), video (T6.2) playing and the similarity graph (T6.3) in this context. After this, we asked the user about what was the excerpt he would label next (T7). Here users found the similarity graph more useful than other components due to their highly similarity and the propagation of previous used labels as suggestions. We also inquired users about the scoring mechanism (T8), and they found it interesting and a great way to stimulate users to participate, although

Table 1. USE evaluation of SoundsLike features in the tasks (scale:1-5). (M=Mean, Δ=Std. Deviation)

Task	Feature	Useful-ness		Satisfac-tion		Ease of Use	
		M	Δ	M	Δ	M	Δ
1.1	Find the current node in the timeline.	4.4	0.7	4.3	1.1	4.5	0.8
1.2	Find the current node in the similarity graph.	2.9	1.4	3.4	1.4	3.7	1.4
2.1	Play of the segment's sound.	3.7	1.1	4.2	0.8	4.4	0.7
2.2	Play of the segment's video.	4.7	0.5	4.6	0.7	4.4	0.8
3.1	Movies Timeline.	4.4	0.8	4.0	1.3	3.6	1.0
3.2	Zoom Timeline.	4.3	1.1	4.2	1.1	4.3	0.9
3.3	Spectrogram timeline.	2.7	1.6	3.5	1.2	4.3	0.8
3.4	Timeline relationships.	4.6	0.5	4.4	0.7	4.0	0.9
3.5	Timeline - Overview	4.6	0.5	3.9	0.7	3.8	0.8
4.1	Similarity Graph.	4.6	0.7	4.0	0.8	4.2	0.9
4.2	Graph dynamism.	3.5	1.2	3.6	0.8	2.5	1.0
4.3	Sound segments colours.	4.6	0.5	3.6	0.8	2.5	1.0
5.1	Choosing suggested tags.	4.6	0.5	4.4	0.5	4.3	0.9
5.2	Add new tags.	4.8	0.4	4.5	0.5	4.2	0.8
5.3	The possibility of tag rejection.	4.7	0.7	4.6	0.7	3.4	1.4
5.4	Adding tags fast.	5.0	0.0	4.4	1.0	2.4	1.4
6.1	Playing of the segment's video on tagging context.	4.8	0.4	4.8	0.4	4.6	0.5
6.2	Playing of the segment's sound on tagging context.	4.9	0.3	4.7	0.5	4.7	0.5
6.3	Using similar sounds for tagging the current sound segment.	4.9	0.3	4.8	0.4	4.7	0.5
7	In game context, choosing the most similar is an efficient way of earning points?	4.5	1.3	4.4	1.1	4.5	1.0
8	Points attribution for sound tagging.	3.9	0.9	3.4	1.3	4.0	1.2
	Soundslike Overall Evaluation	**4.4**	**0.5**	**4.2**	**0.6**	**3.9**	**0.6**
	Total (Mean)	*4.3*	*0.6*	*4.2*	*0.4*	*4.0*	*0.6*

they did not have a full game experience in this short time. We also observed a great user's engagement and immersion within the application, and received compliments and suggestions to be discussed and applied in future developments.

6.2   Overall Evaluation

In the end, users were asked to rate SoundsLike globally. The values obtained were fairly high, with values of 4.4 for usefulness, 4.2 for satisfaction and 3.9 for ease of use. The experience allowed us to control and witness the rapid and fairly easy learning curve and we observed engagement in most users, especially during task 6.

Users pointed the interface fluidity as one of the factors contributing to the engagement felt, and chose the similarity graph, the timelines and the scoring system as the most appreciated features. The least appreciated was the audio spectrogram because some users commented on their lack of expertise in the field of audio analysis.

At the end of the interview, the users classified the application with most relevant perceived ergonomic, hedonic and appeal quality aspects [5] (8 positive

Table 2. Quality terms to describe SoundsLike. H:Hedonic; E:Ergonomic; A:Appeal [5]

# Terms		# Terms	
6 Controllable	H	4 Innovative	H
6 Original	H	4 Inviting	A
5 Comprehensible	E	4 Motivating	A
5 Simple	E	3 Supporting	E
5 Clear	E	3 *Complex*	E
5 Pleasant	A	3 *Confusing*	E
4 Interesting	H	3 Aesthetic	A

and 8 negative terms for each category, 48 in total), as many as they would feel appropriate (most frequent in Table 2). Almost all the terms were positive, the most for Ergonomic qualities which are related with traditional usability practices and ease of use. The most frequent negative terms were "Complex" and "Confusing", although the first is correlated with interesting, powerful or challenging applications (a frequent trade-off, we also recognize in our application), and both terms are also opposite to the terms "Simple" and "Clear", that were selected more often.

7   Conclusions

This paper describes and evaluates SoundsLike, a new Game With A Purpose whose objective is to collect labels that characterize short audio excerpt taken from movies. The interface is designed to entertain the user while pursuing the data collection task. The proposed interface innovates with respect to previous GWAPs with similar objectives by providing a rich context both in terms of temporal aspects through three timelines with different time scales, and in terms of similarities between items by displaying a dynamic force-directed graph where the neighbourhood of the current item is represented. This graph allows the exploration of nearby items in terms of similarity, but it is also used to navigate through the set of audio samples while always keeping track of the corresponding scene in the video document. The application does not restrict the user to a closed set of labels but, by making suggestions, tends to overcome the never-ending vocabulary problem found in other labelling games. The interface lets the user play audio excerpts in several ways: by hovering with the pointer on the representation of the excerpt in the graph, or by clicking it to play the corresponding video in the context of the movie. The user evaluation results were quite good and encouraging. We observed that users had a pleasant experience and found it original, controllable, clear and pleasant. They particularly liked the similarity graph and the timelines. This also provided us with useful feedback and we were able to identify some usability aspects to improve.

Future work includes: 1) the refinement of the interface based on the feedback received and the perceived issues; 2) the refinement of the scoring mechanisms; 3) to remove the constrain of navigation inside a movie at a time, and expand it to allow navigation to other movies, based on audio similarities; 4) a deeper analysis of the user experience and entertainment value, and the evaluation of key design factors and how users perceive the impact of their changes in SoundsLike.

Acknowledgments. This work is partially supported by FCT - Fundação para a Ciência e Tecnologia, through LASIGE Multi-annual Funding.

References

1. Barrington, L., O'Malley, D., Turnbull, D., Lanckriet, G.: User-centered design of a social game to tag music. In: Proceedings of the ACM SIGKDD Workshop on Human Computation, p. 7. ACM Press (2009)
2. Daniel, G., Chen, M.: Video visualization. IEEE Transactions on Ultrasonics, Ferroelectrics and Frequency Control, 409–416 (2003)
3. Deterding, S., Dixon, D., Sicart, M., Nacke, L., Cultures, D., O'Hara, K.: Gamification: Using Game Design Elements in Non-Gaming Contexts. In: CHI EA 2011 Workshop, pp. 2425–2428. ACM, New York (2011)
4. Gil, N., Silva, N., Dias, E., Martins, P., Langlois, T., Chambel, T.: Going Through the Clouds: Search Overviews and Browsing of Movies. In: Proceeding of the 16th International Academic MindTrek Conference, pp. 158–165. ACM, Tampere (2012)
5. Hassenzahl, M., Platz, A., Burmester, M., Lehner, K.: Hedonic and ergonomic quality aspects determine a software's appeal. In: Proceedings of the SIGCHI Conference on Human Factors in Computing Systems, vol. 2, pp. 201–208 (2000)
6. Hauptmann, A.G.: Lessons for the future from a decade of informedia video analysis research. In: Leow, W.-K., Lew, M., Chua, T.-S., Ma, W.-Y., Chaisorn, L., Bakker, E.M. (eds.) CIVR 2005. LNCS, vol. 3568, pp. 1–10. Springer, Heidelberg (2005)
7. Khaled, R.: Its Not Just Whether You Win or Lose: Thoughts on Gamification and Culture. In: Gamification Workshop at ACM CHI 2011, pp. 1–4 (2011)
8. Lund, A.M.: Measuring Usability with the USE Questionnaire. In: Usability and User Experience, vol. 8(2), Usability SIG (2001)
9. Langlois, T., Chambel, T., Oliveira, E., Carvalho, P., Marques, G., Falcão, A.: VIRUS: Video Information retrieval using subtitles. In: 14th International Academic MindTrek Conference, p. 197. ACM Press (2010)
10. Law, E.L.M., Dannenberg, R.B., Crawford, M.: Tagatune: A game for music and sound annotation. In: ISMIR (2007)
11. Mandel, M., Ellis, D.: A Web-Based Game for Collecting Music Metadata. Journal of New Music Research 37, 15 (2008)
12. Turnbull, D., Liu, R., Barrington, L., Lanckriet, G.: A Game-Based Approach for Collecting Semantic Annotations of Music. In: ISMIR (2007)
13. Von Ahn, L., Dabbish, L.: Labeling images with a computer game. In: CHI 2004, vol. 6, pp. 319–326. ACM, New York (2004)
14. Von Ahn, L., Kedia, M., Blum, M.: Verbosity: A game for collecting common-sense facts. In: Knowledge Creation Diffusion Utilization, vol. 1, pp. 75–78. ACM Press (2006)

Creating Immersive Audio and Lighting Based Physical Exercise Games for Schoolchildren

Jaakko Hakulinen[1], Markku Turunen[1], Tomi Heimonen[1], Tuuli Keskinen[1], Antti Sand[1], Janne Paavilainen[1], Jaana Parviainen[2], Sari Yrjänäinen[3], Frans Mäyrä[1], Jussi Okkonen[1], and Roope Raisamo[1]

[1] School of Information Sciences
[2] School of Social Sciences and Humanities
[3] School of Education
FI-33014 University of Tampere, Finland
firstname.lastname@uta.fi

Abstract. We have created story-based exercise games utilizing light and sound to encourage children to participate in physical exercise in schools. Our reasonably priced technological setup provides practical and expressive means for creating immersive and rich experiences to support physical exercise education in schools. Studies conducted in schools showed that the story and drama elements draw children into the world of the exercise game. Moreover, children who do not like traditional games and exercises engaged in these activities. Our experiences also suggest that children's imagination plays a great role in the design and engagement into exercise games, which makes co-creation with children a viable and exciting approach to creating new games.

Keywords: Exergaming, interactive lighting, storytelling.

1   Introduction

There is great need to encourage children and adolescents to engage in physical activity. Childhood obesity is a serious and increasing challenge to public health [1] and regular physical activity in childhood and adolescence is shown to improve health and quality of life [2]. Physical Education (PE) classes in schools play an important role in guiding children to lead a life with healthy amount of exercise, but the actual time available for physical activity can be low [3]. Furthermore, there are children who find physical exercise and sports unpleasant or uninteresting. Supporting the improvement of physical abilities through games could potentially increase the chances of engaging in and benefitting from the positive outcomes of physical activities [4]. One way to foster health-related behavioral change is to use video games designed for this purpose [5]. Especially exertion-based games have been shown to stimulate physical activity in inactive children [3], and to increase energy expenditure over sedentary activities [6].

We have devised a game-based approach to physical exercises, where storytelling and dramatic elements, such as interactive lighting, guide and motivate children. The

D. Reidsma, H. Katayose, and A. Nijholt (Eds.): ACE 2013, LNCS 8253, pp. 308–319, 2013.

aim is to make physical activities more pleasant and motivating for children who find current forms of exercise uninteresting or even intimidating. Our prototype is targeted for 7–12-year-old schoolchildren and is played during a PE class under the supervision of a teacher.

We aimed at a solution that would be economically viable for schools. It consists of a laptop computer, audio speakers, a wireless gaming controller, and a small set of computer controlled lighting fixtures in a mobile trolley. The whole solution can be assembled for about €1000. The setup, augmented with additional hardware like motion sensors and a projector, can be used for many other applications in schools, for example for teaching mathematics or physics in a more immersive way.

The prototype has been studied in situ in PE classes and at an interactive science fair, where several new games were co-designed with children. Our results indicate that it is possible to create immersive and engaging, story-driven exercise games using a small set of lighting hardware and audio. From these simple elements, children's imagination can create rich experiences, which engage even the children who do not enjoy usual PE class activities.

2   Related Work

With the introduction of the Nintendo Wii controller and the Microsoft Kinect, health and activity related games have become popular. Brox et al. [7] differentiate between genres of such games: educational games, persuasive games, and exergames. Educational games are primarily designed for improving health literacy. Persuasive games, on the other hand, attempt to modify players' behavior, be it increases in exercise or adjustments of dietary habits. Finally, exergames are video games that are used in an exercise activity [8]. Definitions of exergames state the games either encourage physical exercise [6] or their outcome depends on the physical activity [9]. Exergames can be categorized according to dimensions such as the nature of the gaming aspects, technological enablers, the type of physical activity, and engagement.

Exergame user interfaces range from free motion interfaces, i.e., games where the players can freely move their body, via exercise equipment to traditional electronic interfaces, and game worlds can be categorized as virtual, like in traditional video games, augmented reality, or reality based [10]. Most of the existing exergames reviewed by Yim and Graham [10] are based on a virtual world or augmented reality, and are either free motion interfaces or utilize some form of equipment.

To be successful, exergames must both make the players exercise effectively and attract them to play long and often enough [8]. Sinclair et al. [8] provide dual flow model, based on the concept of flow state [11], which combines attractiveness and effectiveness, and focuses on challenge level and skill level both from the psychological and physiological sides. Baranowski et al. [5] list features that make games appealing and potentially efficient as behavior change tools, interactivity and personalized, interactive goal setting and tailored feedback being the key aspects. However, they place more focus on the immersive and attention-maintaining nature of games and identify stories and fantasy as tools for reaching this goal.

Many researchers raise the issue of social aspects and feedback in exercise motivation. Bekker et al. [12] raise motivating feedback as their first design value. Allowing players to create their own game goals can be greatly beneficial for the longevity of the exergame, and supporting social interaction patterns is important. Park et al. [13] supported interpersonal synchrony to leverage the positive social effects of "improving rapport and entitativity" and also make exercises more enjoyable. Social aspects are also noted as important for improving motivation by Yim and Graham [10]. They instruct to avoid systemic barriers to grouping and to actively assist players in forming groups. They also suggest that music should be used, and that leadership should be provided for novice players. Players should also be provided achievable short and long-term goals, but at the same time the design should hide players' fitness level to minimize demotivating messages.

The guidelines mentioned above help make the games attractive to players, but to ensure effectiveness, also the physical activity should be appropriately designed. The design should consider physical exercise parameters (intensity); the game must be playable for the required time period (duration); and the game should provide structure, where proper warm-up and cool down take place in addition to the actual exercise [8]. The exercise level can be adjusted per player either by using appropriate sensors, e.g., by a heart rate monitor, or by collecting explicit user input. This way, exercise levels can be balanced according to user's fitness, motivation, and goals.

3   The Lighting-Based Exercise Game Concept

The proposed game concept is designed for physical education classes in grade school where the entire class can play the game together. The game uses lighting hardware that can project light on different parts of the room. The lighting and audio create an immersive story environment. In the games we have built, stories have a central role, and the games ask players to cooperate and work towards a common goal instead of competing with one another. The games do not have direct response from players' actions to game events. Instead, the teacher acts as the intermediary and controls the progress of the game using a wireless controller. Children were often unaware of the human in the loop in our evaluations. The use of human supervisor minimizes technical challenges while keeping the game interactive. This also improves safety since the teacher can stop the game in case of any hazards.

Our main goal is to address the children who do not like the usual activities that take place during the PE classes. The challenge has been addressed before by using exergames by Fogel et al. [3]. Many children can feel that they are not performing well enough in the environment where other children are watching their activities and tend to react by minimizing their participation. This low self-efficacy aspect has been identified as an important factor in demotivating people [14]. Our game design has no explicit goal of behavioral change, but activating inactive children and providing positive exercise experiences will hopefully help them towards a more active lifestyle. To encourage participation, the game asks all players work together towards a shared goal. A single player is never in focus and actively observed by the others. The game is designed to capture the focus and most of the time the players follow the moving lights. The room is dark during the game, except for the lit areas, and the darkness provides some comfort to those shying from attention. Finally, the immersive story draws the players in so that they want to participate.

4   Technical Setup

The system consists of a laptop PC, audio speakers, a Playstation Move® wireless gaming controller, a moving head light fixture, and optionally fixed lights and a projector. The hardware is mounted on a 1 by 1 by 1.8 meters (w, d, h) sized trolley (Fig. 1). The trolley enables easy transportation of the hardware and acts as a physical extension of the virtual characters in the story.

Fig. 1. The trolley with full system setup during a game

The moving head light (Stairville RoboHead X-3 LED) on top of the trolley has three independent 540-degree joints, and can rotate 360 degrees in about 2 seconds. It creates a sharp, round spot with a diameter of 40 centimeters when pointing down on the floor next to the trolley. Light output is about 15,000 lux at one meter. Color filters alter the spot color while brightness can be adjusted gradually. Optional fixed lights include four RGB LED Par lights on the lowest level of the trolley that illuminate the floor on each side, and an RGB LED flood light on the second highest shelf that points upwards to an inverted pyramid shaped reflector.

4.1   Software Architecture

The software consists of an interface component for communicating with the wireless controller, a lighting controller using DMX512 protocol to control the light fixtures [15], a component (AVplayer) that can display graphics, play audio files and control speech synthesizers via Windows SAPI interface, and a central logic component

(Fig. 2). Games are modeled as state machines using XML markup. Entry to each stage can produce sequences of lighting adjustments and audio. Moves to new stages can be triggered with timers and by pressing buttons on the controller. Scripting can be used for more complex logic.

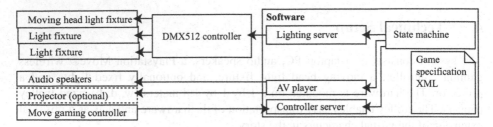

Fig. 2. System architecture

Audio consists of speech generated with a speech synthesizer and a set of audio files to provide music, sound effects and soundscape. In our initial game, a Finnish language synthesizer by BitLips was utilized. The speed and pitch of the voice were modified to create two different voices. In an extended version, audio files pre-generated with BitLips, Acapela and Loquendo synthesizers were used, different synthesizers playing the different roles. Distortion and echo was added to the BitLips files to make it sound more menacing. The use of speech synthesis, as opposed to prerecorded audio with voice actors, enables fast prototyping and quick changes to the game. This was seen more beneficial than the improved dramatic effect of recorded actors' voices. In particular, the use of a synthesizer enabled us to prototype games during workshops, as they were co-created with children (see Section 7).

In addition, background music tracks loop during the different parts of the story, the story characters have identifying soundscapes that play when they enter and there are some sound effects for story and game events.

Playstation Move controller is used to control the progress of the game. At the end of each activity, the operator presses a button when the task is finished. Two buttons are used so that the operator can mark the task success quality ("okay" or "excellent"). Additional button can be used to replay the last instruction in case the players had trouble understanding instructions or there was some mishap, which interrupted the game. This type of controller was chosen because it provides a wireless method of control and does not draw unnecessary attention to technology, but can rather be integrated into stories, for example, as a magic wand.

5   Story and Exercises

We have developed two versions of the game. The initial 10-minute version of the game consists of a story where the "Light" attempts to stop the "Shadow" from destroying the world. It was used in an initial evaluation to validate the fundamental concept and collect initial reactions from children. For the second, extended version, we modified and expanded the story to its full length so that it fills a 60-minute PE class. This version was subject to more extensive testing.

5.1   Initial Version

The first version of the game uses only the moving head light and speakers. The game is played in four groups formed before the game starts. The game starts with an introduction, where the story and characters are presented. Some physical activity is also encouraged at this point. The second part is warming up where participants are instructed (by the Light character) to do some stretching, squatting, etc. Some of the exercises are done simultaneously by all players while others are done group by group so that the light points at the group who is taking turn. Next, four small exercises, each including moving from one place to another (by jumping, one-leg jump, crawling, climbing) are done one group at a time. Motivation for these exercises is given in the story, e.g., crawling is necessary so that the Shadow would not notice the players. Next exercises are done simultaneously by all players participating, e.g., they jump up and down all at the same time to cause an earthquake which would collapse the throne of the Shadow. In the end, the story is wrapped up.

During the game, the two characters are signified by their voice, the soundscape, sound effects, and lighting. Presence of the Light character is signified with white light while the Shadow is represented by a red spotlight. Some exercise sequences also feature colors specific to a group of players. Both the Light and the Shadow address the players directly in their speech, although only the Light tells the players what to do.

5.2   Extended Version

In this version the game starts with an introduction by a narrator. When the actual game starts, the Light character guides the players and the story goes through four stages: awakening, empowerment, calling, and battle. The awakening part consists of four slow stretching and warm-up exercises. Empowerment contains four more active and physical exercises. Calling part is even faster, containing lot of movement around the space in its four activities. Finally, the battle is the most physical part, consisting of four tasks with fast movements in various ways. Once the story part finishes in the end of the battle, the narrator returns and takes the players through a cool-down phase consisting of three slow, relaxing activities. Each part has its own music, and music style and tempo match the level of activity aimed for the part.

The second version incorporates the five fixed RGB lights, four to illuminate areas on the floor and one to provide overall illumination to the room. Use of a reflector pyramid also created a strong visual point in the tower. We also added a projector and projection screen to display a signature image for both the Shadow and the Light characters, stars to signify players' success, and images of animals and elements that are awakened and called to help the players during the story.

In this version, the teacher rates activities on binary scale, each activity rated to be either acceptable or great performance. The feedback is given immediately by speech output and after each exercise set, one, two or three stars are displayed with the projector based on the performance.

6   Evaluations

6.1   Initial Version

The system was evaluated with five groups of 5th and 6th graders (11–13 years old) during two days. The group sizes ranged from 8 to 20 children, some groups consisted of only boys or girls while others had both. In total there were over 60 participants. The system was set up in a small gym in the school. Each group's own teacher was present and the system was operated either by the teacher or a researcher. Two to three additional researchers were also present and the sessions were videotaped. After the initial introduction, which included positioning the participants in groups around the trolley, participants followed the system's instructions. Teacher or researcher instructed the children if they had problems following instructions.

The system was updated after the first day based on our observations. There seemed to be too much waiting without any physical activity during the introduction and some children jumped when the spotlight passed their feet. Therefore an explicit instruction to jump was added.

Method. Subjective questionnaire and interview data was gathered. Almost all participants, 61 in total, filled in a questionnaire and most also participated in interviews, which were conducted in small groups (about 5 persons). The questionnaire included 21 statements which were answered on a scale consisting of three smiley faces, i.e., happy, neutral and sad face. These statements concerned the overall thoughts of the system (e.g., would they like to play again, was it boring), the fluency of the game (e.g., did they understand the instructions, was it too slow), the physical strain of the game (e.g., did they get winded, were the tasks too easy), and the atmosphere of the game (e.g., was the atmosphere good, did they feel outsiders during the game). In addition to the statements, an overall grade between 1 and 10 for the game was inquired, and open-ended questions were asked: the participants were able to tell what was best and worst in the game, and how could it be made more interesting.

Results. Our findings indicated that the basic concept works well: the system received a favorable average overall grade of 6.84 (SD=2.199), and although some of the children testing the system were a bit older than our target age of 10 years, they were still observed to get into the game and enthusiastically participate in the exercises. Both interviews and observation showed that the current design had too much waiting and too little exercise. Addition of feedback on performance was the most common request in the interview feedback: the static structure of the game provided no feedback on players' activities; they could not fail or affect the outcome in any way.

Other opportunities for improvement were also identified. Use of speech synthesizer made the speech somewhat hard to understand, the two characters sounded too similar which reduced the emotional effect of the story. This was found both from player feedback and observations. Also, the group size of twenty was too big for the combination of the activities and the very small gym where the tests took place. Congestion resulted when groups were supposed to move into the same area and especially when all players chased the light spot as one group.

Overall, while many ways to improve the experience were found, our observation of the tests showed that the fundamental concepts, i.e., the use of audio and lighting created a very powerful effect, immersing the players the very moment the game started. Based on the results, we continued the development.

6.2   Extended Version

The second version was evaluated in a different school with 110 participants (56 girls, 54 boys) over the course of a week. The ages ranged from 1st graders all the way to 6th graders, i.e., the participants were 6–11 years old with a mean age of 9.1 years (SD=1.1). The participant groups were classes either as one or two groups. Almost all participants (97%) liked physical exercise and 77% reported to exercise in their free time, while 42% practiced some team sport. These background variables were not affected by gender. However, boys were more active players of videogames than girls out of the participants who reported playing videogames (74% of respondents).

The teacher was present in most cases but the game was introduced and controlled by a researcher. Additional researchers were present and sessions were videotaped. After the introduction, the researcher remained silent, unless there were significant troubles, which occurred only in a few cases. The fact that the researcher was rating the performances was not told to the children. The game was again updated slightly after the first day, shortening or splitting some of the longest instructions. Some were so long, that the players could not remember all the relevant information and got bored. We split such instructions into two parts and included first part of the activity in between, where possible.

Method. We collected subjective experiences with a questionnaire, which was filled in afterwards in class by all the children who played the game. We modified the questionnaire to address some modality-specific statements and shorten it overall. The open-ended questions remained the same but the amount of the experience statements was narrowed down to 13, and they were answered with "Yes", "No" and "I don't know" options. The final statements were (translated from Finnish):

1. Playing was hard.
2. I would like to move this way again.
3. Exercising was now more pleasant than usually on PE classes.
4. I understood the instructions of the exercise tasks well.
5. I understood the speech well.
6. The speech voice sounded pleasant.
7. The music and the voices of the game were compelling.
8. The lights of the game were compelling.
9. I found the game irritating.
10. The story of the game was interesting.
11. The exercise tasks were too easy.
12. I could move with my own style.
13. I felt like an outsider in the game.

The overall grade for the game was reported with a five-step smiley face scale ranging from extremely sad to extremely happy as an answer to the question "How much did you like of the game as a whole?" Background questions included age and gender, do they play videogames, do they like physical exercise, do they do exercise in their free-time and do they practice some team sport (e.g., football, ice hockey).

Results. The median overall grade for the game was 5 out of 5, and almost 60% of the participants gave the system the extremely happy face. Neutral or a little sad face was selected only by 16% and none of the participants selected the extremely sad face. The participants would like to move this way again (76%) and they felt that exercising was now more pleasant than usually on gym classes (72%). The majority (66%) experienced the music and the voices to be compelling, and even more (78%) saw the lights of the game to be compelling. Only 6% of the participants reported they felt like an outsider in the game and only 5% stated playing the game was hard.

There were several statistically significant (p < 0.05) interactions between the experience variables (according to Pearson Chi-Square test, "I don't know" responses set as missing values). For example, whether the participants would like to move this way again had an effect on almost all the other responses as well: only difficulty of playing (statement 1), understanding the speech (5) and feeling an outsider (13) did not interact with willingness to move this way again. Similarly, the overall rating affected almost all other experiences while only difficulty of the game (1), ability to move with own style (12) and feeling an outsider (13) had no interaction with the overall rating of the system.

Remarkably, all 17 participants who did not exercise in their free-time felt that exercising now was more pleasant than usually on gym classes (3). We also observed gender related differences in experiences. Girls felt more often (in fact, all girls) that exercising was now more pleasant than usually on gym classes (X^2=17.848, df=1, p=0.000) and they also liked the game as a whole clearly more than the boys. Boys, on the other hand, experienced the speech sound less frequently pleasant (X^2=4.262, df=1, p=0.039) and the music and voices less compelling than the girls (X^2=5.643, df=1, p=0.018).

Age seems to have had slight effect on almost all of the statements: older participants received the system a bit more negatively. The differences in other statements are not that surprising as the story approach of the game may feel a little childish for the oldest children. The only statements that were not significantly affected by age were difficulty of playing the game (statement 1), easiness of the exercise tasks (11), ability to move with own style (12), and feeling an outsider (13).

7   Co-creation of Games with Children

A set of five workshops was held in a science-themed event to further develop the game concept with children. The event took place in a large, dimly lit indoor arena, which was split into about 80 booths. The workshops took place in a 5 by 8 meter booth, enclosed by 2.5 meter high white walls on three sides. The light setup consisted of one moving head fixture (Martic Mac 300) and four fixed lights RGBW LED fixtures. A pair of active speakers was used for audio and the games were controlled by a researcher operating the laptop where the games were created and run.

In each workshop, a group of 10 to 15 schoolchildren participated and a new game was created. Each workshop lasted 70 to 85 minutes. Participants were free to leave at any time, and in some cases about a third of the participants left after half an hour. Each workshop started with an introduction where the functionality of the lighting hardware was demonstrated. Next, an example game (a 10-minute shortened version of our extended game) was played and after this the actual game design started. The game was designed and implemented during the workshop so that different parts of the game were tested during the development and the full game was played at least once in the end. The created games were finalized after the workshop by adding missing parts like instructions, which were unnecessary for the participants themselves, and fixing other remaining issues. The resulting games were then tested on the last day of the event when interested event visitors were allowed to play the games.

Landry et al. [16] note that it is a challenge to make children aware of the physical and virtual potential of interactive technology. Like them, we made children try out the system to foster understanding of the system, and in addition added an introduction of the technology. However, we went mostly story first and this seemed natural to children. Our process was different from that of Landry et al. in that we worked all the time as one group. This was problematic in larger groups since not everybody could provide their input, and splitting into smaller groups could have worked better. In the end, the exercise and gameplay ideas were less imaginative and followed more on what was in the example game, which suggest the children were biased by their initial exposure to the game environment. However, when testing the games on the last day of the event with interested children, we found that the created games worked well. In particular, the very simple description of the game world (e.g., "You are in the jungle, you are small monkeys."), together with lights, was enough to create immersive environments as children's imagination did the rest. The players also did the necessary interpretations to figure out ambiguous instructions.

8   Discussion and Conclusions

We built light and sound based exercise games for children. Our evaluations showed that it is possible to create strong, immersive experiences with this technology, capable of pulling children into the world of a story. The use of simple graphics did not seem to significantly improve the effect, at times the opposite. Speech was found to be a powerful way to tell a story while sound effects are very important in building the atmosphere. The story does not need to be told in detail; very simple descriptions of stereotypic scenarios are enough as players' imagination takes care of the rest. This means that creating new games does not require particular skills in storytelling. The most important part in writing games is to keep the length of the instructions short and keep players active. The story should incorporate activity and the instructions on what to do should be given at the time the players are supposed to do something.

The basic concepts seemed to work exactly as envisioned, with children participating in the physical activities even if they did not usually like sports and such children reported liking the game more than the usual PE class activities. The facts that the games did not contain strong competitive elements and that the focus is on lighting and the story seemed to help achieve this goal.

The age range of children to which the same game seemed to appeal to was a positive surprise. The original target group was children around 10 years of age. However, even 6-year-olds could easily follow most of the instructions and were very interested in the story. Among children approaching the age of 12, the number of persons considering the game too childish did increase, but many of those who "misbehaved" still did so within the fiction of the game. Only a couple of the most mature children did their best to remain uninterested in the world of the story.

Following the suggestions by Yim and Graham [10] was helpful to the overall success: the application of music clearly made the experience more engaging and guided players toward the tempo we aimed for in the different exercises. The game also gave direct instructions to players, thus providing leadership. Early on, the users did not yet follow the instructions from the system without hesitation. This changed when they noticed that the game progressed when they did what was asked.

The current version of the game has the temporal extent of one exercise session, i.e., less than an hour. This means the goals we provide to users are only short and medium term goals. We plan to introduce long-term goals, for example by creating alternative endings to the game depending on players' performance. This could also provide implicit exercise goals, while still hiding players' fitness levels, which is relevant in helping children with low self-efficacy. In our current solution, we supported players' self-efficacy during group activity by keeping the story at the center of attention and not putting any individuals in focus during the game. Together, the above aspects created an atmosphere where everybody could enjoy the game without worrying about their performance. The overall design focused on the entire group working together to accomplish a common goal. In this sense the game facilitated grouping and group support. In the second version, there were no elements separating the players. This can also be considered a limitation, since the players could not get the kind of support they could get by forming smaller groups.

Above all, exercise games must also be fun in order to be efficient [8, 10]. We feel the game reached this goal. The lighting and audio provide an immersive and novel experience and the spatial nature of the moving spot light naturally encourages physical activity. We also feel that the game matched reasonably well the players' abilities.

Acknowledgements. This work is part of the "Active Learning Spaces" project, funded by the Finnish Funding Agency for Technology and Innovation.

References

1. World Health Organization. Global Strategy on Diet, Physical Activity and Health, http://www.who.int/dietphysicalactivity/childhood/en/
2. U.S. Department of Health and Human Services. Physical Activity Guidelines Advisory Committee report. Washington, DC: U.S. Department of Health and Human Services (2008)

3. Fogel, V.A., Miltenberger, R.G., Graves, R., Koehler, S.: The Effects of Exergaming On Physical Activity Among Inactive Children In A Physical Education Classroom. Appl. Behav. Anal. 43(4), 591–600 (2010)
4. Peer, F., Friedlander, A., Mazalek, A., Mueller, F.: Evaluating technology that makes physical games for children more engaging. In: 10th International Conference on Interaction Design and Children (IDC 2011), pp. 193–196. ACM, New York (2011)
5. Baranowski, T., Buday, R., Thompson, D.I., Baranowski, J.: Playing for real: Video games and stories for health-related behavior change. Am. J. Prev. Med. 34(1), 74–82 (2008)
6. Whitehead, A., Johnston, H., Nixon, N., Welch, J.: Exergame effectiveness: What the numbers can tell us. In: Spencer, S.N. (ed.) 5th ACM SIGGRAPH Symposium on Video Games (Sandbox 2010), pp. 55–62. ACM, New York (2010)
7. Brox, E., Fernandez-Luque, L., Tøllefsen, T.: Healthy Gaming – Video Game Design to Promote Health. Appl. Clin. Inform. 2(2), 128–142 (2011)
8. Sinclair, J., Hingston, P., Masek, M.: Considerations for the design of exergames. In: 5th International Conference on Computer Graphics and Interactive Techniques in Australia and Southeast Asia (GRAPHITE 2007), pp. 289–295. ACM, New York (2007)
9. Mueller, F., Edge, D., Vetere, F., Gibbs, M.R., Agamanolis, S., Bongers, B., Sheridan, J.G.: Designing sports: A framework for exertion games. In: SIGCHI Conference on Human Factors in Computing Systems (CHI 2011), pp. 2651–2660. ACM, New York (2011)
10. Yim, J., Graham, T.C.N.: Using games to increase exercise motivation. In: 2007 Conference on Future Play (Future Play 2007), pp. 166–173. ACM, New York (2007)
11. Csikszentmihalyi, M., Csikszentmihalyi, I.S. (eds.): Optimal experience: Psychological studies of flow in consciousness. Cambridge University Press (1992)
12. Bekker, T., Sturm, J., Eggen, B.: Designing playful interactions for social interaction and physical play. Personal Ubiquitous Comput. 14(5), 385–396 (2010)
13. Park, T., Lee, U., Lee, B., Lee, H., Son, S., Song, S., Song, J.: ExerSync: Facilitating interpersonal synchrony in social exergames. In: 16th ACM Conference on Computer Supported Cooperative Work and Social Computing (CSCW 2013), pp. 409–422. ACM, New York (2013)
14. Hagger, M.S., Chatzisarantis, N.L., Biddle, S.J.: A meta-analytic review of the theories of reasoned action and planned behavior in physical activity: Predictive validity and the contribution of additional variables. J. Sport and Exercise Psychol. 24(1), 3–32 (2002)
15. Hakulinen, J., Turunen, M., Heimonen, T.: Light Control Architecture for Multimodal Interaction in Physical and Augmented Environments. In: DIS 2012 Workshop on Designing Interactive Lighting (2012)
16. Landry, P., Parés, N., Minsky, J., Parés, R.: Participatory design for exertion interfaces for children. In: 11th International Conference on Interaction Design and Children (IDC 2012), pp. 256–259. ACM, New York (2012)

Game Flux Analysis with Provenance

Troy C. Kohwalter, Esteban G. W. Clua, and Leonardo G. P. Murta

Instituto de Computação, Universidade Federal Fluminense, Niterói – RJ, Brazil
{tkohwalter,esteban,leomurta}@ic.uff.br

Abstract. Winning or losing a game session is the final consequence of a series of decisions and actions made during the game. The analysis and understanding of events, mistakes, and fluxes of a concrete game play may be useful for different reasons: understanding problems related to gameplay, data mining of specific situations, and even understanding educational and learning aspects in serious games. We introduce a novel approach based on provenance concepts in order to model and represent a game flux. We model the game data and map it to provenance to generate a provenance graph for analysis. As an example, we also instantiated our proposed conceptual framework and graph generation in a serious game, allowing developers and designers to identify possible mistakes and failures in gameplay design by analyzing the generated provenance graph from collected gameplay data.

Keywords: Game flux, Game analysis, Provenance, Graph Analysis.

1 Introduction

The conclusion of a game session derives from a series of decisions and actions made throughout the game. In many situations, analyzing and understanding the events, mistakes, and fluxes of a concrete gameplay experience may be useful for understanding the achieved results. A game flux analysis may also be fundamental for detecting symptoms of problems that occurred due to wrong decision-making or even bad gameplay design. Besides that, without any formalized process, this type of analysis may be subjective and, depending on the game dynamics and its complexity, it would require playing the game successively, making the same decisions, to intuitively guess which ones were responsible for generating the observed effects. Thus, reproducing the same state can be unviable, making it difficult to replay and identify, in a trial and error approach, the source of the problem. In addition, examining the game flux might allow for the identification of good and bad attitudes made players. This knowledge can be used in future game sessions to avoid making the same mistakes or even to adjust gameplay features.

The analysis process for detecting gameplay issues is done nowadays in an artisanal way by using a popular beta testing [1] approach. The beta test phase is an indispensable source of data for the developers about technical issues or bugs found in the game. Normally, beta testers are volunteers who were recruited to play the game in an early, pre-release, build of the game where they can provide information about

D. Reidsma, H. Katayose, and A. Nijholt (Eds.): ACE 2013, LNCS 8253, pp. 320–331, 2013.

technical issues and provide feedback about the gameplay mechanics. Thus, beta testing is a crucial part of the development to identify important issues in the game. However, developers have little control over the beta testers' gameplay experience or the environment because they can play at home.

The goal of this paper is to improve the game designer's understanding of the game flux, providing insights on how the gameplay progressed and influences in the outcome. In order to improve understanding, we provide the means to analyze the game flux by using provenance. The provenance analysis requires processing the collected gameplay data and generating a provenance graph, which relates the actions and events that occurred during the game session. This provenance graph allows the user to identify critical actions that influenced the game outcome and helps to understand how events were generated and which decisions influenced them. This analysis could be used in conjunction with the beta testing in order to aid in the identification of gameplay or technical issues, allowing the designer to analyze the tester's feedback report and the gameplay data from the game session.

In our previous work [2], we introduced the usage of digital provenance [3] in games. The main goal of the previous work was to propose a framework that collects information during a game session and maps it to provenance terms, providing the means for a post-game analysis. This was the first time that the provenance concept and formalization was used in the representation of game flux. The present paper is based on the conceptual framework definition introduced in the previous paper. However, while in the previous work focused on the provenance gathering, this work focuses on the provenance graph construction and manipulation to support analysis. Even though the scenario used in this paper is over a serious game, we believe that the concepts discussed here are applicable to any kind of game and are useful to support advanced game flux analysis, such as gameplay design and balancing, data mining, and even for storytelling.

This paper is organized as follows: Section 2 provides related work in the area of game flux analysis. Section 3 provides a background on provenance, and Section 4 introduces our framework for provenance gathering. Section 5 presents our approach for provenance visualization through graphs. Section 1 presents the adoption of provenance visualization in a software engineering game, with visualization examples. Finally, Section 7 concludes this work and points out some future work.

2   Related Work

In the digital game domain, Warren [4] proposes an informal method to analyze the game flux using a flux graph, mapping game actions and resources into vertices. By his definition, resources are dimensions of the game state that are quantifiable, while actions are rules of the game that allowed the conversion of one resource into another. Consalvo [5] presents a more formal approach based on metrics collected during the game session, creating a gameplay log to identify events caused by player choices. *Playtracer* [6] allows the user to visually analyze play steps, providing detailed visual representation of the actions taken by the player through the game.

These three approaches are developer-oriented, meaning that they aim to improve the quality of the game by providing feedback to the development team. However, Consalvo [5] presents a template for analysis, acting as guidelines to how the analysis should be done. Meanwhile, *Playtracer* [6] focuses on identifying the player's strategies by visually analyzing play traces instead of using queries.

Lastly, the *Game Analytics* [7] from Unity3D [8] allows visualizing game data as heat maps directly on the scene. This identifies bottlenecks and hotspots, and underused and overused areas of the game. It also measures the game retention rate, where players are stopping playing, and how the game progression develops.

3   Provenance

Provenance is well understood in the context of art or digital libraries, where it respectively refers to the documented history of an art object, or the documentation of processes in a digital object's life cycle [9]. In 2006, at the *International Provenance and Annotation Workshop* (IPAW) [10], the participants were interested in the issues of data provenance, documentation, derivation, and annotation. As a result, the *Open Provenance Model* (OPM) [11] was created during the *Provenance Challenge* [12], which is a collocated event of IPAW. Recently, another provenance model was developed, named PROV [13], which can be viewed as the successor of OPM. Both models aim at bringing provenance concepts to digital data.

Both provenance models assume that provenance of objects is represented by an annotated causality graph, which is a directed acyclic graph enriched with annotations. These annotations capture further information pertaining to execution. According to [11], a provenance graph is the record of a past or current execution, and not a description of something that could happen in the future. The provenance graph captures causal dependencies between elements and can be summarized by means of transitive rules. Because of this, sets of completion rules and inferences can be used in the graph in order to summarize the information.

4   Provenance Gathering in Games

In order to adopt provenance for the context of games, it is necessary to map each type of vertices of the provenance graph into elements that can be represented in games. As mentioned in section 3, OPM and PROV use three types of vertex: *Artifacts/Entities*, *Process/Activities*, and *Agents*. In order to use these vertex types, it is first necessary to define their counterparts in the game context. To avoid misunderstanding, we adopt throughout this paper the terms used in PROV (entities, activities, and agents).

In the context of provenance, *entities* are defined as physical or digital objects. Trivially, in our approach they are mapped into objects present in the game, such as weapons and potions. In provenance, an *agent* corresponds to a person, an organization, or anything with responsibilities. In the game context, agents are mapped into characters present in the game, such as non-playable characters (NPCs), monsters, and players. It can also be used to map event controllers, plot triggers, or the game's artificial intelligence overseer that manages the plot. Thus, *agents* represent beings capable of making decisions, while *entities* represent inanimate objects. Lastly, *activities* are defined as actions taken by agents or interactions with other agents or entities. In the game context, *activities* are defined as actions or events executed throughout the game, such as attacking, dodging, and jumping.

With all three types of vertex mapped into the game context, it is also necessary to map their causal relations to create the provenance graph. The PROV model defines some causal relations that can be used similarly to their original context. However, it also provides rules to extend these relationships or to create new ones. For instance, it is possible to create relationships to express the damage done to a character or relationships that affect specific core mechanics from the game, like attack rolls, healing, and interactions with NPCs or objects. Also, the PROV model deals well with the aspect of time, which can be heavily explored in games, especially on games focused on storytelling.

Each NPC in the game should explicitly model its behavior in order to generate and control its actions, providing an array of behavior possibilities. For example, decision trees [14] can be used to model the NPC's behaviors. With this explicit model, a behavior controller can register information about the action when it is executed. Actions can be represented by a series of attributes that provide a description and the context of the action, allowing the creation of a provenance graph. As illustrated by Fig. 1, every action needs some information: a reason for its existence, why the action was performed, what triggered it, and who performed the action. In addition, the time of its occurrence can be important depending of the reason of using provenance. The main reason of using provenance is to produce a graph containing details that can be tracked to determine why something occurred the way it did. Therefore, with this assumption, the time of the action, the person who did it, and the effects of the action can be recorded for future analysis.

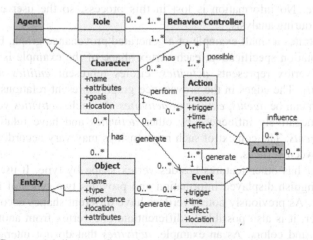

Fig. 1. Data model diagram. Gray classes represent generic provenance classes.

Events also work in a similar way as actions, with the difference in who triggered them, since events are not necessary tied to characters. For objects, its name, type, location, importance, and the events that are generated by it can also be stored to aid in the construction of the graph. Lastly, agents can have their names, attributes, goals, and current location recorded. The information collected during the game is used for the generation of the *game flux log*, which in turn is used for generating the provenance graph. In other words, the information collected throughout the game session is the information displayed by the provenance graph for analysis. Thus, all relevant data should be registered, preferentially at fine grain. The way of measuring relevance varies from game to game, but ideally it is any information that can be used to aid the analysis process.

5   Provenance Visualization

The purpose of collecting information during a game session is to be able to generate a provenance graph to aid the developer to analyze and infer the reasons of the outcomes. In this paper we introduce a provenance visualization tool named *Prov Viewer* (Provenance Flux Viewer), which uses JUNG [15] graph framework and allows detailed analysis of a previously gathered game flux log through a graph. A game using the *provenance in games* conceptual framework is able to generate *a game flux log* that can be analyzed by *Prov Viewer*.

First, the *game flux log*, which contains game events, is processed and used to generate a provenance graph for analysis. After that, our tool creates the graph's edges and vertices following a defined set of rules to build the provenance graph. This graph is a representation of the *game flux log* and is available for the developer to interact and analyze, reaching events and causes about how events occurred during the game, and how they influenced other events. It is also possible to manipulate the graph by omitting facts and collapsing chains of action for a better understanding and visualization experience. No information is lost in this process, so the user can undo any changes made during analysis.

Fig. 2. illustrates a small example of a generated provenance graph. Following the provenance notation specification, each vertex shape of the example is related to its type. Square vertex represents *activities*, circles represent *entities* and octagons represent *agents*. The edges in the provenance graph represent relationships between vertices, which can be *agents*, *entities* or *activities*. As such, *activities* vertices can be positively or negatively influenced by other *activities* and have relationships with *entities* and *agents*. The context of such relationships may vary according to the type of relation between vertices.

Prov Viewer has other features besides vertex shape by type. It uses shapes and colors to distinguish displayed information and provides two types of filters: vertex and edge filter. As previously noted, vertices have different shapes according to their types. However, it is also possible to differentiate one vertex from another with different borders and colors. As an example, *activities* that do not interact with other *activities* are dotted, as illustrated in the upper right corner of Fig. 2.

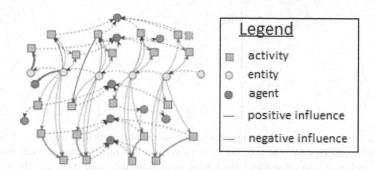

Fig. 2. Example of a generated provenance graph

Different formats can also be used for edges, as well as colors. The thickness shows as how strong the relationship is. A thin edge represents a low influence on the *activity*. On the other hand, the higher the influence is, the ticker the edge. This feature can be used to quickly identify strong influences in the graph just by looking at the edge's thickness. The edge's color is used to represent the type of relationship, which can be any of these three types: positive, which indicates a beneficial relation; negative, which is a prejudicial relation; and neutral, which is neither beneficial nor prejudicial. For each type of relationship (positive, negative, and neutral), a different color is used. Green is used for positive influences, red for negative, and black for neutral. Lastly, dashed edges represent edges without values, which are association edges such as the edges binding activities to an agent. These edge types are also illustrated in Fig. 2, where neutral edges are dashed to emphasize their lack of importance.

In order to better analyze graph data, the vertex filter feature is also available. Since the graph is generated from collected game data, not all collected information is relevant for every type of analysis. Thus, the provenance graph might contain actions that did not provoke any significant change. These elements act as noise and can be omitted during analysis. To do so, it is possible to collapse vertices in order to reduce the graph size by changing the information display scale, grouping nearby vertices together and thus changing the graph granularity. Another usage of collapse is to group *activities* from the same *agent*, improving visibility of all influences and changes that the *agent* did throughout the game. Similar edges that have the same target are also grouped together when collapsing vertices, as shown in Fig. 3. The collapsed edge's information is calculated by the sum or average (depending on the edge type) of the values from the collapsed edges. For example, edges representing expenses uses sum, while edges representing aid modifiers (in percentage) uses average. Another type of filter present in *Prov Viewer* is the edge filter, which filters edges by context and by the type of relationship.

The last feature present is the attribute status display. When selecting the desired attribute, all vertices with the specified status have their colors changed according to their respective values. It uses the traffic light scale [16], which indicates the status of the variable using three colors: red, yellow, and green. As an example, imagine that

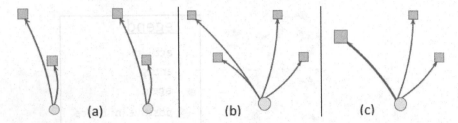

Fig. 3. Collapsing vertices. The original state showing four *activities* and two *entities* with edges of the same type (a), the collapse of both *entities* into one (b), and the collapse of two *activities*, and their respective edges since they were from the same type (c). The size of the resulting edge is bigger than the original ones as a resulting from summing each edge's values.

we desire to analyze the player's financial situation throughout the game. When filtered by this status, all vertices that contain a player financial value have their colors changed according to their values. Activating this type of feature allows the developer to see the player's finances throughout the game, making it easier to identify situations where he might have had financial problems (red color). Section 1 provides more examples of those features.

Using these features for graph manipulation and visualization, the developer is able to interact with the provenance graph, identifying relevant actions that had an impact in the story or in the desired type of analysis. It can also be used to analyze player's behavior, detecting situations that the player had difficulties or didn't behave according to the developer's plan. The next subsection describes alternatives to deal with problems related to graph size and visualization.

5.1   Granularity

Depending on the game style, a game session might take several hours or days to be completed. This makes the size of the provenance graph overwhelming, even when making pre-filtering during the generation of the *game flux log*. One way to avoid such situations is to show the provenance graph with some filters selected instead of its full extension. For example, before showing the graph to the user, it is possible to collapses less relevant vertices to reduce the graph's size. For instance, combats stages can be identified and collapsed into a single vertex for each instance. Places visited in the game can also be collapsed into a single vertex, containing all interactions made in that location. It is also possible to collapse collapsed vertices. In this case, a collapsed combat inside a collapsed area visited by the player may contain other actions aside from the combat, such as interactions with the ambient. This gives an impression of a map from the player's journey, showing vertices for each location visited by the player, while allowing the developer to expand only the situations he desires to analyze.

Instead of collapsing all combats and locations, filters can be used to decide which combats or locations were not relevant to the story, or had no noticeable impact in the player's journey, while keeping important events visible to the developer. This is possible because provenance is analyzed from the present to the past. This way, combats outcomes are known and can be used to decide if they are relevant or not. If the player was victorious with minor challenge, did not suffer severe wounds, or barely used any resources at his disposal, then the entire combat can be simplified into just one vertex representing the combat with the enemy. However, if the combat was challenging or the player lost, it may be interesting to display all actions for a correct analysis, allowing the player to identify important facts that influenced the combat outcome. Note that this type of filter is heavily dependable of the game context, so a specific set of filters should be implemented for each individual game.

6   Case Study

We instantiated this provenance analysis infrastructure, which uses the proposed framework presented in [2] and described in section 4, in a Software Engineering educational strategy game named SDM (Software Development Manager) [17]. The goal of SDM is to allow undergraduate students to understand the existing cause-effect relationships in the software development process. Thus, the adoption of provenance becomes an important instrument to better support knowledge acquisition, allowing tracking mistakes made during a game session or identifying game mechanics that requires tinkering.

6.1   Information Storage

The information structure used on SDM is similar to the one explained in [2]. As such, each project contains a list of employees that are involved in its development. Each employee has a list of actions executed as well as links to other actions in case of external influences. Throughout the game, information is collected and stored for generating the provenance graph used during analysis. Since provenance graphs contains three types of vertex (*activities*, *agents*, and *entities*), the collected information is mapped to each type, according to the data model explained in [2]. Each vertex contains different information according to its type.

Activities vertices, which represent actions executed during the game by employees, store information about their executions. This information includes who executed it, which task and role the employee was occupying, as well as the current morale and stamina status. Worked hours, credits spent to execute the action, and progresses made are also stored. Besides those, if the action had any external influences or used or altered entities, then links to them are also stored.

Agent vertices, representing employees, store the employee's name, his current staff grade, his level, human attributes, which are used in the game, and specializations. *Entities* vertices represent *Prototypes*, *Test Cases*, and instances of the *Project's* development. All information from the game is collected in real time, during the execution of actions and events. Thus it is required to change the method responsible for executing each action and event to also store information. After the data is collected and extracted, a provenance graph corresponding to that scenario is generated and displayed for visual analysis, similarly to the one presented by Fig. 2.

6.2   Provenance Graph

With the adaptations made in the original SDM [2], it is possible to collect data and use it to generate a provenance graph. The collected game data, known as *game flux log*, is exported to *Prov Viewer*. In that application, the data is processed and used to generate a provenance graph to aid in the analysis process.

By analyzing the graph, it is possible to reach some conclusions of why the story progressed the way it did. As an example[1], Fig. 4 illustrates a scenario where the player had financial problems. To simplify the picture, some collapses were made, omitting most of the *agent's activities*. The *entities* represent instances of the development stage and are colored according to the player's financial condition. The *activities* present in the picture represent hiring actions in gray and resigning actions in brown.

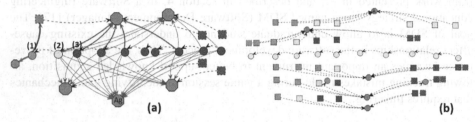

Fig. 4. An example of credits status filter (a) and the non-collapsed provenance graph (b) using filter: Morale. Brown activity vertices represent employees leaving the player's staff.

Fig. 4 was already subject of an attribute status display and a filter to show the player's credits status, both in the edges and in the vertices. In vertex 1, the project had a substantial financial income and a new employee was hired, as marked by the thick green edge to an *agent* and thick red edge to a gray dotted *activities*. The player's credits are also in a green zone as marked by the project's vertex color. However, due to the hiring fee paid in vertex 1 and the resources used by the staff in vertex 2, the player's credits changed to a yellow zone, even with the minor income from *agent* Ag.

In vertex 3, the player's credits changed to red zone due to payments, meaning that his resources are almost empty and he will not have enough credits to keep paying his employees. When that happens, employees' morale is lowered due to the lack of payment and if it reaches red zone, they can resign, as shown by brown *activities*. Observing Fig. 4, we can see the employees' morale getting lower by lack of payment. This helps us to understand why they resigned. Without credits to hire new employees and without a staff, the player loses the game.

This analysis can be used to detect player's behaviors and the reasons of why they lost the game. In the example, the cause was the lack of resources due to hiring a new employee. If it was necessary to hire a new employee, then there is a problem that requires immediate attention. However, hiring an employee causes the player to lose

---

[1]   In order to reduce graph size and provide a quicker understanding for the presented examples, some in game parameters were configured to allow faster state transitions.

the game, leading to the conclusion that if hiring is optional, then some changes might also be required because the penalty is too severe and causes the player to lose, instead of giving only a small setback.

Another example of analysis is checking the employee productivity and understanding why variations occurred by using multiple filters to test theories. In SDM, productivity is defined by the executed task, the amount of outside help, the employee's job (junior, mid-level, and senior), the working hours, and the stamina and morale stats. Fig. 5 illustrates an example scenario. To simplify the graph visualization due to size limits, we focus only on two *agents* and the *entity* known as "project". Those *agents'* roles are programmer and manager, with the manager acting as a supporting role for the programmer.

Analyzing the picture we can see that the programmer's productivity fluctuated throughout vertices 1 to 7. We can also see that the manager did not cause this fluctuation, since his aid bonus did not have much variation. In vertex 2, the programmer maximizes his productivity at the cost of quality. This information, as well as other details about the vertex, is displayed in the vertex's tooltip. The change in vertex 3 can be identified by observing his working hours, which can be done by looking at each individual vertex or by adding a filter, as shown in Fig. 5.

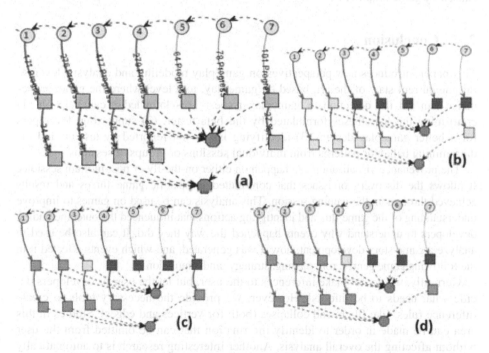

Fig. 5. Example of a provenance graph analysis. The entity is project's stages of the development. Agents are employees from the development staff, with the programmer being the upper agent and the manager the lower one. Graph using different display features: default mode (gray activity vertices) displaying edge values (a), working hours (b), stamina (c), and morale visualization modes (d). Red vertices represent low, yellow represent average, and green represent high values.

In Fig. 5 one can see via the change from yellow to red that the programmer's working hours per day increased. Since the *activity* in vertex 3 is red, it means the employee is doing extra hours, which increases his productivity. From vertices 3 to 7, his working hours remained unaltered. Therefore, the change from vertices 2 to 3 was mainly due the change on his daily working time. However, if we look at vertex 4, we can see a drop in his productivity.

By changing the filter again to show stamina levels, we can see that in vertex 3 the programmer's stamina dropped to yellow because of the extra hours and in vertex 4 it reached red due to exhaustion. Another side effect of his exhaustion was the change on the programmer's morale, which also reached the red zone in vertex 5. Lastly, the small variation from vertices 5 to 7 comes from a random range modifier during productivity computation, since the programmer is already working at minimal levels at the current configuration. With both the morale and stamina at lowest levels, the extra hours were not compensating his productivity loss. As previously shown, if his morale levels do not increase, the programmer might resign. This example of analysis covered all possibilities that affect a programmer's behavior and can be used to further refine game modifiers or state transitions, as well as identifying odd behaviors caused by game modifiers.

7 Conclusion

This paper introduces new perspectives on gameplay modeling and analysis, leveraging the current state of the art, based on gameplay, to a level where the game provenance can aid the detection of gameplay issues. This knowledge can help on (1) confirming the hypotheses formulated by the beta tester, (2) supporting developers for a better gameplay design, (3) identifying issues not reported by testers, and (4) data-mining behavior patterns from individual sessions or groups of sessions.

The provenance visualization can happen on either on-the-fly or post-mortem sessions. It allows the discovery of issues that contributed to specific game fluxes and results achieved throughout the gaming session. This analysis can be used on games to improve understanding of the game flux and identifying actions that influenced the outcome, aiding developers to understand why events happened the way they did. It can also be used to analyze a game story development, how it was generated, and which events affected it in the following game genres: role-playing, strategy, and simulation.

Currently, we do not make inferences to the user, but let the user or developers decide what needs to be inferred. However, we provide the necessary tools to create inference rules, like filters and collapses (both for vertices and edges). Studies in this area can be made in order to identify information that can be omitted from the user without affecting the overall analysis. Another interesting research is to automatically identify patterns in the game flux. Lastly, we are working on different graph visualization layouts and also studying the possibility of using game provenance in educational digital games to aid in the understanding of the concepts taught in the game.

Acknowledgments. We would like to thank CNPq, FAPERJ, and CAPES for the financial support.

References

1. Davis, J., Steury, K., Pagulayan, R.: A survey method for assessing perceptions of a game: The consumer playtest in game design. Game Studies 5 (2005)
2. Kohwalter, T., Clua, E., Murta, L.: Provenance in Games. In: Brazilian Symposium on Games and Digital Entertainment (SBGAMES) (2012)
3. Freire, J., Koop, D., Santos, E., Silva, C.T.: Provenance for Computational Tasks: A Survey. Computing in Science Engineering 10, 11–21 (2008)
4. Warren, C.: Game Analysis Using Resource-Infrastructure-Action Flow, http://ficial.wordpress.com/2011/10/23/game-analysis-using-resource-infrastructure-action-flow/
5. Consalvo, M., Dutton, N.: Game analysis: Developing a methodological toolkit for the qualitative study of games. Game Studies 6 (2006)
6. Andersen, E., Liu, Y.-E., Apter, E., Boucher-Genesse, F., Popović, Z.: Gameplay analysis through state projection. In: Foundations of Digital Games (FDG), pp. 1–8 (2010)
7. Wulff, M., Hansen, M., Thurau, C.: GameAnalytics For Game Developers Know the facts Improve and Monetize, http://www.gameanalytics.com/
8. Higgins, T.: Unity - 3D Game Engine, http://unity3d.com/
9. PREMIS Working Group: Data Dictionary for Preservation Metadata. Implementation Strategies (PREMIS), OCLC Online Computer Library Center & Research Libraries Group (2005)
10. Moreau, L., Foster, I., Freire, J., Frew, J., Groth, P., McGuiness, D.: IPAW, http://www.ipaw.info/
11. Moreau, L., Clifford, B., Freire, J., Futrelle, J., Gil, Y., Groth, P., Kwasnikowska, N., Miles, S., Missier, P., Myers, J., Plale, B., Simmhan, Y., Stephan, E., den Bussche, J.V.: The Open Provenance Model core specification (v1.1). Future Generation Computer Systems 27, 743–756 (2007)
12. Miles, S., Heasley, J., Szalay, A., Moreau, L., Groth, P.: Provenance Challenge WIKI, http://twiki.ipaw.info/bin/view/Challenge/
13. Moreau, L., Missier, P.: PROV-DM: The PROV Data Model, http://www.w3.org/TR/prov-dm/
14. Moret, B.: Decision Trees and Diagrams. ACM Computing Surveys (CSUR) 14, 593–623 (1982)
15. O'Madadhain, J., Fisher, D., Nelson, T.: JUNG: Java Universal Network/Graph Framework, http://jung.sourceforge.net/
16. Diehl, S.: Software Visualization: Visualizing the Structure, Behaviour, and Evolution of Software. Springer (2007)
17. Kohwalter, T., Clua, E., Murta, L.: SDM – An Educational Game for Software Engineering. In: Brazilian Symposium on Games and Digital Entertainment (SBGAMES), pp. 222–231 (2011)

The Challenge of Automatic Level Generation
for Platform Videogames Based on Stories and Quests

Fausto Mourato[1,2], Fernando Birra[2], and Manuel Próspero dos Santos[2]

[1] Escola Superior de Tecnologia – Instituto Politécnico de Setúbal, Portugal
[2] CITI – Faculdade de Ciências e Tecnologia – Universidade Nova de Lisboa, Portugal
fausto.mourato@estsetubal.ips.pt, {fpb,ps}@fct.unl.pt

Abstract. In this article we bring the concepts of *narrativism* and *ludology* to automatic level generation for platform videogames. The initial motivation is to understand how this genre has been used as a storytelling medium. Based on a narrative theory of games, the differences among several titles have been identified. In addition, we propose a set of abstraction layers to describe the content of a quest-based story in the particular context of videogames. Regarding automatic level generation for platform videogames, we observed that the existing approaches are directed to lower abstraction concepts such as avatar movements without a particular context or meaning. This leads us to the challenge of automatically creating more contextualized levels rather than only a set of consistent and playable entertaining tasks. With that in mind, a set of higher level design patterns are presented and their potential usages are envisioned and discussed.

1   Introduction

The way how narratives and videogames are connected is still a topic that is open to debate. Nevertheless, it is undeniable that over the years several videogames have been used to tell stories. In fact, this topic started to catch attention in later years with the appearance of textual adventure videogames, some kind of *Interactive Fiction* [1]. The term *ludology* has been proposed by Frasca [2] as a movement based on *narratology* having different features with distinct merits. Therefore, the main question is not if games are effectively narratives or not but how they relate to narratives. An interesting recent approach on this question is a model presented by Aarseth [3]. Briefly, the author confirms videogames as an interactive fiction medium, whose elements can be characterized in a ludo-narrative dimension. The different elements can have a more meaningful (narrative) effect or a more challenging and amusing (ludic) importance.

In the context of automatic level generation, existing algorithms focus the lower abstraction concepts to provide adequate actions (Section 2), yet higher abstraction concepts must be considered to create more intricate scenarios. We present our studies in how to relate stories and story related concepts with automatic level generation to produce more meaningful content, which include: the definition of a set of abstraction layers in hero-centred stories (Section 3.1); a study on the *platformers'* storytelling capabilities (Section 3.2); the definition of higher level game design patterns for *platformers* (Section 3.3); and a final reasoning on ways to promote more contextualized automatic level generation in platform videogames applied to a prototype (Section 4).

D. Reidsma, H. Katayose, and A. Nijholt (Eds.): ACE 2013, LNCS 8253, pp. 332–343, 2013.

2   Related Work

2.1   Procedural Content Generation (PCG) in Platform Videogames

A possible use of PCG in videogames is automatic level creation. For *platformers*, it may serve either full automatic processes that generate complete levels [4] or semi-automatic processes where some parts are humanly designed [5–7]. This idea was brought to the academic context by Compton and Mateas [8] with a conceptual model that inspired later studies, namely the framework proposed by Smith *et al.* [9] to analyse these videogames. Also, the notions of rhythm and rhythmic pattern were introduced as a "mechanism for grouping individual components into a longer sequence, while still maintaining rhythmic movement for the player", which lead to the implementation of a prototype for a rhythm based generator [10]. This approach has been implemented later in different systems, namely *Launchpad* [11], *Rathenn* [12] and *Endless Web* [13].

An alternative approach consists in the displacement of a set of humanly pre-authored chunks to create the whole level. An effective way to perform that displacement is a technique entitled Occupancy-Regulated Extension [14].

A more direct approach to generate this type of levels was proposed by Pedersen *et al.* [15], focused on *Infinite Mario Bros.*. The authors presented a generator based on an initial parameterization where several level features were defined, such as the number of gaps, their average frequency and amplitude, among several others.

Finally, we have proposed a genetic algorithm implementation [16] to generate more varied types of spaces, including rooms, corridors and mazes. It consists in the integration of a set of simple design patterns to make the algorithm evolve to a set of valid game geometries with different features. To improve content inside those levels, we have also proposed a level adaptation algorithm [17] that is able to fill the main geometry with additional gaming entities, such as enemies or traps. Lastly, an integrated system where those concepts are applied was also implemented [18].

2.2   Game/Level Design Patterns

Game design patterns have been used to understand the rules behind the mind of game creators. This concept was introduced by Björk *et al.* [19] as commonly recurring parts of the design of a game regarding gameplay. Naturally, each genre has particular design patterns, which have been studied lately as this topic is becoming popular. For instance, First-Person Shooters have been examined by Hullet and Whitehead [20] and 'Ville Games such as *Farmville* has been studied by Lewis *et al.* [21].

In the context of platform videogames, besides the first overview that is provided in the previously referred studies by Compton and Mateas, the question of game design patterns was brought by Dahlskog and Togelius [22] in their recent work focusing *Infinite Mario Bros.*. However, the main focus goes once again to the lower abstraction layers, as the authors identify how multiple entities are combined in a sequence. As lower level abstractions are very precise in describing a particular game, they are not likely to be generalized to other titles of the same genre.

An interesting alternative study but yet related to the topic of game design patterns was presented by Sorenson and Pasquier [23]. The authors defined a system based on a genetic algorithm implementation that creates levels by encoding design patterns into the fitness function. Some possible design patterns are given as an example for the videogame *Infinite Mario Bros.* to show how it could be applied.

An adventure *platformer* that allows exploration uses principles from an RPG, where higher abstractions patterns have been defined, and still use action based mechanics. To generate game scenarios that allow this combination, it is important to understand how those higher abstraction patterns can connect to the lower abstraction set of actions.

2.3   Stories and Quests

In order to bring higher abstraction aspects to level generation and provide meaning to the avatar actions representing somehow a story, within a certain context, it is important to understand the key concepts of plot representation. Initial requirements can be identified in Ryan's [24] proposal for the conditions of narrativity. The author refers spatial and temporal dimensions as the essential requirements for a broad concept of story. A mental dimension is defined as the next step to include the human experience in stories, where intelligence and emotions are described with agents, goals, actions and events. A final formal and pragmatic dimension expands the previous semantic concepts to significance, namely regarding the relation among events and their meaning.

Tosca [25] identified the notion of quest as "a way of structuring events in games, and (…) incarnate causality at two levels: a semantic one (how/why actions are connected); and a structural one (plan of actions, interaction of objects and events)". In fact, this concept is natural in videogames mainly because they tend to represent user incarnations on a certain character, the avatar. This hero centred approach that we find in videogames makes them suitable to be represented as quest-based games.

Sullivan *et al.* [26] created a quest browser recalling Howard's definition of quest as "a goal-oriented search for something of value" [27] and stated that quests "give meaning to the player's actions". In addition, authors gathered previous studies based on *World of Warcraft* to identify a set of quest types.

Another perspective to look at quests in videogames was proposed by Aarseth [28], based in a division of the concept into three main axis: place, time and objective.

A practical approach is presented in the playable quest-based story game *Mismanor* [29], where the authors applied their theories about playable stories. The main aspect to refer regards the proposed quest structure, which contains a certain intent and different sets of pre-conditions, starting and completion states.

Finally, a motivating study about quests was presented by Smith *et al.* [30]. Their work regards RPG's, namely the patterns used in that genre of games, which were divided into level patterns and quest patterns. The second type is particularly interesting in the scope of the present work because, as stated, adventure *platformers* can share several principles with RPG's. Authors grouped quest patterns into five main groups: actions, objectives, structure, superstructure and purpose.

In the remaining of this document we will explore how the presented different approaches to describe quests can be merged in the specific genre of platform videogames and how we envision these principles as a way to improve automatic level generation.

3   Platform Videogames

3.1   Quest-Based Stories (for videogames)

As previously stated, our first goal is to understand how platform videogames transmit stories. In this genre, the user controls a character or a set of characters (one at a time) in a certain environment with certain goals. If those goals have some meaning it has to be possible to consider them quests, or parts of quests. For this purpose, it is important to perceive game design patterns for quests in platform videogames. There are different approaches to this challenge, as seen previously. One first issue that might occur when establishing possible patterns and comparing proposals is that the comparison objects might be in different abstraction levels. Consequently, game design patterns must be analysed according to a certain abstraction level and, as we are focusing mainly the game design patterns that are somehow story related, it is important to emphasize that stories have different abstraction levels as well. We propose the following abstraction levels to decompose a character centred story in the context of game design patterns and automatic level generation:

- **Universe**. The higher abstraction is the vague description of the spatiotemporal context, meaning the type of world and physics, among others. It states **when** and **where** the story occurs. Examples: Nowadays, Tolkien's world and Medieval Times.
- **Main Goal**. Defines the ultimate goal and its main motivation. It explains **why** further events will happen. Example: *Find the Holy Grail*.
- **Chapters**. The main goal is naturally divided in sections, normally arranged in chapters in a book or scenes in a movie. In a long story, a grouping mechanism might be used, only for segmentation without any impact on the story itself. This will be the equivalent to dividing a same story into multiple books.
- **Quests**. They represent a non-trivial task with a certain purpose that must be part of the multiple steps to reach the main goal. By some means, this describes **how** the main character reaches the ultimate goal. Depending on how deep the story is, chapters and quests might be similar in abstraction level but they differ especially on the point of view. Example: *Retrieve the sword Excalibur*.
- **Side-quests.** A side-quest has similar principles to a regular quest but it does not have direct implications in the story, and typically it will have a shorter duration. It just endorses the character and his/her personality. Any random heroic action without any additional purpose serves as an example of side-quest.
- **Goals**. Represent the multiple steps to accomplish a quest, and is something that could be continuously expressed by the user meaning what he/she is doing at the moment. Example: Defeating an opponent or a series of opponents.

- **Actions**. As a rule of thumb, one can consider an action as something that can be performed by the avatar and that the player can assign to an input button. Actions do not mean anything in particular and can only be interpreted together with other actions in the context of a goal. Examples: walking, attacking, jumping or running.

Several approaches have been considered for automatic generation on the most concrete layer of the model. On the top layers the common efforts are focused on the narrative and are not suitable for an action game. So, the current goal for automatic level generation is to provide an appropriate bridge between the bottom and the top layers.

3.2   Platform Videogames and Stories

By intuition, *platformers* do not appear to contain an intense and intricate story. Probably, one of the main reasons of their success is that they are typical cases of *easy to play but hard to master* games, where instant action is presented. Normally they have a smaller set of actions and commands than other games and challenges are mainly related to immediate skill. However, content on these games must play an important role as well, as *Sonic* and *Mario* are two of the most popular videogame characters which surely succeeded in the test of time. Therefore, we want to understand how stories have been included in *platformers* and comprehend how different elements are being used regarding ludic and narrative goals. For that purpose, we collected a set of popular platform videogames. Ten titles were selected trying to include a large range of gameplay styles, hardware and themes. Franchises and multi-versioned titles should be considered a global overview over the multiple available versions where the same style is represented. Our list was defined with the following videogames (abbreviations are presented in parenthesis for further references): *Blues Brothers (BB); Braid (Br); The Cave (Ca); Little Big Planet (LBP); Prince of Persia (PP); Rick Dangerous (RD); Sonic (So); Spelunky (Sp); Super Mario (SM); Trine (Tr)*.

The videogames from the previous list were characterized in the already mentioned *ludo-narrative* model proposed by Aarseth [3]. The author identified world, objects, agents and events as the main storytelling elements in a videogame. Those elements can be more narrative if they are stricter to a certain description or more ludic, if their objective is mainly fun without particular relation to an initial narrative. Figure 1 presents that model, where we have positioned our previously referred example titles. The main descriptions proposed on Aarseth's model were used to establish an initial clustered classification. Afterward, similar titles were compared observing the features with more detail to obtain the represented rank. For instance, regarding world structure, both games *Trine* and *Braid* have linear paths but the first contains short bifurcations, hence their different positioning in the scale.

It is noticeable that the elements on those games have features that are more related to the narrative pole rather than the ludic. More than meaning that these games are elaborated stories, this shows that *platformers* tend to be an expression of predefined ideas. Story elements (kernels and satellites) are typically fixed, meaning that the character has an initial strict set of objectives that will lead the whole story development over the game. Hence, it is curious to wonder why *platformers* are not associated with stories and others genres are. The first reason to explain the lack of story association to platform videogames can be found in the previous table regarding agents. *Platformers* tend to use agents merely as ludic elements. Still, some exceptions occur. *Little Big Planet* is one of those cases, mainly because the second title of the game included new characters that accompany the hero in the whole game, manifesting their own personality. *The Cave* also shows interesting dialogs and relations among the playable and the non-playable characters. In *Trine*, there is also a special situation regarding agents. The player controls three different heroes embodied in one single character that can take the physical form of one of them at any time. During the game, the hero's spirits inside the character talk to each other about the adventure that is taking place, exposing their personality. Even though they are not game agents in the common sense of the word, they work as so. Still, this leads us to another aspect that we believe that it is important to consider as a relevant element and that should be included in the previous model, which is the hero himself/herself.

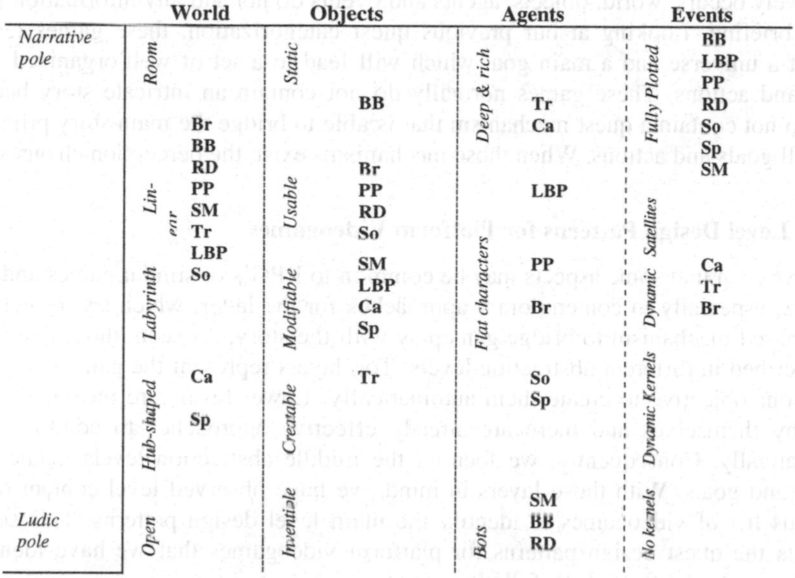

	World	Objects	Agents	Events
Narrative pole	*Room*	*Static* — BB	*Deep & rich* — Tr, Ca	*Fully Plotted* — BB, LBP, PP, RD, So, Sp, SM
	Linear — Br, BB, RD, PP, SM, Tr, LBP, So	*Usable* / *Modifiable* — Br, PP, RD, So, SM, LBP, Ca, Sp	*Flat characters* — LBP, PP, Br	*Dynamic Satellites* — Ca, Tr, Br
	Labyrinth		*Flat characters* — So, Sp	*Dynamic Kernels*
	Hub-shaped — Ca, Sp	*Creatable* — Tr		
Ludic pole	*Open*	*Inventiable*	*Bots* — SM, BB, RD	*No kernels*

Fig. 1. Ludo-narrative positioning of different platform videogames

As we stated, in this quest type of stories, the hero is the centre of all the action and cannot be considered as a simple agent. Considering the hero as a fifth element on the presented model, we propose the following descriptions to define the features from the narrative to the ludic pole:

- A **character with personality** that is presented and explored throughout the game, as the presented case of the videogame *Trine*.
- An **expressive character** that shows his/her current feelings, opinions or suggestions, even though without any particular knowledge about the inner self, such as the *Sackboy* character introduced in the videogame *Little Big Planet*.
- A **living character** that suggests possible feelings but without manifesting them in any way through the game, such as the initial versions of the character *Mario*.

- An **identifiable character** in a somehow adequate level of realism to be majorly accepted as a certain object, such as a car or a spaceship.
- A **simple object** without any particular physical meaning by itself but that will mean something by user contextualization, such as the pads on the game *Pong*.

Excluding *Little Big Planet, Trine* and *The Cave*, which bring up the narrative side on the represented heroes, the remaining games of our sample contain a simple living character as the hero. This is another confirmation on the lack of efforts regarding storytelling in those games, as the hero does not present a particular narrative factor.

Another aspect that may justify the referred disassociation from stories to *platformers* is that they tend to present gaming elements that are disconnected to the main story. Typically, *platformers* contain a briefing mechanism when the level starts (a cut-scene, an animation, a small textual description, or others) and a similar debriefing mechanism on the end of the level. However, *in-between*, where the game action effectively occurs, world, objects, agents and events do not add any information to the initial briefing. Looking at our previous quest categorization, these games tend to present a universe and a main goal which will lead to a set of well-organized small goals and actions. These games normally do not contain an intricate story because they do not contain a quest mechanism that is able to bridge the main story principles to small goals and actions. When those mechanisms exist, the perception changes.

3.3   Level Design Patterns for Platform Videogames

We have seen that some aspects may be common to RPG's or similar games and *platformers*, especially in contemporary approaches for the latter, which try to include a quest based mechanism to bridge gameplay with the story. As seen, those quests can be described in different abstraction levels. Top layers represent the game core and it is not our objective to create them automatically. Lower levels are meaningless actions by themselves and there are already effective approaches to combine them automatically. Consequently, we focused the middle abstraction levels, namely the quests and goals. With those layers in mind, we have observed level content on the previous list of videogames to identify the main level design patterns. This section presents the quest design patterns for platform videogames that we have identified and decomposed into goals as follows:

- *Checkpoint.* This is the most common type of quest in platform games. It consists on reaching a certain part of the scenario with a certain goal. Those goals might be decomposed on the following types:
  - Talk to someone (e.g. in *Little Big Planet* the character breaks one of *Zola*'s creation and is told that should talk to him);
  - Grab a certain item (e.g. in *Prince of Persia* the character has to find a sword);
  - Achieve a milestone on the path (e.g. in *Trine*, characters explicitly state land regions as milestones on the main path);
  - Deliver an item to someone or someplace (e.g. in *The Cave*, each possible character has a certain item of desire to be collected within a chapter);
  - Escort something/someone (e.g. in the *Bride Reception* level in *Little Big Planet* the character finds the groom injured in a cave and is asked to transport him back);

- — Escape a certain enemy or object (e.g. in *Rick Dangerous*, the first level starts with the player escaping a rolling stone ball);
- — Activate (or deactivate) a certain entity (e.g. in the end of the last level of *Rick Dangerous*, the character has to disable a missile);
- *Hostile Zone*. This pattern represents a stop to the main movement mechanics in a particular part of the level. It may be represented by one of the following goals:
- — Defeat *n* opponents (e.g. in *Trine 2* the player encounter hordes of Goblins);
- — Defeat a horde of enemies until a certain condition is reached (e.g. in *Trine 2* the player encounters some situations where enemies are spawned infinitely while he/she tries to accomplish another goal, such as opening a door);
- — Defeat one particular opponent, in the typical form of final *boss* (e.g. in the end of each act, *Sonic* has an encounter with *Dr. Robotnik*);
- *Multiple Checkpoints*. Refers to quests that represent multiple checkpoints that should be performed in a specific order, such as the following:
- — Key/Lock situations, where the character has to take a detour to get a certain item that will allow passage (e.g. in *Braid* the character has to grab keys that open certain doors);
- — Switch/Door, which is a similar situation to Key/Lock but in this case passage is allowed because of a certain trigger. This may lead to a timed challenge, as the trigger might open passage for a short time window (e.g. in *Prince of Persia*, the character frequently presses buttons that open certain gates);
- — Composed Key/Lock, which are the situations where there is a need to gather multiple items to get passage (e.g. in some community levels of *Little Big Planet* we observed doors that open with a set of different keys);
- — Composed Switch/Door situations represent the need to activate several triggers to get passage (e.g. In *Trine*, some contraptions that are controlled with multiple levers that should be pushed in an appropriate order to open some passages);
- — Character modifier situations represent a first stop on a certain entity that will somehow change the characters' features, allowing him/her to reach another checkpoint that otherwise would not be accessible (e.g. in *Spelunky*, the player can get a rope to access additional areas);
- *Puzzle*. A non-trivial combination of game elements to overcome a small part of the level. Puzzle nature, content and difficulty are particularly subjective and we will consider those situations as a quest without a decomposition in different goals.

In addition, we have identified a set of game patterns to promote additional gameplay, which we have previously referred as side-quests, as follows:

- Grab collectible points. Represent the inclusion of scoring elements without any gameplay related reward or with a simple impact on the number of tries (e.g. in *Blues Brothers*, player earns an extra life for every 100 gathered records).
- Reach a secret zone. Represent the inclusion of areas that are not directly identifiable by the player, and that may contain the following type of reward:
- — Collectibles data (game art or videos) that do not have any effect on the game and are mere trophies (e.g. in *Trine*, there are secret arcs that unlock game art);
- — Collectible powers, that enhance the avatar features (e.g. in *Super Mario*, some blocks hide flowers that upgrade the character).

The previous structure of quests and goals allows a designer to sketch the content of a level that represents those concepts. In the next section we will observe how these ideas could be materialized into an automated generation tool.

4   Quest-Based Procedural Content Generation

In this section we briefly present a prototype that is currently being developed to generate platform levels based on the previously described patterns. Although the focus of this article is the previous study, this level editor unveils the potential of the referred ideas. Figure 2 shows the current UI in the creation of an example for the videogame *Prince of Persia*. It consists on a semi-automatic process, where the designer manually defines the sequence of quests with their respective goals and a set of side-quests, as observable on the left part of the figure. The automatic generation process takes those quests as input and generates the geometry using a set of algorithms that differ according to the used patterns. The output is presented on the right part of the window, where the generated segments have been highlighted for comprehension aid.

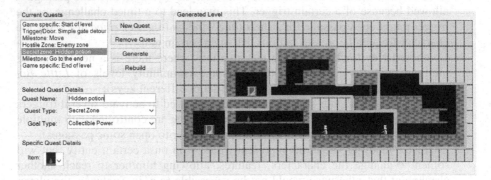

Fig. 2. Prototype application for automated level generation based on quests

It is possible to rebuild a whole level from scratch or only certain quests, allowing a designer to regenerate some parts while keeping others intact. Figure 3(a) shows a sample of multiple variants that were generated for the pattern *Checkpoint* in different full generation runs. For the generation of this specific type of quest in *Prince of Persia*, a composition algorithm was implemented in association with an automatic chunk detection process. *Checkpoint* segments were thus created by retrieving common linear segments from the original set of levels in this videogame.

When the system is rebuilding a specific quest, the algorithm receives the previously existing segment and uses the entry and exit points of that same section as restrictions for the generation process. This gives the algorithm the necessary information to create an alternative geometry that can replace the previous one.

Also, most patterns can be set according certain parameters. As observable back in Figure 2, the side quest *Secret Zone* allows the definition of an item to include in that zone. Moreover, some patterns allow the definition of difficulty based variables. An example is the *Hostile Zone* pattern, which we have implemented to map user skills to the frequency of opponents and respective strength. Figure 3(b) shows different generated alternatives for the same segment with distinct difficulty profiles, in this case using the videogame *Infinite Tux*. A simple terrain displacement generator was used followed by a random inclusion of opponents regulated by the difficulty estimation constraints (roughly, a certain difficulty profile has to match a respective frequency of opponents).

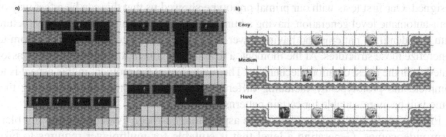

Fig. 3. (a) Alternative geometries generated for a certain patterns and (b) alternative configuration of a certain level part configured for different difficulty settings

As we are decomposing the structure in quests and goals, generation algorithms are responsible for small level parts at each time, reducing the computational complexity. For instance, evolving complete level structures with genetic algorithms as a global process is a time consuming task but generating a small portion to match a certain quest can be achieved promptly. Also, this decomposition into smaller regions potentiate simpler algorithms to be used integrated with more complex techniques. As an example, the referred *Checkpoint* pattern typically consists on a systematic sequence of jumps and/or traps, which can be generated with ease using an *ad-hoc* algorithm. Still, these parts can be merged with other segments representing quests that require more complex algorithms, such as the *Multiple Checkpoint* pattern where paths and routes must be analysed to create those situations.

5   Conclusions and Future Work

We have studied the storytelling capabilities behind platform videogames to identify possible improvements on automatic level generation techniques for this genre. The content in *platformers* tends to be structured in a way that should be considered more narrative than ludic, as most elements have a predefined structure. Yet, these games do not typically contain a rich story because storytelling elements are not explored and, as we stated, agents have not been used properly in that context. This is something that game designers should reason about and consider in the future.

Regarding level design patterns, we identified that the story represented in a videogame can be decomposed in different abstraction layers and level design patterns refer to a certain layer. Different *platformers* were analysed to identify the main containing structures where quest principles were used. A decomposition model was proposed, based on observed situations and recalling existing approaches for other genres. The final result is a set of level design patterns grouped in two abstraction layers, quests and goals, which can lead automatic generation processes to a more contextualized output. Lower abstraction patterns presented in some other works can be integrated to generate level parts where a certain quest or goal is being represented.

As stated, it is important to bridge the higher and the lower abstraction layers of level design patterns in order to improve existing automated generation. With that in mind, a prototype for level construction using the identified patterns in multiple layers has been designed. Our first tests with our primal prototype showed us that this can be a fast way of semi-automatic level generation, having a human to define the main level content structure with the identified patterns and having lower level generation algorithms in the bottom to concretize those structures. At the moment, a few simple generation algorithms were associated with the quest creation mechanism. The main goal at the moment in this aspect is to complete the prototype by including different generation algorithms, considering that some will be more suitable for certain patterns.

Finally, multi-player gameplay is one aspect that has been evidenced in recent platform videogames. Generating a level that is suitable for multiplayer requires to take into account a few more features. For that, one of our current goals is also to map the multiplayer design patterns proposed Rocha et al. [31] and El-Nasr et al. [32] in our prototype, allowing the designers to create levels with specific multi-player situations.

Acknowledgments. This work was partially funded by IPS under FCT/MCTES grant SFRH/PROTEC/67497/2010 and CITI under FCT/MCTES grant PEst-OE/EEI/UI0527/2011.

References

1. Niesz, A., Holland, N.: Interactive fiction. Critical Inquiry 11, 110–129 (1984)
2. Frasca, G.: Ludology meets Narratology: Similitude and differences between (video) games and narrative (1999)
3. Aarseth, E.: A narrative theory of games. In: Foundations of Digital Games, pp. 129–133 (2012)
4. Shaker, N., Togelius, J., Yannakakis, G.N., Weber, B., Shimizu, T., Hashiyama, T., Sorenson, N., Pasquier, P., Mawhorter, P., Takahashi, G., Smith, G., Baumgarten, R.: The 2010 Mario AI Championship: Level Generation Track. IEEE Transactions on Computational Intelligence and AI in Games 3, 332–347 (2011)
5. Smith, G., Whitehead, J., Mateas, M.: Tanagra: A Mixed-Initiative Level Design Tool. In: Foundations of Digital Games, FDG 2010, pp. 209–216. ACM Press, New York (2010)
6. Smith, G., Whitehead, J., Mateas, M.: Tanagra: Reactive planning and constraint solving for mixed-initiative level design. IEEE Transactions on Computational Intelligence and AI in Games 3, 201–215 (2011)
7. Smith, G., Whitehead, J., Mateas, M.: Tanagra: An Intelligent Level Design Assistant for 2D Platformers. Artificial Intelligence and Interactive Digital Entertainment (2010)
8. Compton, K., Mateas, M.: Procedural Level Design for Platform Games. In: Artificial Intelligence and Interactive Digital Entertainment, AIIDE, pp. 109–111 (2006)
9. Smith, G., Cha, M., Whitehead, J.: A framework for analysis of 2D platformer levels. In: ACM SIGGRAPH symposium on Videogames, Sandbox 2008, p. 75. ACM Press, New York (2008)

10. Smith, G., Treanor, M., Whitehead, J., Mateas, M.: Rhythm-based level generation for 2D platformers. In: Foundations of Digital Games, FDG 2009, p. 175 (2009)
11. Smith, G., Whitehead, J.: Launchpad: A Rhythm-Based Level Generator for 2-D Platformers. In: Foundations of Digital Games, vol. 3, pp. 1–16 (2011)
12. Smith, G., Gan, E., Othenin-Girard, A., Whitehead, J.: PCG-based game design: Enabling new play experiences through procedural content generation. In: Workshop on Procedural Content Generation in Games, pp. 5–8 (2011)
13. Smith, G., Othenin-Girard, A.: PCG-based game design: Creating Endless Web. In: Foundations of Digital Games 2012, FDG 2012 (2012)
14. Mawhorter, P., Mateas, M.: Procedural level generation using occupancy-regulated extension. In: Computational Intelligence and Games, pp. 351–358 (2010)
15. Pedersen, C., Togelius, J.: Yannakakis: Modeling Player Experience in Super Mario Bros. In: Computational Intelligence and Games, CIG 2009. IEEE Press (2009)
16. Mourato, F., Próspero dos Santos, M., Birra, F.: Automatic level generation for platform videogames using genetic algorithms. In: Advances in Computer Entertainment Technology, ACE 2011, pp. 8:1–8:8. ACM, New York (2011)
17. Mourato, F., Birra, F., Próspero dos Santos, M.: Enhancing level difficulty and additional content in platform videogames through graph analysis. In: Nijholt, A., Romão, T., Reidsma, D. (eds.) ACE 2012. LNCS, vol. 7624, pp. 70–84. Springer, Heidelberg (2012)
18. Mourato, F., dos Santos, M.P., Birra, F.: Integrated System for Automatic Platform Game Level Creation with Difficulty and Content Adaptation. In: Herrlich, M., Malaka, R., Masuch, M. (eds.) ICEC 2012. LNCS, vol. 7522, pp. 409–412. Springer, Heidelberg (2012)
19. Björk, S., Lundgren, S., Holopainen, J.: Game Design Patterns. Digital Games Research (2003)
20. Hullett, K., Whitehead, J.: Design patterns in FPS levels. In: Foundations of Digital Games, FDG 2010, pp. 78–85 (2010)
21. Lewis, C., Wardrip-Fruin, N., Whitehead, J.: Motivational game design patterns of 'ville games. In: Foundations of Digital Games. 172–179 (2012).
22. Dahlskog, S., Togelius, J.: Patterns and Procedural Content Generation: Revisiting Mario in World 1 Level 1. In: FDG - Workshop on Design Patterns in Games (2012)
23. Sorenson, N., Pasquier, P.: Towards a generic framework for automated video game level creation. Applications of Evolutionary Computation (2010)
24. Ryan, M.: Avatars of story (2006)
25. Tosca, S.: The quest problem in computer games. In: Technologies for Interactive Digital Storytelling and Entertainment, TIDSE (2003)
26. Sullivan, A., Mateas, M., Wardrip-fruin, N.: QuestBrowser: Making Quests Playable with Computer- Assisted Design (2009)
27. Howard, J.: Quests: Design, Theory, and History in Games and Narratives. A K Peters Ltd. (2008)
28. Aarseth, E.: From Hunt the Wumpus to EverQuest: Introduction to Quest Theory. In: Kishino, F., Kitamura, Y., Kato, H., Nagata, N. (eds.) ICEC 2005. LNCS, vol. 3711, pp. 496–506. Springer, Heidelberg (2005)
29. Sullivan, A., Grow, A., Mateas, M., Wardrip-fruin, N.: The design of Mismanor: Creating a playable quest-based story game. In: Foundations of Digital Games, pp. 180–187 (2012)
30. Smith, G., Anderson, R., Kopleck, B., Lindblad, Z., Scott, L., Wardell, A., Whitehead, J., Mateas, M.: Situating Quests: Design Patterns for Quest and Level Design in Role-Playing Games. In: André, E. (ed.) ICIDS 2011. LNCS, vol. 7069, pp. 326–329. Springer, Heidelberg (2011)
31. Rocha, J., Mascarenhas, S., Prada, R.: Game mechanics for cooperative games. ZON Digital Games 2008, 72–80 (2008)
32. El-Nasr, M.S., Aghabeigi, B., Milam, D.: Understanding and evaluating cooperative games. Human Factors in Computing Systems, 253 (2010)

Six Enablers of Instant Photo Sharing Experiences in Small Groups Based on the Field Trial of Social Camera

Jarno Ojala[1], Kaisa Väänänen-Vainio-Mattila[1], and Arto Lehtiniemi[2]

[1] Tampere University of Technology, Human-Centered Technology, P.O. Box 589,
33101 Tampere, Finland
[2] Nokia Research Center, Visiokatu 3, FIN-33270, Tampere, Finland
{jarno.ojala,kaisa.vaananen-vainio-mattila}@tut.fi,
arto.lehtiniemi@nokia.com

Abstract. Mobile photo taking and sharing has become a frequent leisure-time activity for smartphone users. This paper presents a field study of a mobile application called Social Camera, which enables instant sharing of photos within small groups. The application enables collaborative creation of photo collections with shared folders in the cloud and instant connection through the folders and photos. Social Camera was evaluated using four groups (altogether 17 users) in a field trial. The results reveal six enablers of instant photo-sharing experiences within small groups: sense of connectedness and social awareness, presentation and expression of self, lightweight and surprising interaction, collective photography, documentation of experiences, and finally, privacy and user control. This work gives design implications of these enablers for photo-sharing applications.

Keywords: Photo sharing, user study, mobile application, social media interaction, user experience, design.

1 Introduction

Media and entertainment online relies ever more on user-generated content. Social networking services such as YouTube[1], Facebook[2], and Flickr[3] are built on video and photo content from the users [1]. The "interestingness" of content depends on the freshness of the content, the person's relation to the content, personal nature of the content, and whether the content is actually targeted to the receiver [2]. Users currently have solutions for sharing their photos publicly in social networking services (SNS) but lack dedicated solutions for instant sharing within small groups. To this end, novel ideas to support pleasurable user experiences are needed. The private group setting and instant sharing are the key differentiators from conventional photo-sharing tools such as Facebook and Flickr. In our current setup, user's photos are directly uploaded to a shared album, which is accessible to relevant users [3, 4].

This study examines social user experiences enabled by design solutions for small-group photo sharing with mobile devices. A prototype implementation of Social Camera aims to combine the experiences of remote sharing and collocated sharing

D. Reidsma, H. Katayose, and A. Nijholt (Eds.): ACE 2013, LNCS 8253, pp. 344–355, 2013.
© Springer International Publishing Switzerland 2013

into a new way to share photos instantly. The goals of this study are 1) to evaluate the implemented Social Camera prototype, 2) to identify habits of photo sharing within the intimate group, 3) to observe users' interactions with each other during the trial period using the prototype and not using it 4) to identify the needs and wants of the groups that the implementation actually has to fulfill. The results are significant in the area of human-computer interaction since the online sharing of photos in small groups remains a less-studied area, and dedicated solutions for instant sharing with a small group do not exist. This work contributes to the area of social user experience design by introducing enablers of social experience in small-group sharing.

2   Related Work

Development in photo-capturing devices and channels for sharing the content has created a new culture of instant photo sharing. The new culture of digital photo capturing and sharing has also gained interest and sparked rich research in the human-computer interaction community. Kirk et al. has named the whole process of photo taking "photowork" [5]. Frohlich [6] has introduced a model of four categories in the photowork process: co-present sharing, remote sharing, archiving, and sending. The most essential phase needing support in the current online world is the sharing of photos. Data transfer with broader bandwidths and development of cloud computing technology allows new solutions for archiving and sharing photos outside the hard disk and physical drives [7]. The cloud technology has become available for the public audience only recently, by services such as Dropbox[1]. An emerging design trend in mobile photo sharing is automatic upload of photos to a cloud server. Studies by Lucero et al. [8] explore the Image Space application, which allows automatic upload of photos with location tags and sharing the photos within a limited community. A similar cloud-based application called Image Exchange is introduced in work by Vartiainen [9].

As a basis for the design of the small-group–photo-sharing application, several studies were utilized to give background. Previous work has identified a problem in small-group sharing especially after the events a group has attended or trips a group has taken together [10]. Users do not have dedicated services and habits of distributing the photos. Therefore, distribution takes time (and the photos have the greatest value right after the event). Additionally, previous studies suggest that people are willing to share personal content in private circles such as family or close friends [10, 11]. Close-knit groups have needs for demonstrating the group identity and for collectively managing content [10, 12]. A study by Miller and Edwards [13] introduces a culture of "snaprs," photographers that base their photography on sharing with the online community, in the mentioned case Flickr. Snaprs described habits of downloading pictures of others as a part of their own photo collection, where "kodak culture" wanted to have a solution to share to the limited group only [13], which suggests that there is a need for shared or collaborative folders amongst the small groups. Photo sharing using camera phones as the capturing device and the sharing platform is a widely researched area. Frohlich et al. [6] handle photowork on two dimensions: temporal and locational. Photo sharing is handled either instantly or after some time, collocatedly (on the spot) or remotely. Traditional photography requires a certain time gap between the photo capture and the sharing. Digital photography has made the time gap narrower. According to the Kindberg et al. taxonomy [14], there are affective and functional dimensions in photo sharing: mutual task and experiences with the collocated users and remote tasks and shared experiences with those who are absent. Kindberg et al.'s [14] study of camera phone users introduces a taxonomy of six reasons for image capture on a camera phone: individual personal reflection, individual personal task, social mutual experience, social absent friend or family, social mutual task, and social remote task.

The definition of storytelling includes sharing of multiple photos with a textual or oral commentary attached. Collocated sharing and storytelling are the focus of Van House et al.'s work [15, 16, 17]. Van House et al. [16] introduced three motivations for social use of personal photographs: constructing personal and group memory, creating and maintaining social relationships, and self-expression/self-presentation.. Balabanovic et al. [18] have identified patterns of photo-driven and story-driven photo sharing. Sharing with the people who were present in the capturing moment is referred to as "reminiscing" [14, 12], and telling about the event to those who were not present, "storytelling" [6]. Content consumption and creation are often not in balance in communities that are built on user-generated content [19, 20]. Most of the users are eager consumers of content and less willing to produce or especially share the content. However, content production can be motivated by giving users a sense of social interaction and connectedness.

Research on social user experience focuses on the social context of the products, where the presence and actions of other users creates the user experience. Interaction, collaborative creation of content, and reciprocity are essential for the social user experience. Social dimension in the interactive products as a factor of user experience remains a less-studied area. The social user experience is built on the social context in which other users and their presence define the actual interaction. In their study of socially used web services, Väänänen-Vainio-Mattila et al. [21] explored social user experience as UX with services that support social activity through their functionality. The research identifies curiosity, learning, self-expression, suitability of content and functionalities, completeness of networks, and competition as the motivational drivers for social user experience. The study findings presented in this paper contribute to the understanding of social UX with photo sharing in small groups.

3   Design and Field Trial of Social Camera

The design process of Social Camera started with two user studies in 2011 [3, 4, 10]. Relying on the findings from these two studies, the implementation of Social Camera application was completed. Prototype implementation Social Camera aims to combine the experiences of remote and co-located sharing into a new instant way to share photos. The research involved three aspects of interaction design: understanding the users, prototype design, and evaluation [22]. The initial studies related to small group photo sharing raised design framework for the system. It was found out that: 1) small groups have problems in sharing the picture content from many devices between the group, 2) people have suspicions over sharing the data in social media or social networking services, because they are not willing to risk losing their control over their photos 3) people use web folders and cloud services such as Dropbox, although they might not be implemented for sharing and storing photos taken with smart phones 4) the event pictures tend to be most interesting right after the event they are shot into 5) people would like to have dedicated "co-located workspace" for the group photos. In addition to support photo management and sharing, the software aims to support sense of belonging and connectedness and social user experience [2, 21, 12] within the group by as the experience-based design ideology suggests [23].

The Social Camera prototype enables users to create shared photo albums and automatically distribute photographs within a selected group of people. The actual prototype application is divided into four logical sections: shared albums, own photos, notifications, and the camera. Shared albums are the core of the prototype application. The users are able to create and name new albums (Figure 1). The shared album content can be browsed similarly as the local device photo gallery. Users are able to browse by viewing thumbnails under different albums and touching a thumbnail to enlarge the photograph to a full screen size. Under the shared album name a list of users are displayed who share the same folder. Other people can be invited to join the shared albums using NFC i.e. selecting the invite option and bringing the devices in close proximity (Figure 1). The invitation to the shared album is sent automatically to the recipient for acceptance. Under the shared albums, the user is able to select the corresponding album to be default for the camera to assign new photographs to. The assignment can also be changed from the camera section while taking photographs. The captured photographs are distributed automatically to the members of the shared album.

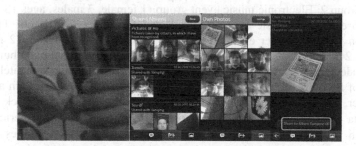

Fig. 1. a) Inviting people to shared albums, b) Shared albums, c) Own photos and d) sharing to albums views in the Social Camera prototype

Alternatively the user is able to access her own photos view from the prototype and share photographs to the shared albums (Figure 1). The own photos view shows a grid view of available photographs in the device as the original photo gallery of the device. The notifications center shows a feed of recent activity to the users, including notifications on new photos in shared albums, new pictures of the user, and group invitations. The aim of the organized field study was to identify the needs for sharing photos instantly within small groups, and to understand the social user experience in such activity. In order to collect actual use experiences of the application, a field trial was organized for four participating small groups. The participant groups included both non-technical photographers who do not use professional equipment and more advanced photographers with semi-pro or pro equipment. The groups were recruited through multiple mailing lists for students of Tampere universities and also through forums of photographers. Fig. 2 shows the events in which the groups participated in.

Fig. 2. Photo taking and sharing activity of the groups during the trial

Background data of the participants was collected by using a web form before the interviews. The participant selection was made on basis of their equipment usage, age and activity of photographing and sharing habits in social networking services. The aim was to have four groups with different backgrounds. Group 1: Skiing family (2 fathers, 3 boys, ages 13-48) took the cameras to the skiing trip to Ylläs in Lapland, where they spend the holiday week, taking and sharing photographs with Social Camera. Group 2: Electronic music event group (1 female, 3 males, ages 18-35) went together to electronic music event, which lasted for twodays in Lahti. The group attended on various smaller events during the trial. Group 3: DJ club (2 female, 2 male, ages 24-27) had a ten days of trial period, where they attended a album release party, a student party cruise and smaller events events together and separately. Group 4: Group of friends (3 female, 1 male, ages 24-25) used the application in a evening get-together, a housewarming party and mostly individually during the week.

The data collection consisted of four different methods: the trial period of 1-2 weeks with the diaries, an individual interview of the trial experiences, a group interview concerning the small group sharing and future feature ideation and a user experience questionnaire with 19 statements. Each group trial started with the session where the test devices were handed out to the participants. In the session, participants were also introduced with the service in detail. Participants were given N9 smartphones with the Social Camera application software installed in the starting sessions, before the trial period. In the starting sessions a brief introduction for the application use was given. Participants were instructed to take photos with the given device throughout the trial period. Findings from the group interviews and diaries were treated as relative notes in the analysis. Comments in the interviews and diaries were transcribed and organized under themes.

4   Results

Creating and managing the collective group folders together was the peak experience of the trial for the most users. Users appreciated seeing the different viewpoints, getting pictures of themself from other photographers, and getting an idea of how others experienced the event. Users saw value in sharing instantly with close individuals and then expanding the audience if desired. There were major differences in the amount of photographing and sharing rates of the photos between the groups during the trial periods. The amount of all pictures captured ranged from 133 pictures in Group 1 to 742 pictures in Group 2. The different natures of the events the groups participated in explain some of the differences. Table 1 shows the photo taking and folder creation activity throughout the trial. For example, on the skiing trip, the wintery weather and poor network connections prevented photo sharing. Sharing rate also varied between the groups, as Table 1 shows.

Table 1. Photo taking and sharing activity of the groups during the trial

	Group 1	Group 2	Group 3	Group 4
Users	5	4	4	4
Photos captured during the trial	133	742	158	264
Photos captured on average by person	26,6	185,5	39,5	66
Folders created	5	7	6	6
Subgroups created	0	1	2	3
Pictures shared	94	298	82	155
Sharing rate of pictures	0,71	0,4	0,52	0,59

Group 2 had the lowest sharing rate, which also was referred to in the interviews, in which the group participants said that they selected the best photos only to be shared. Group 4 was active in creating subgroups and folders that were only shared to some of the users in the group. After the analysis of the diary and interview data, findings were categorized under the following main enablers: 1) connectedness and social awareness; 2) presentation and expression of self: sharing everyday life activities; 3) lightweight communication and surprises; 4) collective photography; 5) documentation of exceptional events; and 6) privacy, user control, and utility. Finding categories include the most promising use cases and motives for small-group sharing in the six categories. The finding categories can be divided into two types of photo experiences: long-term and short-term. The first three categories are short-term enablers, which are related to an instant and spontaneous photo sharing, and the latter three categories are related to long-term experiences and photo storage and archiving.

4.1   Instant Interactions and Social Presence to Support the Sense of Connectedness

The shared folder was a communication channel for the groups during the trial. Even in the cases where group members attended events separately, others were able to follow their photos appearing in the group folder if they decided to carry the device and shoot photos. Since commenting, giving ratings or likes, and similar interaction features were left out of the implementation, people were forming ways to communicate with the photos only The peak experience was seeing the latest photos from others appearing in the system in real time when people were in different locations, it was fun to see what others were doing at the same time. The application created a channel for instant communication throughout the trial, and evidently enriched the social interaction of the participating groups. *"This gave me an excuse to see my friends!" Female, Group 4.* Photos appearing in the application in a real time motivated picture taking and sharing. *"I waited for T. to share his photos from a 'famous people cruise' but unfortunately he didn't have the connection and did not share them instantly onboard!" Female, Group 3.*

Group 3 had an album release event, which they attended together. Before the event, they were getting ready for the event and shared photos each on their own. Two males from the group were having dinner together and watched the photos sent by the female participant from her home, where she was doing programming homework. Afterwards at the album release events the whole group was photographing and speaking about the photos from before the event when they were preparing from the event. *"It was interesting to see the timeline from the members of our group, all on their way to the album release party in the evening. Me and M. were at the wings restaurant and the girls and others on their own route." Male, Group 4.*

The final wrap-up of the event happened at home, where participants watched the collection of photos form the evening. In the user experience questionnaire participants gave an average of 5.77 of 1-7 Likert scale in ratings, in which the standard deviation (SD.) was 1.71, to the statement "It was fun to share the photos with my friends in the service; whereas, "The service offered me a novel way to share photos got an average of 5.16 (SD. 1.87), and "This way to share photos was suitable for me," slightly lower with 4.88 (SD. 1.80).

In order to support a sense of connectedness with the application, the application should offer fresh and real-time content easily and should facilitate visibility for the newest updates. During the trial, participants followed the application, but in the longer term use of the application should give notifications to the user without the user having to actively to seek the newest content.

4.2   Expression and Presentation of Self - Sharing Everyday Life Activities

Participants reported that they saw motivation in sharing their everyday life in the system to the small audience. The application was seen as a channel to distribute random camera snapshots to others. Users shared pictures of details and surroundings or even scenes from the movies they were watching. It was stated that some of these snapshot only have meaning as a creators of social interaction and discussion and in that sense most of the participants also missed lightweight commenting features to the application. Self-expression and presentation of self through the application consisted of sharing new or current information about oneself to the group. Participants shared photos when they shot photos of their face gestures, telling others about their mood. One of the female participants in the group 3 said that all of the members of their group did not know about her musical hobby, so she wanted to tell about it. *"I wanted to send the others photos of my cembalo lessons in Riihimäki. All in our group wasn't aware that I even have such a hobby" Female, Group 3*. Picture blogging or creating a photo diary of everyday activities was also seen as interesting option to utilize the application. Some of the participants shared snapshots of what they are at home. *"I see value if this would be a shared photo diary for our group, so everybody could easily share" Male, Group 4*.

In order to support self-expression the applications should offer clear control of privacy and effortless sharing to the targeted audience. Dedicated folder to one's own pictures in which others can react by adding their responses with photos but still realizing the actual author of the folder offers support for self-expression.

4.3   Photo-Based Communication to Support and Enrich Light-weight and Surprising Interaction

Light-weight communication with pictures was evidently strong in the trial (Figure 3). Participants used the application, for example, negotiating places and for inviting others to certain places.

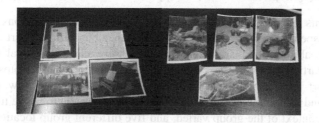

Fig. 3. Example of photo communications in the Group 3

Figure 3 shows examples of the photo communication the participants made in the DJ group. Participants used the application, for example, negotiating places and for inviting others to certain places. Since the classical means to communicate through comments, for example, was removed, users made up creative ways to interact through sending the photos. In some of the cases during the trial, users wanted to *tease* others by showing what they are up to. *"I was waiting for M. and O. to come to the Sunday chill music club. I shared few photos from there to hurry them up!" Male, Group 2*. In the questionnaire users gave averagely 4,06 (SD. 1,65) to the statement "The service offered positively surprising experiences".

A folder that is dedicated for the light interactions and spontaneous photos in addition to event-related, person-related or theme-related folders can support lightweight interactions within the group. Positively surprising experiences can be supported by features that offer targeted photos to the users automatically.

4.4   Shared Cloud Folder to Support Collective Photography

A collective cloud folder was seen as a suitable solution especially for close–knit small groups. The first group in the trial had, however, problems in comprehending fully the shared folder concept. The group had a conceptual model from Facebook: every folder has an author. However, the idea of having many cameras taking trip photos and sending them to the same folder was really appreciated. Currently, they had to wait until each author uploads the photos on Facebook, which they mostly used, or through other means. The users appreciated the experience of seeing photos from all the members of the group put together. Only one of the four participating groups did not see extra value in sharing the photos within their particular group with the presented application. The user experience statement "the service helped me to share the photos within the group" gained an average of 5,98 (SD. 1,79) on the 1-7 Likert scale. "I liked the idea to create shared folders where to upload the photos for the whole group", gained a similar average of 5,98 (SD.1,82). On the concept level, the participants were satisfied with the photo-sharing application.

The group identity was built around the collectively shared folder during the trials. The collective folder in the cloud offered a shared workspace for sharing and storing experiences.

4.5   Sharing Exceptional Events – Support for Documentation

The participants agreed that the application is most suitable in situations in which the group would spend a certain period of time together but still be apart at times. For example, trips abroad, seminars or music events were said to be ideal for using the application. Participants saw the system most suitable for event photos that have a relatively short life span. Physical location of the people and how the group is scattered around define the way to interact through photos. During the trial the social and physical context of the group varied, and five different group location formations were faced: 1) Whole group at the same event physically together, 2) people scattered around at a bigger event, physically nearby, 3) one at home, seeing photos from others in the event, most of the group at the event, 4) one attending and sharing with others and 5) everyone in different locations. Browsing the photos was not as interesting when they all were at the same event, however, seeing the collection of photos from the whole group instantly after the events was an appreciated experience. *"It was nice to see the products of the whole group right after the event! It was nice to see the things that interest others. I would like to share video also though."* Male, Group 2. The electronic music group was documenting the music event at Lahti together, whereas the boys from the Group 1 were shooting photos of their tricks while skiing at Ylläs and instantly sharing them. Storytelling for those who were not present by using the application was seen as an interesting idea. *"If we had this when we were together with the club in Berlin and tried to get in to different clubs. There were 18 of us and only a few got in so they could share the experience and tease others when they get in."* Male, Group 3.

Users had to implicitly select the photos for sharing after the capture. Most of them would like to have an easy sharing mode, where all the captured photos could be automatically transferred to the event folder in special occasions. Event-based folders must be created instantly on the spot of the event or, alternatively, before the event. The access should be granted to the attendees or content contributors. Also features for expanding the group with the acceptance of the group should be included.

4.6   Support for Privacy and User Control

Ahern et al.[24] have identified four factors that affect people's privacy while sharing digital photos: security, identity, social disclosure, convenience. Most of the concerns in the trial were related to questions such as: who can access the content? What if the group is extended by others I do not know? The application included feature of inviting others to the shared folder by holding two devices against each other, which means that every owner of the group folder could invite new users to the group folder. Despite the novelty of the inviting feature, users had concerns that the folder could expand accidentally and on the other hand the feature was said to actually prevent people from spontaneous sharing: creating new event folder and sharing spontaneously is not supported since people need to be physically close to start sharing. Users wanted to remove pictures that they did not like or wanted to give a suggestion for removal if the photo is taken by other user. Also those who are able to view the shared folder need to be visible in the application, so everyone knows how publicly the photos are shared.

Privacy-related statements got relatively low ratings in the user experience questionnaire. " I felt that I'm in control of the privacy of my photos in the service" got surprisingly low average of 1,94 (SD. 1,08), where "I felt my photos are safe in the service" got relatively higher average of 3,03 (SD. 1,51). "I could recommend the service to my friends" gained 4,24 (SD. 1,46). Answers show that users had concerns on the privacy aspects of the technology. Positive comments of the application privacy also occurred, and they mainly related to the possibility to limit the group to share with. Comments from the interview also indicate strong ownership feel of "my folder". *"I want to share my photos to the close friends group that I've selected myself, not everyone in Facebook. That's why I like the privacy thinking."* Female, Group 4. *"I did not like that he posted pictures into my album, I only wanted to give others the viewing rights."* Female, Group 3

Based on the findings in the study privacy of one's photos and especially feel of control is a hygiene factor for positive user experience. Distrust towards the application can prevent users from handing their photos out to the application.

5   Discussion and Conclusion

The results of the field study with Social Camera reveal the following main enablers of photo-sharing experience in small groups: 1) instant interactions and social presence to support a sense of connectedness, 2) expression and presentation of self by sharing everyday-life activities, 3) photo-based communication to support and nrich lightweight and surprising interaction, 4) shared cloud folder to support collective photography, 5) sharing exceptional events for experience documentation, and 6) privacy and user control. The found enablers are in line with the findings in the related work but extend knowledge of the factors of the social user experience. However, their validity should be evaluated in follow-up studies in different group contexts and with different content types. In summary, the study implies the value of the collective online folder on the photo experience for small groups. Implementation of Social Camera lacked aforementioned features such as online sharing with remote people who are not in the formed group, forming groups remotely, commenting and picture descriptions, integration of the application in the native camera, and notifications. Still, users saw value in sharing photos instantly using a lightweight approach.

The evaluated implementation of the application introduced on purpose controversial features for testing the boundaries that users perceive with regard to privacy and the surprise factors. Putting ones' photos or any personal content visible for others online seems to include a motivational aspect of collecting others' comments and also to follow the interaction, discussion, and history around the photos. Users wanted to know which photos got attention from others. Most said that they would like to see others' actions in the folders but maybe not share all of their browsing information. After the study, Social Camera was expanded with a channel for communication through emotional responses [25].

The field trial examined a selection of different events that groups attended. The different group formations at the events gave an idea of the real use of the system, where only a part of the interest group attends the event. The photos are interesting afterwards to these who have attended the event and also in real-time to those who are following the event remotely. Limitations of the implementation and problems with Internet connection prevented peak experiences occurring within some of the groups, but the idea of instant small-group sharing was received positively. The results of this field trial give support to the development of instant photo-sharing solutions for small groups. A promising approach to the group formation theme in the future could be to concentrate more on events and spontaneously created groups.

Acknowledgements. Authors thank Sanna Malinen, Guido Grassel, Jari Kangas, and Yanqing Cui for their valuable contributions to the work.

References

1. Lehikoinen, J., Aaltonen, A., Huuskonen, P., Salminen, I.: Personal Content Experience. Wiley (2007)
2. Malinen, S., Ojala, J.: Maintaining the Instant Connection—Social Media Practices of Smartphone Users. In: International Conference on the Design of Cooperative Systems, pp. 197–211. Springer, London (2012)
3. Vyas, D., Cui, Y., Ojala, J., Grassel, G.: Producing while Consuming: Social Interaction around Photos Shared within Private Group. In: Nijholt, A., Romão, T., Reidsma, D. (eds.) ACE 2012. LNCS, vol. 7624, pp. 133–150. Springer, Heidelberg (2012)

4. Ojala, J.A.O., Vyas, D., Lehtiniemi, A.J.: Technique for evaluating photo sharing interfaces with the early prototypes - group simulation. In: Holzinger, A., Ziefle, M., Hitz, M., Debevc, M. (eds.) SouthCHI 2013. LNCS, vol. 7946, pp. 36–53. Springer, Heidelberg (2013)
5. Kirk, D., Sellen, A., Rother, C., Wood, K.: Understanding photowork. In: CHI 2006, pp. 761–770. ACM, New York (2006)
6. Frohlich, D., Kuchinsky, A., Pering, C., Don, A., Ariss, S.: Requirements for photoware. In: Proceedings of CSCW 2002, pp. 166–175. ACM, New York (2002)
7. Odom, W., Sellen, A., Harper, R., Thereska, E.: Lost in translation: Understanding the posession of digital things in the cloud. In: Proc. CHI, pp. 781–790. ACM (2012)
8. Lucero, A., Boberg, M., Uusitalo, S.: Image Space: Capturing, sharing and contextualizing personal pictures in a simple and playful way. In: Proc. ACE 2009, pp. 215–222. ACM (2009)
9. Vartiainen, E., Väänänen-Vainio-Mattila: User experience of mobile photo sharing in the cloud. In: MUM 2010. ACM (2010), Article No. 4
10. Ojala, J., Malinen, S.: Photo sharing in small groups - identifying design drivers for desired user experiences. In: MindTrek 2012, pp. 69–76. ACM (2012)
11. Kairam, S., Brzozowski, M.J., Huffaker, D., Chi, E.H.: Talking in circles: Selective sharing in Google+. In: Proc. CHI 2012, pp. 1065–1974. ACM (2012)
12. Olsson, T.: Understanding Collective Content: Purposes, Characteristics and Collaborative Practises. In: Communities and Technologies, C&T 2009, pp. 21–30. ACM (2009)
13. Miller, A., Edwards, W.K.: Give and take: A study of consumer photo sharing culture and practice. In: CHI 2007, vol. 20, pp. 347–356. ACM (2007)
14. Kindberg, T., Spasojevic, M., Fleck, R., Sellen, A.: The Ubiquitous Camera: An In-Depth Study of Camera Phone Use. IEEE Pervasive Computing 4(2), 42–50 (2005)
15. Patel, N., Clawson, J., Voida, A., Lyons, K.: Mobiphos: A study of user engagement with mobile collocated-synchronous photo sharing application. International Journal of Human-Computer Studies, IJHCS 67(12), 1048–1059 (2009)
16. Van House, N.: Collocated photo sharing, story-telling and the performance of self. International Journal of Human-Computer Studies, IJHCS 67(12), 1073–1086 (2009)
17. Van House, N.A.: Personal photography, digital technologies and the uses of the visual. Visual Studies 26(2) (2011)
18. Balabanoviç, M., Chu, L.L., Wolff, G.J.: Storytelling with digital photographs. In: Proceedings of CHI 2000, pp. 564–571. ACM, New York (2000)
19. Lehtiniemi, A., Ojala, J.: MyTerritory: Evaluation of outdoor gaming prototype for music discovery. In: MUM 2012. ACM (2012), Article No. 35
20. Ojala, J.: Personal Content in Online Sports Communities: Motivations to Capture and Share Personal Exercise Data. International Journal of Social and Humanistic Computing 2(1-2), 68–85 (2013), doi:10.1504/IJSHC.2013.053267
21. Väänänen-Vainio-Mattila, K., Wäljas, M., Ojala, J., Segerståhl, K.: Identifying Drivers and Hindrances of Social User Experience in Web Services. In: CHI 2010, pp. 2499–2502. ACM (2010)
22. Jones, M., Marsden, G.: Mobile interaction design, 1st edn. John Wiley & Sons Ltd. (2006)
23. Hassenzahl, M.: Experience Design; Technology for all the right reasons. Morgan & Claypool Publishers (2010)
24. Ahern, S., Eckles, D., Good, N.S., King, S., Naaman, M., Nair, R.: Over-exposed?: Privacy patterns and considerations in online and mobile photo sharing. In: Proceedings of CHI 2007, pp. 357–366. ACM (2007)
25. Cui, Y., Kangas, J., Holm, J., Grassel, G.: Front-camera video recordings as emotion responses to mobile photos shared within close-knit groups. In: CHI 2013, pp. 981–990. ACM (2013)

Attack on the Clones: Managing Player Perceptions of Visual Variety and Believability in Video Game Crowds

Sean Oxspring[1], Ben Kirman[2], and Oliver Szymanezyk[2]

[1] Top Notch Studios Ltd.,
UK
[2] Lincoln Games Research Group
University of Lincoln, UK
sean.oxspring@hotmail.com, {bkirman,oszymanezyk}@lincoln.ac.uk

Abstract. Crowds of non-player characters are increasingly common in contemporary video games. It is often the case that individual models are re-used, lowering visual variety in the crowd and potentially affecting realism and believability. This paper explores a number of approaches to increase visual diversity in large game crowds, and discusses a procedural solution for generating diverse non-player character models. This is evaluated using mixed methods, including a "clone spotting" activity and measurement of impact on computational overheads, in order to present a multi-faceted and adjustable solution to increase believability and variety in video game crowds.

Keywords: Crowds, video games, visual diversity, multi-agent systems.

1 Introduction

Procedural crowd generation techniques are increasingly common in the video games industry to simulate large groups of agents. Hordes of zombies have been rendered in games such as the *Left 4 Dead* series (Valve, 2008 and 2009) and *Dead Rising* (Capcom, 2006). Games such as *Hitman Absolution* (IO Interactive, 2012) and *Assassins Creed 2* (Ubisoft, 2009) also rely on the simulation of "realistic" and "believable" multi-agent crowds for the player to interact with.

When simulating crowds in a virtual environment such as a game, it is often hard to produce a great deal of variety in characters. Usually due to the complexity of manual character modelling, it is very time-consuming for a 3D modeller to manually create a great deal of heterogeneous agents [10]. It is common to use a fixed number of template characters to instance into an environment; this, however, may lead to the problem of visually similar 'appearance clones' in the environment [6]. To combat this, procedural generation of characters is becoming a more popular solution [10]. This paper explores techniques in which crowd generation algorithms can be adjusted to better support greater diversity, in order to support more believable play environments. Firstly, a case study of an approach used in a commercial game series is explored, and then we introduce a new, multi-faceted approach to crowd generation, and evaluate it in terms of computational overhead and effect on perception of diversity.

D. Reidsma, H. Katayose, and A. Nijholt (Eds.): ACE 2013, LNCS 8253, pp. 356–367, 2013.
© Springer International Publishing Switzerland 2013

2   Commercial Approaches to Crowd Variety

Procedural Content Generation (PCG) involves the generation of game content in real-time. Randomness is often a key part of procedural generation, allowing a broad range of possibilities to be generated from a small number of parameters. Many games use PCG to generate levels and unique gameplay. *Borderlands* (2K Games, 2009) uses PCG to generate thousands of permutations of guns. *Minecraft* (Mojang, 2011) generates enormous worlds using a procedural algorithm. PCG is also widely applied to the generation of human agents in real-time for use in a crowd of non-player characters (NPCs) in games. Following a simple generation algorithm, hundreds of thousands of unique-looking character models can be created in real time.

2.1   Case Study: Left 4 Dead and Left 4 Dead 2

Left 4 Dead (Valve, 2008) is a cooperative first-person shooter in which players must fight their way through hordes of infected humans during an apocalyptic pandemic. The game uses an artificial intelligence system known as 'The Director' in order to promote replay value and achieve a sense of "Dramatic Game Pacing" [1].

As a zombie game, "infected" characters were designed to be "visible but not memorable" since they appear en masse to challenge the players. Developers reported that one of the early issues was that through lack of diversity, the reuse of models meant that a small set of infected characters became more memorable and familiar. Based on this, additional variation systems were developed [3].

Limited Sharing of Head Textures: Parts of textures would be merged together in order to create a finalised head texture. This would include mouths, eyes and other facial features (see Fig 2). The possible combinations of different features greatly increased potential diversity in absolute terms.

Fig. 1. Left 4 Dead Male Zombie Head Variants

Colour Tinting on Clothes: The clothes on common infected were tinted using a random multiplication of RGB values. This multiplication allowed for the clothing texture to maintain its detailing, as contrast was never lost. Dark parts of the clothes would remain dark no matter what was generated.

Grimes [3] states that fine details and low-contrast areas on textures did not work well to create visual variety amongst members of the horde, as these were difficult to change using colour multiplication techniques and lead to poor-quality textures on models. She declares that geometric variation on the models warped facial features and therefore helped to hide re-used textures. The image below shows two different models with the same facial texture and how they both look visually different from one another:

Fig. 2. Left 4 Dead Facial Geometric Variation and Texturing

Decals such as blood flecks and dirt were also very effective in decreasing the amount of times that playtesters noticed clones of recognisable - the decals obscured recognisable features and allowed one texture to be re-used multiple times without players noticing during play.

Left 4 Dead 2 (Valve, 2009) is the sequel to *Left 4 Dead*. As with the original, it was a first person shooter with an emphasis on four-player teamwork in order to complete missions set in a zombie apocalypse scenario. Focus was put on expanding the game experience and making it more complex than the predecessor. This included the development of an improved system for generating varied common infected [3]. A new shader was developed in order to create even more variance in the common infected models. According to Vlachos [11], the simplest infected has over 24,000 variations. This large amount of visual variation were achieved by a combination of the following methods:

Gradient Mapping in the Luminosity channel was used to tint the textures on the common infected models. It was noted that one single gradient map could not be used for the whole model as having more than one colour in the gradient map caused problem with inappropriate colouration. Grimes [3] describes that the problem was overcome by exclusively masking certain areas of the texture, allowing the tints to be applied to exclusive areas of the final texture.

Blood and Grime Decals were added to the models in a similar technique to that of *Left 4 Dead*. Blood masks were created and were then added on top of the characters tinted texture. Grime was then added on top in the same fashion; since grime did not need to be as defined as blood, this was added using transparencies and a high detail texture [3].

3　　Player Perception of Variety in Commercial Games

In order to better understand the perception of diversity in crowds in games from a player's point of view, a pilot study was conducted. Three groups of randomly chosen people (N=14) were shown two videos of gameplay from commercial games that include crowds. The groups were told to pay particular attention to the crowds, and less about the game itself. They were then asked about what they noticed about the crowds. Gameplay was recorded from *Hitman Absolution* (IO Interactive, 2012) and *Assassins Creed 2* (Ubisoft, 2009). Levels used were specifically chosen to have large crowds of non-player characters.

Fig. 3. Non-Player Crowds in *Hitman: Absolution* (left) and *Assassins Creed 2* (right)

In unstructured discussions, participants shared their thoughts on the crowds in these specific titles. For *Hitman: Absolution*, participants were generally positive about crowd variety, however they did often see repetition of clothing on the models "*I think there were a couple of models that were there a couple of times*". The crowds of people were also described as "*dull and generic*" which was identified as drawing the eye away from looking at the crowd too closely.

For *Assassins Creed 2*, participants were much more negative, repeatedly pointing out the use of the same models for clothing on the characters. They suggested that the game merely manipulated the colours of the clothes and left the models the same. One member of a group pointed out that "*Everyone was the same height*". All three groups were quick to point out the use of similar if not identical clothing models on groups of people such as a group of monks in the video "*[the] attack of the clone monks*". Two of the groups picked out jarring movements and collisions, where characters in the game would crash into each other randomly and not avoid each other correctly.

In both games, participants pointed out noticing motion clones (characters doing the same/similar motion) during the videos. They also described motion of characters in the *Hitman: Absolution* crowd as being 'unrealistic' as they would often pace around randomly with no clear direction.

In all focus group sessions, there was a strong suggestion that appearance clones would impact negatively on the player's sense of believability (and therefore immersion) whilst playing a game.

This activity identified the two major factors affecting believability in these crowds were appearance and movement. This supports by findings of previous work on crowd diversity by McDonnell *et al.* [6] that also suggests that the visual appearance of the characters is more important in creating perceived diversity than their motion.

4   A Procedural Approach to Diversity

As underlined in the previous sections, visual diversity remains a problem in video game crowds. The examples have shown how existing games have approached the task of creating variation. Based upon the suggestions from the focus group, the approaches from the games industry and proposed variety features in the works of Thalmann and Musse [10],.a list of several visual variety-changing factors were collated for inclusion in a proposed multi-dimensional solution. All of these changes are focussed on addressing the variety of appearance of non-player characters in the crowd. Each approach focuses on altering the virtual representation of the game character by altering either the shape of the character model or the post-processing effects used on each character.

4.1   Colouring

One of the simplest approaches to increase visual diversity is through the use of random colouring to different aspects of the character model (i.e. clothing, skin tone, hair). RGB values can be randomly generated and applied to various parts of the character, with the use of a Colour Look Up Table (CLUT) in order to limit potential colours to realistic subsets and distributions. However, Thalmann and Musse [10]. point out that even with techniques of colour change, it does not overcome the feeling of watching the same model - thus physical model changes must be considered as more important than colour changes.

4.2   Body Somatotypes

Somatotype theory is a well-understood framework for the description and categorisation of human body size and shape based on three axes: the ectomorph, mesomorph and endomorph [7]. Each element is defined by a number between 1 and 7, which contribute to a finalised somatotype combination.

Although Somatotypology was originally used in now discredited work on connecting body shape and disease-susceptibility, this system is still useful as a model for generating humanlike figures. Basing the procedural generation of character models on this kind of model ensures that the final models follow shapes that are found in the general population. Implementation of these requires model vertices that allow for deformation of models based on the somatotype elements assigned. An example of this would be deforming a convex stomach area for an endomorph-like character or a concave stomach for an extreme ectomorph.

In addition, character heights can be implemented alongside somatotypes using scaling methods, although careful attention must be made to ensure that the head of the characters is not warped to anomalous dimensions. Additional weight could also be simulated with this method by scaling the characters in the x and z axis.

4.3   Accessories

The addition of possible items such as hats and glasses to characters can also potentially increase variety. Depending on gender, beards, moustaches and other (generally) gender-associated accessories could be added to character models. These accessories would be modelled separately and then instantiated and rendered using the same world transformation as the character that they are assigned to.

4.4   Model Design

The design of the basic/archetypical individual character model itself is a very difficult issue tied to realism and believability. We argue that the believability of crowds is independent of the aesthetic context within which those crowds exist. Specifically, believability is not necessarily the same as realism. Where realism is concerned with the simulation of the real world as accurately as possible, believability is about maintaining a situation that is consistent with the player's expectations within the "magic circle" of the game. For example, it is not realistic that characters in *Super Mario Bros* (1985, Nintendo) exist only within a 2-dimensional space where mushrooms have magical abilities. However, in this context, it would be believable for the consumption of a mushroom to cause a character to greatly grow in size. In contrast, it would be unbelievable if Mario were to move into a third dimension, since (in this title) this behavior is inconsistent with the encompassing game fiction. In terms of visual aesthetics, a consistent visual style is similarly important to maintaining a sense of believability. The massive success of *Minecraft* (2011, Mojang), with its distinctive blocky style, has demonstrated that consistent visual aesthetics can create engaging and consistent (believable) experience [4] in spite of its lack of visual realism.

Based on this argument, the design of model used to demonstrate and evaluate the variety of methods for increasing diversity was specifically chosen to be fairly blocky. In addition, the character models feature no animation, since this research is focused purely on visual diversity rather than movement diversity (as discussed in [10]). Within the fictional world of the test game used to evaluate this methodology, although lack of animation is not realistic, it is believable and consistent with the visual aesthetic.

The model itself is stored within a vertex array. It consists of three cubes with their bottom faces removed (as they do not need to be rendered). The model also makes use of back-face culling, a process in which the back of polygons are not rendered.

The models texture coordinates are stored within another vertex array and are then used to map the texture to its appropriate location in 3D space. Surface normals are also stored in a separate array. This basic model has been extended with extra vertices on the torso in order for deformation of the model to occur. The extra vertices are designed to be moved from their neutral position based on randomly selected somatotype values. When put together these three values and the neutral vertices will produce a complete humanoid body shape. Figure 6 shows the three extreme body types as they would look in the newly designed model.

The *Ectomorphy* value influences the stomach and sides of the character's torso, giving the model a leaner appearance. The *Endomorphy* value affects the vertices in the opposite way, pushing the model's vertices outwards and giving it a more rotund appearance. The *Mesomorphy* value also dampens the effect of the *Endomorph* value on the character model's stomach. It primarily pushes the model's shoulders outwards to create a broader looking model. Examples are shown in figure 6.

The model is therefore capable of being generated based on deformations to model following this approach, and the inclusion of random colour mapping for clothes, hair and skin-colour, height/weight scaling and random accessories as required.

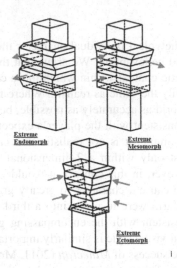

Fig. 4. Extreme Somatotypes and deformations on the character model vertices

5   Evaluation

The multi-faceted nature of the proposed approach to generating diversity creates the opportunity to evaluate the different approaches to introducing variety based on their effect on believability. In addition, it is also important to look at the processing cost of the various approaches, as this will help to evaluate whether or not the changes to a complexity of procedural character generation system are cost-effective in terms of increasing perceived diversity whilst not impacting too heavily on overhead.

5.1   Perception of Variety Evaluation Methodology

Given the argument that lack of variety is associated with negative believability (and therefore engagement/immersion in a game world), we built the evaluation to test player perception of variety in crowds.

Crucially, it is the player's perception of variety that is important, instead of some automated measure of diversity based on combinations of generated models. Although a real crowd has vast diversity based on the millions of differences between individuals, the combination of factors that make a virtual crowd believable may be a much smaller subset. For example, many of the more subtle differences between individuals may have different value in the perception of diversity.

Indeed, it is also exceedingly important that false positives (i.e. player incorrectly identifies a false lack of diversity) are taken into account since it is user perception that is most important (more so than realism, for example). Increasingly subtle changes to the procedural generation of crowds may have no meaningful effect on increasing perceived diversity (i.e. believability).

McDonnell et al. [6] conducted an experiment into the perceptual impact of appearance and motion "clones" in simulated crowds. In their experiment participants were asked to watch a crowd simulation running and then click on clones of characters as and when they noticed them - the time between the start of the simulation and the click was then recorded.

Using elements from the technique described from above, we performed an evaluation to investigate the effectiveness of the variety of factors in the proposed crowd generation algorithms. This does not look at the speed at which participants find clones - instead it looks at the total clones that the player notices within a certain time period as a measure of player perception of variety.

5.2   Procedure

Fifty naive individuals between the ages of eighteen and thirty (26 Male, 24 Female) were asked to take part in the evaluation. They had mixed educational backgrounds and not all had an interest in computer gaming. Each participant was required to provide informed consent and retained anonymity in the study.

Participants were then asked to sit down and watch one of five pre-recorded video sets. These sets of videos had the same six fifteen-second videos in them, but in a randomised order to avoid unintended variables.

Each video featured an animation of a crowd of non-player characters in a virtual test environment (described in [8]), where the generation of character models in each condition used a different combination of approaches. The videos were screen-captures of the crowd simulation in action, but with differences to the way in which the character models were generated.

All videos contain the crowd moving around the environment at an average walking pace as this better recreates a situation in which the crowd would actually be viewed (instead of having all the characters just standing still). The camera was also positioned at eye-level with the other characters in order to simulate the height at which the crowd would generally be viewed. A fixed seed was used to ensure crowds behaved identically between participants.

Participants were individually shown the six videos in random order. They were asked to take a tally whenever they saw two agents in the video that they considered to look the *same*. In this way, perception of variety is recorded based on the number of clones identified, across conditions to allow comparison of the facets of the crowd generation technique.

6   Results

Data collected represent the inverse of the user's perception of diversity in the crowd simulation. The more clones that were spotted suggest less perceived diversity in the crowd regardless of how many "real" clones there were. False positives still lower the perceived diversity in the same way true appearance clones. The population mean calculated from the results suggests that as the models became more varied, it became harder for participants to pick out characters that looked the same within the scene. This supports the case that the improvements made to the basic character generation system (i.e. fixed set of model skins) have been effective; reducing the average of 6.48 clones spotted per session to 3.1 clones.

Table 1. Comparison of clone perceptions across conditions

Condition	Generation Methodology	Mean Clones Spotted (s.d.)
1	Basic – Identical models, skin variants	6.48 (2.79)
2	As condition 1, with height/weight scaling	5.36 (2.66)
3	Model Somatotype generation	4.04 (2.30)
4	As condition 3, with colour tinting	3.56 (1.93)
5	As condition 4, with model accessories	3.1 (2.03)

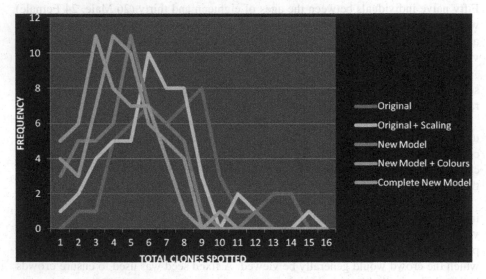

Fig. 5. Distribution of clones identified between conditions

Figure 7 shows the frequency of total clones spotted in each condition. As the model's variation increases, the graph peaks tend towards to lower totals. This shift towards the left implies that it was harder for participants to notice appearance clones as variation increased in the scene.

It is also interesting to note that there is a flatter distribution in the 'original' system's results compared with that of the more complex systems. This increased spread may be due to the inability of some participants to be totally sure that two figures looked entirely the same. As the variation increased it may have been easier for test-subjects to define similar-looking characters due to their more obvious colour changes and similar accessories.

It also appears that basic scaling on the original model (the yellow line on Figure 7) had a dramatic difference to that of its predecessor. This suggests that merely adding the random scaling to each character could provide the greatest benefit on the crowd whilst also being the lowest cost on processing power (compared with the other changes to the model).

It was also noticed that participants spotted many false-positives in the final model version. This may be due to the addition of the accessory hats, which may have made the models look more visually similar to one another than without them (i.e. two men with top hats may have been considered as appearance clones even when they had totally different heads or bodies.) This is an interesting result since it shows that the use of limited accessories such as hats or bags in procedurally generated crowds should be done with great caution since they act as a signifier of lack of diversity.

Unpaired t-Tests were conducted to compare the data collected from the original model test with that of the data collected from the other models. This was done to see whether there was a chance that the models did not actually affect the perceived diversity in the scene. The comparison between the basic (random skin) model and others showed a significant difference in the number of clones identified (therefore perceived diversity) ($p<0.001$) in each condition, except the basic scaling version where $p <0.05$.

In order to see how the extra complexity of additions to the new model (colours and accessories) affected the perceived diversity, t-tests were conducted on the new model and its more complex variations (colour palette alterations and accessories). The results show that while variation of colours was not significant in increasing perceived diversity ($p=0.26$), the addition of random accessories did significantly increase diversity ($p<0.05$).

Fig. 6. High Populations of Agents in crowds (1400+ individuals)

6.1   Model Complexity and Computational Overhead

Having a high frame rate per second (FPS) is an important factor in the fidelity of graphics software and games [2]. Therefore, it was important to analyse the effect that the new model had on the program's frame rate as the number of agents increased.

An experiment was run in which the FPS of the software was recorded as the total number of agents in the scene increased. An agent was instantiated once per frame until reaching a maximum of 1,500 agents at once. Data was recorded once every three frames to reduce the load on the system (see figure 9).

Four tests were carried out based on four conditions: The basic model shape, the "best case" of the new model (lowest possible polygon count), "average case" (normal probability of additional accessories/polygons), and worst cast (all agents have maximum polygons allowed by accessories).

In order to ensure a fair test, the four simulations were run on the same machine with a minimised number of other programs active at run-time. The simulations were carried out using a locked random seed, ensuring that the movement and character generation would be the same each time (the same as with the previous experiment).

Comparing the *average case* of the new model with the *original* model's frame rate shows an average difference of 1.568132 frames per second which at high frame rates is negligible, however the frame rate for the new model drops below twenty-five frames per second at around 376 total agents whereas the frame rate for the original drops at 413, which is a noticeable difference of 37 extra agents.

There is also a dramatic difference between frame rate for the original model and the worst-case scenario (in which every member of the crowd simulation is wearing a hat) however the probability of this case occurring during the simulation is incredibly slim ($P < 0.001$ based approximation using Normal Distribution).

Although the new model does have a slightly lower frame rate than that of the original model, the increased processing overhead is worth the trade-off considering its noticeable effect on the viewer's perception of the crowd (52.16% improvement on the original in terms of participants perception of appearance clones).

7   Conclusion

This paper has investigated the player perception of diversity in video game crowds. In particular, where crowds are procedurally generated, there is a potential gameplay issue where players experience loss of immersion when exposed to game crowds featuring frequently repeated character models. This was confirmed through a pilot qualitative focus group activity where participants watched game videos and commented on lack of diversity in crowds.

Taking inspiration from Sheldon's body somatotype theory a new character generation algorithm was designed with a character model mesh that would deform to represent different body shapes [7], and also vary based on colour, height, weight and accessories (e.g. hats). In experimental conditions, the different facets of the model generation process were tested to understand user *perception* of diversity in virtual crowds. This relative measure is much more important than the absolute measure of diversity since it is based on the personal experience of the player within the game.

With all character generation aspects operating, the new model significantly improved upon the basic version ($P < 0.0001$) in terms of reducing the user's perception of crowd diversity. However, we identified that when the new model was colour-tinted there was no noticeable statistical difference in user perception of diversity. This suggests that colour tinting may not be as effective as previously thought, or that the differences in colours were not vibrant enough for the user to notice.

The new model generation algorithm appears to have reduced the user's perception of appearance clones within the scene. In further tests of computational overhead required by this multi-faceted approach, we highlight the cost/benefit comparison of the approach based on best- and worst-case scenarios, showing how the greatest perceived crowd diversity can be achieved for lowest computational cost.

This work focussed explicitly on appearance clones on moving but not animated models. Although this fits within the visual aesthetic of the game environment chosen (which has a lo-fi style), in other more realistic environments the movement and visual detail of models will no doubt have an effect on user perceptions of clones. The specific factors that are important for different aesthetic styles will vary and as such some aspects of the study may have less or more importance depending on the presentation of a specific game.

References

1. Booth, M.: The AI Systems of Left 4 Dead (pdf) (2009),
   http://www.valvesoftware.com/publications/2009/
   ai_systems_of_l4d_mike_booth.pdf
2. Claypool, M., Claypool, K., Damaa, F.: The effects of frame rate and resolution on users playing First Person Shooter games. In: Electronic Imaging 2006 (2006)
3. Grimes, B.: Shading a Bigger, Better Sequel (pdf) (2010),
   http://www.valvesoftware.com/publications/2010/
   GDC10_ShaderTechniquesL4D2.pdf (accessed January 2, 2013)
4. Kirman, B.: Emergence and Playfulness in Social Games. In: Proceedings 14th Academic Mindtrek Conference, Tampere. ACM (2010)
5. Lewis, M.: Initial Models created by Lewis's Maya Plugin (2000),
   http://citeseerx.ist.psu.edu/viewdoc/
   download?doi=10.1.1.23.3410 (January 3, 2013)
6. McDonnell, R., Larkin, M., Dobbyn, S., Collins, O.C.: Clone attack! Perception of crowd variety. In: SIGGRAPH 2008, Los Angeles (August 2008), Article No. 26
7. Sheldon, W.: Atlas of Men: A Guide for Somatotyping the Adult Image of All Ages. New Edition. Macmillan Pub. Co. (1970)
8. Szymanezyk, O., Dickinson, P., Duckett, T.: Towards agent-based crowd simulation in airports using games technology. In: O'Shea, J., Nguyen, N.T., Crockett, K., Howlett, R.J., Jain, L.C. (eds.) KES-AMSTA 2011. LNCS, vol. 6682, pp. 524–533. Springer, Heidelberg (2011)
9. Thalmann, D., Musse, S.R.: Somatotype Deformation on a Simple Human (2000)
10. Thalmann, D., Musse, S.R.: Crowd Simulation, 1st edn. Springer, London (2007)
11. Vlachos, A.: Rendering Wounds in Left 4 Dead 2 (pdf) (2010),
    http://www.valvesoftware.com/publications/2010/
    gdc2010_vlachos_l4d2wounds.pdf (accessed January 2, 2013)

A Framework for Evaluating Behavior Change Interventions through Gaming

Valentina Rao

Playful Pandas
Galgenstraat 11, 1013LT Amsterdam, Netherlands
v@playfulpandas.org

Abstract. As behavior change interventions increasingly use game and game-like strategies to influence behavior, it seems pressing to develop a specific framework that reconsiders game design practices in a way to include the issue of persuasive effectiveness. This paper presents an overview of current discussion regarding persuasion through games and proposes the category of "game systems" to include different kinds of persuasive strategies that employ gaming such as persuasive games, gamification and gameful design, in order to facilitate the development of design tools that are goal-specific towards behavior change. Current tools focus on game usability or playability, but very few offer usable heuristics for the evaluation of persuasive efficacy. The following pages propose an initial differentiation between persuasive game systems that act as computer-mediated communication and others that instead behave as computer human interaction, to highlight the necessity for different design strategies.

1 Introduction

A growing number of online and mobile software products aim at influencing user behavior through interactions that mimic the dynamics or the aesthetics of (video) games; the diffusion of such phenomenon calls for an increase in attention on what strategies are available to persuade in a gaming context and their efficacy.

In the last years, aside from the already well established practice of video games for persuasive purposes called "persuasive games" or "games for change" (or sometimes by the even more general term of "serious games"), that usually offer a full game experience that is separate from everyday experience, we have witnessed the emergence of other practices, called "gamification" [1] or "gameful design" [2], that instead employ only selected elements from game mechanics, dynamics and aesthetics, often with the final goal of influencing behavior towards a desired goal.

While the boundaries of the above mentioned definitions are subject to ongoing debate, the actual distinctions between these different game forms in practice is quite blurry, and the initial differentiation between persuasive games as systems that use a fictional, immersive environments with rules, goals and a game universe [3] and gamification or gameful design that instead employs only game elements or game

D. Reidsma, H. Katayose, and A. Nijholt (Eds.): ACE 2013, LNCS 8253, pp. 368–379, 2013.

"atoms" [4] doesn't hold anymore as in different databases often the same titles are listed alternatively as gamification or as serious/persuasive games.

In spite of this, persuasive games and persuasive gamification and gameful design continue to develop separately both as academic fields and as design fields. Theoretically and methodologically, the difference between the two is still vast: the definition of persuasive games has been created in conjunction with the definition of procedural rhetoric, a game-specific kind of rhetoric that achieves persuasion by representing ideas and experiences through the computational procedures that recreate the virtual processes portrayed by the game [5].

Maybe because of the theoretical nature of procedural rhetoric, which makes it difficult to empirically measure its results, existing works on procedural rhetoric tend to ignore the design issues that relate to persuasive effectiveness.

On the other side, gamification as a new phenomenon born out of marketing strategies has still to develop as a research field, and while persuasive strategies are an over-mentioned topic, scientific interest is superficial and instrumental to developing some ready made standards to arouse engagement derived from behavioral science, like the popular usage of points, badges and leaderboards, and the strategies themselves are often accused of being manipulative and coercive [6]. The theoretical approach called gameful design tries to give scientific and ethical perspective to gamification principles, supporting designs that produce positive change in the world and that stimulate the better instincts of the players, instead of the worst [7] and expanding the disciplinary boundaries to include officially studies of psychology of persuasion [8].

The approach suggested in this paper is to temporarily set aside definition issues and try to focus on the theme of persuasive goals that is shared by all, considering that a large majority of gamification by definition wants to motivate users towards achieving defined goals [1], and persuasive games use rhetoric for defending a point or opinion and changing the user's attitudes and ultimately behaviors.

In this perspective, both kinds of artifacts can be considered as persuasive "interventions", to borrow the term employed in social sciences to describe initiatives aimed at behavior change [9], and different sorts of game forms can be considered as declinations of the generic category of "game systems", information systems that use the interaction modes of games to achieve a persuasive goal. This angle follows the assumption that video games are first of all HCI principles characterized by shared values (the playful interaction) that reframe the experience in a certain direction [10].

Lockton highlights how persuasive design is *explicitly* intended (my italics) to influence users towards particular behavior [11] to distinguish from other design artifacts that can be susceptible to interpretations that find them persuasive, but in which the implementation of persuasion is not an issue. To the purpose of studying the specificities of such intentional design, Lockton renames persuasive design "design with intent". This explicit intent is what sets aside persuasive games and gamification systems from entertainment games, and what connects them beyond all theoretical differences, together with the frame of reference mentioned above.

For this reason, while the association between the two fields of persuasive games and gamification might still need some theoretical refinement, it is nevertheless proposed here not just for the sake of argument but to offer an interdisciplinary perspective that revolves around the problem of effectiveness, and initiate a research direction in the hope of arousing further discussion about implementation practices that draw equally from game design and persuasive design.

This paper is conceptual in nature, the following pages will offer an overview of the different angles on the topic of persuasion through games, and tentatively propose the notions of game systems as behavior change support systems [12] and of game persuasion through human computer interaction as opposed to procedural rhetoric as the first steps in the development of a theoretical framework.

2   Overview of Disciplinary Perspectives on Persuasion through Gaming

The main obstacle to the development of a research angle specific to persuasive design through gaming lies in the fact that discussion on the topic is scattered among very different disciplinary fields that rarely communicate with each other. In such varied landscape, four main theoretical threads can be identified.

The first thread is characterized by a humanities-oriented approach in which the dominant theory is that of procedural rhetoric [5], theory that describes video games as representational systems to convey ideas, messages or experiences in a symbolic and metaphorical way through the procedures taking place in the game, to the purpose of persuasion. Although the procedural rhetoric theory has been initially developed to explain the processes taking place in persuasive games, in later writings of the same author [13] and in other works following the same line of thought, the focus has been directed towards an interpretation of rhetoric in the sense of meaningful expression rather than persuasive discourse.

Maybe for this reason the procedural rhetoric angle seems to encourage work in the direction of a general theory of meaning production, with the priority of validating digital games as a representational medium and confirm their potential of expressing complex content [14], rather than considering efficacy in rhetorical actions. Even among the critics of the procedural model, there is a definite skepticism about the possibility or utility of evaluating effectiveness [15], because the players' readings are seen as unpredictable and the rhetoric intended by the game design is viewed as dependent on the players' choices. Although a lack of efficacy standards is lamented, especially with regards to games with pragmatic goals such as advertising [16], there is a general diffidence towards measurable persuasion, and specific theories of persuasion such as persuasive technology in this framework are seen as manipulative and ethically redoubtable [6].

The difference between theories of rhetoric and theories of persuasion is mainly a disciplinary one, as rhetoric as a field developed as a literary discipline and grew to encompass not only the "art of persuasion" (Aristotle, in [6]) but also all matters of composition and style in both oral and written communication, while studies of persuasion stemmed from psychology and social sciences and focus much on face-to-face interaction and measurable results.

Not accidentally, the second thread consists in works that instead use methodolo gies from social sciences and focus on the evaluation of efficacy in specific cases. Evaluation in the majority of cases considers the general efficacy of the game medium with respect to other mediums or with respect to the general efficacy of the game experience [17] [18] [19] without further investigations into which design elements contribute to the results. Bang et al. consider persuasion from a learning perspective, and view the persuasive process as a kind of cognitive and behavioral learning [20], while others consider persuasion from the perspective of social cognitive theory and self-efficacy, narrative persuasion and usage of stories [17]. The main problem in this approach is that games developed with very different purposes such as teaching, training, and persuasion are analyzed and assessed with the same tools, leaving re-searchers to denounce the necessity of specific methodologies for different goals [21]. With very rare exceptions [20] [22], available psychological theories of persuasion and evaluation procedures of effectiveness are not employed for game systems, and a tentative agenda for future work on the issue of efficacy evaluation of such systems.

A third thread can be found in those works that instead adopt the persuasive technology framework. Persuasive technology theory [23] maintains that technology can be designed to change attitudes and behaviors, and can employ a large array of channels, including digital games.

One sentence on persuasive tech

Works employing the persuasive technology framework either use games as a platform for the exploration of persuasive strategies in relation to different issues such as for instance culture and persuasive technology, either they focus on a specific subtopic, such as cultural differences in persuasion [24], and a systematic framework in that direction is yet to be defined.

To these three main threads a more recent fourth one can be added, consisting in recent works that consider game-like interactions such as gamification and gameful design; although the focus of most publications is rather on motivational strategies and engagement than on persuasive architecture [25] [1], the persuasive intent and consequent design is recognized and analyzed in single cases (for example, [26]).

A common weakness in otherwise diverse angles can be found in the lack of proper evaluation methodologies, as more often than not the few existing ones are incomplete in relation to both design heuristics and users response. The main obstacle in developing effective methodologies for evaluation seems to lie in the absence of a general framework to conceptualize persuasion in games beyond the more developed model based upon the notion of procedural rhetoric, in which the focus is on artistic expression and interpretation, both difficult to measure.

3   Rhetoric versus Instrumental Play: Two Modalities for Persuasion

The theoretical diversity described in the previous paragraphs is mirrored in the diversity of classification methods both in relation to persuasive games (usually included in more general classifications of "serious games') and gamification products. It is not possible here to go in depth into the arguments surrounding serious games classifications; to summarize, persuasive games suffer from the same classification issues visible in classifications of serious games, in which games are categorized according to market areas, distribution areas, or reception areas [27], but rarely according to their designed intent, to reiterate Lockton's expression.

A more pragmatic classification categorizes games according to their kind of gameplay, the purpose of the design, and the scope of the user contexts in which the game is received (G/P/S model) [28], although this model reduces most serious games to the purposes of message broadcasting, data exchange, and training.

As maintained earlier, a first step in developing a research focus on persuasive design in games is to restrict the field only to games with a stated persuasive intent, and that means creating a very clear distinction between those and other kinds of games such as those for education or training. To this goal, an analysis has been conducted on some of the largest online databases that include persuasive games: the online database of Games for Change, association that focuses on games for social impact, the database of Health Games Research, a US program that supports research and development of health-related digital games, and the database of Gamification.co, official website for gamification and design for engagement (for gameful design unfortunately existing databases consider mostly academic publications and not games).

First, the whole databases have been categorized according to purpose, and subsequently all games with a specific persuasive purpose have been extrapolated.

At first the categories employed to isolate game forms with persuasive purposes have been borrowed from the categories defined by the rhetoric scholar Kinneavy to describe the different communicative purposes of rhetorical discourse, categories that in precedence have been suggested as a useful tool to categorize games according to their intent, rather than by other elements such as context or gameplay. [29]

Such categories that in discourse theory are articulated as referential (educational, scientific), to present, inform of, educate on, or discuss about an existing reality, persuasive (with a persuasive purpose), such as oratory, propaganda, advertising and safety warnings, literary or artistic, when the primary goal is to "be beautiful", such as in literature and theatre, and expressive, when the goal is to express a self or a social unit (diaries, manifestos) (Kinneavy, in [29]).

After applying these categories to the corpus of games examined, the shortcomings of this model were immediately clear in that a percentage of games and especially of gamification projects, outside of wanting to be educational/scientific, rhetorically persuasive, artistic and expressive, were in fact not just supporting a discourse but they were the place of the action, like for instance in games that help children bear painful therapies or gamification systems that help players achieve their house chores (Chore Wars).

By focusing just on those games which intent was overtly persuasive, it was possible to recognize five different strategies to achieve persuasion[1]:

---

[1] A full study reporting all the statistics is to be published soon, with extensive examples.

1) Rhetorical representation: the delivery of ideas or concepts through representational simulations of an experience

2) Product placement: a product is visually inserted within a game experience or otherwise related, to connect the intrinsically gratifying experience of the game with the product

3) Facilitation: the game experience is not separated from real life, but during the game experience some kind of real life action is performed

4) Behavior change systems: similar to facilitation systems, behavior change systems facilitate real actions, but in those there is a conscious design to influence behavior, many gamification add-ons to websites provide this service

5) Aesthetic experience: ideas or concepts delivered by the game are reinforced by the aesthetic experience of the game, in which the goal is not to offer a discourse through experience, but to provide high production values.

These five strategies operate through two main modalities:

a) games that want to transmit a message (rhetorical representation, aesthetic experience, behavior change, product placement), and thus communicate something, and

b) games that instead facilitate a process or organize activities and by doing so influence behavior during the action (facilitation, behavior change, enhancement).

Interestingly enough, this empirical distinction made during the analysis of game examples was more precisely explained in a pre existing text by the persuasive design scholar Oinas Kukkonen, asserting that online persuasive design systems basically utilize two modalities to persuade, either computer-human persuasion, or computer mediated persuasion [30].

Oinas Kukkonen elaborates further, suggesting that persuasive technologies can be categorized by whether they affect attitude and behaviors through *human computer interaction*, which often uses patterns similar to social communication and features the computer system as an actor and interlocutor, or by performing a mediating role and allowing *computer mediated communication* like discussion forums, blogs, chats and similar [30] (my italics) (also in Cassell et al. [31]).

After ulterior analysis, it was clear that the persuasive strategies enacted through gamification systems and persuasive games can be understood through the two modalities of mediated communication, in which the game is a medium to transmit a message (procedural rhetoric, product placement, aesthetic experience) and of human computer interaction, in which the game environment is used to facilitate an action or to influence behavior during a process (facilitation, behavior change support).

By following this logic, then procedural rhetoric qualifies as computer-mediated communication, in which the game system is used to transmit meaning from the designer/author to the player, and when the game experience is over the player ideally takes away an idea, a message that is conceptual in nature, and possibly affects in greater degree attitudes rather than behaviors.

In this view, video games that produce rhetorical discourse on different topics, for instance children's labor [32], or sex change (Dys4ia [33]), perform the role of the medium, one of the three roles that computers can play as persuasive technology, together with tools and social actors [23].

Fig. 1. The game Participatory Chinatown lets citizens provide their real input about city planning in a fictional environment

On the other hand, systems that aim to persuade through direct interaction during the performance of a task (such as breathing correctly with cystic fibrosis [34] or dealing productively with fellow citizens in urban management [35]) or systems that facilitate an action by adding engagement, like many gamified systems do, can be seen at the same time as tools, as they help perform an action, and also as social actors and interlocutors, as the systems engages in dialogue with the player, through feedback, rewards or other tools [23]. To note that such dialogue is not "about" a topic external to the action to be performed, in which case the whole interaction takes the modes of a representation or, as Bogost defines it, "representative simulation" [6] to convey a message, but rather its communication regards the "how" an action is performed during the process itself.

In this second case, the gaming part is instrumental to reaching some goal, giving a new depth to the notion of instrumental play, which happens when hardcore gamers play compulsively to gain points or status in multiplayer games (MMOs) and the act of playing is instrumental to external purposes [36], purposes that can also be not related to the game.

Existing models for persuasive games don't provide the conceptual tools to describe this other approach to persuasion in games, different from procedural rhetoric. To that purpose, it is suggested here to utilize the notion, originally conceived to describe information systems developed for persuasive purposes, of Behavior Change Support Systems.

4   Game Systems as Behavior Change Support Systems

In order to find a model that can accommodate the two kinds of modalities through which games can be persuasive, it seemed appropriate to look for a more generic and flexible way on understanding games. The notion of games as systems is all but new [37], the definition proposed here takes less from the systems of rules games are made of and rather refers to games as one specific kind of information system that incorporates characteristics that are typical of games. Adopting this more general definition makes it easier to visualize different game forms such as procedural games and gamification as nuances of a same phenomenon, and to detach ourselves from pre-existing definitions that might be limiting because of their theoretical baggage. Information Systems (IS) is the theoretical model behind several explanations of online interactions, and behind the notion of behavior change support systems.

Oinas Kukkonen initially proposes the notion of behavior change support systems (BCSS) to describe consumer health applications [38]. Behavior change support systems are socio-technical information systems with psychological and behavioral outcomes designed to form, alter, or reinforce attitudes or behaviors or both without using coercion and deception [12].

The notion of behavior change support systems has been originally ideated in relation to generic interactive systems, but the same concept can be easily adapted to any kind of interactive software system. The specific environment of games, with its qualities of (sometimes feeble) suspension of disbelief, positive attitude, emotional and physical arousal, and compliance to rules and artificial goals [37] [39], requires some preliminary distinction, but overall the definition of behavior change support systems describes very well those games that facilitate behavior, in contrast with "rhetorical" games.

Although all information technology is seen as intrinsically persuasive [12], in behavior change support systems persuasive effects are intentionally caused or facilitated by design. The former statement is even more true in relation to gaming practices, in which the mental opening and positive attitude of acceptance create a favorable dis- position and expectations of enjoyment otherwise difficult to achieve, and game systems also have to confront the ethical fact that they are "always on" with regards to persuasion and never neutral.

The BCSS model underscores how it is preferable to favor the voluntary ways in which people use information technologies to change their attitudes and or behavior through building upon their personal motivation or goal, instead of recurring to manipulation.

The connection with the debate on gamification, also struggling with the issues of manipulation and subliminal communication, is clear, and in this sense BCSSs can provide a model also for the understanding of ethical issues involved in the use of game systems.

Current works on behavior change support systems seem to favor case studies that deal with human-computer persuasion, but in fact the model can be used to consider both computer-mediated persuasive communication and human-computer persuasion.

4.1 Elaboration Likelihood Model and the Many Shades of Game Persuasion

BCSSs offer comprehensive tools to understanding the different modalities of persuasion because they interpret such modalities in the light of the Elaboration Likelihood Model (ELM), in which a general theory of attitude change is developed, by identifying two main processes that underlie the effectiveness of persuasive communications. The first process is called "direct route", and takes place when the message presents a direct argument that takes a long time to be processed. The second process, the "indirect route", employs emotional, almost subconscious heuristics that affect the user in a less conscious (and less effective) way. The term "elaboration" signifies the extent to which a person scrutinizes the persuasive message and its arguments and "the likelihood of elaboration will be determined by a person's motivation and ability to evaluate the communication presented." [40]

An advantage of employing the ELM model as a main model of persuasion (also used to describe and understand behavior change supports systems) is that it comprehends all kinds of persuasive communications, both arguments and facilitation of tasks: "In the ELM, arguments are viewed as bits of information contained in a communication that are relevant to a person's subjective determination of the true merits of an advocated position". [40]

A definition of certain game systems as behavior change support systems doesn't contradict the main theory that sees persuasive games as vehicles for procedural rhetoric, but simply puts that particular kind of game systems on a different point in the spectrum of all the possible persuasive communications that can take place through gaming.

Another advantage of using such model is that it provides a first integration of various classic theories of persuasion, other than the ELM model and puts them to use for the structuring and evaluation of information systems and software development [30].

With regards to game systems, ELM offers the advantage of providing a visualization of how the strategies used in procedural rhetoric and in behavior change support systems can be placed on the two opposite sides of one spectrum: representational procedural rhetoric offers procedural argument that address the central route, by being based on logic and because they embed a message in a game experience and not a game experience in a process, like behavior change support systems do.

Further development of the correlation between game elements and routes of persuasion is in the agenda, and there are indications that such research angle can be useful in finding methodologies for the evaluation of persuasive effectiveness, analogue to the Persuasive Systems Design (PSD) model [41], created to evaluate persuasive strategies in behavior change support systems. The integration of evaluation strategies from video games and persuasion can proceed only after a general model for understanding persuasion through gaming is provided, and this paper hopes to offer a first step in that direction.

5   Conclusions

Existing theoretical limitations of current frameworks of persuasive games, such as the procedural rhetoric framework, affect the development of specific design and evaluation methodologies focusing on persuasive efficacy. These limitations can be overcome by acknowledging other models developed in other disciplinary fields that can also be valid for describing persuasive games, such as Behavior Change Support Systems model, or by conceptualizing new ones. The adoption of such larger scope can improve the chances of better understanding the different ways in which game systems persuade, through both direct routes and indirect routes to persuasion, and it can expand the theoretical tools available to game research for improving de- sign in view of its effectiveness.

The conceptualization of a general framework for the study of persuasion through gaming systems has been pursued in this paper by creating a first differentiation be- tween game systems that facilitate activities (including interpersonal communication) and game systems that communicate concepts or ideas through representation. From such differentiation, hopefully other theoretical developments will follow to specify other modalities employed by games, to create a vast palette of methodologies for use to game designers who design for persuasion.

Future work on the topic will focus on developing specific evaluation heuristics for persuasive game systems to integrate tools for the assessment of game-related issues, like playability (effectiveness of the gameplay experience) [42] and game usability [43], together with tools to evaluate issues related to persuasive design from persuasive design theories.

Acknowledgments. Many thanks to professor Oinas Kukkonen for his long distance support and availability, to Sitwat Langrial and the other colleagues at Oulu research group whose discussions made these theoretical developments possible.

References

1. Zichermann, G.: Game Based Marketing. John Wiley & Sons, New Jersey (2010); Baldonado, M., Chang, C.-C.K., Gravano, L., Paepcke, A.: The Stanford Digital Library Metadata Architecture. Int. J. Digit. Libr. 1, 108–121 (1997)
2. Deterding, S., Dixon, D., Nacke, L.E., O'Hara, K., Sicart, M.: Gamification: Using Game Design Elements in Non-Gaming Contexts. In: Proceedings of the 2011 Annual Conference Extended Abstracts on Human Factors in Computing Systems (CHI EA 2011), Vancouver, BC, Canada. ACM Press (2011)

3. Aarseth, E.J.: Playing Research: Methodological approaches to game analysis. In: Melbourne DAC - the 5th International Digital Arts and Culture Conference. School of Applied Communication, Melbourne (2003)
4. Huotari, K., Hamari, J.: Defining Gamification - A Service Marketing Perspec- tive. In: Proceedings of the 16th International Academic MindTrek Conference, Tampere, Finland (2012)
5. Bogost, I.: Persuasive Games: The Expressive Power of Videogames. The MIT Press, Cambridge (2007)
6. Bogost, I.: Gamification is bullshit. The Atlantic: Technology (August 2011)
7. Deterding, S.: A quick buck by copy and paste: A review of "Gamification by Design". Gamification Research Network (September 15, 2011)
8. Deterding, S.: Gamification: Designing for motivation. Interactions 19(4), 14–17 (2012)
9. Portnoy, D.B., Scott-Sheldon, L.A.J., Johnson, B.T., Carey, M.P.: Computer delivered interventions for health promotion and behavioral risk reduction: A meta-analysis of 75 randomized controlled trials. Prev. Med. 47, 3–16 (2010)
10. Barr, P., Noble, J., Biddle, R.: Video game values: Human- computer interaction and games. Interacting with Computers 19(2), 180–195 (2007)
11. Lockton, D., Harrison, D., Stanton, N.A.: The Design with Intent Method: A design tool for influencing user behaviour. Applied Ergonomics 41(3), 382–392 (2010)
12. Oinas Kukkonen, H.: A foundation for the study of behavior change support systems. Pers. Ubiquit. Comput. (2012), doi:10.1007/s00779-012-0591-5
13. Bogost, I.: Persuasive Games: The Proceduralist Style. Gamasutra.com (January 21, 2009) (accessed September 16, 2012)
14. Treanor, M., Mateas, M., Wardrip-Fruin, N.: Kaboom! is a Many-Splendored Thing: An interpretation and design methodology for message- driven games using graphical logics. In: Proceedings of the Fifth International Conference on the Foundation of Digital Games (2010)
15. Sicart, M.: Against Procedurality. Game Studies 11(3) (2011)
16. Smith, J., Just, S.: Playful persuasion: The rhetorical potential of advergames. Nordicom Review 30, 53–68 (2009)
17. Lavender, T.: Video Games as Change Agents – The Case of Homeless: It's No Game. The McMaster Journal of Communication 7(1), Article 2 (2011)
18. Baranowski, T., Buday, R., Thompson, D., Baranowski, J.: Playing for real: Video games and stories for health-related behavior change. Am. J. Prev. Med. 34(1), 74–82 (2008)
19. Cato, P., Cole, S., Bradlyn, A., Pollock, B.: A Video Game Improves Behavioral Outcomes in Adolescents and Young Adults With Cancer: A Randomized Trial. MPHd Pediatrics 122(2), 305–317 (2008)
20. Bang, M., Torstensson, C., Katzeff, C.: The PowerHhouse: A Persuasive Computer Game Designed to Raise Awareness of Domestic Energy Consumption. In: IJsselsteijn, W.A., de Kort, Y.A.W., Midden, C., Eggen, B., van den Hoven, E. (eds.) PERSUASIVE 2006. LNCS, vol. 3962, pp. 123–132. Springer, Heidelberg (2006)
21. Watt, J.H.: Improving methodology in serious games research with elaborated theory. In: Ritterfeld, U., Vorderer, P., Cody, M. (eds.) Serious Games, Mechanisms and Effects. Routledge, USA (2009)
22. Svahn, M.: Processing Play: Perceptions of Persuasion. In: Digra Conference Proceedings (2009)

23. Fogg, B.J., Cuellar, G., Danielson, D.: Motivating, Influencing, and Persuading Users. In: Jacko, J.A., Sears, T. (eds.) The Human- Computer Interaction Handbook: Fundamentals, Evolving Technologies and Emerging Applications. Lawrence Elbaum Associates, Taylor& Francis, New York (2007)
24. Khaled, R., Biddle, R., Noble, J., Barr, P., Fischer, R.: Persuasive Interaction for Collectivist Cultures. In: Seventh Australasian User Interface Conference (AUIC 2006), Hobart, Australia (2006)
25. Deterding et al: CHI 2011 Workshop Gamification: Using Game Design Elements in Non-Game Contexts. In: CHI 2011 Proceedings, May 7-12, Vancouver, BC, Canada (2011)
26. Inbar, O., Tractinsky, N., Tsimhoni, O., Seder, T.: Driving the Scoreboard: Motivating Eco-Driving Through In-Car Gaming. In: CHI 2011 Workshop Gamification: Using GameDesign Elements in Non-Game Contexts, CHI Conference Vancouver (2011)
27. Klimmt, C.: Serious games and social change. In: Ritterfeld, U., Cody, M., Vorderer, P. (eds.) Serious Games: Mechanisms and Effects. Routledge, USA (2009)
28. Djaouti, D., Alvarez, J., Jessel, J.-P.: Classifying serious games: The G/P/S model. In: Felicia, P. (ed.) Handbook of Research on Improving Learning and Motivation Through Educational Games: Multidisciplinary Approaches. IGI global, Hershey (2011)
29. Rao, V.: How to say things with actions: A theory of discourse for video games for change. In: Digra Conference, Hilversum (2011),
    http://www.digra.org/dl/db/11312.32336.pdf
30. Oinas-Kukkonen, H., Harjumaa, M.: Towards deeper understanding of persuasion in software and information systems. In: Proceedings of the First International Conference on Advances in Human-Computer Interaction (ACHI), pp. 200–205 (2008)
31. Cassell, M.M., Jackson, C., Cheuvront, B.: Health communication on the Internet: An effective channel for health behavior change? Journal of Health Communication 3 (1998)
32. Sweatshop, game, http://www.playsweatshop.com
33. Dys4ia, game, http://www.newgrounds.com/portal/view/591565
34. Ludicross, game, http://www.youtube.com/watch?v=s99Iwe_p3nc
35. Participatory Chinatown, game, http://www.participatorychinatown.org
36. Taylor, T.L.: Power gamers just want to have fun?: Instrumental play in a MMOG. In: Digra 2003 Proceedings Utrecht University, The Netherlands (2003)
37. Salen, K., Zimmerman, E.: Rules of Play, Game Design Fundamentals. MIT Press (2004)
38. Räisänen, T., Lehto, T., Oinas-Kukkonen, H.: Practical findings from applying the PSD model for evaluating software design specifications. In: Ploug, T., Hasle, P., Oinas-Kukkonen, H. (eds.) PERSUASIVE 2010. LNCS, vol. 6137, pp. 185–192. Springer, Heidelberg (2010)
39. Petty, R.E., Cacioppo, J.T.: The elaboration likelihood model of persuasion. In: Berkowitz, L. (ed.) Advances in Experimental Social Psychology, pp. 123–205. Academic Press, New York (1980)
40. Räisänen, T., Lehto, T., Oinas-Kukkonen, H.: Practical findings from applying the PSD model for evaluating software design specifications. In: Ploug, T., Hasle, P., Oinas-Kukkonen, H. (eds.) PERSUASIVE 2010. LNCS, vol. 6137, pp. 185–192. Springer, Heidelberg (2010)
41. Isbister: Game Usability. Elsevier, Burlington (2008)
42. Bernhaupt, R. (ed.): Evaluating User Experience in Games Concepts and Methods. Springer, London (2010)

eVision: A Mobile Game
to Improve Environmental Awareness

Bruno Santos, Teresa Romão, A. Eduardo Dias, and Pedro Centieiro

CITI, DI-Faculdade de Ciências e Tecnologia, Universidade Nova de Lisboa
2829-516 Caparica, Portugal
bmsjobs@me.com, tir@fct.unl.pt, {aed.fct,pcentieiro}@gmail.com

Abstract. A significant part of the population is still not aware of the sustainability problems that our planet is facing, so it is important to inform the citizens while persuading them to change their behaviour and to acquire pro-environmental attitudes. The work presented in this paper describes an environmental scanner, named eVision, which combines augmented reality and mobile computing technologies to allow users to inspect their surroundings with their mobile devices in search for pollution sources. When detected, eVision provides users with additional information regarding those environmental threats and allows users to virtually eliminate them. eVision also works as an entertaining and persuasive game, incorporating a rewarding system and a virtual game character that interacts with the users and positively reinforces their pro-environmental actions. The paper also presents the user studies performed so far to evaluate the application's usability and impact on the users' environmental awareness and attitudes.

1   Introduction

The modern society has evolved in many aspects in the recent years, but people still lack routines and behaviours that support and help the environment. In our everyday life, we are confronted with situations that compromise our planet's sustainability, sometimes without even noticing them. Making people aware of this kind of situations is crucial to change their perspective, concerns and attitudes. With that objective in mind, we conceived eVision, an application which tries to persuade users to have a pro-environment behaviour. eVision uses mobile devices and augmented reality technology to provide users with information regarding the environmental threats in their surroundings and to offer a game-based activity where users are rewarded when completing tasks of interest. To engage users, Snowkin, a customizable virtual character, interacts with the users encouraging them to proceed.

It is unrealistic to think that everyone will change his or her behaviours day over night. However, making people aware of the problems and their possible solutions helps to engage them in activities that contribute for these solutions. Moreover, social influence and peer pressure help to disseminate and reproduce desirable behaviours [1]. Therefore, users activities and achievements while using eVision can also be

D. Reidsma, H. Katayose, and A. Nijholt (Eds.): ACE 2013, LNCS 8253, pp. 380–391, 2013.

disseminated through social networks (Facebook) in order to capture the attention of even more citizens.

Our goal is to use a familiar and powerful device that people frequently carry with them everywhere, the smartphone, to augment their ability to explore the surrounding environment and encourage them to perform pro-environmental activities. User studies were conducted to evaluate the application's usability and impact on users environmental awareness and attitudes.

eVision has been developed in the scope of Project DEAP, which aims to introduce new paradigms for environmental awareness, helping to motivate citizens to become more environmentally responsible in their everyday lives and engaging them in environmental preservation activities.

This paper is organized as follows: section 2 addresses the state of the art related to the main areas covered by the presented work; section 3 describes eVision, the design process, implementation and interface; section 4 presents the conducted usability evaluation and impact tests, and finally, section 5 presents the conclusions and a blueprint for the future work.

2   Related Work

Persuasive Technology purposefully applies psychological principles of persuasion to interactive media, aiming at changing users' attitudes and behaviours without coercion or deception. Its application in the field of Human-Computer Interaction (HCI) is quite diversified from Health, to Commerce, Safety, Management and other fields [3]. B.J. Fogg coined the term Captology as a new word that described the study of computers as persuasive technologies [4]. Eckles and Fogg [6] mention that mobile phones are an excellent persuasion tool. Mobile phones include a wide range of features and most people own them and carry them everywhere. eVision was designed to take advantage of the inherent features of smartphones, making them a bridge to apply persuasion.

Social networks enable people to establish social links with other people according to their motivations and interests and are highly depend on being able to hold the users attention and desire to continue participating. This started a new phenomenon, which Fogg calls "Mass Interpersonal Persuasion" (MIP) [7]. MIP brings together the power of interpersonal persuasion with the reach of mass media, by creating applications that allow people to interact and cooperate on a non-personal level, allowing them to reach a massive number of people. Social networks allow the exploration of the principles of influence (such as social proof) on a larger scale [1]. This type of persuasion was applied to eVision's design giving it the ability to share information through Facebook.

Persuasive technology can also be used to promote pro-environmental behaviours. eVision includes a game activity to reinforce its persuasive potential since games may influence players to take action through gameplay [8]. Games can not only deliver messages, but also simulate experiences and may become rhetorical tools for persuading players. Applications with a social presence can also be persuasive by making users respond to computers as if they were living beings, even when they are not given explicitly anthropomorphic interfaces. This allows computers to persuade by rewarding people with positive feedback, modelling a target behaviour or attitude and providing social support. When designing eVision, efforts were made to create a bond between the users and the virtual character, augmenting the chances of applying persuasion.

Augmented Reality (AR) is a technology in which the user's view of the real world is enhanced with virtual objects that appears to coexist in the same space as real objects. This type of technology allows computer products to narrow the gap between the real physical environment and the information concerning it. Sean White explores this ability and studies how to implement it on persuasive systems. He proposes that if augmentation affects the way we perceive the environment and our world, and if we can control that augmentation, then we can affect behaviour [9]. This type of visual cue was used when designing the eVision's environmental scanner, using AR to highlight the environmental threats surrounding the user.

eVision combines the many advantages of mobile devices, AR and persuasive technologies and explores the potential of social networks with the intent of making people aware of Earth's environmental problems and changing their attitudes towards environment in a fun and entertaining way.

3   eVision

eVision is a mobile game designed to improve environmental awareness and change people's attitudes or behaviours towards environment in a fun and entertaining way, through the use of mobile devices, augmented reality and persuasive technology. It was conceived to be an iPhone application which works like an environmental scanner, that allows users to use their mobile devices to detect and gather information regarding air quality and environmental threats around their current geographical position. Users are invited, by the eVision virtual character, Snowkin, to participate in a game activity that consists in detecting and cleaning environmental threats, such as cars, airplanes and factories, which will then be automatically overlaid with pro-environmental objects (e.g.: overlaying a car with a bicycle). For this cleaning operation, the users just need to use their finger to rub the mobile phone display over the detected threat (Fig. 1). When completing each activity, users are awarded with points and green leaves (eVision's virtual currency), as well as with environmental information regarding the corresponding threat. eVision's green leaves can then be spent to buy items, in the in-game store, that can be used to customize the Snowkin. Positive reinforcement techniques are also used to keep the user engaged. This aspect is very important and it is achieved with the assistance of Snowkin by establishing motivating and pro-environmental dialogues every time the users clean a threat.

The main objectives of the developed application were to: inform users about the environmental threats in their surroundings and their consequences for the environment; encourage them to change their behaviour towards the environment; offer digital rewards for completing pro-environment tasks; create a bond between the users and the virtual character to make them more receptive to his advices and suggestions and to enable data sharing through social networks.

Fig. 1. User Interaction: (1) Detection, (2) Cleaning, (3) Overlaying of the Environmental Threat

After the user and task analysis, eVision development followed an iterative design process that started with the design of a paper prototype, which was informally evaluated by several users in 3 iterations. According to the results achieved during this evaluation, the original design was improved and a second computational prototype was implemented as described below in this paper.

3.1 Paper Prototype

The eVision paper prototype was an interactive mock-up used by participants to perform several scenarios. The tests were conducted in three phases: the first was executed with a paper prototype freshly finished without user feedback (8 participants with ages between 23 and 46 years old), the second was made with an improved paper prototype based on the user feedback from the first phase (8 different participants with ages between 13 and 56 years old) and the last one was conducted only to make sure everything was fixed (2 participants with 17 and 51 years old). At the end of every test, users were informally inquired about their experience and requested to give feedback about future improvements.

The paper prototype greatly helped the computer implementation of eVision by allowing the detection of some interaction design problems. The most notable one (detected in the first phase) occurred in the scanner mode of the application and it concerned the act of cleaning the detected environmental threats. Some users expressed their concern regarding the viability of cleaning the threats on a live setting situation. Consider the following situation: *The user was walking home and aims the device high to capture a moving airplane. While he is walking and the airplane is moving he has to rub is finger on the iPhone screen while still aiming to the sky.* As can be seen, the task would be complex and frustrating from the user standpoint. Being the detection of environmental threats a core eVision feature, a solution had to be found. Our approach to handle this issue was to change the dynamic threat detection from the real time video to a snapshot. Instead of performing threats' detection and cleaning over the real time video captured by the mobile device camera, the users need to first take a snapshot of the scene which is then used by the system to identify the threats. This way the user could detect the environmental threats presented on his surroundings in a more relaxed way without having to do complex and simultaneous actions.

During the second phase, the most important detected issue was related to the interface used to customize the Snowkin. A slot machine interface element was included to allow users to select Snowkin customizing items (e.g. sweatshirts, hats).

The third phase demonstrated that the system development could proceed to the implementation of the computational prototype.

Regarding the informal questions asked in the end of each test, most feedback was positive and, generally, the participants felt that eVision was an interesting and innovative application.

3.2   Implementation

eVision was developed for iPhone 4 using iOS 5.1. All the implementation code was written using Apple's Xcode IDE in Objective-C. The eVision's interface elements were made on Xcode Interface Builder, with some exceptions generated through specific code. The image processing module was developed using the OpenCV library compiled for iOS 5.1, using C++ to write the module responsible to detect the dynamic environmental threats present on the snapshots. Facebook mobile API for iOS was used for Facebook integration, with minor refinements. Figure 2 illustrates the system's architecture.

eVision current implementation allows users to detect different pollution sources: cars, airplanes and factories. Knowing the static location of factories, GPS was used to identify factories in the users surroundings. Although it was not the main focus of this work, image detection methods had to be investigated in order to detect the dynamic position of cars and airplanes during eVision's game activity. In conjunction with the OpenCV library, one airplane detection method was designed and for car detection tests were conducted using two different methods.

The airplane detection method is based on contour detection and analysis. It worked quite well, since tests were conducted in a controlled environment (always on a clear sky). Limiting the sky appearance we could achieve successful airplane detection based on contours.

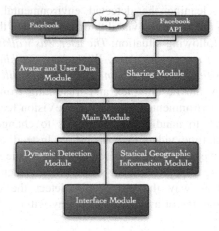

Fig. 2. Software architecture

Regarding vehicle detection, two different methods were tested, being the first one based on Cascade Classifiers and Haar-like features. This method was considered since it has been demonstrated to be successful detecting cars from various angles [2]. Unfortunately, when testing this method in eVision two problems arose: cars' side views would always produce unsatisfactory results and the method was extremely slow on iPhone 4 hardware.

A contour based method for cars' detection was then designed. Several problems were immediately identified: different cars had different contour shapes and the background did not have a uniform colour, introducing a lot of noise when processing the image. To overcome these problems, we decided to detect cars' registration plates instead. This would guarantee that the application would always search for something with a rectangular shape independently from the car type and background.

The mobile device accelerometer was used to detect if the users were aiming at an airplane on the sky or a car, in order to activate the appropriate image detection process. After some optimization procedures, the image detection accuracy was sufficient to ensure the validity of the conducted tests It is worth mentioning that image detection is not the main focus of this work and any improved methods can easily replace the currently used by eVision.

3.3   Interface and Features

Figure 3a illustrates the eVision's main menu interface, which is used to navigate through all the features of the application. The help menu (Fig. 3b) provides the user with an introduction and a tutorial. The Scanner mode is the eVision's main feature, leading the users to the core game activity, where they can inspect their surroundings and gather information regarding environmental threats. Different types of environmental information are presented, being the data regarding air quality in the user's location shown on the upper right corner of the screen. When the user touches the screen Snowkin appears to invite him to participate in the game cleaning activity. Snowkin always addresses the user by his name (Facebook login needed) and with a happy and cheerful tone to persuade the user to engage in the activity.

Fig. 3. eVision: (a) Main menu and (b) Help menu

When the user accepts the invitation to participate on the game activity, a countdown will appear and the activity starts. A score gauge appears on the upper right corner and a "capture image" button with the eVision's logo shows up on the bottom left corner, allowing users to take a snapshot (Fig. 4a). Snowkin assumes his motivational role and pushes the user to find environmental threats.

Fig. 4. (a) Activity start, (b) Threat Detected

While the user scans his surroundings with the mobile device, static environmental threats (currently factories) are represented on the screen, in real time, in the correct direction of their location. Information about factories is given on a smoke cloud to represent the pollution effect caused by them.

When a threat is detected on a snapshot taken by the user, Snowkin warns the user so he can clean it (Fig. 4b). After the detected threat is cleaned (the users just need to use their finger to rub the mobile phone display over the detected threat, as shown in Fig. 1), it disappears or it is automatically overlaid with a pro-environmental object (e.g.: overlaying a car with a bicycle) and Snowkin immediately congratulates the user and motivate him to keep going. The score gauge is also filled depending on the value of the threat cleaned (a greater area will be filled according to the score value of the eliminated threat).

It is important to notice that Snowkin's face expression changes according to the game contextual situation (Fig. 5). After cleaning threats, Snowkin's expression changes to a happy face.

Fig. 5. Snowkin's face expressions

After the score gauge is fully filled, the current game level ends and Snowkin praises the user. A score table is shown, discriminating the values that were factored to calculate the final score in green leaves. This moment, when the user is focused on the screen, is exploited to persuade the user by providing him with information regarding the effects of his actions on the environment.

The eShop interface allows the user to spend the green leaves earned playing eVision's game activity. A list of items to customize Snowkin is presented in an appealing way using a small icon to represent each item, showing the item's name and slot, as well as its price in green leaves (Fig. 6a). The user's green leaves balance is shown on the upper right corner of the screen and the items that were already purchased have a Snowkin icon.

Fig. 6. Customization: (a) eShop and (b) Snowkin Menu (c) Facebook

After buying items the user can visit the Snowkin interface and customize its appearance. The commitment and time the user puts on building Snowkin's appearance makes him more likely to follow the character's advices and recommendations regarding the environment, thus being persuaded by the application. In figure 6b every column represents an item slot (head, torso, legs, feet and hands). The slot machine style selection is very intuitive and avoids the danger of simultaneous choosing two different items of the same slot. The Statistics menu option allows the users to keep track of their game progression and to access data related to the application, such as time spent cleaning threats or the number of each kind of threat cleaned.

Finally, the Facebook interface (Fig. 6c) is responsible for handling the Facebook features available on eVision, allowing users to connect and share their activity. After verifying the user's credentials, the button to publish statistics and the "Like" button for Project DEAP's Facebook page become available. A user's profile picture also appears in the frame held by Snowkin.

4   Evaluation

User tests were performed in order to evaluate eVision's usability, persuasive potential and impact on users environmental awareness and attitudes.

4.1   Usability Test

Throughout eVision's development some small-scale usability tests were conducted to assert specific interface components and functionality. Although useful, these tests were not enough to proper evaluate how people would use and be affected by the application. To overcome these shortcomings and evaluate how people were affected by eVision, usability tests based on a live setting were carried out with a diverse group of twenty participants (50% male) aged 18-56 years old (mean = 30.9). 10% of the participants had MSc degrees, 40% had BSc degrees and 50% had high school education. 30% of the participants were students, 20% were unemployed and 50% were full time workers. All participants were familiar with new technologies. Most of them use mobile phone, computer and Internet on a daily basis.

The tests took place, in the outdoors, in a location where some road and air traffic were expected, in the afternoon during a clear sky day. These circumstances allowed us to control the experience, providing the users with appropriate conditions to use eVision during the period of the test, and to focus on the main objectives of the user tests (we were not testing the performance of the image detection algorithms).

Before starting to use eVision, each participant was briefed on the context and functionalities of the mobile application. The participants had twenty minutes to use the application at their convenience. In the end of each test, a questionnaire was given to each participant to evaluate the eVision's usability and potential persuasive effect.

Questionnaire

Five sections composed the questionnaire. First section comprised questions on participants' personal data, such as age, gender, background and familiarity with new technologies. In section two, participants evaluated eVision's general aspects, as well as its usability and ease of use based on the rate of agreement with three statements using a five-point Likert scale ranging from 1 (totally agree) to 5 (totally disagree). Users also rated how easy it was to execute the ten main eVision functionalities using a five-point Likert scale ranging from (1) very easy and (5) very difficult.

The third section of the questionnaire was based on the Microsoft "Product Reaction Cards" [5]. The purpose of using this method was to collect feedback on desirability and to measure the users' emotional involvement during the test. Thus, the users were asked to choose the words that best describe their experience while using eVision, from a selected set of words. They could select as many words as they wished from a list of 19 words, consisting of about 60% of words considered positive and 40% considered negative.

The fourth section refers to Snowkin and comprises eight questions. In six of them, users had to indicate their agreement with a statement using a five-point Likert scale ranging from 1 (totally agree) to 5 (totally disagree). The interaction with the Snowkin was evaluated with a five-point Likert scale ranging from 1 (extremely nice) to 5 (extremely unpleasant). At the end of this section, the participants indicated their perception of Snowkin role (e.g. a friend, a team mate, a teacher or other).

In the last section of the questionnaire users were invited to contribute with suggestions, comments or recommendations to improve the application.

Results

Participants agreed that eVision responded quickly to the various actions and that it required just a few steps to perform each task. They also found very easy to detect a vehicle, while the detection of a polluting infrastructure or a plane was more difficult, because the former ones were more frequent to find in the area where the application was tested. Anyway, the participants considered easy to obtain information relating to the environment, as well as to clean any detected threats. Buying items and customizing Snowkin, as well as consulting statistics regarding users' performance were also perceived as being easy to execute.

Most of the participants (45%) did not sign in to Facebook, mainly because they didn't feel comfortable entering their credentials on a mobile device which was not their own. This made the experience less customized for these users and this also might have decreased the persuasive capacity of eVision due to a minor tailoring effect (e.g. Snowkin could not address the user by his name). Those who signed in found it easy to publish statistics on their "wall".

Users enjoyed the experience when using the eVision (mean = 2.25, in a scale 1-5 where 1 represent excellent). The fact that 55% of participants considered that the use of the application contributed to increase their awareness regarding environmental issues demonstrates the eVision's persuasive potential.

From the analysis of the question based on the Microsoft "Product Reaction Cards" we concluded that all users held positive feelings when classifying their experience using eVision. The most selected word was "interesting" (80%), followed by the words "curiosity" (70%), "fun" (55%), "friendliness" (35%), "empathy" (25%) and "joy" (15%). Emotions such as friendliness and empathy show a relational dimension that demonstrates the social role assigned to Snowkin, consequently ensuring him a greater persuasive power. Fun and joy are also relevant characteristics for a game application. Negative emotions such as boredom, frustration and disappointment were also experienced but only by a very small number of participants (5%).

We also wanted to study the Snowkin design and role to understand how his appearance, face expressions, and dialogs could influence users feelings and perception. In general, the feedback from users was positive and congruent with the image that we wanted to create for the virtual character. Users agreed that Snowkin cares about the environment (mean = 1.1 (male), 1.3 (female)), it is a friendly character (mean = 1.2 (male), 1.2 (female)) and they felt good when the Snowkin praised their progression (mean = 1.3 (male), 1.2 (female)). Users also agreed that Snowkin is expressive (mean = 1.8 (male), 1.7 (female)), the information given by Snowkin was credible (mean = 1.8 (male), 1.7 (female)) and that they will take into account the information provided by Snowkin (mean = 2.0 (male), 1.9 (female)). The participants' opinion about the Snowkin was not significantly different between men and women ($\rho > 0,05$ for all the statements, using Mann-Whitney U test).

These results showed the considerable potential of persuasion present in eVision through Snowkin, which can put into practice several persuasion principles, such as tailoring and conditioning. As a social actor, Snowkin is also very effective: it has not only the right physical cues (e.g. expressiveness), but also the right psychological (e.g. cares about the environment) and social traits (e.g. friendly). The Snowkin was considered a teacher or advisor for the majority of women (60%). Women considered it also a friend (20%), a teammate (10%) and "a friendly character" (10%). On the other hand, men considered it a teammate (50%) and a teacher or advisor (40%) – 10% of men have not answered this question. Anyway, it is important to note that in all cases, it was clear that the users always established a positive relationship with the virtual character.

Most participants felt motivated to go on and wanted more time to continue experiencing the eVision. The Snowkin character had a particular strong impact, driving the participants to keep scoring, so they could buy more items to customize the virtual character. Some participants became sad when the test was over and they had to say goodbye to Snowkin.

Finally, the participants made suggestions and recommendations to improve the application, such as; the boxes used to highlight the detected threats should be more appealing; and the icons that appear after the cleaning of the detected environmental threats should be more diverse. Other users expressed their satisfaction with eVision: "I really enjoyed playing this game, because it gave me more information about the environment", "the idea is quite original and well developed", "I really enjoyed the experience".

4.2   Impact Test

To better evaluate the persuasive effect of eVision and to check if it still holds sometime after the eVision experience, an impact test was performed. Roughly one month after the usability tests were conducted, participants were asked to answer a new questionnaire, expressing their opinions regarding four statements. They had to indicate their degrees of agreement using a five-point Likert scale ranging from 1 (totally agree) to 5 (totally disagree).

Participants agreed that eVision played an important role in alerting them to Earth's sustainability problems (mean = 2.25) and they also reported that their experience with eVision influenced their daily life decisions, such as what type of car they should buy (mean = 2.3). They felt that Snowkin's dialogues and information were still relevant to them a month after the experience (mean = 2.35). Curiously, they also reveal that they missed Snowkin after interacting with it (mean = 2.05), showing the importance of the virtual character for the goal of this mobile application.

Although the results were fairly positive it is necessary to perform further tests with a larger number of users and allowing them to use the application for a longer period of time to better evaluate the persuasive power of the application.

5   Conclusions and Future Work

This paper presented eVision, a persuasive mobile game designed to change people's attitudes or behaviours towards environment in a fun and entertaining way, through the use of mobile devices, augmented reality and persuasive technology. It was conceived to work like an environmental scanner that allows users to inspect their surroundings, detecting and gathering information regarding environmental threats with their mobile devices. eVision also introduced a virtual character named Snowkin, which interacts with users encouraging them to play, helping to persuade them to adopt pro-environmental behaviours and making them aware of environmental threats in their surroundings. The paper also presents the user studies performed to evaluate the application's usability and impact on users environmental awareness and attitudes.

eVision is making a contribution to increase people environmental awareness through an engaging experience. The results from the user tests were very positive, regarding both the gameplay and eVision's persuasive ability. Although it is difficult to evaluate behaviours since these are complex and non-linear, we believe, from the feedback we got, that eVision can help to shape people's attitudes and behaviours towards a better environmental conscience.

Despite the positive and encouraging results there is room for improvements. Future work includes the detection of additional environmental threats, as well as the optimization of existing image detection methods and algorithms. To better evaluate the persuasive effect of the application, further user tests that include the use of the application by the participants during a longer period of time (e.g. a few days or weeks) will be performed.

Acknowledgments. This work is funded by Fundação para a Ciência e Tecnologia (FCT/MEC), Portugal, in the scope of project DEAP (PTDC/AAC-AMB/104834/2008) and by CITI/DI/FCT/UNL (PEst-OE/EEI/UI0527/2011). The authors thank Bárbara Teixeira for her contribution on the graphic design.

References

1. Cialdini, R.: Influence: Science and Practice. Allyn & Bacon, Boston (2001)
2. Horta, R., Jonna, K., Krishna, P.: On-road vehicle detection by cascade classifiers. In: Proc. of the Third Annual ACM Bangalore, Compute 2010, Bangalore, India, January 22-23. ACM Press (2010)
3. Fogg, B.J.: Persuasive Technology: Using Computers to Change What We Think and Do. Morgan Kaufmann, San Francisco (2003)
4. Fogg, B.J.: Captology. The Study of Computers as Persuasive Technologies. In: Abstracts CHI 1998, Los Angeles, USA, April 18-23, p. 129. ACM Press, NY (1998)
5. Benedek, J., Miner, T.: Measuring Desirability: New Methods for Evaluating Desirability in a Usability Lab Setting. In: Proc. of Usability Professionals' Association 2002 Conference, UPA 2002, Orlando, USA, July 8-12 (2002), http://www.microsoft.com/usability/UEPostings/DesirabilityToolkit.doc (accessed on June 8, 2013)
6. Eckles, D., Fogg, B.J.: The Future of Persuasion is Mobile. In: Mobile Persuasion: 20 Perspectives on the Future of Behavior Change, pp. 5–11. Stanford Captology Media, Stanford (2007)
7. Fogg, B.J.: Mass Interpersonal Persuasion: An Early View of a New Phenomenon. In: Oinas-Kukkonen, H., Hasle, P., Harjumaa, M., Segerståhl, K., Øhrstrøm, P. (eds.) PERSUASIVE 2008. LNCS, vol. 5033, pp. 23–34. Springer, Heidelberg (2008)
8. Bogost, I.: Persuasive Games: The Expressive Power of Videogames. MIT Press, Cambridge (2007)
9. White, S.: Augmented Reality: Using Mobile Visualization to Persuade. In: Mobile Persuasion: 20 Perspectives on the Future of Behavior Change, pp. 55–62. Stanford Captology Media, Stanford (2007)

Why Does It Always Rain on Me? Influence of Gender and Environmental Factors on Usability, Technology Related Anxiety and Immersion in Virtual Environments

Mareike Schmidt[1,*], Johanna Xenia Kafka[1,2,*], Oswald D. Kothgassner[1,3], Helmut Hlavacs[3], Leon Beutl[3], and Anna Felnhofer[1,3]

[1] University of Vienna, Faculty of Psychology, Department of Applied Psychology: Health, Development, Enhancement and Intervention
[2] University of Vienna, Faculty of Social Sciences, Department of Sociology
[3] University of Vienna, Faculty of Computer Science, Research Group Entertainment Computing

Abstract. Collaborative virtual environments and technical possibilities in general are still a growing and more and more important influence on everyday life. According to corresponding studies it seems that context conditions as well as individual factors such as gender play an important role in the experience of virtual environments (i.e. immersion and technology-related anxiety) and in the rating of the used technology (i.e. its perceived usefulness). Thus, the objective of the current study was to evaluate the above mentioned factors in a group of 14 women and 14 men using two different emotionally charged collaborative virtual environments. The corresponding results indicate that there are in fact gender differences: Women reported higher levels of technology-related anxiety and immersion. In general, participants in the rainy condition rated the usefulness of the virtual environment higher. Also, women in the rainy condition rated the perceived usefulness higher than women in the cheerful condition whereas in the group of men it was vice versa.

1 Introduction

We live in a world surrounded by technological equipment. The technical possibilities have developed massively during the last decades and changed our everyday lives and communication patterns. In the field of so-called collaborative virtual environments there are many possibilities of application ranging from gaming, or educational purposes to health care. There are several promising attempts to integrate virtual environments effectively into therapy [13]. Virtual environments are increasingly used as emotion-inducing stimuli for exposure therapy. Yet, women and men seem to differ regarding their perception of virtual environments [6], and their behavior in virtual environments [28]. Thus far however, there is lack of research combining both, environmental factors of

---

* Mareike Schmidt and Johanna Xenia Kafka contributed equally to this paper.

D. Reidsma, H. Katayose, and A. Nijholt (Eds.): ACE 2013, LNCS 8253, pp. 392–402, 2013.
© Springer International Publishing Switzerland 2013

emotion-inducing stimuli and the effect of gender on key aspects of technology usage.

2 Related Work

The technology acceptance model [3] which is based on the Theory of Reasoned Action by Fishbein and Ajzen [8] is one of the most commonly used models to evaluate computer technology systems like communication and entertainment applications for educational and/or therapy purposes (cf. [5,13,17,24,27]). It has been shown that perceived usefulness and ease of use strongly influence the behavioral intention to actually use virtual environments. Interestingly, Fetscherin and Lattermann [7] found that technology-related anxiety has no significant impact on the behavioral intention to use the technology; instead, a strong relationship between the possibility to interact or collaborate with others and a person's intention to use the technology was reported.

Immersion: Considering this, other factors possibly influencing the acceptance of virtual environments are the constructs of immersion and the sense of presence. While the sense of presence refers to the experience of actually being there in a virtual environment which is based on a perceptional illusion of non-mediation [15], immersion can be regarded a characteristic of a technology [22]. As this, immersion describes the extent to which a computer interface is capable of transporting a vivid, surrounding and inclusive experience to the user, who feels enveloped by the presented environment. This approach has been criticized as it implies that every user should experience the same level of immersion when using the same technology. Studies however have shown that users seem to differ in their extent of experienced immersion even when using the very same interface (c.f. [12,29]). Here, immersion seems to depend on one's ability to fully focus on and engage in the virtual environment, thus "forgetting" the outside world.

Environmental factors: When watching a movie, the scenery can become so vivid and compelling that we start feeling for the characters and we place ourselves into those artificial settings. It can be assumed that a true life depiction of environmental factors plays an important role on whether we perceive something as realistic or lifelike. There is some evidence that environmental factors, such as lighting or weather conditions, in virtual reality would be effective as mood induction procedures with anxiety-inducing and relaxing stimuli. It seems that a medium must be able to induce a feeling of presence in order to provoke affective responses [19]. Yet, some other studies showed that the lighting level of the virtual environment alone has no effect on the affective state of the users [25].

Gender: Gender differences are a widely researched field. Unsurprisingly, the inclusion of the gender perspective when studying usability factors or the experience of immersion is gaining more importance in research and the game industry [28]. It is estimated that 48% of video game purchasers are women [4]. Thus, computer games can no longer be seen as an exclusively masculine domain, yet some studies still show an advantage of male over female gamers regarding reported game experience [9]. However, individual differences such as gender and personality seem to have a valuable impact on how information technology systems are perceived and used [26]. According to the growing body of research males rate computer technology as more useful and easier to use, because of their higher self-efficacy regarding computer usage [2,17,21]. Surprisingly, there is only little knowledge about how gender influences the usage of technologies like virtual environments. Some results indicate that on the one hand males seem to be more task-oriented than females when using virtual environments, while on the other hand females focus more on collaborative aspects during their game play [5,23,28]. Yet, there is still little research considering a gender perspective when studying the experience of immersion in virtual reality. Some studies indicate that men both, perceive virtual environments as more realistic and show higher degrees of spatial presence than their female counterparts [6,16].

3 Aim of the Study

Following the presented literature above the study focuses on the two following research questions:

- *Research question 1:* Are there differences between women and men regarding technology usage factors (ease of use and perceived usefulness), immersion or technology-related anxiety?
- *Research question 2:* Are there differences between two different emotionally charged context conditions (i.e., a sunny outdoor scene vs. a rainy outdoor scene, see Section 4.4) regarding technology usage factors (ease of use and perceived usefulness), immersion or technology-related anxiety?

4 Experiments

4.1 Methods

The study took place at the Department of Psychology at the University of Vienna. All participants signed an informed consent form within which they were informed about the course of the experimental procedure and their right to discontinue their cooperation at any time. Statistical analyses were performed using SPSS Version 19 (SPSS, Inc. Chicago, USA). An alpha error of 5% was chosen.

4.2 Participants

28 undergraduates (14 women, 14 men) were recruited from several psychology courses at the University of Vienna and received course credit for their participation. The mean age was 24.93 (SD = 5.120) years with a range between 19 and 43 years. Participants were randomly assigned to one of the two experimental conditions (see Section 4.4), with n = 14 in the sunny condition and n = 14 in the rainy condition. Mean age in the sunny condition was 26.14 (SD = 5.696;

range $20 - 43$) years, in the rainy condition the mean age was 23.71 (SD $= 4.340$; range $19 - 34$) years. All participants had normal or corrected to normal vision and were fluent German speakers. Table 1 and Figure 1 show the participants computer and computer gaming experience for women and men separately.

Table 1. Means (M) and standard deviations (SD) for computer gaming hours per week for males and females seperately

Male			Female		
M	Range	SD	M	Range	SD
2.46	$0 - 12$	3.39	2.22	$0 - 20$	5.92

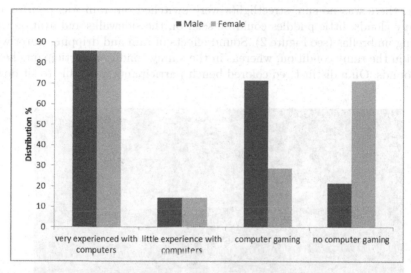

Fig. 1. Distribution of experience with computers and computer gaming by gender in percent.

4.3 Procedure

The study was described to the participants as an experiment about the usage of virtual realities and was conducted on weekdays between 9 a.m. and 2 p.m. Upon their arrival, the participants signed the informed consent form and then filled out a short demographic survey. Subsequently, they were guided to the laboratory and after resting five minutes an experimenter explained to them how to navigate through the virtual environment using a smart phone device (HTC Desire SV, Taoyuan) and later set up the head-mounted-display (HMD, Sony HMZ-T1 3D Visor, Tokyo, Japan). Head movement in the virtual simulation was tracked with an externally applied head tracking system (TrackIR 5, NaturalPoint, Corvallis, USA). The dwell time in the simulation was five minutes during which the participants were free to explore the park without instructions or tasks. Participants were only asked to memorize self-selected objects in the virtual environment. After the experimental phase the psychological questionnaires were administered (see Section 4.5).

4.4 The VR-Park

During the experiment participants were free to explore a virtual scenario, which was modeled on a common urban park. There were two conditions, a sunny and a rainy park. Both of them included benches, trees, a little pond, bins, grass etc., but differed regarding the degree of lighting. The sunny park was filled with sunlight, and a bright blue sky could be seen and there were birds on the sidewalks, butterflies flying around and ducks on the pond (see Figure 3). In the rainy condition there were no birds, butterflies or ducks, instead the park was darker, there was no sun, streetlights were switched on, rain was pouring out of heavy clouds, little puddles could be seen on the sidewalks and avatars were carrying umbrellas (see Figure 2). Sound effects of rain and dripping water were played in the rainy condition, whereas in the sunny condition participants heard bird sounds. On a distinct red colored bench participants were able to sit down.

Fig. 2. Park in the rainy condition with NPC holding an umbrella

The non-playing characters (NPCs) strolling through the park were modeled on the photographs of the research staff involved in this study. GIMP and Blender 3D were used as modeling tools, as well as the render engine OGRE3D for real time rendering. To control the avatar, participants used an Android smart phone as input device. Subjects could steer their avatar, seen from the first person perspective, by tilting the phone.

Fig. 3. Pond with ducks and resting NPC in the sunny condition

4.5 Measures

To measure the participant's evaluation of the virtual environment the self-report questionnaire *Technology Usage Inventory* (*TUI*, [14]) was used. The TUI comprises the following four factors: (1) *Ease of Use* (three items referring to the perceived user-friendliness, e.g. "The application of this technology is easy to understand"), (2) *Immersion* (four items assessing the absorption in a virtual environment, e.g. "I could forgot my real problems in the virtual situation"), (3) *Perceived Usefulness* (four items related to the perceived benefit of the technology, e.g. "This technology would help me cope better with my daily duties") and (4) *Technology-related Anxiety* (four items regarding mistrust towards the use of a specific technology, e.g. "I think that the use of this technology is always associated with a certain risk"). After the experimental phase in the virtual environment participants were asked to respond to the 15 items, which were scored on a seven-point Likert scale (does apply – does not apply). The reliability (Cronbach's alpha) for the scales ranged between $\alpha = .70$ (*Technology-related Anxiety*) and $\alpha = .84$ (*Immersion*).

5 Results

5.1 Manipulation Check

To validate the emotion-inducing content of the virtual environments, a short manipulation check including a single item on a 4-point Likert scale ("I feel happy in this environment" – "I feel sad in this environment") was implemented.

The results of the manipulation check indicate that the participants reported a significantly higher level of happiness in the sunny environment than in the rainy environment ($T = 2.212$; $p = 0.036$).

5.2 Effects of Gender and Environmental Factors

In Table 2 means and standard deviations for the four factors *Ease of Use, Immersion, Perceived Usefulness* and *Technology-related Anxiety* divided by group and gender can be found.

Table 2. Means (M) and standard deviations (SD) for the scales of the TUI for the sunny and rainy condition and for gender

	Gender				Condition			
	Male		Female		Sunny		Rainy	
	M	SD	M	SD	M	SD	M	SD
Perceived usefulness	10.79	5.63	11.36	6.29	9.00	5.05	13.14	5.65
Ease of Use	15.93	3.71	17.00	3.08	16.64	4.08	16.29	2.67
Immersion	12.43	4.03	18.64	5.12	13.86	4.94	17.21	5.72
Technology-related Anxiety	12.57	3.43	15.86	4.33	13.79	4.40	14.64	4.06

To assess the influences of gender and group on technology usage factors, immersion and technology-related anxiety a two-way ANOVA was performed. The four TUI scales *Perceived Usefulness, Ease of Use, Immersion* and *Technology-related Anxiety* constituted the dependent variables. The condition participants were assigned to and their gender appeared as the between-group factors. A main effect of the factor gender was found for *Immersion* ($F(1, 24) = 13.87$; $p = 0.001$) and for *Technology-related Anxiety* ($F(1, 24) = 4.737$; $p = 0.040$). The only main effect regarding the rainy condition was found for *Perceived Usefulness* ($F(1, 24) = 6.029$; $p = 0.022$). Additionally there was an interaction effect of group and gender for *Perceived Usefulness* ($F(1, 24) = 16.516$; $p < 0.001$). There were no significant effects or interactions found for the other scales. Overall, women scored higher in both, *Immersion* and *Technology-related Anxiety*. Moreover participants in the rainy condition rated the *Perceived Usefulness* of the technology higher than those in the sunny condition. And finally, there was an interaction effect on the judgement of the usefulness of the technology. Men perceived the technology as being more useful when they were assigned to the sunny condition, whereas women rated the technology as more useful when they were part of the rainy condition.

6 Discussion

Given the fact, that virtual environments are increasingly adopted in all areas of life for all kinds of purposes – ranging from entertainment applications to therapeutic programs – studying the effect of these virtual environments seems crucial. Specific aspects of a virtual experience in particular, such as immersion, technology-related anxiety and the perceived usefulness of a technology, promise to be valuable tools in explaining individual differences concerning the handling and perception of these virtual environments. Additionally, environments differing in their level of lighting and/or affective content, have been shown to affect users differently. Thus, the main objective of the present study was to evaluate specific technology usage factors with regard to possible gender differences and diverging influences of two contrasting virtual environments (rainy vs. sunny).

The results imply that men and women experienced the virtual park differently: while women reported higher levels of immersion and technology-related anxiety in both (sunny and rainy) virtual environments, men overall tended to rate the technology as more useful. These findings correspond with previous results, which found women to be more anxious when using technology [21] and men to generally rate technology as more convenient and easier to use than women [17]. This phenomenon is mostly explained with a generally lower computer self-efficacy in women as opposed to their male peers [21]. In the current sample, men and women both reported to be very experienced with computers, yet women stated to play significantly less computer games than men. This is in line with the current literature on computer gaming, which reports an advantage of male over female gamers [9]. For the present study it can be interpreted as a lack of familiarity with gaming environments in female participants. This lack of acquaintance in turn can be seen as a possible cause for more timid reactions in women when handling the equipment (such as the HMD and the HTC-phone) and steering their avatar through the environment.

Interestingly though, in the present study women were also found to be more immersed in the virtual park than men. There is no consensus in the current literature [15] regarding the question, whether an unfamiliarity with a virtual environment discourages the engagement with it and thus, hinders the experience of immersion or whether the opposite is true and more experienced users underlie the well-known habituation effect. Nonetheless, it has been suggested that so called experts, i.e. more experienced users of virtual environments (e.g. frequent game players), tend to look for and notice more flaws in the programming of the virtual environment and therefore compromise their optimal experience of immersion and presence. In the present study, female participants might have been more impressed with the novelty and unfamiliarity of the virtual environment, and thus experienced greater immersion, whereas male participants might have constantly been evaluating and comparing the virtual park to their knowledge of common computer games and thus, inhibited their ability to fully engage in the environment.

It is remarkable however, that there were also clear differences between both, the two conditions (sunny vs. rainy) and men and women regarding their ratings of the technology's usefulness. The rainy park was altogether evaluated as more useful than the sunny park. Additionally, female participants rated the technology as being significantly more useful and beneficial when they were assigned to the rainy condition, whereas male participants found it to be more convenient and suitable when they experienced the sunny condition. The fact, that previous studies did not find a significant effect of lighting conditions on the experience of the virtual environment [25], yet instead indicated the efficacy of virtual environments as affective tools for shaping the virtual experience [19], underlines the importance of emotional processes in this context. In the present study, the sunny park indeed seemed to evoke more positive emotional responses, whereas the rainy park seemed to be associated with rather negative emotional states (see Section 5.1). It has widely been argued, that content factors, such as story line and emotionally engaging stimuli, are very likely to have an impact on the extent of immersion and presence the user experiences [11]. In other words, the emotional response (e.g. anxiety) is believed to be interpreted by the user as a sign of presence and/or immersion. High levels of immersion and presence in turn are thought to be associated with better ratings of a technology's usefulness and usability (see [1] for studies regarding the link between cognitive absorption and technology acceptance). Hence, the possibly more intensely felt negative emotions in the rainy park could have led women to more strongly perceive the technology as more useful in the rainy as opposed to the sunny condition. Again, the rainy environment could have been experienced as more novel, unique and impressive than the plain, ordinary sunny environment and may have therefore led to a stronger identification with it in women. In men, this relationship was reversed, providing ground for the assumption that men were less influenced by the affective nature of the presented environment.

One of the main limitations of this study pertains to the relatively small sample size. Bearing this in mind, generalizations should be undertaken with caution and the reported results should be considered as a ground for the conceptualization of future studies. Especially the highly interesting relationship between emotional content, immersion and the individual evaluation of a technology are worth further investigation since they pave the path for future developments, which are even more suited to individual needs and preferences and thus, make the experience of a virtual environment even more compelling and satisfying.

References

1. Agarwal, R., Karahanna, E.: Time Flies When You're Having Fun: Cognitive Absorption and Beliefs about Information Technology Usage. MIS Quarterly 24(4), 665–694 (2000)
2. Braak, J.: Domains and determinants of university students' self-perceived computer competence. Computers & Education 43(3), 299–312 (2004)
3. Davis, F., Bagozzi, P., Warshaw, P.: User acceptance of computer technology - a comparison of two theoretical models. Management Science 35(8), 982–1003 (1989)
4. ESA. Essential Facts about the Computer and Video Game Industry 2012: Sales, Demographic and Usage Data (2012), http://www.theesa.com/facts/pdfs/esa$_$ef$_$2012.pdf (May 29, 2013)
5. Fallows, D.: How women and men use the Internet (2005), http://www.pewinternet.org/Reports/2005/How-Women-and-Men-Use-the-Internet.aspx (May 29, 2013)

6. Felnhofer, A., Kothgassner, O.D., Beutl, L., Hlavacs, H., Kryspin-Exner, I.: Is virtual reality made for men only? Exploring gender differences in the sense of presence. In: Annual Proceedings of the International Society on Presence Research. Philadelphia, USA (2012)

7. Fetscherin, M., Lattemann, C.: User acceptance of virtual worlds. Journal of Electronic Commerce Research 9(3), 231–242 (2008)

8. Fishbein, M.A., Ajzen, I.: Belief, Attitude, Intention, and Behavior: An Introduction to Theory and Research. Addison-Wesley (1975)

9. Hartmann, T., Klimmt, C.: Gender and computer games: Exploring females' dislikes. Journal of Computer-Mediated Communication 11(4), article 2 (2006)

10. Hsu, C.L., Lu, H.P.: Why do people play on-line games? An extended TAM with social influences and flow experience. Information & Management 41(7), 853–868 (2004)

11. IJsselsteijn, W.A.: Presence in Depth. Eindhoven: Technische Universiteit Eindhoven (2004)

12. Jennett, C., Cox, A.L., Cairns, P., Dhoparee, S., Epps, A., Tijs, T., Walton, A.: Measuring and defining the experience of immersion in games. International Journal of Human-Computer Studies 66, 641–661 (2008)

13. Kothgassner, O.D., Felnhofer, A., Beutl, L., Hlavacs, H., Lehenbauer, M., Stetina, B.: A virtual training tool for giving talks. In: Herrlich, M., Malaka, R., Masuch, M. (eds.) ICEC 2012. LNCS, vol. 7522, pp. 53–66. Springer, Heidelberg (2012)

14. Kothgassner, O.D., Felnhofer, A., Hauk, N., Kastenhofer, E., Gomm, J., Kryspin-Exner, I.: TUI. Technology Usage Inventory. FFG, Wien (2013), http://www.ffg.at/sites/default/files/allgemeine_downloads/thematische%20programme/programmdokumente/tui_manual.pdf

15. Lombard, M., Ditton, T.: At the heart of it all: the concept of presence. Journal of Computer-Mediated Communication 3(2) (1997)

16. Nicovich, S.G., Boller, G.W., Cornwell, T.B.: Experienced Presence within Computer-Mediated Communications: Initial Explorations on the Effects of Gender with Respect to Empathy and Immersion. Journal of Computer-Mediated Communication 10(2) (2005)

17. Ong, C.S., Lai, J.Y.: Gender differences in perceptions and relationships among dominants of e-learning acceptance. Computers in Human Behavior 22(5), 816–829 (2006)

18. Papastergiou, M., Solomonidou, C.: Gender issues in internet access and favourite internet activities among Greek high school pupils inside and outside school. Computers & Education 44(4), 377–393 (2005)

19. Riva, G., Mantovani, F., Capideville, C.S., Preziosa, A., Morganti, F., Villani, D., Alcaiz, M.: Affective interactions using virtual reality: The link between presence and emotions. CyberPsychology & Behavior 10(1), 45–56 (2007)

20. Sanchez-Franco, M.J.: Exploring the influence of gender on the web usage via partial least squares. Behaviour & Information Technology 25(1), 19–36 (2006)

21. Schumacher, P., Morahan-Martin, J.: Gender, internet and computer attitudes and experiences. Computers in Human Behavior 17(1), 95–110 (2001)

22. Slater, M., Usoh, M.: Body centred interaction in immersive virtual environments. Artificial life and Virtual Reality 1, 125–148 (1994)

23. Szell, M., Thurner, S.: How women organize social networks different from men. Scientific Reports 3 (2013)

24. Terzis, V., Economides, A.A.: Computer based assessment: Gender differences in perceptions and acceptance. Computers in Human Behavior 27(6), 2108–2122 (2011)

25. Toet, A., van Welie, M., Houtkamp, J.: Is a dark virtual environment scary? CyberPsychology & Behavior 12(4), 363–371 (2009)
26. Venkatesh, V., Morris, M.G., Davis, G.B., Davis, F.D.: User acceptance of information technology: Toward a unified view. MIS Quarterly Archive 27(3), 425–478 (2003)
27. Whitley, B.E.: Gender differences in computer-related attitudes and behavior: A meta-analysis. Computers in Human Behavior 13(1), 1–22 (1997)
28. Williams, D., Consalvo, M., Caplan, S., Yee, N.: Looking for gender: Gender roles and behaviors among online gamers. Journal of Communication 59(4), 700–725 (2009)
29. Witmer, B.G., Singer, M.J.: Measuring presence in virtual environments: A presence questionnaire. Presence: Teleoperators and Virtual Environments 7, 225–240 (1998)

Meaning in Life as a Source of Entertainment

Robby van Delden and Dennis Reidsma

Human Media Interaction, University of Twente,
P.O. Box 217, Enschede, The Netherlands
{r.w.vandelden,d.reidsma}@utwente.nl

Abstract. In this paper we mean to introduce into the field of entertainment computing an overview of insights concerning fundamental human needs. Researchers such as Hassenzahl and Desmet, discuss design approaches based on psychological insights from various and varied sources. We collect these and expand them with a focus on meaning in life as seen in humanistic philosophy. We summarise the various roles that these insights can play in our research on new technology, and illustrate the discussion with examples from the field of computer entertainment.

1 Introduction

Successful entertainment technology is all about achieving the right user experience. When we think about new computer entertainment, we explore new experiences that we can offer to the user through the invention of new technology and interfaces, or through the development of interesting new application concepts. However, we should also not forget to think about when and how these experiences are worthwhile. Not just because the interaction targets useful secondary goals (e.g. edutainment applications) but also because the interactive experiences themselves fulfil certain needs.

Designing for user experience is a challenging endeavour. As Hassenzahl says, experiences are elusive and ephemeral, and resist engineering. His solution is to similarly look below the surface of the experiences: underlying fundamental human needs engender and determine to a large extent the experience resulting from interaction with technology. He suggests that by properly understanding these fundamental needs, and understanding how they relate to user experiences, we can more easily systematically design for experience by designing for fundamental needs [1].

In the current paper we mean to introduce into the field of entertainment computing an overview of insights concerning fundamental human needs. Researchers such as Hassenzahl, Desmet, and others, discuss design approaches based on psychological insights from various and varied sources [1,2]. We collect these and expand them with a focus on meaning in life as seen in humanistic philosophy, following the suggestion by Cockton [3]. We summarise the various roles that these insights can play in our research on new technology, and illustrate the discussion with examples from the field of computer entertainment.

D. Reidsma, H. Katayose, and A. Nijholt (Eds.): ACE 2013, LNCS 8253, pp. 403–414, 2013.

2   Fundamental Human Needs and HCI

As early as 1997 there was a workshop to advance the HCI research agenda with a perspective on human needs and social responsibility (largely focused on accessibility and usability issues) [4]. At a later time, Cockton stressed the urgency to look at psychological well-being, motivation and needs in order to design beyond the task-efficiency oriented origins of HCI and the superficiality of much non task focused entertainment at the time. He proposed an approach aimed at designing for worth and value [3]. Hassenzahl et al. turned to fundamental human needs as a basis for their "design for user experience" approach because these needs allowed them to describe and understand individual user experiences in all their variety [1]. In computer entertainment, Wyeth et al. built upon a set of fundamental needs to develop guidelines for whole body gaming experiences for people with intellectual disabilities [5].

If we have a closer look at these approaches we see similar, but not quite the same, bases of needs, as can be seen in Fig. 1. In the remainder of this section we explain these approaches and the human needs they identify in some more detail, but first we briefly describe what human needs are: Human needs are motivations for our actions, signify what makes life worthwhile and what gives meaning to our lives. Baumeister and Leary specified that needs produce effects and affect, apply to all people, direct cognitive processing and behaviour, have implications that go beyond psychological functioning, and lead to ill effects if not satisfied [6].

2.1   Hassenzahl and the Needs of Sheldon et al.

Hassenzahl et al. aim to design for *user experience* for products and technology. They approach this from the premise that experiences are very personal and ephemeral and thus, to address those, one might benefit from starting with an underlying set of more universal fundamental human needs [1]. They base the underlying needs of their "design for experience" approach largely on the work of Sheldon et al. [7].

Sheldon et al. describe a set of fundamental human needs based on four pillars [7]. The first pillar is Deci and Ryan's self-determination theory which stresses *autonomy, competence* and *relatedness*. The second is Maslow's view, adding *physical thriving, security, self-esteem,* and *self-actualisation,* (with Maslow's *love-belongingness* taken as similar to Deci and Ryan's *relatedness*). The third pillar is Epstein's cognitive-experiential self-theory (CEST), which adds pleasure (described as *pleasurable stimulation*).[1] The fourth pillar contains needs fitting the "American Dream" assumption: *money-luxury,* and *popularity-influence.* This results in a set of ten fundamental human needs.

From these needs the first three (autonomy, competence and relatedness), originating from the self-determination theory, were hypothesised by Sheldon

---

[1] On a side note, the theoretical framework of CEST contains the assumption that if a need is fulfilled at the cost of another need it will result in intensification of fulfilling the other needs. In extreme cases this may result in maladaptive consequences [8].

et al. to be the most essential ones. Based on questionnaires with self-reported rates of the selected needs, indeed these three but also self-esteem seemed to be important. Security emerged as an important need based on experience of unsatisfying events, the other identified needs were found to be less important, with money-luxury having the lowest need status [7].

It is worthwhile to notice that out of the four basic needs from Epstein's theory pillar they choose to exclude *self-consistency*, which is supposed to bring a sense of stability. Sheldon et al. found it too similar to Maslow's security need, but in our opinion it resembles more a set values to live by, or a sense of morality, a belief in what is good and bad that plays a central role in humanistic approaches to meaning in life. We will come back to this in Section 4.

2.2   Cockton and Aldorf's ERG Theory

Cockton writes about value centred design (VCD) [3]. He places an emphasis on looking at value as represented in and produced by products. He distinguishes between two definitions of value: (1) the capitalist notion, and (2) moral value(s) as in the morally oriented approach of value sensitive design (VSD) [9,10] and the embedded (moral) values of design of the "values at play" approach [11]. VCD acknowledges the importance of both, but focuses more on the first than on the second.[2] Cockton turns to Alderfer's ERG theory to address what people might find worthwhile. Alderfer's ERG theory consists of three (categories of) needs: (1) *existence*, including physiological and safety needs, (2) *relatedness*, including social and external esteem, and (3) *growth*, including self-actualisation and internal esteem [12,3].

2.3   Wyeth et al. and the Self-determination Theory of Deci and Ryan

Wyeth et al. proposed a set of guidelines for designing for whole body interaction for people with intellectual disabilities that is based on the Self-Determination Theory (SDT) of Deci and Ryan [5,13,14]. SDT is one of the most influential contemporary psychological models for human motivation and revolves around three primary needs: competence, autonomy and relatedness [13,15,14]. Self acceptance, personal growth and purpose in life are taken into account in the postulates of the theory [16]. Wyeth et al. also focused on the underlying principles of SDT and their intrinsic motivation factors such as free choice, interest, optimal challenge and the mentioned psychological needs but also including effectance and personal causation. Furthermore, in their work they apply three fundamental dimensions of supporting social contexts: autonomy support, structures, and involvement [5]. An important statement —exemplified by Wyeth's choice of the user group— is that fundamental human needs are universal and are relevant for any target user group.

---

[2] To prevent confusion with the second meaning, which plays a more central role in the humanistic tradition, Cockton later changed terminology to describe his method as Worth Centred Design.

Although many acknowledge the value of SDT, there are of course some discussion points on the SDT in the psychological field. Some point to the aspect of the subjective-perceived need fulfilment instead of actual fulfilment which seems to be addressed in SDT [17]. Others suggest a more central social comparative aspect of need fulfilment, people tend to see their fulfilment with respect to others [18]. Furthermore, according to Andersen et al., relatedness plays a more important role and they acknowledge autonomy and compentence as important needs [19]. However, they also point to an explicit need for meaning and security and safety -a notion of stability and perceived future psychological and physiological states [19]. Also, Andersen suggests it would be valuable to look at the coherence with social-cognitive theory of Baumeister and others. Therefore, in the next section we look at such a theory of Baumeister on the meaning of life, and the humanistic view of van Houten.

3   Adding Two Humanistic Viewpoints

Fig. 1 summarises the fundamental needs from the HCI literature discussed above. The secondary references on which they base their work, however, suggest that it will also be useful, or even necessary, to look more explicitly at humanistic philosophy and its view on meaning in life. In this section we take a look at the seminal work of Baumeister, and the work of Van Houten, leading to additional entries in the overview in Fig. 2.

3.1   Baumeister

Baumeister wrote extensively about meaning in life and proposed a set of fundamental universal human needs for meaning in life [21]. His theory is based on a meta-analyses over several fields, including history, sociology and anthropology. We choose to incorporate this meta-study as it is based on a broad range of disciplines, has not yet been mentioned in HCI context, and in our opinion gives an insightful addition to both the theoretical framework and the list of fundamental needs that can be addressed in our work.

Baumeister states that human need for meaning in life can be divided into four basic needs: a need for purpose, a need for efficacy, a need for self-worth and a need for (moral) values in life. If someone does not satisfy one or more of the needs to satisfaction, it will lead to negative connotations such as depression or sadness. In general, if people are faced with a reduction in fulfilment of one (or several of) the need(s), they will cope by intensifying other activities in order to fill the gap. Besides this they might be more open at that point to engage in new activities that might satisfy one or more needs. Below, we discuss the four needs in some more detail.

3.2   Purpose

Purpose concerns the interpretation of one's activities and how these seem to influence future states. Directly linked to this are *goals* and *fulfilment*. Fulfilment

This table has been based on several viewpoints, looking at the same question of "what makes somebody tick" using different terms: fundamental human needs, intrinsic motivation, and meaning in life.

	#	Model	Psychological needs	Hassenzahl (2010) [6] for UX	Wyeth et al. (2011) for whole-body gaming with ID	Flanagan & Nissenbaum (2007) VAP [4]	Cockton (2006) for worth	Desmet & Hassenzahl (2012) for UX
	2	Deci & Ryan (1991[1], 2000),	autonomy	x	x	x 10		x
	3	*Ryan & Deci (2000)* [1]	competence	x	x			x
	4	*related to Maslow, Alderfer,*	relatedness	x	x	x 10	x 10	x
	A	*Csikszentmihalyi, Lepper,*	*effectance* [1]	x	x			x
	A	*Baumeister & Leary, Reiss*	*personal causation* [1]		x			
Sheldon et al.	6		physiological / physical thriving[2]	left out			x	
Sheldon et al.	8		safety / security[2]	x			x	
Sheldon et al.	=4[2]	Maslow (1943 / 1954**)	love(-belongingness[2])	x	x 10	x 10	x	x 10
Sheldon et al.	=1[2]		esteem	left out	x 10	x 10	x	x 10
Sheldon et al.	7		self-actualization (-meaning[2])	x			x	x 10
Sheldon et al.	1		self-esteem	x	x 10	x 10		x 10
Sheldon et al.	=4[2]		relatedness	x	x 10	x 10	x 10	x 10
Sheldon et al.		Epstein (1990)	pleasure (vs. pain)					
Sheldon et al.	5		/ pleasure stimulation[2]	x	x 10			x 10
Sheldon et al.			self-concept consistency					
Sheldon et al.	=8[2]		/sense of stability[2]	x				
Sheldon et al.	9	American Dream	popularity influence	x				
Sheldon et al.	10		money luxuries	left out				
		Rokeach (1973)[3]				x 10	x	

[1] Wyeth et al. used an extended interpretation of Deci & Ryan(1991) and Ryan & Deci (2000) as a starting point, resulting in these two additional mentioned needs: *personal causation* , that is the intention to produce change in the environment, and *effectance,* which they describe as dealing effectively with an environment. Whereas, competence and autonomy are central in mastery behaviour to develop interests and capacities.

[2] As used, mentioned and interpreted in Sheldon et al.'s list

Fig. 1. Overview of human needs in HCI

	Model	Desmet & Hassenzahl (2012) for UX	Cockton (2006) for worth	Flanagan & Nissenbaum (2007) VAP⁴	Wyeth et al. (2011) for whole-body gaming with ID	Hassenzahl (2010)⁶ for UX
Psychological needs	**Alderfer⁷**					
	Existence (physiological and safety) or Identity	X¹⁰	X			X¹⁰
	Relatedness (social and external esteem) or Belonging	X¹⁰	X	X¹⁰	X¹⁰	X¹⁰
	Growth needs (self-actualization and internal esteem)		X	X¹⁰		
	Friedman and Kahn (2003)⁵			X⁹		
	Baumeister (1991)					
	Purpose		X⁸,¹⁰	X⁸,¹⁰		
	Values			X¹⁰	X¹⁰	X¹⁰
	Self-worth			X¹⁰	X¹⁰	X¹⁰
	Efficacy			X¹⁰	X¹⁰	
Other humanistic views	**van Houten (1999)**					
	solidarity (other-relatedness)			X¹⁰	X¹⁰	X¹⁰
	artistic dimension of aesthetics e.g. creatively active and open-mindedness	X¹⁰			X¹⁰	X¹⁰
	self-consciousness (reflecting on one's life)	X¹⁰				X¹⁰

3 Rokeach proposed two sets of universal values (although differing in strength), (1) *terminal values*, those to be fulfilled before death: a comfortable life, an exciting life, a sense of accomplishment, a world at peace, a world of beauty, equality, family security, freedom, happiness, inner harmony, mature love, national security, pleasure, salvation, social recognition, true friendship, wisdom, and (2) *instrumental values*, those modes of behaviour to attain end-state of existence: ambitious, broadminded, capable, cheerful, clean, courageous, forgiving, helpful, honest, imaginative, independent, intellectual, logical, loving, obedient, polite and self-controlled

4 Flanagan and Nissenbaum proposed some values relevant to games, those underlined were targeted in their case study of Rapunsel: gender equity, environmentalism, security/safety, creativity and expression, cooperation, sharing, trust, authorship, liberty, diversity, justice, inclusion, equality, privacy, and personal autonomy

5 They refer to Value Sensitive Design and discuss a set of 12 human values with ethical import: human welfare, ownership and property, privacy, freedom from bias, universal usability, trust, autonomy, informed consent, accountability, identity, calmness, and environmental sustainability

6 We omitted the in the paper present set of items from Jordan and Tiger, Gaver and Martin, and Hassenzahl's earlier work. These were reflecting more experiences or were design solution oriented.

7 We use two terminologies here as described in Cockton's work

8 "values" can be interpreted in many different ways as Cockton makes clear, e.g. worth, morality, being of personal or monetary value etc.

9 Referenced to Friedman's 2003 paper only in a related publication of Flanagan, Howe and Nissenbaum (2005)

10 Seems to be addressed in their approach (to some extend) but not based specifically on this literature on needs

Fig. 2. Overview of human needs in HCI (ctd.)

deals with positive affect and achieving the goals. Goals are more related to extrinsic motivations. An activity might be unpleasurable in itself but is done to reach or to come closer to a goal. When the entertaining value or fulfilment results from performing the activity itself it is an intrinsic motivation.

3.3 Self-worth

The need for Self-Worth concerns the fact that people need to feel that they have something to contribute. This often results in people having the tendency to feel better than others. This can be done by showing-off, engaging in competition or scraping together small details to form a superior identity. It has some overlap with value and especially having positive value. Nonetheless, it is a distinct need and the two can even conflict.[3]

3.4 Efficacy

Efficacy, control and competence are very important feelings about being capable and being strong in life. Remarkably, it is especially about the *perception* hereof. An illustrative example is given from Rodin and Langer [22]. In this experiment elderly were made aware of their responsibilities for themselves and were given the task to care for a plant. It gave them a sense of efficacy and being needed. Results showed that this group felt better and lived longer.

Primary and Secondary Control – A subitem of the need for efficacy is *primary control*. It is a form of control in which the environment is changed for one's own benefit. *Secondary control* means that one adjusts to the environment or situation. An sub-category of this latter is *interpretive control*. This means that merely understanding something already provides a sense of control. Furthermore, even the illusion of having control over negative aspects of an environment can have beneficial results.

3.5 Values

Having values, a belief in what is good and bad, can be a source of a sense of meaning in one's life – independent of whether one actually manages to live according to the values. Also, people want to justify their behaviour even if it is not a key factor of a choice. Morals are generally stated in negative ways, like *"Thy shall not kill"*. Positive morals or values such as sharing, helping others and defending the group, exist as well in most societies. A specific type of value is a "value base". This kind of value, according to Baumeister, are values that need no further justification. Typical examples are doing something *"for God's sake"* or *"for the children's sake"*.

---

[3] When the self-worth of a person is raised by things that actually conflict with their own values, this discrepancy may negatively influence the *self-consistency* discussed by Epstein.

Value Gap – The Judeo-Christian religion that shaped western society do no longer provide the uniform, unquestioned set of values to live by, to the majority of people. According to Baumeister this hollowing of value bases resulted in a "value gap", no longer everyone knows what to live by (e.g. the ten commandments) and for (e.g. to enter heaven). Moreover, many traditions have been stopped as their reasons for existence were questioned; in a diminishing amount one uses *"because we've always done it that way"* as a value. The capitalist work ethos, *"because your boss tells you to"*, seems to have further weakened morality. As a result financial values have become more dominant, but these are often inadequate and unsatisfying. According to Baumeister a response is to turn to the other needs, finding a basis for values from these. In modern society this especially seems to be the self or self-identity, but also work ethic and the sacredness of family.

3.6   The Humane Life of van Houten

We see the view of Van Houten as a second important source representing a more humanistic side of human needs [23]. He noticed that the Dutch society has been classifying, standardising, normalising and discriminating. In current society being able to work has seem to been established as a central value. Even for those who are not able to work, attempts at work are more or less imposed and ultimately expected. If they can't, they are felt sorry for and are excluded of parts of life. As an alternative approach to this, he proposes three main lines for values for a humane life and society: three necessities for a good life, "beyond the common man".

The first is centred around *solidarity* and can be described as other-relatedness; it is based on the social nature of humans. An important role is played herein by the autonomy of the person, respect for others and responsibility. Being cut-off, manipulated or used are identified as threats to this.

The second is an artistic dimension: *aesthetics*. In other words making something beautiful, being creatively active and open-mindedness help one to lead a fulfilling life.

The third is *self-consciousness*. This concerns the attempt to reflect on one's life and aim for a "prudent" (well-considered and well thought-out) way of life. This latter, according to Van Houten, should not only hold for individuals but for companies and society as a whole as well. Although we understand the relevance for this need, we are somewhat hesitant to incorporate it as a core need because it relies heavily on cogitation and a high level of rational, cognitive ability. We would prefer instead to turn to expression of oneself one's identity and especially becoming that what one can be as part of the self-actualisation of Maslow [24].

4   Needs in Entertainment

In this section we briefly explain the identified needs of the several models that can be targeted and fulfilled with entertainment. We address the needs from Figure 1 and 2. The mentioned examples are not exhaustive but are intended to show that entertainment on itself can fulfil a wide array of human needs. Although the several models are not easily fitted into a universal model of everything, turning to these needs in the design and development process for new (entertainment) technology still yields worthwhile and interestingly new applications.

Autonomy. Autonomy as mentioned here is about the need to be self-consistent and feeling a sense of volition. Not merely about free-choice, for which it is often mistakenly interpreted [15]. The need as such, is targeted often in games. People have been playing games in which there are no clear pre-defined goals and part of the game is the goal creation or selection. In our experience this gives a feeling of volition, experimenting with odd goals, and finding those fitting one's identity. In this line of work one could think of open-ended entertainment in which players come up with their own interpretations and rules [25].

Efficacy. Efficacy, control and competence focus on the need of feeling capable, and being strong in life. As stated in Baumeister, merely understanding something helps to fulfil this need of efficacy. The whole edutainment movement signifies the importance of this.

Social-Relatedness. Social-relatedness, to feel connected to other people, preferably in a reciprocal way, is a very strong and important need in life [6]. For example, interactive playgrounds for children can (actively) encourage social interactions [25,26].

Physiological Thriving. The need for physiological thriving focuses on aspects of feeling healthy, including the need for food, water and exercise. With the recent introduction of controllers, platforms and devices for whole body interactions, such as the Wii and Kinect but also mobile devices integrating GPS, games have been used to target fitness. Another aspect is the need for the right nutriments. No realistic entertainment alternatives exist for these but entertainment has been used to increase the enjoyment of eating and drinking by combining it with other needs [27].

Safety/Security. The need for safety and security is about perceived threats for future need fulfilment. Related to the need for efficacy mentioned earlier, learning to deal with such threats might increase security as well as efficacy. There are several serious games targeting security with the use of virtual reality to train police officers and the military, and to help people with a variety of phobias [28].

Self-esteem. To feel worthy, good and in some cases better compared to others, are essential in the need for self-esteem. Again this need is related to efficacy and competence but has its own specifics. In practice, in games this aspect is often limited to the use of high-scores, bulletin boards, levels and solving puzzles.

Self-actualisation, Creativity, Open-mindedness and Self-Expression.
The need to express one self and to become who one really is, many see it as
an artistic dimension, although this is only a part of what self-actualization is
about. Many game designers make use of this expressiveness, the joy of creation
and personalization in their games, allowing for exploration and creativity, some
even explicitly target self-actualisation of Maslow's hieracrchy of needs [29], or
make creativity and self-expression the main point of the game (e.g. minecraft
and other sandbox games).

Pleasure Stimulation. The enjoyability of beautiful things, the aesthetics,
(passively) undergoing a pleasant experience, the hedonic quality of things, these
are the basis for the need for pleasure stimulation. The increase in performance
of computer technology allows for more and more sensual stimulating experiences, ranging from artpieces, to virtual worlds or virtual tours through existing
landscapes. Moreover, pleasant experiences such as enjoying humour, the thrill
of being scared and reliving enjoyable memories help to fulfil this need.

Purpose. Purpose is about having goals and attaining fulfilment, to do things
for a reason and the expected influence of this on future states. The turn to gamification to solve hard problems with humans, for instance via crowdsourcing is
one of the ways in which the need for purpose is satisfied through entertainment.

Values. Having certain values to live by, moral standards and things to measure
up to, the 'basics' that can give guidance to one's life, those are central in the
need for values. Traditional board games, take into account values in a indirect
way. Many allow and depend on a set of house rules, additional rules to make
the game *fair*, *age appropriate* or enhancing the aspect of *personal causality*
by reducing randomness. These rules make such values explicit. Values could
also be targeted through contemplation. For instance, the game series of GTA
and Molleindustria contain a set of explicit values (although odd and perhaps
morally crooked) that could encourage the gamer to contemplate on their own
set of values.

5   Conclusion

In this paper we looked at fundamental human needs in an HCI perspective,
looking at existing work in this direction, and adding work from humanistic
philosophy. This provided us with an overview of fundamental needs that might
be addressed through new technology as well as some general insights from the
various underlying theoretical frameworks. By linking entertainment examples
to the list of identified needs, based on a variety of theories, we showed that
entertainment can be more than mere fun. We conclude that entertainment
can be a welcome addition for intrinsic motivation, mental well-being, and for
increasing meaning in life. Turning to needs in the design and development

process for new (entertainment) technology might also be useful in setting up requirements, during design, and evaluation and help in selecting projects and activities to engage in. Entertainment can be a very valuable tool and an outlook on needs adds to life.

Acknowledgments. This publication was supported by the Dutch national program COMMIT. We would like to thank Marloes Arends for sharing her knowledge and viewpoints. Last but not least, we would like to thank reviewers of our work for their insightful comments.

References

1. Hassenzahl, M., Diefenbach, S., Göritz, A.: Needs, affect, and interactive products - facets of user experience. Interacting with Computers 22(5), 353–362 (2010)
2. Desmet, P., Hassenzahl, M.: Towards happiness: Possibility-driven design. In: Zacarias, M., de Oliveira, J.V. (eds.) Human-Computer Interaction. SCI, vol. 396, pp. 3–28. Springer, Heidelberg (2012)
3. Cockton, G.: Designing worth is worth designing. In: Proceedings of the 4th Nordic Conference on Human-Computer Interaction: Changing Roles, NordiCHI 2006, pp. 165–174. ACM, New York (2006)
4. Muller, M.J., Wharton, C.: Workshop on HCI research and practice agenda based on human needs and social responsibility. In: Proceedings of CHI 1997, CHI EA 1997. ACM, New York (1997)
5. Wyeth, P., Johnson, D., Sweetser, P.: Motivating Whole Body Gaming for People with Intellectual Disability. In: Proceedings of 4th International Workshop on Whole Body Interaction at ACE 2011 (2011)
6. Baumeister, R.F., Leary, M.R.: The need to belong: Desire for interpersonal attachments as a fundamental human motivation. Psychological Bulletin 117(3), 497–529 (1995)
7. Sheldon, K.M., Elliot, A.J., Kim, Y., Kasser, T.: What Is Satisfying About Satisfying Events? Testing 10 Candidate Psychological Needs. Journal of Personality and Social Psychology 80(2), 325–339 (2001)
8. Epstein, S.: Cognitive-experiential self-theory of personality. In: Milton, T., Lerner, M.J. (eds.) Comprehensive Handbook of Pscycholgy, pp. 159–184. Wiley & sons, Hoboken (2003)
9. Friedman, B.: Value-sensitive design. Interactions 3(6), 16–23 (1996)
10. Friedman, B., Kahn Jr., P.H.: Human values, ethics, and design. In: Jacko, J.A., Sears, A. (eds.) The Human-Computer Interaction Handbook, pp. 1177–1201. L. Erlbaum Associates Inc., Hillsdale (2003)
11. Flanagan, M., Nissenbaum, H.: A game design methodology to incorporate social activist themes. In: Proceedings of CHI 2007, pp. 181–190. ACM Press, New York (2007)
12. Alderfer, C.P.: Existence, relatedness, and growth: human needs in organizational settings. The Free Press, New York (1972)
13. Deci, E.L., Ryan, R.M.: A motivational approach to self: Integration in personality. In: Nebraska Symposium on Motivation, vol. 38, pp. 237–288 (1991)
14. Ryan, R.M., Deci, E.L.: Self-determination theory and the facilitation of intrinsic motivation, social development, and well-being. American Psychologist 55(1), 67–78 (2000)

15. Deci, E.L., Ryan, R.M.: The "what" and "why" of goal pursuits: Human needs and the self-determination of behavior. Psychological Inquiry 11(4), 227–268 (2000)
16. Coleman, G.C.: Aging and satisfaction of psychological needs. Psychological Inquiry 11(4), 291–295 (2000)
17. Pyszczynski, T., Greenberg, J., Solomon, S.: Toward a dialectical analysis of growth and defensive motives. Psychological Inquiry 11(4), 301–305 (2000)
18. Buunk, B.P., Nauta, A.: Why intraindividual needs are not enough: Human motivation is primarily social. Psychological Inquiry 11(4), 279–283 (2000)
19. Andersen, S.M., Chen, S., Carter, C.: Fundamental human needs: Making social cognition relevant. Psychological Inquiry 11(4), 269–275 (2000)
20. Rokeach, M.: The nature of human values. The Free Press (1973)
21. Baumeister, R.F.: Meanings of Life, 1st edn. The Guilford Press (1992)
22. Rodin, J., Langer, E.J.: Long-term effects of a control-relevant intervention with the institutionalized aged. Journal of Personality and Social Psychology 35(12), 897–902 (1977)
23. van Houten, D.: De standaardmens voorbij. Elsevier/De Tijdstroom (1999)
24. Maslow, A.: A Theory of Human Motivation. Psychological Review 50, 370–396 (1943)
25. Bekker, T., Sturm, J.: Stimulating physical and social activity through open-ended play. In: Proceedings of the 8th International Conference on Interaction Design and Children, IDC 2009, pp. 309–312. ACM, New York (2009)
26. Moreno, A., van Delden, R., Poppe, R., Reidsma, D.: Socially aware interactive playgrounds: Sensing and inducing social behavior. IEEE Pervasive Computing 12(3), 40–47 (2013)
27. Wei, J., Nakatsu, R.: Leisure food: Derive social and cultural entertainment through physical interaction with food. In: Herrlich, M., Malaka, R., Masuch, M. (eds.) ICEC 2012. LNCS, vol. 7522, pp. 256–269. Springer, Heidelberg (2012)
28. Gamito, P., Oliveira, J., Morais, D., Rosa, P., Saraiva, T.: Serious games for serious problems: From ludicus to therapeuticus. In: Kim, J.J. (ed.) Virtual Reality. InTech (2010)
29. Schell, J.: The art of game design: A book of lenses. Morgan Kaufmann Publishers (2008)

D-FLIP: Dynamic and Flexible Interactive PhotoShow

Chi Thanh Vi[1], Kazuki Takashima[2], Hitomi Yokoyama[2], Gengdai Liu[3],
Yuichi Itoh[4], Sriram Subramanian[1], and Yoshifumi Kitamura[2]

[1] University of Bristol, UK
[2] Tohoku University, Japan
[3] OLM Digital Inc., Japan
[4] Osaka University, Japan

Abstract. We propose D-FLIP, a novel algorithm that dynamically displays a
set of digital photos using different principles for organizing them. A variety of
requirements for photo arrangements can be flexibly replaced or added through
the interaction and the results are continuously and dynamically displayed. D-
FLIP uses an approach based on combinatorial optimization and emergent
computation, where geometric parameters such as location, size, and photo angle are considered to be functions of time; dynamically determined by local relationships among adjacent photos at every time instance. As a consequence,
the global layout of all photos is automatically varied. We first present examples of photograph behaviors that demonstrate the algorithm and then investigate users' task engagement using EEG in the context of story preparation and
telling. The result shows that D-FLIP requires less task engagement and mental
efforts in order to support storytelling.

Keywords: Dynamic PhotoShow, Emergent Computing, EEG.

1 Introduction

Pervasiveness of digital cameras has led to large collections of digital photos that
users often browse on computer displays, by rearranging them to gather similar ones
based on specific features/ meta-data. While several techniques to do this efficiently
exist, most of them are somewhat systematic or goal-driven in terms of applying principles for displaying photos. These methods are useful in systematically organizing
and finding photos but previous studies suggest that users often browse their photo
collections without a specific search goal (e.g. [1]) but a more general purpose such as
looking back at previous memories. Moreover, users often browse photos with actions
such as displaying/enlarging photos randomly or starting a slideshow for personal
gratification and pleasure. To support these behaviors, the presentation of photos
should be flexibly and dynamically adapted with visual effects based on user's input.

Consequently, we propose a novel method to flexibly display a set of photos by
showing each of them in a dynamic and continuous motion like a living object. It
allows users to replace or add displaying principles interactively and flexibly. In
order to achieve such flexibility, we introduce an approach based on emergent computation. Geometric parameters (i.e. location, size, and photo angle) are considered to be

D. Reidsma, H. Katayose, and A. Nijholt (Eds.): ACE 2013, LNCS 8253, pp. 415–427, 2013.
© Springer International Publishing Switzerland 2013

(a) Photos arranged by Geotags   (b) Finding someone's photos   (c) Photos corrected by meta-data

Fig. 1. Examples of arrangements by tags

functions of time. Photos are dynamically moved toward the directions determined by local relationships with adjacent photos at each time instance. As a result, the global layout of all photos varies automatically and converges gradually with time. These dynamic behaviors provide users enjoyable interactions with less effort to recall good story from the photos. This will enhance one of the most enjoyable parts of personal photos, which is to share memories and reminisce with friends or relatives.

We illustrate example behaviors of photos and then do a user study to evaluate D-FLIP against Windows Explorer, a photo managing program familiar to Windows users. The evaluation involved two participants, a narrator and a listener to prepare and share a story. We measured both participants EEG to quantitatively measure users' metal effort/ task engagement. In addition, NASA-TLX forms were also collected from the narrators and listeners after each task.

The contributions of this paper are: (1) a proposed method to dynamically and flexibly display photos; and (2) an evaluation method using EEG which can be used to evaluate interactive applications.

2   Related Work

2.1   Browsing Digital Photos and Photo Collages

Many efforts were proposed to arrange photos effectively. For example, a browser that arranges multiple photos in folders by grouping them with different magnification levels [2], or by categories with different hierarchy depths [3]. Other examples are arranging photos calendar by using their shooting dates [4], displaying them on a digital geographical map at their shoot locations using meta-data [5], grouping photos with shoot locations and persons [6], and browsing large image datasets using Voronoi diagrams [7]. A technique for browsing large image collections was presented by [8] using the rectangle-packing algorithm, and by [9] using hierarchical tree structured organization of images with level of details. However, most of these methods lack flexibility in displaying with mixtures of requirements based on user's input.

Digital photo collages, which summarize meaningful events or memorabilia, are widely used to display photos. This is efficient because users can view multiple photos at once. However, it requires two types of treatment: (1) a geometric treatment concerning about arranging multiple photos in a pre-determined area but avoids overlapping and empty regions, and (2) a semantic treatment concerning about content of the photos. Several authoring tools have been proposed to create photo collages easily (i.e. AutoCollage [10], Picture Collage [11], and Digital Tapestry [12]).

2.2   The Effect of Animation on Users' Interest

Compared to static method, dynamic photo displaying seems to be more interesting and aesthetically appealing [13]. Previous studies have shown that animation can boost users' performance in learning and teaching such as understanding Newton's law of motion [14]. In other words, animations can help users perform the task (e.g. learning) easier and with a better performance in learning and teaching. In terms of users' interest, animation are likely to increase emotional interest (created by events that are arousing) while static graphics are likely to trigger more cognitive interest (related to the connections between incoming information and background under-standing [15]). As the result, D-FLIP may trigger emotional interest from users be-cause of its dynamical and interactive movements. This will help to achieve the goal of D-FLIP which is letting users viewing photos interactively with ease and interest.

2.3   Evaluating Using Neural Signals

Traditionally interactive programs are evaluated by investigating performance or us-ers' behaviors. However, with programs designed for using with ease and pleasure, an evaluation method measuring users' affective or inner states is preferred. Although this can be done by questionnaires answered by participants, they occur after the event when important issues may be forgotten. Neural signals, measured from the brain can better reflect a users' current state and provide an evaluation metric.

There are many methods to detect neural signals such as fMRI, MEG, fNIRS and EEG. A brief summary of those techniques are discussed in [16]. In addition, EEG devices are portable and have high temporal resolution. EEG signals have been also shown to capture the affective state (such as arousal [17] and task engagement [18]).

As one purpose of D-FLIP is to help user browse photos with ease and interest, measuring task engagement can help to evaluate. [19] defined task engagement as the *effortful concentration and striving towards task goals* where task demands and per-sonal characteristics may influence this pattern of processing. Previous studies have shown a positive correlation between EEG engagement and task demands including stimulus complexity processing and the requirement for attentional resources alloca-tion [20]. Consequently, if an application requires low level of task engagement in using, can be considered easier to use when compared with applications requiring higher task engagement. Moreover, [21] present a measure of task engagement from EEG as $\beta / (\alpha + \theta)$. Given this evidence of measuring users' task engagement/ work-load, we used it to evaluate D-FLIP by comparing with a competitive program.

3   Algorithm of Dynamic Display of Photos

3.1   Algorithm Overview

Each photo has three parameters: its position, size, and rotational angle. They are considered as functions of time and are controlled to arrange multiple photos simulta-neously on a display. The photo movement is shown by gradually changing the values of these parameters at every time instant. The algorithm is explained by Eq. (1):

$$dx / dt = f(\vec{x}) + \eta \tag{1}$$

Here, $\vec{x}$ is a set of the three parameters above and its variation dx/dt is derived by $f(\vec{x})$, the principle to achieve the photo arrangement, and noise term η. Larger amplitude noise increases the fluctuation and is useful for escaping local optimum. Furthermore, Eq (1) can be re-written in another form with the weight coefficients:

$$\frac{dx}{dt} = \sum_i \{w_i f_i(\vec{x}) + \eta_i\} \tag{2}$$

In here, $f(\vec{x})$, a variety of principles, is used to achieve the photos arrangement or layout. Let P represents the data of a photo, I represents the information of certain input or output devices, $\vec{P}$ is all the photos in the environment, $Position(P)$ is the photo position, $Size(P)$ is its size, and $Rotation(P)$ is its rotational angle. Assuming that the number of principles related to position, size, and rotational angle are l, m, and n, respectively. Eq. (3) is obtained by modifying Eq. (2). It controls the parameters of photo P and is calculated from all photos. Here, $f_{Pi}(\vec{x})$, $f_{Si}(\vec{x})$ and $f_{Ri}(\vec{x})$ are functions that represent the changes of position, size, and rotation, respectively:

$$\frac{d}{dt}Position(P) = \sum_i^n \{f_{Pi}(I,\vec{P}) + \eta_i\}; \frac{d}{dt}Scale(P) = \sum_i^m \{f_{Si}(I,\vec{P}) + \eta_i\}; \frac{d}{dt}Rotation(P) = \sum_i^l \{f_{Ri}(I,\vec{P}) + \eta_i\} \tag{3}$$

3.2   Principles of Photograph Arrangement

There are two types of principles that are important for photo arrangement: *packing* and *mapping*. *Packing* is a geometric problem concerning about arranging multiple photos with different sizes and rotational angles in a pre-determined area; it avoids overlaps and empty regions as much as possible. On the other hand, *mapping* is a semantic concerning about locating each photo based on its content and interaction with users. Here, each function can be established independently based on an individual principle as well as to be implemented without paying attention to the global coordination. Certain feature values of each photo are assumed to be calculated and stored in the tag beforehand (e.g. to specify a person, taken location, etc.). Different photo arrangements can be achieved flexibly by replacing or adding functions that correspond to the displaying principles.

Geometric Packing: Here we explain principles related to geometric packing. First, the principle to avoid overlaps with adjacent photos is represented by Eq. (4). Here, N is the number of photos, $Avoid(P, Pi)$ is P's vector for escaping when P and Pi overlap. $Adjacency(P)$ is the set of photos overlapping with P.

$$f_{translatio}(I,\vec{P}) = \sum_i^N Avoid(P, P_i) \quad if \ P_i \in Adjacency(P)$$
$$\tag{4}$$

Second, a photo moves toward the inside of the window based on Eq. (5) if its position exceeds the displaying window's border. Here, L, B, R, and T are the left, bottom, right, and top coordinates of the window, $L(P)$, $B(P)$, $R(P)$, and $T(P)$ are the corresponding photo coordinates, and A_l, A_b, A_r, and A_t are their coefficients:

$$f_{mold}(I,\vec{P}) = \sum_{i}^{N} \begin{cases} A_l \cdot \{L - L(P_i)\} & if\ L(P_i) < L \\ A_b \cdot \{B - B(P_i)\} & if\ B(P_i) < B \\ A_r \cdot \{R - R(P_i)\} & if\ R(P_i) > R \\ A_t \cdot \{T - T(P_i)\} & if\ T(P_i) > T \end{cases} \tag{5}$$

Fig. 2 illustrates how photos avoid overlapping. Without overlaps, each photo becomes larger until it reaches the predetermined maximum scale when Eq. (6) is applied (Fig. 2a). If two adjacent photos overlap, the larger photo becomes smaller until it reaches the predetermined minimum scale when Eq. (7) is applied (Fig. 2b); they move to opposite directions when Eq. (4) is applied (Fig. 2a), or rotate in opposite directions when Eq. (8) is applied (Fig. 2c). Here, A_{s1} and A_{s2} are coefficients, and $Ang(Pi, Pj)$ is the rotational angle with which Pi and Pj avoid overlapping:

$$f_{enlarge}(I,\vec{P}) = \sum_{i}^{N} A_{s2}\{Scale_{max} - Scale(P_i)\} \tag{6}$$
$$if\ Adjacency(P_i) = \varphi \wedge Scale_{max} > Scale(P_i)$$

$$f_{shrink}(I,\vec{P}) = \sum_{i}^{N} A_{s1}\{Scale_{min} - Scale(P_i)\} \tag{7}$$
$$for\ all\ P_j \in Adjacency(P_i),$$
$$Scale(P_j) < Scale(P_i) \wedge Scale_{min} < Scale(P_i)$$

$$f_{rotation}(I,\vec{P}) = \sum_{i}^{N} Ang(P,P_i) \tag{8}$$

The upper-right photo in Fig. 2b will become as large as possible by referring to environmental parameters indicating the positions and sizes of adjacent photos. However, when two photos collide, the larger one becomes smaller (shown in the lower-left corner) based on Eq. (7) if these two equations are simultaneously applied. Thus, all photos are gradually arranged without empty space while their sizes become almost equal. Even if these two principles conflict, the algorithm will find a solution. Other principles related to geometric packing can be obtained similarly.

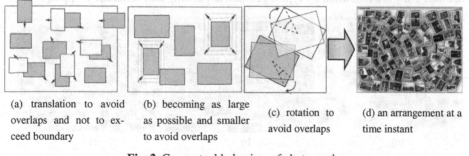

(a) translation to avoid overlaps and not to exceed boundary

(b) becoming as large as possible and smaller to avoid overlaps

(c) rotation to avoid overlaps

(d) an arrangement at a time instant

Fig. 2. Conceptual behaviors of photographs

Semantic Mapping: One of the simplest examples of semantic mapping, a function to enlarge an interesting photo, is represented by Eq. (9). Here, *Attention* is a set of interesting photos given by an input device as a mouse or a gaze input device:

$$f_{attention}(I,\vec{P}) = A_{a1} \cdot \{Scale_{max} - Scale(P)\} \tag{9}$$
$$if\ P \in Attention$$

Eq. (10) shows how a focused photo attracts other ones with similar attributes. Here, *Similarity(Pi, Pj)* is the similarity between photos *Pi* and *Pj*, and if this value is larger than a threshold, *Pj* moves toward *Pi*, and away otherwise. The similarities are assumed to be calculated by feature values obtained by image processing or from tags of photos. Other related principles of semantic mapping can be obtained similarly.

$$f_{attraction}(I, \vec{P}) = \begin{cases} \sum_{i}^{N} A_{a2}\{Similarity(P, P_i) - Threshold\} \\ \quad \cdot \{Position(P_i) - Position(P)\} \\ \quad if\ Similarity(P, P_i) \geq Threshold \\ \sum_{i}^{N} A_{a2}\{Similarity(P, P_i) - Threshold\} \\ \quad /\{Position(P_i) - Position(P)\} \end{cases} \quad (10)$$

Viewer's Interactions: Even after the system reaches the balanced condition, the photograph behaviors can be observed when parameters of the display environment vary (e.g. when new photos are added or the size of the displaying window is changed). Also if a cursor (operated by a mouse, for example) is used, the photo overlaid by the cursor becomes larger using Eq. (8) with certain weight coefficients.

Users can observe the displayed photos and interact simultaneously with separate input devices (i.e. touch or gaze input devices). In addition, the display resolution, the number of displays, their positions, orientations, and sizes are variables of the output. Such information about input and output is treated as I in previous equations.

4   Behaviors of Photographs and Performance

4.1   Behaviors of Photographs

The experimental system was developed in C#, using Windows User API and Microsoft .NET Framework 3.5. Some photograph behaviors using the principles explained in the previous section are illustrated here as well as to show the flexibility of our method. They are classified by types: geometric packing and semantic mapping.

a)   b)   c)

Fig. 3. Geometric packing: a) original layout; b) final layout without rotation, c) with rotation

Fig. 4. Sequence when size of the displaying window is changed

Photograph Behaviors with Geometric Packing: Fig. 3 (a, b) shows how photos avoid overlaps when Eqs (4)(5)(6)(7) are applied. Fig. 3a shows the initial state where 75 photos are located randomly and overlapped. However, they gradually move to avoid overlaps and occupy the empty regions (using Eqs. (4)(5)), as shown from (a) to (b). At the same time, the photos' sizes are varied (using Eqs. (6)(7)), then soon become almost equal (Fig. 3b). Fig. 3 (a, c) is an example of photos avoiding overlaps by rotating in addition to the equations used in Fig. 3 (a, b). In Fig. 3a is the original layout, and Fig. 3c is the layout with collision-free arrangement with rotation. This is useful when photos are shown on tabletop surface displays shared by several users.

Fig. 4 shows an example of photograph behaviors when one of the environmental parameters, the window size, is changed. Once the window is enlarged (left figure), the contained photos steadily move to the empty space (middle figure), according to Eq. (5). This is gradually convergent with time so that the sizes of all photos become almost equal but avoid overlapping (right figure).

Photograph Behaviors with Semantic Mapping: Fig. 5a shows an example where one photo is focused by overlaying a cursor (at the bottom center of the photo). Fig. 5b shows photos arranged by color and user interests using the principles of geometric packing (i.e., Eqs. (4)(5)(6)(7)). Here, two cursors (magenta and green) point at two photos (bottom-left night scene and upper-right daylight scene). Soon photos with similar colors are moved toward the focused ones. The final layout is achieved by Eq. (9) with semantic mapping principles. Similarly, other feature values calculated by image processing can be used to a group of photos by applying this principle.

(a) A photo is focused by overlaying a pointer   (b) Photos are arranged by color and interest

Fig. 5. Examples of geometric packing (a) and semantic mapping (b)

Fig. 1a shows an example of photos arranged using Geotags. In this example, photos arranged without overlapping (using the Eqs. (4)(5)(6)(7)) are attracted by their geographical identification metadata (latitude and longitude coordinates) based on Eq. (9) and moved to their corresponding positions on a world map.

Fig. 1b shows an example of finding someone's photos. Given a photo set of a social relationship, when a human face in a photo is selected, the size of that photo becomes larger by Eq. (8). Also, all photos containing the selected person are attracted and gathered around the focused photo dynamically by Eq. (9). Here, a face recognition function is assumed to be working and tags for the faces are adequately given in advance. Similarly, Fig. 1c displays examples of grouping photos with closed curves drawn by a mouse using meta-data given to each of the photos in advance. In this figure, photos having meta-data of Mr. A and Mr. B are gathered in the red closed curve in the left and the green closed curve in the right, respectively. In the overlapping area of these closed curves there are photos belonging to both Mr. A and Mr. B.

4.2   Discussions

Our proposed method has each photo arrangement generated at every time instant which may not always optimally satisfy all principles. However, these arrangements provide viewers a dynamic photo-viewing environment where they can observe the smooth transitions of photos layout and the behaviors caused by their interactions.

Theoretically, the displayed photos by our algorithm are slightly vibrated because the function inherently includes a noise term in Eq. (1) that causes the system to be constantly in motion. In the above examples, a fixed small amplitude was used for the noise. Larger amplitude noise increases the fluctuation of the environmental parameters, and such fluctuation is often useful for escaping local optimum. However, the vibrations can be removed using a filter before rendering if not suitable. Moreover, the amplitude can be varied during photo arrangement to obtain a better performance.

A performance evaluation confirms that the proposed algorithm provides about 60 FPS to show 700 photos with 512x320 pixels on a Windows 7 64-bit PC with Intel Core i7 CPU (3.20 GHZ), 12.0 GB memory, NVIDIA GeForce GTX 285. The system performance drops quickly when the number of photos exceeds 700. However, this is a reasonable number for photo browsing because of: (1) screen resolution (all photos are displayed on a screen and should be large enough to view individually); and (2) common number of photos belonging to an event. However, this number can be increased with different implementation (parallel run, multi-core CPU usage, etc.).

5   User Evaluation of D-FLIP

Photo arrangements with dynamic motions, shown in previous section, are expected to be effective in many situations such as viewing many photos at once, surveying a set of photos from different layouts, and finding pictures from the dynamic motions. Moreover, the smooth visual effect caused by interactions will keep up users' motivation to actively see and interact with photos. Our study investigates this further and explores whether it helps users perform browsing/sharing tasks easier.

We compared D-FLIP to the Windows Explorer (Explorer), a default Windows program. This is because although existing software (such as PhotoMesa, PhotoFinder, etc.) incorporate some of D-FLIP's animated properties, none of them supports animation of all photos in the collection. Instead, Explorer (of Windows 7) was chosen to be the most suitable candidate because: (1) it can be easily customized to have a separate area to store selected photos but still show the non-selected ones to support the story; (2) it includes many features of other photo browsing software such as: view all photos of the collection, sort or group photos (i.e. by name, tags, rating, etc.); and (3) it is a Windows built in software which is familiar and easy to use for users.

5.1   Task Design

The experiment is a modified version of [22] where a user shares a story with a friend by showing her photo collections. Each experiment session required two participants:

one narrator and one listener who sat beside each other in front of a 27-inch monitor (2560x1440 resolutions) displaying the narrator's personal photos. We measured task engagement from both narrator and listener to investigate the effect of the interactive application on the person who actually interacted with the program (the narrator) and on the person who only observed the interaction and listened to the story (the listener). Participants wore Emotiv EEG headset during the study.

There was a storyboard in D-FLIP to support the storytelling mode. The area had ten equal boxes which held ten selected photos (Fig. 6, left). In case of Explorer, we used two Explorer windows with one window above another. The bottom window was used to store 200 photos and the top window was used to store the selected 10 photos (Fig. 6, middle). In Windows 7, filenames, all bars and additional panes (e.g. Library, Details, and Navigation) were hidden to make Explorer comparable to D-FLIP in term of visualization and functions. Features of D-FLIP in this experiment included dynamic arrangement when overlaying a pointer, attraction for photos with similar colors. These features were chosen as they are comparable with Explorer.

5.2   Method

14 participants (9 males) between the ages of 19 and 32 volunteered for the study and were arranged into 7 pairs. The narrators brought to the experiment their 400 photos divided into 2 sets of 200 each. Photos were resized to 640x480, rotated if necessary by the experimenter before beginning the study.

Fig. 6. Storytelling mode with D-FLIP (left) and Windows Explorer (middle); An example of a narrator's task engagement changes in time in one session (right)

First, the narrator had adequate time to practice with D-FLIP and Explorer using a sample photoset (Fig. 6, left & middle). After this both users wore the Emotiv headsets. Each experiment session had two blocks each with either D-FLIP or Explorer. In each block, the narrator prepared a story in 5 minutes by selecting 10 photos from her first photoset. Then she told the story to the listener within 5 minutes. Both participants had a 2-minute break before the same procedure was repeated with the next program. NASA-TLX forms were given to both participants after each block.

In the storytelling step, we only recorded EEG signals from the listener. This was because the narrator needed to speak freely with facial, hand, and body movements which would contaminate the EEG signals. Narrators were instructed to use the software as normally as possible. This includes free using any desired features (including sorting, grouping, etc.). They were also encouraged to use the non-selected photos in the collection to enrich their story. In addition, all users were asked to sit comfortably.

5.3   Data Acquisition and Analysis

We used an Emotiv EPOC for measuring EEG signals. Its signals quality have been validated by previous studies (e.g. detecting and classifying Event Related Potentials

[16], evaluating visualization effectiveness [23], exploring the nature of decision making [4], and designing a BCI controlled video game [24]). It is portable, easy to setup, and most users can wear it comfortably for at least an hour [25].

We adapted the "sliding window technique" which is commonly used to process EEG signals (e.g. [26]). The recorded EEG signals (output at 128Hz) were segmented into 4s epochs with 2s overlaps between them. To remove artifacts, we adapted a decontamination process [20] with eye blink events detected by Emotiv SDK. Following this procedure, we removed totally 7.83% of collected signals in which 5.13% due to excessive signals and 2.7% due to high changes in combined power spectral.

Engagement index was calculated as in Pope et al. [21]. β, α, and θ, are the combined power in the ranges of 13-22Hz, 8-12Hz and 5-7Hz frequency bands: *Engagement Index* $= \beta / (\alpha + \theta)$. We used F3, F4, FC5, FC6, P7, P8, O1, and O2 channels as they are the surrounding channels of Cz, Pz, P3, and P4 which were used by Pope et al. [21]. Engagement indexes were calculated in 4s window for each task & user separately and then normalized for the narrator or listener.

6   Results and Discussion

Table 1 summarizes the results, which are the averaged task engagement during the session, for two types of tasks (Preparation/ Telling), two types of programs (Explorer/ D-FLIP), and with two participant types (Narrator/ Listener). Fig. 6 (right) shows a time series sample of engagement during the preparation task of one narrator. Fig. 7 (left) shows the task engagement values of narrators in each experiment session between two programs. T-test shows that there is a significant difference between those two (t = 2.95, p < 0.05). However, we found no significant differences between two types of program in listeners (p > 0.5). The details are shown in Fig. 7, middle (Story Preparation) and Fig. 7, right (Storytelling). This may due to the individual differences where the listeners did not directly interact with the programs hence the measured task engagement depended more on the storytelling skills of the narrators.

Table 1. Averaged task engagement for narrators and listeners

Tasks	Story Preparation		Story Telling	
Programs	Explorer	D-FLIP	Explorer	D-FLIP
Narrator	0.603	0.554		
Listener	0.480	0.436	0.512	0.440

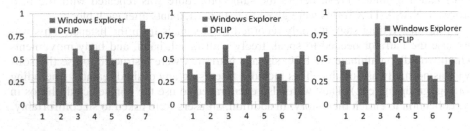

Fig. 7. Task Engagements of narrators in Story Preparation task (left); and listeners in the Story Preparation task (middle) and Story Telling task (right).

For the NASA-TLX, only mental demand (for narrator) presented with a significant difference ($p < 0.05$) between two tasks: Explorer (mean: 9.14) and D-FLIP (mean: 5.00). For the listener, there was no significant difference ($p > 0.05$) for any of the NASA-TLX questions. These results showed that the narrators had higher engagement when using the Explorer compared to D-FLIP. This implies that narrators need to put in more effort with Explorer than D-FLIP to complete the same task in the same amount of time. Consequently, besides the benefit of having more interest, D-FLIP makes the task easier to perform. The results of NASA-TLX (for both participant types) are consistent with the task engagement results.

Users had adequate practice time with D-FLIP. However, the familiarity with Explorer may result in a more skilful performance. Hence, the actual difference between measured task engagements of two programs might be larger if a less famous program (e.g. PhotoMesa) was used instead of Explorer. Our results show that even if there are effects of familiarity, D-FLIP still requires less task engagement and mental demands.

7   Discussion

An interesting finding from our user evaluation is that D-FLIP requires less mental effort and task engagement compared to Explorer in narrators but not listeners. A probable cause is that only the narrators physically actually interact with the programs. Hence, with less task engagement or workload in performing the task, interacting with D-FLIP is easier and more pleasurable.

Several factors of D-FLIP may contribute to this result viz.: high visibility with variety of layout, dynamic and smooth motions of photos, gathering photos based on similar attributes. Consequently, users can focus on interactions with other users and the story contents with less effort in performing the task. Additionally, D-FLIP keeps motivation and interest in users due to the dynamic, flexible, and interactive motions of photos produced by the proposed principles, thus making D-FLIP a particularly powerful system for visualizing large collections of images.

Our next step is to improve the algorithm categorizing the parameters and optimizing it for different types of interactive applications. Besides existing content types (i.e. text, broadcasts, movies, etc.), our algorithm can adapt to work with new and emerging content types such as dreams visualization [27] where values of parameters from fMRI patterns for an image. This can also help to build an ecosystem of photos which includes various promising features such as pigeonholing, printing, automatic acquisition of meta-data, evolving into photo sharing sites, and coordinating with social network services. We can also explore other interaction devices such as multi-touch digital tables, voice recognition, brain-machine interface, and other sensing devices to further enhance the fluidity of interaction in different application contexts.

Although the focus of this paper is not on a novel evaluation methodology, we believe that our way of measuring task engagement using EEG offers greater insights into workings of an application. Our measured task engagement is consistent with the NASA-TLX results; providing a source of external validity to our measurement mechanism. It can also be improved to capture emotions (e.g. relaxation, meditation) and other users' inner states (e.g. error awareness).

8   Conclusion

We presented D-FLIP a program which displays a set of photos flexibly, dynamically, and interactively. The underlying algorithm adjusts the displaying principles adaptively when users interact with the program. Our performance evaluation shows it can handle smoothly at least 700 photos. Our user evaluation shows that D-FLIP requires less task engagement and mental effort from users allowing them to enjoy the content rather than manage it.

References

1. Kirk, D., Sellen, A., Rother, C., Wood, K.: Understanding photowork. In: CHI (2006)
2. Bederson, B.B.: PhotoMesa: a zoomable image browser using quantum treemaps and bubblemaps. In: UIST (2001)
3. Dachselt, R., Frisch, M., Weiland, M.: FacetZoom: a continuous multi-scale widget for navigating hierarchical metadata. In: CHI (2008)
4. Graham, A., Garcia-Molina, H., Paepcke, A., Winograd, T.: Time as essence for photo browsing through personal digital libraries. In: JCDL (2002)
5. Ahern, S., Naaman, M., Nair, R., Yang, J.H.-I.: World explorer: visualizing aggregate data from unstructured text in geo-referenced collections. In: JCDL (2007)
6. Gomi, A., Itoh, T.: A personal photograph browser for life log analysis based on location, time, and person. In: SAC (2011)
7. Brivio, P., Tarini, M., Cignoni, P.: Browsing Large Image Datasets through Voronoi Diagrams. IEEE Trans. Vis. Comput. Graph. 16(6) (2010)
8. Itoh, T., Yamaguchi, Y., Ikehata, Y., Kajinaga, Y.: Hierarchical data visualization using a fast rectangle-packing algorithm. IEEE TVCG 10(3) (2004)
9. Gomi, A., Miyazaki, R., Itoh, T., Jia, L.: CAT: A Hierarchical Image Browser Using a Rectangle Packing Technique. In: Book CAT: A Hierarchical Image Browser Using a Rectangle Packing Technique (2008)
10. Rother, C., Bordeaux, L., Hamadi, Y., Blake, A.: AutoCollage. SIGGRAPH (2006)
11. Wang, J., Quan, L., Sun, J., Tang, X., Shum, H.-Y.: Picture Collage. In: CVPR (2006)
12. Rother, C., Kumar, S., Kolmogorov, V., Blake, A.: Digital Tapestry. In: CVPR (2005)
13. Kim, S., Yoon, M., Whang, S.M., Tversky, B., Morrison, J.B.: The effect of animation on comprehension and interest. JCAL 23(3) (2007)
14. Rieber, L.P.: Animation, incidental learning, and continuing motivation. Journal of Educational Psychology 83(3) (1991)
15. Kintsch, W.: Learning from text, levels of comprehension, or: Why anyone would read a story anyway. Poetics 9 (1980)
16. Vi, C., Subramanian, S.: Detecting error-related negativity for interaction design. In: CHI (2012)
17. Hagemann, D., Hewig, J., Walter, C., Schankin, A., Danner, D., Naumann, E.: Positive evidence for Eysenck's arousal hypothesis: A combined EEG and MRI study with multiple measurement occasions. J. of Personality and Individual Differences (2009)
18. Berka, C., Levendowski, D.J., Lumicao, M.N., Yau, A., Davis, G., Zivkovic, V.T., Olmstead, R.E., Tremoulet, P.D., Craven, P.L.: EEG Correlates of Task Engagement and Mental Workload in Vigilance, Learning, and Memory Tasks. ACEM 78(5) (2007)

19. Matthews, G., Campbell, S.E., Falconer, S., Joyner, L.A., Huggins, J., Gilliland, K., Grier, R., Warm, J.S.: 'Fundamental Dimensions of Subjective State in Performance Settings: Task Engagement, Distress, and Worry'. Emotion 2(4) (2002)
20. Berka, C., Levendowski, D.J., Olmstead, R.E., Popovic, M.V., Cvetinovic, M., Petrovic, M.M., Davis, G., Lumicao, M.N., Westbrook, P.: Real-time Analysis of EEG Indices of Alertness, Cognition, and Memory with a Wireless EEG Headset. IJHCI 17(2) (2004)
21. Pope, A.T., Bogart, E.H., Bartolome, D.S.: Biocybernetic system evaluates indices of operator engagement in automated task. Biological Psychology 40 (1995)
22. Rodden, K., Wood, K.R.: How do people manage their digital photographs? In: CHI 2003 (2003)
23. Anderson, E.W., Potter, K.C., Matzen, L.E., Shepherd, J.F., Preston, G.A., Silva, C.T.: A user study of visualization effectiveness using EEG and cognitive load. In: EuroVis (2011)
24. Ames, M.G., Manguy, L.: PhotoArcs: ludic tools for sharing photographs. In: MM (2006)
25. Ekandem, J.I., Davis, T.A., Alvarez, I., James, M.T., Gilbert, J.E.: Evaluating the ergonomics of BCI devices for research and experimentation. Ergonomics 55(5) (2012)
26. Lee, J.C., Tan, D.S.: Using a low-cost electroencephalograph for task classification in HCI research. In: UIST (2006)
27. Horikawa, T., Tamaki, M., Miyawaki, Y., Kamitani, Y.: Neural Decoding of Visual Imagery During Sleep. Science (2013)

PukaPuCam: Enhance Travel Logging Experience through Third-Person View Camera Attached to Balloons

Tsubasa Yamamoto, Yuta Sugiura, Suzanne Low, Koki Toda,
Kouta Minamizawa, Maki Sugimoto, and Masahiko Inami

Graduate School of Media Design, Keio University
4-1-1 Hiyoshi, Kohoku-ku, Yokohama 223-8526, Japan
{sugar283,y-sugiura,suzannedbel,kmd-std.8979,
kouta,sugimoto,inami}@kmd.keio.ac.jp

Abstract. PukaPuCam is an application service that utilizes a camera attached to balloons, to capture users' photo continuously from a third-person view. Then, users can glance through their photos by using PukaPuCam Viewer. PukaPuCam records the interaction between users and their surrounding objects or even with the people they meet. As balloon experiences air resistance, it can change its inclination according to the user's speed and thus, capture pictures from different direction or angles. This gives rise to interesting and unusual records to be added to the user's collection. As compare to other similar devices, PukaPuCam uses a common design people are familiarize with – a balloon; making it an interesting application to be used at tourist spots. As balloons are cute, we aim to give users a more enjoyable, delightful experience.

Keywords: life logging, third-person view, balloon, sightseeing.

1 Introduction

People goes through many daily experiences which invokes numerous emotions – from happy, sad, angry etc. One way to express themselves is through logging their daily events; either through a blog, diary or other archives. As technology advances, there exist many networking services that help people connect with each other through these loggings such as Twitter and Facebook.

Sumi et al. mentioned that one of the meanings to recording experience is to share the records of memories [7]. Yamashita et al. mentioned that the popularization of the web log or web diary is to allow one to learn more and to understand oneself -- to express their satisfaction or emotion. They analyzed that feedbacks from the readers can result in satisfaction psychologically [10]. In recent times, contents through SNS such as daily recordings or pictures have been developing at great speed as it holds great values and high demands from the society. Especially interesting contents or experiences such as travelling, visits to the museum, or even outing at an amusement park. Through these activities, we can observe new sceneries and meet new people

D. Reidsma, H. Katayose, and A. Nijholt (Eds.): ACE 2013, LNCS 8253, pp. 428–439, 2013.

from different places. From these experiences, we build up new emotions, reactions and expressions. When we look back at those times, we can recall the feelings we felt.

In this project, we call these experiences as a "Journey". Normally, when one look back at their albums, most pictures found have similar sceneries, poses or facial expressions. Many of these pictures do not reflect the interaction that took place at that time. Therefore, we propose PukaPuCam, a camera to capture pictures of different moments, from different angle and direction, to give the user a better recap of those moments when they view the pictures. This camera would capture the user's pictures from a third-person view without the user being conscious about them. As the camera is placed on a balloon, it enhances an exciting journey experience (Fig.1).

Fig. 1. PukaPuCam is a service to capture users' photo continuously from a third-person view

2   Related Work

There are several attempts to record user's activity from a third-person view. Flying Eyes is a system that utilizes AR.Drone to follow and record user's activity by recognizing their cloth's color [2]. However, as the system requires lots of power to keep flying, it faces challenges to follow the user for a long period. Hasegawa et al. developed a system whereby a camera is mounted at the end of a pole that is attached to skydiver's waist, to capture the user and project it real-time in a HMD [1]. This way skydiver can see and adjust his body movement accordingly. Pfeil et al. created ball camera, a throw-able sphere device embedded with 36 small cameras to shoot from a panorama view when the user throws the ball [5]. Sugimoto et al. designed Time Follower's Vision, a robot control interface based on third-person view which combines past images taken by a camera mounted on a robot with CG [6]. Dog-Leash Interface is a robot that follows its user to capture the user's image. Similar to walking a dog, user will pull its string to control its route [11].

NHK Balloon Camera is an anchored floating body system with a camera mounted on a balloon ship to take pictures from a birds-eye view without the need of a crane [4]. Our approach differs from these researches, as our system is not proposed to act together with users in their everyday environment. Floating Eye is known as a media art, equipped with a spherical dome screen to project images in the sky, taken from a camera attached to an airship in real-time [3]. Although these systems are similar to our study, our aim is to give user a new travel logging experience. Therefore, our system differs in terms of user experience awareness.

In terms of life logging, Vicon Revue is a wearable camera system equipped with different sensors (temperature, luminance, accelerator etc.), which automatically captures the user's pictures [9]. This system is suspended on the neck and captures from a first-person view at every 30 seconds intervals or from the influences of the surroundings it detects.

While most experience recording system's approach is to take videos and images from a first-person view, Sumi et al. proposed a combination of wearable sensors and environmental sensors to provide multiple camera view system: first-person view (mounted on the user), second-person view (mounted on the person the user is interacting with) and third-person view (placed in the surrounding environment) [8]. They observed that pictures from first-person view lack many things for users to learn more about their behavior and expression. Second and third-person view are equally important to remind users of their feelings and actions at a particular situation.

However, most of the proposed system faces challenges to be used frequently when user goes for a walk. Or it may be hard to blend in with the surroundings. Among the researches in life logging, many can be mounted on the neck or blend into daily wearable. However, most of these systems captures from a first-person view and thus, one's own figure is hardly reflected in the shots. Our thought of an ideal life logging system is where users are projected in the pictures while is unconscious about being photographed. This way, the records reveal the user's natural expression. To achieve this, we propose the design of a camera system that captures in a third-person view and can blend easily into the surroundings.

3   Concept

3.1   PukaPuCam's Concept

This project aims to create a "Camera that continuously records your journey". PukaPuCam is a design service to create a personal photographer that will capture the users' journey experience and fun interactions between the users and their best friends. Here, we emphasize on three main design guidelines.

(1)   Users can take pictures that differs from the common first-person view camera – pictures from a bird's-eye view
(2)   Users can easily look back at their journey and explain to others.
(3)   Users can enjoy a fun journey experience.

From these aim, we aim to accomplish (1) with a system utilizing a camera attached to balloons, (2) with a viewer where users can glance through back at their recorded pictures to recall their surrounding environment as well as the route they have taken and lastly (3), by using balloon to increase the fun experience.

3.2   Balloon

Our proposal of using a balloon to generate a third-person view is mainly because

- Balloon does not produce any sound and it is non-disturbing to the surroundings.
- Balloon can easily blend in the surroundings, preventing user to feel out of place.
- Majority has held a balloon during their childhood period. Therefore, its usage allows easy prediction of behavior.

PukaPuCam will fit into places where balloons are commonly used such as theme park or tourist attractions. One advantage is that a balloon has high resistance against air resistance as it is filled with helium gases. This is beneficial to record the surrounding environment and the users' behavior at that moment, such as their interest or interactions. In addition, it can also capture the surrounding conditions, such as the wind's direction or weather. Besides that, people have different curiosity, actions or expression which many would not take notice of normally. These unusual moments would too be a great part of the users' collection.

An example of an interaction with the PukaPuCam system is shown in Fig. 2 whereby when the user stops, the balloon will be on top of the user (Fig.2 left), or when the user moves, the balloon incline backwards and record sceneries from the user's back (Fig.2 right). The angle will change according to the user's walking speed. In order for the balloon to automatically record form a third-person view at any place, there are 2 design points needed to be taken into account: the mooring method for the camera to capture the user's field of view continuously and the length of the string.

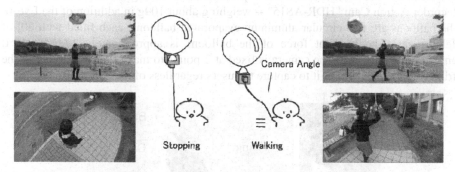

Fig. 2. The camera angle will change depending on the user's walking speed

4   Implementation of PukaPuCam

Fig. 3 shows the configuration of PukaPuCam system. This system is composed of "PukaPuCam" (the balloon and a camera) and "PukaPuCam Viewer" (iPad application). By attaching a SD memory card "Eye-fi", the picture data will be transferred to the iPad whenever the camera captures a picture. These data will then be arranged on "PukaPuCam Viewer" in combination with the GPS information.

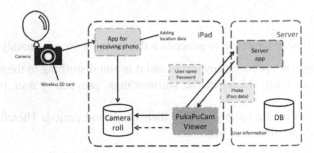

Fig. 3. System configuration of PukaPuCam

4.1   Design and Implementation for Spontaneously Shooting

Balloon is highly influenced by air resistance. Due to this, the balloon may waver and cause blurriness effects to the shootings. If the recordings are in video form, the user may feel sick when they glance back at the records. In addition, many may skip forward bits and parts of the video. Therefore, we decided to test with short interval shootings while placing importance on the journey's time. To find an optimum timing for each shot so that user can feel the journey's flow when they look at the records, we decided to experiment with 5 seconds intervals. For example, if users look at 4 continuous pictures taken at a similar scene, it reflects that they were there for 20 seconds or so.

We want to implement a camera that captures at a wide angle and is less affected by vibration. Our selection for the experimentation is Digital HD Video Camera Recorder Action Cam "HDR-AS15" -- weighing about 109g in addition of the Eye-fi. The balloons are two circular aluminum evaporated balloons, each filled with 80l of Helium gas. The buoyant force of the balloons is approximately 172g at 10°C temperature and 1 atm. The camera is fixed at 2 points to make its lens parallel to the string (Fig.4). This allows it to capture the users regardless of the balloon's position.

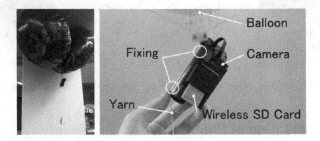

Fig. 4. Overview of balloon system (left), detail of camera (right)

4.2   Design and Implementation of the String's Length

The string's length places much importance in the system as it determines the angle of the camera's view. To find the optimum length, we did an experimentation with 3 volunteers in their 20's. During this experiment, the angle was fixed at 120°. Here, the users will adjust the string's length accordingly and from these records, we will decide the maximum length by calculation.

Then, from the results, we developed a hand-held device whereby user can adjust the string's length up till 210 [cm] (between the camera and the spool). If the thread is extended to its limit, and the height of the hand from the ground is 1[m], it is possible to shoot approximately 532 [cm] (310 [cm] × √3 = 532 [cm]) radius around the users, assuming that the balloon and the camera are right above the users.

4.3   PukaPuCam Viewer

PukaPuCam Viewer is an iPad application, consisting of 2 main pages: My Page and pictures inspection. When users log in, My Page screen will appear and there will be folders indicating the place and time of the journey. The main screen of the viewer is illustrated in Fig. 5. It consists of 3 elements: a scroll view, map and main view. In the map view, the route the users took will be shown, whereby each picture is placed at the location it was taken. Therefore, by touching and tracing the route, user can see the pictures like a flipbook. Thumbnail images are arranged on top in a scroll view and users can zoom in the picture when they tap it.

Fig. 5. PukaPuCam Viewer: Scroll View (above), Map View (left), Enlarge View (right)

5   User Experience

We conducted a user study, to observe how PukaPuCam can enhance the user's journey experience. In this study, participant will use PukaPuCam and the viewer during their journey. We will observe their interaction and receive their feedback of the system.

5.1   Participants

H: Female in her 20s. She loves travelling around by train.
B: Female in her 20s. She hardly takes a walk but she loves places with lots of nature.
M: Male in his 20s, H's best friend. He learns about the journey from H's user study.

5.2   User Study Contents

On 12th December 2012 (sunny), H visited the Yume Migasaki Zoo. During her visit, she used both PukaPuCam and her own digital camera to take pictures (Fig. 6). After walking for 10 minutes, she met up with B and they walk together. We observed the whole situation. Four days later, H explained her journey using pictures from both her own digital camera and the viewer app "PukaPuCam Viewer". We observed the situation again and lastly we interviewed her for her feedback.

Fig. 6. Scenes of user experience recorded by PukaPuCam

5.3   Result of Interview

We interviewed the participants about their experience of using PukaPuCam, focusing on both the usage of PukaPuCam and PukaPuCam Viewer, which will be discussed in section 6.

6   Discussion

PukaPuCam is a service proposal, to give users a new journey experience never experienced before. Here, we will discuss the results from the user study dividing then into 3 main points.

(1) Users can take pictures which differs from the common first-person view camera – pictures from a bird's-eye view.
Air resistance and wind

As balloon receives air resistance, it changes direction depending on the wind and the user's walking speed. However, thanks to this, when the balloon moves to the front, H was able to get a shot of a pose with her friend as shown in (Fig. 7). H was really fond of this picture when she looked through the viewer. H also mentioned that the balloon was really easy to use. Even situations where the wind was strong, she can intuitively aim to record different scenes.

Fig. 7. Photo taken by PukaPuCam when participants were posing

Due to the wind, some of the pictures taken were blurred. However, this blurriness gave a touch of difference to the pictures such as in Fig. 8 where both users introduced the picture to M as "interesting pictures". They mentioned happily, *"It doesn't feel look like a picture taken when it is windy right?"*

Fig. 8. Blurred picture

Natural Expression

As PukaPuCam captures from a third-person view, it can capture pictures of oneself naturally – to capture the expressions of the users, giving great pictures where the users can learn more about themselves. For example, *"the type of expressions the user usually have"* or *"how the user smiles in daily conversations"* etc. From this, users can learn the type of atmosphere that can lift up their own happiness.

When H met up with B, many of the pictures captured reveals their smile and happy faces. H mentioned, *"I am really glad to be able to capture my natural smile, as I am quite camera shy and I hardly smile in most pictures."* She also added, *"If the picture was taken from my own camera, most of the time I will not be part of the picture. However, when taken from a third-person view, both our pictures and the surroundings are taken as well. We can really feel the atmosphere of the journey."*

Besides, some of the other interesting pictures which were captured unexpectedly by the camera are such as, user looking up at the balloon when the wind blows slightly, or when there was a strong wind, user was pulling and looking at the direction of the balloon. Therefore, PukaPuCam allows capturing these interesting expressions caused by the balloon.

Interest

PukaPuCam can capture scenes which the users themselves hardly notice, such as what type of objects which the user are interested in or when user sees object which do not catch their interest, they would just walk by them quickly. Some examples are B's figure who was engross in taking pictures or H's figures peeping at the animals.

Cute

This is attracts a lot of attention from females and children as by using balloons, PukaPuCam can capture pictures which can increase the cuteness values. Balloon can capture pictures such as H's face looking up (Fig. 9) or H posing with her friend B (Fig.7). The two participants really like these two pictures. Other than that, as the camera follows and captures a lot of picture from the back of the participant, it was able to capture the "cute unprepared moments". Fig. 10 shows the picture taken from the front by the user's camera where the user posed for it together with a picture of back captured by PukaPuCam.

Fig. 9. User looking up at the balloon

Fig. 10. Photo by the user's camera (Left), Photo by PukaPuCam at same place (Right)

(2) Users can easily look back at their journey and explain to others.
Video sequence

The pictures captured by the camera shows the subtleties of emotion, movement and behavior of the users with the surrounding. While browsing through the viewer, M said, *"As PukaPuCam captures the pictures at short intervals, we can feel the flow of the journey recorded."* He added that, *"I can really understand their interaction and relationship such as how did they feel when they were walking or what interests them the most."* H commented, *"It was really fun to look at pictures taken at different moments as there are many interesting things I had missed or had never known."*

Participants reviewed that the Viewer was really smooth and interesting to use. They also commented that this system really guides them to explain their journey to people. Therefore, from our observation, having interval shot recorded from a third-person view supports the story telling of the users' behavior in their journey.

Indexing the Location

The MapView on the PukaPuCam Viewer record the location and each picture taken will be added to the photographing point using GPS information. By having an index of the location, it can easily help recollect one's memories. We questioned H on her opinion on whether is it a useful guide for explanation. H replied, *"It was a great assistance. The viewer shows the whole map of Japan and when you click on the zoo's location, it will zoom in and show the route that you have taken in your journey."*

Feedback due to Limited Field Vision

However, there were feedbacks that participants had challenges in explanation due to limited field of vision captured. At places where people tend to stop often, the balloon captures pictures from right above the head. These pictures do not reflect the reason the user stopped as the scene is outside the camera's field of view. Although, it advantages over first-person view pictures, as the recordings were interesting and users are always reflected in the pictures. Therefore, a combination of both will be a great complementary to the journey's story telling. For example, (Fig. 11 left) shows the user pointing her finger, taken at a third-person view and (Fig. 11 right) which is taken a while later by the user. From the combination of both pictures, we can tell that the user is really interested in flamingo and was telling her friend about it.

Fig. 11. Photo by PukaPuCam lleft), Photo by user's camera at the same place (right)

(3) Users can enjoy an exciting journey experience

Reaction from Children and Animals

Among the pictures taken by PukaPuCam, many reveal that children were gazing at the balloon from afar. Fig 12 (left) shows a picture of a child following behind. Animals too, gain interest in the balloon. For example, a deer was staring and moving its eyes according to the balloon's movement and a lesser panda was climbing to the edge of the cage while staring at the balloon (Fig.12 right). Therefore, thanks to the balloons, we are able to capture these kind of interesting animal reactions.

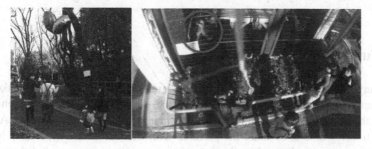

Fig. 12. Reactions from children and animals

Heart-shape balloon

We also observed that when the participants noticed that the shadow of the balloon was a heart shape, they jumped with excitement and took a picture together with their shadow (Fig.13). This lifted up the atmosphere of the journey.

Fig. 13. Balloon makes a heart-shaped shadow

Usability

H gave some feedbacks regarding the length of the string whereby she mentioned, *"As there is wind and lots of trees at the surroundings, it was hard to handle the string as it may get entangled between the trees. However, it was easy to get used to it after a while."* We questioned H and M that from their short experience, would they be interested to use PukaPuCam service in the future or would they recommend the service to others. Both excitedly replied *"Yes, we would love to."* *"Especially, if we go to theme parks such as Disney Land, it would be really cool to take recordings of when we meet and shake hands with the characters. We would like many people to use it as well."*

Summary

To summarize the above, participants were really happy with the pictures and when others look at the pictures, they get to learn about their journey, their expression, the surroundings etc. without asking the participants beforehand. From our user study, walking with a balloon can produces a fun experience for users as they can have new interaction with children and animals. Therefore, by using PukaPuCam, it is possible to record a new journey experience that differs from recordings from a first-person view.

7   Future Work

First, many pictures do not reflect the surrounding environment as it was taken from straight up or when the users walked by too fast. Therefore, the combination of both first and third-person view images will be a great tool for journey logging. A second possible future works is to share the pictures with friends. This way, it may lead to a new perspective or findings. Finally, one of the participant commented that it would be a great motivation for travelling if users can save and store the picture on a national map, rather than just the route they have taken.

8   Conclusion

In this project, we propose a balloon camera system PukaPuCam to give users a new journey experience that differs from the ordinary way of travelling. As a result of our user study from both interview and observation, PukaPuCam has exceeded our expectation. Participants had a fun journey and PukaPuCam was very useful for participants to glance back through their journey. Furthermore, this system can record the atmosphere and can bring out the "cuteness" of the users.

Acknowledgment. This work was supported by the Strategic Information and Communication R&D Promotion Programme (SCOPE) of the Ministry of Internal Affairs and Communications, Japan.

References

1. Augmented Ski, http://haselab.net/~hase/ski/ski.php
2. Higuchi, K., Ishiguro, Y., Rekimoto, J.: Flying eyes: free-space content creation using autonomous aerial vehicles. In: Proc. CHI EA 2011, pp. 561–570. ACM (2011)
3. Iwata, H.: Floating Eye, ARS ELECTRONICA (2001),
   http://90.146.8.18/en/archives/prix_archive/
   prix_projekt.asp?iProjectID=11055
4. NHK Balloon Camera Shoots Stable Aerial Footage,
   http://www.diginfo.tv/v/12-0020-r-en.php
5. Pfeil, J., Hildebrand, K., Gremzow, C., Bickel, B., Alexa, M.: Throwable panoramic ball camera. In: Proc. SIGGRAPH Asia 2011 Emerging Technologies, Article 4, 1 page. ACM (2011)
6. Sugimoto, M., Kagotani, G., Nii, H., Shiroma, N., Inami, M., Matsuno, F.: Time follower's vision. In: Elliott-Famularo, H. (ed.) ACM SIGGRAPH 2004 Emerging Technologies, p. 29. ACM, New York (2004)
7. Sumi, Y.: Tatsuyuki Kawamura. Towards Experience Medium: Technical Survey for Record and Utilization of Experiences. In: The 20th Annual Conference of the Japanese Society for Artificial Intelligence (2006) (in Japanese)
8. Sumi, Y., Ito, S., Matsuguchi, T., Fels, S., Mase, K.: Collaborative capturing and interpretation of interactions. In: Pervasive 2004 Workshop on Memory and Sharing of Experiences, pp. 1–7 (April 2004)
9. Vicon Revue, http://viconrevue.com
10. Yamashita, K., Kawaura, Y., Kakami, Y., Asako Miura, A.: The psychology of the weblog. In: NTT Shuppan (2005)
11. Young, J.E., Kamiyama, Y., Reichenbach, J., Igarashi, T., Sharlin, E.: How to Walk a Robot: A Dog-Leash Human-Robot Interface. In: Proc. Ro-Man 2011, pp. 376–382 (2011)

Advances in MASELTOV –
Serious Games in a Mobile Ecology of Services for Social Inclusion and Empowerment of Recent Immigrants

Lucas Paletta[1], Ian Dunwell[2], Mark Gaved[3], Jan Bobeth[4],
Sofoklis Efremidis[5], Patrick Luley[1], Agnes Kukulska-Hulme[3],
Sara de Freitas[2], Petros Lameras[2], and Stephanie Deutsch[4]

[1] JOANNEUM RESEARCH Forschungsgesellschaft mbH, Institute DIGITAL
Graz, Austria
lucas.paletta@joanneum.at
[2] Coventry University, Serious Games Institute,
Coventry, United Kingdom
idunwell@cad.coventry.ac.uk
[3] The Open University, Institute of Educational Technology
Milton Keynes, United Kingdom
mark.gaved@open.ac.uk
[4] CURE – Centre for Usability Research and Engineering
Vienna, Austria
bobeth@cure.at
[5] Athens Institute of Technology
Athens, Greece
ser@ait.gr

Abstract. Immigration imposes a range of challenges with the risk of social exclusion. As part of a comprehensive suite of services for immigrants, the MASELTOV game seeks to provide both practical tools and innovative learning services via mobile devices, providing a readily usable resource for recent immigrants. We introduce advanced results, such as the game-based learning aspect in the frame of recommender services, and present the rationale behind its interaction design. Benefits and implications of mobile platforms and emergent data capture techniques for game-based learning are discussed, as are methods for putting engaging gameplay at the forefront of the experience whilst relying on rich data capture and analysis to provide effective learning solutions.

Keywords: Mobile serious game, social inclusion, incidental learning framework, recommender system, human factors.

1 Introduction

Immigration imposes a range of challenges, including successful communication with members of the local society and understanding the culture of the host nation. Failure to overcome these challenges can lead to social exclusion from the information society

D. Reidsma, H. Katayose, and A. Nijholt (Eds.): ACE 2013, LNCS 8253, pp. 440–455, 2013.
© Springer International Publishing Switzerland 2013

(Halfman 1998) and difficulties of integration leading to fragmented communities and a range of social issues. With a comprehensive suite of services for immigrants, the European project MASELTOV[1] (Mobile Assistance for Social Inclusion and Empowerment of Immigrants with Persuasive Learning Technologies and Social Network Services) seeks to provide both practical tools and innovative learning services via mobile devices, providing a readily usable resource for recent immigrants. The services will support the development of communication skills, situated incidental learning of the target language and culture, and finally foster employability. The prototypical service implicitly has the potential to scale up to a very large number of end users, complementing popular online social networks for language learning.

Game-based components of education have been widely used in pedagogical approaches such as those of Vygotsky (1970) as a means for allowing learners to develop their understanding through abstraction; however, the emergence of digital technologies has played a key role in defining the notion of "serious" games, a term which broadly recognizes the use of digital technologies and parallels to digital gaming for entertainment purposes as having educational potential when aligned with a set of pedagogical goals. Context is of central relevance when seeking to deploy game-based learning (Muratet et al., 2012), as it can drive decisions regarding how much intrinsic motivation can be expected on the part of the learner, and in turn how much the game must foster the desire amongst learners to engage with the game as a recreational activity rather than a formal educational pursuit.

Fig. 1. Using the MASELTOV app (MAPP) for mixed reality gaming in the streets

---

[1] http://www.maseltov.eu

In the particular case of cultural learning amongst immigrants, MASELTOV addresses the specific challenge of providing mobile services to immigrants via a suite of Android applications. By providing immediate support in addressing day-to-day challenges, whilst simultaneously allowing immigrants to learn key skills, these immediate supports become less required over time: they provide "scaffolding" to learning that can fade into the background when no longer required. The role of game-based learning in such a context must be carefully considered; the suite of MASELTOV services will provide on-demand educational content, and therefore caution must be taken to prevent game-based learning services simply presenting a more obtuse representation of this educational content. The MASELTOV game may also go beyond its target audience of immigrants, involving and raising awareness amongst the general population through the provision of an entertaining game. Finally, we provide more background into the target audience, and existing games targeted at raising cultural awareness or conveying cultural learning content.

In the case of game-based learning within MASELTOV, it is suggested that a game may provide a resource which allows users to identify through analogy areas in which cultural differences are most prominent, the form these differences might take, and strategies to address them. A game-based resource might also have appeal to audiences with little willingness to engage with more formal educational content, such as structured language lessons. This synergizes with the gamified, social approach to language learning presented by other services within MASELTOV such as those provided by social network based language learning communities, though also presents challenges in developing a game design suitable for this usage context and target audience. In Section 3, these challenges and the design approaches taken to address them are outlined. Sections 4 and 5 then present an early prototype design of the MASELTOV game, and discuss how it aims to synergize with the other MASELTOV services whilst providing a playful environment for cultural learning.

We introduce recent results, based on the initial game-based learning concept of the MASELTOV project presented in Dunwell et al. (2013).The benefits and implications of mobile platforms and emergent data capture techniques for game-based learning are discussed, as are methods for putting engaging gameplay at the forefront of the experience whilst relying on rich data capture and analysis to provide an effective learning solution. We specifically introduce a recommender system that proposes activities and content in the context of an ever progressing learning journey. Language lessons, communication in social fora as well as interaction with local citizens are activities recommended by the system, and, if successfully mastered, at the same time may foster progress in the serious game.

2   MASELTOV – A Suite of Playful Services

The European MASELTOV project recognizes the major risks for social exclusion of immigrants from the local information society and identifies the considerable potential of mobile services for promoting integration and cultural diversity:

Everywhere/anytime (pervasive) assistance is crucial for more efficient and sustainable support of immigrants. Language understanding, local community building, as well as awareness and knowledge for bridging of cultural differences will be fostered via the development of innovative social computing services that motivate and support informal learning for the appropriation of highly relevant daily skills.

A mobile service based assistant embeds these novel information and learning services such as ubiquitous language translation, navigation, administrative and emergency health services that address activities towards the social inclusion of immigrants in a pervasive and playful manner. MASELTOV is developing a mixed reality game in which the user applies her language skills in various situations, such as in dialogues during shopping, or for navigation in the urban environment (cf. Figure 1). The mobile service supports her in the situation as well as receives feedback from the user in order to measure or estimate performance.

The ecology of mobile services of MASELTOV includes:

Peer reviewed language learning: language exercises focusing around everyday tasks. The service is offering learning materials set at the Common European Framework of Reference for Languages (CEFR) A1 and A2 standard, but also some more elementary material to help very recent immigrants with their immediate needs. When an exercise is completed, it will be assessed by a peer learner. Further discussion will be possible via linked social forums. Progress will be recorded by a user profile system.

Mobile navigation tool: to help with directions, indicating local places of interest and services. The navigation tool will support pedestrian as well as public transport travel giving orientation information, distance to location and best route. Information about important services in the nearby environment will be shown (e.g. doctors, libraries, public transport stops). If selected by the learner, proximity to particular locations or types of buildings may trigger learning exercises or in-context language support.

Profile system: the user's details and learning progress will be recorded to enable personalized learning. The MASELTOV system will recommend particular types of content or learning exercises to support each learner's particular needs. Learners will be able to personalize their learning journey, indicating what is important to them.

Geo-social radar: A volunteer helper service allowing users to find nearby volunteers who can help them with a problem, for example acting as a translator at a doctor's appointment, or negotiating local bureaucracy.

TextLens: allows a learner to take a photo of a sign, and have this converted to text. This can then be coupled with a language translation tool such as Google Translate. Images and text can be uploaded for help when the meaning is ambiguous, and if the learner wishes to discuss their social, cultural or legal implications.

3   User Centred Design

When adopting user-centered design (UCD), the involvement of target users in the design and development process of a new service is crucial for its success (Vredenburg et al. 2001). Based on frequent user feedback addressing ideas, scenarios and prototypes the service concept is iterated and refined in order to match and satisfy users´ needs. However, former research has shown that cultural differences (e.g. perceptual and cognitive processing) matter in interface design and affect the quality of user generated feedback within a UCD process (Callahan 2005). A precondition to any user involving activity is to know who the users of the service will be. MASELTOV and the serious game aim at supporting immigrants to approach sociocultural conditions of the host country and successfully integrate themselves (and their relatives) into the foreign societal system.

Immigrants moving to countries within the European Union come from all over the world and form a very heterogeneous group (Eurostat 2013). Due to great variety of user characteristics depending on maternal language, cultural background, motivation, education, profession, religion and duration of stay, immigrants´ needs (such as individual, social as well as security related) differ widely. Hence, approaching all immigrants in Europe at once seems to be unreasonable, especially when supporting social integration. Keeping the cultural diversity in mind, we explicitly target three large immigrant groups within the European Union (Eurostat 2013): Arabic-speaking immigrants from North Africa, Turkish-speaking Turks and Spanish-speaking Latin Americans. These groups are meant to have a perceptibly different cultural background than Western cultures, especially in the cultural dimensions of power-distance and collectivism/ individualism (Hofstede 2001) which should be addressed within the serious game.

Working with immigrant users requires the consideration of some special challenges for the process of UCD: (i) in general the impact of the cultural orientation of the immigrants toward the home and the host country on the design process is unclear, (ii) designers might not be familiar with relevant particularities within the cultural orientation of the home country (e.g. basic values, attitudes), (iii) recruitment processes for the successful acquisition of participating volunteers from a vulnerable user group according to pre-defined criteria are complex and laborious (Aykin et al. 2006), and (iv) mistrust towards involved experts from design and research might lead to a lack of frankness on the part of the immigrants (Hynes 2003). These issues and challenges emphasize the importance of user involvement as otherwise no accurate predictions can be made whether immigrants of the defined target group would be able and willing to use the developed services. To reduce the mentioned issues we created a framework for the requirements analysis of the UCD process (Bobeth et al. 2013) and collaborated with three nongovernmental organizations (NGOs) in Graz (Austria), London (UK) and Madrid (Spain) who provide support services for immigrants and organized the recruitment of the participants for user involving activities in MASELTOV.

3.1   Procedure for Requirements Analysis

To gain deeper insights into barriers and problems in everyday life of immigrants, we conducted semi-structured interviews with 20 participants (10 Arab, 3 Ecuadorian and 7 Turkish immigrants). Based on the interview data and previously elaborated concepts the MASELTOV service scenarios were formulated. Aiming to earn valuable feedback and to create additional input, we discussed the service scenarios within focus groups with overall 37 immigrants at the NGOs. In contrast to the interviews, we invited more accommodated immigrants who had lived in the host country for more than three years. The goal of the focus groups was to discuss the service concepts and further ideas by benefiting from participants´ experience and retro perspective reflection. Participating immigrants appreciated the idea of having a serious game to become aware of cultural differences in the host countries. They found playful explanations motivating and believed that the acquired knowledge could help them to feel more comfortable in everyday life.

3.2   Usability Studies for Feedback on Design

Based on the results of the requirements analysis user interfaces for the MASELTOV services including the serious game were designed following an iterative process. At first, elementary user interface concepts were elaborated and discussed with usability experts. The updated mock-ups were evaluated by immigrants within a usability evaluation study, whose purpose was to identify usability issues of the current user interfaces and to gather suggestions for improvement. By performing a set of tasks and interacting with the gaming application on one and the same mobile device the participants were encouraged to talk to each other about the system's behavior (Wildmann 1996). The results of the evaluation showed that the idea of the game was in general assessed very positively as the participants welcomed the playful approach to learn about cultural differences. User feedback and elaborated design suggestions served as input for the next design iteration when the concepts were refined and finalized.

4   Incidental Learning and Progress Indicators

4.1   Incidental Learning

Incidental learning has been defined as "unintentional or unplanned learning that results from other activities", and it is an emerging paradigm in mobile language learning (Song & Fox, 2008). Incidental learning occurs during everyday activities, and while it may be triggered by events or incidents and solve an immediate problem (Silva, 2007), it can also happen in more reflective moments, such as while engaging in leisure activities like game playing, or in the course of observation, conversation or social interaction (Le Clus, 2011). Incidental learning is often triggered by context, and is therefore a particularly suitable mode of learning for mediation via mobile devices such as smart phones that are ubiquitous in daily lives and enhanced by sensors that can make sense of the environment and trigger recommendations. For example, in a typical MASELTOV scenario, an inbuilt GPS sensor may register that the user is in the locality of a train station, and may offer to provide a language learning lesson based around travelling. Knowledge gained from incidental learning has been argued to develop self-confidence and increase self-knowledge in learning (Ogata & Yano, 2004) and is hence particularly suitable for recent immigrants who may not have had previous positive experiences with formal education.

Flexibility in educational provision and delivery is crucial to support these learners, who may also struggle to attend regular classroom based learning due to constraints of work and family lives. Mobile ICT based learning may therefore provide a very suitable form of education for immigrants (Kluzer et al. 2011, pp.9-10). Mobile phones are known and trusted by many people, and 'domesticated' into their everyday practices. This integration with everyday life is beneficial for language learning. Second language acquisition is perceived by adult migrants as well as host governments, "as a crucial factor for socio-economic and cultural integration", with language acquisition and social integration closely intertwined (Van Avermaet & Gysen, 2009). For example, knowledge of specific terminology is required to sit a driving licence exam, which then opens up opportunities for employment (Farinati et al., 2012).

However, a challenge with incidental learning is that, since it occurs in everyday life during other activities, it may occur in "fragments" or small learning episodes that are weakly structured and disconnected from each other. It is therefore necessary to understand how such fragmented learning episodes can be reconceived by users as elements of a more coherent, longer term learning journey towards social inclusion. We argue that timely and appropriate feedback and progress indicators may encourage this shift towards a more reflective learning process.

4.2   Feedback and Progress Indicators

We propose that feedback and progress indicators (FPIs) may play an instrumental role in helping learners reflect upon the individual learning episodes and conceive them as constituting elements of a longer learning journey (Gaved et al., 2013). Furthermore, educational research suggests that timely and appropriate feedback and indicators of progress can motivate learners (Nix and Wyllie, 2009). We define 'feedback' as responses to a learner's performance against criteria of quality and as a means of directing and encouraging the learner; and 'progress indicators' as responses indicating the current position of a learner within a larger activity or. Well-presented feedback can help learners to take responsibility for their own learning. In addition, learners' activity using a computer mediated set of learning tools (such as the MASELTOV serious game and other apps) can be captured and held within the system to act as feedback to the software and educational developers, who can act on patterns of use to iteratively improve their services, for example recognizing that learners struggle with particular tasks, either because the user interface requires further design or because the content itself is at an inappropriate level.

FPIs provided to the learners can be instantiated in a range of ways and can be cognitive (such as knowledge achieved, assessment results), affective (praise, emotional reflection) and social (peer ratings of quality of participation, support). FPIs are recognized as an important aspect of learning, and have been well described for both formal and informal learning. We have identified previously (Gaved et al., 2013) that there is a scarcity of FPIs present in incidental learning, notably with respect to goal setting, planning, structured feedback from peers, and reflection on improving performance for specific activities. Encouraging these specific types of feedback and progress indicators may enable the transition from isolated, sporadic learning on a problem by problem basis towards a more reflective learning process and enable the recent immigrant to consider their broader social inclusion goals. However, feedback has to be managed sensitively since the effects of feedback on performance are highly variable: "under some conditions, feedback may improve performance, and under other conditions, feedback may reduce performance (Kluger and DeNisi, 1996)" (in Garris, 2002). Gibbs' model of reflection (see Figure 2) indicates cognitive, affective and social aspects of the process, and we can see that these could form the basis for feedback prompts to the MASELTOV user to encourage them to both look back on what they have done, as well as forward to plan what they might do next.

Summaries of a MASELTOV learner's progress and feedback to and from the learner will be stored and displayed in a personal space to enable the learner to reflect and monitor their own progress. Many services offer a "progress dashboard" which shows users a report of their progress across a number of tasks, often as a summary of all their activities. The information in this dashboard is presented as a list, or as a graphical representation; it may be presented in an initial 'home page' for the software or alternatively held on a personal profile page. Such dashboards enable learners to 'own' their user profile and use it as a tool for self-reflection and modifying future goal planning. This approach is being considered for implementation in MASELTOV.

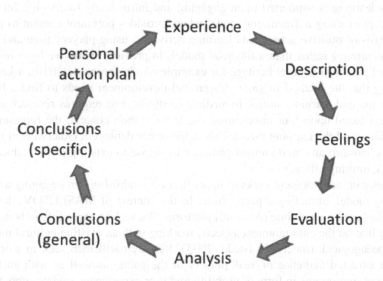

Fig. 2. Gibbs' model of reflection (1988)

5   A Serious Game for Cultural Learning

The first generation of serious games focused more on high priority learning environments such as first response training, levee patrolling and medical simulation (Knight et al., 2010). But more recently, games have been regarded not only as a basis for learning through simulation, but also as a tool for the development of a wider range of skills such as communication, through more diverse and abstract forms of play (Zielke et al., 2009; de Freitas & Routledge, 2013). The main reason that games can be so effective in cognitive-based areas of training arises from the way in which games allow for negotiated meanings to be developed within individuals; as part of group activities, shared realities can be negotiated and derived. This characteristic is mainly affected through game design mechanics that allow for individual tasks and practices to be blended with social elements and services. One way in which games can offer this capability is to have the learner assume the role of an avatar, embodying them within the environment and thus allowing for subjective relations to be associated with the behaviors of their own and other avatars. This individual connection between gameplay and the player or learner then consequently placed at the heart of the relationships set up in such a game, making it an effective tool for both replicating real, and projecting imagined environments. Both support higher cognitive learning and can be a valuable tool in how games as learning tools can be deployed to support formal and informal learning and training.

Serious games have demonstrated capabilities for supporting a diverse range of pedagogical models. The cultural learning space is a complex and intricate environment, which must take into account many different aspects such as language learning skills, interpersonal skills, team skills and problem-solving. Within the MASELTOV project, the design seeks to encompass both the notions of 'playful' cultural learning, whereby learning is supported in an engaging and intrinsically motivating form, and the concept of using a 'freemium' model which provides premium content to players on the basis of positive actions and learning activities, using players' time and activities as a currency rather than a financial model. In previous work, we have reviewed the use of games in cultural heritage for example (Anderson et al., 2010), a key finding being that the method of game design and development needs to find a balance between fun and learning, utilize immediate feedback, and requires research and development based upon four dimensions: the learner, their context, the representation of the game, and the learning theories and approaches deployed. Otherwise, it may be either too close to an entertainment game, or too close to existing formal educational materials, limiting efficacy.

To this end, development seeks to focus first on establishing an engaging and 'fun' gameplay model, attracting a player base. In the context of MASELTOV, the game will be deployed on a mobile (Android) platform. We seek to exploit these benefits by focusing first on the entertainment aspects, working with an existing cultural model to ensure pedagogical aspects (Hofstede, 2005). Research will then seek to work with both the attracted audience of 'real' players of the game, as well as with an invited audience of immigrants in form of usability and user experiences studies supported by non-government organizations who provide support to immigrants on a daily basis.

Working with this target group to evolve the game and ensure pedagogical requirements are met aims to address the careful balance between engagement and education, allowing the various methods of conveying learning content and encouraging behavioral changes to be evaluated, refined, and validated. This will be achieved through both direct metrics obtained from the game engine, for example time spent with certain content elements and the extent to which external resources within the MASELTOV platform are used, as well as through qualitative feedback and surveys.

An image taken from the prototype game is shown in Figure 3. Whilst the environment seeks to immerse the player in a pseudo-realistic context, a game-based narrative and 'dimension flip' mechanic, coupled with playable platform levels, it wraps cultural learning through dialogues with an immersive storyline and platform gameplay which seeks to engage the player and to generate a perceived value for character upgrades and game progression. The game then intends to use this perceived value to explore how the currency for these upgrades might be earned through positive actions using other MASELTOV services: for example rewarding use of the social network, posting on the forums, using information sources, or engaging with mixed-reality challenges using the context awareness services or text lens. The dimension flip also plays a central role in the game, allowing the player to observe two distinct, fictional cultures at opposite poles informed by Hofstede's model of cultural differences, and via scaffolding provided by other learning services within MASELTOV, to learn incidentally how, where, and why differences in cultures can cause issues.

Fig. 3. Image from the MASELTOV game, currently in development for Android

In particular, the MASELTOV project seeks to explore the benefits of integration within the comprehensive suite of its mobile services. By integrating educational content with service provision, the platform seeks to support both tools for immediate assistance, and deeper learning over time to lessen reliance on these tools, and promote integration. There are several roles a game could play which capitalize on the strengths of game-based learning: a game might reach a wider audience than purely pedagogical or service-based content; it may offer a means to provide feedback and rewards to learners and hence stimulate certain actions; and it may allow for a different perspective on cultural learning than that provided by more conventional forms of education such as text-based content. Effective integration, therefore, demands the ability to capitalize on these advantages, whilst similarly leveraging the strengths of the other services to provide a comprehensive and integrated mobile solution.

6   User Profile and Recommender System

The User Profile is a central component of the MASELTOV game platform that maintains information about personal data and user preferences, as well as collected knowledge on user usage behavior, progress and user context recognitions (Dimakis et al., 2010) that enable the personalization of used services, for example triggering of personalized recommendations on MASELTOV functionalities, targeted services and assistance. The feedback and progress indicators that are maintained with the User Profile will facilitate the overall learning journey, allowing the monitoring of the user satisfaction for the offered services and the offering of advanced personalized targeted services.

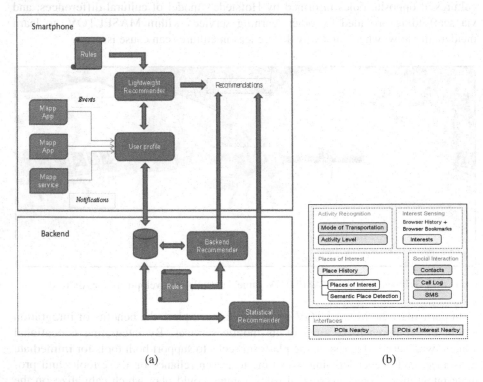

(a)

(b)

Fig. 4. (a) Architecture of the User Profile and the Recommender System. (b) Modes of geo-contextual awareness applied in MASELTOV.

Recommendations can feed into serious game components, such as, recommending to play a specific component of the mobile serious game, e.g., buying a ticket at the virtual bus stop. The objective of the recommender system is to issue useful personalized recommendations to its user based on the events and notifications it receives from other MASELTOV app (MAPP) applications. The information that is carried through the events and notifications allow the recommender system to formulate the required level of context awareness, and, in combination with a set of rules that specify the preconditions under which actions should be taken, allow it to issue targeted recommendations. The functioning of the recommender system depends on (a) events received from MAPP applications, which are application dependent and reflect the current user activity and context, (b) notifications received from MAPP platform services, like the current user location, (c) the information contained in the user profile, like user preferences and progress indicators, and (d) a set of defined rules, which may also be specialized to specific user groups.

The architecture that is presented in Figure 4a shows the two platforms, namely the smartphone and the backend, and the components that run on each of the two. The user profile makes use of a backend database to store user preferences data and information that is communicated to it, like events coming from MAPP applications and notifications coming from MAPP services. The stored information can also be used by more advanced recommender systems, either rule based ones or based on statistical processing of data. The architecture shows a lightweight rule based recommender system that runs on the smartphone and a fully-fledged rule based recommender system that runs on the backend server.

The recommender makes use of a set of rules, which specify actions (recommendations in this case) to be taken when certain conditions are satisfied. A general form of a rule is *Predicate → Action [expiration specification]*. The interpretation of this rule is that when the predicate is satisfied the rule fires and the action is taken. A typical recommendation for language learning, for example, would take status features from a geo-contextual event ('at the bus station') to trigger an appropriate recommendation action 'propose language lesson on vocabulary/expressions used at a bus station'.

7   Context Awareness and Human Factors

7.1   Geo-Contextual Context Sensing and Classification

MASELTOV embeds an easily scalable context recognition framework (Dimakis et al., 2010) that receives contributions from various context feature generating services; it evaluates the user behavior and from this maps to appropriately motivating actions in the form of recommendations. In MASELTOV, user behavior is evaluated in terms of progress indicators in the frame of the various services. An important progress indicator for language learning is the capability in leading a dialogue for a specific purpose, and the capability to memorize vocabulary and apply it at the spot of interest. Activities such as effectively finding the point of interest in the urban environment (job centre, doctor, shop, tourist sight), successful interaction in the geo-social radar, or the visiting of a local event, are further indicators for progress. The context module is implemented as background module on the smartphone and analyses continuously data from build-in sensors, user interactions and entries as well as location based data from online resources to finally generate hypotheses on a user's current situation, their overall daily behaviour and to identify their interests and preferences. Any context information is consequently sent to the local user-profile and will be used to trigger context sensitive recommendations.

The system consists of the following main components, shown in Figure 4b: activity recognition, interest sensing, places of interest, social interaction and an interface for querying nearby points of interest (POIs) and nearby places of interest. *Activity recognition*: The mode of transportation module returns the type of movement of a person. Modes that can be detected are on foot, on bicycle, in a vehicle, still, tilting and unknown, including confidence values for the detected mode. The activity level represents the intensity of the physical activity of a person, measured by the number of times a certain threshold of the accelerometer magnitude has been exceeded within a specific time window. *Places of Interest:* Interests are determined by analyzing the frequency of occurrences of specific terms within the browser bookmarks and browser search history on the mobile phone. The recognition of social interaction is realized by detecting the amount and duration of communications on the phone. Statistics about the call behavior, SMS messages and contacts are collected. *Interfaces*: An interface method for querying nearby POIs is provided by the context module. Places with a longer staying time are compared to the POI database and added to a place history. *Interest sensing:* If a place is regularly visited it will be assumed that the place is of interest to the person. Frequently visited places are added to the place history with the number of visits updated. With the help of the semantic place detection module, categories of places can be detected, such as, being "at home" and "at work". An interface for querying places of interest nearby is provided. Categories of nearby places are compared to the interests collected in the user profile and can be filtered accordingly.

7.2   Mobile Human Factors Sensing and Classification

In addition, in MASELTOV we consider long-term communication assessments with multimodal mobile context awareness on the basis of affect and attention sensitive services in order to classify the language learning behavior of the recent immigrant. The recommender system then instantiates – according to the individual human factors profile and the measured performance – personalized motivating games, in order to change the behavior of the user. For example, to reinforce the training on interaction with local citizens, the rewarding of dialogue supporting activities will be increased, such as, by doubling virtual credits in return for dialogue specific language learning and measured communication in shopping scenarios. The success of an applied dialogue in terms of the emotion and frustration of the user is sensed with the smartphone in situ, using recent computational audio-based affective computing. Advanced human factors studies with wearable interfaces are further applied to extract the decisive parameters of affective and attention oriented content in audio. Next, wearable eye-tracking glasses data are interpreted with semantic 3D mapping of attention (Paletta et al., 2013), bio-signal sensing, and classification to automatically extract from a huge data analysis the decisive parameters for behavior analysis (Schuller et al., 2013), such as the evaluation of dialogues. An important aspect in short dialogues is attention as manifested by eye-contact between subjects. In a first study we provided quantitative evidence that visual attention is evident in the acoustic properties of a speaker's voice (Figure 5), and extracting a significant relation between the acoustic features and the distance between the point of view and the eye region of the dialogue partner. Mobile service components detecting eye contact, the speaker's capability in controlling the host language, and the user's satisfaction will become available to evaluate the progress of applying language knowledge in-situ.

(a)   (b)

Fig. 5. Progress indicator underlying the mobile game based language learning. Dialogues are evaluated using voice analysis and its relation to eye contact.

8   Conclusion and Outlook

The approach taken to game-based learning development in MASELTOV intends to capitalize on both the strengths of the mobile platform, in terms of the ability to capture data on users and adapt the game accordingly. In this paper, we have suggested that such an approach could benefit from focusing first on entertainment and engagement aspects, and then work with the resultant user base to implement and assess pedagogical goals. Validating this approach will be a central goal of future work, as will comparing the efficacy of the resultant solution to approaches which place pedagogical design at the forefront. Such an approach can be particularly challenging to communicate to stakeholders with expectations of a game which "appears" immediately educational at the earliest stage, such as a simulation-driven approach. However, for the reasons outlined in Section 3 it is difficult to define how a ubiquitous simulation-driven solution might be achieved. The more abstract approach proposed by this paper reflects on the context of mobile gaming for cultural learning alongside, and blended with, a wide range of other educational and practical tools for immigrants. Achieving this integration effectively requires reflection on the limitations of game-based learning as well as its strengths: in contexts where information is needed urgently, a game is likely to prove a cumbersome means of transferring this information. However, in contexts in which mobile games are commonly played, for example during travel, a chance to reflect upon cultural differences in a gamified form, with immediate access to educational resources if requested, may prove an effective combination.

Defining the means by which efficacy can be established and measured is another central topic of research. The nature of learning, which includes a temporal component as well as multiple levels of comprehension, can only be assessed to a limited degree by existing instruments such as surveys. In this project, it has also been posited that game-based learning deployed on a mobile platform represents an ideal opportunity to move the evaluation process away from smaller-scale trials, and towards a larger community of active players. Provided ethical requirements can be met, interesting future potential exists in understanding the rich volume of data these communities might generate in their online interactions, both in-game and in the wider context of the MASELTOV services and social network.

Acknowledgments. The research leading to these results has received funding from the European Community's Seventh Framework Programme (FP7/2007-2013) under grant agreement n° 288587 MASELTOV, and by the FFG - Austrian Research Promotion Agency, contract n°832045, Research Studio Austria FACTS.

References

1. Aykin, N., Honold Quaet-Faslem, P., Milewski, A.E.: Cultural Ergonomics. In: Salvendy, G. (ed.) Handbook of Human Factors and Ergonomics, pp. 1418–1458 (2006)
2. Bobeth, J., Schreitter, S., Schmehl, S., Deutsch, S., Tscheligi, M.: User-Centered Design between Cultures: Designing for and with Immigrants. In: Kotzé, P., Marsden, G., Lindgaard, G., Wesson, J., Winckler, M. (eds.) INTERACT 2013, Part IV. LNCS, vol. 8120, pp. 713–720. Springer, Heidelberg (2013)
3. Callahan, E.: Interface design and culture. Annual Review of Information Science and Technology 39(1), 255–310 (2006)
4. de Freitas, S., Routledge, H.: Designing leadership and soft skills in educational games: The e-leadership and soft skills educational games design model (ELESS). British Journal of Educational Technology (2013)
5. Dimakis, N., Soldatos, J., Polymenakos, L., Bürkle, A., Pfirrmann, U., Sutschet, G.: Agent-based architectural framework enhancing configurability, autonomy and scalability of context-aware pervasive services. Autonomous Agents and Multi-Agent Systems 21(1), 36–68 (2010)
6. Dunwell, I., Lameras, P., Stewart, C., Petridis, P., Arnab, S., Hendrix, M., de Freitas, S., Gaved, M., Schuller, B., Paletta, L.: Developing a Digital Game to Support Cultural Learning amongst Immigrants. In: Proc. IDGEI 2013, SASDG (2013)
7. Eurostat Migration & Migrant Population Statistics,
   `http://epp.eurostat.ec.europa.eu/statistics_explained/`
   `index.php/Migration_and_migrant_population_statistics`
   (last access: July 11, 2013)
8. Farinati, L., Masseroni, M., Vimercati, M.: Parliamoci Chiaro: an online opportunity to learn Italian for immigrants. In: Pixel (ed.) Proc. ICT for Language Learning, Padova, Italy, pp. 65–68 (2012)

9. Garris, R., Ahlers, R., Driskell, J.E.: Games, motivation, and learning: a research and practice model. Simulation and Learning 33(4), 441–467 (2002)
10. Gaved, M., Kukulska-Hulme, A., Jones, A., Scanlon, E., Dunwell, I., Lameras, P., Akiki, O.: Creating coherent incidental learning journeys on mobile devices through feedback and progress indicators. In: Proc. mLearn (2013)
11. Gibbs, G.: Learning by doing: a guide to teaching and learning methods (1988)
12. Halfman, J.: Citizenship Universalism, Migration and the Risks of Exclusion. The British Journal of Sociology 49(4), 513–533 (1998)
13. Hofstede, G., Hofstede, G.J.: Cultures and Organisations: Software of the Mind (2005)
14. Hofstede, G., Hofstede, G.H.: Culture's consequences: Comparing values, behaviours, institutions, and organizations across nations. Sage, Beverly Hills (2001)
15. Kluger, A.N., DeNisi, A.: The effects of feedback interventions on performance: A historical review, a meta-analysis, and a preliminary feedback intervention theory. Psychological Bulletin 119, 254–284 (1996)
16. Kluzer, S., Ferrari, A., Centeno, C.: Language learning by adult migrants: policy challenges and ICT responses. JRC-IPTS, Seville (2011)
17. Knight, J., Carly, S., Tregunna, B., Jarvis, S., Smithies, R., de Freitas, S., Mackway-Jones, K., Dunwell, I.: Serious gaming technology in major incident triage training: A pragmatic controlled trial. Resuscitation Journal 81(9), 1174–1179 (2010)
18. LeClus, M.A.: Informal learning in the workplace: a review of the literature. Australian Journal of Adult Learning 51(2), 355–373 (2011)
19. Muller, M.J.: Participatory design: the third space in HCI. In: Sears, A., Jacko, J.A. (eds.) The Human-computer Interaction Handbook, pp. 1061–1081 (2009)
20. Muratet, M., Delozanne, E., Torguet, P., Viallet, F.: Serious game and students' learning motivation: effect of context using prog&play. In: Cerri, S.A., Clancey, W.J., Papadourakis, G., Panourgia, K. (eds.) ITS 2012. LNCS, vol. 7315, pp. 123–128. Springer, Heidelberg (2012)
21. Nix, I., Wyllie, A.: Exploring design features to enhance computer-based assessment: learners' views on using a confidence-indicator tool and computer-based feedback. British Journal of Educational Technology 42(1), 101–112 (2009)
22. Ogata, H., Yano, Y.: Context-aware support for computer-supported ubiquitous learning. In: Roschelle, J., Chan, K.T., Yang, S. (eds.) Proc. WMTE 2004, pp. 27–34 (2004)
23. Paletta, L., Santner, K., Fritz, G., Mayer, H., Schrammel, J.: 3D Attention: Measurement of Visual Saliency Using Eye Tracking Glasses. In: Proc. CHI 2013, pp. 199–204 (2013)
24. Schuller, B., Dunwell, I., Weninger, F., Paletta, L.: Pervasive Serious Gaming for Behavior Change – The State of Play. IEEE Pervasive Computing 3(12), 48–55 (2013)
25. Silva, P.M.: Epistemology of Incidental Learning. PhD, Virginia Polytechnic and State University (2007), http://scholar.lib.vt.edu/theses/available/etd-10162007-224008/unrestricted/silva.pdf (retrieved)
26. Song, Y., Fox, R.: Uses of the PDA for undergraduate students' incidental vocabulary learning of English. ReCALL 20(3), 290–314 (2008)
27. Van Avermaet, P., Gysen, S.: Language policies for citizenship and integration: the Belgian case. In: Extra, G., Spotti, M., Van Avermaet, P. (eds.) Language Testing, Migration and Citizenship: Cross-national Perspectives on Integration Regimes (2009)
28. Vredenburg, K., Isensee, S., Righi, C.: User-Centered Design: An Integrated Approach (2001)
29. Vygotsky, L.: Mind in Society. Routledge, London (1970)
30. Wildman, D.M.: Getting the most from paired-user testing. Interactions 2(3), 21–27 (1995)
31. Zielke, M.A., Evans, M.J., Dufour, F., Christopher, T.V., Donahue, J.K., Johnson, P., Flores, R.: Serious games for immersive cultural training: Creating a living world. IEEE Computer Graphics and Applications 29(2), 49–60 (2009)

Building an Intelligent, Authorable Serious Game for Autistic Children and Their Carers*

Kaśka Porayska-Pomsta[1], Keith Anderson[2], Sara Bernardini[3],
Karen Guldberg[4], Tim Smith[5], Lila Kossivaki[4], Scott Hodgins[6], and Ian Lowe[7]

[1] Institute of Education, London Knowledge Lab, 23-29 Emerald Street, London
WC1N 3QS
K.Porayska-Pomsta@ioe.ac.uk
[2] Tandemis Limited
[3] King's College London
[4] University of Birmingham, School of Education
[5] Birkbeck College, Department of Psychological Sciences
[6] Acuity ETS Limited
[7] Topcliffe Primary School, Birmingham

Abstract. This paper introduces the SHARE-IT project, which leverages serious games paradigm to motivate and engage children with autism diagnosis in interactive activities, based on the state-of-the-art autism intervention practices. The aim of SHARE-IT is to formulate, in partnership with schools, parents and industry, the requirements for a robust, intelligent and authorable environment for supporting children in exploring, practicing and acquiring social interaction skills. SHARE-IT focuses on two key challenges: (i) developing robust system architecture and implementation, able to support both continuing development of a serious game for children with autism and its real world use; and (ii) selecting appropriate technologies and techniques to allow for (a) multi-device and operating system deployment, (b) the development of an *intelligent* serious game for supporting social interaction while (c) allowing the flexibility for the environment to be authored by lay persons. SHARE-IT's architecture is presented and several considerations of importance to enabling the engineering of an intelligent and authorable serious game are discussed. Examples of technologies developed to date are given throughout and a discussion of future challenges offered.

1 Introduction

Autism Spectrum Conditions (ASCs) are neuro-developmental conditions affecting an increasing number of individuals globally, with conservative estimates reporting approximately 6 per 1000 autistic children under 8 years [1]. Children with ASCs have marked difficulties in social interaction and communication and

---

* This project is funded by the EPSRC, grant number: EP/K012428/1. We thank Cathy Ennis and Arjan Egges (Univerity of Utrecht) for their advice about agent animations and for a set of motion-captured animations for our agent.

D. Reidsma, H. Katayose, and A. Nijholt (Eds.): ACE 2013, LNCS 8253, pp. 456–475, 2013.

in initiating and responding to social actions, including imitation, turn-taking and collaborative (joint) actions. Early intervention and consistent support that is also sustained over time and contexts is paramount to improving children's ability to cope with social situations and to enhancing their and their caregivers' quality of life [2]. Modern interventions emphasise the need for consistent support across contexts, and for teachers and parents to share the management of goals for each child through co-creation of learning experiences [3].

Increasingly, teachers and parents look to technology as a complimentary support. Unfortunately, there is a notable paucity of autism related applications that would allow parents or teachers to author and modify the existing software according to the specific needs of individual children, without reliance on software developers. Furthermore, despite the growing number and availability of technology-enhanced interventions (TEIs) for autism, as with previous teaching-learning innovations, design and research have evolved with little direct influence on practice and limited research in real-world classrooms and homes. Many TEIs are research prototypes, which are rarely robust enough for a researcher-free deployment *in-the-wild* and they often lack substantial evaluations to demonstrate their role and efficacy as intervention tools [4].

SHARE-IT's aim is to formulate, in partnership with schools, parents and industry, the requirements for a robust, intelligent and authorable serious game for supporting children with ASCs in exploring, practicing and acquiring social interaction skills. SHARE-IT builds on the ECHOES project, in which a serious game for children with ASCs was designed and evaluated [5]. ECHOES facilitated interactions through a multitouch screen and it employed a semi-autonomous agent, which was underpinned with AI techniques, including automated planning and user modelling for real-time tracking of the child's progress.

The outcomes of ECHOES motivate SHARE-IT: (1) ECHOES provoked children to manifest social behaviours that they did not exhibit in the classroom and observing such behaviours allowed teachers to appreciate the child's hidden potential and to tailor the support accordingly, (2) it demonstrated a potential to improve key skills for social communication, such as turn-taking, sharing of attention with others, and initiating and responding to bids for interaction; and (3) highlighted the real demand for affordable TEIs for Autism [5]. ECHOES also highlighted several key design and engineering challenges, specifically: (4) the need for robust system architecture and implementation, able to support both continuing development of a serious game such as ECHOES and its real world use; (5) the need for considered selection of appropriate technologies and techniques to allow for (a) multi-device and operating system deployment, (b) the development of an *intelligent* serious game needed in the context of supporting social interaction while (c) offering the flexibility for the environment to be authored by lay persons.

SHARE-IT's chief focus lies in addressing challenges (4) and (5). It targets children's *social communication* competences, including the ability to coordinate and share attention, intentions, and emotions with others, and engaging in reciprocal interaction through verbal and non-verbal means. Crucially, SHARE-IT investigates the question of the appropriate infrastructure that is needed to foster independent and sustainable engagement and flexibility of the serious game use by stakeholders, at the component, device and operating system levels.

The remainder of the paper is structured as follows: Section 2 provides a brief introduction to the trends in serious games for social skills training for autism as well as in *intelligent* games. In Section 3, we present SHARE-IT's pedagogical underpinnings and how these are reflected in the SHARE-IT's activities and design decisions, including the need for autonomous agents and real-time user modelling, which we argue are essential for developing serious games that foster social skills in children with ASCs. In Section 4, we present SHARE-IT's architecture and discuss several considerations of importance to enabling the engineering of an intelligent serious game. Section 5 is dedicated to examining the decisions that are of relevance to making a game such as SHARE-IT authorable by teachers and parents. In Section 6, we offer some conclusions and outline the future work.

2   Background

2.1   Serious Games for Autism

Serious games are increasingly employed as *tools* for supporting a wide range of activities, from therapy, e.g. for pain management and rehabilitation, to training of specific skills, such as literacy and numeracy [6]. Educational games based on virtual reality are believed to offer particular benefits for children with ASCs [7], because they can help alleviate children's stress associated with real social interactions and because they allow the child to repeatedly rehearse behaviours in different scenarios, from simple and structured situations to increasingly more complex and unpredictable ones. Studies show that autistic children who were taught by a virtual human experience higher levels of retention than those in traditional classroom settings [8] and that virtual agents may promote generalisation [9] - a holy grail of any autism intervention. There is also some evidence that both role-play and practice of behaviours across different contexts can contribute to increasing the chances of transferring the learned skill from the virtual to the real world [10].

The majority of serious games for autistic children have focused mainly on the following domains of social communication:

Language Skills. Games targeting these skills range from systems that aim to increase the fluency of speech [11] to systems that improve the intelligibility of speech [12]. Since understanding child speech is still technologically challenging, some of the more successful applications involve a "Wizard of Oz" approach, where a human experimenter manipulates the system [9]. Recent improvements in speech recognition allow for technologically more sophisticated support (e.g. TouchStory [13]), and open up the possibility of focusing on literacy skills and expanding children's vocabulary [14,15].

Affective Skills. The focus of games in this category is on training recognition of facial expressions and body gestures, e.g. cMotion [16] and LIFEisGAME [17], both of which aim to help children recognise contextualised facial expressions through manipulation of an interactive virtual character [18]. Commercial games, include FaceSay [19] or Society [20], which provide children with opportunities to practice key skills, e.g. attending to eye gaze, discriminating facial expressions and recognising faces and emotions with the help of interactive avatar assistants, or which teach how to recognise and control their emotions and cope with social challenges such as handling bullying and talking to strangers.

Interaction Skills. Turn-taking, imitation and collaborative play provide the focus for games in this category. The tabletop interactive Collaborative Puzzle Game [21] aims to foster collaboration skills. It revolves around an interaction rule, called "enforced collaboration", where puzzle pieces must be touched and dragged simultaneously by two players in order to be moved. Barakova et al. [22] proposed a multi-agent system composed of autonomous interactive blocks that can express emergent behaviours through change in their colours and light intensity based on how they are manipulated by the users. Teaching interaction skills to autistic children through robotic toys is an area of emerging interest. Examples include a silicone robot, called Keepon [23] and different robotic platforms used in the AuRoRa project [24], from simple mobile robots to more anthropomorphic creatures.

2.2   Intelligent Serious Games

With the growing sophistication of user expectations, a demand emerges also for more convincing game characters and plots, which can be adapted in real-time based on the knowledge that the system can acquire about the user behaviours, also in real-time. Artificial Intelligence techniques and paradigms increasingly provide a research and application focus in this context, with autonomous agents and user modelling emerging as two areas of special interest to games design.

Autonomous Agents. Social interaction involves social partnership. This creates a demand for characters which can act as such partners to the user in a believable way. We argue that credible social partnership requires an investment into the creation of autonomous or at least semi-autonomous agents, i.e. agents that are able to decide independently how to act best to achieve a set of high-level goals that have been delegated to them. Autonomy involves a broad spectrum of behaviours with *no autonomy* and *full autonomy* lying at its extremes. Autonomous agents carry a significant potential for autism intervention because they can contribute to the intensive one-on-one support needed while easing the demand for such support from practitioners and parents. Such agents can complement the traditional interventions allowing human practitioners to focus on the most complex aspects of face-to-face interventions, while supporting repetitive tasks and on-demand access.

Although in the last ten years there has been a growing interest in the potential of artificial agents in the area of autism intervention, both virtual and physically embodied, the efforts have focused primarily on agents with little or no *autonomy*. Typically, in such contexts, virtual agents are either authored *a priori* or controlled by a practitioner through a control panel, while robots are tele-operated. The approaches which form the exceptions in this respect include the Thinking Head project [25], which focuses on developing a talking head that teaches social skills, through realistically portraying facial expressions, and the virtual peers, Baldi and Timo, [14] – 3D computer-animated talking heads for language and speech training. The limited effort in the area of autonomous agents for autism intervention can be in part explained by the fact that, in line with some behaviourist clinical intervention frameworks, most technologies in this context focus on *training* children with respect to specific skills, e.g. recognising a predefined set of facial expressions, rather than on creating believable social interaction experiences, which can be freely explored by the child.

Planning techniques are crucial to enriching virtual characters with autonomy. Path planning, for example, is extensively used in action games to avoid collisions between multiple characters and to allow characters to inhabit and move around architecturally complex environments [26,27]. Task planning is used to enhance the quality of individual moves in puzzle games [28] and to help coordinate actions by multiple characters [29]. Narrative and storytelling planning are of particular relevance to serious games for supporting social interaction, because their aim is to support the generation of evolving contexts and stories within which characters are able to manifest intentionality and emotions [30]. Such emergent narratives are useful in contextualising the behaviours of characters and the training of social skills as reviewed in Section 2.1

User Modelling. In general, user modelling consists of: (1) static profile of the user, containing information such as gender, age, preferences etc., and (2) a diagnostic system responsible for inferring the user's hidden psychological states from behaviours observable online. Specifically to games, recent reviews discuss modelling players' behaviours in terms of their actions vis á vis the games' objectives, their tactics (short-term behaviours) and strategies (long-term action planning) and player profiling in terms of their psychological predispositions based on the detected actions, tactics and strategies [31]. In this context, the player modelling applications tend to focus on adult players in shoot-them-up or strategy games. Relatively little effort is available in relation to modelling children as players, with the notable exception of work by [32], who create and evaluate user models that predict 8-11 year old children's entertainment of games.

The recent recognition of serious games as a genre with substantial potential in complimenting traditional education motivates the need for user modelling in the context. Much work that is relevant to modelling players of serious games comes from the related fields of Intelligent Learning Environments and Affective Computing. Many accounts exist of the nature of mental states that relate to user motivation and learning. Malone [33] highlights factors such as *challenge*, *curiosity* and *fantasy* that impact on users' enjoyment of and learning with digital environments and these factors are also increasingly investigated in relation to users of serious games. Csikszentmihalyi [34] discusses *flow* as crucial to users' ability to immerse themselves in virtual worlds, with the specific dimensions of flow in relation to children game playing, being identified as users' *endurability*, *engagement* and *expectations* [35]. Flow refers to users' sustained focus of attention which psychologists link to children's improved memory, learning and increased ability to self-regulate emotionally [36]. Burleson [37] discusses the state of *stuck* as a factor potentially detrimental to users' enjoyment and learning. User *achievement of the goals* within a specific environment and the user's *personal goals* that emerge from a combination of their mental states and personality traits was examined by Ortony et al. [38] and most notably implemented in a learner model of 6th and 7th grade students (in the US) by Conati [39]. Research in Artificial Intelligence in Education provides further insights into the older children's mental states that are important for learning with technology (e.g. [40]), how these may relate to the specific forms of digital environments and contexts of use (e.g. [41]) and types of help provided to the child (e.g. [42]).

Research in affective computing and use of sensors for detecting users' behaviours in games and education, is thriving. Most existing approaches rely on a combination of cues, such as touch, eye-gaze, facial expression tracking and voice recognition [43]. A recent example of user modelling that relies on cue detection in the context of serious games for social interaction include the work by the TARDIS project, which focuses on developing a technology for training young adults at risk of social exclusion to self-regulate emotionally and to self present to potential employers [44].

3   SHARE-IT's Pedagogical Underpinnings

SHARE-IT focuses on enhancing the social communication competences of children with ASCs, because this is the domain with which they typically have the most difficulty [3]. Social communication involves the ability to coordinate and share attention, intentions, and emotions with others and a capacity for engaging in reciprocal interaction by understanding and using verbal and non-verbal means. SCERTS [3] provides SHARE-IT with a comprehensive approach to social communication assessment and intervention in autism. Based on several established methods in clinical and educational interventions, it identifies the particular skills that are essential for successful social communication: (i) *Social Communication*: spontaneous and functional communication, emotional expression, and secure and trusting relationships with others; (ii) *Emotional Regulation*: the ability to maintain a well-regulated emotional state to cope with stress and to be available for learning and interacting; (iii) *Transactional Support*: caregivers' ability to respond to the child's needs and interests, to adapt the environment, and to provide tools to enhance learning.

3.1   SHARE-IT's Learning Activities

SHARE-IT serious game is organised around discrete scenes, each with a definite pedagogic purpose. For example, a child might be encouraged to turn-take to grow flowers by shaking the cloud (Fig. 1) or stack pots to build a tower (Fig. 2).

SHARE-IT uses the design of the ECHOES learning activities, which have been created over several years through participatory design workshops with teachers, practitioners and children, e.g. [5]. The activities are set in a sensory garden, which is populated by an agent, called Andy, and by interactive objects that react in different ways, sometimes transforming into other objects when the agent or the child act upon them through specific touch gestures or through gaze. For example, tapping on a flower can turn it into a floating bubble or a bouncy ball. The child can pop the bubbles simply by looking at them. The relationship of action-reaction implemented through touch and gaze is intended to support children's understanding of cause and effect, which is often impaired in individuals with ASCs, while the gaze controlled interface also supports children's development of attentional control.

The choice of a magic garden as the setting for the learning activities serves a number of purposes - mainly encouraging the child's imagination through the unusual properties of the objects which can do things that are not possible in the real world, and through exploration, since it is not obvious to the children from the outset how the different objects will behave and react to their gestures. In addition, the use of the magic garden builds on the SCERTS principle that learning activities need to share an obvious unifying theme in order to support shared attention [3].

Fig. 1. A child interacting with the ECHOES system through multi-touch interface. In SHARE-IT, we reuse the types of the activities and most of the skin (appearance) of the objects and the environment.

Fig. 2. Andy, the SHARE-IT agent demonstrates pot stacking to the child. The idea is that the child will imitate Andy's action and take turns with Andy in subsequent moves.

SHARE-IT's agent, Andy, acts as a social partner to children, prompting them to take their turn. This requires the agent to be aware of when the child has completed an action and to be capable of taking their own turn. In addition the agent needs to be able to assess the appropriateness of the action for the activity and with respect to the agent's own actions. Finally, Andy needs to deal with the unexpected, e.g. the user not responding, not taking turns, or interacting with the environment in ways unrelated to the activity. Unlike in many games, the difficulty levels in SHARE-IT do not correspond to the different activities, but rather they are organised around the different types of pointing, from relatively ambiguous distal pointing with gaze (i.e. looking at an object), to proximal pointing by touching an object of interest. A combination of several types of pointing, such as distal pointing through gaze and finger point, as well as the agent's verbal request, e.g. "Pass me that pot" is considered the least difficult in SHARE-IT. Prompting and verbal guidance, such as Andy reminding the child of their turn is also used to regulate the difficulty level within activities. Children who respect turn-taking will get fewer prompts, whereas more scaffolding is needed for children who have difficulties in this area.

4   Engineering SHARE-IT's Serious Game

SHARE-IT is essentially a complex system (Fig. 3), combining multimodal user data, specifically – screen touch and eye-tracking data, with facial recognition data being planned as additional input, and requiring for all of these data to be routed to its relevant subsystems. The primary subsystems are the planner and the user model and both of these are consumers of the user data. From a purely engineering point of view, of importance to building robust complex systems for real world use, this leads to questions of synchronisation and prioritisation, specifically – which subsystem should receive the inputs first and then how should the outputs from that subsystem be combined with the results of feeding the data to the other subsystems?

Many systems such as ECHOES are based on a distributed architecture using middleware like ICE [45] to handle inter-process communication. This approach allows for different languages to be used (e.g. ECHOES used Java and Python primarily) and, depending on the languages chosen, it can provide cross-platform

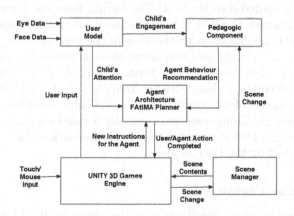

Fig. 3. SHARE-IT's system architecture

support. However there are major drawbacks with this approach, which can hinder long-term extendibility of the system, its computational efficiency and consequently its real world robustness. Specifically, developing a system that relies on a distributed architecture is very resource heavy, because a separate process is needed for each component (and possibly Java Virtual Machine). Furthermore, debugging such an architecture is difficult, because a separate debugger is needed for each component. Based on our experience and evaluation of the ECHOES system, we opine that a distributed architecture in this context increases system complexity without adding any significant gain.

The idea behind SHARE-IT is to deliver a platform for authorable game development and this, coupled with the fact that there is already significant complexity involved in implementing an autonomous agent, leads to our adopting the philosophy to keep the SHARE-IT system architecture and code design as simple as possible at every level, with additional layers of abstraction being avoided wherever possible. To this end, the whole system is designed around a single process, using just one language. All system resources are kept in one location avoiding the problem of contention as all threads in the system are managed from the one process. Additionally, using a single language allows us to maintain a high degree of code consistency making the project easier to maintain and extend.

Another decision relates to the use of an existing games engine to generate the SHARE-IT game. While the system could have been written from scratch, as indeed it was for ECHOES, a lot of unnecessary work and complexity is added to the project for no appreciable gain. There are many commercial and freeware games engines that can handle all the rendering, audio file handling, character animation, 3D effects and physics that are required for projects like SHARE-IT. Any games engine of this type will automatically handle user input from mouse and touch screen. However, eye-tracking and facial expression recognition need to be handled separately. Since the User Model is the primary consumer of these data, which it uses to make judgements about the child's level of engagement with the system and the frequency and consistency of the desired behaviours, these inputs are routed directly to it. The output from the User Model is then routed to the Planner to allow it to make more informed decisions about how the agent should collaborate with the user in the task at hand. In addition to the User Model, the Pedagogic Component also communicates with the Planner providing a top level control over what forms of support should the agent provide to the individual children along with the frequency and the kind of prompting, thereby being responsible also for setting the difficulty levels for each individual child. The Pedagogic Component is essentially a rule-base expressing SCERTS recommendations, which it executes based on information about the child's engagement supplied by the User Model.

4.1   The Game Engine

At the heart of an agent based game is the agent itself. While such a game requires an environment, this generally consists of background artwork and foreground 3D objects. Although the objects may be animate, they are so in very simple ways compared to an agent. An agent itself comprises a physical embodiment: a number of manifest behaviours – generally animated movement and speech, and rules to control these behaviours.

The choice of artwork to be used for the agent and the environment is critical for the success of a game. However life-like the agent's behaviour or enticing the activities, the child will not be drawn in unless the physical environment of the game is comfortable and attractive. Ideally, the appropriate art design should involve a participatory effort between children, practitioners and designers to ensure that the design is attractive to children, while lending itself to supporting the pedagogical aspects of the game. For example, in activities focused on improving children's attentional control, it is important that the number, the type and the interactive nature of objects acting as distractors are in line with the pedagogic requirements of the task. This paper does not address the creation of artwork, since its focus is on game development. In SHARE-IT, we re-use the artwork that has been inspired by the children and teachers themselves, and which proved very successful with most of almost a hundred children who used the ECHOES environment over the years.

However, it is important to consider that in the context of serious games for social interaction, there is an increased need for precision in the execution of certain gestures of the agent and facial expressions, especially if the expectation is for the child to recognise emotions in such expressions, follow pointing by the agent or imitate the behaviours modelled by the agent. Large libraries of resources are available for choosing artwork, for example TurboSquid[1] and RocketBox[2] and both provide rigged characters that can be animated for use as agents. Motion capture offers the best results, especially for fine-grained hand gestures such as one-finger pointing needed by an agent to unambiguously point to objects, e.g. in initiating bids for interaction with the child, as well as Makaton sign gestures, often used to support instructions and communication with children with autism (see Fig. 4).

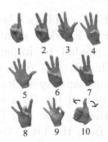

Fig. 4. Makaton numbers gestures illustrate detail that may be needed

---

[1] http://www.turbosquid.com/

[2] http://www.rocketbox-libraries.com/

To address the multi-platform requirement of SHARE-IT (Windows, Mac OS, IOS and Android), needed to facilitate access to the SHARE-IT technology by different stakeholders and in different contexts, various games engines were evaluated. Some open source engines, like Ogre[3] are graphics engines only, others like Panda[4] are full games engines, but do not support the range of operating systems required. There are a bewildering number of commercial games engines available (Game Maker Studio, LibGDX, Unity, Blender, Leadwerks, Source, CryEngine). Many do not support all platforms and most are designed for the creation of shoot-them-up style games. Unity 3D was chosen on the basis that it supports the four platforms of interest and that it comes with Mono built-in, which means that JavaScript or C# can be used for the development. The latter is the obvious choice for the complex system such as SHARE-IT, because it offers a fully object-oriented development language rather than a scripting language. Although some would argue that this choice is a matter of preference, we argue that this decision impacts the ease of maintaining the large and complex code-base required by the system like SHARE-IT and which would have been very difficult to achieve with JavaScript.

Another reason that led to the choice of Unity concerned the source of the 3D characters and animations required for the agent. There are a number of systems available (3ds Max, Maya, SketchUp, Realsoft3D, Cheetah3D), but few offer as complete end-to-end support for creating and then animating characters as the AutoDesk products. Furthermore the 3ds Max biped used in 3DS Max is one of the main industry standards and off-the-shelf characters rigged with this biped are widely and cheaply available. There are large libraries of motion capture data available, such as the Carnegie Mellon repository,[5] which can be readily imported onto the 3DS Max biped, and AutoDesk MotionBuilder product provides rich support for the import of motion capture and animation data of different formats. The resulting animations can be exported (using the FBX file format) so that they can be directly imported into Unity3D. All this provides a seamless workflow that further justifies the choice of these technologies.

4.2   SHARE-IT's Intelligence

Agent Development. SHARE-IT employs FAtiMA [46] domain-independent architecture to underpin its agent. FAtiMA combines the type of *reactive* and *cognitive* capabilities that are needed to implement an autonomous, *socio-emotionally* competent agent that is also proactive and reactive. The cognitive layer of FAtiMA is based on *planning* techniques, specifically a variant of PDDL2.1 [47], and it is characterised by: (i) a set of internal goals; (ii) a set of action strategies to achieve these goals; and (iii) an affective system, while the emotional model is derived from the OCC theory of emotions [38] and the appraisal theory [48]. A FAtiMA agent builds an affective system from emotional reaction rules, action tendencies, emotional thresholds and emotion decay rates.

---

[3] http://www.ogre3d.org/

[4] http://www.panda3d.org

[5] http://mocap.cs.cmu.edu/

Appraisal and *coping* are mechanisms controlling a FAtiMA agent, which is able to "experience" one or more of the 22 emotions of the OCC model, based on its appraisal of the current state of the world and its subjective tendencies to experience certain emotions instead of others. The agent deals with these emotions by applying problem-focused or emotion-focused coping strategies. Both the appraisal and the coping work at the *reactive* level, which affects the short-term horizon of the agent's behaviour, and at the *deliberative* level, which relates to the agent's goal-oriented behaviour.

Similar to ECHOES, in SHARE-IT, each learning activity has an associated FAtiMA agent model. All these models share the same specification of the agent's affective system, to enable the agent to maintain the same 'personality' between sessions, in order to establish a trusting relationship with the child. Andy was designed to have a positive, motivating and supportive character, to be happy and to not get frustrated easily. Such behaviours were obtained through manipulating Andy's emotional reaction rules, thresholds and decay rates of the OCC emotions available. For example, the child looking at an object pointed to by the agent has a very high desirability to it, whereas the child looking away has low desirability. Currently the agent's happiness threshold is set to low, its frustration threshold is high, its happiness decay is slow, while its frustration decay is fast, leading to the agent's tendency to be happy and to not become easily frustrated regardless of the child's actions. Although ECHOES' evaluation, especially the analysis of children's engagement showed that children did interact with Andy as if with an intentional being [49], it also highlighted a possible need to make our agent more interesting, by furnishing it with more moods and emotions, both positive and negative. Our current discussions with teachers and parents are consistent with this analysis, suggesting that a more modulated behaviour is required of the agent within activities to make him more credible and enticing to children, as well as to introduce different levels of difficulty for children, whereby the child is exposed to unexpected and varied behaviours on the part of the social partner. For example, in an activity where the child can shake the cloud to make rain and to grow flowers, children often flout the implicit expectation that cloud ought not to be shaken on the agent. Yet, naturally, children find trying to make the agent wet very funny. Currently, the agent's reaction to this is to smile and continue in good humour. However, following teachers' assessments, by not having the agent progressively become sad or angry, is a missed opportunity for demonstrating to the child the cause-effect relationship between their actions and emotional reactions of others.

Following teachers' suggestions, in SHARE-IT we are developing the agent as an emotional being able to express complex emotions. To this end we have developed authoring tools (discussed in Sec.5; see Fig. 5) for displaying the agents emotions and are in the process of linking those to the more complex specification of its action tendencies in the FAtiMA model, which then control the agent's facial expressions and gestures. With the need for a more sophisticated real-time emotional display by the agent, we are presently working with teachers and parents on articulating: (i) the high-level *pedagogic goals* on which the individual

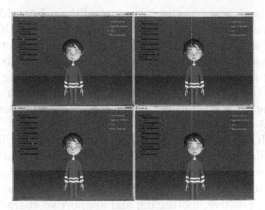

Fig. 5. SHARE-IT authoring tool for morphing the agent's emotional expressions

activities ought to focus and (ii) the specific *narrative content* of the activities itself. These will be incorporated in the Pedagogic Component of the system and will be used to inform the goals for the agent to actively pursue along with appropriate action strategies for each learning activity.

User Modelling. SHARE-IT also reuses ECHOES' user model, which estimates the child's cognitive and affective states in real-time and feeds back this information to the Pedagogic Component and the Planner whenever a change in a given state is detected. In SHARE-IT, the model receives real-time information from the touch and eye-gaze systems and, based on this data, it interprets the current level of child's engagement as well as the level, consistency and desirability of the child's attention vis á vis the goals of a given activity or specific agent actions. The cognitive assessment is facilitated by a *rule-based engine* which estimates the extent to which the child has achieved the goals associated with the session, e.g. based on the number of the child's responses to the agents bids for interaction in a pre-specified time frame. The rules are based on SCERTS guidelines and precise timing constraints for establishing the child's mastery of joint attention and symbolic use skills. For example, the behaviour "shifts gaze between people and objects" is satisfied if the child shifts gaze spontaneously between a person and an object at least three times and the entire sequence occurs within two seconds. Detailed real-time eye-gaze data is essential to enable the interpretation outlined.

In ECHOES, the assessment of the child's engagement was based on a combination of supervised and unsupervised learning techniques [49]. Engagement is defined in terms of: *very engaged, engaged* and *not engaged*. The children are considered "very engaged" when they are fully absorbed by the learning activity; "engaged" when they are interested in the current learning activity, but are not immersed in it; "not engaged" when they do not interact with the system at all, either *via* gaze or touch.

In SHARE-IT our efforts to date focused on practicalities of improving the reliability of gaze detection to enhance the estimation of children's engagement. Specifically, we have incorporated a portable Tobii eye-tracker (X2-30 compact) with the rest of the system. Tobii provides us with high precision of gaze detection in different lighting conditions and can cope with different face occluders, such as glasses. Another advantage of this technology is that it comes with an SDK that supports .Net version 2 allowing for a direct integration into a Unity build. SHARE-IT's User Model provides a callback function that gets called by the eye-tracker each time there is new data.

One challenge involved in using eye-trackers in this context relates to calibration. This typically consists of drawing calibration objects on the screen that the user has to stare at in the order they are displayed. Keeping track of our ambition to create a game for children, in SHARE-IT we turned the calibration task into a game-like activity, where the agent instructs and prompts the child where to look. However, there is still the possibility that the child may be unable or unwilling to follow the process, in which case the eye-tracker informs the system that the calibration was unsuccessful. In this case, the process can be retried, or this form of input to the system can be disabled. Since it is envisaged that the system will run on a variety of systems, where eye-trackers may not always be available, the use of this data needs to be optional to the system. The system was thus designed in such a way that the eye-tracker is used to refine the estimates of engagement reached from processing input from mouse/touch and facial expression processing.

The SHORE object recognition engine will be used in SHARE-IT for simple image recognition based on the output from a webcam, such as the built-in camera that features in laptops and tablets, to extract features such as facial locations and a range of emotional expressions. The engine is reasonably good at detecting happy (smiling), sad (downturned mouth) and surprised (open mouthed) expressions, without the need for over-exaggeration [44]. This will provide another source of useful input to the User Model, for example an unhappy looking user may require more intervention and support from the agent. SHORE's SDK supports Mac/IOS and Windows, but not Android, so again this input will be made optional to the system. The data produced by SHORE is of a less definite nature than the other inputs - mouse/touch and eye-tracking data can tell us exactly which objects, or parts of the scene are currently engaging the user. Facial expressions need to be collated over time to provide meaningful data. We are currently developing a suite of activities that will rely on SHORE, involving mimicking the agents' expressions (as can be produced in the tool shown in Fig. 5) and in turn having the agent to mimic the child's facial expressions. Apart from the logs of this data contributing to the training of emotion interpretation capabilities of our User Model, they are also intended to support important skills, such as recognition of emotions from other people's faces and imitation skills.

5   Authoring Tools

The authoring environment for SHARE-IT is intended for use by teachers and parents, so that they can tailor the game according to the needs of the individual children in their care. The authoring environment is designed to allow existing activities to be chosen and new ones to be created from a palette of components. A great deal of effort in constructing the Unity game for the project was spent creating a range of objects and agent animations and speech to provide the building blocks for this tool. Ease of use is a primary consideration given the non-specialist nature of the end users and is a continuing focus of participatory design workshops with teachers and parents.

The authoring application consists of three components: (1) **A scene selector tool** (Fig. 6) that allows the scenes and their order to be selected. It also controls display of a scene selection menu in the game which permits the user free choice of scenes. Furthermore, basic object properties, such as object transformations can be set from this too; (2) **A scene creator/editor window** (Fig. 7), which is used to setup or alter the physical components of a scene - how many of each object and where they are placed, their colour and size, and the scene background; (3) **A rule creation dialogue** (Fig. 8), which is used after the scene creator to set up the planner rules which will govern the agent's behaviour in the scene.

The first two of these components write the XML initialisation file for Unity to read on startup. This allows Unity to create all the required scenes at runtime.

Fig. 6. SHARE-IT authoring tool for selecting and ordering learning activities

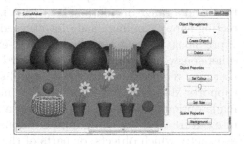

Fig. 7. SHARE-IT authoring tool for choosing the objects, their properties and number

The rule creation component is somewhat more involved, as it has to map the elements selected by the scene author into rules that the FAtiMA planner can consume. As shown in Fig. 8 this might be an activity to throw bouncy balls through the cloud to turn them different colours and in which the agent and user take turns with each ball. Each action type has an XML template that forms the basis of the rule in Fig. 9, which then gets filled in with the details of the objects

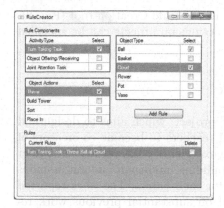

Fig. 8. SHARE-IT authoring tool for creating planner rules.

Fig. 9. XML rule relating to the rule created in the editor shown in Fig. 8

selected. In the example in Figs. 8 and 9, the "indicatedTurn()" property means that this is a turn taking activity and "BallThrowing(isChosenActivity)" means that this rule only applies to the Throwing activity.

Mapping of user friendly representations to the rules governing the planner required a simple set of rule categories to be chosen such that an automatic translation mechanism could be set up. This set needed to be rich enough to allow for the pedagogic aims of the system to be expressed. The rule base for the SHARE-IT planner consists of a number of fixed rules which govern the low-level behaviours of the agent that are common to all activities: (1) Rules that govern the low-level behaviours of the agent, e.g. types of movement and interaction strategies, e.g. whether and when to prompt, correct or encourage the child. These are part of the psychological makeup of the agent and are currently hard-coded. (2) General scene-related activities, e.g. walking on/off scene, starting an activity, detecting and acknowledging the end of an activity, manipulating objects (throwing, stacking, etc.). These are common to all activities and are also hard-coded. (3) Higher-level behavioural traits of the agent, such as types of greeting, speech and movement used for the prompting and encouragement and one-off behaviours, such as giggling or falling around, designed to relax or entertain the child, and not linked to any particular activity.

SHARE-IT authoring tools allow for a specification of higher level rules that determine how the agent behaves during a particular activity. For example, an activity that involves turn taking in stacking objects to build a tower would involve specifying the object type, the action permitted (stacking) and the fact that turn-taking is required. In order to keep the rule base manageable and to prevent the authoring tool itself from becoming too complex, the activities were constrained to the following categories: (i) Turn taking activities, (ii) Object offering/receiving, e.g. allowing the user to hand an object to the agent, for instance, (iii) Joint activities, e.g. carrying an object together. For each of these categories XML templates have been created that can be modified to construct individual activities as specified by the user in the Rule Creation tool (Fig. 8). In this way any combination of objects and actions on objects can be specified to create an activity.

6   Conclusions and Future Work

In this paper, we introduced the SHARE-IT project, which aims to design and implement an infrastructure for parents and teachers to become co-creators of their children's technology-enhanced learning experiences. We outlined a number of practical considerations of importance to building intelligent and autonomous serious games for children with autism and for their carers. The work reported is very much in progress, albeit it is based on substantial previous work related to the ECHOES project, which it extends. The considerations are therefore grounded in our extensive experience of developing an intelligent serious game for social interaction. Much work still remains to be done, particularly in relation to enriching our virtual character with more interesting and varied behaviours, extending the range of characters available to include females and those representing different ethnicities. A major limitation in the agent's intelligence is that the agent cannot currently deal with inappropriate or unexpected behaviour from the user, such as not responding to the agent, not honouring turn taking, being occupied with objects in the scene not related to the activity, complete disengagement, etc. We are currently adding further rules to the planner's actions to cover the most obvious cases, although in the longer term it would be desirable to make these behaviours part of the agent's personality, so that they would vary with the affective system parameters. We are also focusing on improving the accuracy of the SHARE-IT modelling tools. Incorporating a robust eye-gaze tracking system is of special importance in this context because the ability to follow gaze by social partners provides the foundations of successful social communication. While the Tobii technologies currently employed are still unaffordable by most, they are set to enter the mainstream market as part of ordinary PCs in the next 12 months. We are currently working with parents and teachers on refining the design and the variation of the SHARE-IT learning activities to make them more flexible to extend and we are testing the authoring tools to assess their usability and robustness. In the next 3 months studies with children, parents and teachers are planned, where the SHARE-IT technologies will be piloted simultaneously in school and home contexts and the authoring tools will be tested in-the-wild, with a special attention being paid to the relevance and feasibility of the activities across the two contexts. While children are the main beneficiaries of the game developed, providing parents and teachers with authoring powers is also expected to enhance parents-school communication and continuity, consistency and coherence of the experience provided to children. The results of the planned studies will be reported in due course.

References

1. Medical Research Council: Autism - Research Review (2001) (accessed October 20, 2012)
2. Knapp, M., Romeo, R., Beecham, J.: The economic consequences of autism in the uk. Foundation for People with Learning Disabilities Report (2007)
3. Prizant, B., Wetherby, A., Rubin, E., Laurent, A., Rydell, P.: The SCERTS® Model: A Comprehensive Educational Approach for Children with Autism Spectrum Disorders. Brookes (2006)
4. Wass, S., Porayska-Pomsta, K.: The uses of cognitive training technologies in the treatment of autism spectrum disorders. Autism: International Journal of Research and Practice (in press)
5. Bernardini, S., Porayska-Pomsta, K., Smith, T.J., Avramides, K.: Building autonomous social partners for autistic children. In: Nakano, Y., Neff, M., Paiva, A., Walker, M. (eds.) IVA 2012. LNCS (LNAI), vol. 7502, pp. 46–52. Springer, Heidelberg (2012)
6. de Freitas, S.: Learning in immersive worlds. Technical report, Joint Information Systems Committee, Bristol (2006) (accessed October 20, 2012)
7. Parsons, S., Cobb, S.: State-of-the-art of virtual reality technologies for children on the autism spectrum. European Journal of Special Needs Education 26(3), 355–366 (2011)
8. Grynszpan, O., Martin, J.C., Nadel, J.: Multimedia interfaces for users with high functioning autism: An empirical investigation. International Journal on Human-Computer Studies 66(8), 628–639 (2008)
9. Tartaro, A., Cassell, J.: Playing with virtual peers: bootstrapping contingent discourse in children with autism. In: Proceedings of the ICLS 2008, pp. 382–389 (2008)
10. Parsons, S., Mitchell, P.: The potential of virtual reality in social skills training for people with autistic spectrum disorders. Journal of Intellectual Disability Research 46(5), 430–443 (2002)
11. Anwar, A., Rahman, M., Ferdous, S., Anik, S., Ahmed, S.: A computer game based approach for increasing fluency in the speech of the autistic children. In: Proceedings of the 11th IEEE International Conference on Advanced Learning Technologies (ICALT), pp. 17–18 (2011)
12. Rahman, M.M., Ferdous, S., Ahmed, S.I., Anwar, A.: Speech development of autistic children by interactive computer games. Interactive Technology and Smart Education 8(4), 208–223 (2011)
13. Davis, M., Otero, N., Dautenhahn, K., Nehaniv, C., Powell, S.: Creating a software to promote understanding about narrative in children with autism: Reflecting on the design of feedback and opportunities to reason. In: IEEE 6th International Conference on Development and Learning, Proceedings of the Development and Learning, ICDL 2007, pp. 64–69 (July 2007)
14. Bosseler, A., Massaro, D.: Development and evaluation of a computer-animated tutor for vocabulary and language learning in children with autism. Journal of Autism and Developmental Disorders 33(6), 653–672 (2003)
15. Massaro, D.W.: Embodied agents in language learning for children with language challenges. In: Miesenberger, K., Klaus, J., Zagler, W.L., Karshmer, A.I. (eds.) ICCHP 2006. LNCS, vol. 4061, pp. 809–816. Springer, Heidelberg (2006)
16. Finkelstein, S.L., Nickel, A., Harrison, L., Suma, E.A., Barnes, T.: cMotion: A new game design to teach emotion recognition and programming logic to children using virtual humans. In: Proceedings of the 2009 IEEE Virtual Reality Conference, pp. 249–250 (2009)

17. Abirached, B., Zhang, Y., Aggarwal, J., Tamersoy, B., Fernandes, T., Miranda, J., Orvalho, V.: Improving communication skills of children with asds through interaction with virtual characters. In: 2011 IEEE 1st International Conference on Serious Games and Applications for Health (SeGAH), pp. 1–4 (2011)
18. Schuller, B.: ASC-Inclusion Project (accessed October 20, 2012)
19. Hopkins, I.M., Gower, M.W., Perez, T.A., Smith, D.S., Amthor, F.R., et al.: Avatar assistant: Improving social skills in students with an asd through a computer-based intervention. Journal of Autism and Developmental Disorders 41(11), 1543–1555 (2011)
20. Beaumont, R., Sofronoff, K.: A multi-component social skills intervention for children with asperger syndrome: The junior detective training program. Journal of Child Psychology and Psychiatry 49, 743–753 (2008)
21. Battocchi, A., Pianesi, F., Tomasini, D., Zancanaro, M., Esposito, G., Venuti, P., Ben Sasson, A., Gal, E., Weiss, P.L.: Collaborative puzzle game: a tabletop interactive game for fostering collaboration in children with autism spectrum disorders (asd). In: Proceedings of the ACM International Conference on Interactive Tabletops and Surfaces, ITS 2009, pp. 197–204. ACM, New York (2009)
22. Barakova, E., van Wanrooij, G., van Limpt, R., Menting, M.: Using an emergent system concept in designing interactive games for autistic children. In: Proceedings of the 6th International Conference on Interaction Design and Children, IDC 2007, pp. 73–76. ACM, New York (2007)
23. Kozima, H., Michalowski, M., Nakagawa, C.: Keepon: A playful robot for research, therapy, and entertainment. International Journal of Social Robotics 1(1), 3–18 (2009)
24. Dautenhahn, K., Werry, I.: Towards interactive robots in autism therapy: Background, motivation and challenges. Pragmatics and Cognition 12(1), 1–35 (2004)
25. Milne, M., Luerssen, M., Lewis, T., Leibbrandt, R., Powers, D.: Development of a virtual agent based social tutor for children with autism spectrum disorders. In: Proceedings of the International Joint Conference on Neural Networks, pp. 1–9 (2010)
26. Snape, J., Guy, S., Lin, M., Manocha, D.: Local and global planning for collision-free navigation in video games. In: Proceedings of the 3rd International Planning in Games Workshop, ICAPS 2013 (2013)
27. Jaklin, N., van Toll, W., Roland, G.: Way to go - a framework for multi-level planning in games. In: Proceedings of the 3rd International Planning in Games Workshop, ICAPS 2013 (2013)
28. Do, M., Tran, M.: Blocksworld: An ipad puzzle game. In: Proceedings of the 3rd International Planning in Games Workshop, ICAPS 2013 (2013)
29. Menif, A., Guettier, C., Cazenave, C.: Planning and execution control architecture for infantry serious gaming. In: Proceedings of the 3rd International Planning in Games Workshop, ICAPS 2013 (2013)
30. Riedl, M., Young, M.: Narrative planning: Balancing plot and character. Journal of AI Research 29, 217–268 (2010)
31. Bakkes, S., Tan, C.T., Pisan, Y.: Personalised gaming. Creative Technologies 3 (2012)
32. Yannakakis, G., Hallam, J.: Modeling and augmenting game entertainment through challenge and curiosity. International Journal on Artificial Intelligence Tools 16(6), 981–999 (2007)
33. Malone, T.W.: Guidelines for designing educational computer games. Childhood Education 59, 241–247 (1983)

34. Csikszentmihalyi, M.: The Psychology of Optimal Experience. Harper Perennial, New York (1990)
35. Read, J., McFarlane, S., Cassey, C.: Endurability, engagement and expectations: Measuring children's fun. In: Proceedings of the International Conference for Interaction Design and Children (2002)
36. Safyan, L., Lagattuta, K.H.: Grownups are not afraid of scary stuff, but kids are: young children's and adults' reasoning about children's, infants', and adults' fears. Child Development 79(4), 821–835 (2008)
37. Burleson, W.: Affective Learning Companions: strategies for empathetic agents with real-time multimodal affective sensing to foster meta-cognitive and meta-affective approaches to learning, motivation and perseverance. PhD thesis, Massachusetts Institute of Technology (2006)
38. Ortony, A., Clore, G.L., Collins, A.: The Cognitive Structure of Emotions. Cambridge University Press (1988)
39. Conati, C.: Probabilistic assessment of user's emotions in educational games. Journal of Applied Artificial Intelligence, Special Issue on Merging Cognition and Affect in HCI 16 (7-8), 555–575 (2002)
40. Arroyo, I., Beack, J., Beal, C.R., Woolf, B.P.: Learning with the zone of proximal development with the animalwatch intelligent tutoring system. In: Proceedings of the American Educational Research Association annual meeting, Chicago, IL (2003)
41. Kerawalla, L., O'Connor, J., Underwood, J., du Boulay, B., Holmberg, J., Luckin, R., Smith, H., Tunley, H.: The homework system: using tablet pcs as tools to support continuity of numeracy learning between home and primary school. Educational Media International 44(4), 289–303 (2007)
42. Chen, Z.H., Deng, Y.C., Chou, C.Y., Chan, T.W.: Active open learner models as animal companions: motivating children to learn through interaction with mypet and our-pet. International Journal of Artificial Intelligence in Education 17, 145–167 (2007)
43. Pantic, M., Rothkrantz, L.J.M.: Towards an affect-sensitive multimodal human-computer interaction. Special Issue on Multimodal Human-Computer Interaction (HCI) 91, 1370–1390 (2003)
44. Damian, I., Baur, T., Gebhard, P., Porayska-Pomsta, K., André, E.: A software framework for social cue-based interaction with a virtual recruiter. In: Proceedings of the 13th International Conference on Intelligent Virtual Agents, Santa Cruz (2013)
45. Henning, M.: A new approach to object-oriented middleware. IEEE Internet Computing 8(1), 66–75 (2004)
46. Dias, J., Paiva, A.: Feeling and reasoning: A computational model for emotional characters. In: Bento, C., Cardoso, A., Dias, G. (eds.) EPIA 2005. LNCS (LNAI), vol. 3808, pp. 127–140. Springer, Heidelberg (2005)
47. Fox, M., Long, D.: PDDL 2.1: An extension to PDDL for expressing temporal planning domains. Journal of Artificial Intelligence Research 20, 61–124 (2003)
48. Smith, C.A., Lazarus, R.S.: Emotion and adaptation. In: Vlahavas, I., Vrakas, D., Pervin, L.A. (eds.) Handbook of Personality: Theory and Research, pp. 609–637. Guilford, New York (1990)
49. Bernardini, S., Porayska-Pomsta, K., Sampath, H.: Designing an intelligent virtual agent for social communication in autism. In: Proceedings of the Ninth Annual AAAI Conference on Artificial Intelligence and Interactive Digital Entertainment (2013)

The TARDIS Framework: Intelligent Virtual Agents for Social Coaching in Job Interviews

Keith Anderson, Elisabeth André, T. Baur, Sara Bernardini, M. Chollet,
E. Chryssafidou, I. Damian, C. Ennis, A. Egges, P. Gebhard, H. Jones, M. Ochs,
C. Pelachaud, Kaśka Porayska-Pomsta, P. Rizzo, and Nicolas Sabouret

The TARDIS consortium

Abstract. The TARDIS project aims to build a scenario-based serious-game simulation platform for NEETs and job-inclusion associations that supports social training and coaching in the context of job interviews. This paper presents the general architecture of the TARDIS job interview simulator, and the serious game paradigm that we are developing.

1 Introduction

The number of NEETs[1] is increasing across Europe. According to Eurostat[2], in march 2012, 5.5 million of 16 to 25 years old European youngsters were unemployed, amounting to 22.6% of the youngster global population. This unemployment percentage is 10 points above the entire world's population, highlighting European youth unemployment as a significant problem.

Current research reveals that NEETs often lack self-confidence and the essential social skills needed to seek and secure employment [BP02]. They find it difficult to present themselves in a best light to prospective employers, which may put them at further risk of marginalization. Social coaching workshops, organized by youth inclusion associations across Europe, constitute a common approach to helping people in acquiring and improving their social competencies, especially in the context of job interviews. However, it is an expensive and time-consuming approach that relies on the availability of trained practitioners as well as the willingness of the young people to engage in exploring their social strengths and weakness in front of their peers and practitioners.

The TARDIS project[3], funded by the FP7, aims to build a scenario-based serious-game simulation platform that supports social training and coaching in the context of job interviews. It participates in the Digital Games for Empowerment and Inclusion initiative[4]. The platform is intended for use by young people, aged 18-25 and job-inclusion associations. Youngsters can explore, practice and improve their social skills in a diverse range of possible interview situations. They interact with virtual agents, which are designed to deliver realistic socio-emotional interaction and act as recruiters.

---

[1] NEET is a government acronym for young people not in employment, education or training.
[2] `ec.europa.eu/eurostat`
[3] `http://www.tardis-project.eu`
[4] `http://is.jrc.ec.europa.eu/pages/EAP/eInclusion/games.html`

D. Reidsma, H. Katayose, and A. Nijholt (Eds.): ACE 2013, LNCS 8253, pp. 476–491, 2013.
© Springer International Publishing Switzerland 2013

The use of serious games for job interview simulations has two advantages: 1) repeatable experience can be modulated to suit the individual needs, without the risk of real-life failure; 2) technologies are often intrinsically motivating to the young [MSS04] and may be used to remove the many barriers that real-life situations may pose, in particular the stress associated with engaging in unfamiliar interactions with others. In this context, the originality of the TARDIS platform is two-fold. First, TARDIS is able to detect in real-time its users' emotions and social attitudes through voice and facial expression recognition, and to adapt the game progress and the virtual interlocutor's behaviour to the individual users. Second, it provides field practitioners with unique tools for 1) designing appropriate interview scenarios without reliance on researchers and 2) measuring individuals' emotion regulation and social skill acquisition (*via* the user modelling tools), thus enabling a more flexible and personalized coaching for young people at risk of social exclusion.

This paper presents the TARDIS architecture and game design. The next section briefly presents some related work in serious games and affective computing. Section 3 presents the TARDIS architecture. Section 4 presents the TARDIS game itself.

2 Related Work

Addressing social exclusion of marginalized young people is a key issue that must be tackled on a wide range of different levels. The INCLUSO project [EDVDB10] outlined two main directions in supporting social integration: (1) to encourage and support personal development and (2) to encourage and support social participation. The TARDIS project focuses on the first challenge, *i.e.* on improving communication skills in one-on-one interactions. Based on the analysis that computer games as well as serious games are intrinsically motivating to users (e.g. see [MC05]), we have developed a virtual social coaching platform that follows a serious games paradigm, in which the youngster can train and evaluate his/her social interaction skills with a virtual agent.

The use of virtual agents in social coaching has increased rapidly in the last decade. Projects such as those by Tartaro and Cassell [TC08] or e-Circus [APD+09] provide evidence that virtual agents can help humans improve their social skills and, more generally, their emotional intelligence [Gol06]. In job interview situations, emotional intelligence of both the applicant and the recruiter plays a crucial role: in human to human job interviews, the personality of the applicant is inferred by the recruiter according to the mood, the emotions and the social attitudes expressed by the youngster [HH10]. Furthermore, visual and vocal perceptions of the interviewer have been shown to affect their judgments of the applicants during job interviews [DM99]. Youngsters' emotional intelligence, in particular their ability to self-regulate during the interview will affect the outcome of the interview.

In the TARDIS project, we address two challenges. First, in line with the objectives of the field of *Affective Computing* [Pic97], we aim to build virtual agents that react in a coherent manner (see also [MGR03, PDS+04, PSS09]). Based on the non-verbal inputs (smiles, emotion expressions, body movements) and their goals (making the applicant at ease or, on the contrary, trying to put him/her under pressure), the agent must select relevant verbal and non-verbal responses. Second, the model presented in this paper seeks to take into account all the different dimensions of the socio-affective interaction, in the context of a job interview situation, including indepth real-time understanding of the individual youngsters emotional states while they are interacting with the system.

A number of serious games exist that relate to different aspects of TARDIS. First, the utilization of Microsoft Kinect has become popular as an affordable markerless motion capture system, and has been utilized successfully in many games with serious applications. Mostly, however, these games tend to be applied in the medical field, with applications for stroke rehabilitation patients [JYZ12] and people suffering with Parkinsons [SS12]. However, when it comes to reading more complex parameters, such as emotions, regular cameras are also frequently used.

Some examples of serious games that infer complex paradigms about the state of mind of the user from visual and audio inputs are *LifeIsGame* [Orv10] and *ASC Inclusion* [SMBC+13]. Both are ongoing projects within the EC framework and focus on helping children on the Autism spectrum to recognize and express emotions through facial expressions, tone of voice and body gestures. While these games access the facial expressions and behaviour of the user in a similar manner to TARDIS, virtual humans will interact based on low-level signal analysis as opposed to the virtual recruiter in TARDIS who will respond to high-level socio-emotional behaviours and mental states' representations.

Some serious games also focus on employment and the work place. A serious game with some similar objectives to TARDIS is interview training game *Mon Entretien D'embauche* [dR13]. Released by telecoms company SFR, the user is represented by an avatar and progresses through a number of events before the interview itself by selecting appropriate responses to interactions with other avatars. While the goal to relieve stress or anxiety is similar to that of TARDIS, the approach is quite different. While Mon Entretien D'embauche assesses progress based on the verbal responses of the player, TARDIS focuses on whether the player is completely engaged and displaying appropriate non-verbal social behaviours. Another workplace focused game is *iSpectrum* [Ins13], which aims to help people on the Autism Spectrum to prepare themselves for working in a new environment and increase their employability. It can also educate employers, increasing their knowledge about integrating someone with Autism within their company.

My Automated Conversation coacH, *MACH* [HCM+13] utilizes a virtual human to coach the user's social communication skills. While one of the applications of this game is for interview situations, the focus here is on the facial expressions, speech and prosody. The intelligent agent here will mimic the users behaviour and respond verbally and non-verbally, as was done in Semaine [BDSHP12]. However, while TARDIS focuses on the underlying emotion or state-of-mind, MACH provides feedback on physical behaviours such as explicit facial expressions and tone and volume of voice.

3   The TARDIS Architecture

3.1   General Architecture

Social coaching involves three actors: the participant (the youngster), the interlocutor, which is replaced by an intelligent virtual agent in the TARDIS game, and the coach or

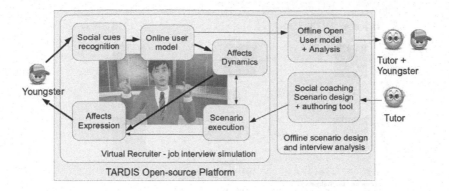

Fig. 1. TARDIS general architecture

practitioner from the social inclusion association. In this context, the TARDIS system architecture includes four main components:

- **The Scenario module** controls the discourse during the interview. It tells the virtual recruiter the expectation in terms of emotions and attitudes expressed by the youngster, depending on the stage of the interview (*Scenario Execution* in Fig. 1, Section 3.2).
- **The Social Signal modules** provide the affective model with information about the youngster's emotions and social attitudes (we refer to them as *mental states*) that are detected by the system (*Social Cues Recognition and Online User Model* in Fig. 1, Section 3.3 and 3.4).
- **The Affective Module** is responsible for building a model of beliefs and intentions (for the virtual recruiter) about the mental states of the youngster (in terms of affects) and about the course of actions in the ongoing interview (*Affects Dynamics* in Fig. 1, Section 3.5).
- **The Animation module** is responsible for expressing the virtual recruiter's affective state built by the affective model through verbal and non-verbal behaviour, both in terms of facial animation and body movements (*Affects Expressions* in Fig. 1, Section 3.6).

The interaction is recorded and post-game debriefing sessions can be organized between the practitioner and the youngster. Fig. 1 gives an overview of this architecture. The following subsections briefly present the different components of the platform. Section 4 presents the TARDIS game paradigm.

3.2 The Scenario Module

For the authoring of our interactive virtual recruiter's behaviour, we rely on an authoring tool [GMK12] that allows to model and to execute different behavioural features at a very detailed and abstract level. A central authoring paradigm of this tool is the separation of dialog content and interaction structure, see Fig. 2.

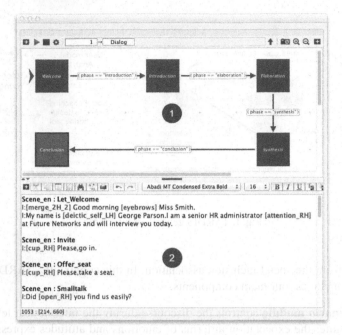

Fig. 2. Main five stages of the recruitment scenario modelled as HSFMs

The multimodal dialog content is specified with a number of scenes that are organized in a *scenescript* (see Fig. 2, panel 2). The scene structure, which can be compared to those in TV or theatre playbooks, consists of utterances and stage directions for the actors. In our scenes, directions are animation commands for the non-verbal behaviour of the virtual recruiter (e.g. gestures, facial expressions, or postures). The (narrative) structure of our interactive recruitment simulation and the interactive behaviour of our virtual recruiter is controlled by parallel hierarchical finite state machines (HFSM) specifying the logic of the scenes played and the commands executed according to a user reactions and a given state of the interactive performance, see Fig. 2, panel 1.

In contrast with a linear theatre scene arrangement, an interactive presentation comes along with another degree of freedom, *i.e.* the reactions of the system to user's detected affects or to the virtual recruiter's mental state. Such reactions have to be considered in the scenario control. In order to realize this, we have enhanced a linear five stage recruitment story (see Fig. 2, panel 1.) with reactions to user input. During the five stages, depending on the attitude that the virtual recruiter wants to convey (see Section 3.5), the virtual recruiter may mimic specific behaviours of the user. For this task, we use two HFSMs (modelled within each recruitment stage) that allow the character to react in a similar way as the user's behaviours. The state machines react to the detected social cues and trigger an overlay behaviour. This behaviour is blended with any ongoing animation that the virtual recruiter is performing at any time (Section 3.6). For example, if a user smiles while the virtual recruiter asks a question, the recruiter will also smile. Similar behavioural reactions are modelled in the case of head movements.

In order to detect and interpret the social cues expressed by the youngster during the interview, we have integrated social signal modules. In the next section, we first present the module for the recognition of the youngster's social signals. In section 3.4, the module for the interpretation of the recognized social signals are introduced.

3.3   The Social Signal Recognition Module

The social signal recognition module is able to record and analyze social and psychological signals from users and to recognize predefined social cues, i.e. behaviours of the interviewee, conscious or unconscious, that have a specific meaning in a social context such as a job interview, in real-time. Examples of such signals are smiles, head nods and body movements. These social cues will allow us to determine the mental state of the user (Section 3.4) in real-time and will act as a basis for debriefing sessions between youngsters and practitioners after the interviews.

In TARDIS the social cues were selected based on two criteria: pertinence to the job interview context and automatic recognition viability from a technological point of view. In order to determine what social cues are pertinent to the desired context, we evaluated the data from multiple user studies involving real NEETs and practitioners. The technological viability was determined using a literature review as well as in-depth analysis of available state-of-the-art sensing hardware. This is an ongoing process and we are continuously looking to extend the list of social cues.

The system uses a combination of sensors and software algorithms which offer good results in terms of accuracy and low intrusion. High accuracy ensures that a youngster's social cues are correctly recognized and allows the virtual recruiter to react to them correctly. It is equally important that the approach has a low intrusion factor. For example, biological signal sensors are not feasible in this scenario because attaching various sensors to the skin of the users will most likely result in an increase in stress which might have a negative effect on the user's job interview performance, but may not be actually indicative of the user's actual abilities. Therefore, in the context studied, remote sensors are preferred.

Fig. 3. Examples of the gestures our system can recognise

For recording and pre-processing human behaviour data, our system relies on the SSI framework[5] which was developed as part of our previous work [WLB+13]. It provides a variety of tools for the real-time analysis and recognition of such data. Using SSI and the Microsoft Kinect sensor we are able to recognize various social cues [DBA13], such as *hand to face*, *looking away*, *postures* (arms crossed, arms open, hands behind

---

[5] http://openssi.net

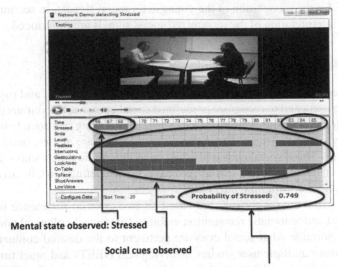

Mental state observed: Stressed

Social cues observed

Probability inferred for the last second of observation

Fig. 4. Video playback facility, with the annotation data and Bayesian network output in the bottom-right corner of the screen

head), *leaning back, leaning forward, gesticulation, voice activity, smiles* and *laughter*. In addition to these, our system is also able to compute the expressivity [CRKK06] of the user's movements (i.e. energy, overall activation, spatial extent and fluidity of the movement). Fig. 3 exemplifies some of the recognized social cues.

Given the recognized social signals, the next step consists in interpreting these signals to determine the socio-affective state of the youngster. In the next section, we present the process to interpret the youngster's social cues.

3.4   The Social Signal Interpretation Module

Inferring youngsters' mental states in real-time is important to determine the behaviours of the virtual recruiters. In order to gain an understanding of the social cues that occur in job interview situations and how these correspond to youngsters' mental state (in terms of affects and attitudes such as relaxed, stressed, enthusiastic...), we conducted a study at Mission Locale in Goussainville, France, with 10 real job seekers and 5 practitioners engaged in mock interviews. The data was video recorded and annotated manually.

Episodes as in Fig. 4 were annotated for fine-grained behaviours, *e.g.* looking away, lack of direct eye contact, smiling, etc. The annotations were mapped onto eight mental states, identified by the practitioners during post-hoc video walkthroughs and semi-structured interviews, as relevant to this context: *Stressed, Embarrassed, Ill-at-ease, Bored, Focused, Hesitant, Relieved*. The annotations have been fed through and used by a suite of four TARDIS bespoke C# applications: *Annotation Analyzer*, which calculates the frequencies of the co-occurrences of groups of social cues with each mental state;

Net Populator, which infers the probability tables of the Bayesian Networks (BNs), representing the mental states; *Net Demonstrator*, which allows to playback a video of an interaction along with the annotations used to train the networks and the real-time output of the network for a given mental state; *Net Tester* – a facility that feeds the annotations through the Bayesian Networks and produces statistics about the network's performance in terms of correct and incorrect classifications.

The BNs and the Social Cue Recognition component (Section 3.3) are integrated , so that the inferences about mental states can occur in real-time. While the accuracy of the BNs themselves is relatively high when tested with video data, real-time recognition of social cues that would provide a sufficient and necessary evidence for the BNs remains a challenge for TARDIS and for the field of affective computing as a whole. Presently, we are testing several solutions which leverage and combine continuous stream of information from the Social Cue recognition module along with information about contextual information, in particular the type of question being asked by the recruiter and the expectations that relate to appropriate response on the part of the youngster.

Based on the inferred youngster's mental states and based on the course of the interaction, the virtual recruiter should determine its affective behaviour. For this purpose, we have developed an Affective Module presented in the next section.

3.5   The Affective Module

The Affective Module for the virtual recruiter has two main computational functions:

- it will periodically compute the new affective states of the virtual recruiter, based on the perceptions, expectations from the scenario and its current affective states.
- it will select actions (*i.e.* different forms of utterances and specific branching in the scenario) according to its intentions following the youngster's mental state.

Figure 5 illustrates the different elements of the Affective module as well as the links to the other modules.

The Affective model. This module is detailed in [JS13]. It provides a reactive model based on expectations from the youngster and perceptions (by Social Signal Interpretation) on the youngster. It allows a computation of the virtual recruiter emotions, moods and social attitudes. Emotion computation relies on the difference between expectations and perceptions. Emotions are modelled with OCC categories [OCC88]. Moods evolve on a middle term dynamic and are directly influenced by emotions following Mehrabian *Pleasure, Arousal, Dominance* framework [Meh96]. One of the originality of this model lies in the proposal for a computational model of the virtual recruiter social attitudes that rely on its personality and its current mood.

The Decision module. The goal of this module is to build a representation of the youngster's beliefs (*a.k.a.* Theory of Mind or ToM [Les94]). The virtual recruiter considers the affective dimensions of the youngster's answers (computed by the Social Signal Modules, see section 3.3 and 3.4) in a particular context (the question that has just been asked by the recruiter) to derive the positive or negative attitude the youngster has with

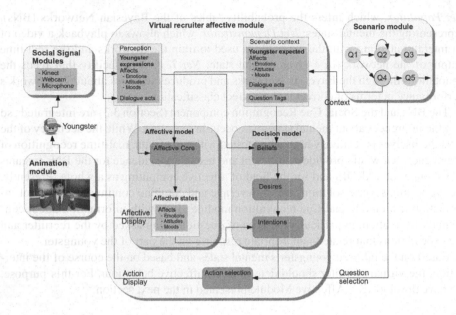

Fig. 5. The Architecture of the Affective Module

respect to the considered topic. For instance, if the youngster reacts with too high a detachment to a question about the technical requirements for the job, then the agent might deduce that, on the topic *skill*, the user is not very confident. It will lower the value of $B_{Young}(skill)$. This model will, in turn, influence the next utterances of the virtual agents in function of the recruiter high-level intentions. The agent will select in the scenario subjects where the youngster is at ease (helpful/friendly) or not (confrontational/provocative).

3.6   The Animation Module

A person's affective state is mainly expressed through their non-verbal behaviour (e.g. facial expressions, body postures, audio cues, and gestures). In order to give the capability to the virtual recruiter to display its emotions and attitudes computed by the Affective Module (Section 3.5), we use the Greta system [BMNP07] to compute the animation parameters for the multimodal expressions of emotions [NHP11]. Moreover, the virtual recruiter will be animated using a combination of hand-animated gesture outputs (based on the animation parameters) and posed facial expressions, along with motion-captured animation techniques. This allows us to exploit the both methods: the essential flexibility relates to the character's gestures and movements when reacting to the input of the youngster, and the innate naturalness and subtleties of human motion that can be displayed through motion-captured data.

In order to ensure that the emotions conveyed by the virtual character are interpreted as intended, a number of studies on the perception of emotion through body motion

Fig. 6. Stimuli from one perceptual study showing, from left to right synchronized facial and body motion, body motion alone and facial motion only for the basic emotion *fear*

have been carried out, with conversing virtual characters as the stimuli. We have found that some complex and subtle body motions are difficult to convey through body motion alone, and so have highlighted the importance of the appropriate combination of facial and body motions [EE12]. The literature suggests that the combination of facial and body motions does increase the perception of expressiveness of such emotions on video game characters (Figure 6). To this end, one major research challenge for the animation of the virtual character is the integration between the gestures, facial and body motions of the recruiter to ensure the maximum effectiveness of expressing emotions, while ensuring the character maintains a sense of naturalness about his/her motions. One way of making our virtual recruiter appear as natural as possible is through the inclusion of inherent human behaviours such as idle movements and interaction with objects and the environment around them.

The attitude of the virtual recruiter may be also expressed through non-verbal signals (such as smiles) but also through the dynamics of the behaviour. The global behaviour tendency (e.g. the body energy), the combination and sequencing of behaviours (e.g. order of display of smile and head aversion) as well as the mimicry of the the youngster's behaviour may convey different attitudes [KH10]. In order to identify the non-verbal behaviours that the virtual recruiter may express to display different attitudes, we are analyzing the videos that were recorded at Mission Locale (Section 3.4). For this purpose, annotations have been added to consider the interaction context (e.g. turn-taking and conversation topic), the non-verbal behaviour of the recruiter (e.g. gestures, facial expressions, posture) and his expressed attitudes (friendliness of dominance using a bi-dimensional scale based on Argyle's attitude dimensions [Arg88]). In order to give the capability to the virtual recruiter to display attitudes, we are extracting patterns and characteristics of behaviours associated with different levels of friendliness and dominance.

4   The TARDIS Game

The TARDIS game is being developed with the aim to ensure that it meets both the educational and entertainment demands of the associated youngsters. The user will play him/herself applying for a fictional job, and is expected to behave as he/she would in real life. To this end, there is no "player" avatar and the input device used most frequently is the player him/herself. The movements and sounds made by the player will be the main method of input deciding how the game progresses.

Fig. 7. Our two different game settings: (top) flipchart/presentation scene with our male character and (bottom) our office desk environment with female recruiter

4.1   Game Setting and Assets

The user will be seated in the real world, in front of a computer. Two different settings will be available in the game; a conference room and a typical office environment. In these settings, the virtual recruiter will be seated at a desk or standing in front of a flip-chart or use a presentation wall. The office/desk setting will be used as a prototypical interview arena, whereas the flip chart/conference room setting can be used for training purposes or feedback sessions, where information can be presented to the user. Small objects will also be present in the environment for the virtual character to interact with and present some variety for the youngster.

There will be two different character models in the TARDIS game, one male and one female. Different aspects of each character's appearance can be modulated to give the impression of variety across interviews and scenarios; such as skin or hair colour, glasses, clothing and age. This is important as the practitioners will have some control over the virtual recruiter and they will ensure that it is appropriate the individual scenarios. Examples of the TARDIS game assets can be seen in Figure 7.

4.2 Game Modes

There will be a number of different game modes for TARDIS, to allow maximum interaction between the user and practitioner to permit the youngster to obtain the best results:

- Menu mode: Here, the user is presented with a menu and can select whether to modify settings or practice or play the game. There is also an option for the practitioner to enter edit mode.
- Settings/Options mode: Here, the user can select the level of difficulty at which they wish to play the game in, as well as set sound/visual options and check that their equipment is working adequately.
- Practice mode: Here, the user can practice a virtual interview, which does not count towards their progress. This mode will include a virtual interview as in the Play mode, but will allow for a "Pause" function, and will also include visual feedback to inform if their actions have been read by the system.
- Play mode: Here, they will be able to select which position they wish to interview for and take part in the virtual interview.
- Edit mode: This opens the editor for the practitioners, where they can modify interview scenarios to tailor individual needs of the user or job descriptions. They will also have access to change some dialog of the interaction, such as small-talk. This will result in a more varied experience for the youngster, but will not affect the expectations of the scenario.

4.3 Progress and Advancement

During the virtual interview, the user will receive "credits" for a range of properties concurrent with appropriate behaviour in job interviews. These credits will contribute to an overall score upon the conclusion of the interview. Completing a level will occur once a specified score has been achieved. They can then attempt a job interview at a more challenging level.

As the user progresses within the game, "levels" will not result in a different location in the physical world as in a platform game. Rather, the setting will remain the same, and the internal states of the virtual recruiter will reflect an advancement. For instance, the recruiter may become less patient, or more reactive to inappropriate behaviours. This can be reflected in the agent's reaction to individual behaviours or movements of the player. It can also be built into the agent's internal state. For instance, they could be aggressive or docile, friendly or aloof, and become less facilitative or forgiving of mistakes as the player progresses.

Since the objective of TARDIS is to achieve a sense of independence and inclusion for the youngsters who use it, we encourage players to assess their own progress, and will provide them with useful feedback to do so as the game progresses. To this end, as well as a final score when the interview comes to an end, we will provide the player with a breakdown of how well they performed over a number of relevant factors. Physical parameters such as body or hand movement, head gaze or the evenness of the vocal intonation can be obtained from our SSI and reported to the user. So, the youngster can identify which aspects of their social interaction are satisfactory and they can acknowledge other areas where they may need to focus on improving. We also plan to translate the physical parameters calculated from the SSI in non-technical terms, such as gestures, posture, vocal, head gaze, or even more abstract personality traits like openness or professionalism. Then the user can be provided with further details about their performance along with suggestions on how to improve. For example, "you have scored xx% on comfort, maybe next time try to ensure that you keep your voice even and do not fidget too much to appear more at ease". Any such feedback will be provided from a source outside of the virtual recruiter.

4.4   Post Interview Analysis

After each Game Session, the users receive feedback regarding their performance using our NOnVerbal behaviour Analysis tool (NovA) [BDL+13]. It enables the playback of the audiovisual recording of the interaction and visualizes recognized social cues, as well as continuous data streams in several modalities, such as graphs, time line tracks, heat maps, pie- and bar charts and others. Typically, different kinds of behaviours are coded on different parallel tracks so that their temporal relationships are clearly visible. Additionally, a series of statistics regarding the user's performance is automatically computed which is meant to help users track their improvements over time.

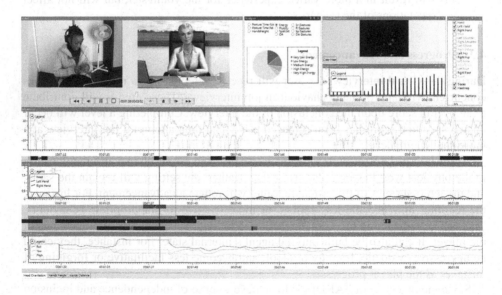

Fig. 8. NovA Analysis Tool

The analysis tool is designed to help youngsters reflect on their behaviour as well as to support the practitioners in identifying problems in the youngsters behaviour. The design of the tool has been informed during a workshop conducted in association with the practitioners at Mission Locale Goussainville. During the workshop, several key design points have been discussed. For instance, the practitioners pointed out that the ability of reviewing the performance of the user in parallel to the performance of the virtual agent is critical to interpreting the user's behaviours correctly. The discussions also yielded that it is equally important that the tool gives the practitioners information regarding when a certain behaviour of the user happened relative to the scenario's progress.

5 Conclusion

The originality of the TARDIS platform is threefold. First, we consider a participatory design for both the game and the simulator architecture. Workshops with practitioners and mock interviews with youngsters facing either human beings or virtual agents was used to define the expectations of the system. Second, the system is able to detect in real-time user's emotions and social attitudes through voice and facial expression recognition, and to adapt the progress of the game and the virtual interlocutor's behaviour to the individual users. Third, TARDIS gives practitioners new instruments to measure individuals' progress in being able to self-regulate emotionally and their social skill acquisition, thus facilitating reflection on their own practice and enabling a more flexible and personalized coaching for young people at risk of social exclusion.

We are currently evaluating the first prototype of the project and working on the next iteration of our opensource platform, implemented in C++ and Java using the Semaine[6] framework with EmotionML[7] messages.

Acknowledgement. This research was funded by the European Union Information Society and Media Seventh Framework Programme FP7-ICT-2011-7 under grant agreement 288578.

References

[APD+09]   Aylett, R., Paiva, A., Dias, J., Hall, L., Woods, S.: Affective agents for education against bullying. In: Affective Information Processing, pp. 75–90. Springer, Heidelberg (2009)
[Arg88]   Argyle, M.: Bodily Communication. University paperbacks, Methuen (1988)
[BDL+13]   Baur, T., Damian, I., Lingenfelser, F., Wagner, J., André, E.: Nova: Automated analysis of nonverbal signals in social interactions. In: Human Behavior Understanding (HBU) Workshop at 21st ACM International Conference on Multimedia (2013)
[BDSHP12]   Bevacqua, E., De Sevin, E., Hyniewska, S.J., Pelachaud, C.: A listener model: introducing personality traits. Journal on Multimodal User Interfaces 6(1-2), 27–38 (2012)

---

[6] http://www.semaine-project.eu
[7] http://www.w3.org/TR/2010/WD-emotionml-20100729/

[BMNP07] Bevacqua, E., Mancini, M., Niewiadomski, R., Pelachaud, C.: An expressive eca showing complex emotions. In: Proceedings of the AISB Annual Convention, Newcastle, UK, pp. 208–216 (2007)

[BP02] Bynner, J., Parsons, S.: Social exclusion and the transition from school to work: The case of young people not in education, employment, or training (neet). Journal of Vocational Behavior 60(2), 289–309 (2002)

[CRKK06] Caridakis, G., Raouzaiou, A., Karapouzis, K., Kollias, S.: Synthesizing gesture expressivity based on real sequences. In: Workshop on Multimodal Corpora: from Multimodal Behaviour Theories to Usable Models, LREC Conf., Genoa, Italy (May 2006)

[DBA13] Damian, I., Baur, T., André, E.: Investigating social cue-based interaction in digital learning games. In: Proceedings of the 8th International Conference on the Foundations of Digital Games, SASDG (2013)

[DM99] DeGroot, T., Motowidlo, S.J.: Why visual and vocal interview cues can affect interviewers' judgments and predict job performance. Journal of Applied Psychology 84(6), 986–993 (1999)

[dR13] Société Française de Radiotéléphonie. Mon entretien d'embauche game (June 2013)

[EDVDB10] Engelen, J., Dekelver, J., Van Den Bosch, W.: Incluso: Social software for the social inclusion of marginalised youth. Social Media for Social Inclusion of Youth at Risk 1(1), 11–20 (2010)

[EE12] Ennis, C., Egges, A.: Perception of complex emotional body language of a virtual character. In: Kallmann, M., Bekris, K. (eds.) MIG 2012. LNCS, vol. 7660, pp. 112–121. Springer, Heidelberg (2012)

[GMK12] Gebhard, P., Mehlmann, G., Kippo, M.: Visual scenemaker - a tool for authoring interactive virtual characters. Journal on Multimodal User Interfaces 6(1-2), 3–11 (2012)

[Gol06] Goleman, D.: Social intelligence: The new science of human relationships. Bantam (2006)

[HCM+13] Hoque, M.E., Courgeon, M., Martin, J., Mutlu, B., Picard, R.W.: Mach: My automated conversation coach. In: Proc. ACM International Joint Conference on Pervasive and Ubiquitous Computing, UbiComp 2013 (to appear, 2013)

[HH10] Hareli, S., Hess, U.: What emotional reactions can tell us about the nature of others: An appraisal perspective on person perception. Cognition & Emotion 24(1), 128–140 (2010)

[Ins13] Serious Games Insitute. ispectrum game (June 2013)

[JS13] Jones, H., Sabouret, N.: TARDIS - A simulation platform with an affective virtual recruiter for job interviews. In: IDGEI (Intelligent Digital Games for Empowerment and Inclusion) (2013)

[JYZ12] Jiao, Y., Yang, X., Zhang, J.J.: A serious game prototype for post-stroke rehabilitation using kinect. Journal of Game Amusement Society 4(1) (2012)

[KH10] Knapp, M.L., Hall, J.A.: Nonverbal Communication in Human Interaction. Cengage Learning (2010)

[Les94] Leslie, A.M.: ToMM, ToBy, and agency: Core architecture and domain specificity. In: Hirschfeld, L.A., Gelman, S.A. (eds.) Mapping the Mind Domain Specificity in Cognition and Culture, ch. 5, pp. 119–148. Cambridge University Press (1994)

[MC05] Manske, M., Conati, C.: Modelling learning in an educational game. In: Proceeding of the 2005 Conference on Artificial Intelligence in Education: Supporting Learning through Intelligent and Socially Informed Technology, pp. 411–418 (2005)

[Meh96]   Mehrabian, A.: Pleasure-arousal-dominance: A general framework for describing
             and measuring individual Differences in Temperament. Current Psychology 14(4),
             261 (1996)
[MGR03]   Marsella, S., Gratch, J., Rickel, J.: Expressive behaviors for virtual worlds. In: Life-
             like Characters Tools Affective Functions and Applications, pp. 317–360 (2003)
[MSS04]   Mitchell, A., Savill-Smith, C.: The use of computer and video games for learning:
             A review of the literature (2004)
[NHP11]   Niewiadomski, R., Hyniewska, S.J., Pelachaud, C.: Constraint-based model for
             synthesis of multimodal sequential expressions of emotions. IEEE Transactions
             on Affective Computing 2(3), 134–146 (2011)
[OCC88]   Ortony, A., Clore, G.L., Collins, A.: The Cognitive Structure of Emotions. Cam-
             bridge University Press (July 1988)
[Orv10]   Orvalho, V.: Lifeisgame: Learning of facial emotions using serious games. In: Proc.
             Body Representation in Physical and Virtual Reality with Application to Rehabili-
             tation (2010)
[PDS+04]   Paiva, A., Dias, J., Sobral, D., Aylett, R., Sobreperez, P., Woods, S., Zoll, C., Hall,
             L.: Caring for agents and agents that care: Building empathic relations with syn-
             thetic agents. In: Proceedings of the Third International Joint Conference on Au-
             tonomous Agents and Multiagent Systems, vol. 1, pp. 194–201. IEEE Computer
             Society, Washington, DC (2004)
[Pic97]   Picard, R.W.: Affective Computing. Emotion TR 221(321), 97–97 (1997)
[PSS09]   Pareto, L., Schwartz, D.L., Svensson, L.: Learning by guiding a teachable agent to
             play an educational game. In: Education Building Learning, pp. 1–3 (2009)
[SMBC+13]   Schuller, B., Marchi, E., Baron-Cohen, S., O'Reilly, H., Robinson, P., Davies, I.,
             Golan, O., Friedenson, S., Tal, S., Newman, S., Meir, N., Shillo, R., Camurri, A.,
             Piana, S., Bölte, S., Lundqvist, D., Berggren, S., Baranger, A., Sullings, N.: Asc-
             inclusion: Interactive emotion games for social inclusion of children with autism
             spectrum conditions. In: Proc. 1st International Workshop on Intelligent Digital
             Games for Empowerment and Inclusion, IDGEI 2013 (2013)
[SS12]   Siegel, S., Smeddinck, J.: Adaptive difficulty with dynamic range of motion ad-
             justments in exergames for parkinson's disease patients. In: Herrlich, M., Malaka,
             R., Masuch, M. (eds.) ICEC 2012. LNCS, vol. 7522, pp. 429–432. Springer, Hei-
             delberg (2012)
[TC08]   Tartaro, A., Cassell, J.: Playing with virtual peers: bootstrapping contingent dis-
             course in children with autism. In: Proceedings of the 8th International Conference
             on International Conference for the Learning Sciences, vol. 2, pp. 382–389. Inter-
             national Society of the Learning Sciences (2008)
[WLB+13]   Wagner, J., Lingenfelser, F., Baur, T., Damian, I., Kistler, F., André, E.: The social
             signal interpretation (ssi) framework - multimodal signal processing and recogni-
             tion in real-time. In: Proceedings of ACM MULTIMEDIA 2013, Barcelona (2013)

Development of a Full-Body Interaction Digital Game for Children to Learn Vegetation Succession

Takayuki Adachi[1,*], Hiroshi Mizoguchi[1], Miki Namatame[2], Fusako Kusunoki[3], Masanori Sugimoto[4], Keita Muratsu[5], Etsuji Yamaguchi[5], Shigenori Inagaki[5], and Yoshiaki Takeda[5]

[1] Tokyo University of Science, 2641, Yamazaki, Noda, Chiba, Japan
j7512602@ed.tus.ac.jp, hm@rs.noda.tus.ac.jp
[2] Tsukuba University of Technology, 4-3-15, Amakubo, Tsukuba, Ibaraki, Japan
miki@a.tsukuba-tech.ac.jp
[3] Tama Art University, 2-1723, Yarimizu, Hachioji, Tokyo, Japan
kusunoki@tamabi.ac.jp
[4] Hokkaido University, Kita 14 Nishi 9, Kita, Sapporo, Hokkaido, Japan
sugi@ist.hokudai.ac.jp
[5] Kobe University, 3-11, Tsurukabuto, Nada, Kobe, Hyogo, Japan
126d103d@stu.kobe-u.ac.jp, inagakis@kobe-u.ac.jp

Abstract. In this study, we developed a simulation game called "Human SUGOROKU" that simulates vegetation succession of the real forest area in the virtual world. This game consists of a full-body interaction system to enable children to enjoy and learn vegetation succession by playing with their body movement. We conducted an experiment with children and investigated the effects of the full-body interaction through interviews. The results showed that the full-body interaction promotes a sense of immersion in the game. This paper describes the structure of this system and the interview results.

Keywords: Interactive Content, Ultrasonic Sensor, Embodiment, Learning Support System.

1 Introduction

Elementary school students often find it difficult to understand environmental problems because they cannot easily experience the knowledge they gain at school. In this light, we are aiming to collaborate with schools to teach elementary school students about environmental problems.

Toward this end, we have developed a simulation tablet game based on the digital SUGOROKU board game for vegetation succession [1][2]. Multiple players can participate in a SUGOROKU game. There are grids around the board and each player handles a piece. Players move their own pieces on the grids according to dices or

---

* Corresponding author.

D. Reidsma, H. Katayose, and A. Nijholt (Eds.): ACE 2013, LNCS 8253, pp. 492–496, 2013.
© Springer International Publishing Switzerland 2013

cards, with their aim being to have the most advanced piece. In our game, a piece corresponds to a plant and grids, to the succession phase of the plant. In other words, the children play the role of plants in the simulation. We conducted an experimental evaluation that revealed that our game effectively stimulated the interest of students and supported their learning.

However, one drawback is that it is digital and is therefore played on a computer screen; we found that the virtual world did not well approximate the real world. The experimental evaluation suggested that students were not enough immersive in the virtual world and making the virtual world more immersive would not only further motivate the students but also enhance their further understanding. To immerse students in the digital game, we focused on realizing operations via body movements.

Accordingly, we developed a new learning support system called "Human SUGOROKU." To make this game immersive, a full-body interaction interface was realized by combining a human detector interface to measure a person's movement and the digital SUGOROKU game. In Human SUGOROKU, the students themselves move on the board as pieces and play the digital game.

2   Human SUGOROKU

2.1   Structure

In "Human SUGOROKU", people operate the pieces of the digital game by moving on the grids. To realize this operation, technology to measure a people's position and to identify them in the room is necessary. A technology to measure people's 3D position through attached ultrasonic sensors has already been proposed [3]. Accordingly, we used ultrasonic sensors as the human detector interface.

This system is composed of ultrasonic sensors, two computers, and a projector (Figure 1). Receivers are placed on the ceiling and transmitters are attached to people moving on the grids. A server computer is connected to the ultrasonic sensor. Another client computer runs the digital game that is projected by the projector. Because the transmitters have unique identifiers, the ultrasonic sensors can identify them. The 3D position and ID measured by the ultrasonic sensors is sent over the network (Figure 2). Therefore, by setting transmitters that correspond to a type of plant piece in advance, we can understand the position of a learner and type of plant.

2.2   Digital Game

This game simulates the real forest area of Mt. Rokko in Japan. Figure 3 shows a screenshot of the game. The plant pieces represent the characteristic plants that grow on Mt. Rokko. The surrounding part is the grid area. There are event cards that disturb or promote plant growth. Pieces move on the grids accordingly. The window visualizes vegetation succession according to the progress in the game.

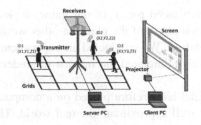

Fig. 1. Structure of Human SUGOROKU

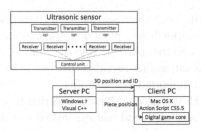

Fig. 2. System Configuration

In the digital game, there are 3 types of plant pieces: vertebral, red pine, and *Rubus microphyllus*. These plants have different growth rates and size. There are 6 types of event cards: sunny, rainy, wild boar, insects, landslides, and felling. The extent of disturbance depends on the characteristics of each event card, and they affect plant breeding. Vegetation succession is expressed by the relative progress of each plant piece. Players can visually understand the state of vegetation succession from the visualization.

3　Experiment

The subjects comprised 35 Japanese sixth-grade elementary school students aged 11–12 years (Figure 4). The evaluation task was to investigate students' subjective impressions of playing 'Human SUGOROKU' based on individual interviews.

On the basis of the interview records, we created categories for classifying students' statements and counted the number of student responses in each category (Table 1). Table 2 shows the statements relating to the most common category in Table 1. Subject 1 pointed out a feature of "Human SUGOROKU" that allowed him to be a piece on the game board, stating that he was able to pretend to be a real plant. Table 3 highlights the statements relating to the second most common category in table 1. Subject 2 had a sense of being inside the game, because his/her own movement was reflected in the movement of the piece displayed on the screen. Table 4 shows the statements relating to the third most common category in table 1. Subject 3 said that it was great to be able to learn the name of plants while playing SUGOROKU.

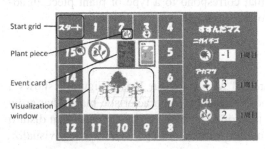

Fig. 3. Screenshot of Digital Game

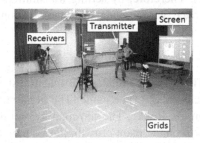

Fig. 4. Playing Human SUGOROKU

Table 1. Number of students responding to each category

Category	No. of students
I had a real sense of being a plant because my own body was a piece on the game board.	16
I could feel that I was in the game because the movements of my body were linked to the movements of the plant on the computer screen.	14
It was good that I could learn various things about vegetation succession.	11

N = 35, includes multiple answers.

Table 2. Statement relating to a student's feeling of being a plant

I:	Please tell us what you liked about the 'Human SUGOROKU'.
S1:	Since I can be a piece on the game board, [...] I had fun making moves while pretending to be a real plant.

I: Interviewer, S1: Subject 1

Table 3. Statement relating to the movement linking the students' body and the plant on the computer screen

I:	Please tell us what you liked about the 'Human SUGOROKU'.
S2:	Because I have a sensor on my head and the piece displayed on the screen moves as I move, it was as if I were inside the game.

I: Interviewer, S2: Subject 2

Table 4. Statement relating to learning various things about vegetation succession

I:	Please tell us what you liked about the 'Human SUGOROKU'.
S3:	I thought it was great that I was able to learn about plants, such as their names, while being a piece on the game board and playing.

I: Interviewer, S3: Subject 3

4   Conclusion

The results of the evaluation indicated that many students were immersed in the virtual world of vegetation succession by becoming a piece on the game board and having their own movement linked to the movement of the piece displayed on the screen. On the basis of these results, we can conclude that 'Human SUGOROKU' is effective for facilitating students' immersion in the virtual world of vegetation succession.

Acknowledgments. This research was partly supported by the Grants-in-Aid for Scientific Research (B) (No. 24300290).

References

1. Deguchi, A., Inagaki, S., Kusunoki, F., Yamaguchi, E., Takeda, Y., Sugimoto, M.: Vegetation interaction game: Digital SUGOROKU of vegetation succession for children. In: Yang, H.S., Malaka, R., Hoshino, J., Han, J.H. (eds.) ICEC 2010. LNCS, vol. 6243, pp. 493–495. Springer, Heidelberg (2010)
2. Deguchi, A., Inagaki, S., Kusunoki, F., Yamaguchi, E., Takeda, Y., Sugimoto, M.: Development and evaluation of a digital vegetation interaction game for children. In: Natkin, S., Dupire, J. (eds.) ICEC 2009. LNCS, vol. 5709, pp. 288–289. Springer, Heidelberg (2009)
3. Nishida, Y., Aizawa, H., Hori, T., Hoffman, N.H., Kanade, T., Kakikura, M.: 3D ultrasonic tagging system for observing human activity. In: IEEE International Conference on Intelligent Robots and Systems (IROS 2003), pp. 785–791 (2003)

Assessing Player Motivations and Expectations within a Gameplay Experience Model Proposal

Samuel Almeida[1,2], Ana Veloso[1], Licínio Roque[2], and Óscar Mealha[1]

[1] CETAC.MEDIA, Dept. of Communication and Art, University of Aveiro, Aveiro, Portugal
{sja,aiv,oem}@ua.pt
[2] CISUC, Dept. of Informatics Engineering, University of Coimbra, Coimbra, Portugal
lir@dei.uc.pt

Abstract. This work explores a Gameplay Experience Model proposal centered on the dynamic interaction and interplay that exists during video game play. Two elements are key in the model – the Video Game and the Player – defined by a group of dimensions and characteristics that can influence each other during game play. A study was carried out with 40 individuals that played a video game during multiple rounds. After each round players answered a questionnaire on their experience and how the model characteristics manifested during the game. Results collected from the questionnaires were analyzed to assess how game related characteristics influence player Expectations and Motivations.

Keywords: Gameplay Experience, Video Game, Player, Expectations, Motivations, Model.

1 Introduction

Among the many discussions within the realm of video games, one of the most widely debated relates to the experience of playing games. Commonly used concepts to describe game experiences are *immersion* [1–3] and *flow* [4], for example. Other studies [2, 5, 6] have developed specific models that characterize the nature of the gameplay experience. We consider these examples do not fully grasp the extent of the gameplay experience and our interpretation of its key actors: the video game, the player and the multiple relations that result from their interplay and work towards creating, ideally, a satisfying gameplay experience. Furthermore, there lacks a model that equally balances and characterizes the dynamic interaction described. The work presented here seeks to fill the identified gap, by presenting a conceptual model that characterizes our interpretation of the gameplay experience – a twofold experience, considering it both the process and the outcome – and which attributes equal importance to the video game and the player. Furthermore, we present results from a study steered towards partially validating the *Motivations* and *Expectations* dimension of the model within a specific context.

D. Reidsma, H. Katayose, and A. Nijholt (Eds.): ACE 2013, LNCS 8253, pp. 497–500, 2013.
© Springer International Publishing Switzerland 2013

2   Gameplay Experience Model Proposal

The model proposed here identifies the key characteristics that help construct the gameplay experience. The model looks to equally balance the two elements we believe are essential in the construction of the gameplay experience – the video game and the player – and is sustained on the initial premise that gameplay experiences result from the interaction between a game and the player [2]. Fig. 1 represents the proposed Gameplay Experience Model, including the video game and player elements, and respective supporting dimensions and characteristics.

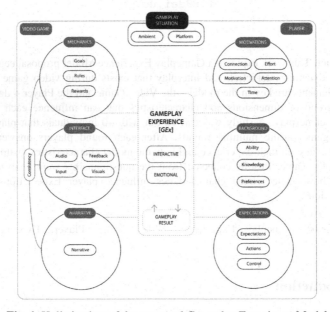

Fig. 1. Holistic view of the proposed Gameplay Experience Model

Developed from a literature review analysis and focus group results, the model considers the gameplay experience as a twofold experience: it is both an interactive experience (process) and an emotional experience (outcome). During game play, these experiences can influence each other and are shaped by the multiple characteristics of the model, defining the outcome of the experience. Initially, the model considers a *Gameplay Situation*, characterized by an 'ambient setting' (e.g. time of day) and a 'platform setting' (e.g. PC or console). The **Video Game** element incorporates four dimensions: *Mechanics* (Goals, Rules, Rewards), *Interface* (Visuals, Audio, Input, Feedback), and *Narrative* (is itself a dimension and characteristic). Connected to the video game element is *Consistency*, a characteristic that refers to the balance established between the three dimensions. The **Player** element incorporates three dimensions: *Motivations* (Motivation, Attention, Effort, Time, Connection), *Background* (Preferences, Ability, Knowledge) and *Expectations* (Expectations, Action, Control).

3   Model Validation through Case Study

A study was carried out to demonstrate possible connections among dimensions and characteristics of the model, focusing mainly on *Motivations* and *Expectations*. We hypothesized that *(i)* changes in rules and visuals influence player expectations; and *(ii)* changes in rules and visuals influence player motivations. Data was collected with a *Pre-Questionnaire (PQ)* and a *Gameplay Experience Questionnaire (GExQ)*, including 27 items (measured on a 5-point Likert scale) and developed specifically to measure the presence of each characteristic in participants' interpretation of the experience. The game – 'ReCylce', a multi-player First-Person Shooter developed by Moura [7] – consisted in three game maps with differences among them. Each map M1 (base map), M2 (more energy loss) and M3 (smaller map) was played twice. After the first three rounds (M1$_1$, M2$_2$, M3$_3$), players responded to the *GExQ*.

4   Preliminary Results

Data from the *PQ* and *GExQ* was processed from 40 participants with different playing experiences. In order to measure the possible evolution of the *Motivations* and *Expectations* dimension, multiple statistical tests were applied using SPSS.

Three *Expectations* dimension (ED) variables (ED$_{M1}$, ED$_{M2}$, and ED$_{M3}$) were computed based on four questionnaire items. Based on the mean scores results, there was a small increase in *Expectations* from the first round M1 (*M=3.556, SD=0.627*) to the second M2 (*M=3.594, SD=0.627*) and the third M3 (*M=3.656, SD=0.757*), suggesting changes in rules (M2) and visuals (M3) reflected on players' expectations. Three Paired-Samples *t-tests* were applied to statistically compare the means for three variables (ED$_{M1}$, ED$_{M2}$, ED$_{M3}$). In the first test (M1/M2), *t=-0.422, p=0.675*, which is not statistically significant. For the second test (M1/M3), *t=-0.75, p=0.458*, indicating the differences in means for MD$_{M1}$ and MD$_{M3}$ are not statistically significant. In the third test (M2/M3), *t=-0.527, p=0.601*, which is also not statistically significant. Considering our hypothesis (Hyp. 1) and study sample, there is no statistical evidence that alterations in game rules (M2) or visuals (M3) have an effect on player expectations. Three *Motivations* dimension (MD) variables were computed based on 10 questionnaire items. Based on the mean scores results, there was an evident increase in the mean value of *Motivations* from the first round map M1 (*M=3.633, SD=0.494*) to the second M2 (*M=3.715, SD=0.540*) and third M3 (*M=4.010, SD=0.705*), also suggesting that the changes in game rules and visuals increased player motivations. Three Paired-Samples *t-tests* were applied to compare the means for the three variables (MD$_{M1}$, MD$_{M2}$, MD$_{M3}$). In the first test (M1/M2), *t=-1.159, p=0.253*; which is not statistically significant. In the second test (M1/M3), *t=-3.798, p=0.000*; indicating the differences in the means for MD$_{M1}$ and MD$_{M3}$ are statistically significant. In the third test (M2/M3), *t=-2.899, p=0.006*, which is also statistically significant. Considering our hypothesis, there is statistical evidence to show that game visuals (M3) alone or combined with rules (M2) influence player motivations. However, rules (M2) alone do not influence motivations.

5   Conclusion

The work explored here presents a gameplay experience model proposal that equally balances two key elements in our interpretation of the gameplay experience: the video game and player, each considering several dimensions and respective characteristics.

In order to demonstrate the relation between multiple dimensions of the model, a study was carried out with a video game and 40 participants. Based on collected data, despite a visible increase in both players' *Expectations* and *Motivations* across all three game maps, these results do not have statistical significance with *Expectations*, but are significant with *Motivations* in two statistical tests. Further studies showed no statistically significant differences between genders in terms of *Motivations*, while *Expectations* did significantly differ according to gender.

With this study we have looked to initially validate multiple dimensions of the model. While initial results show some relation among the dimensions, further statistical studies are recommended to continue looking into these relations. Also, the model can be further explored and its potential studied, namely looking into the 'Interactive Experience' based on game metrics. Analyzing metrics can possibly provide further insight into the questionnaire results and how they reflect in the multiple dimension variables and the emotional experience of the game.

Acknowledgments. Thanks to Labs.SAPO, Arnaldo Moura and Rui Rodrigues; thank you to those that participated in the study. Our acknowledgment to the institution 'FCT' for funding this project PhD grant no. SFRH/BD/66527/2009.

References

1. Brown, E., Cairns, P.: A grounded investigation of game immersion, pp. 1297–1300 (2004), doi:http://doi.acm.org/10.1145/985921.986048
2. Ermi, L., Mäyrä, F.: Fundamental Components of the Gameplay Experience: Analysing Immersion (2005)
3. Jennett, C., Cox, A.L., Cairns, P., et al.: Measuring and defining the experience of immersion in games. Int J. Hum. -Comput. Stud. 66, 641–661 (2008), doi: http://dx.doi.org/10.1016/j.ijhcs.2008.04.004
4. Csíkszentmihályi, M.: Flow: The Psychology of Optimal Experience (1990)
5. Gámez, E.H.C., Cairns, P., Cox, A.L.: Assessing the Core Elements of the Gaming Experience 288 (2010)
6. Fernandez, A.: Fun Experience with Digital Games: a Model Proposition. In: Leino, O., Wirman, H., Fernandez, A. (eds.) Extending Experiences: Structure, Analysis and Design of Computer Game Player Experience, pp. 181–190. Lapland University Press, Rovaniemi (2008)
7. Moura, A., Roque, L.: ReCycle Report. Universidade de Coimbra (2011)

OUTLIVE – An Augmented Reality Multi-user Board Game Played with a Mobile Device

Edward Andrukaniec, Carmen Franken, Daniel Kirchhof, Tobias Kraus,
Fabian Schöndorff, and Christian Geiger

University of Applied Sciences Düsseldorf, Germany
geiger@fh-duesseldorf.de

Abstract. We present a mobile augmented reality that combines elements of traditional board games with digital game content. We designed a multi-user game play inspired by "Settlers of Catan" with real game elements and use a mobile device as "magic window" to enable the currently active player to see things that the other players can not see and to act without letting others know. This supports our objective to integrate a mobile device as central element for a "magic circle of play".

1 Introduction

Mobile technologies and interactive digital media allow to collaborate in a large number of application domains and apply digital content in real life scenarios. Technology-mediated games have greatly increased and many of them claim to build on everyday experiences. However, many commercially available games simply add a virtual dimension to an existing game concept. On the other hand, advanced game prototypes often focus on the technological issues of the digital augmentation of games. The design of handheld augmented reality game interfaces is a complex endeavor and effective solutions should significantly expand the "magic circle of game play" [3]. This concept is often used as a short-hand for a dedicated place in space and time where a game takes place. Players enter the magic circle of a game and enter a new virtual world that separates them from reality. It is not necessary to create this new world with digital means and traditional games often use physical artifacts to create these worlds using cards, tokens, boards, etc. Digital games are well known and in recent years the combination of real and virtual elements, also known as mixed reality games, gained much attention as they try to increase the game experience by using digital technologies. Many of these approaches focus on pervasive gaming to provide a ubiquitous gaming experience and thus offer a game play logic that is suitable for the special requirements of pervasive gaming. Considering game play, such games are more simple than traditional games (e.g. board games) taking into account the location-based properties and the very special game concepts that pervasive mixed reality games require [3]. In this work we developed an augmented reality board game that is played with real tokens on a physical board. To enhance the user experience of the "magic circle of the game" we apply a smartphone as "magic window" to show individual information to each player.

D. Reidsma, H. Katayose, and A. Nijholt (Eds.): ACE 2013, LNCS 8253, pp. 501–504, 2013.

Fig. 1. OUTLIVE real game play (left) and smartphone view (right)

2   Related Work and Requirements

We looked at a number of examples to derive requirements for an appropriate mobile augmented reality game. **AR! Pirates** is a simple AR ego shooter game for IOS. Using three coins placed on a table for reference the goal is to shoot and sink virtual ships. The game is available at Apple's app store. The tracking works sufficient as long as the coins are visible. But the game does not exploit reality-based interaction or the advanced combination of real and virtual game elements. The real table is simply used as surface for the virtual boats. **Art of Defense** is cooperative handheld AR board game highlighting the design rationale and design process to create AR games with tangible interaction elements [2]. It is a strategic "Tower Defense" gameplay that provided a positive gameplay experience for users. **NerdHerder** is a recent AR game of the same research group featuring the herding of a flock of nerd characters to their cubicles by leveraging the players' physical movement. In [4] the authors identified trade-offs when designing mobile AR game interfaces for this prototype. These include exploration vs goal-directed behavior, own and other's presence and different levels of body movement. **AR Bamboleo** was an AR board game prototype that featured a strong relation of virtual and real objects [1]. The user places objects on a tilting board balanced on a cork ball and moves a virtual sorcerer towards the board's center of gravity. The character is commanded by gestures and voice to cast an evil spell at the opponent's virtual castle. The new **Sphero AR games** (www.gosphero.com) like "Sharky the Beaver" show that actively controlled physical objects combined with high-quality character animation could be an attractive player experience even if the gameplay is rather limited as in most AR games. Summarizing, we found that related mobile AR games can create an interesting game experience with robust AR technology and advanced digital media content. But most mobile AR games have a limited game play and focus on the AR technology as main feature. Selected examples of AR board games show that this mix of traditional and digital game element may provide a new game play experience.

3   Game Play Walkthrough

The key objective of this project is the useful combination of a traditional board game and a digital computer game and to combine the benefits of both gaming experiences. At the beginning of each game, players find themselves stranded on a tropical island. An active volcano in the centre of the island and a tribe of natives threaten the players and lead them to try to escape the island as fast as possible. To achieve this they have to collect several raw materials to build a raft. Whoever escapes the island first wins the game. The game consists of the following physical objects: a game board, a volcano mounted on a wheel of fortune, and small tiles each representing a virtual player. Virtual objects include animated players, raw material, the raft shown in different stages of its building progress, and some animals moving around the island. A central game design concept was to employ the mobile device as a "magic window". The main advantages of combining the board game concept with a mobile AR device is that only the active player is able to see his/her resources and discover fields. Other players do not know which raw materials the player has gathered. This encourages players to explore the whole island and think of an efficient strategy how to get their required items first.

The prototype runs on an Android smartphone, we currently use a Samsung Note II running on Android 4.1. The required physical elements include a board game and tokens. The virtual scene is realized in Unity3D V4 and the tracking is implemented using the Unity plug-in Vuforia SDK v2.5. It uses the built-in camera of the smartphone and takes physical objects such as game board and tokens as tracking reference for virtual objects. Once the game board is tracked the software sets its coordinate system in the centre of the volcano and player movements are calculated and validated with regard to this global coordinate system. The physical volcano placed in the centre of the game board is also used as 3D tracking reference to trigger game events after the user has spun it. The wheel consists of two small wooden hexagon plates. The top one is mounted on the bottom plate via ball bearing, which allows spinning the top plate independently from the bottom one. In the upper plate there are twelve magnetic bolts screwed in which will react to a magnet attached under the bottom plate. This results in the wheel stopping shortly after it is spun. After it has stopped, the volcano will reveal one symbol representing an event occurring in the game. While playing, the user holds the camera in his hands and points the camera towards the game board. Looking at the display of the smartphone enables the player to look through a magic window. S/he is able to turn the camera around the game board and to see the virtual objects such as the parrot in a correct angle. The virtual object's size is scaled according to the camera's distance to the tracking references, as it would be if the user moved

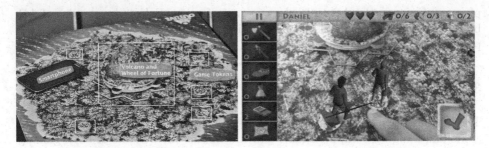

Fig. 2. OUTLIVE real game elements and AR user interface

closer to real objects. Besides graphics, sound is arranged spatially in the virtual environment. So while holding the camera close to the game board the ambient sounds of the wood become louder than while the camera is in the sky. If the user holds the device close to the water image of the physical game board, s/he can hear the sound of the waves. During a turn the user sees an interface presenting all of his possible actions, his/her health and resources in addition to the augmented camera image. The user is able to choose between the different options. After s/he finishes her/his turn the device is handed to the next user.

4   Conclusion

We showed that it is possible to integrate a smartphone as integral part of a game play experience. The prototype is fully functional and preliminary internal tests indicate an interesting game play. However, in future work we need to evaluate the OUTLIVE game using game evaluation questionnaires like GEQ.

References

1. Geiger, C., Stöcklein, J., Klompmaker, F., Fritze, R.: Development of an Augmented Reality Game by Extending a 3D Authoring System. In: Proc. of the International Conference on Advances in Computer Entertainment Technology, ACE 2007, Salzburg, Austria, June 13-15 (2007)
2. Huynh, D.-N.T., Raveendran, K., Xu, Y., Spreen, K., MacIntyre, B.: Art of defense: a Collaborative Handheld Augmented Reality Board Game. In: Spencer, S.N. (ed.) Proceedings of the 2009 ACM SIGGRAPH Symposium on Video Games (Sandbox 2009). ACM, New York (2009)
3. Montola, M.: A Ludological View on the Pervasive Mixed Reality Game Research Paradigm. Personal Ubiquitous Computing 15(1) (January 2011)
4. Xu, Y., Mendenhall, S., Ha, V., Radu, I., MacIntyre, B.: Trade-Offs for Designing Handheld Augmented Reality Game Interfaces. In: Workshop on Mixed Reality Games at CSCW 2012, Seattle, Washington, February 11-15 (2012)

Onomatrack: Quick Recording of User's Rhythmic Ideas Using Onomatopoeia

Jo Arima, Keiko Yamamoto, Itaru Kuramoto, and Yoshihiro Tsujino

Kyoto Institute of Technology, Matsugasaki, Sakyo-ku, Kyoto, Japan
{arima,kei,kuramoto,tsujino}@hit.is.kit.ac.jp

Abstract. While creating music, musicians often want to record their rhythm pattern ideas. If this cannot be done quickly and with minimum effort, their ideas could be forgotten or documented unclearly. In this paper, we propose a system named Onomatrack, which uses onomatopoeias to easily record complicated rhythmic ideas. Using onomatopoeias, users can choose their desired sound quickly and intuitively without searching for it in lists of sound databases. Users can input sounds by writing down onomatopoeias directly to the system as a "rough sketch" of their rhythmic ideas, and can adjust musical parameters by changing the size and position of the onomatopoeias.

Keywords: music production, onomatopoeia, idea recording.

1 Introduction

When musicians play guitar or other instruments, they often come up with rhythmic ideas. In this situation, they would like to write down their ideas quickly, before they forget them. This can be difficult, however, especially when the ideas involve complicated rhythm patterns. These can be made up of many different sounds, such as electronic glitch sounds or ambient sounds, rather than conventional drum set sounds. They can also include frequent changes of musical parameters such as volume and pan.

Musicians often record their musical ideas using Digital Audio Workstations (DAW). However, the use of conventional DAWs for recording such complicated rhythm patterns often takes a lot of time. Recording with DAW needs 1) time for searching and selecting sounds with the tone that they want to use, 2) time for large inputs with a mouse or some other MIDI (Musical Instrument Digital Interface) input devices, and 3) time for adjusting parameters for each sound. If the rhythm pattern recording process takes too long, the original musical ideas can be forgotten. This becomes more serious as the complexity of the ideas increase.

There are some systems that allow users to record musical ideas quickly. Voice Drummer[1] allows users to input rhythm patterns by voice percussion. In this system, however, users cannot use more than two sounds, such as a bass drum and a snare drum sounds, and they cannot input multiple sounds at the same time. Therefore, it does not suit recording complicated rhythmic ideas. The

D. Reidsma, H. Katayose, and A. Nijholt (Eds.): ACE 2013, LNCS 8253, pp. 505–508, 2013.

Music Notepad[2] allows users to write down their musical ideas quickly by entering music notation on the interface as they sketch music with pen and paper. However, in order to use the system, users must be able to understand and write music notation.

In this paper, we propose a system named Onomatrack, in which users can use onomatopoeias to record their complicated rhythmic ideas quickly and easily.

2   Onomatrack

We propose Onomatrack which is a system to allow a user to record complicated rhythmic ideas and to create the rhythm track by inputing onomatopoeias[1] . Onomatrack includes features to reduce the three time problems related to using a DAW as identified in Introduction.

1) With Onomatrack, users can easily choose a specific tone by representing it with an onomatopoeia. This feature allows users to save the time of searching a certain sound with their desired tone in a database. Musicians often express a rhythm pattern using onomatopoeias like "don-tan-don-don-tan...." In this case, a musician would imitate a base drum sound with the onomatopoeia "don" and a snare drum sound with "tan." The use of an onomatopoeia to express a specific sound is more natural and quicker than a conventional DAW.

Another value of using onomatopoeias is the ease of re-choosing or changing of the tone. It is generally known that the vowel of an onomatopoeia has a relationship with the pitch[3]. That is, a sound pitch changes from high to low according to the change of the vowel of the onomatopoeia as follows: $/i/ \rightarrow /e/ \rightarrow /a/ \rightarrow /u/ \rightarrow /o/$. Using this property of onomatopoeias, users can easily re-choose or change the tone by changing the vowel of the onomatopoeia.

For example, if the user inputs a sound with a tone of an onomatopoeia "dang," but after the playback wants to change the tone to one with a lower pitch, he or she can change the "dang" to "dong," which is similar to the former onomatopoeia, but has a different vowel making the pitch lower.

2) Users can input the sound by writing down the onomatopoeia of the tone directly on the screen. This feature allows users to input their desired sound more intuitively compared to conventional inputs using a mouse or some other MIDI devices. They can record their rhythmic idea as quickly as drawing a "rough sketch." When people come up with an idea, they often take a note or draw a rough sketch to remember it. With Onomatrack, users can draw such a "rough sketch" as a rhythm track that can be played back.

3) Users can adjust the volume of the sound by changing the size of an onomatopoeia and adjust the panning of the sound by changing the vertical position of an onomatopoeia on the screen. This feature allows users to adjust these parameters more quickly than with conventional DAWs.

We implemented a prototype of Onomatrack on an Apple iPad®. It allows users to input sounds by drag-and-drop from a list of onomatopoeias. We chose

---

[1] The use of words which sound like the noise they refer to. Japanese usually use a lot of onomatopoeias.

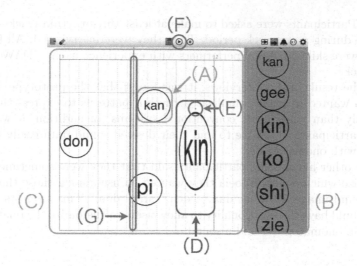

Fig. 1. Prototype interface

this method so that we could test the effectiveness of point 1) described previously in this section for making complicated rhythm patterns. In this prototype, users can select from 40 onomatopoeias. These onomatopoeias include electronic glitch sounds, ambient sounds, and conventional drum set sounds.

Fig. 1 shows the prototype interface. (A) is an example of an onomatopoeia icons that represents a sound with a specific tone. Users select their desired onomatopoeia icon from (B) and drag-and-drop it to the field (C). The vertical position of an onomatopoeia is related to the sound pan, which is volume balance between left and right speakers. The field (C) is divided into five horizontal regions. These regions represent the position of the sound in the stereo sound field. If an onomatopoeia icon is placed in the top region, the sound for the onomatopoeia appears in only the right channel. The second region represents a 45 rightward angle. If an onomatopoeia icon is placed here, the sound appears at an angle of 45 to the listener. Other regions are similar.

Users can adjust the sound volume by changing the size of the onomatopoeia icon. The onomatopoeia icon (D) shows an example of adjusting volume. The size of an onomatopoeia icon is changed by dragging the adjustment handle (E).

When users want to check a rhythm track they have created, they can listen to it by pushing the play back button (F), at which point the play head (G) begins to move. By default, the rhythm track is played repeatedly. Users can add new onomatopoeia icons while listening to the rhythm track.

3   Discussion

An empirical evaluation of our prototype was conducted to confirm the effectiveness of inputting sounds with onomatopoeias for recording complicated rhythm patterns. Participants were asked to make at least three rhythm tracks with the prototype during a one week period. Then they were interviewed. All four participants were skilled musical performers with experience using a DAW to make sound track.

From the result of the interviews, it was found that the prototype did allow users who wanted to make complicated rhythm patterns to express their ideas more easily than when using conventional systems. In addition, it was found that all participants were able to find their desired sound data easily from the database with onomatopoeia.

On the other hand, some participants said that they were sometimes unable to recognize which onomatopoeia they wanted to use among those that have a similar sound image, such as "dan," "den," and "don." This suggests that our system should have the functionality to allow users to customize the relationships between an onomatopoeia and a sound.

4   Conclusion

In this paper, we proposed Onomatrack which is a system to record complicated rhythm pattern ideas quickly and easily. Onomatrack allows users to specify their desired sound with onomatopoeias. We implemented a prototype of Onomatrack allowing users to input sounds by drag-and-drop of onomatopoeias. We conducted an empirical evaluation of the prototype to confirm the effectivness of onomatopoeias for making complicated rhythm patterns.

From the results of the evaluation, it was found that users were able to express their rhythmic ideas more easily with the prototype as compared to conventional systems and find their desired sound using onomatopoeias.

As a future work, we plan to implement the ability to input onomatopoeias with hand drawings, and then evaluate whether the system with this function makes it quicker and easier for the users to specify and to input the sound that they want. In addition, we plan to implement a function that allows users to customize relationships between an onomatopoeia and a sound.

References

1. Nakano, T., Goto, M., Ogata, J., Hiraga, Y.: Voice Drummer: A Music Notation Interface of Drum Sounds Using Voice Percussion Input. In: Proceedings of the ACM Symposium on User Interface Software and Technology, pp. 49–50 (2005)
2. Forsberg, A.S., Dieterich, M., Zeleznik, R.C.: The Music Notepad. In: Proceedings of the ACM Symposium on User Interface Software and Technology, pp. 203–210 (1998)
3. Hiyane, K., Sawabe, N., Iio, J.: Study of Spectrum Structure of Short-Time Sounds and its Onomatopoeia Expression. Technical Report, IEICE, no. SP97-125, pp. 65–72 (1998) (in Japanese)

Musical Interaction Design for Real-Time Score Recognition towards Applications for Musical Learning and Interactive Art

Tetsuaki Baba, Yuya Kikukawa, Toshiki Yoshiike, and Kumiko Kushiyama

Graduate School of System Design, Tokyo Metropolitan University
6-6, Asahigaoka, Hino, Tokyo, Japan
baba@sd.tmu.ac.jp
http://ideea.jp

Abstract. Not only in childhood but also adulthood, we need some training to read music scores, which sometimes make music hard to learn and enjoy. In this article, we shall propose the system that enables users to play their handwritten musical notations by our musical interface. Since 1960's, Optical Music Recognition (OMR) has become mature in the field of printed score. In recent, some products were released on market that uses OMR for music composition and playing. However, few research on handwritten notations have been done, as well as an interactive system for OMR. We combined notating with performing in order to make the music more intuitive for users and give aid for learning music. Furthermore, we applied our technique to an interactive work, which is kind of vision based record disc.

Keywords: Musical Interface, Musical Notation, Interactive Art, Interaction Design, Computer Vision.

1 Introduction

We are interested in developing tools that support the enjoyable education and performing music. Since so many digital musical instruments have been developed, The interface of electronic musical instrument has been evolved to new types, such as gestural, wearable, computer vision, etc. From the imitation of the classic musical instrument to a totally new one, these kinds of digital instruments provide new possibility for performance and education of music. To learn and performing some piece of music, we generally use staff based score that consists of five horizontal lines and notes. The staff originated from musically annotated text, though the Gregorian Chants around the 12th to 13th centuries. It is a basic and important literacy that not only professional musicians but also beginners can use staff based score for learning, playing and composing.

We have developed an interactive system that enables users to write and play their handwritten musical score[1](see Fig.1). In this study, we applied our interactive technique to digital pen interaction and record disc, Gocen Record which is a kind of interactive artwork.

D. Reidsma, H. Katayose, and A. Nijholt (Eds.): ACE 2013, LNCS 8253, pp. 509–512, 2013.

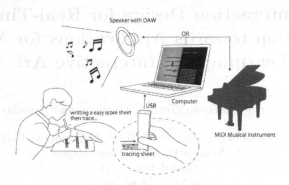

Fig. 1. Our system abstract

2   Related Works

In the field of media art or tangible UI, many researchers reported kinds of new musical instruments. Especially several research or works are focused on enhancing comprehensibility for music performing and learning as a motif of the music score.

Bottelo proposed Tangible user interface for music learning to help children learning the music theory. He developed the software system that enables users to create music by putting objects labeled optical marker on the table[2]. A user can not only put objects but also rotate or extend objects to make change pitch or length of the note.

Noteput by Jonas Friedemann Heuer[3] is an interactive music table based on five line staff, which combines all three senses of hearing sight and touch to make learning the classical notation of music for children and pupils easier and more interesting. These kind of timeline based musical interface is already well known by Golan Levin[4] , Toshio Iwai[5] and et al. Drawn by Liberman[6] presents a whimsical scenario in which painted ink forms appear to come to life, rising off the page and interacting with the very hands that drew them. Inspired by early filmic lightning sketches, in which stop-motion animation techniques were used to create the illusion of drawings escaping the page, drawn presents a modern update: custom developed software alters a video signal in real-time, creating a seamless, organic and even magical world of spontaneous and improvised performance of hand and ink. Calligraphy is one of art form and it is the supreme art form in China. So we could not separate writing and paper. This kind of primitive and intrinsic interaction between human and paper is important for our creative activity.

Tsandilas and et al. [7] focus on the creative use of paper in the music composition process and proposed Musink to provide composers with a smooth transition between paper drawings and OpenMusic as a flexible music composition tool by using the Anoto pen.

Our goal is to develop music performing and learning system that do not require mouses, keyboards and displays on a computer and design user interaction between users and a paper or real object.

3   Gocen

Gocen is our project name which is derived from a Japanese word of musical staffs. We have already developed scanning device type system shown[1]. Furthermore, we created a digital pen based system and an interactive art work.

3.1   Digital Pen Mode

On our previous system, users need to look at the display to play, while they operate the handheld device. It is unnatural for users to use this kind of separated interface. Therefore, we found a solution to adopt a digital pen[1], which makes realize system without displays.

First, a user set a digital pen receiver on a paper, then he write musical notations on a paper. His writing strokes are stored on computer via digital pen and receiver. The data of strokes processed in real-time by SVM algorithm, then recognized positions of staff lines and notations.. A user can make sound by putting the tip on a notation after writing(see Fig.2).

Fig. 2. Snapshot of Gocen Digital Pen which is consist of a digital pen system with a computer

3.2   An Interactive Art Work: Record Disc

Record disc, MD, CD, WAV/MP3..., ways to memorize music has been changed. This work is a kind of homage to record disks for discovering the border of "recording" and "playing". We applied our computer vision library to this work(see Fig.3).

---

[1] We used Airpen by PENTEL CO., LTD.

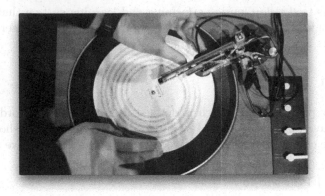

Fig. 3. Snapshot of Gocen Disc which is consist of musical notation engraved on record disc, computer vision system and a turn table

References

1. Baba, T., Kikukawa, Y., Yoshiike, T., Suzuki, T., Shoji, R., Kushiyama, K., Aoki, M.: Gocen: a handwritten notational interface for musical performance and learning music. In: ACM SIGGRAPH 2012 Emerging Technologies (SIGGRAPH 2012), Article 9, 1 page. ACM, New York (2012), http://doi.acm.org/10.1145/2343456.2343465, doi:10.1145/2343456.2343465
2. Bottello, L.: Tangible user interface for music learning (2010), http://lorisbottello.it/ (last accessed, June 2013)
3. Heuer, J.F.: Noteput is an interactive music table with tangible notes, that combines all three senses of hearing, sight and touch to make learning the classical notation of music for children and pupils more easy and interesting, http://www.jonasheuer.de/index.php/noteput/ (last accessed, June 2012)
4. Levin, G., Lieberman, Z.: Sounds from Shapes: Audiovisual Performance with Hand Silhouette Contours in "The Manual Input Sessions". In: Proceedings of NIME 2005, Vancouver, BC, Canada, May 26-28 (2005)
5. Toshio, I.: Chess on the table (1997)
6. Zachary, L.D.: http://thesystemis.com/projects/drawn/ (last accessed, June 2013)
7. Tsandilas, T., Letondal, C., Mackay, W.E.: Musink: composing music through augmented drawing. In: Proceedings of the 27th International Conference on Human Factors in Computing Systems, CHI 2009, pp. 819–828. ACM, New York (2009)

How to Make Tangible Games and Not Die in the Attempt

Eva Cerezo, Javier Marco, and Sandra Baldassarri

GIGA-Affective Lab, Computer Science Department, Engineering Research Institute of Aragon
(I3A), Universidad de Zaragoza, Spain
{ecerezo,javi.marco,sandra}@unizar.es

Abstract. Tabletop devices offer an attractive environment to create tangible
games that seamlessly integrate physical and digital game interaction. However,
the prototyping of Tangible User Interfaces (TUI) challenges designers, preventing the rapid exploration of richer physical interactions with the game. In spite of
the toolkits that are emerging in the TUI domain the development of an application is not easy, since it usually implies to "hardcode" complex algorithms to
process raw data from tabletop in order to detect and track each playing piece manipulated on the active surface. This situation brings a gap between designers and
developers. The aim of the workshop is to give attendants an opportunity of gathering experiences from both the designing and the implementation perspectives,
making community and discussing current challenges and future perspectives.

1   Workshop Topics and Themes

Horizontal computer-augmented surfaces (tabletops) enable simultaneous and co-
located access to digital content to multiple users around the table. Until recently, the
use of these devices were restricted only to research environments, but now private
companies are offering tabletop solutions [8], and also there is a growing community
of hobbyist designers of tabletops [9] thanks to new affordable hardware techniques
[10]. Games and entertainment emerge as very promising applications for these devices, since tables are popular spaces for social games due to their physical affordances that engage face to face interaction between players [11].

Most of the tabletop games are based on multitouch interaction in which playing
pieces are virtually projected on the surface and players manipulate them dragging
their fingers on the table. But several tabletop devices are not only capable of detecting user fingers and hands, but also of supporting the identification and tracking of
conventional objects placed on the active surface. By keeping playing pieces in the
player's physical environment, emotional impact of videogame is reinforced [3] [2]
and digital technology becomes accessible to other user profiles such as very young
children [7], users with disabilities [5] and the seniors [1].

However, despite the rich functionality afforded by such systems, prototyping and
creating designs for conceptually complete Tangible User Interfaces (TUI) remains a
challenging task requiring advanced technical skills such as low level programing and
dealing with electronic sensors and actuators. Recently, toolkits are emerging in the
Tangible User Interfaces (TUI) domain [4] [6], in order to make more accessible the

D. Reidsma, H. Katayose, and A. Nijholt (Eds.): ACE 2013, LNCS 8253, pp. 513–515, 2013.
© Springer International Publishing Switzerland 2013

creation of physical-based computer applications to non-experts designers and developers. However, current TUI toolkits are not covering equally all the tasks involved in the design and implementation of tangible systems. Therefore, there is still a gap between the game design process and the implementation of the game, preventing designers to explore new ways of Tangible Interaction with the computer. We argue that this is largely due to a lack of high-level design and modeling tools linked to executable software frameworks oriented to support designers in exploring rich, expressive and complete tangible interactions in computer augmented board-games.

This workshop aims to address this issue by discussing different experiences in designing and building physical based computer games, and proposing solutions to reduce the mentioned gap between designers and developers. It is complemented by the ACE tutorial "The ToyVision Toolkit for Tangible Games", a practical session in which participants will have a hands-on experience creating a tangible game.

2   Expected Outcomes

The workshop will be an excellent opportunity of gathering experiences from both the designing and the implementation perspectives, making community and discussing current challenges and future perspectives.

Acknowledgements. This work has been partly financed by the Spanish Government through the DGICYT contract TIN2011-24660.

References

1. Al Mahmud, A., Mubin, O., Shahid, S., Martens, J.B.: Designing and evaluating the tabletop game experience for senior citizens. In: 5th Nordic Conference on Human-Computer Interaction (NordiCHI 2008), pp. 403–406. ACM, New York (2008)
2. Hinske, S., Langheinrich, M.: W41K: digitally augmenting traditional game environments. In: Proceedings of the 3rd International Conference on Tangible and Embedded Interaction, TEI 2009, pp. 99–106 (2009)
3. Iwata, T., Yamabe, T., Poloj, M., Nakajima, T.: Traditional games meet ICT: a case study on go game augmentation. In: Proceedings of the Fourth International Conference on Tangible, Embedded, and Embodied Interaction (TEI 2010), pp. 237–240. ACM, New York (2010)
4. Kaltenbrunner, M.: reacTIVision and TUIO: a tangible tabletop toolkit. In: Proceedings of the ACM International Conference on Interactive Tabletops and Surfaces, 2009, pp. 9–16. ACM (November 2009)
5. Li, Y., Fontijn, W., Markopoulos, P.: A Tangible Tabletop Game Supporting Therapy of Children with Cerebral Palsy. In: Markopoulos, P., de Ruyter, B., IJsselsteijn, W.A., Rowland, D. (eds.) Fun and Games 2008. LNCS, vol. 5294, pp. 182–193. Springer, Heidelberg (2008)
6. Marco, J., Cerezo, E., Baldassarri, S.: ToyVision: a toolkit for prototyping tabletop tangible games. In: Proceedings of the 4th ACM SIGCHI Symposium on Engineering Interactive Computing Systems, pp. 71–80. ACM (June 2012)

7. Marco, J., Cerezo, E., Baldassarri, S., Mazzone, E., Read, J.: Bringing Tabletop Technologies to Kindergarten Children. In: 23rd BCS Conference on Human Computer Interaction, Cambridge University, September 1-4, pp. 103–111. British Computer Society, Swinton (2009) ISBN:978-1-60558-395-2
8. Microsoft surface, http://www.microsoft.com/surface/en/us/default.aspx
9. NUI Group web, http://nuigroup.com
10. Schöning, J., Hook, J., Motamedi, N., Olivier, P., Echtler, F., Brandl, P., Muller, L., Daiber, F., Hilliges, O., Löchtefeld, M., Roth, T., Schmidt, D., von Zadow, U.: Building Interactive Multi-touch Surfaces. JGT: Journal of Graphics Tools (2009)
11. Rogers, Y., Rodden, T.: Configuring spaces and surfaces to support collaborative interactions. In: O'Hara, K., Perry, M., Churchill, E., Russell, D. (eds.) Public and Situated Displays, pp. 45–79. Kluwer Publishers (2004)

Touch, Taste, and Smell: Multi-sensory Entertainment

Adrian D. Cheok, Jordan Tewell, Gilang A. Pradana, and Koki Tsubouchi

1   Introduction

This workshop's purpose is to gain awareness of using all five of our senses for creating multimedia artifacts such as in entertainment. We are interested in the user's emotional feedback from using the addition of touch, smell, and taste in entertaining activities. The workshop organizers will present a background review for each of the three senses and their key projects for each: RingU, a wearable fashion interface for sending virtual hugs, "Digital Taste Interface", a device that transmits a sense of taste without chemicals, and ChatPerf, an accessory that actuates scent from a user's mobile phone (Fig 1). We also welcome attendees to discuss work of their own that exhibits one or a combination of these three senses in a fun and novel way.

Fig. 1. Left to Right: RingU, Digital Taste Interface, and ChatPerf

2   Touch

2.1   Background

Touch effects our emotions and social relationships with one another. Not only to help us complete motor tasks, the sensation of touch also provides the scaffold upon which we build our judgments and decisions of others [1]. While touch expressions can be seen in game controllers for haptic feedback, few works explore the use of touch for communicating emotions like love to the user. Some examples of this are "Hug Over A Distance" [2], "Hug Shirt" [3], and "Huggy Pajama" [4].

D. Reidsma, H. Katayose, and A. Nijholt (Eds.): ACE 2013, LNCS 8253, pp. 516–518, 2013.

2.2   RingU

Touch expressions can be utilized in small artifacts that we can wear like fashion accessories. RingU is our ring-shaped, wearable fashion system for sending hug messages tactilely via internet communication [5]. When paired with a user's smartphone, the ring can send a small squeeze to their loved one anywhere in the world, and the recipient can feel the squeeze with a color coded light accompanying it on their ring. By touching the top of their ring or by pressing a button within our app, users can send the message to anyone in their friend list. With the system, two people can communicate more intimately remotely than with plain text messaging.

3   Taste

3.1   Background

While the sense originally evolved from a primary need for survival to differentiate edible food, taste is now reserved for pleasure in dining. Taste is vastly underexplored in the paradigm of entertainment from one person to another. Taste will be important as internet bandwidth increases to extend the internet to all of our senses. We explore the research carried out to gauge response from chemically stimulating users using a variety of tasting displays. "Food Simulator" [6], "Taste Screen" [7] and "Meta Cookie" [8] will be reviewed. We also review Nakamura's work [9] which closely parallels our own with regards to electric taste.

3.2   Digital Taste Interface

We will demonstrate a unit that stimulates a tongue by electric and thermal means [10]. Inspired by Volta's observation of a salty sensation felt during his experiments [11], this device can send a current through the tongue when placing it between electrodes. By varying the parameters of the current and the temperature of the electrode, we can simulate some basic taste sensations such as sour and bitterness. We call this "digital taste" and we can use this to easily send taste information over the internet.

4   Smell

4.1   Background

Smell is perhaps the most fundamental sense to all living organisms and was probably the first sense developed. Smell evolved from finding food and mates, deciding whether to flight or fight, and helped establish social hierarchies [12]. Like taste, it is now reserved for pleasure such as perfuming or adding aroma to food. We present some background on instruments of scent delivery such as early work with the "Smell O Vision" [13] and "iSmell" [14], and experimental work such as "Virtual Cocoon" [15] and "olfaction printer" [16].

4.2   ChatPerf

Koki Tsubouchi and his company in Tokyo have created Chatperf [17], a self contained accessory that can be attached to a mobile phone device. Together with the SDK, it can allow app developers to bring a new dimension of sensory enhancement to their apps. The development cycle of ChatPerf will be explored as well as the business model of product delivery to the consumers.

References

1. Morton, A.H., Schiff, W.: The Psychology of Touch. Lawrence Erlbaum Associates, Hillsdale (1991)
2. Mueller, F., et al.: Hug over a distance. In: CHI 2005 (2005)
3. Hug shirt, http://www.cutecircuit.com/hug-shirt/
4. Teh, J.K.S., Cheok, A.D., Choi, Y., Fernando, C.L., Peris, R.L., Fernando, O.N.N.: Huggy pajama: a parent and child hugging communication system. In: Proc. IDC 2009, pp. 290–291 (2009)
5. RingU, http://ringu.mixedrealitylab.org/
6. Kortum, P.: HCI Beyond the GUI: Design for Haptic, Speech, Olfactory and Other Non-Traditional Interfaces, pp. 291–306. Morgan Kaufmann, Burlington (2008)
7. Maynes-aminzade, D.: Edible bits: seamless interfaces between people, data, and food. In: Proceedings of the 2005 ACM Conference on Human Factors in Computing Systems, CHI 2005, Portland, OR, April 2-7, pp. 2207–2210 (2005)
8. Narumi, T., Kajinami, T., Tanikawa, T., Hirose, M.: Meta cookie. In: ACM Siggraph 2010 Emerging Technologies, Siggraph 2010, Los Angeles, CA, July 25-29, p. 143 (2010)
9. Nakamura, H., Miyashita, H.: Augmented gustation using electricity. In: Fourth Augmented Human International Conference, AH 2011, Tokyo, Japan, March 12-14, p. 34 (2011)
10. Nimesha, R.: Digitally stimulating the sensation of taste through electrical and thermal stimulation. Ph.D. dissertation, National University of Singapore, Singapore (2012)
11. Volta, A.: On the electricity excited by the mere contact of conducting substances of difference kinds. Abstracts of the Papers Printed in the Philosophical Transactions of the Royal Society of London 1, 27–29 (1800)
12. Herz, R.: The Scent of Desire. HarperCollins, New York (2007)
13. A Sock in the Nose. Review, Behind the Great Wall. Time Magazine, 57 (December 21, 1959)
14. How internet odors will work, HowStuffWorks (January 5, 2012), http://computer.howstuffworks.com (accessed November 20, 2012)
15. Derbyshire, D.: Revealed: the headset that will mimic all five senses and make the virtual world as convincing as real life. Mail Online (March 5, 2009), http://www.dailymail.co.uk (accessed November 19, 2012)
16. Bannai, Y., Noguchi, D., Okada, K., Sugimoto, S.: Ink jet olfactory display enabling instantaneous switches of scents. In: Proceedings of the International Conference on Multimedia, MM 2010, New York, pp. 301–310 (October 2010)
17. ChatPerf, http://chatperf.com/

Between Music and Games: Interactive Sonic Engagement with Emergent Behaviors

Insook Choi and Robin Bargar

Columbia College Chicago
600 S. Michigan Ave., Chicago, IL, 60605 USA
{ichoi,rbargar}@colum.edu

Abstract. Data from an interactive simulation of dynamic agents' social behavior is applied to the control of real-time sound synthesis. User engagement models present the application of sound in parallel with visualization in a simulated environment where content is generated dynamically and is playable. Computational models for the simulation and for sound synthesis are discussed, including requirements and constraints for interactive applications. Design principles for interactive sound are introduced and implementations of three models of sonic engagement are compared.

Keywords: evolutionary interface, agents, swarms simulation, sound synthesis, interaction, playable media, engagement, sound authoring, client-server, multimodal correspondence.

1 Introduction

The current investigation explores a space between games and music with intent to generate alternative play experience leveraging a common simulation. The method is focused on rendering interactive media events or content dynamically generated or transformed by data from a simulation, controlling both audible and visible attributes of the media.

To design a system between games and music there are two criteria, one for computation and one for sound design. Computational criteria are consulted for an interaction method with sound, and then consulted again in relation to sound design to elucidate a simulation's salient features. This project compares the two criteria and analyzes their relationship. What makes sound interactive, and what makes it relevant to engagement? The structural model for this investigation uses a common simulation as the sole data source coordinating sound and visual media.

The experimental system minimizes peripherals concerns such game rules or narrative and focuses on implementing two requirements in sound design. The first requirement is to establish a relationship between sound and simulation such that the temporal model of sound synthesis is compatible to the temporal model of the simulation dynamics. The second requirement is that the sound synthesis model corresponds to visual rendering of the simulation. This correspondence requires understanding how the simulation properties are visualized in the graphical display. Here the graphics and sounds are rendered in parallel as both graphics and sounds receive data from the simulation. This means visual media are not a source for sound control. The system is neither a musical instrument nor a game, yet is playable and performable [1].

D. Reidsma, H. Katayose, and A. Nijholt (Eds.): ACE 2013, LNCS 8253, pp. 519–523, 2013.
© Springer International Publishing Switzerland 2013

2   Interactive Systems for Simulation with Visualization and Sound

Procedural sound replaces sound reproduction as a conceptual apparatus. By eliminating the prescriptive protocol of "sound track," a whole paradigm of how sounds play in media is transformed. While a sound track engages a listener as third hand in discovery, procedural interactive sound engages a listener as first hand in discovery: Interactive sound is generated for the first time, every time when it is being heard.

The current investigation uses a system optimized for procedural sound, and minimizes prerecorded sounds. There is no dialogue or sound effects. Engagement changes when sound protocols are not description or narrative as implied by a sound track model. In the resulting interactions, listeners may glean consistent or divergent patterns from images and sounds, yet both can be consistent with a simulation that is controlling their attributes.

2.1   Experimental Use of a Swarm Simulation

Sayama [2] developed the swarm simulation based upon Reynold's 'boids' flocking algorithm [3]. A number of agents (usually 100 to 300) are initialized at random positions in a bounded virtual space and are set in motion at random initial velocities. The motion is defined by social engagement with other agents. Each agent is given a perceptual field defined in virtual distance units, and also given parameterized responsiveness rules for interactions with other agents. An agent's rules determine the agent's movement with respect to others within the agent's perceptual field at the current time step.

Among the salient features, the most prominent is the formation of clusters. Regardless of agents' species, cluster formation informs the summary of interaction at given instances. As each agent is limited to its perceptual boundary, clustering and de-clustering behaviors are overall effects of spontaneous spatial distribution of agents. A *superagent* enables control determined by a player. As the superagent moves independently the other agents respond as they would to all other agents, enabling the player to influence the swarm.

2.2   Requirements for Procedurally Driven Sound from an Interactive Simulation

Continuous sample buffering is required to deliver sound samples in an uninterrupted stream. The ability to control and vary computation is required at micro scale of individual sound samples and macro scale of extended musical passages or audio extended scenarios. Event computation processing is required to be asynchronous to interactive control data generation and asynchronous to graphics computation. Capacity is required to selectively synchronize sound events at perceptible time scales. Selective synchronization should be extensible for selected sound events to synchronize with selected interactive control data or graphics events. Auditory diversity is required: sound synthesis algorithms must support a requisite variety of sound types. Computer memory is required sufficient to host prerecorded sounds as source material for procedural computation. A programming language for sound is required in a syntax that is accessible to sound designers. This language must be able to designate sound synthesis signal pathways and control data routing and gating. A development and application environment is required to connect procedural sound programming with simulation environments, graphics computation, interactive control devices, and related processes.

3   Procedural Models for Sonic Engagement

In sound design the balance between predetermined and interactive control data can be analyzed along two design dimensions: (1) the direct relationship between sound and simulation dynamics, and (2) the cross-modal relationship [4] between sound and visualization of the simulation data. Dimension (1) has to do with compatibility between temporal models in sound and temporal models in simulation dynamics. The models define ranges: primarily frequency ranges including pitch and spectral structure, also metric ranges including beat and rhythmic structure. Dimension (2) has to do with correspondences that emerge dynamically between features in sound and features in visualization.

The two most important design properties of sounds are ranges and features. These can be designed with different combinations of sound parameters such as amplitude, frequency and spectral domain, granularity (adjacent onset with concurrent duration), and beats and rhythms. Sound synthesis becomes interactive when continuous control ranges are designated from the simulation data, and covariation is applied to corresponding synthesis ranges for transforming audible features. When design is applied to an audible range, it is not just a matter of mapping simulation dynamics into audible range. To ensure audibility the first order mapping requires a perceptual scale applied to frequency ranges: this is relatively trivial. The second order mapping requires *a priori* experience with simulation dynamics to optimize all possible frequency areas into differentiable areas with consistency.

3.1   Three Procedural Models of Sonic Engagement with Swarm Data

Three procedural models apply swarm data for interactive control of sound synthesis: a Literal, a Statistical, and a Feature-based interpretation. Each uses different preconfigured control data to create the audible framework for the interactive control data. As a baseline the Literal model uses minimal preconfigured control data, and each dynamic agent's position data is applied for interactive control. The other two interpretations apply preconfigured control data and analysis of the simulation data with increasing complexity and refinement. Each interpretation applies a different sound synthesis design, establishing alternative ranges and features. In each case the sound's temporal model provides a unique level of detail reflecting the simulation's temporal characteristics. And in each case the sound's audible features establish a unique correspondence to the swarm visualization. Control rate and latency of interactive data are constant in all three cases.

3.2.1   Literal Model

The Literal interpretation creates an individual sound source—a "voice"—for each of 100 agents in the swarm, and sustains a texture of agents' voices corresponding to their continuous movements. The result is a dense layer of simple and mostly uniform sounds that change individually without regular tempo or rhythm.

"Literal" means there is a baseline for correspondence with visual features: each agent produces an individual sound at a rate of ~1 Hz with duration of ~3ms. Persistence in sound by repetition of small multiples is aligned with agent persistence in the visual field. Give 10 or more agents the outcome of this granular approach is a layered sound texture. The experiment in this approach is to observe whether audible clusters emerge as features in the sound texture. Audible ranges in frequency (pitch) and horizontal position (stereo panning) were tuned to optimize for this model.

Result: The Literal interpretation produces mixed results in terms of correspondence with visual information. Agents' density and distribution are echoed in the granular sound texture, which intuitively reflects the swarm visualization. But clusters formed clearly on the screen do not emerge distinctively in sonic clusters, except when a cluster's vertical distribution generates a narrow frequency range, such that a pitch center can be heard. As the spatial area of a cluster increases the corresponding sound is less differentiated from the swarm's overall audible texture. So while the sound texture provides suitable audible "wallpaper" for the swarm experience, the engagement is not particular to many of the cluster transformations that a player can generate in the visualization.

3.2.2   Statistical Model

The sound synthesis model provides two sound sources—two "voice streams"—using an auditory summarization model. One sound stream is a "Persistent" voice that responds to the overall swarm dynamics. Statistics of the state of swarm agents are applied to the Persistent voice. The second sound stream is a "Transient" voice that responds to data from the current largest cluster. Cluster analysis is applied to identify cluster size. When no cluster is present the Transient voice is silent. The Persistent voice is tuned at a lower frequency range than the Transient voice. Musically the Persistent voice corresponds to a *rhythmic/harmonic bed* (popular); the Transient voice to a *lead*.

Result: Cluster data produces the most audible features, as there is a clear correspondence to the size of the largest cluster, in particular when a player divides a cluster or leads two clusters to merge, and the audible frequency region immediately shifts. This is highly engaging in narrow regions of emergent behavior, as transformations of the largest cluster control the Transient voice. The swarm-level statistical background data establishes a general audible correspondence between the Persistent voice and the tempo and regularity of simulation events. However the audible interpretation in the Persistent voice does not carry strong associations to the other swarm features, therefore the focus on the largest cluster generates somewhat of a miscue when players expect similar results upon interacting with other clusters.

3.2.3   Feature-Based Model

To establish correspondence between sound and visualization, symmetry data is included in the cluster analysis of 3.2.2. Four audible voices are created and respond to control data from the four largest clusters. The voices have music-based attributes: discrete tone sequences with tempo and rhythmic patterns. Data from clusters' transformations is applied to transform the musical tone and pattern attributes.

This cluster-analysis interpretation represents a significant shift in method. The Literal and Statistical models scaled sound data based upon the dispositions of agents in relation to the simulation space, with the intent that emergent features will be audible through an accumulation of many brief sound events. Feature-based method extracts simulation features using targeted analysis then scales the sound to the attributes of the features that have been recognized. Overall this model shifts from an absolute measurement scale to a relative measurement scale. Feature extraction is applied to identify clusters, and clusters provide independent control data relative to other clusters' data.

Result: Because the interactive control data is related to the four largest clusters, the data extraction may shift abruptly from cluster to cluster as noted above. "Cluster-hopping" in control data streams is a discontinuity in the sense of measurement. However from the players' perspective these hops generate continuity for players' engagement by providing an audible articulation and associated cluster interaction. Players rapidly determine which clusters are controlling sounds and this ongoing discovery process becomes as aspect of engagement.

4   Future Work

Future work begins with user validation for generalization of the engagement models developed for swarm simulation. In many applications playability with sound could be greatly facilitated by libraries and interfaces for iterative design workflow coupled a capacity to select from and develop interactive sound synthesis palettes. To extend the engagement model beyond single users, currently under development is a peer-to-peer mechanism for passing simulation control and sounds between mobile devices.

References

1. Choi, I., Bargar, R.: A Playable Evolutionary Interface for Performance and Social Engagement. In: Camurri, A., Costa, C., Volpe, G. (eds.) INTETAIN 2011. LNICST, vol. 78, pp. 170–182. Springer, Heidelberg (2012)
2. Sayama, H.: Decentralized Control and Interactive Design Methods for Large-Scale Heterogeneous Self-organizing Swarms. In: Almeida e Costa, F., Rocha, L.M., Costa, E., Harvey, I., Coutinho, A. (eds.) ECAL 2007. LNCS (LNAI), vol. 4648, pp. 675–684. Springer, Heidelberg (2007)
3. Reynolds, C.: Flocks, herds and schools: A distributed behavioral model. In: SIGGRAPH 1987: Proceedings of the 14th Annual Conference on Computer Graphics and Interactive Techniques, pp. 25–34. Association for Computing Machinery (1987)
4. Frassinetti, F., Bolognini, N., Làdavas, E.: Enhancement of visual perception by crossmodal visuo-auditory interaction. Experimental Brain Research 147(3), 332–343 (2002)

Linear Logic Validation and Hierarchical Modeling for Interactive Storytelling Control

Kim Dung Dang, Phuong Thao Pham, Ronan Champagnat, and Mourad Rabah

University of La Rochelle - L3i, Avenue Michel Crépeau, 17042 La Rochelle, France
{kim_dung.dang,phuong_thao.pham,ronan.champagnat,
mourad.rabah}@univ-lr.fr

Abstract. The games are typical interactive applications where the system has to react to user actions and behavior with respect to some predefined rules established by the designer. The storytelling allows the interactive system to unfold the scenario of the game story according to these inputs and constraints. In order to improve system's behavior, the scenario should be structured and the system's control should be validated. In this paper, we deal with these two issues. We first show how to validate Interactive Storytelling (IS) control using Linear Logic (LL). Then we present "situation-based" hierarchical scenario structuring which allows the state space reduction.

Keywords: Video game, Linear Logic, Interactive Storytelling, scenario validation, game controller, situation-based scenario.

1 Introduction

Video games, nowadays, are considered as one of the most popular media that has important contribution to the edutainment domain. Indeed, [6] demonstrated that, thanks to the effects of interactivity, video games brought a learning support that was more efficient than the traditional supports (non-interactive media formats such as text, oral presentation, video). However, the unfolding of a game (the unfolding of the story corresponding to the game) and its level of interactivity are commonly thought to be opposite [2]. The first relates to a designer's control on the game s/he has created as the second relates to a player's control on the game s/he is playing. In order to deal with this opposition, we have proposed an approach based on a LL model (an executable formal model) [1], which allows balancing these two controls.

The weakness of this approach is the explosion of state space for complex scenarios. Furthermore, a game designer cannot plan all the possible actions that a player can realize. To handle this issue, we propose to contextually structure the application execution into interaction sequences, called "situations". Each situation corresponds to a contextual resource-centered sequence of activities/events, and it is characterized by pre-conditions and post-conditions. That enables the system to control the execution and to establish casual links between the situations. Thus, the model confines actors' interactions according to shared contexts allowing hierarchical view of the scenario.

D. Reidsma, H. Katayose, and A. Nijholt (Eds.): ACE 2013, LNCS 8253, pp. 524–527, 2013.

In this paper, we present briefly the usefulness of LL in modeling, validating and controlling an IS. We explain then the hierarchical situation-based modeling that we use to reduce the overall state space. We applied our approaches to build a video game: Little Red Cap (LRC) adventure game. In this game, the player plays the LRC character and the game controller adapts the scenario unfolding to her/his actions regarding game designer's desired effects.

2   Modeling, Validation and Control of Game Scenarios Using LL

In order to create interactive video games whose scenario (a set of all the possible discourses) satisfies the designer's intention, our approach is to model game scenarios by canonical narrative schemas introduced in Greimas' semiotics [1]. These schemas may be directly formalized by a LL model and thus we can validate game scenarios by proving the received LL model. This valid LL model is then used as the input of a game controller. The game controller aims to manage correctly the unfolding of the game by taking into account player's action choices and calculations executed on the LL model. Thanks to the modeling process, the game designer may determine the required goals or a structure of discourse that the game has to obtain. In other words, the LL model represents a predefined scenario of the game (interested readers can get more information in [1]). Thus, the game controller is able to follow the execution track, and hence will operate correctly: avoid incoherent states, guarantee the player's freedom and the consistency of the generated discourses.

Discussion: The scenario modeling by LL shows a lot of advantages. The game designer may balance between both the discourse point of view and the character point of view for the created games by taking into account both system's choices and player's choices thanks to additive connectors in LL [1]. Moreover, the modification of the modeled scenario is simple: we are able to make more or less discourses by adding or deleting events/actions, which allows increasing the adaptability of the scenario. However, this approach may lead to a state space explosion if there are a lot of events/actions in the story. Besides, the current LL approach does not use the interaction context, user's states, resource constraints... Finally, it is not really suitable for applications where interactions are totally unplanned. For these reasons, we propose the notion of situation that can be seen as a scene in a scenario. It encompasses not only interaction execution but also interaction management and resource use. The situations, as basic narrative elements, respect the overall scenario structure and facilitate interaction planning and management by characterizing, contextualizing and confining them.

3   Situation-Based Scenario

In general, in an interactive system, the execution is composed of a succession of activities and actions performed by the actors or a sequence of events affecting their behavior. Hence, a story is defined as a set of partially ordered events that solve the storytelling problem. That leads us to organize a scenario into a set of interaction sequences called "situations" [5].

3.1   Situation Model

The interactions are split into a set of situations. Each situation is a sequence of interactions between two or more actors in a precise context to achieve a predictive objective. It is characterized by: the pre-conditions, the post-conditions, a set of actors, and a set of resources. Due to the fact that actors' behaviors, especially human behaviors, are not always precisely modeled, and due to the influence of the external events, the progression of a situation can be considered as an "execution and adaptation black box" where the interactions are executed in a non-predictable way. To theses components we add a "consistency management component": set of mechanisms devoted to prevention, detection and treatment solutions, to adjust the situation's progression in spite of misunderstanding and inconsistency problems.

3.2   Application Execution and Adaptation

The situations are considered as the plot structuring elementary blocks. Each application provides a set of situations defining all the possible interaction sequences that can happen during the application execution. They can be grouped and linked together to build the overall application scenario. The scenario is then represented by a directed graph of situations. Each node is a situation and each edge is a transition from one situation to another. The situation graph shows causal relationships between scenario situations, without taking into account used resources and event management. A given situation can be followed by multiple situations. A scenario may then have several beginnings and some possible endings. This allows expressing complex scenarios with a lot of paths. Moreover, the situations are defined regardless of the scenario conception and gathered in a situation library. The scenario definition by the application designer then consists in combining these available situations.

The advantage of the situation-based model against the LL approach and some existing story representation models [3, 4] is that it enhances the execution control and interaction adaptation. The application progression becomes the scenario unfolding from one starting node to one final node on the predefined situation graph. The drawback of this static chaining is its rigidity that does not allow the graph modification once the scenario execution begins. Therefore, in order to increase the adaptability, the second method is proposed: no predefined graph where situation choices are made according to the pre-conditions that best satisfy the global state and decision criteria. Thus, this method is more flexible, adaptive, and applicable in "real time" during the application execution.

4   Case Study: Little Red Cap Video Game

We have built a video game on the LRC story to which we have added multiple options for the non-player and player characters to increase the unpredictability as well as the interactivity of the game. The game scenario is modeled and validated by the LL approach to guarantee the objectives that the game has to reach. In order to reduce the state space explosion, we have also applied our situation-based structuring on the created scenario by reorganizing it with "situation" blocks. The starting point of this transformation comes from the fact that these two approaches are based on common notions such as events/actions, states, state transitions... Our idea is to reorganize the scenario graph by regrouping the events/actions, happening in a same context and relating to each other as a chain of different interactions, into one same situation. Therefore, we can eliminate the interaction sequences repeated in the graph obtained after the initial modeling for the LL validation. Thus, we are able to avoid the redundancy in the scenario graph. As a result, we have obtained a situation graph with 20 nodes instead of the initial graph with 56 nodes in the LL approach.

5   Conclusion

In this paper, we addressed the IS control from the validation and structuring points of view. We have tried to combine the user choices with the game designer's intentions. To this purpose, we use a LL model to express the causality of the story and the distinction between player's choices and game controller's choices. LL is also well suited to prove the correct scenario execution and properties such as the reachability of predefined system states and the absence of deadlock.

However, the drawback of this approach is the state space explosion. In order to deal with this problem, we propose a hierarchical model based on the notion of "situation". A "situation" encloses a set of interactions related to a shared context of several actors. In addition, each situation contains a set of management components that ensure a correct termination of the enclosed sequence. Compared to the state diagram, the situation can be seen as a higher level block representing several initial states and transitions. This approach allows us to reduce the state space by eliminating the redundancy in the interaction sequences in the modeled scenario.

References

1. Dang, K.D., Champagnat, R., Augeraud, M.: Modeling of Interactive Storytelling and Validation of Scenario by Means of Linear Logic. In: Aylett, R., Lim, M.Y., Louchart, S., Petta, P., Riedl, M. (eds.) ICIDS 2010. LNCS, vol. 6432, pp. 153–164. Springer, Heidelberg (2010)
2. Juul, J.: A Clash Between Game and Narrative. In: Digital Arts and Culture Conference, Bergen (1998)
3. Magerko, B.: Story Representation and Interactive Drama. In: 1st Artificial Intelligence and Interactive Digital Entertainment Conference, Los Angeles, California (2005)
4. Mateas, M.: Interactive Drama, Art, and Artificial Intelligence. PhD Thesis, School of Computer Science, Carnegie Mellon University (2002)
5. Trillaud, F., Pham, P.T., Rabah, M., Estraillier, P., Malki, J.: Online Distant Learning Using Situation-based Scenario. In: CSEDU 2012 (2012)
6. Wong, W.L., Cuihua, S., Nocera, L., Carriazo, E., Tang, F., Bugga, S., Narayanan, H., Wang, H., Ritterfield, U.: Serious video game effectiveness. In: Proceedings of the ACE 2007 Conference, Salzburg (2007)

GlowSteps – A Decentralized Interactive Play Environment for Open-Ended Play

Linda de Valk, Pepijn Rijnbout, Mark de Graaf, Tilde Bekker,
Ben Schouten, and Berry Eggen

Department of Industrial Design, Eindhoven University of Technology
P.O. Box 513, 5600 MB Eindhoven, The Netherlands
{l.c.t.d.valk,p.rijnbout,m.j.d.graaf,
m.m.bekker,b.a.m.schouten,j.h.eggen}@tue.nl

Abstract. In this paper we present the interactive play environment GlowSteps. GlowSteps consists of ten flexible tiles that respond with light feedback on player's actions. The play environment is developed to support both social and physical play and is designed with the intention to encourage children to create their own play and games. The tiles can be programmed with different interaction behaviors leading to a variety of play experiences. This showcase illustrates our design approach for such interactive play environments, combining the fields of decentralized systems and open-ended play.

Keywords: Play Environment, Open-ended play, Decentralized Systems.

1 Introduction

Play is an important activity in children's lives. It gives them an opportunity to practice skills and explore imaginary worlds [1]. Players can immerse themselves in a world different from everyday life, with its own boundaries and rules [4]. In our research, we are interested in how to design for play, focusing on developing decentralized play environments that support open-ended play. Such environments consist of multiple players and interactive objects and aim to encourage physical play and social interaction.

Within the field of play, we focus on open-ended play. This means that the designs we develop do not offer predefined game rules or goals but instead provide local interaction opportunities that children can attach meaning to and create their own games with [2, 7]. In this way, children can play with the design in different ways, which enhances the play experience. The design intention is to support different goals, rules, stories, roles and so on to enhance children's imaginations and creativity. Designing for open-ended play differs from designing a game with predetermined rules and goals. Open-ended play leaves room for improvisation; for players to create their own games. Therefore, designers have to clearly define their design space and make conscious decisions on which properties to design and which to leave open for players to interpret themselves [7].

D. Reidsma, H. Katayose, and A. Nijholt (Eds.): ACE 2013, LNCS 8253, pp. 528–531, 2013.
© Springer International Publishing Switzerland 2013

Instead of designing play environments incorporating video projection or virtual reality, we focus on tangible objects that embody mechanics for interaction. In this way, we want to emphasize both spatial (environment) as well as personal (object) interaction between players and objects as well as between objects. These players and objects together form a decentralized environment. In previous work, we have developed a framework for designing decentralized interactive play environments [5]. Such environments are a collection of interactive elements, each with their own interaction rules. These elements decide on actions based on locally available information and can communicate with each other. As play can have a high degree of unpredictability, we believe that the properties of scalability, robustness and self-organization [3] of a decentralized system can be very useful.

2   GlowSteps

In this section we present our design called GlowSteps. We describe the design and the different interaction behaviors. Next, we discuss several recent user evaluations.

2.1   Design and Interaction

GlowSteps is a set of interactive tiles that responds with light output on input measured by pressure sensors. If someone stands on a tile or touches it with their hands, the lights react depending on the current interaction behavior. The tiles are autonomous objects that together form a decentralized play environment. They can be picked up and moved around. In this way, children can create their own play spaces. GlowSteps is an improved version of an earlier prototype called FlowSteps [6].

Fig. 1. Impression of children playing with GlowSteps

The following scenario describes how children might play with GlowSteps:

Peter and Jessica are playing with GlowSteps. They place the tiles in a path and jump on them one after another. The tiles light up in different colors. "We have to make them all red!" shouts Jessica. She continues to jump on one tile until it is red. "No," says Peter, "I make a rainbow and you have to repeat it." Suddenly, one tile lights up in blue. "Did you see that?" asks Jessica. Peter nods. "I think we have to catch it!" Together they run towards the tile with the blue light.

So far, three interaction behaviors have been designed for GlowSteps: Catch, Create and Toggle. We will now describe these behaviors in more detail. *Catch* is designed to encourage physical active play. One tile lights up in a certain color for a short amount of time. In this time, players must step on that tile to 'catch' the light. All tiles then flash to communicate that the light has been caught. If the players are not quick enough, the light disappears and then appears again at another tile. Players can prevent the light to come to a certain tile by stepping on that tile. In this way, they 'block' the tile. *Create* is focused on expression and creativity. This interaction behavior is more reactive than active, i.e. the tiles themselves do not light up but they react on the players stepping on them. When a player steps on a tile, this tile starts to cycle through a range of colors (e.g. from red to blue to green to yellow to purple and so on) and a player can 'stop' this by stepping down the tile again. This tile then 'freezes' in the last color. After a while, it fades out. In this way, players can 'draw' and create patterns, or they can come up with a sequence of colors that other players need to repeat as in the scenario above. Lastly, *Toggle* is developed to stimulate both competitive and cooperative play. All tiles light up in red, green or blue. By stepping on a tile, this tile moves to the next color in the sequence (e.g. red, then green, then blue and then red again). Players can decide to turn all tiles into one color; but if one player is aiming for red and the other for blue, they have to compete against each other. All three interaction behaviors are rather simple but have the potential to lead to diverse forms of play.

2.2   User Evaluations

On several occasions, children played with GlowSteps in both formal and informal settings. The Catch scenario was tested in a user study with 36 children in the age of 6 to 9 years old at a primary school. Children played in groups of three with the design. The teacher set up these groups and the children could play for a fixed amount of time (about ten minutes) in an unused room in their school. Early analysis showed us that children played in various ways with the design, moving the tiles around and creating games involving stepping on the tiles and catching the lights. The study also gave us important insights in how to improve the interaction behavior of GlowSteps, as children did not seem to understand or use all interaction opportunities. For example, some children were not aware of the fact that they could 'block' tiles.

The Create and Toggle scenarios were developed more recently. They have been exposed at a public 'open' day event at our university. At this occasion, children could engage with GlowSteps in a more informal setting. They could play alone or with other children for as long as they wanted. During this day, all three different interaction behaviors were tried out. Throughout the day, many children (and adults) played enthusiastically with GlowSteps. The different interaction behaviors resulted in various forms of play as stepping on the tiles, catching the light or playing hopscotch.

We plan to do more, mostly formal, studies in the near future, in which we want to evaluate the interaction behaviors in more detail and further improve them. Exploring how children interact with our design gives us important insights that are extremely valuable in our iterative design process.

3 Proposal for Demo

The proposed installation for ACE 2013 will include GlowSteps with various interaction behaviors. We aim on presenting the three interaction behaviors described in this paper, although they might be improved depending on user evaluations performed in the meantime. During the conference, participants can try out the different versions, compare their experiences and give us feedback. Furthermore, we hope to discuss our design approach focusing on decentralized systems and open-ended play in more detail.

Acknowledgements. This research is part of the Creative Industry Scientific Programme (CRISP), which is funded by Dutch government FES funding.

References

1. Acuff, D.S., Reiher, R.H.: What Kids Buy and Why; the Psychology of Marketing to Kids. Free Press (1997)
2. Bekker, T., Sturm, J., Eggen, B.: Designing Playful Interactions for Social Interaction and Physical Play. Personal and Ubiquitous Computing 14(5), 385–396 (2010)
3. van Essen, H., Rijnbout, P., de Graaf, M.: A Design Approach to Decentralized Interactive Environments. In: Nijholt, A., Reidsma, D., Hondorp, H. (eds.) INTETAIN 2009. LNICST, vol. 9, pp. 56–67. Springer, Heidelberg (2009)
4. Huizinga, J.: Homo Ludens: A Study of the Play Element in Culture. Beacon Press, Boston (1955)
5. Rijnbout, P., de Valk, L., Vermeeren, A., Bekker, T., de Graaf, M., Schouten, B., Eggen, B.: About Experience and Emergence – A Framework for Decentralized Interactive Play Environments. In: 5th International Conference on Intelligent Technologies for Interactive Entertainment (2013)
6. de Valk, L., Rijnbout, P., Bekker, T., Eggen, B., de Graaf, M., Schouten, B.: Designing for Playful Experiences in Open-ended Intelligent Play Environments. In: IADIS International Conference Games and Entertainment Technologies, pp. 3–10 (2012)
7. de Valk, L., Bekker, T., Eggen, B.: Leaving Room for Improvisation: Towards a Design Approach for Open-ended Play. In: 12th International Conference on Interaction Design and Children, pp. 92–101 (2013)

Eat&Travel: A New Immersive Dining Experience for Restaurants

Mara Dionísio[1,2], Duarte Teixeira[1,2], Poan Shen[1,2], Mario Dinis[3], Monchu Chen[1],
Nuno Nunes[1], Valentina Nisi[1], and José Paiva[3]

[1] Madeira Interactive Technologies Institute, University of Madeira, Funchal, Portugal
{monchu,njn,valentina}@uma.pt
[2] Entertainment Technology Center, Carnegie Mellon University, PA, USA
{mdionisi,dteixeira,poans}@andrew.cmu.edu
[3] Eat&Travel, Lisboa, Portugal
{mario.dinis,jose.paiva}@eatandtravel.pt

Abstract. Modern society is moving towards a busier lifestyle, people have less time to enjoy themselves despite the increasing leisure options. Also, many countries around the world are facing a financial crisis, making people less willing to travel abroad. In this paper we describe Eat&Travel, an interactive solution that ties dining and traveling together, offering restaurants the possibility to offer their customers an opportunity to enjoy a unique regional meal combined with a virtual trip in a river, where they can appreciate the landscape and learn more about the country and the culture, using an immersive CAVE environment, without the need to travel abroad.

Keywords: CAVE, Dining Experience, Virtual Travel, Local Culture, River Cruising.

1 Introduction

Today's society is moving towards a busier lifestyle despite of the available leisure options. Hence, people look for options to recover the energy spent with their busy lives, get rest and enjoy meaningful moments. One of the ways that people can do this is by traveling. In order to travel, people need to be in good health, financially fit, available time wise, and ultimately willing to explore unknown places. Having all these factors working together is very hard, especially for families with children.

So people in order to fulfill this search for meaningful moments turn to their meal breaks. With this in focus, we see a relevant opportunity to bring together the meal-time with the desire of fleeing from stressful routine in seeking engaging activities and unique environments, such as touristic destinations. Along goes the customer's desire to try out new things, novel experiences or new sources of stimulation.

In the current competitive economy, the restaurant industry seeks to provide memorable experiences, constant novelties, aiming for customers' loyalty and satisfaction. Studies indicate that the service's atmosphere is an essential aspect to customer satisfaction as well as determining repeated patronage [1, 2]. The physical set-up of a

D. Reidsma, H. Katayose, and A. Nijholt (Eds.): ACE 2013, LNCS 8253, pp. 532–535, 2013.

CAVE enables the development of immersive environments in which users can engage with each other as well as with the images projected within the CAVE [3]. We identified that little attention has been paid to the potential of CAVEs in creating a new and memorable experience in traditional places such as restaurants.

Eat&Travel creates a solution that ties dining and traveling to offer restaurants, the ability to provide their customers with the novelty of memorable experiences by allowing them to travel the world while enjoying a unique menu.

2   Eat&Travel

The setting of the Eat&Travel restaurant consists of a "cruise ship" like dining space divided in two different spaces: the waiting area and the dining area. The Waiting Area is where the customers arrive and wait until the "trip" starts. The Dining Area is a space enclosed by screens that replicates exactly an 180° view of the landscape through video projections thus creating an immersive environment. It enables customers to visit off-location destinations in an immersive journey through the rivers around the world. A cruise ship in a river is the perfect setting since it provides a calm journey that can cross many famous cities. Therefore becoming the ideal setting to enjoy a meal and sightseeing. The menu is specifically designed with reference to the destination's gastronomy for a whole experience. Consequently, customers are led in a multi-sensory experience where taste plays an important role in driving the experience into the visited location.

Additionally, this experience will enable customers to interact with their journey by self-indulged curiosity with venue-specific information. The outcome is a pervasive learning process.

2.1   Dining Experience: Captain Jack Jones and His Journal

It's a known fact that every cruise ship must have a captain and that a captain uses a log to record his traveling's. Therefore, we designed the whole experience around Captain Jack Jones and his Journal. Usually cruise ship captains are experience sailors, who traveled around the world many times and certainly, in most of the cases, have many experiences to share. The first contact that customers will have is in the waiting area where the captain will welcome the guests and arouse the customer's curiosity about the trip. Once the captain is ready to embark, one of his assistants, a waiter, leads the customers to the dining area. Along the trip Captain Jones will appear several times to highlight places of interests appearing on the panoramic screen. Customers could also learn more about the surrounding area using a copy of his journal, a digital tablet, placed on every table in the restaurant.

In the journal, Captain Jones wrote interesting facts and stories about the places, people, fauna, flora and food. His deep passion for food is well documented through the journal in his meticulous notes and recipes. To support various needs from different customers, the journal will provide customers with information they can relate to (for a celiac customer it is important to know what contains gluten and the available gluten-free options) and information they seek for (cooking process, food origin, historic info about dishes, curiosities).

3   Implementation

For our prototyping purpose, we used the CAVE room in our lab for implementation and testing. The prototyping platform consisted of a CAVE with four 135-inch screens four projectors, a surround sound system, two LCD screens, a webcam and a tablet. The set up enabled us to create a fully unified and immersive experience. It is planned to implement the system in a real restaurant in the near future.

3.1   The Waiting Area

The LCD screen in the waiting area is equipped with a webcam that can detect the presence of people. When any customer approaches, the captain immediately appears and interacts with the customers. During the idle mode, (i.e. when no customers are around) it shows the map of the trip, highlighting the different locations along the river.

Fig. 1. Waiting Area

3.2   The Dining Area

Each table will have a tablet displaying the Captain Jones' journal where the customers can learn more information related to the food and the journey by flipping through the pages of the journal. Customers can also order the food and access the order and to change at any time. Finally when done with their selections they can send the order to kitchen and enjoy the trip while their food is being prepared.

Fig. 2. Screenshot of the interface of the journal

In order to make the Captain visible to all customers for the entire dining area, four LCD screens are to be placed in the four different corners of the room. Whenever the Captain feels there something worth mentioning to the customers, he will appear on the LCD screens and talk to the customers. All the systems are interconnected, in that way to synchronize the projections with the captain appearing on the LCD screens highlighting the points of interest so that the customers can see it at that precise moment in the projections.

Fig. 3. Dining room

4   Conclusion and Future Work

Our findings highlight the success of our prototype. The Eat&Travel restaurant provided an immersive experience that engaged visitors to interact and explore. Visitors felt immersed with our CAVE like environment highlighting the feeling on being on a cruise ship. Customers also felt tempted to learn more about the food, reading and sharing trivia information as well as the recipe. Having the captain appearing at predetermined moments in the trip to point out places of interest, such as castles and monuments as well a fauna and flora helped to guide the visitors along the trip and to built a meaningful connection between customers and the captain. We aim to continue our work to test the Eat&Travel experience tested in a real restaurant, and to have a menu specifically designed with reference to the destination gastronomy for a whole experience.   With this prototype, we achieved the goal to deliver an immersive and unified experience.   We believe that this platform can provide a significant breath of fresh air to the current competitive restaurant industry.

References

1. Bitner, M.J.: Evaluating service encounters: the effects of physical surroundings and employee responses. Journal of Marketing 54 (1990)
2. Wakefield, K.L., Blodgett, J.G.: The importance of servicescapes in leisure service settings. Journal of Services Marketing (1994)
3. Cruz-Neira, C., Sandin, D.J., DeFanti, T.A.: SurroundScreen Projection-Based Virtual Reality: The Design and Implementation of the CAVE. In: Proceedings of the ACM SIGGRAPH 1993 Conference, pp. 135–142 (1993)

Evaluation of the Dialogue Information Function of Interactive Puppet Theater: A Puppet-Show System for Deaf Children

Ryohei Egusa[1,*], Kumiko Wada[2], Takayuki Adachi[3], Masafumi Goseki[3], Miki Namatame[4], Fusako Kusunoki[2], Hiroshi Mizoguchi[3], and Shigenori Inagaki[1]

[1] Kobe University, Tsurukabuto, Nada, Kobe, Hyogo, Japan
126d103d@stu.kobe-u.ac.jp, inagakis@kobe-u.ac.jp
[2] Tama Art University, Yarimizu, Hachioji, Tokyo, Japan
viscount-ff@hotmail.co.jp, kusunoki@tamabi.ac.jp
[3]Tokyo University of Science, Yamazaki, Noda, Chiba, Japan
{j7512639,j7511629}@ed.tus.ac.jp, hm@rs.noda.ac.jp
[4] Tsukuba University of Technology, Amakubo, Tsukuba, Ibaraki, Japan
miki@a.tsukuba-tech.ac.jp

Abstract. We have developed Interactive Puppet Theater, a puppet-show system designed for use by deaf children. For this study, we conducted evaluation experiments to determine whether Interactive Puppet Theater helps these children to have an enriched viewing experience. The evaluation results showed that Interactive Puppet Theater could be an effective way to ensure that deaf children understand the characters' dialogue as they watch the puppet-show, and that it enables them to have an enjoyable viewing experience.

Keywords: Puppet show, Balloon, Kinect sensor, Deaf children.

1 Introduction

It is difficult for deaf children to enjoy the contents of a puppet show as much as children with normal hearing do. The reason for this is that some of the contents, the characters' dialogue, the sound effects, and the background music consist of aural information. To help these children, we developed Interactive Puppet Theater (IPT) [1], is a puppet-show system designed use by deaf children.

IPT has two features. One is a function regarding the presentation of dialogue information, which supplements the characters' dialogue as text. The other is a function in which the audience participates in the theater, using physical movement. In IPT, the story progresses as the actors perform the puppetry while the children watch the show. What is different, though, is that the children can actually participate in the puppet-show by acting as facilitators of the story. This interactive experience amplifies their appreciation and promotes their understanding of the story's content and characters, thus allowing them to have an enjoyable viewing experience.

---

* Corresponding author.

D. Reidsma, H. Katayose, and A. Nijholt (Eds.): ACE 2013, LNCS 8253, pp. 536–539, 2013.

We have previously evaluated the function of audience participation via physical movement to determine its effectiveness [2]. However, the effectiveness of the function of the presentation of the dialogue information has not yet been evaluated in detail. Therefore, this study aims to evaluate the effectiveness of this function to determine whether it helps deaf children watch a puppet show with enjoyment.

2   Design

2.1   Framework of the System

Fig.1 shows the stage setting. It is composed of a 180-inch screen, paper puppets, a Kinect sensor (hereafter referred to as Kinect), and a short-focus projector. Two operators operate the paper puppets, which are maneuvered in between the screen and the desk, which serves as a blindfold. Two voice actors are in charge of the dialogue and are also responsible for operating background animation at the same time.

IPT, which is called a paper theater, has a total of two paper puppets as characters. Background animation, created using Adobe Flash, is projected using a short-focus projector, which can be set up near the screen. This prevents the puppets and the background from interfering with one another.

2.2   Presentation of the Dialogue Information

It is important to ensure the accuracy and the identification of the speaker at supplementing dialogue information as text [3]. We use balloons to present dialogue information regarding the text spoken by the characters. Our intention was for the balloons to help deaf children to understand the characters' dialogue, and which character is speaking. Fig.2 illustrates a scene how the dialogue information is displayed. The figure shows two puppets on the stage, and the dialogues in the balloons are displayed behind the puppets. The dialogue used for this study consisted of simple sentences that can be understood by a 3rd grade elementary school student.

2.3   Audience Participation by Using Physical Movement

During the story, a point at which the story's development branches out is presented to the children. Fig.3 shows a flowchart of the story's development at this time. Icons

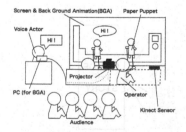

Fig. 1. Stage Setting

Fig. 2. Speech Balloon

and a cursor appear on the screen. Operating the cursor, the children choose one icon they like that corresponds to the story's development. The operation of the cursor is effected via the measurement of physical movement by a range image sensor. We selected Kinect as a range image sensor for two reasons: first, it is compact and easy to carry and set up, and second, the depth sensor installed in the device is compatible with IPT. This depth sensor is able to accurately sense human bodies in a dimly lit room. Thus, this type of function is effective during the performance of IPT, because the lights in the room are dimmed in order for the animation to be projected clearly.

When a person's hand is moved toward Kinect, it detects his/her hand, making it possible to trace the hand movements. Kinect traces these hand movements and measures their three-dimensional positions.

3   Evaluation Experiment

Target: This study targeted 17 deaf students from the 3rd to 6th grade at the T Prefectural School for the Deaf, Elementary School Division.

Task and Procedures: After the students viewed IPT, they were given a questionnaire survey, whose aim was to collect their subjective evaluations of emotional and design aspects of IPT. Items, which the questionnaire had, were about enjoyment of IPT and the effectiveness of the textual dialogues. For each item on the survey, the following 5-point scale was used: "strongly agree," "relatively agree," "neither agree nor disagree," "relatively disagree," and "strongly disagree." We investigated the trends of the responses obtained after separating them into two groups: positive responses ("strongly agree" and "agree") and neutral or negative responses ("neither agree nor disagree," "disagree," and "strongly disagree"). The difference between the positive and the neutral or negative evaluations was computed using Fisher's exact test (1×2). The results are summarized in Table 1.

The results for three survey items regarding emotional aspects of IPT (Table 1. 1-3) and six items regarding design aspects (Table 1. 4-8) indicate that the participating students gave more positive than neutral or negative responses. Significance tests showed that the number of positive responses significantly exceeded the number of neutral or negative responses.

Taken together, these results indicate that our system ensures that the text dialogue information in IPT functions effectively and helpfully, enabling deaf children to understand the story and enjoy their viewing experience via the dialogue balloons that supplement the dialogue information.

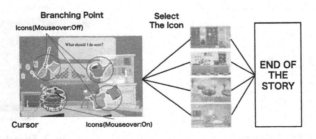

Fig. 3. Flowchart of the Story

Table 1. Investigation of Subjective Results - Emotional and Design Aspects of IPT

	Positive	Neutral Negative
1.The puppet theater was fun. **	16	1
2.The story was easy to understand. **	17	0
3.I was focused on watching the puppet theater until the end. **	16	1
4. I was able to read each dialogues in the balloons correctly. **	15	2
5.I was able to identify quickly which dialogues belonged to the apprentice (*character's name) by looking at balloons. **	15	2
6.I was able to identify quickly which dialogues belonged to the teacher (*character's name) by looking at the balloons.**	15	2
7.I was able to understand the apprentice's feelings by reading the dialogues in balloons. **	16	1
8. I was able to understand the teacher's feelings by reading the dialogues in balloons. **	16	1

$^{**} p < 0.01$

4   Conclusion

In this study, the results obtained from our experiments showed that the function of presenting dialogue information could be an effective way for deaf children to acquire dialogue information as they view a puppet show, and assists them in having an enjoyable viewing experience.

Acknowledgments. This research was supported by a JSPS the Grants-in-Aid for Scientific Research (B) (No. 23300309).

References

1. Egusa, R., Wada, K., Namatame, M., Kusunoki, F., Mizoguchi, H., Inagaki, S.: Development of an Interactive Puppet Show System for Hearing-Impaired People. In: The Fourth International Conference on Creative Content Technologies, pp. 69–71 (2012)
2. Adachi, T., Goseki, M., Mizoguchi, H., Namatame, M., Kusunoki, F., Egusa, R., Inagaki, S.: Puppet Theater System for Normal-Hearing and Hearing-Impaired People. In: Nijholt, A., Romão, T., Reidsma, D. (eds.) ACE 2012. LNCS, vol. 7624, pp. 461–464. Springer, Heidelberg (2012)
3. Lambourne, A., Hewitt, J., Lyon, C., Warren, S.: Speech-Based Realtime Subtitling Services. The International Journal of Speech Technology 7, 269–279 (2004)

Music Puzzle: An Audio-Based Computer Game That Inspires to Train Listening Abilities

Kjetil Falkenberg Hansen[1], Rumi Hiraga[2], Zheng Li[1], and Hua Wang[1]

[1] KTH Royal Institute of Technology
Lindstedtsvägen 24, 10044 Stockholm, Sweden
kjetil@kth.se
[2] Tsukuba University of Technology
4-3-15, Amakubo, Tsukuba 305-8520, Japan

Abstract. The Music Puzzle is a computer game for tablets and smartphones using sounds for the gameplay. Just like an original picture is reconstructed from pieces with jigsaw puzzle, an original sound is reconstructed from musical segments with Music Puzzle. Each segment is distorted by shifting the pitch and equalization. To finish the game, the user listens to each segment visualized as pieces on the screen, reorders them, and corrects their pitch and equalization. The game has a possibility for deaf and hard of hearing people to improve their residual hearing ability since the observation shows their concentrating the game with sounds and preference for music.

Keywords: tablet game, hearing ability, audio based game, training.

1 Introduction

Our experiences tell that deaf and hard of hearing young people like to listen to music, and they enjoy using smartphones. Also, we are aware of the well-documented beneficial effects of music [5], and that it is possible to train one's hearing to recover sensory abilities and thus music appreciation (e.g. [3,4]). Recently we conducted an experiment using an audio-based computer game called the "Music Puzzle", and preliminary results have been reported in [2]. The experiment showed positive results concerning how much time persons with hearing losses are willing to invest in playful hearing training, and that playing the game potentially can improve sound perception and thus appreciation of music.

In this paper we will briefly describe the gameplay and the experiment set-up and game settings. Also some of the more aesthetic considerations and choices will be discussed. For experiment results, see [2]. The novelty of the work is how we use music for gaming, and how we investigate differences between solving a task with music stimuli, speech stimuli or the combination of speech and music.

2 The Music Puzzle Game

The likeness to a traditional jigsaw puzzle game is clear as the task is to reconstruct a complete picture from smaller pieces, or in our case, a sound file from

D. Reidsma, H. Katayose, and A. Nijholt (Eds.): ACE 2013, LNCS 8253, pp. 540–543, 2013.

distorted sound fragments. This was chosen for several reasons, but mainly it can be argued that a familiar game can be easier to get started with. Our experiment group, consisting of students with hearing losses, were not used to audio based games and therefore we chose to keep the task simple, but challenging.

In a jigsaw, the *puzzle* is the complete picture; traditionally a well-known image divided into many small pieces. We use a sound recording divided into several small sound segments. The user can start by listening to the full recording or even start without knowing the target sound; the latter could be compared to laying a puzzle without looking at the picture on the box. The puzzle thus becomes more of a riddle or secret message to be deciphered. The *pieces* of the jigsaw must be hooked together correctly in two dimensions with fitting forms, but in our case the pieces must be ordered temporally. To introduce a further challenge than just finding the correct order in one dimension, each piece is randomly changed in pitch and tone quality (hi-pass and lo-pass filtering). This makes it more complex than a jigsaw puzzle while keeping the concept.

To solve the puzzle the player has to listen very carefully to each sound fragment, choose correct audio filtering and reorder the pieces. This task has proved to be quite complex involving focussing on details in the sounds to get it right, which corresponded perfectly with our ambition of making a motivational hearing training game based on sounds, speech and music from everyday life.

The game was written for smartphones with Android 2.2 or above, and later including other Android devices. Audio programming was done in Pure Data (Pd) with the *libpd* library for mobile systems. Pd is a programming environment for audio and has the necessary functions for pitch shifting and filtering.

2.1   Game Play

The game provides a simple user interface with only a few visual objects in order for players to concentrate their efforts to listening to the sounds. First, the user sets the game mode by choosing a predetermined sound set (First–Fourth) as shown in Figure 1(a), and the type of puzzle—speech, music, or mixed, Figure 1(b). These options were made for the experiments and can be changed to suit other purposes. After that, a ball appears in the center of the display, Figure 1(c). When the user presses the ball, the target sound is played. The user is requested to shake the tablet to "break" the ball into several smaller pieces, as illustrated in Figure 1(d). The number of pieces that are created depends on both the force of the shaking and the chosen difficulty level.

The created pieces contain a segment of the original sound and have equal durations; in a typical scenario, a 15 seconds long puzzle (sound recording) is divided into six 2.5 seconds long pieces. The user can then press to listen to a piece, drag and reorder it. Since pitch and equalization shifts are applied to each piece, the user also has to correct the pitch and equalization for each piece individually. Correcting options appear when the user presses and holds a piece on the screen. Radio buttons for these options have random color and order each time the window opens to prevent giving visual cues to the player. Besides interacting with the sound pieces, users can use two cheat buttons for

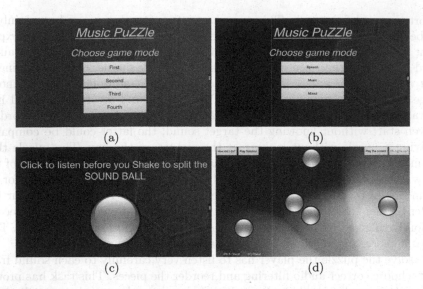

Fig. 1. The user interface. (a-b) The user sets the game mode by selecting between four sets of sounds and then between three puzzle types. (c) The user initiates the game by listening to the sound then shaking the tablet. (d) The game starts with the pieces randomly positioned on the screen.

automatically correcting pitch and filtering, found at the left bottom corner in Figure 1(d), and also use four buttons on the top row of the screen to evaluate a game session, play the original sound, play the current sequence as ordered on the screen, or dismiss the game.

2.2 Difficulty Settings and Sounds

The difficulty level is determined by several parameters: the length of the sound file, the number of pieces possible to create from shaking, the range of the pitch shift, the equalization's filtering settings, and not least the sound itself. These parameters impact greatly on each other in a complex way. For instance, a game consisting of more pieces is not always harder than a game with fewer pieces, and likewise a short sound file is not always harder than a longer one. Also, the change of pitch can make two pieces that in the original sounded differently appear very similar. Furthermore, symmetry effects caused by the division (for instance when dividing a 4-bar music segment into 2 or 4 pieces) or silent pieces (due to gaps in the original sound) file can make the task unexpectedly demanding.

Sounds are placed in folders, and settings are defined in a text file. Any sound recording can be used, depending on the experiment. In our experiments in [2] we have used read poetry, instrumental music and a combination of the reading and the music piece (A, B, A+B). In all, we had four sets of each which were not particularly different. In the earlier experiments [1] we used speech and music recordings of more varied character. Our experience from selecting the stimuli is that before dividing the sound, it is hard to know how difficult the task will be, and this demands that each game and sound should be tested for all the possible number of pieces. Sounds that seem overly easy, such as a read count-down of the numbers 5–4–3–2–1, can still be sufficiently challenging.

3   Summary of Preliminary Studies

We have conducted several preliminary experiments [1,2] with hearing Swedish university students, and with Japanese university students with and without hearing losses. Most of them reported that they enjoyed playing the game. An interesting result was that most hearing participants preferred to play with speech, whereas most participants with hearing impairments showed a preference for music. Players without hearing loss perform overall slightly better than persons with hearing impairments, but less so than expected. The game seems to be challenging for all.

Further studies have been initiated, and we aim to reveal possible long-term training effects of using the game. Two other aims are to study how different sound stimuli are perceived and appreciated, and to see how difficulty settings (rates of pitch and filter changes, duration of pieces) can provide knowledge about sound perception in a playful way.

Acknowledgements. The authors want to thank the experiment participants, game testers and the paper reviewers for constructive feedback. This work is supported by a Grant-in-Aid for Scientific Research (C), the Japan Society for the Promotion of Science, and The Swedish Post and Telecom Authority (PTS).

References

1. Hansen, K.F., Li, Z., Wang, H.: A music puzzle game application for engaging in active listening. In: SIG Technical Reports: Proceedings of 97th Information Science and Music (SIGMUS) Research Conference, vol. (7), pp. 1–4 (electronic). Information Processing Society of Japan, Tokyo (2012)
2. Hiraga, R., Hansen, K.F.: Sound preferences of persons with hearing loss playing an audio-based computer game. In: Proceedings of the IMMPD and ACM Multimedia 2013, Barcelona, Spain. ACM Press (in press, 2013)
3. Kraus, N., Skoe, E., Parbery-Clark, A., Ashley, R.: Experience-induced malleability in neural encoding of pitch, timbre, and timing. Annals of the New York Academy of Sciences 1169, 543–557 (2009)
4. Särkämö, T., Pihko, E., Laitinen, S., Forsblom, A., Soinila, S., Mikkonen, M., Autti, T., Silvennoinen, H.M., Erkkil, J., Laine, M., Peretz, I., Hietanen, M., Tervaniemi, M.: Music and speech listening enhance the recovery of early sensory processing after stroke. Journal of Cognition and Neuroscience 22(12), 2716–2727 (2010)
5. UK Department for Education. Annex 3: The benefits of music (academic literature review). In: Department for Culture, Media and Sport (ed.) The Importance of Music. A National Plan for Music Education, pp. 42–44. Crown Copyright (2011)

Enabling Interactive Bathroom Entertainment Using Embedded Touch Sensors in the Bathtub

Shigeyuki Hirai, Yoshinobu Sakakibara, and Hironori Hayashi

Faculty of Computer Science and Engineering, Kyoto Sangyo University
Department of Frontier Informatics, Graduate School of Kyoto Sangyo University
Department of Science, Graduate School of Kyoto Sangyo University

Abstract. We propose a new entertaining bathroom environment with applications controlled via capacitive touch sensors embedded in the bathtub. The bathtub touch sensor system, called TubTouch, provides a new touch user interface near to the edge of the bathtub for persons who are bathing. TubTouch can be used to control both existing bathroom equipment, such as water heaters, jacuzzis, TVs, audio, and lighting, and a variety of new applications. In this paper, we give an overview of the TubTouch system and discuss its entertainment applications used in daily life.

Keywords: Capacitive Touch Sensor, Bathroom, Bathtub, Everyday Life.

1 Introduction

With network-enabled household appliances now a reality, ubiquitous computing research to enhance the convenience and comfort of everyday life in the home has become very active. To date, most of the research has been focused on the living room and kitchen, where electrical appliances are easily installed. The focus of our research is to bring various ubiquitous computing technologies into bathrooms and to enhance the everyday act of bathing so that it is more entertaining. In this paper, we present a number of entertainment applications for the bathroom that are controlled via embedded touch sensors in the bathtub.

2 TubTouch System Overview and Design

TubTouch provides an integrated user interface and several interaction features in the bathtub for the control of various equipment and applications. As illustrated in Fig. 1, capacitive touch-sensors are attached on the inside edge of the bathtub to enable a bather to interact by touching the bathtub. A video projector installed above the bathtub projects virtual buttons and/or a screen for applications over the touch sensors, shown in the picture on the right side of Fig. 1. In Japan, standardized bathroom systems are widespread in homes, including houses, condominiums, and apartments. The bathrooms are constructed from

D. Reidsma, H. Katayose, and A. Nijholt (Eds.): ACE 2013, LNCS 8253, pp. 544–547, 2013.
© Springer International Publishing Switzerland 2013

unit elements, for instance wall, floor, ceiling, bathtub, and are relatively easy to assemble and remove. The space on the inside of the side of the bathtub can be accessed by removing a side panel; resulting in easy installation of capacitive touch-sensors, shown in the picture on the left side of Fig. 1. This space in the side of the bathtub was designed specifically for additional equipment such as a Jacuzzi. The picture on the left side of Fig. 1 also shows several electrodes on the upper inside edge of the bathtub, and a sensor box containing a touch sensor controller board. This arrangement means that TubTouch can be installed as an additional system in any such existing bathroom. In addition, electrodes can be freely installed on the rear side of surfaces, including curved surfaces. Another advantage is the flexibility of the interactive display and its compatibility with conventional household environments.

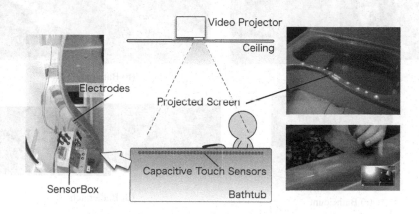

Fig. 1. TubTouch System Overview

Capacitive sensors usually respond to contact with water and are therefore used to measure water levels in tanks. Hence, recent multi-touch input devices tend to be incompatible with wet environments. However, the basic function of a capacitive sensor is to react to the presence of dielectric objects. Since water and the human body have different relative permittivities, TubTouch can indeed be used to detect human touch, even when wet, in response to each sensor signal.

Japanese bathroom systems also have space in the ceiling to install equipment such as ventilators, dryers, mist generators, loudspeakers, and audio units. In the bathroom ceiling, an access hatch is provided for easy access to this space; thus, a projector can very easily be installed there.

There are three ways to interact with TubTouch: touching, sliding, and proximity to the edge of the bathtub.[1,2] As mentioned above, the proximity value is measured by reaction to the presence of dielectric objects, such as fingers and hands in this case. Touch detection is a proximity state that can be determined

---

[1] TubTouch Example 1: http://www.youtube.com/watch?v=1DKR6rTwobM
[2] TubTouch Example 2: http://www.youtube.com/watch?v=oiKocZ1IORw

quite simply using a threshold. Sliding motions can be detected by transitions of proximity values from multiple electrodes.

3   TubTouch Entertainment Applications

TubTouch has several entertainment applications, including control of some bath equipment such as lighting, audio, and TV. In this section, we introduce four entertainment applications that, in particular, provide new experiences during baths.

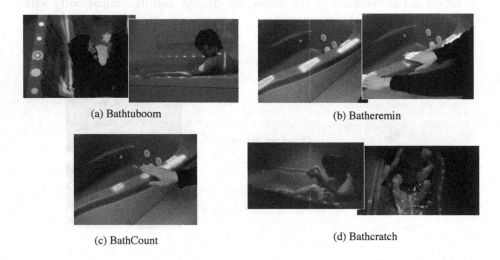

(a) Bathtuboom   (b) Batheremin

(c) BathCount   (d) Bathcratch

Fig. 2. TubTouch Entertainment Applications

3.1   Bathtuboom

Bathtuboom, shown in Fig. 2(a), is a kind of interactive art system. Each colored ball projected on the edge of the bathtub is a button that is able to activate sound phrases and move light shapes on the top of the bathtub. When a bather touches these buttons simultaneously, the overlapped sound phrases generate music that can be listened to. Bathers, especially kids who dislike bathing, can experience some amount of pleasure by touching these balls and listening to the resulting music.

3.2   Batheremin

Batheremin, shown in Fig. 2(b), is a theremin application. The theremin is a very famous electronic musical instrument that is controlled by the proximity of the two hands via capacitive sensors. We designed a bathtub embedded touch sensor system as a theremin that can be played using two hands.

3.3 BathCount

When taking a bath, many Japanese children play a game, while in the tub of water, in which they count from one to a few tens until the end of the bath. Children learn numbers and counting through these experiences with their parent(s) in the bathroom. BathCount, shown in Fig. 2(c), is a kind of support system for this counting experience. When a button is touched, BathCount displays the number on the bathtub, and speaks the number or plays some sounds. Children using this system can count numbers with/without a parent, resulting in more fun at bathtime.

3.4 Bathcratch

Bathcratch[1], shown in Fig. 2(d), is a DJ scratching entertainment system that partially utilizes TubTouch. Using this application, a bather can scratch like a DJ by rubbing the edge of the bathtub with a hand, and touching TubTouch buttons to select rhythm tracks, scratching sounds, and phrases.

4 Conclusion

In this paper, we presented the TubTouch bathroom system, which enables a bathtub to become an interactive controller using embedded capacitive touch-sensors, and a number of new entertainment applications associated with it. We described four of these applications in detail. The TubTouch system and these applications have been exhibited and demonstrated at several exhibitions and conferences. The general feedback from people who experimented with the applications has been very positive; they usually state a desire to have the TubTouch system and its applications in their own homes.

As a future work, we plan to develop middleware for TubTouch in order to make applications easier to develop. The middleware will use the TUIO protocol [2] to divide TubTouch into hardware and software platforms. We hope to spread this technology, and also hope that more and varied entertainment applications will be developed for both kids and adults to enhance bathing activities and make the act of bathing more fun.

Acknowledgment. This research was partially supported by a grant from the Hayao Nakayama Foundation.

References

1. Hirai, S., Sakakibara, Y., Hayakawa, S.: Bathcratch: Touch and sound-based DJ controller implemented on a bathtub. In: Nijholt, A., Romão, T., Reidsma, D. (eds.) ACE 2012. LNCS, vol. 7624, pp. 44–56. Springer, Heidelberg (2012)
2. Kaltenbrunner, M.: reacTIVision and TUIO: a tangible tabletop toolkit. In: Proc. of ITS 2009, pp. 9–16 (2009)

Audio-Haptic Rendering of Water Being Poured from Sake Bottle

Sakiko Ikeno[1], Ryuta Okazaki[1], Taku Hachisu[1,2],
Michi Sato[1,2], and Hiroyuki Kajimoto[1,3]

[1] The University of Electro-Communications, Tokyo, Japan
[2] JSPS Research Fellow
[3] Japan Science and Technology Agency
{ikeno,okazaki,hachisu,michi,kajimoto}@kaji-lab.jp

Abstract. The impression of food can be affected by "rendition"—i.e., the surrounding environment such as the appearance of the food and the dish—not just by its taste. We focused on the sound and vibration of liquid being poured from a Japanese Sake bottle as a haptic rendition of liquid. Sake bottles are known for their unique "glug" sound and vibration which we believe affects the subjective impression of the liquid in the bottle. To examine this idea, we proposed a method that reproduces the vibration of pouring liquid from a Japanese Sake bottle by measuring and modeling real vibrations. We measured the vibration of water by tilting a Sake bottle at different angles, and created a model consisting of two decaying sinusoidal waves of different frequencies. To verify the appropriateness of the model, we developed two types of devices; a bottle-shaped device with embedded vibrators and an attachment type device for any plastic bottle.

Keywords: haptic rendering, pouring water, tactile display, tang.

1   Introduction

Several studies have suggested that the impression of food can be affected by "rendition", i.e., the surrounding environment such as the appearance of the food and the dish, not just by its taste [1]. While most renditions are limited to visual effects, we focused on the aural and haptic rendition of the eating environment. Some studies have reported on the audio-haptic effects during biting or drinking [2] [3], but we speculate that we first encounter food with our hands, where there is a room for new type of audio-haptic rendition.

In this study, we focused on the sound and vibration of liquid being poured from a Japanese Sake bottle as an audio-haptic rendition of liquid. Sake bottles are known for their unique "glug" sound and vibration. We believe that these sounds and vibrations affect the subjective impression of the liquid in the bottle. To examine this idea, we propose a method that reproduces the vibration of pouring liquid from a Japanese Sake bottle by measuring and modeling real vibrations.

D. Reidsma, H. Katayose, and A. Nijholt (Eds.): ACE 2013, LNCS 8253, pp. 548–551, 2013.
© Springer International Publishing Switzerland 2013

2   Method

One of the ways to reproduce sensation caused by vibration is to create a model by measuring a vibration and reproducing it. Okamura et al. created a vibration model that uses a decaying sinusoidal wave to reproduce the vibro-tactile sensation of tapping an object by measuring the real vibration and modifying reality-based vibration parameters through a series of perceptual experiments [4]. We extended this method to reproduce the vibration of pouring water.

3   Measuring and Modeling the Vibration of Water Being Poured

We surmised that the vibration of water being poured is a function of tilt angle of the Sake bottle. Fig. 1 shows the measured vibration of a pouring-water bottle with a tilt angle of 180° (i.e. the bottle was upside down). We took a single group of waves from the measured data, which resembled a decaying wave, and observed the spectrum of the wave using the Fast Fourier Transform (FFT) (Fig. 2 (Left)).

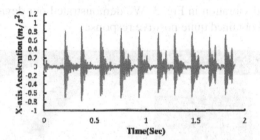

Fig. 1. Vibration of a bottle pouring water (Bottle angle 180°)

We found two peaks in the frequency spectrum. The higher peak was around 250Hz, which we speculated was caused by Helmholtz resonance [5]. The lower peak was around 20 - 40 Hz, which we presumed was caused by water surface fluctuation. Interestingly, while both frequency peaks can be perceived aurally, both can also be perceived by two types of mechanoreceptors in the skin (the Pacinian corpuscle senses the higher peak, and the Meissner corpuscle the lower peak) [6], which implies that these peaks not only aurally but also haptically characterize the pouring water experience.

We reproduced the wave by the following model consisting of two decaying sinusoidal waves of different frequencies:

$$Q(t) = \sum_{n=1}^{2} A_n \exp(-B_{nt}) \sin(2\pi f_n t) \qquad (1)$$

Here, A_1 and A_2 are the wave amplitudes, B_1 and B_2 are the attenuation coefficients, f_1 and f_2 are the frequencies of the sinusoidal waves, and t is time. Parameters were determined by the least-squares method to fit the measurement result. The modeled waveform is also shown in Fig. 2 (Right).

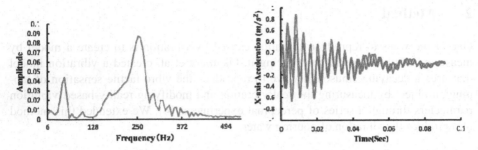

Fig. 2. (Left) Spectrum density of a single wave at 180°, (Right) Red: Original single wave. Blue: Modeled wave.

4   Reproducing Vibration on the Haptic Device

4.1   A Sake Bottle Type Device

To verify the appropriateness of the created model, we manufactured a Sake bottle shaped device with a vibro-tactile actuator (Haptuator Mark II , Tactile Labs Inc.) and present the modeled vibration in Fig. 3. We demonstrated our device at some domestic conferences and obtained quite positive response.

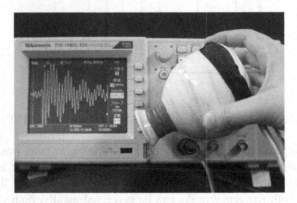

Fig. 3. Sake-bottle-shaped device with a vibro-tactile actuator

4.2   An Attachment Type Device

Our model can also be used to alter the impression of real liquid being poured from various containers. We manufactured a device that can be attached to the neck of any plastic bottle, as shown Fig. 4. The same algorithm as a sake bottle type device was employed to overwrite the impression, so that users felt as if they were really pouring from a sake bottle.

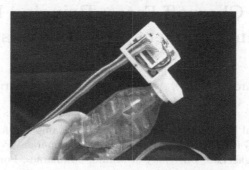

Fig. 4. The device attached to a plastic bottle

5   Conclusion

We proposed a method that reproduces the vibration of pouring liquid from a Japanese Sake bottle by measuring and modeling real vibrations. We measured the vibration of water by tilting a Sake bottle at different angles, and created a model consisting of two decaying sinusoidal waves of different frequencies. To verify the appropriateness of the model, we developed a Sake bottle type device and generated the modeled vibration. We also developed an attached device to alter the impression of real liquid being poured from various containers.

Our future works will include a more realistic rendering of pouring liquid, by monitoring and reflecting the remaining amount of water, which will cause a gradually diminishing effect. We will also add a multimodal cue such as a tabletop display to enhance the realism. Participants incline the bottle, feel the liquid aurally and haptically, and then, a few seconds later, visually observe the poured water on the table.

References

1. Ban, Y., Narumi, T., Tanikawa, T., Hirose, M.: Modifying an Identified Size of Objects Handled with Two Fingers Using Pseudo-Haptic Effects. In: Joint Virtual Reality Conference of ICAT - EGVE - EuroVR 2012, pp. 1–8 (2012)
2. Zampini, M., Spence, C.: The Role of Auditory Cues in Modulating the Perceived Crispness and Staleness of Potato Chips. J. Sensory Studies 19(5), 347–363 (2004)
3. Hashimoto, Y., Inami, M., Kajimoto, H.: Straw-like User Interface: Virtual experience of the sensation of drinking using a straw. In: Ferre, M. (ed.) EuroHaptics 2008. LNCS, vol. 5024, pp. 484–493. Springer, Heidelberg (2008)
4. Okamura, A.M., Cutkosky, M.R., Dennerlein, J.T.: Reality-Based Models for Vibration Feedback in Virtual Environments. IEEE/ASME Trans. on Mechatronics 6(3), 245–252 (2001)
5. Selamet, A., Lee, I.: Helmholtz resonator with extended neck. J. Acoust. Soc. Am. 113(4), 1975–1985 (2003)
6. Kandel, E.R., Schwartz, J.H., Jessell, T.M.: Principles of Neural Science, 4th edn. McGraw-Hill (2000)

Living Chernoff Faces: Bringing Drama and Infotainment to Public Displays

Ido Aharon Iurgel[1,3], Andreas Petker[1], Björn Herrmann[1],
Christina Martens[1], and Pedro Ribeiro[2]

[1] Rhine-Waal University of Applied Sciences, Kamp-Lintfort, Germany
[2] CCG (Computer Graphics Center), Guimarães, Portugal
[3] EngageLab, University of Minho, Guimarães, Portugal
ido.iurgel@hochschule-rhein-waal.de,
{andreas.petker,bjoern.herrmann,christina.martens}@hsrw.org,
pribeiro@ccg.pt

Abstract. Interactive public displays are already widespread without being yet ubiquitous. With advances in computer vision technologies and falling prices for displays and sensors, we assume considerable growth in the upcoming years, in particular for publicity and related areas. This motivates our exploration of Living Chernoff Faces. Chernoff Faces represent data as features of an abstract face. The Chernoff Faces for digital signage that we are currently developing are alive; They are displayed in public spaces and are equipped with a camera. They look at users and passers-by and communicate with them non-verbally, thus combining the presentation of information, attention seeking, interaction, and fun.

Keywords: Chernoff-Faces, Storytelling, Anthropomorphic Interface Agents, Public Displays, Digital Signage, Entertainment, Publicity, Infotainment.

1 Introduction

Interactive public displays are already widespread without being yet ubiquitous. With advances in computer vision technologies and falling prices for displays and sensor systems, it seems like a safe bet to assume considerable growth in the upcoming years, in particular for publicity and related areas. Cameras or other sensors enable proactive behavior of the display and foster implicit and explicit interaction of users with it. We are currently studying ludic concepts for public displays that will combine entertainment, storytelling and transmission of information, based on Living Chernoff Faces that represent data as features of an abstract face, e.g. the happiness of a mouth correlating to low unemployment rates. This study shall contribute to an understanding of how emerging proactive informative or advertising public displays can be designed to joyfully attract, engage and convince passers-by without being excessively intrusive.

D. Reidsma, H. Katayose, and A. Nijholt (Eds.): ACE 2013, LNCS 8253, pp. 552–555, 2013.
© Springer International Publishing Switzerland 2013

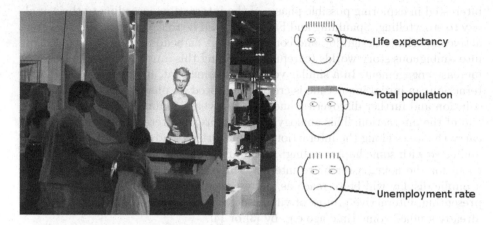

Fig. 1. Left: Photo of the proactive avatar of our information kiosk during the shoe fair of Milano in Fall 2012. Right: a screen shot of currently implemented Chernoff Faces, with exemplary explanations.

2   Related Work

A starting point for our work has been our own experiences with avatars (anthropomorphic user interface agents) for public spaces, for instance the proactive kiosk that we have created for attracting visitors at the 2012 Milano shoe fair in the context of the Portuguese SHOEINOV project, cf. Fig. 1. There, we employed our own high-quality rendering technology together with a movement detecting camera to drive a very realistic looking, proactive female avatar, aiming to attract potential customers to the boot of our partner. The customers could then interact with the avatar via a touch screen displaying the shoe catalog, but the expected intermediate climax of the interaction was only achieved when a human representative of the manufacturer initiated the contact to the curious visitor. As expected (cf. [2]), informal reports of our partner confirm the high efficacy of the avatar for non-verbally attracting attention and generating curiosity. Now we are trying to transfer this sensible usage scenario of the avatar to other situations, and to improve the experience design of such interactive digital publicity instruments.

Chernoff Faces (cf. [1]) are a way of representing multivariate data on abstract faces, where facial features such as the shape of the mouth or of the eye brows stand for the value of data, e.g. the curvature of a mouth that amounts to a sad expression will stand for a poor average income per person of a certain country. To the best of our knowledge, this is the first attempt at such a ludic and pro-active transformation of Chernoff Faces.

Müller et al. [5] describe, along with other interaction design issues, how passers-by need a motivation to pass from a distinct phase to the next phase, while coming closer to and intensifying their interaction with a public display. Our thoughts follow the lines drawn by these authors, but we are particularly interested in exploring possible phases of the interaction according to their analogy to storytelling. Spaulding and Faste analyzed he role of storytelling for interactive experience design [6], and concluded that embedding provocative designs into ambiguous story worlds (carefully balancing this ambiguity) will effectively increase engagement. In a similar vein, we assume that, in the course of the interaction, an initial inquietude is created, followed by phases of attempting at a solution and further discoveries, and a final revealing climax, which leads to an end of the interaction. This analogy shall explore an interaction design that will carry the users along the interaction phase barriers, lead to a rewarding climax, and close with some happy ending; A delimited end is often required for leaving room for the next passer-by to interact, since one of the requirements of such a public display will be to reach as many persons as possible. The potential for presenting, interactive groups of virtual characters along storytelling ideas was already studied some time ago e.g. by [3] or [4].

3   Living Chernoff Faces

Certainly, there are many situations in which future public displays in some sort of publicity context will possess a decoy function, attracting people proactively in the first place, and then involving them into some premeditated path that will ideally lead to a desired climax, e.g. to the sale of a good or to the transmission of some information or message. We expect to soon see more public displays addressing individuals proactively, and involving them subsequently according to their goals. We are currently investigating scenarios for airports or train stations, where you can find many passers-by who might be attracted by such a display while waiting. Since the most natural way to intentionally and individually address a passer-by is to employ some anthropomorphic entity that is capable of communicative and deictic gestures as to look at, we are now exploring the potential of Chernoff Faces for such proactively involving public displays. Our toy application indeed visualizes current contrasting economic data of European countries in the current debt crisis, e.g. unemployment, debt rate, size of population, economic growth of for instance Germany, Spain, and Greece. The message of this application is the disturbingly disparate current economic situation in Europe. Chernoff Faces are particularly appropriate for representing this data in a public context because they allow integration of emotional and polemic aspects to the data visualization without lying about the data; Thus, if unemployment is represented by the curvature of the mouth, the face of Greece will become sad, and Germany will be quite happy. The main distinctive feature of our Chernoff Faces is that they are alive and move eyes, mouth and brows, and react to the presence of passers-by, detecting their movement and directing their gaze at them. At the first contact, they appear to the passer-by as a group of avatars seeking attention (similarly to the aforementioned avatar of the SHOEINOV project), each in strange emotional disconnection from the other; They keep their secret as data representations and reveal it only at a later phase of the interaction.

With our work, we would like to contribute to two issues: Firstly, we consider the venerable Chernoff Faces to carry considerable potential to be revitalized with current technologies as proactive and interactive faces; We would like to initiate this exploration, starting with a simple case. Secondly, we want to understand how to design the interaction in analogy to the dramatic arc of a story. We believe that the faces carry a natural potential for storytelling. In our simple initial toy scenario, the climax is reached when the passer-by comes close, and then a legend is revealed that explains the meaning of the faces, solving the puzzle of the dissonant group of faces. More complex scenarios would allow the faces to set a short interactive story into scene that engages and involves the user. By talking to each other and commenting on the facts, they might lead the user to more information and might encourage him/her to explore the data in detail during the course of the story and the interaction.

Our initial implementation employs Processing, with a standard web cam and standard Blob detection algorithms to register presence and proximity of passers-by.

4   Conclusion

Future studies should comprise possible benefits of employing more realistic faces for improved emotional expression, movements and behavior that reflect these emotions, as well as text-to-speech with lip-sync and emotional voices. Our current scenario with economic data can be easily extended to a publicity context, and adapted to the entertaining, proactive, interactive comparison of the efficacy of skin moisture creams, say: a scenario where even the skin textures of the avatars could be exploited for representation.

References

1. Chernoff, H.: The use of faces to represent points in k-dimensional space graphically. Journal of the American Statistical Association 68, 361–368 (1973)
2. Christian, A.D., Avery, B.L.: Speak out and annoy someone: experience with intelligent kiosks. In: Proceedings of the SIGCHI Conference on Human Factors in Computing Systems (CHI 2000), pp. 313–320. ACM, New York (2000)
3. Iurgel, I.: From Another Point of View: Art-e-Fact. In: Göbel, S., Spierling, U., Hoffmann, A., Iurgel, I., Schneider, O., Dechau, J., Feix, A. (eds.) TIDSE 2004. LNCS, vol. 3105, pp. 26–35. Springer, Heidelberg (2004)
4. Klesen, M., Kipp, M., Gebhard, P., Rist, T.: Staging Exhibitions: Methods and tools for modelling narrative structure to produce interactive performances with virtual actors. Special Issue of Virtual Reality on Storytelling in Virtual Environments (2003)
5. Müller, J., Alt, F., Michelis, D., Schmidt, A.: Requirements and design space for interactive public displays. In: Proceedings of the International Conference on Multimedia (MM 2010), pp. 1285–1294. ACM, New York (2010)
6. Spaulding, E., Faste, H.: Design-driven narrative: using stories to prototype and build immersive design worlds. In: Proceedings of the SIGCHI Conference on Human Factors in Computing Systems (CHI 2013), pp. 2843–2852. ACM, New York (2013)

Character Visualization in Miniature Environments with an Optical See-through Head-Mounted Display

Dongsik Jo, Daehwan Kim, Yongwan Kim, Ki-Hong Kim, and Gil-Haeng Lee

Electronics and Telecommunications Research Institute, Daejeon, Korea
dongsik@etri.re.kr

Abstract. In this paper, we present a visualization method of virtual characters to provide augmented reality (AR) experiences for a user wearing an optical see-through head-mounted display (HMD). First of all, we execute plane detection to find position of a user's real desk. Second, we perform position update of virtual characters to connect real-time location information for reflecting the height of miniature objects on the desk. Finally, we visualize virtual characters that is involved in environmental properties with the optical based see-through HMD. Our method can be applied to AR contents with respect to contexts of environmental information surrounding the user such as miniature elements.

Keywords: Augmented reality, virtual character, see-through HMD.

1 Introduction

Recently, augmented reality (AR) systems to overlay virtual objects on the real world have been widely used for the purposes of location based service, and many researchers have many efforts to study interaction design of AR objects to support an intuitive sense of the user [3]. In particular, realistic operation about the virtual character with context-aware interfaces of real-world environments are also introduced with a view to offering a seamless environment beyond the barrier between virtual space and real one [4]. In recent years, markerless-based tracking with a depth sensor such as Microsoft Kinect have extensively increased, which allowed user interaction to manipulate the virtual character with detection of the users motion in real-time [2]. Sam et al. proposed an augmented reality system to visualize virtual spiders that were controlled behavior and interactivity using a depth camera [5]. Ha et al. presented a miniature AR system to help exhibition visitors and to provide DigiLog experience by interactive storytelling. Here, position of virtual objects was determined by 3D reconstructed models, and AR objects were visualized with devices such as a phone and an e-book [7].

In this paper, we present a visualization method of virtual characters in relation to real situations such as miniature environments with wearing an optical see-through HMD. Our method is capable of executing updated location of the virtual character through real-time height information of the miniature topography estimated by a depth camera. Specially, we combine the sensors among

D. Reidsma, H. Katayose, and A. Nijholt (Eds.): ACE 2013, LNCS 8253, pp. 556–559, 2013.
© Springer International Publishing Switzerland 2013

an optical-based see-through HMD, a depth camera, and a optical based tracker to provide real-time visualization and tracking. We also develop activity animation of the virtual character to apply with various contexts of the composed miniature environments such as the miniature element involving position of the virtual character.

2 Character Visualization System

2.1 Position Detection to Visualize Virtual Characters

First of all, we execute plane detection to identify an active desk in real environments and execute height estimation of the desk with the basis of the installed depth camera. The virtual character for visualization can be updated continuously with correct position based on a height map to consider not only the desk but also miniature elements.

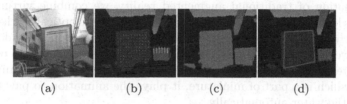

(a)   (b)   (c)   (d)

Fig. 1. Active plane detection to find the real desk as an interaction space: (a) real environments of the desk; (b) normal map to extract using depth information; (c) candidates among plane areas; and (d) the result to detect an active plane

Figure 1 shows the overall procedure of the active plane detection to find an interaction space on the real desk using a depth camera. First, we calculate the normal vectors of all pixels in a depth image by doing cross product of three neighboring 3D point [1]. Second, we divide all depth pixels into spatially several neighboring components which can be easily classified by gathering same normal directions. In order to reduce the depth noise, we simply smooth each depth value by meaning of around nine pixels before the division. Third, we select our active plane as a component in the middle of the image as an interaction space. Fourth, we take the 3D plane equation using randomly selected three points among given N points obtained from the interaction space. Let P1=(X_1, Y_1, Z_1), P2=(X_2, Y_2, Z_2), and P3=(X_3, Y_3, Z_3) be the three points. Three typical plane equations can be described using P1, P2, and P3 as follows. Here, k represents the number of a selected point.

$$aX_k + bY_k + cZ_k + d = 0 \tag{1}$$

We solve these equations using Cramers rule. Last, we convert the xyz coordinate for the active plane into the criteria coordinate by calculating the transformation matrix T and multiplying all 3D pixel values P by the matrix.

$$Pc = T * P \tag{2}$$

2.2   Visualization of Virtual Characters with the See-through HMD

We install our miniature environments including an optical see-through HMD, a MS Kinect depth camera, and an optical-based tracker. In particular, the depth camera for real-time height calculation is installed over the top of miniature. As a precise tracking to obtain the data of head position, we use NatualPoint OptiTrack rigid-body markers and an object-tracking toolkit that can calibrate and track 6DOF (six degrees of freedom) objects related to head motion of the user. To visualize virtual images, we also use Silicon Micro Display ST1080 HMD to support see-through visualization [6].

To adjust position of the virtual character with height information, we use the method by the extraction of height values with real-time depth information since this is able to reflect positional movement of dynamically movable objects. Figure 2 shows real-time character visualization to apply height information of movable elements in miniature such as a pond and a bridge. Unlike visual tracking with pose estimation of traditional augmented reality, we combine virtual objects with 3-axis location based on the coordinate system of the optical tracker and the value coverted real-time depth information into tracker coordinate. Additionally, we also develop generation of automatic animation to consider local position of the character on the miniature. For example, when the virtual dinosaur falls out the pond which is a part of miniature, it plays the animation to paw the air to get out of the water automatically.

As a software development platform, we use the Unity 3D tool to render the virtual content, and C# language to integrate the movement and animation of virtual characters with the depth camera on a Microsoft Windows 7 operating system. The quantitative evaluation of the distance about average errors to compose 3D virtual objects had less than 0.3mm in tracking accuracy that was considered with the combination of the optical tracker and the depth camera. Moreover, our estimated results of achieved accuracy about the height position with the AR characters had less than 1cm, and online detection speed for interaction to apply the height of the users hand had more than 20 frame per

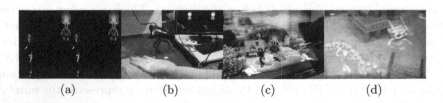

(a)   (b)   (c)   (d)

Fig. 2. Character visualization with the see-through HMD in relation to real-world height of the miniature: (a) virtual characters generated by computer and reflected stereoscopic visualization. The virtual dinosaur was transformed with position to consider hill height of our miniature system; (b) The virtual dinosaur to reflect height position of the users hand; (c) a concept of character visualization to overlay virtual objects on the optical see-through HMD under miniature environments; (d) the result of character visualization to capture inner images of the HMD using a webcam.

second (FPS). Our system is built on a PC with a 3.07GHz Intel Core i7 CPU, 12 gigabytes of main memory, and a NVIDIA GeForce GTX 260 graphics chip.

3 Conclusion and Future Work

An augmented reality system using an eyewear based device such as a see-through HMD needs to reflect visualization involving real environments for the purposes of providing realistic experience. In this paper, we proposed a constructed system including the see-through HMD to visualize virtual characters on the miniature with coordinate correspondence. We also presented visualization methods of virtual characters living real worlds to consider positional information such as the height of real objects, and the dominant plane. In our future work, we need to work towards the expansion of improving an algorithm for a depth camera which can locate random position away from regular position on the top of the miniature to support wearable technology. we will also develop interaction methods of virtual characters with finger gesture.

Acknowledgments. This work was supported by the R&D program of Ministry of Science, ICT & Future Planning (MSIP) and Korea Evaluation Institute of Industrial Technology (KEIT) (10039923, Development of Live4D contents platform technology based on expansion of realistic experiential space).

References

1. Holz, D., Holzer, S., Rusu, R.B., Behnke, S.: Real-time plane segmentation using RGB-D cameras. In: Röfer, T., Mayer, N.M., Savage, J., Saranlı, U. (eds.) RoboCup 2011. LNCS, vol. 7416, pp. 306–317. Springer, Heidelberg (2012)
2. Jo, D.S., Kim, Y.W., Cho, E.J., Kim, D.H., Kim, K.H., Lee, G.H.: Tracking and Interaction Based on Hybrid Sensing for Virtual Environments. ETRI Journal 35(2), 350–359 (2013)
3. Hannah, S., Bruce, T., Rudi, V.: Tangible User Interaction Using Augmented Reality. In: Proceedings of the Third Australasian Conference on User Interfaces, pp. 13–20 (2002)
4. Nadia, M.T., George, P.: Virtual Worlds and Augmented Reality in Cultural Heritage. In: Proceedings of the International Workshop on Recording, Modeling and Visualization of Cultural Heritage (2005)
5. Sam, C.D., Andreas, D., Adrian, C.: An Interactive Augmented Reality System for Exposure Treatment. In: Proceedings of the 11th IEEE International Symposium on Mixed and Augmented Reality. IEEE Xplore Digital Library (2012)
6. Silicon micro display, http://www.siliconmicrodisplay.com
7. Ha, T.J., Kim, K.Y., Park, N.Y., Seo, S.C., Woo, W.T.: Miniature Alive: Augmented reality based interactive digilog experience in miniature exhibition. In: Proceedings of CHI 2012, pp. 1067–1070. ACM Press (2012)

MARIO: Mid-Air Augmented Reality Interaction with Objects

Hanyuool Kim[1], Issei Takahashi[1], Hiroki Yamamoto[1], Takayuki Kai[1],
Satoshi Maekawa[2], and Takeshi Naemura[1]

[1] The University of Tokyo,
7-3-1 Hongo, Bunkyo-ku, Tokyo, Japan
{hanyuool,issei,yamahiro,kai,naemura}@nae-lab.org
[2] Parity Innovations Co. Ltd.,
3-5 Hikaridai, Seika-cho, Soraku-gun, Kyoto, Japan
maekawa@piq.co.jp

Abstract. This paper proposes a novel interactive system that supports augmented reality interaction between mid-air images and physical objects. Our "Mid-air Augmented Reality Interaction with Objects (MARIO)" system enables visual images to be displayed at various positions and precise depths in mid-air. For entertainment purposes, a game character appears in mid-air and runs around and over "real" blocks which users have arranged by hands. Users thereby enjoy interaction with physical blocks and virtual images.

Keywords: Mid-air Image, Interactive Blocks, Tangible User Interface, Mixed Reality, Augmented Reality.

1 Introduction

To see Mario [1], the star character of Nintendo's Super Mario Brothers games, jumping on bricks in a video display is no surprise. However, to see him jumping on real blocks would be quite surprising. Such a feature in a game would enable the player to interact more intuitively with the virtual characters and thus enjoy the game with a higher sense of reality.

Aiming at more seamless spatial mixing of physical objects and virtual images, we developed a system that provides a tangible and interactive interface for such mixing. Our "Mid-air Augmented Reality Interaction with Objects (MARIO)" system enables virtual images to be displayed at various positions and precise depths in mid-air in combination with physical objects. A game character appears in mid-air and runs around and jump over the physical blocks which users have arranged by hands (Fig.1).

With MARIO system, mid-air images can be displayed anywhere inside a rectangular parallelepiped space (35 cm (W)×30 cm (D)×25 cm (H)). A high sense of reality is achieved due to three types of consistency between the mid-air images and physical objects: high-speed processing for temporal consistency, image display at precise positions for geometrical consistency, and shadow projection for optical consistency.

D. Reidsma, H. Katayose, and A. Nijholt (Eds.): ACE 2013, LNCS 8253, pp. 560–563, 2013.

Fig. 1. Proposed MARIO system. Users can interact with physical objects and mid-air images. A virtual character (Hiyoko, a chick) is displayed in mid-air on wooden blocks. A coordinate system is defined as x for width, y for height, and z for depth.

2   Related Work

Kato and Naemura's floating image display [2] forms a mid-air image on physical objects that the user has arranged by hand. The use of a Fresnel lens and display enables the resulting image to float and move in the vertical plane (the xy-plane) but not in the horizontal one (the z-axis).

In contrast, Tablescape Plus [3] supports horizontal movement (in the zx-plane) of visual images on a tabletop interface through the use of image projection. Users can move tiny stand-up screens on the table to interact with visual images. However, the images are tethered to the screen surface, so that they cannot "jump" vertically (the y-axis movement).

The Augmented Urban Model [4] realizes simple object detection through the use of a depth sensor, enabling ordinary blocks to be used for a tabletop application. However, the projected images are displayed only from the table surface (in the zx-plane), not in mid-air.

In contrast to these previous systems, MARIO system enables the display of images in mid-air that can freely move in both the horizontal and vertical directions. A mid-air image is displayed in a volumetric area (the xyz-space) through the combined use of a novel real imaging optics [5] and a linear actuator. A depth sensor detects the positions and orientations of the physical objects, and thus mid-air images are seamlessly mixed with the physical objects.

3   System Design

As illustrated in Fig.2, a depth sensor (Kinect) is suspended 80 cm above the table to detect shapes and positions of physical objects on a table. The detectable area is set as a rectangular parallelepiped space (35 cm (W)×30 cm (D)×25

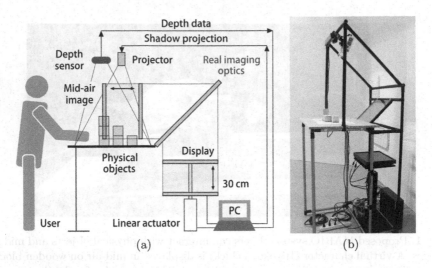

Fig. 2. (a) System overview; (b) implemented MARIO system

cm (H)). The shapes of objects which enter this area are estimated from the depth data. A thin and compact real imaging optics (AIP-350) is used for mid-air imaging display. The imaging optics is fixed at a 45° angle to the table surface. A 19-inch color display (S1903-TBK) is placed below the optics. A linear motor actuator (RCP4-RA5C, maximum stroke: 30 cm) connected to the display changes the imaging position with vertical movement. An LED projector (GP10) is installed 65 cm above the table to project shadow covering the interaction area. The coordinate systems of physical objects, mid-air images, and projected shadows are aligned using manual calibration.

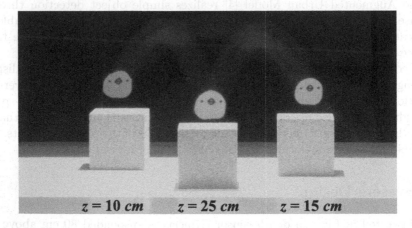

Fig. 3. A mid-air image moves in various depths (10 cm, 25 cm, 20 cm). This picture is taken with a long exposure to express the movement (ISO100, f/36, 25 sec).

4   Implementation

An image of a Hiyoko character appears in mid-air to run across and jump over wooden blocks arranged and stacked by the user as a physical terrain (Fig.1). The character appears to move back and forth in different depths due to the change of imaging position by the actuator (Fig.3). The movements and positions of the character change in accordance with the shape of the terrain, so users can play with Hiyoko by re-arranging the blocks.

5   Conclusion

In this paper, we present a new interactive system combining mid-air images and physical objects. On the basis of its novelty of interaction, MARIO system was selected for regular exhibition in Japan National Museum of Emerging Science and Innovation starting from July 2013. During the exhibition, the system will be evaluated in terms of mid-air image display and user interaction. Future work includes more volumetric expression by using integral photography and light field displays.

Acknowledgments. We are sincerely grateful to Yasuko Mori and Ryota Yoshi-hashi for their support in system implementation. Part of this research was funded by the JST-CREST "Harmonized Inter-Personal Display Based on Position and Direction Control" project.

References

1. Nintendo, Super Mario Bros., http://mario.nintendo.com
2. Kato, N., Naemura, T.: Floating Image Display with Dual Imaging Optics for Mixed Reality Environment. Trans. of the VRSJ 12(3), 323–329 (2007) (in Japanese)
3. Kakehi, Y., Naemura, T., Matsushita, M.: Tablescape Plus: Interactive Small-sized Vertical Displays on a Horizontal Tabletop Display. In: The 2nd IEEE International Workshop on Horizontal Interactive Human-Computer Systems, pp. 155–162 (2007)
4. Knecht, K., König, R.: Augmented urban model: Bridging the gap between virtual and physical models to support urban design. In: The 11th International Conference on Construction Applications of Virtual Reality, pp. 142–152 (2011)
5. Maekawa, S., Nitta, K., Matoba, O.: Transmissive optical imaging device with micromirror array. In: Proc. of SPIE, vol. 6392, pp. 63920E:1–8 (2006)

A Face-Like Structure Detection on Planet and Satellite Surfaces Using Image Processing

Kazutaka Kurihara[1], Masakazu Takasu[2], Kazuhiro Sasao[3], Hal Seki[4], Takayuki Narabu[5], Mitsuo Yamamoto[6], Satoshi Iida[7], and Hiroyuki Yamamoto[8]

[1] National Institute of Advanced Industrial Sci. and Tech.
qurihara@gmail.com
[2] teamLab. INC
takasu@team-lab.com
[3] Nico-TECH
k.sasao@gmail.com
[4] Georepublic Japan
hal@georepublic.de
[5] NTT DATA CCS CORPORATION
tnarabu@nttdata-ccs.co.jp
[6] Denso IT Laboratory, Inc.
miyamamoto@d-itlab.co.jp
[7] Nico-TECH
nyampire@gmail.com
[8] DENSO CORPORATION
hyamamyto1981@gmail.com

Abstract. This paper demonstrates that face-like structures are everywhere, and can be detected automatically even with computers. Huge amount of satellite images of the Earth, the Moon, and the Mars are explored and many interesting face-like structure are detected. Throughout this fact, we believe that science and technologies can alert people not to easily become an occultist.

Keywords: Face detection, google map, NASA.

1 Introduction

"Face-like" structures have been found in many provinces on the earth or other stars [5][2]. They are rocks or other geographical structures that look like a human face.

Fig. 1. Face on Mars ©Google

D. Reidsma, H. Katayose, and A. Nijholt (Eds.): ACE 2013, LNCS 8253, pp. 564–567, 2013.

Because it is quite rare for such shapes to be made without artificial efforts, people tend to think that they derived from such as unidentified ancient civilizations or space aliens.

One of the most popular examples of face-like structures is "Face on Mars" (Figure 1) [5]. Some people say that is an ancient ruin made by Martians, and other people say that is an artifact made by human beings. This mysterious face has been inspired many sci-fi stories [1][3], even after it turned out just an optical illusion by later analyses in detail.

Our goal of this research is to demonstrate that such face-like structures are every-where, and can be detected automatically even with computers. Throughout this fact, we believe that science and technologies can alert people not to easily become an occultist.

2   Related Work

Onformative[1] shows a similar idea in 2013, but our project is original as the upload date of a Youtube video[2] shows that we demonstrated our early result in 2010. In addition our project includes exploration of not only the Earth, but also the Moon and Mars.

3   System Description

Fig. 2. Positive examples for training

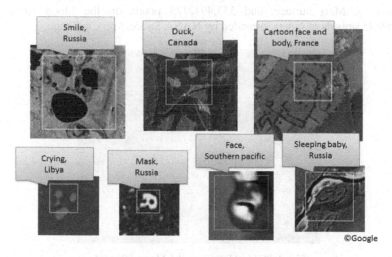

Fig. 3. Example results ©Google

---

[1] http://www.onformative.com/lab/googlefaces/
[2] https://www.youtube.com/watch?v=ooKFEmE6JXQ

3.1   Prototype #1 for the Earth Surface

The object detector of OpenCV with Haar-like features was used to detect face-like structures. This was a commonly used classifier to detect human faces. Since features of face-like structures such as Figure 1 were slightly different from those of original human faces, we have trained our classifier with some simplified illustrations of human faces like Figure 2 as positive examples.

In 2010, we collected thousands of satellite images per day using Google Static Map API [4] and applied our classifier[3]. Figure 3 shows some examples of our results.

With this prototype, we learned that our detection result included many false positives: face-like clouds, and simple mis-recognitions that were not recognized as human-faces with human cognition, and need some improvements to refine detection algorithm.

3.2   Prototype #2 for the Mars and the Surfaces

We developed our prototype #2 as a project for International Space App Challenge hosted by NASA[4]. The major functional updates are (1) applying multiple detection algorithms in parallel, and (2) applying the detector to the Mars and the Moon surfaces that has less obstacles such as clouds.

Applying Multiple Detection Algorithms in Parallel
We applied three algorithms in parallel to our face detector: OpenCV Haar-like feature detection, Anime face detection[6], and Brightness Binary Feature[7][8]. 50 instances of Windows Asure were used for the computation.

Applying Detector to Mars and Moon Surfaces
We explored face-like structures from 11,829,761,106 pixels, including 10,059,979,678 pixels on the Mars surface, and 533,491,975 pixels on the Moon surface, and 1,236,289,453 pixels of others, provided by NASA Space App Challenge.

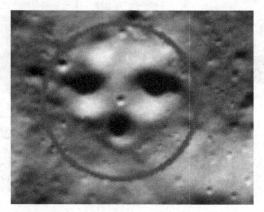

Fig. 4. "Grey Aliens" on the Moon ©NASA

---

[3] https://sites.google.com/site/geofaceproject/
[4] We won the third place award in the Tokyo local competition.
http://marproject.org/

Results

Figure 4 shows a detection example that looks like a famous alien called "Grey Aliens" [9]. This structure is located on the south pole of the moon [10]. We could find many face-like structures in the polar area because the incidence angle of sunlight was smaller in high latitude and inside of craters were mostly dark with shadows. Other examples of faces on the south and north poles of the moon were shown in Figure 5.

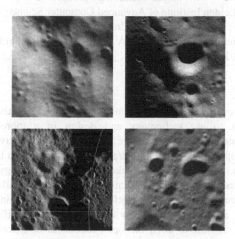

Fig. 5. Face-like structures on the south and north pole of the Moon

4   Conclusion and Future Work

In this paper we demonstrated that face-like structures are everywhere and can be detected automatically on varieties of star surfaces, even with computers. Out next step is to manage our web service that allows people to vote "face candidates" to refine automatic detection results and obtain better and interesting face-like structures with collaborative intelligence.

References

1. Hoagland, R.C.: The Monuments of Mars: A City on the Edge of Forever. Frog Books (1987)
2. http://ryukyushimpo.jp/news/storyid-2333-storytopic-5.html
3. Asuka, A., Mikami, T.: Messiah, a Mystery of Lost Face on Mars. Gakusyu Kenkyusya (2002)
4. https://developers.google.com/maps/documentation/staticmaps/
5. http://en.wikipedia.org/wiki/Cydonia_(region_of_Mars)
6. http://ultraist.hatenablog.com/entry/20110718/1310965532
7. Huang, C., et al.: High-Performance Rotation Invariant Multiview Face Detection. IEEE Trans. Pattern Anal. Mach. Intell. 29(4), 671–686 (2007)
8. http://libccv.org/
9. http://en.wikipedia.org/wiki/Grey_alien
10. http://wms.lroc.asu.edu/lroc_browse/view/SP_Mosaic

Tinkering in Scientific Education

Maarten H. Lamers, Fons J. Verbeek, and Peter W.H. van der Putten

Media Technology group,
Leiden Institute of Advanced Computer Science,
Leiden University,
Niels Bohrweg 1, 2333CA Leiden, The Netherlands
{lamers,fverbeek,putten}@liacs.nl

Abstract. In recent years in arts, technology and science there appears an increasing push to use technology and design in a more personal and autonomous context, integrated with the physical world. Creative platforms are developed that open up personal digital/physical technology to larger groups of novice tinkerers, allowing people to take control of technology and prototype solutions to personal problems and aims. Likewise, education benefits by providing students with tools and platforms to learn by doing and making. However, these advances lead to new challenges for scientific research and education, such as how to align the open-endedness of tinkering with more fixed education and research agendas. This is the first scientific workshop to identify and discuss such issues, and provide a platform for future collaboration and dissemination of results.

1 Scale of the Individual

Many of today's technology heroes and aficionados started their careers by what can be considered as *tinkering*. Bill Gates and Steve Jobs are well-known examples, surrounded by anecdotes of working in garages with small, enthusiastic teams, supposedly working under playful conditions. For many they exemplify what tinkering and grass-roots initiatives could lead to. But also the Wii Remote tinkering projects by Johnny Chung Lee (www.johnnylee.net), shown on Youtube.com, have captured and sparked the imagination of many.

At the level of today's technology consumer, there appears to be an increasing desire to interface our technological power-machines to the real physical world. And power-machines they are, our personal computers, tablets and smart phones – equipped with highly advanced man-machine interaction technologies, communication possibilities, location-determining hardware, acceleration sensors, and more. However, for all their strengths and possibilities, they do not offer the connectivity to the physical world around us that many dream of. No smart phone is currently on offer that drives itself around the house to play with the cat. No tablet is equipped with motors and sensors that make it suitable to steer a child's soap-box cart. No current iPhone models have a user-accessible digital thermometer to play with. And in a way, this is what we more-and-more expect our technology to do (well,

D. Reidsma, H. Katayose, and A. Nijholt (Eds.): ACE 2013, LNCS 8253, pp. 568–571, 2013.
© Springer International Publishing Switzerland 2013

perhaps not exactly this, but similar things) – to connect our computational devices to the physical world.

This desire to connect may have been always present, but there appears to be more of a push towards closing the gaps between human and technology, by leveraging technology in a more personal, private and autonomous manner, under control of the user.

As a result, tinkering with digital/physical computing systems has gained much attention over the last few years. For example the Wiring (www.wiring.org.co) and Arduino (www.arduino.cc) projects offer immensely popular tools for lower- to intermediate-level software and hardware tinkerers (e.g. [1],[2]), spawning thousands of interesting home-grown projects. Similar projects are Raspberry Pi (www.raspberrypi.org), MaKey MaKey (www.makeymakey.com) and, more in the creative coding domains, Processing (www.processing.org) and OpenFrameworks (www.openframeworks.cc).

These initiatives gave rise to low-cost rapid prototyping tools that offer rich, if not full functionality, while hiding complex underlying structures from the developer. The frequent open-source nature of the projects kindles what is in essence a community-like support structure, and the ongoing generation of example code and libraries. All this makes it possible for single medium-skilled developers to master complex (physical) digital prototyping tools.

> **Observation 1.** In recent years, (physical) digital prototyping was fitted to the scale of the individual. After years of increasing technological complexity in the systems around us, the right combination of technological abstraction and openness has re-enabled individuals to understand, own and prototype solutions to their own problems and aims.

2   Scientific Education

The adoption of digital/physical tinkering by individuals has had its effect on science and education. Scientists increasingly use publicly available low-cost digital prototyping systems to create measurement tools and other experimental devices (e.g. [3]). To witness, a Google Scholar (scholar.google.com) query for articles containing the word "Arduino" in their title, excluding legal document, patents and citations, yielded a result of 490 scholarly articles[1].

Naturally, developments in science and technology resonate in science education (e.g. [4],[5]) and scientific education (e.g. [6],[7]), although not all experiences are always positive. Tinkering is found in curricula worldwide, and students realized a plethora of projects that are disseminated via the web.

An example of successful tinkering by academic students that stands out in our opinion, is the Amplino project (www.amplino.org), in which students developed a low-cost Arduino-based polymerase chain reaction (*PCR*) diagnostic tool for malaria.

---

[1] Query result on September 2, 2013.

Naturally, not all student projects are as successful as the Amplino project. However, they nonetheless have educational value.

> **Observation 2.** Tinkering projects in education typically strive to teach various technical objectives such as programming skills, understanding of digital hardware, and rapid prototyping skills. Moreover, scientific education may benefit from the tinkering approach also by inducing playful interaction with scientific knowledge, exploration of a problem domain, and solution ownership by students.

Particular attention should be given to the role of educational tinkering within a research-oriented environment. Scientific research is a knowledge-driven activity, geared towards answering questions and generating new knowledge. Although exploration is an important force in science [8], typically scientific research is brought about through rigorous and methodical work, in which the exploratory and playful nature of tinkering has only limited place. The emphasis in science is typically on testing the validity of theories, hypotheses, methods, tools and other scientific end products, as opposed to providing the creative process and tools to discover and generate these. Furthermore, research agenda's may be based on timed delivery of knowledge products, something that does not evidently match the open-ended nature of tinkering. Finally, in research-based education, one may be uncertain how to evaluate the end results of tinkering – should evaluation be based on knowledge discovery, on work methodology, or on aspects of exploration?

> **Observation 3.** Aspects of tinkering in research-oriented education require special attention. Existing insights must be collected and further insight may be developed.

3   Current State and Future

It is the position of the authors that tinkering as a mode of knowledge production has great value, as acknowledged by the theme of the 10th International Conference on Advances in Computer Entertainment Technology (ACE 2013). Moreover we propose that this value extends into the realm of scientific education. As argued above, particular attention is required for implementing tinkering within research-oriented education. We are not aware of any initiatives to collectively deal with this topic.

> **Observation 4.** There exists an unfulfilled need to collect and share experiences, views, and thoughts about the future of tinkering in scientific education.

4   Workshop Objectives, Format and Output

The workshop "Tinkering in Scientific Education" aims at bringing together those who adopted tinkering as part of their scientific education, and those who wish to learn more about it. Participants share experiences, develop strategies and tackle problems, with the explicit goal of consolidating what is known and what is desired, and building a network for future collaboration.

Participants are encouraged to bring their own experiences and questions into the discussions. To this end, applicants are invited to fill in a short questionnaire prior to the workshop. After a plenary introduction and review of issues/questions posed by participants, separate issues are dealt with by sub-groups within short consecutive sessions. In a final plenary session, the results are aggregated and possible plans for future collaboration among participants can be discussed. If possible, the organizers will aggregate all material into (a) separate paper(s) to be published, consolidating the workshop results.

References

1. Thompson, C.: Build It. Share It. Profit. Can Open Source Hardware Work? Wired Magazine 16(11) (2008)
2. Banzi, M.: Getting Started with Arduino. Books & O'Reilly Media, Make (2008)
3. D'Ausilio, A.: Arduino: A Low-cost Multipurpose Lab Equipment. Behavior Research Methods 44(2), 305–313 (2012)
4. Dougherty, D.: Learning by Making: American Kids Should be Building Rockets and Robots, Not Taking Standardized Tests. Slate / Future Tense Article (June 4, 2012) (online resource)
5. Gerstein, J.: The Flipped Classroom: The Full Picture for Tinkering and Maker Education. Post on User Generated Education Blog (June 16, 2012) (online resource)
6. Brock, J.D., Bruce, R.F., Reiser, S.L.: Using Arduino for Introductory Programming Courses. Journal of Computing Sciences in Colleges 25(2), 129–130 (2009)
7. Jamieson, P.: Arduino for Teaching Embedded Systems. Are Computer Scientists and Engineering Educators Missing the Boat? In: Proc. FECS, pp. 289–294 (2010)
8. Doherty, P.C.: The Beginner's Guide to Winning the Nobel Prize: Advice for Young Scientists. Columbia University Press (2008)

Modeling Player-Character Engagement in Single-Player Character-Driven Games

Petri Lankoski

Södertörn University,
141 89 Huddinge, Sweden
petri.lankoski@sh.se

Abstract. This pilot study looks at how the formal features of character-driven games can be used to explain player-character engagement. Questionnaire data (N=206), formal game features (in 11 games), and ordinal regression were used in the analysis. The results show that *interactive dialogue* and *cut-scenes showing the romances* between the player-character and another character relates to higher character engagement scores, while *romance modeling* and *friendship modeling* relate to lower character engagement scores.

Keywords: ordinal regression, player-character, engagement, identification.

1 Introduction

This is a pilot study that aims to isolate formal game features that contribute toward player-character engagement. The focus of this study is on single-player character-driven games. Lankoski's theory [1] is used as the basis of the study. In order to evaluate connection between games and engagement, the formal game features are classified and then evaluated by using ordinal regression and self-reported engagement scores.

Lankoski [1] argues that player-character engagement relates to goal-driven engagement and empathic engagement. Here I focus only on empathic engagement. Lankoski suggests that character engagement depends on how the character is presented; the kind of access that the player has to the characters actions, thoughts, and emotions; and how the player evaluates the character in terms of morals and aesthetics. [1]

The following formal features where selected (c.f., [1]): dialogue vs interactive dialogue, moral choices (no–yes), supporting different play styles (no–yes), cut-scenes with romantically content – romance in cut-scenes, appearance customization (no; possibility to change some aspects of the character, e.g., cloths, hair style); customizing sex and appearance, character development (no, scripted character development, player-guided character development), player character dialogue is voice acted (no–yes), romance/friendship modeling (some modeling, complex modeling as in *Dragon Age: Origins)*) and moral choices (no–yes).

D. Reidsma, H. Katayose, and A. Nijholt (Eds.): ACE 2013, LNCS 8253, pp. 572–575, 2013.

Most of these features relate to the kind of access the player has to the character except for appearance customization, play styles, and character development that relate more to the aesthetical and moral evaluation of the character (c.f., [1]). It is possible that this list does not include all the features that are relevant to player-character engagement and, hence, the analysis below reveals only the information on these features in relation to the feature set.

2 Method

Player-character engagement is measured by using a single 5-point Likert scale question: I identified with my player-character (1: totally disagree, 5: totally agree). Here the concept of identification is used in the questionnaire as I assumed that the term is more familiar to players than that of engagement.

A non-proportional quota sampling method was used. The target was to set to 20 answers for each game. In addition the target for female respondents was set to 25%.

Respondents were gathered by advertising the study in Facebook, Twitter, Google+, and pelilauta.fi as well as in two forums dedicated to *Assassin Creed: Brotherhood* and *Uncharted 2: Among Thieves* whenever there was a need to gather more answers about those games. In addition, to get more answers from females, the study was advertised in a Finnish girl gamer forum.

The data was gathered by using two questionnaires. One-half of the games was in the first questionnaire and the other half in the second questionnaire.

I selected popular, rather new games for the study to ensure that the sufficient amount of answers were obtained. The games are listed in figure 1. The games were played and judged base on whether they have the aforementioned formal features.

The data were analyzed by using ordinal regression and mixed effect models. R [2] and cumulative link mixed models (clmm) from the ordinal package [3] were used. The Gauss-Hermite quadrature approximation with ten points was used in the analysis. No structure (except that $1 < 2 < ... < 5$) were assumed in the ordinal scale. Subjects were modeled as a random effect.

Stepwise model selection by using Aikake's Information Criterion (AIC) was used. The model with the lowest AIC was selected, However, simpler model was preferred when the models were not statistically different (by using the likelihood ratio test).

3 Results

The total number of subjects in the study is 206. However, there can be overlap, as the data was collected through two anonymous questionnaires. The mean age of the respondents of the questionnaires is 28.49 (min = 13.00, max = 51.00). 68.9 % of the respondents are male and 31.1 % female. 66% of the respondents are from Finland, 15 % from Sweden, 4 % from the US, and the rest from different countries. 21.4 % of the respondents had obtained high school eduction, 5.5 %

	Romance in cut-scenes	Moral choices	Perspective	Different play styles	Apppearance customization	Romance modeling	Interactive dialogue	Character development	Voice-acted PC dialogue	Friendship modeling
Fallout 3	no	yes	1st*	yes	yes	no	yes	yes	no	some
Dragon Age: Origins	yes	yes	3rd	yes	yes	yes	yes	yes	no	yes
Red Dead Redemption	yes	yes	3rd	yes	some	no	no	no	yes	no
Dragon Age 2	yes	yes	3rd	yes	yes	yes	yes	yes	yes	yes
Elder Scrolls V: Skyrim	yes	yes	1st*	yes	yes	some	yes	yes	no	some
Mass Effect 2	yes	yes	3rd	yes	yes	yes	yes	yes	yes	yes
Deus Ex: Human Revolution	yes	yes	mixed	yes	no	no	yes	yes	yes	some
Assassins Creed: Brotherhood	yes	yes	3rd	no	some	no	no	some	yes	no
Batman: Arkham Asylum	no	no	3rd	yes	no	no	no	yes	yes	no
Grand Theft Auto IV	yes	yes	3rd	no	some	yes	no	no	yes	yes
Uncharted 2: Among Thieves	yes	no	3rd	no	no	no	no	no	yes	no

Fig. 1. Categorization of games. The games with perspective *1st** have a default of a 1st person perspective, but allow playing using a 3rd person perspective.

vocational, 23.3 % college, 24.0 % bachelor, 18.5 % masters, 6.0 % doctoral, and 1.1 % other education. Figure 1 shows the various features of the games.

The predictor variables of the optimal model are *interactive dialogue, romance modeling, friendship modeling,* and *romance in cut-scenes* and *subject* is a random effect.[1]

The optimal model is significantly better ($p < .001$) than the null model containing only a random effect *subject*. This means that the data is explained better with the optimal model than by assuming that the player preferences would explain the data.

The random effect subject has a variance of 2.219 and a standard deviation of 1.489. The strongest positive effect is by *interactive dialogue* (2.1274, $CI_{95} = 1.4789 - 2.7759$). This means that the games having of interactive dialogue are estimated to have higher player engagement with their PCs. Showing romantic engagement in the cut-scenes emph(romance in cut-scenes: 0.6932, $CI_{95} = 0.1553 - 1.2310$) relates to higher scores in the terms of identification. The effect is considerably smaller than the effect of interactive dialogue. The games having romance (*yes*: -1.2650, $CI_{95} = -1.9054 - -0.6245$) or friendship modeling (*some*: -1.4392, $CI_{95} = -2.2342 - -0.6444$) have lower player-character engagement than the games without those features. As an effect, limited romance modeling (*romance some*: 0.0843, $CI_{95} = -0.6242 - 0.7929$) does not differ from

---

[1] Two models with lower thhe AIC was rejected, because there are problems in the models: Adding sex to the model decreases the AIC, but this model is not significantly better ($\Delta AIC = .493, p = .1143$) and the confidence interval for *sex* crosses zero (males and females are not significantly different). Hence, a simpler model is preferred. A model having a fixed effect with an interaction between *table-top role playing hobby, sex,* and *romance modeling* is significantly better than the optimal model ($\Delta AIC = 9.648$, p=.0009), but the confidence intervals of the interaction terms are very wide and cross zero. Hence, the model with interactions was rejected.

no romance modeling in a significant fashion (because the 95 % confidence intervals cross zero). The effect of limited friendship modeling (*friendship some*) could not be estimated because the model design is column rank deficient if the level is not dropped.

4   Discussion

As nonprobability sampling was used, the results are not directly generalizable by using probability theory. However, the optimal model indicates that the different backgrounds has no significant role in the results. However, the study includes only 11 games. The implementation of formal features can have an impact on the results. Finally, if some formal feature that is relevant to player-character engagement is *not* included in the list of features used in the model selection, the relevance of the feature cannot be evaluated (e.g., the set of games does not contain pure 1st person games such as *Half-Life*). To conclude, I believe that the results are somewhat generalizable to the population outside the sample, but it is likely that the results are tied to the implementation of the formal features within the games in this study.

The results indicate that interactive dialogue and showing romantic episodes in the cut-scenes relate to a higher player-character engagement. Interactive dialogue in all the games in this study contains dialogue options that can be used to present different types of personalities (e.g., in *Dragon Age 2* one can select from diplomatic/helpful, humorous/charming, and aggressive/direct lines). This allows the players to modulate the character towards their preferences. This can contribute towards positive evaluation of the character and a higher engagement (c.f., Lankoski[1]). Surprisingly, romance and friendship modeling relate to lower player-character engagement scores. This might relate to the quality of the modeling.

In this study I am able to connect formal game features to the identification oclf-evaluation scores by using ordinal regression. However, using only one question in the questionnaire is being simplistic. Using more nuanced measurements for evaluating player-character engagement remains to be done in a future work.

References

1. Lankoski, P.: Player character engagement in computer games. Games and Culture 6, 291–311 (2011)
2. R Development Core Team: R: A Language and Environment for Statistical Computing. R Foundation for Statistical Computing, Vienna, Austria (2012) ISBN 3-900051-07-0
3. Christensen, R.H.B.: Ordinal—regression models for ordinal data (2122) R package version 2012.01-19, http://www.cran.r-project.org/package=ordinal/

Paintrix: Color Up Your Life!

Dimitri Slappendel, Fanny Lie, Martijn de Vos, Alex Kopla, and Rafael Bidarra

Delft University of Technology

Train stations, shopping malls and airports: all public places where we spend a lot of time, waiting for the train, for our friends and for the gate to open. While waiting, we get bored and we would like to entertain ourselves in order to kill time. The first thing that comes to our minds is playing a game or socializing using our smartphone. People around you are doing the exact same thing. Wouldn't it be great if you could play a game with those people, a game which requires collaboration and interaction with your surroundings?

This is exactly where Paintrix comes into play: gather people, form two teams and let them collaborate and compete at the same time. Teams have to solve the same puzzle against the clock. Be faster than your opposing team to win! How does this work?

Gameplay

The objective of the game is to recreate a colored picture that previously has been shortly visible on a screen. See Figure 1 for example pictures.

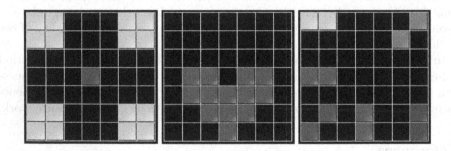

Fig. 1. Example Paintrix levels

Memorizing the grid is of great importance, as the picture will disappear once the game starts. Armed with their smartphones as paintbrushes[1] they start painting. The tiles on the field represent the pixels. In order to paint a tile, the player must first get one color from one of the three available 'color buckets' that can be found in the corners of the grid: red, blue or yellow. There is also

---

[1] The app required for this game is called 'Paintrix Live', which can be downloaded from the Apple App Store and the Android Play Store.

D. Reidsma, H. Katayose, and A. Nijholt (Eds.): ACE 2013, LNCS 8253, pp. 576–579, 2013.

a special erase bucket available in order to erase a painted tile if a mistake has been made. After that, they walk (or run) to the tile to be colored and paint it. A generic arrangement of a field is shown in Figure 2.

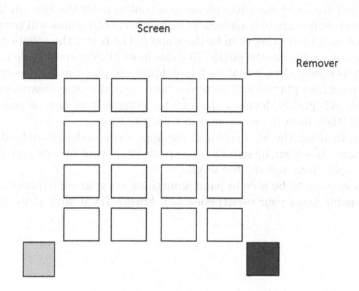

Fig. 2. Arrangement of a 4x4 Paintrix field

Currently, the game is played with two teams competing against each other. The team that recreates the picture first wins. This means players should first agree on who does what in order to work efficiently together. Players can leave and join a team at any moment: making Paintrix ideal for places like train stations and airports. The picture grid is very scalable and several configurations are possible to adjust the difficulty of the game. For example, a larger grid could be used for places that have more space. Sometimes secondary colors are needed. Just like real paint, secondary colors can be created by combining two primary colors. See Figure 3 at the end of this document for gameplay photo's.

At the end of every game each team recieves an amount of Paintrix Points: these points are calculated and displayed on the screen after a game. The Paintrix Points are stored in the app where the player can get an overview of their played games and the earned Paintrix Points. Players can also create their own levels with the build-in level editor in the app: after approval, their created boards have a chance to appear when a game starts!

What Makes Paintrix Standing Out?

Nowadays, multiplayer games are very popular. Paintrix is a multiplayer game that lets you play with both familiar and unfamiliar people in a competitive setting. This way, collaboration is more fun because you need to beat the opponents together.

In contrast to regular apps, Paintrix is not a game where you are glued to the screen of your smartphone and seperated from your environment and bystanders. Instead, you are using the smartphone as a tool to paint the tiles on the field.

When two teams are playing against each other, both teams will try their best to win, but only one of them can be the winner. The better the collaboration, the faster the team will solve the puzzle. Because most players are very determined to win, there is a good chance that each individual will play the game very actively: it is a game where players will be tested both mentally (they have to memorize the board and quickly devise a strategy to recreate it as fast as possible) and physically (they need to run around to color the tiles).

Finally, by using the level editor in the app, you can design and submit your own pictures. Use your imagination to create some cool boards and you might be able to play your self-created level!

It's no surprise to be able to paint something *on* your smartphone... But did you ever paint *using* your smartphone as a *brush*? Try it with Paintrix!

Fig. 3. Gameplay photo's. Watch the video here.

The ToyVision Toolkit for Tangible Games

Javier Marco, Eva Cerezo, and Sandra Baldassarri

GIGA-Affective Lab, Computer Science Department,
Engineering Research Institute of Aragon (I3A), Universidad de Zaragoza, Spain
{javi.marco,ecerezo,sandra}@unizar.es

Abstract. "ToyVision" is a software toolkit aimed to make easy the prototyping of tangible games in visual based tabletop devices. Compared to other software toolkits, ToyVision provides designers and developers with intuitive tools for modeling innovative tangible controls and with higher level user's manipulations data. Tutorial participants will create a Tangible board-game by using ToyVision. Thanks to it, they will be able to develop a functional prototype without the intrinsic difficulties of managing electronic sensors, actuators and machine vision algorithms. The goal of this tutorial is to give ACE attendants the opportunity of having a first contact on the new possibilities that the Tangible Interaction paradigm can bring to videogames.

1 The ToyVision Toolkit

The increasing popularity of tabletop devices is bringing a new generation of entertainment and game applications that mix traditional face to face gaming with computer augmentation on the active surface [7]. At present, most of these tabletop games are based on multitouch interaction [1], However, several tabletop devices are not only capable of detecting user fingers and hands, but also of supporting the identification and tracking of conventional objects placed on the surface. This also enables the use of physical playing pieces in tabletop games [3], and so reinforcing the emotional impact that the activity has in the players [2].

The creation of a Tangible tabletop game usually implies to "hardcode" complex algorithms to process raw data from tabletop in order to detect and track each playing piece manipulated on the active surface. One way to transition Tangible User Interfaces (TUI) into the mainstream is to provide prototyping tools that support designers to generate their own functional Tangible experiences.

This tutorial addresses this issue by presenting ToyVision [6], a software toolkit that lowers the threshold for prototyping both the bits and the atoms of tangible tabletop games. ToyVision is based on Reactivision open-source toolkit [4] and includes a GUI assistant (see fig.1) that enables the designer to graphically model each playing piece and its active and passive manipulations involved in the tabletop application. Modelling of playing pieces in the GUI is made using a specification language based on Shaer and Jacob [8] Tangible User Interface Modelling Language (TUIML), which has been adapted to the tangible board-games context. ToyVision classifies playing pieces into four categories:

D. Reidsma, H. Katayose, and A. Nijholt (Eds.): ACE 2013, LNCS 8253, pp. 580–583, 2013.
© Springer International Publishing Switzerland 2013

- Simple Tokens: Simple Tokens are the most common playing pieces in board-games(e.g. Checkers, Ludo, Stairs and Ladders, Roulette...). Players arrange a limited amount of playing pieces on the board according to game rules
- Deformable Tokens. Some playing-pieces do not have a constant shape, as they are made of malleable materials, such us clay, cardboard, cloth...
- Named Tokens. Other kind of playing pieces has a unique role in the game, which are perceived by the player through their physical appearance. For example, in the Chess game, the Tower piece has a different appearance and rules than the Pawn.
- Constraint Tokens. A Constraint Token can be described as a playing piece that acts as a physical constraint of a set of smaller Tokens. Players fill, empty, rearrange or move the little pieces inside the Constraint Token. For example, in the Trivial Pursuit game, players fill their playing pieces with little chips in order to represent their status in the game.

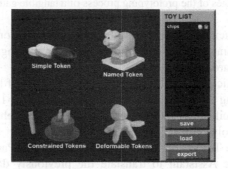

Fig. 1. Graphic Assistant: Main menu

Participants will be introduced to TUIML and ToyVision in order to be able to create a complete functional tangible game for the NIKVision tabletop [5], a visual-based active horizontal surface especially designed for young children.

2   Tutorial Organization

The tutorial will last three hours. Participants will follow the complete process of creating a predefined tangible tabletop game. The game is a Tangible version of the

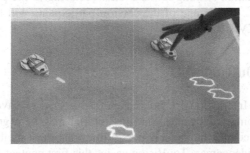

Fig. 2. Tangible Asteroids game to be created by participants during the tutorial session

classic Asteroids video game from Atari. Playing pieces will consist on cardboard space-ships that players will manipulate on the tabletop surface in order to clean the virtual star-field from asteroids by shutting missiles (see fig. 2).

The tutorial will be organized following the different stages that any designer should follow in order to prototype a game using ToyVision (see fig. 3).

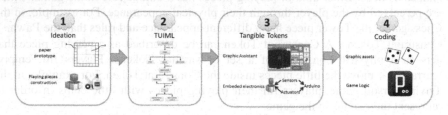

Fig. 3. Different stages of the prototyping process of a tangible game using ToyVision

- 13:30 - 14:30. Participants will be introduced to a NIKVision tabletop. Organizers will explain the game concept to be prototyped and playing pieces will be hand-made using cardboard.
- 14:30 – 15:00. Participants will draw a visual abstraction of the previously created playing pieces using the Tangible User Interface Modeling Language (TUIML), a pen and paper specification tool designed for modeling behaviors and manipulations of objects involved on a TUI.
- 15:00 – 15:30. The ToyVision toolkit will be introduced. Participants will use the ToyVision Graphic Assistant to translate the previously draw TUIML into the ToyVision application. ToyVision will use this info to provide the required visual markers to be attached to the base of the playing pieces in order their manipulations can be tracked by the tabletop visual hardware. Participants will be able to test the playing pieces on the tabletop.
- 15:30 – 16:30. Participants will code the game in Processing development environment. Any programing language can be used to develop games in ToyVision. We are proposing Processing since it is an open-source environment that is becoming very popular for developing graphic and interactive applications. Participants will first create and import to Processing al the graphic and audio assets required for the game, and then they will code the game logic. ToyVision will provide with high-level information relating to the events occurring to the playing pieces while running the game. At the end of the session participants will be able to test their games in the NIKVision tabletop.

3   Tutorial Outcomes

Attendants to ACE International Conference are expected to have experience in designing and developing videogames, but this tutorial may be a great opportunity for them to have a first contact on the new possibilities that the Tangible Interaction paradigm can bring to videogames. ToyVision easies this first contact with the developing of tangible games for tabletop devices by offering designers and developers of video-games with an intuitive environment that isolated them for the technical issues of involving physical objects into a Tangible system.

This tutorial complements the ACE'13 workshop "How to Make Tangible Games and not Die in the Attempt"; a discussion panel with experts around their experiences designing and implementing Tangible games for children.

Acknowledgements. We would like to Elisa Ubide, for her help developing the Toy-Vision Toolkit during her final degree project. This work has been partly financed by the Spanish Government through the DGICYT contract TIN2011-24660.

References

1. Cooper, N., Keatley, A., Dahlquist, M., Mann, S., Slay, H., Zucco, J., Smith, R., Thomas, B.H.: Augmented Reality Chinese Checkers. In: Proceedings of the 2004 ACM SIGCHI International Conference on Advances in Computer Entertainment Technology, ACE 2004, vol. 74, pp. 117–126 (2004)
2. Iwata, T., Yamabe, T., Poloj, M., Nakajima, T.: Traditional games meet ICT: a case study on go game augmentation. In: Fourth International Conference on Tangible, Embedded, and Embodied Interaction (TEI 2010), pp. 237–240. ACM (2010)
3. Heijboer, M., van den Hoven, E.: Keeping up appearances: interpretation of tangible artifact design. In: 5th Nordic Conference on Human-Computer Interaction: Building Bridges (NordiCHI 2008), pp. 162–171. ACM (2008)
4. Kaltenbrunner, M.: reacTIVision and TUIO: a tangible tabletop toolkit. In: Proceedings of the ACM International Conference on Interactive Tabletops and Surfaces, pp. 9–16. ACM (November 2009)
5. Marco, J., Cerezo, E., Baldassarri, S.: Playing with toys on a tabletop active surface. In: Proceedings of the 9th International Conference on Interaction Design and Children, pp. 296–299. ACM (June 2010)
6. Marco, J., Cerezo, E., Baldassarri, S.: ToyVision: a toolkit for prototyping tabletop tangible games. In: Proceedings of the 4th ACM SIGCHI Symposium on Engineering Interactive Computing Systems, pp. 71–80. ACM (June 2012)
7. Rogers, Y., Rodden, T.: Configuring spaces and surfaces to support collaborative interactions. In: O'Hara, K., Perry, M., Churchill, E., Russell, D. (eds.) Public and Situated Displays, pp. 45–79. Kluwer Publishers (2004)
8. Shaer, O., Jacob, R.J.K.: A specification paradigm for the design and implementation of tangible user interfaces. ACM Trans. Comput.-Hum. Interact. 16(4), Article 20, 39 pages (2009)

Ball of Secrets

Ben Margines[1], Raunaq Gupta[2], and Yoram Chisik[2]

[1] HCII, Carnegie Mellon University, Pittsburgh, PA, USA
benjamin.margines@gmail.com
[2] M-ITI, University of Madeira, Funchal, Portugal
{raunaq.rg,ychisik}@gmail.com

Abstract. With this creative showcase titled the Ball of Secrets, we demonstrate an interactive prototype consisting of a unique user interface with an emphasis on pure play. Through this prototype we created a device that encourages playfulness and explore sharing and communication via anonymous message posting.

In this paper we describe the concept and the technology used to create the interface in order to evoke the necessary user experience.

Keywords: Design, Experimentation, Human Factors, Natural tangible interfaces.

1   Introduction

Play is a form of exploration. While playing a player explores the range of possibilities made possible by a toy, token or controller within a set of constraints.

Within the context of games the "toy" is an element of the gameplay (in football a ball is kicked around towards a goal post) and the explorations are goal oriented, governed by a set of rules, bounded by the dimensions of the board or the playing field and driven by an element of competition.

In pure play situations, that is play that takes place for its own rewards with no specific goal in mind the toy is the object of play and the explorations are driven by curiosity and are only bounded by the imagination of the player and the constraints of the physical and social environment. For example, bouncing a ball around allows the player to coax the ball to reveal its secrets, e.g. how bouncy it is while learning about his own strength (how far can I throw the ball), the environment (will the ball bounce higher from a concrete floor or from a grass field?), and the limits of social acceptability (bouncing a ball where or when you are not supposed to).

Digital artifacts are on the whole far less amenable to this type of playful exploration as their digital innards reveal little about their contents and capabilities and their interfaces are often designed with a specific set of aims and an exact set of instructions. The Ball of Secrets is a digital device designed to encourage pure play exploration. Using the familiar and highly tangible shape of a ball and a set of buttons wired to a fast acting audio board, the Ball of Secrets offers a myriad set of opportunities through which the player can explore the physical shape and digital functionality of the ball itself and the secrets in the form of audio recordings that lie within it.

D. Reidsma, H. Katayose, and A. Nijholt (Eds.): ACE 2013, LNCS 8253, pp. 584–587, 2013.
© Springer International Publishing Switzerland 2013

Our aim in designing the Ball of Secrets is twofold. First, we want to understand how people interact with the device given its form, functionality and lack of an explicit purpose or instruction. Second, we want to see whether people would use the "secret" nature of the ball as a communication medium or leaving messages and personal details which they might not share otherwise, similar to a digital version of PostSecret.com[2].

We wish to explore the effect of setting and context on the ways in which people will interact with the Ball of Secrets. By placing it in different environments such as shopping malls, schools, conference halls and old age homes, etc., the Ball of Secrets may take on different interactions and forms of use; it may be a communication device of the future, an avenue to share stories, disclose secret crushes, or just be an ambiguous and fun device. We hope to observe the ways in which context, environment, personality and society impact and encourage play and exploration.

2   Concept

The Ball of Secrets provides a tangible user interface with memory capabilities to store audio clips. The prototype is a spherical shaped ball close to the size of a standard bowling ball. It has two rows of buttons equally aligned across its surface in the pattern of fingers which are gripping the ball. As the ball is held, subtle holes cover a microphone facing the player. A speaker positioned on the bottom of the ball is similarly obscured. There are no other visible markings on the surface.

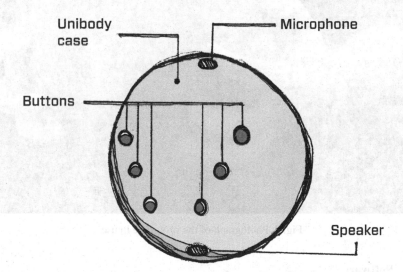

Fig. 1. Components of the prototype

The ball has the ability to store a 10 second audio clip for each combination of buttons that is pressed. As the user holds the sphere in his hands, his fingers can press any combination of the buttons. If there is no audio file stored for a particular combination of buttons, the microphone activates and displays its status with a red LED. This audio clip termed a "secret" can only be heard on pressing the same combination of buttons. With six buttons in the initial prototype, the total number of combinations which can be stored is 63.

3   Implementation

3.1   Hardware

The Ball of Secrets was built using an Arduino Uno microcontroller[3] together with an audio wave shield[4], using a SD memory card to store the audio recordings. The wave shield takes input from an electret microphone, and outputs to a small speaker mounted on the bottom of the sphere. The Arduino is also connected to six pushbutton switches, both for powering an internal LED within each switch and for receiving input.

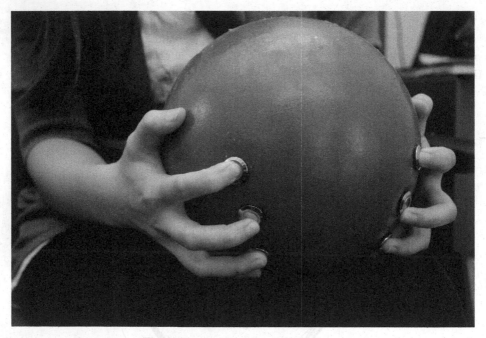

Fig. 2. Photograph of the prototype in use

3.2   Software

The Ball of Secrets primarily uses an adaptation of the already developed WaveRP library[5]. When activated, the Arduino is constantly reading and debouncing the digital input coming from each pushbutton. Each pushbutton is assigned to one of the following values: 1, 2, 4, 8, 16, 32. As the Arduino passes through the debouncing code, it sums the values of the pressed switches, which will be unique for that combination. It then passes that integer to the WaveRP library to search for a track at that index, and, if it does not find one, the recording function is triggered. After an audio file is played or recorded, the Ball of Secrets returns to its default state afterward.

4   At the Conference

As the ball was designed to be primarily used amongst a gathering of people, we see the creative showcase section of the conference as an ideal place to observe how the conference-goers will interact with the device. We propose to display the ball with minimal supervision and ready to be explored by curious attendees. It will be placed with instructions to use it and will not be supervised to encourage creative interaction and reduce discussion about the ball itself. This will help us observe how people approach the ball, learn about its functions and then use it as per an implicit understanding that they arrive at. To aid in providing context to first-time users the ball will also be pre-loaded with messages for certain combination of buttons.

References

1. Caillois, R.: Man, Play and Games. University of Illinois Press (2001)
2. PostSecret, http://www.postsecret.com
3. Arduino Uno, http://arduino.cc/en/Main/arduinoBoardUno
4. Wave Shield, http://www.ladyada.net/make/waveshield/
5. Waverp, https://code.google.com/p/waverp/

'P.S.(Postscript)' : Hearing of Your Heartstring

Myongjin Moon and Yeseul Kim

KAIST(Korea Advanced Institute of Science and Technology)
335 Gwahangno, Yuseong-gu
Daejeon, Korea
cie19@kaist.ac.kr, yeseulkm@kaist.ac.kr

Abstract. " 'P.S.': Hearing of your Heartstring " is the interactive installation creating collaborative sound with users' voices. Through this artwork 'P.S.', we want to ease the people who have a huge wave of nostalgia because of remaining words in mind and sympathize with each other's nostalgia through hearing their voices carefully.

Keywords: Interactive Installation, Interface for Artistic Expression, Tangible Interface, Sound Installation.

1 Introduction

Do you have remaining words or messages that you have deep in your heart? Unsent letter and remaining words bother people's hearts because of tormenting yearnings. 'P.S.' gives people a chance to deliver their inner mind genuinely.

This installation consists of two parts. One is recording the remaining words by users' voices. Second is exploring the words on the elastic surface screen with hand gestures. Through this experience, participants can feel healed by opening and hearing their heartstrings.

2 Related Works

Elastic screen has been explored by a few researchers as a tool for artwork or data visualization display. Cassinelli et.al.[1] have implemented the elastic screen as an interactive art installation. By deforming the screen, the space and time of video sequence transform. Meanwhile, Yun et al.'s work[2] presents intuitive exploration through complex and multi-dimensional data structure. It suggests several interaction methods navigating the human body, or searching with a force directed graph visualization. An elastic screen also can be a deformable workspace for manipulating 3D virtual objects.[3] Also, recently, Hemsley et.al.[4] designed a set of principles and interaction examples utilizing the elastic nature of surface. Even though various researches about elastic screen have been introduced, the majority of them have got focus on the technical aspects. We developed abstract interaction with physical changes on the screen. It suggests pushing into an elastic surface as a metaphor for

D. Reidsma, H. Katayose, and A. Nijholt (Eds.): ACE 2013, LNCS 8253, pp. 588–591, 2013.

digging deeper into a 'forest' of sound and finding thoughts. This work suggests elastic screen as a multisensory searching space and intuitive tool for finding sounds and visual data.

3   Purpose- 'P.S.': Hearing of Your Heartstring

In our lifetime, sometimes we have a moment not to send our own mind to someone who we cherish - maybe your old teddy bear, friend or family. Whenever you recall remaining words in your heart, you feel nostalgia for all the things about your friend and want to talk genuine mind with someone.

If people tell their remaining minds to the microphone, 'P.S.' collects voices. All the collected voices could be explored on the elastic surface screen which is similar to lake surface for feeling of wave of nostalgia. Through this artwork 'P.S.', we want to ease people who have a huge wave of nostalgia because of remaining words in mind and sympathize with each other's nostalgia through hearing their voices carefully.

4   Design

'P.S.' consists of two parts - recording booth and multisensory display. First, an user enters the recording booth and there is a mailbox which looks like a letter envelope. When an user opens mailbox, he or she can say what's on one's mind through the mailbox that records the voice. Recorded voices are sent to the multisensory space and elastic screen presents messages with selected voices responding to a finger.

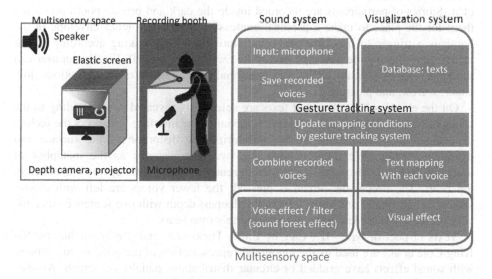

Fig. 1. 'P.S.' System overview

4.1   System Overview

Efficiency is important in computing process for an interactive work to be immersive. Overall process is designed with Processing and MaxMSP. Relative depth value of the elastic screen is acquired using depth camera(KINECT).

1) Sound recording/control part:
Recording system collects voices and stored them from recoding booth. Then, in the sound control system, stored voices are combined and applied sound effect on each voice. An algorithm created with MaxMSP controls the number of voices to combine and various sound effects, based on the depth. This provides a very expressive multisensory experience with visual and tangible interaction on the elastic screen.

2) Visualization control part:
Recorded voices are saved in the sound control part and mapped to the text randomly in the visualization control part. Processing is used for water effect of lake in the heart by gestures and controls text size bigger and smaller, based on the depth.

3) Hand tracking part:
To capture the change of depth value without heavy delay, only selected area from maximum resolution is actuated for detecting. A X, Y, Z position of the point that is closest from depth camera means the deepest dent on screen since the camera is located below the screen. For increased stability and accuracy of tracking, we use the average value of 10 frames.

4.2   Interaction

A participant in the work is both the person directly involved of a story and explorer of it. Stories of participants are recorded inside the dark and private booth providing them for the place to make a personal confession. Opening a letter envelope in the booth is a trigger to make the recording status on. After talking according to the instructions, closing the envelope makes the recording status off. Finally, an user can send the voice by pressing one of 4 expressional buttons which mean 4 emotions- joy, anger, sorrow, and pleasure.

On the elastic screen, 4 sets of texts are selectively revealed corresponding to the status of buttons. We suggest an elastic material as the interface to express the feeling of instigation by remaining words considering the distortion of the surface and dynamic reaction. We use touching and sweeping gestures as the metaphor of touching the heart. Also, pressing is used to reach genuine words deeply embedded in the heart. The deeper the screen is pressed, the fewer voices are left with clearer sentences and finally one voice lefts in the deepest depth with one sentence since the very secret words are left in the deepest of one's own heart.

Texts of poet or lyric -'If I Can' by Emily Dickinson, and 'Unforgettable' by Nat King Cole et al.- are used as the emotional representation of recorded words. Voices with sound effects have gridded or circular distribution spatially on screen. An user can hear 7 voices, which are randomly or sequentially selected among overall 20 voices, maximally at once when touching but not pressing.

Table 1. Interaction mapping by gestures

Gesture	Interaction
Touch	*sound: water drop sound effect* *visual: blurring text, wave visual effect*
Sweep	*sound: wave sound effect, controlling voices volume* *visual: controlling positions of texts, wave visual effect*
Press	*sound: adding or reducing voices by depth* *visual: controlling text size bigger or smaller by depth*

Fig. 2. 1st step of depth: an user touches the elastic screen and hears mixed 4 voices(left)

Fig. 3. 2nd~3rd step of depth: an user presses the screen and hears mixed 3~2 voices (middle)

Fig. 4. 4th step of depth: an user presses the screen and hears 1 voice (right)

5   Conclusion

The 'P.S' suggests the collaborative interaction system that gathers people's normal voices and transforms them into a real-time generative artwork. The elastic interface and the way of interaction make participants connected to the concept of the work. By digging the surface which is similar to finding or accessing something, a participant can hear and share the heartstrings.

References

1. Cassinelli, A., Ishikawa, M.: Khronos projector. In: ACM SIGGRAPH (2005)
2. Yun, K., et al.: ElaScreen: exploring multi-dimensional data using elastic screen. In: CHI 2013 Extended Abstracts on Human Factors in Computing Systems. ACM (2013)
3. Watanabe, Y., Cassinelli, A., Komuro, T., Ishikawa, M.: The Deformable Workspace: a Membrane between Real and Virtual Space. In: 3rd IEEE International Workshop on Horizontal Interactive Human Computer System (TABLETOP), Amsterdam, the Netherlands, October 1-3 (2008)
4. Hemsley, R., Dand, D.: Obake: Direct Interactions with Deformable Shape Changing Surfaces. In: CHI, Paris, France, April 27-May 2 (2013)

Children Ideation Workshop

Creative Low-Fidelity Prototyping of Game Ideas

Christiane Moser

HCI & Usability Unit, ICT&S Center,
University of Salzburg,
Salzburg, Austria
christiane.moser2@sbg.ac.at

Abstract. Player's enjoyment is one of the most important goals for games. Without this, children will not repeatedly play them. In order to meet children's needs, it is important to consider them in the development process, for example, by enabling them to participate actively in the process. Therefore, children will be enabled to participate in ideation workshops to create creative low-fidelity prototypes of game ideas that inspire game designers.

Keywords: Game design, user-centered design, participatory design, low-fidelity prototyping, child-computer interaction.

1   Introduction

Children are becoming experienced and frequent users of software, services, and technology and are emerging as an important user group [4]. They encounter and use software or technologies in their daily lives through, e.g., mobile phones to communicate, computer games for individual or collaborative entertainment, and educational technologies for learning [7].

As there is not a lot of literature available for the involvement of children throughout the whole development process of games (next to [7] or [10]), children are rarely involved. In order to meet their needs, an adequate consideration of them in the development process of technologies is necessary [1]. For game developers, it would thus be an advantage to work together with children to satisfy their range of desires and needs (e.g., [2], [11]) and not to see them only in the role of game consumers.

2   Objectives/Aims of the Workshop

The child-centered game development (CCGD) approaches [7] offer different ways to integrate children throughout the different phases of game design within the context of the school (i.e., analysis, conceptualization, design phases, prototyping/development and evaluation phase). Suitable HCI approaches from user-centered and participatory design, as well as educational principles and approaches, were used

D. Reidsma, H. Katayose, and A. Nijholt (Eds.): ACE 2013, LNCS 8253, pp. 592–599, 2013.
© Springer International Publishing Switzerland 2013

as a foundation. The CCGD approaches illustrate how to guide the involvement and participation of children aged 10 to 14 years in school classes within the development process of games. The children's ideation workshop for the design phase uses game progress storyboards and creative low-fidelity prototyping and aims at:

- enabling participatory design with children for a better game design;
- creating creative and tangible game prototypes of game ideas that provide game designers, as well as developers' insights about children's thoughts on possible game play, in order to better meet their expectations. This in turn should inspire the final game design.

3 Approaches for the Workshop

In the following game progress storyboards and creative low-fidelity prototyping, two CCGD approaches are described in more detail to provide a better understanding about these approaches for the application in the workshops. Afterwards, the requirements for conducting such a workshop are specified and an overview about the breakdown of activities (steps) is given.

3.1 Game Progress Storyboards

Storyboards are typically used in the film industry for sketching or mocking up shots before they are actually filmed. They are also used for concept sketches or mock-ups of game levels (see [5], [8]). Game progress storyboards aim at illustrating or highlighting certain aspects within games (e.g., game play scenes). One advantage of using these types of storyboards is that they allow children to experiment with changes in the storyline of the game and discuss, as well as describe, different outcomes (see Fig. 1 showing example of game menu design or [7]).

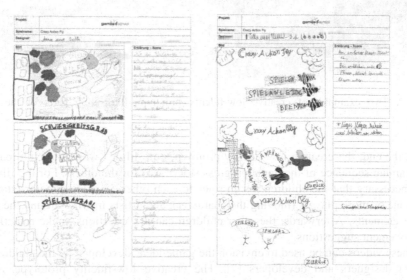

Fig. 1. Two examples of game progress storyboards illustrating parts of the game menu

3.2   Creative Low-Fidelity Prototyping

Creative low-fidelity prototypes can be built in groups of four to six children. They are sketchy, incomplete, and quickly built working models of game aspects. Druin [3] mentioned in her work that *"there is never a need to teach people how to prototype, since using basic art supplies comes naturally to the youngest and oldest design partners"*. Nevertheless, children need a starting point for prototyping [9]. Therefore, this workshop starts with explaining the game idea and the creation of storyboards to illustrate a short sequence of interactions within the game to build the game prototype afterwards.

Similar to Knudtzon et al. [6] 'bags of stuff' approach, the children are provided with Playmais, Playdough, Lego, and other creative material to create the prototypes. The prototypes are used to illustrate parts of game levels (see Fig. 2) and re-enact scenes of the previously created game progress storyboard. Children can try out game procedures/mechanics and actively discover problems or challenges in the game play. For very complex game concepts, the low-fidelity prototypes might be problematic, as the implementation might be too difficult or simply impossible for children [7]. Therefore, the game idea should be easy to explain and understand, but also not too detailed in order to leave room for imagination (i.e., children should easily come up with design ideas for the game).

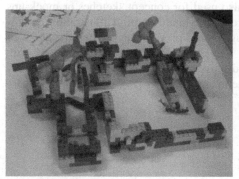

Fig. 2. Two examples of creative low-fidelity prototype illustrating parts of the game world

In the end, the creative low-fidelity prototypes are filmed while the children play the gaming sequence of the game progress storyboard for the others. For the filming, it is necessary that the children assign roles to each other, i.e., one director (storyteller), one or more players (moving the character), and artists moving around the other game elements. Afterwards, the other children can ask questions, make remarks, or improvement suggestions.

These videos can be used to envision the game ideas developed by the children for absent designers and developers [7]. The creative low-fidelity prototype videos provide insights about children's thoughts on possible game play, which can help to better meet their expectations about the game idea and thereby inspire the development process.

3.3   Requirements (Room Specification/Materials/Facilitators)

For the workshop, a multi-purpose room for the amount of children is needed, where tables for group work can be formed and the children can craft. Two people (i.e., the workshop lead and assistant) organize and conduct the workshop. The following materials have to be prepared in advance:

- Hand-outs with the game idea/concept
- Storyboard templates printed in A3 (black and white)
- Matt/Pasteboard and colors (e.g., water colors, acrylic paint or finger paint) for the ground of the game scene (paper to put on the ground and work coats might be useful as well)
- Playmais, Playdough, Lego, and other creative material (e.g., colored paper, felt, foam rubber, pipe cleaners, balloons, pearls, wood, shells, scissors, glue, colored pencil, felt pens or markers) to construct game elements
- Video camera and tripod for recording (an extension wire should also not be forgotten)

3.4   Breakdown of Workshop Activities

In order not to lose the motivation of children, each workshop should be split into steps/activities and questions or explanations should be prepared if possible unknown terminology is used. Furthermore, it is essential to give an introduction with clear instructions to reach the defined goal of the workshop. During the group work phases, there is also the need to provide ongoing support for each group. As soon as the children know what to do, they are very creative and develop many interesting game scenes. However, they sometimes also get lost in details. When working with children, it has also to be considered that they get bored faster than adults and, therefore, require variations [7].

The following table illustrates how the workshop should be broken down in single varying steps/activities. Activities highlighted in grey are either pre or post activities to be conducted by the organizers and are not included in the 120 minute duration of the workshop. For the different activities, there are timeframes dependent on the pre-experience of the workshop organizers (e.g., pre-experience with user-centered or participatory design approaches or pre-experience when working with children like organizing workshops), the amount of children involved, the complexity of the game idea, etc. Nevertheless, most of the time should be spent on creating the creative low-fidelity prototypes and nearly the same time together for the game progress storyboards and the final filming of the workshop outcome.

Table 1. Activities for the Workshop

Step	Time in Minutes	Activities
0.	5-10	• Prepare the multi-purpose room, i.e. arrange tables for group work of 4 to 6 children
1.	2-3	*Welcome and preparation* • Welcome the children to the workshop • Formation of groups of 4 to 6 children o Either let the children choose themselves or use creative techniques[1] o This should be done before the introduction, in order to let the children start work immediately afterwards and avoid troubles later on
2.	2-3	*Introduction to the workshop and goals* • Explain the steps of the workshop to the children (it is necessary to break down the workshop in workable and memorable steps) • Introduce and discuss the game idea with the children • Hand out a written version of the game concept to the groups
3.	15-20	*Create 1-2 pages of storyboards in the group to illustrate a game scene* • Explain the outcome of this step and what will happen afterwards • Handout 1-2 A3 pages of the storyboard template and different kind of pens to each group and explain that the scenes sketched on the left side should be described on the right side • Walk around from group to group and help them o Briefly discuss their storyboard with them to assure it goes along with the game idea and that they did not get stuck in details
4.	70-90	*Creation of creative low-fidelity prototype* • Explain the outcome of this step and what will happen afterwards • First hand out the matt/pasteboard and colors for the ground to each group (this activity should not take longer than 10 minutes) • Afterwards, make a 5 to 10 minutes break and use to the time to put the matts away in order to let them dry • Next provide the other creative material on a table where the children are allowed to pick up what they need in order to create game elements (e.g., characters, obstacles, opponents or other game world elements) and return the rest not needed • Use the last 5-10 minutes to clean up (i.e. all unused creative material is brought back to the table it was provided)

---

[1] http://pubs.iied.org/pdfs/G01508.pdf

Table 1. (*continued*)

5.	15-20	*Preparation for filming (study the scene of the storyboard)* • Explain the outcome of this step and what will happen afterwards • Put the game world ground (the matt/pasteboard) on the different tables and let the children place the other created materials on top of it (this should not take longer than 5 minutes) • Children should assign roles in the group: 1 director (storyteller), 1 or more player (moving the character) and the rest are artists moving around the other game elements o Help the children to assign roles, if this takes more than 2-3 minutes, in order to have enough time to study the play according to their storyboard • Let them practice the game scene from the storyboard according to the directors instructions
6.	10-15	*Filming (recording of the played gaming scene)* • Explain the outcome of this step and what will happen afterwards • Walk from group to group with the video camera and tripod • Let the children act their gaming scene, if necessary let them react parts of it • Meanwhile let the other children stand around the table, watch the play and ask questions afterwards, if there were obscurities
7.	5-10	*Closing* • Wrap-up the workshop • Ask children about their experiences • Summarize your own experiences and the outcome of the workshop
8.	30-90	• Edit recorded videos and provide them to the designers as well as developers

4   Outcomes of the Workshops

The objectives of the workshop, the expected outcome, and outcomes of previously conducted workshops are described in the following sections.

4.1   Objectives of Workshops

The workshop should enable participatory design with children, i.e., children are enabled to develop about four different game play scenes for each game idea that will be prototyped by them. The outcomes of the workshop should provide the game designers and developers more insights about children's thoughts on possible game play (i.e., understanding) in order to better meet their expectations about game ideas when building games.

4.2 Expected Outcomes of the Workshops

The outcomes of the workshop should be different visualization of game ideas in form of game progress storyboards and creative low-fidelity game prototypes. Short narrative videos showing possible game play scenes to the game designers and developers should enable them to get a better understanding and feeling of how children envision the game idea and what they expect from it. Additionally, they should inspire the final game design that game designers and developers develop and implement in a next step.

4.3 Outcomes of the Conducted Workshops

This toolkit was already successfully applied with 3 school classes in the Games4School Project[2]. This was the activity most loved by the children (among other workshops that were previously conducted with them). The videos enabled the game designers and developers (in this project master students) to get familiar with how children understand and envision the different game ideas. Together with the researchers, they decided how to prototype the games in order to best meet their expectations. The final design was greatly inspired by the provided the videos and creative low-fidelity prototypes. The children of the workshops were proud of their ideas included in the final game design and had a lot of fun while playing the game like others.

5   Conclusion

The need for child-centered design methods for game development is there. As the suggested approaches for the children's ideation workshops have already been successfully applied with children ages 10 to 14 years, the proposed workshop holds the potential for actively involving children in the development process of games with a win-win situation. On one hand, children are enabled to actively participate. On the other hand, game designers get insights regarding children's need and inspiration from the produced videos of the creative low-fidelity prototypes.

Acknowledgements. Special thanks go to the cooperation partner the secondary school of Wals-Viehhausen for the support in the Games4School Project (funded by the Austrian Ministry of Science in course of the educational project "Sparkling

---

[2] http://www.sparklingscience.at/de/projekte/508-games4school-wissenschafter-innen-entwickeln-spiele-mit-und-f-r-sch-ler-innen/ or http://www.icts.sbg.ac.at/content.php?id=1851&m_id=1011&ch_id=1039&ch2_id=1452

Science"). This work is supported by the Austrian project "AIR – Advanced Interface Research" funded by the Austrian Research Promotion Agency (FFG), the ZIT Center for Innovation and Technology and the province of Salzburg under contract number 825345.

References

1. Antle, A.N.: Child-based personas: need, ability and experience. Cognition, Technology & Work 10(2), 155–166 (2008)
2. Brederode, B., Markopoulos, P., Gielen, M., Vermeeren, A., de Ridder, H.: Powerball: the design of a novel mixed-reality game for children with mixed abilities. In: Proceedings of the 2005 Conference on Interaction Design and Children (IDC 2005), pp. 32–39. ACM, New York (2005)
3. Druin, A.: The Role of Children in the Design of New Technology. Behaviour and Information Technology 21(1), 1–25 (2002)
4. Jensen, J.J., Skov, M.B.: A review of research methods in children's technology design. In: Proceedings of the 2005 Conference on Interaction Design and Children, IDC 2005, pp. 80–87. ACM, New York (2005)
5. Jones, C., McIver, L., Gibson, L., Gregor, P.: Experiences obtained from designing with children. In: Proceedings of the 2003 Conference on Interaction Design and Children (IDC 2003), pp. 69–74. ACM, New York (2003)
6. Knudtzon, K., Druin, A., Kaplan, N., Summers, K., Chisik, Y., Kulkarni, R., Moulthrop, S., Weeks, H., Bederson, B.: Starting an intergenerational technology design team: a case study. In: Proceedings of the 2003 Conference on Interaction Design and Children (IDC 2003), pp. 51–58. ACM, New York (2003)
7. Moser, C.: Child-Centered Game Development (CCGD): Developing Games with Children at School. Personal and Ubiquitous Computing, Special Issue on Child Computer Interaction, 1–15 (2012)
8. Rouse, R.: Game Design Theory and Practice, 2nd edn. Wordware Publishing Inc., Plano (2000)
9. Scaiffe, M., Rogers, Y.V.: Kids as Informants: Telling Us What We Didn't Know or Confirming What We Knew Already? In: The Design of Children's Technology, pp. 27–50. Morgen Kaufman, San Francisco (1999)
10. Tan, J.L., Goh, D.H.L., Ang, R.P., Huan, V.S.: Child-centered interaction in the design of a game for social skills intervention. Computers Entertainment 9(1), 17 (2011)
11. Tychsen, A., Canossa, A.: Defining personas in games using metrics. In: Proceedings of the 2008 Conference on Future Play: Research, Play, Share (Future Play 2008), pp. 73–80. ACM, New York (2008)

Dosukoi-Tap: The Virtual Paper *Sumo* Game

Yuta Nakagawa, Kota Tsukamoto, and Yasuyuki Kono

Kwansei Gakuin University, 2-1 Gakuen, Sanda city, Hyogo, Japan
{nakagawa717a,tsukamoto,kono}@kwansei.ac.jp

Abstract. We have developed a virtual paper *sumo* game, "*Dosukoi*-Tap", a Japanese traditional game using paper figures. A player taps on his/her own-side of the *sumo* ring board. He/she lets his/her own wrestler rush and fight with its opponent. Our system simulates the feature of actual paper *sumo* and has solved some of the problems of actual one by employing multi-finger tracking and pressure-sensitive device.

Keywords: virtual game, multi finger tracking, pressure sensitive.

1 Introduction

Paper *sumo* game is one of the popular tabletop games in Japan. This game follows *sumo* rules by using paper figures. Two players play this game with each *sumo* wrestler figure made of paper as depicted in Fig.1. Each player puts his/her own paper wrestler facing each other on the *sumo* ring board that is typically made of a paper box. The player taps on his/her own-side of the *sumo* ring board and lets his/her own wrestler rush and fight with its opponent. The match is decided when either wrestler has been out from the *sumo* ring or lost balance and fallen down. Because of the simplicity, many of Japanese children have played the game. However, it cannot be played well when paper wrestlers don't collide or fall down before the game heated.

Fig. 1. Paper *sumo* game

D. Reidsma, H. Katayose, and A. Nijholt (Eds.): ACE 2013, LNCS 8253, pp. 600–603, 2013.
© Springer International Publishing Switzerland 2013

We propose the virtual paper *sumo* game "*Dosukoi*-Tap" which solves following problems of the actual paper *sumo* game:

- The wrestler will fall down easily.
- The wrestlers do not push each other.
- It is difficult to find out a strategy.

This simulation is reproduced by the system employing the multi-finger tracking and pressure-sensitive device.

2   Dosukoi-Tap

Dosukoi-Tap basically simulates paper *sumo* employing a multi-finger tracking and pressure-sensitive touch pad as an input device. This game solves many of the paper *sumo* problems while inheriting the pleasure of the actual paper *sumo* and is more interesting than actual one on the following features:

- The wrestler does not accidently fall down.
- The wrestlers basically face and push each other.
- Original swipe operations and the strategies are introduced.

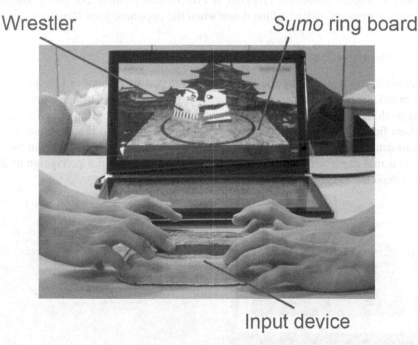

Fig. 2. Dosukoi-Tap's over view

2.1   The Rules and Strategy

Dosukoi-Tap provides simple operation similar to the actual paper *sumo*. Each player chooses his/her favorite wrestler character in the selection screen and the wrestlers are arranged as facing each other on the *sumo* ring board on the screen. Each player lets his/her wrestler move by tapping on his/her own-side of the ForcePad as depicted in Fig.2. The wrestlers move forward and push each other in response to the repetition of tapping. Tapping affects not only wrestler's motion but also their balance. A wrestler loses when it is pushed out from the *sumo* ring or it loses its balance and falls down.

This game provides not only the actual paper *sumo* operations but also the following original operations to heat up a match:

Tsuppari. When a player does swipe toward the opponent, his/her wrestler does an offence action to push strongly. However it's easy to lose balance.

Harai. When a player does swipe toward oneself, wrestler moves back to avoid the *Tsuppari* of it's opponent.

In this game, the tapping and the two original operations involve players' strategic behaviors. In order to win a match, they must repeat tapping while considering wrestler's balance. Although *Tsuppari* is effective in pushing out an opponent, the operation carries the risk of falling down when the opponent does *Harai*.

2.2   Interactive System

In *Dosukoi*-Tap, we employ the ForcePad developed by Synaptics [1], as the *sumo* ring board. In the actual paper *sumo* game, a player controls his/her paper wrestler using both strength and frequency of tapping so we need the input device that can measure finger locations and their pressure strength. ForcePad is a touchpad which is able to detect multiple fingers of variable pressure. Furthermore, it is about the same size as actual paper *sumo* ring board so players can have similar perception as actual one as depicted in Fig.3.

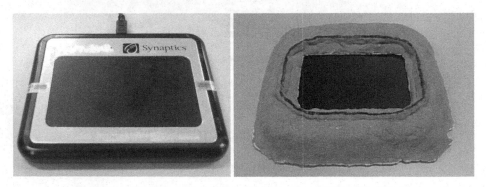

Fig. 3. ForcePad: a multi-finger tracking and pressure-sensitive device

Tapping operation moves the wrestler. In actual paper *sumo*, the motion of wrestlers is not stable because tapping operations vibrate only *sumo* ring board made of paper. The wrestlers fall down easily and also do not easily grapple with each other so it is difficult for a player to let his/her wrestler fight. The wrestler moves and pushes one another in response to the force of each tap. The force also affects the wrestler's center of gravity balance according to the position of each tap on the ForcePad. Players must keep the left-right balance to win a match.

3   Concluding Remarks

Dosukoi-Tap has been realized Japanese traditional game paper *sumo* by employing multi-finger tracking and pressure-sensitive device. This game can be played by simple tapping operation like actual paper *sumo* and solved some of the problems of it. The original operations have also increased the excitement of the "paper *sumo*". The users who know or do not know actual paper *sumo* rules easily understand the operation method, and the strategy is considered because of these simple operations. In recent years, many traditional games including paper *sumo* have not been played frequently. These games can be reborn in a more interesting game by solving some of problems and giving new technology. It will lead us to rediscovery of the fun that we had lost in these days.

Reference

1. ForcePad, http://www.synaptics.com/solutions/products/forcepad

DropNotes: A Music Composition Interface Utilizing the Combination of Affordances of Tangible Objects

Musashi Nakajima, Hidekazu Saegusa, Yuto Ozaki, and Yoshihiro Kanno

Department of Intermedia Art and Science, Waseda University
3-4-1 Okubo, Shinjuku-ku, Tokyo, 169-8555 Japan
634.nakajima@aoni.waseda.jp, saku-fin@ruri.waseda.jp,
bjp-nct@suou.waseda.jp, ykanno@waseda.jp

Abstract. The design principle of Tangible User Interfaces has been applied to musical interfaces for more accessible usage of computers for musical expression. This paper proposes DropNotes, a tangible user interface for music composition, which utilizes the combination of affordances of familiar objects as metaphorical procedures to manipulate digital audio. By creating more accessible and intuitive user interface for music composition, we target opening up a novel interactive musical expression.

Keywords: Tangible User Interface, Music Composition, Digital Audio Workstation, Affordance.

1   Introduction

Tangible music interfaces have eased user experiences to leverage computers for musical expression, having made digital audio information more accessible. The design philosophy behind Tangible User Interfaces (TUI) [1] emphasizes representing digital information manipulation in natural affordances of objects in the physical world, in an effort to enable users to intuitively interact with the information world. Based on this concept, a number of tangible music interfaces has been designed. A natural affordance is assigned in an action to manipulate digital audio information, such as playing audio with a sequencer, arranging musical constructions, or changing parameters in a synthesizer [2-6]. Design principles of these interfaces have enabled more accessible and intuitive audio manipulation, and have opened up a new frontier of musical performances.

Tangible music interfaces have been mainly focused on playing, modifying and arranging preset sound sources [2, 4-6]. However, to augment capacities of feasible musical expressions, users need to have an option to jack up sound materials, not confined using only ready-made ones, so that users can express their versatile intentions and nuances on composing music. Thus, it is significant to offer users a means to record sound materials according to their musical nuances, in order to ensure potential diversity for musical expression by means of a tangible music interface. Furthermore, all procedures for music composition, including recording, choosing,

D. Reidsma, H. Katayose, and A. Nijholt (Eds.): ACE 2013, LNCS 8253, pp. 604–607, 2013.
© Springer International Publishing Switzerland 2013

arranging and effecting, should be represented by a seamless sequence of metaphorical natural affordances, which conform to the design philosophy of TUI.

In this research, we present DropNotes, a new tangible user interface for music composition. It features all requisite procedures for composition (recording, choosing, arranging, and effecting), utilizing the combination of relative multiple affordances of objects that represent each procedure for audio manipulation.

Each metaphor for a kind of audio manipulation is represented in an affordance of familiar objects, a funnel, a dropper, a bottle and a table, so that users can take advantage of their own lifelong acquired experiences when utilizing the system. In this paper, we have designed four procedures for music composition as metaphors of familiar affordances: putting a funnel in a bottle as recording a sound, tapping off a liquid with a dropper as choosing a sound source, dropping liquids on the glass table as arranging sound sources, and changing the color of liquids as processing sound sources. By combining all these metaphorical actions, music composition, which entails a lot of technical procedures, is intuitively achieved as a mere accumulation of natural affordances of familiar objects.

The system offers users more variety of means to reflect their intentions and nuances on the outcome (especially by the recording function) as metaphors of familiar affordances. It works as an accessible, intuitive, and collaborative audio workstation for music composition, following the design principle behind TUI. DropNotes embodies a new experience of music composition by means of a tangible user interface, and eventually suggests a new direction for interactive musical expression.

2   The DropNotes System

2.1   System Overview

DropNotes consists of a liquid bottle stand, a glass table, a web camera, a projector, a speaker, and a PC as shown in Figure 1. In this system, multiple procedures to compose music are assigned in metaphorical familiar affordances. Sound source recording, source choosing, musical construction arrangement, and effecting are represented as putting a funnel into a bottle, tapping off a liquid from the bottle with a dropper, dropping liquids onto the table, changing the color of droplets, respectively.

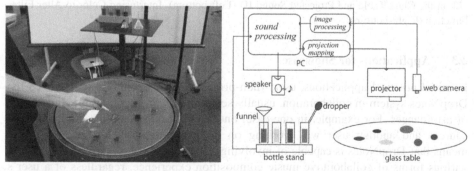

Fig. 1. DropNotes System in Use (Left), and System Configurations Diagram (Right)

2.2   Metaphorical Affordances Description

Figure 2 shows appearances of system usage. To begin with, users record sound sources to bottles. The trigger to start recording is represented as putting a funnel into a bottle, and the sound is recorded through a microphone within the bottle stand, and the recorded audio is stored in the PC with an ID. Users can pick up an intended sound source with the dropper, and put it onto the glass table. The web camera captures arrangement and color of droplets on the table. It then triggers both to play sound sources with corresponding IDs and to display each droplet's sound ID on its surface through the projector. Users may also change the color of a droplet to control the filter function afterward. In this paper, distance between the center of the table and the position of a droplet determines playback timing for its corresponding sound, and a droplet's angle on the polar coordination shifts the pitch of corresponding sound source. The sequence of playbacks is repeated in   certain duration.

Fig. 2. Recording (Left-top), Choosing and Picking up Sources (Right-top), Dropping the Liquid on the Glass Table and Projected Sound ID (Left-bottom), Interfusing Color to Alter Filter Function (Right-bottom)

2.3   Applications for Showcase

In initial practical applications, users (non-professionals of composition) utilized the DropNotes system in collaboration, usually separating their own roles based on kinds of affordances. For example, in one case, one user concentrated on recording sound sources and another user was working on arranging droplets on the table. That means that DropNotes is capable of involving users in diverse ways, and of realizing various forms of collaborative music composition experience, regardless of a user's proficiency in composition. In addition, the atmosphere of outcome music could be widely varied due to the user's preferences of sound, from a jazz-like song, an industrial one, to ambient music.

3   Conclusions & Future Works

In this research, we have designed a novel tangible music interface for more accessible, intuitive and collaborative music composition, especially emphasizing the importance of recording function. We have represented all procedures to manipulate audio information in relevant metaphorical affordances of familiar objects, based on the design principles of TUI. Users can intuitively leverage their own acquired experiences for audio manipulations. In initial applications, users were capable of collaboratively composing music with the system. Even non-professional users are successfully involved in a music composition procedure due to familiarities of metaphorical affordances. Moreover, initial applications also indicated that the system also has potential to work as a platform for diverse kinds of music, because users can express their musical nuances on sound materials by the recording function.

As to the next study, we need to pursue appropriate interpretations for a set of droplets to seek more transparent interaction between users and the system. It is also necessary to grasp the inclination of outcomes of this system through more user experience studies, for envisioning the potential of novel interactive musical expressions.

References

1. Ishii, H., Ullmer, B.: Tangible bits: towards seamless interfaces between people, bits and atoms. In: Proceedings of the SIGCHI Conference on Human Factors in Computing Systems, Atlanta, Georgia, March 22-27, pp. 234–241 (1997)
2. Jordà, S., Kaltenbrunner, M., Geiger, G., Bencina, R.: "The reacTable*". In: Proceedings of the International Computer Music Conference (ICMC 2005), Barcelona, Spain, pp. 579–582 (August 2005)
3. Cameron, A.: Systems Design Limited, "The Art of Experimental Interaction Design". Gingko Press (2005)
4. Ishii, H., Mazalek, A., Lee, J.: Bottles as a minimal interface to access digital information. In: Proceeding of the CHI EA 2001, CHI 2001 Extended Abstracts on Human Factors in Computing Systems, New York, NY, US, pp. 187–188 (2001)
5. Levin, G.: The Table is The Score: An Augmented-Reality Interface for Real-Time, Tangible, Spectrographic Performance. In: Proceedings of the International Conference on Computer Music (ICMC 2006), New Orleans, November 6-11 (2006)
6. Blaine, T., Fels, S.: Collaborative Musical Experiences for Novices. Journal of New Music Research, Swets&Zeitlinger 32(4), 411–428 (2003)
7. Klügel, N., Frieß, M.R., Gloh, G., Echtler, F.: An Approach to Collaborative Music Composition. In: Proceedings of the International Conference on New Interfaces for Musical Expression, pp. 32–35 (2011)

Could the Player's Engagement in a Video Game Increase His/Her Interest in Science?

Stéphane Natkin[1], Delphine Soriano[1], Grozdana Erjavec[2], and Marie Durand[2]

[1] CNAM, CEDRIC, ILJ Team, Paris
{stephane.natkin,delphine.soriano}@cnam.fr
[2] University of Paris 8, CHART Laboratory, Paris
grozdana.erjavec@etud.univ-paris8.fr,marie.ec.durand@gmail.com

Abstract. Our work is to analyze how the practice of chosen video games may influence the player's interest. A set of video games was selected by a group of experts according to their qualities as games and their relations with scientific knowledge. A focus test experiment has been set up to evaluate the correlation between teenagers engagement and their interest in scientific domains. The analysis of the results shows that the desire to pursue the game and the sentiment of responsibility has, respectively, a direct and an indirect influence on the player's scientific interest. Considering that interest is known to be an important motivational factor in learning, these results have important implications for the serious games design.

Keywords: Video games, scientific knowledge, player's engagement, serious game, focus test.

1 Introduction

The present study is a part of the project, Recensement /INMEDIATS[1], which main goals are to understand the relationship between digital entertainment and the interest in scientific knowledge. Our work is to analyze how the practice of chosen video games may influence the player's interest.

Interest is defined to be an emotional and motivational variable [1]. Furthermore, it has been established that the student's personal, situational and topic interest influence positively his/her learning outcomes [2,3]. Finally, in cognitive science, interest is considered to be very closely associated to a person's engagement in a given cognitive activity [4].

Engagement is associated with sensations such as immersion or, even more so, presence: Essentially, the sensation to "be there" [5,6,7]. In particular, Brockmyer & al. establish the relation between engagement and emotions, as fear, in their game engagement questionnaire. Furthermore, some theoretical video game studies observed that emotion can be considered as a component of engagement [8,9]. On the

---

[1] Recensement/INMEDIATS is partly funded by the Government agency ANRU with Universcience, CNAM, the University of Paris 8 as partners.

D. Reidsma, H. Katayose, and A. Nijholt (Eds.): ACE 2013, LNCS 8253, pp. 608–611, 2013.

other hand, Natkin [10] defined engagement in video games as a feeling of responsibility and Shoenau-fog [11] came to the conclusion that engagement can be conceived as a desire to pursue the game. Engaging the user in his/her experience of the product should be, among others, facilitative of cognitive efforts associated with serious aspects which might be presented in the product [12].

However, the manner in which a fun and engaging nature of an application, notably a video game, influences cognitive processes of the user has not yet been established. One way to think of such a relationship is to conceive it as being mediated by some other variable, for example the player's interest. Considering All these points of view, the present study attempts to explore the relationship between the player's engagement in a videogame and his interest in the scientific domain presented in the game.

2   Method

2.1   Video Games Selection

A set of video games has been selected by a group of experts. That was divided in two steps: first, from a dedicate data base, games were chosen according to their scientific aspects and gameplay qualities; Then, these shortlisted games were played by a group of scientific popularization experts and a pedagogical expert[2]. The final games chosen are: The Bridge (Ty Taylor and Mario Castaneda, 2013), World of Goo (2D Boy, 2008), Angry Birds Space HD (Rovio, 2012), Puddle (ENJMIN, Neko/Konami 2012) and Sim City 4 (Maxis, 2003).

2.2   Participants

One hundred and thirty three teenagers participated in the study, 23 girls and 110 boys. They were ranging in age from 14 to 18 years old ($M =15 360$; $SD =1.292$), were all native speakers of French and had the habit to play video games at least three hours per week.

2.3   Questionnaires

For this study we designed a pre- and a post-questionnaire. The pre-questionnaire was designed to assess video games habits and school interests. It consisted of multiple-choice questions. The post-questionnaire was designed to assess the level of engagement that the video game incited in the participants, as well as participants' interest in the scientific domain that was suggest by the video game a given participant has played. The participant's engagement in the video game was assessed on three separate dimensions; the player's presence during the game, the desire to pursue playing the video game and the feeling of responsibility.

---

[2] More details on http://www.cite-sciences.fr/inmediats/
seriousgame/projet.php

Each section of the post-questionnaire contained several questions to which participants were asked to answer by choosing one modality on a scale going from 1 to 10 : 1 being either a highly negative answer or an answer with the lowest degree of agreement. The questions corresponding to the different sections of the post-questionnaire were conceived based on theoretical and methodological elements from previous studies [1,2,10,11].

2.4   Procedure

The study consisted of 3 stages. In the first stage, the participant was asked to answer the pre-questionnaire. In the second stage, the participant was assigned to a video game related to a scientific domain different than his/her favorite school subject. He/she was asked to play the game autonomously for 30 minutes. In the third and final stage the participant was invited to answer, right after they played the game, at the post-questionnaire.

2.5   Results

The post-questionnaire internal stability was tested with the use of Cronbach's alpha statistics[3]. For further analysis, only the data from sections with high reliability (Cronbach's alpha was superior to .650) were retained (*Desire to pursue the game*, *Feeling of responsibility* and *Interest in scientific domain*), while those from section *Presence* were excluded (Cronbach's alpha was inferior to .500).

In order to assess the influence of the two compound variables of player's engagement on his/her interest in the scientific domain presented in the video game he/she has played, a multiple regression analysis using a step-wise method was conducted with the *Desire to pursue the game* and the *Feeling of Responsibility* as predictor variables, and the *Interest in the scientific domain* as a predicted variable.

The multiple regression[4] analysis results revealed a moderate to middle positive correlation among the variables ($r=.483$ for the correlation between *Desire* and *Interest*; $r=.357$ for the correlation between *Responsibility* and *Interest*; $r=.504$ for the correlation between *Desire* and *Responsibility*)[5]. Furthermore, *Desire*, but not *Responsibility*, was found to have a significant contribution to predicting Interest. ($F(1,131)= 39.861$; $p<.001$) and to account for approximately 23 per cent of the variance of the predicted variable ($R^2 =.233$; *delta* $R^2 =.227$)[6].

---

[3]   Coefficient providing a measure of the internal stability of a given questionnaire..

[4]   *F*-test (*F* and *p* values): In multiple regression, it explore whether the variables thought of as predictors have a significant effect on the predicted variable.

[5]   *r*: Pearson product-moment correlation coefficient which is a measure of dependence between two variables. Its values vary between +1 -1; the higher the absolute value of *r*, the stronger the dependence/correlation.

[6] R^2: Coefficient of determination which provides a measure of how well observed outcomes are replicated by the model.

2.6   Discussion and Conclusion

Roughly speaking, these results show that the *Desire to pursue the game* has a direct impact on the *Interest in the scientific domain*, while the *Feeling of responsibility* influences this same variable through its relation to *Desire to pursue the game*. *Desire* directly affects *Interest* with a very likely causal link. Similarly, *Responsibility* indirectly affects *Interest*, through *Desire* but this link might not be causal.

As theorized by Natkin [10], it might be linked to the *Feeling of responsibility* thus seems to be a component of the player's engagement. Following this research, it is necessary to validate the game questionnaire engagement on presence and to include it in our study [5]. It may help to understand better the potential relationships between the quality of a game in term of engagement and its implicit contents and messages (in our case, the scientific content) included in the same game. Finally, further research is needed in order to identify other factors influencing the player's interest for serious contents of a video game.

References

1. Ainley, M., Hillman, K., Hidi, S.: Gender and interest processes in response to literary texts: Situational and individual interest. Learning and Instruction 12(4), 411–428 (2002)
2. Renninger, K.: Individual interest and its implications for understanding intrinsic motivation (2000)
3. Schiefele, U.: Topic interest, text representation, and quality of experience. Contemporary Educational Psychology (1996)
4. Besley, J.C., Roberts, M.C.: Qualitative interviews with journalists about deliberative public engagement. Journalism Practice 4(1), 66–81 (2010)
5. Brockmyer, J.H., Fox, C.M., Curtiss, K.A., McBroom, E., Burkhart, K.M., Pidruzny, J.N.: The development of the Game Engagement Questionnaire: A measure of engagement in video game-playing. Journal of Experimental Social Psychology 45, 624–634 (2009)
6. Gamberini, L., Barresi, G., Maier, A., Scarpetta, F.: A game a day keeps the doctor away: A short review of computer games in mental healthcare. Journal of Cyber Therapy and Rehabilitation 1(2), 127–145 (2008)
7. Regenbrecht, H.T., Schubert, T.W., Friedmann, F.: Measuring the sense of presence and its relations to fear of heights in virtual environments. International Journal of Human-Computer Interaction 10(3), 233–249 (1998)
8. McMahan, A.: The Video Game, Theory Reader (2003)
9. Prensky, M.: Digital game-based learning. Comput. Entertain. 1, 21 (2003)
10. Natkin, S.: Interactivity in Games: The Player's Engagement. In: Nakatsu, R., Tosa, N., Naghdy, F., Wong, K.W., Codognet, P. (eds.) ECS 2010. IFIP AICT, vol. 333, pp. 160–168. Springer, Heidelberg (2010)
11. Schoenau-Fog, H.: Hooked! Evaluating Engagement as Continuation Desire in Interactive Narratives. In: André, E. (ed.) ICIDS 2011. LNCS, vol. 7069, pp. 219–230. Springer, Heidelberg (2011)
12. Zichermann, G.: Fun is the Future: Mastering Gamification (October 2010), http://www.gamesfornature.org/

Block Device System with Pattern
Definition Capability by Visible Light

Huu Nguyen Nguyen Tran and Junichi Akita

Kanazawa University, Kanazawa, 920–1192, Japan
{nguyen,akita}@ifdl.jp

Abstract. This paper describes an interactive block device – LED Tile – utilizing 8x8 dot-matrix LEDs which obtain pattern drawing capability. It also applies magnet connectors for physical connections and signal transmissions, as well as interacts with accelerometer sensor and audio signal device. The function of the block device can be defined by the drawn pattern on the matrix LED, and this capability extends the block system applications. In this paper, we describe the hardware and software configurations of this block device, as well as several fundamental and high-level functions of alphanumerical character recognition. We also describe two applications of this device, such as magic square and character arrangement.

Keywords: Block Device; Pattern Drawing; Function Definition.

1 Introduction

Block device systems, which have contained many simple component block devices, have been evolving from the simple structural devices, such as traditional LEGO blocks, to the intelligent devices that have small computer, sensors, actuators and communication channels [1], [2], [3]. Such intelligent block devices allow to build interactive systems. Each intelligent block device obtains fixed functions such as photo sensor, microcontroller, while operations in controller can be externally programmed.

The authors have been proposing and developing the block device with 8x8 dot-matrix LED unit as display output as well as input device by using visible light source, "LED Tile" system and its applications [4], [5].

In this paper, we propose a new type of block device system where each block can recognize alphanumerical characters for function definition drawn by visible light on the matrix LEDs. Each block behaves as it is defined by the drawn patterns, although it is identical in hardware. We also describe the implementations of two application games using this capability i.e. Magic Square and Character Arrangement.

2 Function Definitions by Visible Light

In this section, we describe both the hardware and software configurations of the developed block device, as well as the function definition algorithms by visible light.

D. Reidsma, H. Katayose, and A. Nijholt (Eds.): ACE 2013, LNCS 8253, pp. 612–615, 2013.
© Springer International Publishing Switzerland 2013

2.1   Hardware Configuration

Hardware Specification

Figure 1a shows the developed matrix LED block device named as "LED Tile (LT)". The microcontroller (ATmega640, Atmel) and tri-axis acceleration sensor (MMA7455, Freescale) are mounted on the board that accommodates to the 8x8 dot matrix LED unit size. The LT accompanies by the four magnet connectors located at the four edges for easing to connect and disconnect among blocks. The communication among the connected LTs is carried out in the asynchronous full-duplex serial protocol to implement system operations across the LTs. The LT unit also holds Lithium-Polymer battery (3.7V, 110mAh) and Piezo sounder.

A dot matrix LED unit is applied for displaying and also for photo sensing[6], and users can 'draw' patterns on the dot matrix LED unit surface by visible light like LED light or laser pointer, by the time-divided operation of display and sensing.

(a)   (b)

Fig. 1. Developed matrix LED block device, LT

Principle of Light Detection

By using the procedure in [5], the device can detect the drawn pattern by the visible light, and display the desired pattern independently.

The photosensitivity of LED, or saturated voltage of LED for incident light, depends on the wavelength (color) of the light and the structure of LED. The sensitivity becomes maximum for the incident light whose wavelength is equal to that of LED itself. The structure of LED also defines the saturated voltage for incident light; the generated photo current by incident light will increase the voltage of LED by charging the junction capacitor, while the leakage current decreases the voltage, which is larger than voltage of LED, and finally becomes an equilibrium state. The photosensitivity of LED is basically low compared with the photo sensor (photo diode), and the voltage change of LED by environmental light can be ignored; the voltage change by the 'bright' incident light by the user's intension can be detected to enable user's interaction with LED by visible light.

2.2   Software Configuration

The microcontroller (ATmega640) of LT device operates under an Arduino boot loader, and it can be programmed by the standard Arduino IDE.

The Basic Software Library: This library involves several fundamental sub libraries such as detecting where the light strikes to individual LED in 8x8 dot matrix LED surface and then turning on/off of each suitable LED, and displaying patterns such as alphanumerical characters in the matrix LED. The acceleration parameter can be used for implementing the user's interaction, such as shaking.

The Character Recognition Library: This library implements a high level code – mainly alphanumerical character recognition. The algorithm is to use vector directions and Euclidean distances established by two consecutive extracted feature points [7], to distinguish different characters which resemble a vector set. We map an individual LED dot corresponding to a unique coordinate. When drawing the patterns on the matrix LED surface, all points will be saved in an array with the chronological order. They will be then processed and extracted to a few feature points in the same order. Finally, two consecutive feature points establish an array of vectors whose every element grasps one in eight different directions such as up, down, right, left, upleft, upright, downleft, and downright. This information will be compared with the stored dictionary data to decide which characters should be recognized. Figure 2a illustrates a typical example that is vector's order numbers when drawing number '1' on the surface of matrix LED.

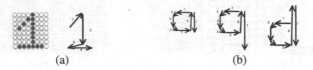

(a)   (b)

Fig. 2. Drawn character and its corresponding vectors

In the case, some characters have the identical directions of all vectors such as 'a', 'd', 'q' characters provided in Figure 2b, the Euclidean distance will be applied to distinguish all of them. In this example, the 6th and 7th vectors will be considered to calculate the Euclidean distance.

Figure 3 shows some examples of actually drawn patterns as well as the recognized and displayed suitable numerical characters.

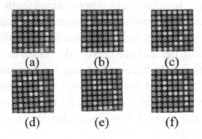

(a)   (b)   (c)

(d)   (e)   (f)

Fig. 3. Drawn ((a)(b)(c)) and recognized ((d)(e)(f)) patterns. (a)(d) Number 3, (b)(e)Number 5, and (c)(f) Number 9.

The Communication Library: We propose a protocol with three-byte command for interacting between two neighbor block devices using built-in UARTs for four directions; the first byte indicates a command such as PLUGNPLAY or ACK, the second one denotes the address of LT in the system, and the third one is the transmitted data. Figure 1b shows the connection among four LED Tile modules through magnets.

3   Application

The character recognition capability for the drawn pattern on LED can be used for defining the block function, with the identical device hardware. This is worth to extend the application of the block devices. In this section, we describe ideas and implementations of two applications using the LT device and the recognition capability.

3.1   Magic Square 3x3

We build the system connected to matrix-like 3x3 whose one element tantamount to one LT unit. Every block LT device firstly recognizes the specific drawn number from 0 to 9. The master unit located at the left top matrix's corner is manually chosen. Then, the system gradually established by plugging other devices which send formatted data to the master one. Finally, the master device verifies the matrix is a *magic square* where sums of value in all columns, rows and diagonals are equal.

3.2   Character Arrangement

We give a word in a specific field such as education, animal, or other areas. It contains several out of order characters drawn and recognized in every LT. Players should arrange all characters to form a meaning word. All nodes will automatically be plugged and played, and send the message to the node 1 – the left most node - which is a default brain of the system. Node 1 will examine the word correctness based on the small dictionary and feedback to other nodes with indication for 'YES' or 'NO'.

4   Conclusion

In this paper, we described the matrix LED block device with pattern draw capability by visible light, and the character recognition algorithm. We also described two applications of function-definable block system.

References

1. Gorbet, M.G., Orth, M., Ishii, H.: Triangles: Tangible Interface for Manipulation and exploration of Digital Information Topography. In: Proc. of CHI 1998, pp. 49–56 (1998)
2. Lee, J., Kakehi, Y., Naemura, T.: Bloxels: Glowing Blocks as Volumetric Pixels. ACM SIGGRAPH 2009 Emerging Technologies ET 331 (2009)
3. Suzuki, H., Kato, H.: AlgoBlock: a Tangible Programming Language for Collaborative Learning. In: Proc. of ED-Media, p. 770 (1994)
4. Akita, J.: Matrix LED Unit with Pattern Drawing and Extensive Connection. In: Proceedings of SIGGRAPH 2010, Emerging Technologies, CD-ROM (2010)
5. Akita, J.: Interactive Block Device System with Pattern Drawing Capability on Matrix LEDs. In: The ACM SIGCHI Conference on Human Factors in Computing Systems (CHI) 2012, Interactivity, in DVD-ROM (2012)
6. Hudson, S.: Using Light Emitting Diode Arrays as Touch Sensitive Input and Output Devices. In: Proc. UIST 2004, pp. 287–290 (2004)
7. http://www.ccs.neu.edu/home/feneric/charrec.html

Multi-sensor Interactive Systems
for Embodied Learning Games

Nikolaos Poulios and Anton Eliens

Computer Science. Multimedia Group – Vrije Universiteit Amsterdam, The Netherlands
ni.poulios@gmail.com, eliens@cs.vu.nl

Abstract. This paper explores the use of modern sensor technologies for physical interaction in educational games and interactive spaces. The paper presents a prototype of an educational game developed using a motion capture controller and two biofeedback sensors (EEG, ECG), proposing a generic architecture for multi-sensor interactive spaces. Target of this research is to study further the potential effect of such technologies on educational interactive games, in two aspects: i) on the involvement of human body and motion in the process of learning, and recall of knowledge, ii) on assisting the development of basic social emotional competencies, through the enhanced social affordances of embodied games.

Keywords: multi-sensor systems, educational games, embodied learning, physical interaction, motion interaction, interactive spaces, affective interaction, biofeedback sensors.

1 Introduction

The use of computer games in education has been an active field of academic research for the last twenty years, providing considerable evidence to support the positive effects of the use of games on the learning outcomes of students. Up until recently, based on the capabilities of the given technology, academic studies focused mainly on the conceptual engagement of learners in games. At the same time, scientists have highlighted the importance of psychological factors that influence children's learning, placing the development of social-emotional competences at the core of modern pedagogy, and creating a growing need in education for tools and instruments to support and assess these skills. Central to the development of social-emotional competences is the individual in relation to his or her social environment using all possible expressive forms. The human body can be seen as part of the human cognition (Dourish 2001 [1]), and a medium of self-expression and interaction with the environment and other people, thus its involvement in learning is of key importance.

The use of motion controllers and biofeedback sensor technologies has great potential for educational games, contributing to the conceptual engagment of learners [2], as well as to the social interaction affordances of the game [3]. Motion controllers, offer more

D. Reidsma, H. Katayose, and A. Nijholt (Eds.): ACE 2013, LNCS 8253, pp. 616–621, 2013.

freedom to move and to self express, leading to an effective kinesthetic experience. Additionally, body sensors, and their use inside game dynamics, provide us an instrument to observe and quantify in real time, the reflection of our actions, or stimuli of the surrounding environment, to our body, physical and mental condition, helping us to understand ourselves better. For spectators who can monitor player's performance and physical effort, player becomes an active physical part of the game creating a theatrical atmosphere around his performance, the game's story and virtual environment. As players and spectators exchange roles, the overall experience leads to increased self-awareness and awareness of others.

This paper showcases a prototype developed during a study in the design of multi-sensor interactive systems for learning games. This study was conducted for the master thesis project of the author, during an internship at the Waag Society institute for arts, science and technology in Amsterdam, and as preliminary research for a project called the Embodied Playful Learning Theater (EPLT). EPLT is meant to be a highly immersive environment, providing an open platform for research and development of applications and games featuring multiple sensor technologies. EPLT is part of the institute's involvement in the COMMIT P4[1], "virtual worlds for well-being" project. COMMIT program is a large, national wide program for innovation, bringing together leading research institutes and the high technology industry.

2   A Prototype for a Multi-sensor Interaction Physical Learning Game

Targets of the prototype presented were: i) the testing and demonstration of the capabilities of some selected commercial sensors, ii) the basic implementation of a multi-sensor system's, generic architectural design, and iii) to provide a base for the collection of some first body and motion data for further study of the concept of using these data in game interactions.

Inspired by simple traditional children games like hopscotch or jumping rope, main idea of the prototype conceptualized and developed by the author, was to use a motion capture sensor to create a board game that would blend characteristics of such games, such as physical social interaction and body motion, with those of modern video games, like dynamic computer graphics, sound effects, and fantastic virtual environments.

2.1   The Technology

The prototype uses the Microsoft Kinect sensor, the Neurosky Mindwave EEG sensor, and the Zephyr HxM ECG sensor. The selection of these devices was based on their availability as ready-made solutions, their technical specifications, their suitability to be used in a physical installation, and the level of support in the programming development of the game.

---

[1] http://waag.org/en/project/commit

Microsoft Kinect is a real-time motion capture sensor, which based on an infrared depth camera, and advanced computer vision algorithms, is capable of tracking at 30Hz the position of 20 joints of the body in space, for two players simultaneously. Kinect was chosen as a state of the art commercial motion sensor, an economic solution with previously proven performance and reliability.

Neurosky Mindwave is a wireless EEG based sensor, designed mainly to be used for games. The sensor uses a single electrode on the forehead of the player to capture voltage fluctuations in specific frequencies that have been related to brain activity, providing as output two values of "attention" and "meditation", that indicate the mental state of the player. An EEG sensor was chosen as new in commercial level technology, with promising features that would add novelty to the game, and intrigue the player. Mindwave was selected specifically for its ease of use in an installation, requiring short time to wear and calibrate, and the ability to maintain position and signal even under intense motion.

Zephyr HxM is a wireless ECG sensor placed near the chest of the player measuring his heartbeat rate. Heartbeat rate was chosen as a value that in contrast with the EEG signals, all people and even children are quite familiar with, because large enough fluctuations are internally sensed by our senses. The visualization of the heartbeat rate, and the interaction based on it, creates another link between the physically sensed body, and the virtual environment, that will enhance the feeling of immersion.

The combination of these two selected body sensors creates a good first base to collect data and study possible indications of correlation of physical activity and mental state.

The prototype was developed using the Unity 3D game engine for the game, OpenNI SDK for communication with the Kinect Sensor, and cinder C++ library for communication with the other sensors, visualization and storage of the data collected. All game artwork was taken from Unity's community and example projects.

2.2   The Game – NumHop

In the final game prototype developed, named NumHop, the player is placed in a virtual large hall [Fig. 1]. In front of the player placed on the floor, there is a board of 16 numbered tiles. The player is called to answer questions on simple multiplication matrices, for example the result of 6 x 7. The tiles of the board are numbered to values close to the correct result with at least one containing the correct number. The player then has some seconds to select his answer by stepping onto a tile. The faster the player responds correctly, the more points he gains. If the player does not respond, the game moves automatically to the next question. If on the other hand the player selects a wrong answer, the board moves to the next question, and an enemy robot is teleported in the scene through one of the 6 chambers, and starts approaching the player with bad intensions. The player can defend himself against the robots by activating his "superpower beam" (activated by raising both hands above shoulder level) and direct it against the robots. The player starts the game with a certain level of superpower that it is reduced by use. When however the EEG sensor that player

Fig. 1. View of the NumHop prototype game scene

wears on his head, detects high level of attention, the superpower level starts to charge and the player can use it again. If the player runs out of superpower, he has to suffer the robot's hits, which reduce the player's health level. If the player survives the attack he can step back for a moment and try to relax. When the EEG sensor detects high level of meditation, the health level of the player is increased. The player is given 3 lives in the beginning of the game, and bonus lives are awarded after a number of consecutive correct answers.

The heart rate value is not directly connected to any element of the game play. There are two reasons that led to this decision. The first one is that because the heart sensor has to be a little moisturized and worn under player's clothes, it might prove to be impractical, and time consuming to use in a school test session. The second one is that designing a certain interaction based on heart rate, and mapping this to a crucial element of the game, required to know in advance the expected range of values during the game, knowledge and expertise that was not available at the time of development. The presence of the heart rate value however was thought to be useful as also explained earlier, first for collection of the data for further use, and second to see how players respond to this information, if for example by placing the heart rate value of the player, appearing on the GUI, as what could be conceived by someone as another form of scoring points, motivates the player to raise his heart rate by moving more intensively.

3   Multi-sensor Interactive System Architecture

NumHop prototype was developed following a design pattern that demonstrates a generic architecture for multi-sensor interactive spaces, such as the Embodied Playful Learning Theater project. As described in the introduction of this document the EPLT is meant to be an open platform to be used by developers, artists and researchers for experimentation, testing and support of multi-sensor interaction technologies. As such, the EPLT should feature a flexible, extendable and scalable architecture that can be adapted according to the application built upon it, and the equipment used.

Based on the above system requirements, characteristic of the proposed architecture is the separation of the system and its interactions in three levels. The first level is the world level including the physical setup of the installation, the sensor devices used, and the various output devices of the system, such as projectors, sound and lighting systems.

The second level is the device level, describing low-level hardware and software acting as middleware, responsible for the collection and transmission of data coming from the various sensors to the application, and other sub-systems controlling the output mechanisms used by the application.

The third level, the application level corresponds to the system accepting data from the sensors as input and process them to the corresponding output. Components composing the different parts of the device and the application level can correspond either to processes running on the same computer, or processes running distributed over a network, each one implementing a different part of the interactive system. In order to provide this flexibility, a common messaging service is established between the two levels.

Following this architecture, NumHop consists of two applications, the game itself developed in the Unity game engine (C#), and a second one, developed in cinder (C++) library, implementing the device level. That second application is responsible for the connection with sensor devices, the collection, over time visualization, and permanent storage of the sensor data, along with the transmission of those data to the game engine. The two applications communicate using the Open Sound Control (OSC) protocol. OSC features include URL-style symbolic naming, high-resolution numeric argument data, pattern matching language to specify multiple recipients of a single message, high-resolution time tags, and "bundles" of messages whose effects must occur simultaneously. Due to its flexibility and simplicity, OSC has become an "industry standard" in the field of interactive installations, and has been implemented in a lot of programming languages, real time multimedia processing software and hardware, sound and light consoles, and various tangible interfaces. This makes OSC an ideal solution to be used in the system's middleware, as it allows the use of sensors, even with applications and devices used by non-programmers. Another advantage of this scheme is that it allows the deployment of an input control system that makes it easier for the whole system to handle and recover from errors. Errors like sensors losing contact with player's body, or dropped connections, are easier to diagnose by monitoring the data collected, outside of the game, and if possible, to restore normal function without interruption.

4   Conclusions – Further Study

The experience of a preliminary evaluation of the prototype (12 participants, 20-40 years old) showed us that these technologies add a certain level of novelty to the game, triggering people's curiosity and offering and engaging experience. On the negative side, it also showed us that even in a simple game, designing interactions based on multiple sensors might lead to some degree of difficultness to understand game mechanics.

Previous studies in the field of sensor technologies and affective interaction have found various real-time modalities and bio-signals that reveal information about the emotional state of a person. Expanding this research and intergrading those finding in games, will allow us to work towards more ambient forms of interaction, where sensor data is not directly mapped to certain actions, but used by an adaptive game environment and virtual actors with basic signs of emotional intelligence. Elements like these would enhance the immersive experience of an interactive story, with robustly interactive characters, that by extension would help the player to express and control her own emotions.

References

1. Dourish, P.: Where the action is: The foundations of embodied interaction. MIT Press, Cambridge (2001)
2. Lindley, S.E., Couteur, J.L., Berthouze, N.L.: Stirring up experience through movement in game play: effects on engagement and social behaviour. In: Proceedings of the Twenty-sixth Annual SIGCHI Conference on Human Factors in Computing Systems (CHI 2008), pp. 511–514. ACM, New York (2008)
3. Johnson-Glenberg, M.C., Birchfield, D., Savvides, P., Megowan-Romanowicz, C.: Semi-virtual Embodied Learning – Real World STEM Assessment. In: Annetta, L., Bronack, S. (eds.) Serious Educational Game Assessment: Practical Methods and Models for Educational Games, Simulations and Virtual Worlds, pp. 225–241. Sense Publications, Rotterdam (2010)

Photochromic Carpet: Playful Floor Canvas with Color-Changing Footprints

Daniel Saakes[1], Takahiro Tsujii[1], Kohei Nishimura[2],
Tomoko Hashida[3], and Takeshi Naemura[1,2]

[1] Graduate School of Information Science and Technology, The University of Tokyo
[2] Graduate School of Interdisciplinary Information Studies, The University of Tokyo
[3] The Department of Intermedia Art and Science, Waseda University
{daniel,tsujii,nishimura,hashida,naemura}@nae-lab.org

Abstract. Natural environments record their past and reveal usage in subtle cues such as erosion and footprints. In modern society of concrete cities and dynamic touch screens, this richness is lost.

We present a large size interactive floor display that captures visitors' footsteps in playful prints to make a modern environment into a canvas of past activities. The implementation consists of a carpet coated with color changing ink and shoes that activate color changes. Each step a visitor makes results in a dynamic print that slowly fades away.

Keywords: color changing material, interactive floor display.

1 Introduction

In the classic fairy tale, Hansel and Gretel safely return home by tracing back their path using a trail of pebbles. Natural environments capture history in various ways from valleys carved out by rivers to the broken twigs that trackers use to locate animals. Man-made products depict their most frequent used functionally in wear, such as chipped off paint or the greasiness of buttons. However, in modern society of concrete buildings and dynamic touchscreen interfaces, these environmental clues of use are lost. With the photochromic carpet, we aim to re-introduce the concept of subtle recording of history in the environment and visualize patterns-of-use that interact with the user in a ludic way.

The system consists of a large floor painted with passive, mono-stable color changing ink that is excited by footsteps of custom indoor shoes with build-in LEDs. Wearing the shoes, users leave trails of dynamic generated patterns. The patterns persist for minutes and invite users to use the carpet as an expressive canvas. Using smart materials in the floor, and the shoe as an activation medium, the system easily scales to very large surfaces, without the limitation of installing a camera-projector system or sensor networks.

Our current demonstration serves no other purpose than an experiential prototype. Through exhibits we aim to gather user feedback for future applications in schools and hospitals.

D. Reidsma, H. Katayose, and A. Nijholt (Eds.): ACE 2013, LNCS 8253, pp. 622–625, 2013.
© Springer International Publishing Switzerland 2013

Fig. 1. The carpet is made from photochromic material that temporarily becomes dark purple under UV radiation. As shown, near UV LED embedded in shoes activate the color change long enough to create playful patterns.

2   Related Work

Our effort spans two different research areas: projects that aim to enrich human interaction with physical objects and projects that augment shoes and floors for sports, entertainment and as user interface.

The History Table Cloth by Gaver et.al. [2] consists of a table top embedded with electroluminescent material. The table senses objects placed on the table and lights up around the objects for hours visualizing the flow of objects. They so investigate digital technologies that aim to engage their users in playful open-ended interactions rather than functional. Like wise, in "Material Traces" Rosner et.al. [7] discuss the practice of materiality and implications for HCI, illustrated by a number of provocative ideas, such as paint that traces rodent movement in the house. These projects relate to our aim, but ideas are prototyped on objects. In contrast, the technology proposed in this demonstration makes these concepts experiential on large scale environments and includes a practical way of realization. In computer entertainment interactive floors are made popular with dance dance revolution [4] in which a floor functions as a input device for a dancing game. Various interactive floors have been proposed. For instance, the magic floor [5] aims to capture user motion, however require complex sensor networks. Other projects take reverse approach by embedding the sensor technology in the shoe rather than environment. Expressive footware [6] embeds sensors in various ways to capture sport and dance performance.

An early example of a floor as input and output medium is the artwork Boundary Functions by Scott Snibbe [9]. Using a webcam and projector setup, visitor activity is captured and graphics are projected accordingly. To address the limitations of resolution and occlusion, the multitoe floor [1] aims to build a floor with multitouch displays. In that way they explore various interaction techniques activated by feet rather than by fingers. However, current display and projector technologies have various shortcomings when applying for large surface, high resolution or daylight applications. Using mono-stable color changing materials solves these issues by exploiting the persistence of image as a physical frame buffer. In that way, no digital representation is involved in the process of

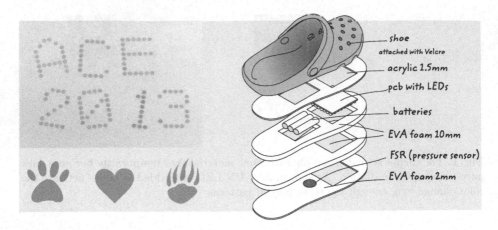

Fig. 2. The indoor shoes have custom soles attached with Velcro. The soles have an embedded LED array, and contain an accelerometer and pressure sensor for activation. Dynamic and static patterns are shown on the left.

capturing and displaying content. Because the photochromic carpet consists of a large area, sparsely populated with footprints, we can use the human as an actuator by embedding the color change activation mechanism in the shoe.

3   Design and Implementation

Various techniques are suitable for color changing floors to be used under daylight conditions [3,8]. Liquid floors react to pressure in interesting ways, but have only limited resolution. Thermochromic materials change with temperature, however activation technology is difficult to achieve in a small form factor. Therefore we've selected the photochromic material Spiropyran that is activated with near UV radiation.

Spiropyran produces color under UV light and returns gradually to colorless and transparent when the UV light is blocked. For the prototype we selected deep purple because of its high contrast color change. Shown in Figure 1. , the prototype floor spans $3x3m^2$ and is made out of 9 tiles. Each tile consists of a sandwich of the Spiropyran ink protected in 2mm acrylic sheet that is transparent for UV wavelengths.

The activation mechanism consists of a LED array embedded in the sole of shoes, as shown in Figure 2. The LEDs (Nichia NSPU510CS) have a peak wavelength of 375nm and in our setup an irradiance value of 4.642 μW/cm^2. For static patterns we use a 14 LED array, the dynamic pattern consists of a 64 LED array, driven by a constant current display driver that duty cycles the LEDs. We tuned the radiation duration to a maximum of 0.5 second per step, so that the color change in the floor that is persistent for approximately 5 minutes, depending on lighting conditions. The shoe sole is powered by three rechargeable aaa batteries. In practice, the batteries last for a few hours of use.

Because UV radiation is not safe for skin and eye contact, each shoe includes a safety mechanism driven by an Arduino. A FSR (Force Sensitive Resistor) detects whether shoe is pressed against a surface, and the accelerometer detects if the shoe is flat on the floor and without user induced acceleration. These two conditions have to be met in order to turn on the LEDs.

4   Future Work and Conclusion

In this project, human motion activates color changes that are spatially captured to make floors into a creative canvas that captures history. The system is implemented in the Miraikan National Museum of Emerging Science and Innovation in Tokyo and the exhibition will run for six months. Early feedback indicates that the system is popular by all ages.

Future versions could include wireless communication between all the shoes to coordinate dynamic patterns. In addition to shoes, other activation mechanisms could be explored such as autonomous or rc-vehicles.

Another avenue of research is to generalize the system for data visualization to represent transient data of the time domain, spatially on floors or walls.

References

1. Augsten, T., Kaefer, K., Meusel, R., Fetzer, C., Kanitz, D., Stoff, T., Becker, T., Holz, C., Baudisch, P.: Multitoe: high-precision interaction with back-projected floors based on high-resolution multi-touch input. In: Proceedings of UIST 2010, pp. 209–218. ACM, New York (2010)
2. Gaver, W., Bowers, J., Boucher, A., Law, A., Pennington, S., Villar, N.: The history tablecloth: illuminating domestic activity. In: Proceedings of DIS 2006, pp. 199–208. ACM, New York (2006)
3. Hashida, T., NIshimura, K., Naemura, T.: Hand-rewriting: automatic rewriting similar to natural handwriting. In: Proceedings of the 2012 ACM International Conference on Interactive Tabletops and Surfaces, ITS 2012, pp. 153–162. ACM, New York (2012)
4. Konami: Dance dance revolution, http://www.konami.com/ddr (accessed: June 10, 2013)
5. Paradiso, J., Abler, C., Hsiao, K.Y., Reynolds, M.: The magic carpet: physical sensing for immersive environments. In: CHI 1997 Extended Abstracts on Human Factors in Computing Systems, CHI EA 1997, pp. 277–278. ACM, New York (1997)
6. Paradiso, J., Hsiao, K., Benbasat, A., Teegarden, Z.: Design and implementation of expressive footwear. IBM Systems Journal 39(3.4), 511–529 (2000)
7. Rosner, D.K., Ikemiya, M., Kim, D., Koch, K.: Designing with traces. In: Proceedings of CHI 2013, pp. 1649–1658. ACM, New York (2013)
8. Saakes, D., Chiu, K., Hutchison, T., Buczyk, B.M., Koizumi, N., Inami, M., Raskar, R.: Slow display. In: ACM SIGGRAPH 2010 Emerging Technologies, pp. 22:1–22:1. ACM, New York (2010)
9. Snibbe, S.: Boundaryfunctions, http://www.snibbe.com/projects/interactive/boundaryfunctions/ (accessed: June 10, 2013)

Mood Dependent Music Generator

Marco Scirea

IT University of Copenhagen

Abstract. Music is one of the most expressive media to show and manipulate emotions, but there have been few studies on how to generate
music connected to emotions.

Such studies have always been shunned upon by musicians affirming
that a machine cannot create expressive music, as it's the composer's
and player's experiences and emotions that get poured into the piece. At
the same time another problem is that music is highly complicated (and
subjective) and finding out which elements transmit certain emotions is
not an easy task.

This demo wants to show how the manipulation of a set of features
can actually change the mood the music transmits, hopefully awakening
an interest in this area of research.

1 Music Mood Taxonomy

The first issue we had to deal with mood generation was the mood taxonomy. The
set of adjectives that describe music mood and emotional response is immense
and there is no accepted standard; for example Katayose *et al.*[4] use a set of
adjectives including *Gloomy, Serious, Pathetic* and *Urbane*.

Russell [9] proposed a model of affect based on two bipolar dimensions: *pleasant-
unpleasant* and *arousal-sleepy*, theorizing that each affect word can be mapped in
this bi-dimensional space by a combination of these two components. Thayer [10]
applied Russel's model to music using as dimensions *stress* and *arousal*; although
the name of the dimensions is different from Russell's their meaning is basically the
same. Also, we find different names in different research while the semantic value
stays the same. Since valence and arousal are the most commonly used terms in
many affective computing research, we will use these terms in this paper.

Thus the music is divided in four clusters: **Anxious/Frantic** (Low Valence,
High Arousal), **Depression** (Low Valence, Low Arousal), **Contentment** (High
Valence, Low Arousal) and **Exuberance** (High Valence, High Arousal).

These four clusters have the advantage of being explicit and discriminable;
also they are the basic music-induced moods (even if with different names) as
discovered by Kreutz [5] (*Happiness, Sadness, Desire* and *Unrest*) and Lindstrom
[6] (*Joy, Sadness, Anxiety* and *Calm*).

2 The Mood Modifying Features

Following Liu *et al.*[7], our current system employs three factors as the features
that characterize mood: **Intensity**, **Timbre** and **Rhythm**. Liu's study was

D. Reidsma, H. Katayose, and A. Nijholt (Eds.): ACE 2013, LNCS 8253, pp. 626–629, 2013.
© Springer International Publishing Switzerland 2013

about mood information extraction, we applied the principles they worked with to instead generate music.

2.1   Intensity

Intensity is defined by how strong the volume of the music is; in music with low arousal we generally have a lower volume than in the ones that have high arousal.

2.2   Timbre

Timbre is what we could call the brightness of the music: how much of the audio signal is composed by bass frequencies. In previous literature MFCC (Mel-Frequency Cepstral Coefficients) and spectral shape features have been used to analyze this. For example the brightness of *Exuberance* music is generally higher than in *Depression*, this will result in greater spectral energy in the high subbands for *Exuberance*. It's generally a factor that is very dependent on the instrumentation choice; in our case we act on the synthesizers, our instruments, to generate brighter and darker sounds.

2.3   Rhythm

Finally Rhythm has been divided in rhythm strength, regularity and tempo [7]. For example in a high valence/high arousal piece of music we can observe that the rhythm is strong and steady, while in a low valence/low arousal the tempo is slow and the rhythm cannot be as easily recognized. We act on these features in different ways. To influence rhythm strength we change how much the drums are prominent in the music.

Having the notes generators create notes on the beat or the upbeat creates different feeling of regularity and irregularity, for example in Contentment music we will favor a steady rhythm with notes falling on the beats of the measure while in a Depression one we will give more space to upbeat notes. Finally to influence the tempo we just act on the BPMs (Beats Per Minute) of the music.

2.4   Remarks

We noticed that these features, originally devised to extract mood information, were enough to generate different moods. But we also realized that we could strengthen the impression by introducing dissonances in the music: for *Exuberance* and *Contentment* we use a diatonic scale while for *Anxious* and *Depression* an alterated one.

3   The System

The demo has been realized using PD (aka Pure Data) [8], a real-time graphical programming environment for audio, video, and graphical processing. In PD, programs are written as graphical graphs called *patches*, in our demo we used some patches taken from Brinkmann's website [3].

The generated music is played by 3 instruments (synthesizers) and a drum machine. The system consists of five random number generators: four of these numbers will be converted into notes for the instruments and the drums, while the last one is used as a sound effect controller. Additionally each of the 4 notes generators also generate another number that will determine the volume the note will be played.

These generators create semi-random numbers by adding (in decimal) from a start value a certain step each tick. Then each generator converts the number to another base and adds the digits of the result. This value will then become the note we'll play; at the same time through a slightly different sum we generate another number that will control the volume the note will be played.

The numbers, before being sent to the synthesizers that will generate the note, are filtered so that we can control which notes we want and which we don't. This allows us to use dissonances or maintain a diatonic feel to emphasize moods. The numbers at this point represent notes in MIDI (Musical Instrument Digital Interface) notation (they can span from 0 to 127), so to filter them we just use a modulo operation to understand what note they represent. For example, as there are 12 notes in an octave, we can see that 60 modulo 12 equals 0, this means that 60 represents a C.

At this point the synthesizers generate the note, by converting the MIDI notation to a frequency and using PD's built-in audio wave generator. The synthesizers we use are constructed in a way that we can choose the waveform of the sound, modulation and if we want to transpose octaves.

After the notes are actually generated we have a patch that controls their volumes so that we can decide if we want some instruments more prominent than the others: a mixer. Now we have all the notes at the desired intensity but before playing them we apply some effects.

At the moment we have implemented only the music generation for the four quadrants of the bi-dimensional space, we plan to expand it so that the music can be generated by choosing a point in the plane.

4   Potential Application Domains and Future Work

This project generates music in real time with seamless transition between moods, this could be used in the making of games (where, unlike in a movie, events unfold in response to the player's input) to have a dynamic soundtrack. This can be done by using libraries to interface the game engine and PD. Also, music therapy could be another possible application since music manages to transmit moods immediately and in a non ambiguous way (at least for the four quadrants). Interesting future work includes the usage of words as input, using sentiment analysis tools such as SentiWordNet [1] to extract emotional value from them. This could in the end allow us to create music generated by texts that would reflect the different moods inside it. In the future we'll have a population sample describe their emotional state using SAM (Self Assessment Manikin)

[2] before and after interacting with the demo, this will yield important data in understanding how effective our generator is.

5 The User Experience of the Demo

The demo doesn't require any specific hardware, only a computer with Pure Data installed and speakers. The users will be able to interact with it by specifying the mood they are in (or they want to listen to) and the program will generate the music.

Ideally we will have the user's mood extracted by facial recognition, but at the time of this writing this part has not been implemented yet. By interacting with the demo we hope the users to get interested in experimenting with dynamic music in various media.

The demo can be downloaded at http://goo.gl/TAW2K9.

References

1. Baccianella, S., Esuli, A., Sebastiani, F.: Sentiwordnet 3.0: An enhanced lexical resource for sentiment analysis and opinion mining. In: Proceedings of the 7th Conference on International Language Resources and Evaluation (LREC 2010), Valletta, Malta (May 2010)
2. Bradley, M.M., Lang, P.J.: Measuring emotion: the self-assessment manikin and the semantic differential. Journal of Behavior Therapy and Experimental Psychiatry 25(1), 49–59 (1994)
3. Brinkmann, M.: Pure data patches, http://www.martin-brinkmann.de/
4. Katayose, H., Imai, M., Inokuchi, S.: Sentiment extraction in music. In: 9th International Conference on Pattern Recognition, 1988, pp. 1083–1087. IEEE (1988)
5. Kreutz, G., Ott, U., Teichmann, D., Osawa, P., Vaitl, D.: Using music to induce emotions: Influences of musical preference and absorption. Psychology of Music 36(1), 101–126 (2008)
6. Lindström, E., Juslin, P.N., Bresin, R., Williamon, A.: Expressivity comes from within your soul: A questionnaire study of music students' perspectives on expressivity. Research Studies in Music Education 20(1), 23–47 (2003)
7. Liu, D., Lu, L., Zhang, H.-J.: Automatic mood detection from acoustic music data. In: Proceedings of the International Symposium on Music Information Retrieval, pp. 81–87 (2003)
8. Puckette, M., et al.: Pure data: another integrated computer music environment. In: Proceedings of the Second Intercollege Computer Music Concerts, pp. 37–41 (1996)
9. Russell, J.A.: A circumplex model of affect. Journal of Personality and Social Psychology 39(6), 1161–1178 (1980)
10. Thayer, R.E.: The biopsychology of mood and arousal. Oxford University Press on Demand (1989)

A Tangible Platform for Mixing and Remixing Narratives

Cristina Sylla[1], Sérgio Gonçalves[1], Paulo Brito[1], Pedro Branco[2], and Clara Coutinho[3]

[1] EngageLab/CIEd, University of Minho, Portugal
{sylla,sgoncalves,pbrito}@engagelab.org
[2] Department of Information Systems, University of Minho; Portugal
pbranco@dsi.uminho.pt
[3] Institute of Education, University of Minho; Portugal
ccoutinho@ie.uminho.pt

Abstract. This work discusses a tangible interface for storytelling that targets pre-school children and offers a playful experimental space where children can create their own narratives by placing tangible picture-blocks on an electronic board. We present the system and report on the findings, describing the extent to which this interface can motivate and engage children, both in creating narratives, as well as in experimenting different solutions to solve conflicts created during the story plot.

Keywords: Tangible Interfaces, Storytelling, Oral Expression, Emergent Literacy, Collaboration, Children.

1 The Importance of Exploring Narratives

Storytelling plays a major role in children's lives, offering them a universe where their most adventurous fantasies become true, providing opportunities for social interaction and innovative thinking [5]. The familiarity of stories may facilitate creativity and generation of ideas helping children practice important literacy skills, such as language development, story comprehension and sense of the structure [4]. In the platform presented here, children have the possibility of animating the stories they know, or remixing elements from familiar stories, playing with characters, and objects and exploring different storylines. The interface was developed following an iterative participatory design process [2] together with preschoolers and their teachers.

2 An Interface for Remixing Narratives

The system is composed by different sets of picture-blocks and an electronic board that identifies the blocks placed on it. The blocks are placed on slots marked on the board. Each block has an image of what it represents on the upper side and an electronic tag on its backside that provides the system its identification. The electronic board is connected to a computer. Placing a block on the board displays the image and triggers an animation on the computer screen according to the combination of blocks that are on the board.

D. Reidsma, H. Katayose, and A. Nijholt (Eds.): ACE 2013, LNCS 8253, pp. 630–633, 2013.

Taking into account results and observations from previous studies [6] the system animates the elements on the screen following the order in which the picture-blocks are placed, and not their position on the board. When a block is removed from the platform it just disappears from the screen (fig.1).

The story engine was implemented to animate the elements according to the rules devised from situations that typically arise in traditional children stories. As the animations play, children can add or remove elements further developing the narrative. For example, how can children help the little pig to escape from the witch? Maybe they decide to place a house where the little pig can hide, hum... or ask other characters for help? Maybe the fairy... but will she be able to defeat the bad witch?

Fig. 1. Children creating a narrative

2.1   Story Engine

The concept behind the story engine was to model a world that would be understandable for young children. The goal is to allow children to bring their knowledge into play, while fostering their curiosity by playing out different situations where they might want to figure out what would happen if...

The story engine is implemented on top of the Unity game engine and it is developed based on behavior trees, a concept well known in the field of computer games to model character behavior, reactive decision-making and control of virtual characters. Each entity on the scene has a corresponding behavior tree that defines the actions of that element. When the users place the blocks on the platform, the behavior tree gets the inputs of the entities that are present. The behavior triggered for each entity depends on the other entities that are also in the scene, and the properties of those entities.

Adittionally, by pressing the Enter Key, the system automatically generates snapshots of the created narrative, saving them as digital images.

Fig. 2. Automatically generated snapshots of a narrative

The created images, which resemble comic book representations, are stored on the computer and can be directly uploaded to a blog or printed and shared with family and friends, thus extending the way to share stories with other people involving them into a collaborative storytelling experience (fig. 2).

3   First Pilot User Study

A qualitative user study was carried with a group of 15 children, during four sessions, with the duration of one-hour and a half each. The study revealed that one of the strongest affordances of the platform is the extent to which it promoted collaboration, showing that the children were highly motivated to engage and collaborate in different storytelling activities, exploring different story plots (fig. 3).

Fig. 3. Children collaborating in the creation of a story

Children engaged in teamwork, collaborating together in the creation of different stories, they personalized the figures giving them names and character traits. The tangible blocks acted as anchors for the creative process, helping children to shape their ideas. Children were able to begin their stories by situating them on particular sceneries; they used characters and created moments of tension, involving fights and the resolution of upcoming conflicts. Children explicitly expressed the wish to create their narratives with their peers, stating that it would be "more fun". The children quickly understood and used the various mechanisms behind the blocks, applying different strategies to achieve a certain goal, such as using a particular   combination of blocks, or removing others.

In line with [3] the tangibility of the input literally placed the story in children's own hands, so they negotiated, divided, and shared the blocks among them.

4   Conclusions and Future Development

By engaging with each other focusing on creating stories together, children may develop interpersonal language use, as they externalize their feelings and thoughts, learning to express themselves and to communicate with others, with time becoming more fluent in their language use [1]. The interaction and collaboration supported by the system creates a micro-world where children socialize with each other, learning to share, handle, divide, respect and accept the opinions from each other.

Future development involves a version to run on tablets connecting via Bluetooth, as well as to broaden and diversify different stets of blocks that explore other themes.

Acknowledgments. A very special Thank You to Colégio Teresiano, Braga the preschool children and teachers. This work is funded by FEDER funds through the Operational Competitiveness Factors Program - COMPETE and by National Funds through the FCT – Portuguese Foundation for the Science and the Technology within the Projects: PTDC/CPE-CED/110417/2009, FCOMP-01-0124-FEDER-022674 and the Doctoral Grant: SFRH /BD/62531/2009.

References

1. Ackermann, E.: Constructing Knowledge and Transforming the World. In: Tokoro, M., Steels, L. (eds.) A Learning Zone of One's Own: Sharing Representations and Flow in Collaborative Learning Environments, pp. 15–37. IOS Press, Amsterdam (2004)
2. Druin, A.: Cooperative inquiry: Developing new technologies for children with children. In: Proceedings of CHI 1999, International Conference on Human Factors in Computing Systems, pp. 592–599. ACM Press, New York (1999)
3. Hunter, S., Kalanithi, J., Merrill, D.: Make a Riddle and TeleStory: Designing Children's Applications for the Siftables Platform. In: Proceedings of IDC 2010 International Conference of Interaction Design and Children, pp. 206–209. ACM Press, New York (2010)
4. Morrow, L.M.: Literacy development in the early years: Helping children read and write, 5th edn. Allyn and Bacon, Boston (2005)
5. Paley, V.G.A.: Child's Work: The Importance of Fantasy Play. Chicago University Press, Chicago (2004)
6. Sylla, C., Branco, P., Coutinho, C., Coquet, M.E., Škaroupka, D.: TOK – a Tangible Interface for Storytelling. In: Proceedings of CHI 2011, International Conference on Human Factors in Computing Systems, pp. 1363–1368. ACM Press (2011), doi:10.1145/1979742.1979775.

Network Shogi Environment
with Discussion Support after Games

Yoshikazu Tagashira, Hiroyuki Tarumi, and Toshihiro Hayashi

Kagawa University, Takamatsu, Kagawa 761-0396, Japan
s12g467@stmail.eng.kagawa-u.ac.jp, tarumi@acm.org

Abstract. Japanese chess called *shogi* is the most complex variant of chess-like games. Several services are provided to play *shogi* on the Internet, but they do not provide enough functions for *kansousen*, which is a reviewing discussion session after games. SAKURA, a network *shogi* environment developed by us, provides supports for *kansousen*.

Keywords: Shogi, Network Game Community, Discussion Support.

1 Introduction

Shogi [1] is a variant of chess-like games, which is very popular in Japan. Among all chess variants, *shogi* is the most complex one because it allows reuse of captured pieces as well as its board size is 9x9. *Shogi* has 10^{226} possible positions, whereas the western chess has 10^{120}. Here, a *position* (in *shogi*, called *kyokumen*) refers to a status of the game board, defined by locations of all pieces and a turn of the next move (black or white).

Researchers have been developing many AI programs to play *shogi* and some of them defeated professional human players in 2013. Today, stronger programs are not required by most amateur players but they need improved environments to enjoy *shogi*.

Playing *shogi* on the Internet is very popular. For example, a web service "Shogi Club 24" [2] provides a networked gaming environment and has more than 200 thousands registered members. However, it does not provide enough functions for *kansousen*. *Kansousen* is a reviewing discussion after a game. In case of *shogi*, *kansousen* is more popularly conducted than other board games including the western chess or *Go*. "Shogi Club 24" only provides text chatting for *kansousen*. In case of "81 Dojo" [3], which is an international service for shogi, it has graphical interfaces to discuss alternative moves (*variations*). However, it does not support users to organize and save the discussion records.

2 Project SAKURA

We have been developing a network-based environment for *shogi*, including features to support *kansousen* [4]. It is called SAKURA (Shogi Archives and Kansousen Utilities for Research and Advice) [5].

D. Reidsma, H. Katayose, and A. Nijholt (Eds.): ACE 2013, LNCS 8253, pp. 634–637, 2013.

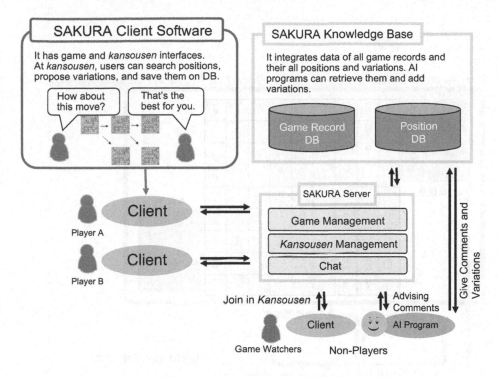

Fig. 1. Configuration of SAKURA

Figure 1 shows the configuration of SAKURA. It has a server system and a connected knowledge base. Players use client software to play games and have *kansousen* for their played games. Other users who did not play the game can also join in any *kansousen* using the client software. An AI program refers to a software to play *shogi*, which is generally strong as stated above. In the SAKURA project, AI programs are not developed by us but we provide interfaces with which external AI programs can connect with SAKURA.

SAKURA Knowledge Base consists of two databases. One is a game record (*kifu* in *shogi* terminology) database and another is a position database. Having a position database is a unique design among all *shogi* related systems. In the western chess, similar databases are supported for mainly opening and endgames. However, due to the complexity of *shogi*, huge position databases have not been provided by other systems.

3   Kansousen Features

In order to realize the *kansousen* features, we have designed (a) a set of communication protocol for group discussion and (b) a set of user interfaces for discussion and to append variations (i.e. candidates of alternative moves that should be taken at a particular position in the game) and comments to any positions.

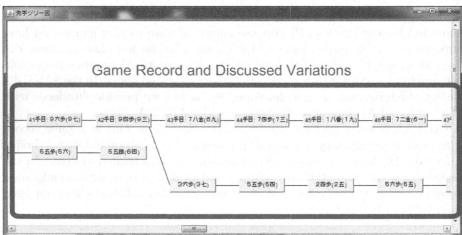

Fig. 2. Sample User Interface for Kansousen

The protocols provide many functions to create a *kansousen* discussion session, to participate in or leave a session, for floor (turn-taking) control, to propose a particular position to discuss, and to append comments and variations. In the design of protocols, participation of non-players is considered.

The user interface support users to join in a *kansousen* discussion session, to append comments and variations, to chat, and to edit shared and private game boards.

Figure 2 shows a part of the user interface for players joining in an *kansousen*. Red rectangles and texts are appended for this figure. The upper window is a shared board with comments field; the lower is a tree-chart of a game record and discussed variations appended while a *kansousen*. Other user interfaces such as chatting are omitted here due to the limit of space.

To validate the design, we have simulated a recorded oral *kansousen* session conducted by two professional players on our designed protocol. It has been confirmed that the protocols are enough to implement discussions in *kansousen*.

Records of discussion can be saved on SAKURA Knowledge Base so that the players or other users are able to refer to them.

4   Conclusion

SAKURA provides unique features to support *kansousen* of *shogi*, which have not been given by other services.

We are currently implementing interfacing software with which AI programs can give comments to players in the discussion. In the design, we are paying attention to the amount of comments and timing when they are given by AI. Basically *shogi* players like to consider by themselves for training. Hence comments by AI are given when they are explicitly requested by players and when the players are closing the discussion without noticing very bad mistakes.

Acknowledgments. This research is partially supported by KAKENHI (25540169).

References

1. Russel, J., Cohn, R. (eds.): Shogi. Book on Demand Ltd. (2012)
2. Shogi Club 24, http://www.shogidojo.com/
3. 81 Dojo, http://81dojo.com/
4. Tarumi, H., Hiraga, Y., Hayashi, T.: Groupware Support for Kansousen of Shogi. In: Proceedings of Fifth International Conference on Collaboration Technologies, IPSJ, pp. 58–59 (2009)
5. Yamamoto, K., et al.: Database Support for Shogi Learners. In: Proceedings of 2012 Fourth IEEE International Conference on Digital Game and Intelligent Toy Enhanced Learning, pp. 126–128. IEEE (2012)

Hospital Hero: A Game for Reducing Stress and Anxiety of Hospitalized Children in Emergency Room

Sara Tranquada, Monchu Chen, and Yoram Chisik

Madeira Interactive Technologies Institute, University of Madeira, Funchal, Portugal
st89nikon@hotmail.com, {monchu,ychisik}@uma.pt

Abstract. A visit to a hospital emergency room is often a traumatic and anxiety inducing experience for children (as well as their parents). Hospital Hero is game developed with the aim of helping children familiarize themselves with the hospital environment and the instruments/equipment that they will undergo while focusing their attention on positive feedback thereby alleviating their anxiety and easing the work of hospital staff and the burden on parents and care givers leading to better treatment and a better experience.

Keywords: Games, Children, Hospital, Games for Health, Anxiety Reduction, Children's Emergency Room.

1 Introduction

Hospitals are not the most hospitable of places at the best of times and for a child already suffering from the effects of an illness or an injury they can be downright antagonistic. It is not only the shock of a new and often noisy place and the assortment of people prodding and asking probing questions that is disturbing it is also the shuttling from one examination room to another via a maze of doors, corridors and elevators and the often visible nervousness of accompanying family members.

Hospitals have invested a great deal of effort in making the emergency room a more welcoming environment for children by building separate emergency room facilities equipped not only with specialist doctors but with colorful walls, dressed up equipment, and a variety of toys, games and music intended to calm and distract the child [1,2] however all of these efforts regardless of their rates of success treat the symptom (agitation and anxiety) and not the cause (fear and unfamiliarity).

Hospital patients (adults as well as children) are anxious and agitated not only due to the pain and discomfort brought about by their medical condition but also by their lack of familiarity with the hospital environment, their lack of knowledge of the medical procedures they are about to undergo and at times their mistrust of hospital staff.

Hospital Hero is a game designed to help children familiarize themselves with the hospital environment, staff and various medical procedures thereby reducing their anxiety and making them more cooperative. This in turn enables faster treatment and better experience for the patient, hospital staff and accompanying family members.

D. Reidsma, H. Katayose, and A. Nijholt (Eds.): ACE 2013, LNCS 8253, pp. 638–641, 2013.
© Springer International Publishing Switzerland 2013

2   Design Rational

Agitation and anxiety brought about by fear and unfamiliarity can be addressed by making the unknown known and by providing positive feedback. In the "Teddy Bear Hospital", Bloch and Toker [2] have shown that inviting children to bring their teddy bears to a mock hospital and helping them examine and apply treatments to the teddy bear, e.g. check the teddy bear heartbeat with a stethoscope, apply bandages and administer injections lower the perceived anxiety of the children about the prospect of having to go to the hospital and undergo such procedures themselves. Baldwin's MindHabits Trainer game [3] has shown that it is possible to develop games that help people focus on positive feedback such as smiling faces thereby boosting their self-confidence and reducing anxiety.

Hospital Hero builds on these earlier works by creating a 3D virtual environment of a hospital through which the player can familiarize himself with the hospital environment, staff, patients and equipment. The gameplay consists of finding lost patients and collecting a set of medical supplies and equipment, portrayed in the form of cartoon characters and objects through the maze of corridors and rooms that make up a cartoon version of a hospital. As the player traverses through the corridor of the virtual hospital they will encounter various characters. Characters with positive expressions provide clues about the lost patients and medical supplies and equipment.

The characters players encounter in the game serve two purposes. The first purpose is to familiarize children with the hospital staff and they type of patients they are likely to encounter. The second purpose is to get the players to actively seek out and focus on smiling faces in a crowd in an effort to gain the same positive effect shown by Baldwin in MindHabits [4]. Whenever a sub-task is accomplished (e.g. obtaining a stethoscope), a positive feedback is also provided in the form of a cute animation.

3   Implementation

The game was developed using the Unity game engine for deployment on tablets and kiosks. Although developed in Portugal, the game is designed to be bilingual and can be easily ported to other languages. To cover the wide range of kids, the game requires minimal language ability. Relaxing ambient sounds and positive sound effects, upon correct movements, are provided.

A short anxiety test, based on the Modified Short State-Trait Anxiety Inventory and Talking Mats [5], was added before and after the game to test the effectiveness. The anxiety test was designed as a part of the game to be non-intrusive. Four expressions (happy, sad, calm and scared) were created and used in pre- and post-game anxiety tests. A neutral face was also created for the purpose of showing neutral results. Approximate results are also shown after each test with three different faces (sad-with high anxiety, happy-with low anxiety and neutral-middle anxiety) as a form of feedback. All characters, 3D objects as well as the environment were created in Autodesk Maya.

Fig. 1. Screen captures of the *Hospital Hero* during language selection at the beginning of the game session (left), and during pre-game anxiety test (right)

Fig. 2. Shows a corner of the virtual hospital where a kid will encounter avatars of hospital staffs and patients with either happy faces or sad faces. When touching a avatar with a happy face, the avatar offers hints as positive feedbacks, whereas a sad avatar will offer neutral feedback (right).

4   Discussion

Although the game has not been formally deployed to kiosk in the hospital, the proto-type has already been tested on tablet with university students to identify usability problems and interface design issues. A revised prototype was also tested with some children in a local elementary school to gather preliminary results and to evaluate the experimental design.

For statistic analysis, the game automatically keeps track a player's activities in a log file. In addition to the log file, the front camera of the tablet also records the facial expression of the player. Another regular video camera was also setup to capture the whole area in order to study player's behaviors outside of the game. The Yale Preoperative Anxiety Scale Modified (YPAS-m) test [6] was conducted by a shadowing experimenter before/after the game to compare and correlate to the results from the self-report anxiety level of the in-game anxiety test.

Children reported that they enjoyed the game and did learn new knowledge about the emergency room. The preliminary results indicate some improvements in terms of anxiety level. However, we do not have enough subjects for the result to be signifi-cantly meaningful. The test at the elementary school shows that the system and expe-rimental setup is ready for deployment at the Children's Emergency Room. We are positive about the effectiveness of the game once installed. And we are very eager to deploy the system in the local hospital in order to collect the real world data for our long-term study.

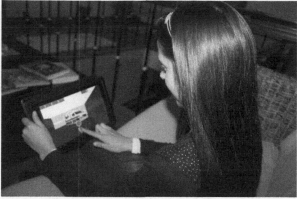

Fig. 3. A kid with a transplanted kidney playing the kiosk at the Children ER of Funchal Hospital (left), and another kid play-testing an early prototype of the game on an Andriod tablet (right)

References

1. Weiland, T.J., Jelinek, G.A., Macarow, K.E., Samartzis, P., Brown, D.M., Grierson, E.M., Winter, C.: Original Sound Compositions Reduce Anxiety in Emergency Department Patients: A Randomised Controlled Trial. Medical Journal of Australia 195(11-12), 694–698 (2011)
2. Bloch, Y.H., Toker, A.: Doctor, Is My Teddy Bear Okay? The "Teddy Bear Hospital" As A Method To Reduce Children's Fear of Hospitalization. Israel Medical Association Journal 10(8-9), 597–599 (2008)
3. Baldwin, M.: Mindhabits: Games for a Positive Outlook. Mindbits (2012)
4. Electric Owl Studios. Interactive Kiosks,
   http://www.electricowlstudios.com/interactive-kiosks/kick
5. Nilsson, S., Buchholz, M., Thunberg, G.: Assessing Children's Anxiety Using the Modified Short State-Trait Anxiety Inventory and Talking Mats: A Pilot Study. Nursing Research and Practice (2012), doi:10.1155/2012/932570
6. Kain, Z.N., Mayes, L.C., Cicchetti, D.V., Bagnall, A.L., Finley, J.D., Hofstadter, M.B.: The Yale Preoperative Anxiety Scale: How Does It Comparewith a "Gold Standard"? (1997)

Toinggg: How Changes in Children's Activity Level Influence Creativity in Open-Ended Play

Bas van Hoeve, Linda de Valk, and Tilde Bekker

Department of Industrial Design, Eindhoven University of Technology,
P.O. Box 513, 5600 MB Eindhoven, The Netherlands
b.j.s.v.hoeve@student.tue.nl, {l.c.t.d.valk@,m.m.bekker}@tue.nl

Abstract. This paper describes an explorative study with an open-ended play environment called Toinggg that consists of three interactive trampolines and was developed for children aged 6-8 years old. Toinggg was used to evaluate the change of children's activity level on creativity in open-ended play. With this exploration, we aim to gain a better understanding of the balance between physical activity and creativity in play. In a user evaluation twenty-one children played in groups of three with Toinggg. Results show an increase in development of new game play and creativity after a moment of rest concerning the activity level of the interaction behavior.

Keywords: Open-ended Play, Physical Play, Creativity, Design Research.

1 Introduction and Related Work

Imagine yourself being a 7 year old child again for one day, playing around and exploring freely without any limits. Play is considered as an intrinsically motivated activity with no direct benefit or goal that is situated outside of daily life that triggers creativity [2]. In our research, we aim at designing interactive playful solutions with simple interaction rules that enable children to create their own play and games. We call this open-ended play [1]. In previous research we have focused on designing open-ended play objects that stimulate both social and physical play [1, 8]. We experienced that physical high active play has a possible negative effect on the creativity of the children. In this paper we therefore investigate the relation between physical play and creativity in open-ended play. How can we design for a proper balance between the right physical activity level and children still having enough energy to be creative? An open-ended play installation named Toinggg was developed, consisting of three interactive trampolines. A change in the interaction behavior of Toinggg is built in which should support moments of less active open-ended play to stimulate creativity. This leads to our research question: Can changes in children's activity level influence creativity in an open-ended play environment?

The research presented in this paper is related to open-ended and physical play. An example of free play is FeetUp [4], a playful accessory integrated in a pair of shoes. Children get audiovisual feedback whenever they jump or are off the ground. They

D. Reidsma, H. Katayose, and A. Nijholt (Eds.): ACE 2013, LNCS 8253, pp. 642–645, 2013.
© Springer International Publishing Switzerland 2013

can freely play with FeetUp anywhere and anytime. It is however a wearable play object that does not specifically focus on the level of creativity. Concerning physical play, a related design is the Interactive Trampoline [3], which is a large trampoline with four satellites, sixteen LEDs build-in in the outer curve and a speaker. The interaction rules of these elements differ per game. Research with the trampoline studied physical activity, safety and technology to enrich the play value of the trampoline. The main differences between Toinggg and the Interactive Trampoline are the number of trampolines and their size. Instead of one large trampoline, Toinggg consists of multiple intelligent play objects that create a play environment.

2   Design

We applied a research through design process [9] consisting of several design iterations. In most of these iterations, children were involved in pilot tests and exploratory evaluations. The design developed in these iterations is called Toinggg. Toinggg is designed for children in the age of 6-8 years old. It consists of three small trampolines (96cm diameter) with three modules underneath that have integrated RGB LEDs and distance sensors that can detect a jump. The interaction rules of Toinggg are developed around four animals: a mouse, a cat, a dog and an elephant, represented by different sounds and colors of light. Jumping on a trampoline will trigger an animal sound, a color of light and the intensity influences the brightness. A child jumping on another trampoline gets a different animal. When children jump in the same rhythm, one animal will win (depending on the hierarchy of the animals) and replace the losing animal. In this way, all trampolines can be set to the same animal. After five minutes, all lights will fade out and the system will not react anymore to temporarily discourage high activity physical play. For one minute, a combination of snore and cricket sounds creates the experience of sleeping animals. The children can use this moment to review their acts and think of new playful solutions.

3   Evaluation and Conclusion

An explorative study was conducted to examine the influence of an intentionally activity output change on creativity in open-ended play. This user evaluation took place at a gymnastics room (10x10m) of a primary school. Twenty-one children aged 6-8 years old participated in the play sessions. For each session, three children (mixed in age and gender) were invited to play with Toinggg. Children were told that the animals can get tired for a short period of time but will be willing to play again afterwards. Each session took 15-20 minutes including some quick open questions at the end to reflect on children's play behavior. All sessions were video recorded.

Analysis of the sessions was done by coding the videos of each session per minute on number of new developed games, classified by four types of play [5]: Functional play (simple physical active play), Explorative play (play to explore), Dramatic play (play involving fantasy) and Games-with-rules (actual rule-based games). To measure the level of creativity we scaled the three aspects Fluency (based on the number of interpretable, meaningful, and relevant ideas generated), Originality (based on the uniqueness, non-common way of thinking and level of detail) and Enjoyment (based on the enjoyment of the users during the test) on a scale from 0-7 [6, 7].

Results show that children played enthusiastically with Toinggg in various ways. They responded quickly to the sounds of the modules, both verbally: "I am an elephant", or non-verbally by expressing a smiling face when an animal sound played. Sounds were interpreted in many ways and sometimes triggered the imagination of the children (e.g. the mouse sound was interpreted as a chicken or a Tyrannosaurus). After individual explorations, the children started to play together. This led to games-with-rules like changing trampolines and guessing which animal you are.

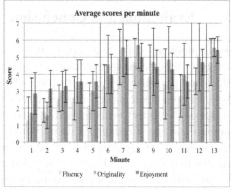

Fig. 1. Children playing with Toinggg during the evaluation sessions

The children tended to play very physical in the first minutes of the sessions. This could be related to Functional play. Regarding this type of play, the rest moment was necessary since the children became very tired. Earlier pilot tests showed that in this case, children tend to become less concentrated and inspired. As can be seen in Figure 2a, the games (specified in different types) changed clearly on the moment of activity output change. A peak in the amount of new created games can be found during the rest moment (minute 6) and even more right after it (minute 7). These are both situations in which the interaction rules changed. Overall the types of play appeared in the following order: Functional play, Explorative and Dramatic play and Games-with-rules and

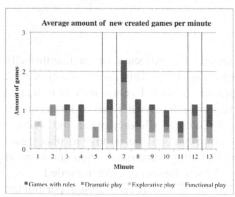

Fig. 2. These charts show (a) the average amount of new games created, divided in types of play (vertical), counted per minute (horizontal) and (b) the average scores and standard deviation rated per minute of the seven play sessions scored from 0-7. The vertical lines on the beginning and end of minute 6 and 12 show the sleep interaction moment.

Dramatic play. The second rest moment (minute 12) created less new games compared to the first rest moment. This can be related to the fact that the users became familiar with the interaction rules in both situations (rest and active).

The aspects Fluency, Originality and Enjoyment gave a good impression about the play behavior of the children. This analysis on the quality of gameplay showed a similar peak compared to the amount of created games. As can be seen in Figure 2b, the quality of creativity tended to remain after the rest moment. Observations showed that this occurred since the richness of the games was explored instead of creating a new game. Enjoyment seemed to grow even more every time the interaction rules changed which was visible during the sessions; the children understood the game better and better. The Originality in games slightly decreased over the rest moments, since the new situation needed to be explored again. This was for the children a moment to check if everything was still the same: "Let's check if the animals didn't change position during the night!"

Our results show a positive change in amount of creativity after a change of activity level. However, the actual peak can be found when the rest moment ends and the initial interaction rules start again. It seems like the rest moment created a 'reset button' for the children to rest and think about the situation. After the rest moment, the interaction rules were explored again and creativity of children increased. We believe these insights can help designers in developing engaging playful solutions.

References

1. Bekker, T., Sturm, J., Eggen, B.: Designing Playful Interactions for Social Interaction and Physical Play. Personal and Ubiquitous Computing 14(5), 385–396 (2010)
2. Huizinga, J.: Homo Ludens: A Study of the Play Element in Culture. Beacon Press, Boston (1955)
3. Karoff, H.S., Elbæk, L., Hansen, S.R.: Development of Intelligent Play Practice for Trampolines. In: 11th Int. Conf. on Interaction Design and Children, pp. 208–211 (2012)
4. Rosales, A., Arroyo, E., Blat, J.: FeetUp: A Playful Accessory to Practice Social Skills through Free-Play Experiences. In: Campos, P., Graham, N., Jorge, J., Nunes, N., Palanque, P., Winckler, M. (eds.) INTERACT 2011, Part III. LNCS, vol. 6948, pp. 37–44. Springer, Heidelberg (2011)
5. Rubin, K.H.: The Play Observation Scale (POS). Centre for Children, Relationships and Culture. University of Maryland (2001)
6. Silva, P.A., Read, J.C.: A Methodology to Evaluate Creative Design Methods: A Study with the Bad Ideas Method. In: 22nd Conference of the Computer-Human Interaction Special Interest Group of Australia on Computer-Human Interaction, pp. 264–271 (2010)
7. Torrance, E.P.: The Torrance Tests of Creative Thinking: Norms-Technical Manual. Personnel Press (1966)
8. de Valk, L., Rijnbout, P., Bekker, T., Eggen, B., de Graaf, M., Schouten, B.: Designing for Playful Experiences in Open-ended Intelligent Play Environments. In: IADIS International Conference Game and Entertainment Technologies, pp. 3–10 (2012)
9. Zimmerman, J., Forlizzi, J., Evenson, S.: Research through Design as a Method for Interaction Design Research in HCI. In: SIGCHI Conference on Human Factors in Computing Systems, pp. 493–502 (2007)

ZooMor: Three Stages of Play for a Sleeping Creature

Daniël van Paesschen, Mark de Graaf, and Tilde Bekker

Department of Industrial Design, Eindhoven University of Technology
P.O. Box 513, 5600 MB Eindhoven, The Netherlands
d.e.v.paesschen@student.tue.nl,
{m.j.d.graaf,m.m.bekker}@tue.nl

Abstract. This paper presents a design case of an interactive zoomorphic play object for open-ended pretend play, based on De Valk's three stages of play framework. It was designed to invoke pretend play around a sleeping object. Design iterations were tested in a public play environment.

Keywords: open-ended play, pretend play, stages of play, zoomorphic.

1 Introduction

A sleeping being – animal, human - is intriguing for many children. It is tempting to wake it up to see how it reacts, but there is the risk of a negative reaction. This was the inspiration for ZooMor: a 'sleeping' zoomorphic object placed in an open play space, designed to invite children to play with it, moreover, to develop pretend play around it.

With the last question, we position ZooMor as an interactive object that aims to support open-ended pretend play, like for example [1]. Design for open-ended play aims to support children in creating their own play, without predefining the rules of play [2].

ZooMor is an object that has much similarity to relational artifacts. Turkle defines relational artifacts as 'objects presenting themselves as having "states of mind" that are affected by their interactions with human beings' [3].

The challenge of designing for interactive open-ended play is to provide opportunities to players. This is fundamentally different from for example game design, in which the play activity is largely predefined. De Valk's Stages of Play provides a framework to design for this open-ended play. In this framework, an interactive experience in play goes through three stages. First, a potential player must be attracted to start playing. This first stage is called the *invitation phase*. Once a player is attracted to the play design, she or he explores opportunities for interaction and play in the '*exploration stage*', wanting to understand aspects such as rules and affordances. Once a player has acquired sufficient understanding of possibilities for play, immersion in play may occur: the '*immersion stage*'.

2 Design Iterations

ZooMor was designed to be a zoomorphic creature, its form giving leaving room for interpretation in order to support open-ended pretend play. Its basic form was symmetric, with a 'leg' part at front and back side, and a heightened back. The form allowed children to sit on it and crawl underneath it.

D. Reidsma, H. Katayose, and A. Nijholt (Eds.): ACE 2013, LNCS 8253, pp. 646–648, 2013.

In total three design iterations have been done. All iterations were completed with a field test in 'De Ontdekfabriek', an open play environment. Children from ages ranging from 3 to 9 could enter freely to play. ZooMor was available for play for about two hours per study. In every test, 5 to 10 children played with the prototypes for 5 to 30 minutes. Evaluation of play was done in two ways: analysis of video and semi-structured short interviews with the children leaving the place. The interactivity of ZooMor was tested with the Wizard of Oz technique. [4A]

In the first design iteration, emphasis was on the first stage of play, invitation [5]. Applied to ZooMor, it had to sleep but arouse curiosity of children nearby. It is known that life-like sounds like pulse, breath, snore or cough are strong triggers of zoomorphic perception [5]. To invite children to interact, we chose the sound of snoring.

The experimenter followed a strict protocol in controlling ZooMor's behavior. The initial state in all tests is asleep. After 5 seconds of sleep, it starts snoring loudly. It wakes up if a child does at least one of the following things: crawl under the belly, climb on top of it, stroke or pet it, or kick or hit it. It does not react to sound. When it wakes up, it stops snoring and to give further feedback to the child a blue light under the belly is switched on. When no one is touching ZooMor for more than 10 seconds, it will go back into the asleep-state.

The snoring did invite children to come to ZooMor and start playing with it. Interaction comprises petting, lying down next to it, and sometimes more aggressive interactions like hitting, kicking, hopping on top of it and shouting occurred. The sleeping state was very well understood; the awake state with the blue light was not. Children referred to ZooMor as "sleeping beast", "giant", "horse". One child did not dare to enter the space because there was "a monster sleeping".

Fig. 1. The final version of ZooMor

In the second iteration, the emphasis was on De Valk's exploration phase. Several changes were made to the design. First, the poorly understood blue light was replaced by abstract eyes on one side of the form, to appeal more to zoomorph identification. Second, the interaction opportunities were extended somewhat: the possibility to 'wiggle' the back perpendicular to the spine of ZooMor. This movement could for example lead to rubbing, stroking, shaking or wiggle while sitting on top of it. The wiggling movement was also defined as an input that could wake up the creature, when repeated at least 3 times. Finally, a second ZooMor was added to the scene, having the same affordances, but in a different color. These changes were successful in invoking a stronger zoomorphic perception: children were talking about the two creatures as living things frequently, and started having "inappropriate expectations" [6]: attributing capabilities to them they did not have. The second design did stimulate children effectively to explore ZooMor's behavior. It was not however interesting enough to create a long lasting and playful experience.

Therefore, the third iteration focused on De Valk's *immersion* stage. We aimed for richer behavior than be awake or asleep, to elicit more variety in play. This was done through a redesign of the eyes, Fig. 1. These now could be anything in between fully open and fully closed. The expectation was that this would allow for perceptions like drowsy, tired, dreamy, and so on. We indeed observed richer and more lasting play, children assigning meaning to the intermediate states of the eyes.

3   Conclusion

In 3 iterations, ZooMor was developed as a zoomorphic creature that invited children to play with it. The stages of play framework proved to be very useful for the systematic development of ZooMor. The last iteration, addressing all stages of play including immersion, indeed led to the most sustained pretend play.

References

1. Beukering, A., De Valk, L., Bekker, M.M.: Wobble: How an Open-ended Play Environment Supports Different Levels of Social Play. In: Reidsma, D., Katayose, H., Nijholt, A. (eds.) ACE 2013. LNCS, vol. 8253. Springer, Heidelberg (2013)
2. Bekker, M.M., Sturm, J.: Stimulating Physical and Social Activity through Open-Ended Play. In: Interact 2009, Uppsala, Sweden, pp. 952–953 (2009)
3. Turkle, S., Breazeal, C., Dasté, O., Scassellati, B.: Encounters with kismet and cog: Children respond to relational artifacts. In: Digital Media: Transformations in Human Communication (2006)
4. Green, P., Wei-Haas, L.: The Rapiud Development of User Interfaces: Experience with the Wizard of Oz Method. In: Proceedings of the Human Factors and Ergonomics Society Annual Meeting (1985)
5. Schmitz, M.: Concepts for Life-Like Interactive Objects. In: Proceedings of the 5th International Conference on Tangible, Embedded, and Embodied Interaction, pp. 157–164 (2011)
6. DiSalvo, C., Gemperle, F.: From Seduction to Fulfillment: The Use of Anthropomorphic Form in Design (2003)

Social Believability in Games

Harko Verhagen, Mirjam Palosaari Eladhari, Magnus Johansson, and Joshua McCoy

Department of Computer and Systems Sciences, Stockholm University
{magnus,verhagen}@dsv.su.se
Institute of Digital Games, Malta University
mirjam.eladhari@um.edu.mt
Center for Games and Playable Media, University of Southern California
mccoyjo@soe.ucsc.edu

Abstract. The Social Believability in Games Workshop intends to be a point of interaction for researchers and game developers interested in different aspects of modelling, discussing, and developing believable social agents and Non-Player Characters (NPCs). This can include discussions around behaviour based on social and behavioural science theories and models, social affordances when interacting with game worlds and more. The intention is to invite participants from a multitude of disciplines in order to create a broad spectrum of approaches to the area.

Keywords: social believability, NPCs.

1 Introduction

From the beginning of digital games, AI has been part of the main idea of games containing acting entities, which is to provide the player with "worthy" opponents (NPCs). The development of multiplayer games has increased the demands put on the NPCs as believable characters, especially if they are to cooperate with human players. However, the social aspect of intelligent behaviour has been neglected compared to the development and use AI for e.g. route planning. In particular, the interplay between intelligent behaviour that is task-related, the emotions that may be attached to the events in the game world and the social positioning and interaction of deliberating entities is underdeveloped. This workshop aims to address this deficiency by putting forward demonstrations of work in the integration of different aspects of intelligent behaviour, as well as models and theories that can be used for the emotional and social aspects.

1.1 Non Player Characters

Non-player characters (NPCs) are the ever-present inhabitants of online games so often visited by players. Games, and game worlds in particular, have to be populated to be interesting (Bartle, 2003) and one strategy is to create a computer-generated population of NPCs to make them come alive. NPCs typically play a role in the story of the world they populate, and their sole reason for being in that world is to create a value or a function for players. Amongst those functions or roles Bartle (2003, p.87)

D. Reidsma, H. Katayose, and A. Nijholt (Eds.): ACE 2013, LNCS 8253, pp. 649–652, 2013.
© Springer International Publishing Switzerland 2013

lists the following: 1) Buy, sell and make stuff. 2) Provide services. 3) Guard places.4) Get killed for loot. 5) Dispense quests. 6) Supply background information. 7) Do stuff for players. 8) Make the place look busy.

From one perspective the goal of games AI is to support game designers in providing players with a compelling game experience that supports interactivity and player choices and adds to replay ability (Bailey and Katchabaw, 2008). The current way in which people play games might indicate either that players do not easily become immersed in the games they play or that they play games differently today: "As more and more people actually finish fewer and fewer games, the opportunity to extend the life of games becomes important." (Consalvo, 2007, p. 62)

Game research has a growing interest in NPCs. In (Afonso and Prada, 2008) social relationships between NPCs are seen as the most important for improving the gaming experience of players. Merrick and Maher (2006) discuss the seemingly static representation and behavioural repertoire of NPCs in cases where the game world constantly changes (MMOGs), changes that should also be reflected in the NPCs in order to be believable, a view that is shared by Lankoski and Björk (2007). One view that is shared by all referenced sources in this section is that 'Believability is a basic requirement for non-player characters of videogames' (Gomez-Gauchía and Peinado, 2006, p.1).

Game developers develop different aspects of NPCs in new directions as well. In L.A Noire (Team Bondi, 2011) NPCs' facial expressions add both immersion and believability, and the behavioural repertoire of the NPCs in Skyrim (Bethesda Game Studios, 2011) is an example of complex NPC behaviour as are the strategic elements of the NPCs in Rage (id Software, 2011).

1.2   Believable NPCs

What is believability, and what makes a believable NPC believable? This is perhaps one of the most important considerations as regards the conceptualization of character for games that exceed the behavioural repertoire of current NPCs, since believability is currently lacking (Gomez-Gauchía and Peinado, 2006). For many people, the phrase believable agent conjures notions of an agent that tells the truth or an agent you can trust. But this is not what is meant at all. Believable is a term coming from the character arts. A believable character is one who seems lifelike, whose actions make sense, who allows you to suspend disbelief (Bates 1994).

In our interpretation, one of the most important aspects of believability deals with actions situated in a context where NPCs are lifelike, 'whose actions make sense' in a certain situation. There are indeed many suggestions about what makes an NPC seem lifelike and believable, and the Oz group at Carnegie Melon University have been working on the following set of requirements for characters to be believable (Loyall, 1997, pp. 15-26; Mateas, 1999):

- Personality –have a rich personality that is reflected in all their actions.
- Emotion –exhibit personality-specific responses to the emotions of others.
- Self-motivation – a measure of the character's own internal drives and desires that the character pursues whether or not others are interacting with them.
- Change – a believable character should change and grow with time.
- Social relationships – a believable character should also engage in detailed interactions in manners consistent with that social relationship, a relationship that in turn changes as a result of the interaction.

- Consistency of expression –facial expression, body posture, movement, voice intonation, etc.
- The illusion of life – a collection of requirements dealing with a character's reaction to stimuli in the environment.
- Well-integrated (capabilities and behaviours) – believable characters should be well-integrated, smoothly moving from one activity to the next (Mateas, 1999, p.4)

Processing Increasingly Limited Capabilities	Knowledge *Increasingly Rich Situation*					
	Nonsocial Task (NTS)	Multiple Agents (MAS)	Real Interaction (RIS)	Social Structural (SSS)	Social Goals (SGS)	Cultural Historical (CHS)
Omnipotent Agent (OA)	goal directed models of self produces goods uses tools uses language	models of others turn taking	face-to-face timing constraints	socially situated class differences	social goals organizational goals	historical motivation
Rational Agent (RA)	reasons acquires information	learns from others education	scheduling	social ranking social mobility competition	disillusionment	social inheritance social cognition
Boundedly Rational Agent (BRA)	satisfices task planning adaptation	group making	social planning coercion priority disputes mis-communication	restraints on mobility uses networks for information corporate intelligence	party line voting delays gratification moral obligation cooperation altruism	gate keeping diffusion etiquette devience roles sanctions
Cognitive Agent (CA)	compulsiveness lack of awareness interruptability automatic action	group think	crisis response	automatic respence to status cues	clan wars power struggles	develop language role development institutions
Emotional Cognitive Agent (ECA)	intensity habituation variable performance	protesting courting	mob action play rapid emotional responce	campaining conformity	nationalism patriotism	norm maintenance ritual maintenance advertising

Fig. 1. Social fractionation matrix (Carley and Newell 1994)

If we take a closer look at the Oz group's list of requirements for believability, we can see that there are many common traits compared with what other researchers have reported as important aspects of believability, and this coincides with Carley and Newell's (1994) fractionation matrix (Figure 1).

The work of Lankoski and Björk has many overlaps with the Oz group, particularly as regards the following traits: emotional attachment, contextual conversational responses, and goal-driven personal development, where the interpretation might differ slightly but indicates the necessity for emotions, character development/change and social aspects on an individual plane. Most other traits as identified by Lankoski and Björk (2007, p.1) fall under the category of the Oz Group's 'the illusion of life'.

Fig. 2. Social believable NPCs

One thing that stands out is that whereas the Oz group details the individual behaviour of believable characters the social fractionation matrix has little to add to our understanding of believability in individual characters. The social fractionation matrix does however add a lot to our understanding of the fine-grained details about the social believability of and interactions between characters, adding an important focus to the social dimension. Figure 2 depicts the relation between these sources, where the theories from the Oz –group (Loyall, 1997, pp. 15-26; Mateas, 1999) end up in the 'individual NPC' part of the figure, accompanied by the overlaps identified in Lankoski and Björk (2007). Lankoski and Björk also touch upon 'narrative', a subject that has also been studied in depth by Mateas and Stern (2003). It is obvious that these theories deal with different parts of Figure 2. Little attention, however, is paid to how the behaviour of groups of NPCs influences immersion, indicating a gap that needs to be discussed further.

In summary, we look forward to the workshop to discuss the matters outlined here as well as other topics relevant to increased social believability in games.

References

Afonso, N., Prada, R.: Agents That Relate: Improving the Social Believability of Non-Player Characters in Role-Playing Games. In: Stevens, S.M., Saldamarco, S.J. (eds.) ICEC 2008. LNCS, vol. 5309, pp. 34–45. Springer, Heidelberg (2008)

Bailey, C., Katchabaw, M.: An Emergent Framework. In: FuturePlay 2008, Toronto, Ontario, Canada, November 3-5 (2008)

Bartle, R.: Designing Virtual Worlds. New Riders, Indianapolis (2003)

Bates, J.: The Role of Emotions in Believable Agents (1994)

Bethesda Game Studios. Skyrim (PC). Bethesda Softworks (release date November 11, 2011)

Carley, K.M., Newell, A.: The nature of the social agent. Journal of Mathematical Sociology 19(4), 221–262 (1994)

Consalvo, M.: Cheating: Gaining advantage in videogames. The MIT Press, Cambridge (2007)

Gómez-Gauchía, H., Peinado, F.: Automatic Customization of Non-Player Characters Using Players Temperament. In: Göbel, S., Malkewitz, R., Iurgel, I. (eds.) TIDSE 2006. LNCS, vol. 4326, pp. 241–252. Springer, Heidelberg (2006)

Id Software. RAGE (PC). Bethesda Softworks (release date October 4, 2011)

Lankoski, P., Björk, S.: Gameplay design patterns for believable non-player characters. In: Proc. 3rd Digital Games Research Association International Conference (2007)

Loyall, A.B.: Believable Agents. Ph.D. thesis. Tech report CMU-CS-97-123, Carnegie Mellon University (1997)

Mateas, M.: An Oz-Centric Review of Interactive Drama and Believable Agents. Carnegie Mellon University, Pittsburgh (1999)

Mateas, M., Stern, A.: Façade: An Experiment in Building a Fully-Realized Interactive Drama. In: GDC 2003 (2003)

Merrick, K., Maher, M.L.: Motivated Reinforcement Learning for Non-Player Characters in Persistent Computer Game Worlds. In: ACE 2006, June 14-16 (2006)

Team Bondi, Rockstar Leeds, Rockstar Games. L.A. Noire (PC)

Computer Entertainment in Cars and Transportation

David Wilfinger[1], Alexander Meschtscherjakov[1], Christiane Moser[1],
Manfred Tscheligi[1], Petra Sunström[2], Dalila Szostak[3], and Roderick McCall[4]

[1] University of Salzburg
[2] Mobile Life Center
[3] Intel
[4] University of Luxembourg
{david.wilfinger,alexander.meschtscherjakov,christiane.moser2,
manfred.tscheligi}@sbg.ac.at petra@sics.se,
dalila.szostak@intel.com, roderick.mccall@uni.lu

Abstract. This workshop deals with the potential that entertainment systems
and games hold for the transportation context. Travelling by car, bus, plane or
by foot can be frustrating and full of negative experiences, but also holds great
potential for innovative entertainment application. New off the shelf technology
offers great potential beyond old-fashioned rear seat entertainment systems with
the sole purpose of keeping kids quiet. The richness of contextual factors and
social situations have so far not sufficiently been exploited, which is why this
workshop aims at discussing potentials for gaming in transportation.

Keywords: games, transportation.

1 Introduction

Since the early days of mankind, games were used to reduce stress, support
amusement, strengthen social ties and simply to have a good time. All of this is often
missing in cars and transportation although especially when we are on the move,
playing a game might cheer us up or relive us from boredom.

Working towards gaming in transportation this workshop is a forum for researchers
and practitioners interested in games & entertainment approaches for the
transportation and automotive domain. We believe that this is an emerging field, since
entertainment technology has the potential to not only entertain travellers but also to
reduce frustration, aggression, and foster positive behavior in all travelling situations.
Games or Gamification can also help shaping the traveller's behavior for the better
by, for example, keeping them of from driving during rush hour or using less fossil
energy getting from A to B. The potential for entertainment in transportation is also
growing, as (semi) autonomous vehicles will, for example, free up time for drivers
and make opportunities for interactive technology even larger. The potential for
entertainment in public transportation is also great for it being a social place. Gaming
can change the way we travel, make it more fun but also have a societal impact by
directing travelers' behavior.

D. Reidsma, H. Katayose, and A. Nijholt (Eds.): ACE 2013, LNCS 8253, pp. 653–655, 2013.
© Springer International Publishing Switzerland 2013

2   Motivation

Although the potential for games in transportation is obvious, there are challenges as well as opportunities that distinguish gaming in transportation from gaming in other contexts. Gaming in transportation cannot be like gaming in the living room, but it also should not be the same. Designing successful entertainment applications for transportation requires a solid body of research as well as creativity making gaming in the transportation context a fun experience.

The context of playing games in transportation is highly influential on the experience that the game elicits. When travelling between locations, the context the game is played in, changes. Some of these changes affect what can be called environmental context. Changes in light for example will occur, the landscape moves past the player and although often not moving the body itself, players move through an environment with different speeds [1].

Also to consider for games in transportation is the social context. Other travellers can be a source of annoyance when, for example, space is limited during rush hour. On the other hand, the presence of other players can allow flexible multiplayer games that are more entertaining than a single player game can be. But there are still issues to be solved, for example privacy concerns when playing games in public places with strangers where we cannot keep our identity hidden and simply log out as it is possible in online gaming.

Apart from that the space that the game is played in can create very distinct situations. Playing games in the car requires the usage of a very limited space, most of which is not reachable when children are seated in child seats. Sharing a space like the car cabin also holds potential for conflict, since not all passengers might be interested in listening to the same sound that the game for one player creates [5].

Also in matter of time, transportation is different from playing games in living rooms or other more traditional contexts. Travel duration is flexible and thus needs an adaption of the game. Thinking of multiplayer games in public transport, players need to have the opportunity to join an ongoing game but also to leave it at every moment when they have reached the stop to get of.

From a more technology driven perspective, the transportation context is rich of data starting, for example timetables that are public available in many countries through open data initiatives. Also cars offer a vast amount of sensor data that can also serve as input for games and related applications. Even when walking we create data that can be used for meaningful and entertaining games. The challenge is to use this data in games and therefore make them unique for the context they are played in. In a way, the transport modality can be seen as controller of future games. This inclusion of transportation data and the context has the potential to make games meaningful but needs to be explored further.

This non-exhaustive list of challenges gives a first impression on research questions and topics that entertainment researchers face in the transportation context. Solutions must be found on how to use these very special characteristics of the transportation context and make them a feature in entertainment applications. It is necessary to create a better understanding of what makes a good game for the transportation context and which strategies of game design can be applied for games while travelling. Travelling on the daily commute, for example, is very repetitive and thus causes boredom [2]. This is an aspect that a game has to take into account so that a context dependent game, for example, does not get boring simply because the traveller passes by the same place every day.

While there are promising approaches for gaming in transportation such as exergames for playing in the tramway [4], more has to be done to use the potential for gaming when people are on the move.

3   Workshop Objectives

Therefore this workshop is a forum to discuss how to enrich technology in transportation through aspects of entertainment and gaming. The goals of the workshop are twofold.

First, we want to bring researchers with interests in this topic together and have them present their work in order to inspire others. This goes in line with our efforts to create a community of researchers who are interested in the emerging topic of entertainment technology while travelling. We are convinced that the large body of research that is done in both the gaming and the transportation fields can be brought together to some extend, informing the work of researchers in both fields.

Second, we believe that the potential for entertainment applications in transportation is far from being sufficiently exploited; new off the shelf technology offers great potential beyond old-fashioned rear seat entertainment systems with the sole purpose of keeping kids quiet. Creative ideas are needed and this workshop can build a base for future collaboration and sharing ideas will help create a vision and contribute to the formation of a community.

References

1. Brunnberg, L., Juhlin, O.: Keep your eyes on the road and your finger on the trigger - designing for mixed focus of attention in a mobile game for brief encounters. In: Fishkin, K.P., Schiele, B., Nixon, P., Quigley, A. (eds.) PERVASIVE 2006. LNCS, vol. 3968, pp. 169–186. Springer, Heidelberg (2006)
2. Obrist, M., Wurhofer, D., Krischkowsky, A., Karapanos, E., Wilfinger, D., Perterer, N., Tscheligi, M.: Experiential perspectives on road congestions. In: CHI 2013 Extended Abstracts on Human Factors in Computing Systems, CHI EA 2013. ACM (2013)
3. Sundström, P., Wilfinger, D., Meschtscherjakov, M., Tscheligi, M., Schmidt, A., Juhlin, O.: The Car as an Arena for Gaming. In: Adjunct Proc. MobileHCI 2012 (2012)
4. Toprak, C., Platt, J., Mueller, F.: Designing Digital Games for Public Transport. In: Fun and Games: Extended Proceedings of the 4th International Conference on Fun and Games, pp. 29–31. IRIT Press (2012)
5. Wilfinger, D., Meschtscherjakov, A., Murer, M., Osswald, S., Tscheligi, M.: Are we there yet? A probing study to inform design for the rear seat of family cars. In: Campos, P., Graham, N., Jorge, J., Nunes, N., Palanque, P., Winckler, M. (eds.) INTERACT 2011, Part II. LNCS, vol. 6947, pp. 657–674. Springer, Heidelberg (2011)

Possibility of Analysis of "Big Data" of Kabuki Play in 19th Century Using the Mathematical Model of Hit Phenomena

Yasuko Kawahata[1,*], Etsuo Genda[1], and Akira Ishii[2]

[1] Department of Contents and Creative Design, Graduate School of Design, Kyushu University
6-10-1 Hakozaki, Higashi-ku, Fukuoka 812-8581, Japan
purplemukadesan@gmail.com
[2] Department of Applied Mathematics and Physics, Tottori University, Koyama,
Tottori 680-8554, Japan
ishii.akira.t@gmail.com

Abstract. Kabuki was a popular entertainment in the Edo period in the 19th century from the 17th century. Kabuki in the Edo period was different from standing position as a traditional performing arts in modern. Methods of mathematical models in Nowadays has been selected topics in SNS through the Internet, they do not exist in the Edo period. In order to perform the calculation and measurement of popular artists of the Edo period, we were subject to publication of the paper medium is the only media at the time (Ukiyoe, poem, haiku,book) to there. With this approach, the study of past popular actor, with respect to the reputation of masterpiece can be also from the perspective of current.

Keywords: Hit phenomena, Stochastic process, Kabuki, Senryu, Ukiyo-e.

1   Mathematical Model of Hit phenomenon in the Edo Period

The mathematical model accepts the number of performances as input, and predicts the extent of public interest. We consider that the model should be applicable to historical as well as current trends. To test this idea, we investigated the culture and fashion in the Edo period, which flourished approximately 200 years ago. We focused on the presumed cultural center of Edo, the Kabuki. Kabuki was a popular Edo-period entertainment from the 17th to the 19th centuries. Unlike modern culture, Kabuki in the Edo period was a traditional performing art form.   The number of topics in SNS calculated by the proposed mathematical model is based on modern hit phenomena. The media available to the modern public can access media did not exist in the Edo era. Thus, to adapt the model to popular Edo-period Kabuki actors, an examination of paper media being the only available media is required.[1] We selected the book of Kawaraban, haiku poem, and Ukiyo-e as appopriate paper media for analyzing the reputation of Kabuki actors. [2] Model inputs were news source data published in the

---

* Corresponding author.

D. Reidsma, H. Katayose, and A. Nijholt (Eds.): ACE 2013, LNCS 8253, pp. 656–659, 2013.

Fig. 1. We went to the English translation further the modern translation of the word green line of ancient documents in the figure. Process of a modern translation of this ancient document is part of an important method of this study. The following text is an English translation of the statement process. In the capital, all take their fashion cues from kabuki-particularly those of high rank, but even the lower orders look to these to pattern their clothing, to the point even of learning how to tie their obi belts. "From Onnachō Hōki ("A Treasury for Women"), by Sunbokushi Kusada (aka Jōhaku Namura), 1692 Fig.4 from National Diet Library.

Kawaraban and the number of stage performances described in the rankings. The database used to investigate Edo period trends comprised approximately 630000 publications from 1855 to 1849 owned by museums and individuals, and held in libraries and universities in Japan and overseas. [1,2] Data duplications and errors are prevented by applying a numerical value for human operators. We will show the data which we collected in this study on Web by cooperation of Professor Hideaki Takeda of National Institute of Informatics in future.[5] The period selected for the study is of historical importance, covering natural disasters such as the Ansei earthquake (in which many popular actors perished)and other highly topical events. [3-5]

Fig. 2. Namazu-e

The catfish picture (Fig. 2) was published in large quantities during the great Ansei earthquake. Therefore, to investigate the number of different Ukiyo-e themed publications, we must focus on the persons or items of the Edo period. We identified popular Edo-period Kabuki actors by a variable called "actor reputation mentioned." The quality of actors at that time was recorded in Osaka, Kyoto, and Edo Kabuki publications. However, because the content of the performance differed from one locality to another, the reputation rankings of Osaka, Kyoto and Edo were biased by their regional differences. Therefore, we restricted our study to Edo regional literature and the most commonly found relics of that time, Ukiyo-e.[1-5]

2   Methods-Hit Phenomena in Edo-

In this theory, we present the equation to calculate the intention which is the intentions for people in the society for a certain entailment in Edo. In the case of this paper, the intention to each actor of Edo Kabuki. Based on the observation of the hit phenomena in Japanese market, we present a theory to explain and predict hit phenomena. First, instead of the number of people N(t), we introduce here the integrated intention of individual customer in Edo, Ji(t) defined as follows,

$$N(t) = \sum_i J_i(t)$$
(1)

Kabuki are the very important factor to increase the intention of each person for enjoying entertainment in Edo. Kabuki are done at 3 Hall in 1849-1855.[5,7,8]We consider the advertisement effect as an external force term A(t) to the intention as follows,

$$\frac{dI_i}{dt} = C_{adv}A(t) + \sum_j D_{ij}I_j(t) + \sum_j \sum_k P_{ijk} I_j(t)I_k(t)$$
(2)

where D_{ij} is the factor for the direct communication and P_{ijk} is the factor for the indirect communication. The factor Cadv corresponds to the strength of the impression of the media or Concerts exposure for each advertising campaign. Because of the term of the indirect communication, this equation is a nonlinear equation. If we consider Kabuki, we can solve the equation by including several effect of the advertisement in the following way,

$$C_{adv}A(t) \Longrightarrow \sum_i C_i A_i(t)$$
(3)

where each coefficient C_i corresponds to the each advertisement and Concert's counts and can be determined by using the random number technique introduced in Ref. [6]. The actual formula used in the calculation to analyze the Edo prints response are introduced in detail in Ref.[6-8]

3   Result

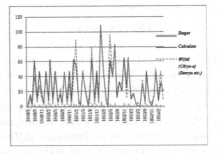

Fig. 3. Plot the results for Danjuro Ichikawa. Fig.3 The number of documents pertaining to Danjuro Ichikawa as a function of time.[4-8].

4   Conclusion

We have been able to use exactly the same mathematical model to analyze and predict hit phenomena in the past and present as well as the reputation of the artists. While problems remain with our method in the sense that it is difficult to say that our sample numbers are complete, we invite the cooperation of volunteers and readers interested in our study's attempt, in the hopes that this will lead to the discovery of a new historical understanding, and that the application of this technique elsewhere in the world might lead to the appearance of new discoveries and fruitful suggestions. We expect that in future, the potential of past media for the study of archeology will be unlocked, leading to a new point of departure for research in the field of archeological research.

References

1. Gerstle, C.A.: Flowers of Edo: Eighteenth-Century Kabuki and Its Patrons. Asian Theatre Journal 4, 52–75 (1987)
2. Leiter, S.L.: A Kabuki reader: History and performance, pp. 3–359. ME Sharpe Inc. (2002)
3. Edo Kabuki Ukiyo-e for Bigdata database, http://data.linkedopendata.jp/storage/f/2013-08-30T04%3A47%3A01.086Z/edokabukirefernces.pdf
4. Library and Art Gallery and Museum and database of Ukiyo-e subject of investigation, http://data.linkedopendata.jp/storage/f/2013-08-30T05%3A05%3A52.332Z/library-and-art-gallery-and-museum-and-database-of-ukiyo.pdf
5. Matsumura, F., Kobayashi, I., Kato, F., Kamura, T., Ohmukai, I., Takeda, H.: Producing and Consuming Linked Open Data on Art with a Local Community. In: Sequeda, J.F., Harth, A., Hartig, O. (eds.) Proceedings of the Third International Workshop on Consuming Linked Data (2012)
6. Ishii, A., et al.: The 'hit'phenomenon: A mathematical model of human dynamics interactions as a stochastic process. New Journal of Physics 14, 063018 (2012)
7. Kawahata, Y., Genda, E., Ishii, A.: Revenue Prediction of Music Concerts Using the Mathematical Model of Hit Phenomena. In: ICBAKE 2013 (unpublished 2013)
8. Ishiil, A., Ota, S., Koguchi, H., Uchiyama, K.: Quantitative analysis of social popularity for Japanase pop girl group AKB48 using mathematical model for hit phenona. In: ICBAKE 2013 (unpublished 2013)

Ouch! How Embodied Damage Indicators in First-Person Shooting Games Impact Gaming Experience

James E. Young, Ibrahim Shahin, and Masayuki Nakane

Department of Computer Science, University of Manitoba, Canada
young@cs.umanitoba.ca, {i.j.shahin,msyknakane}@gmail.com

Abstract. In this paper we present results from an exploratory study on first-person shooting game damage indicators, comparing a *red flash*, a *paper doll*, and an *x-ray* mechanism, observing impact on gaming experience.

1   Introduction and Related Work

In first-person shooting games players interact with virtual worlds through multiple modalities (first-person graphics, spatial sound, movement) from the perspective of a virtual character, with the aim of enabling the player to experience the game as the character. While creating a first-person gaming experience it is not entirely feasible to cause pain to a player when the character receives an injury, and so games attempt to replicate aspects of getting an injury without actually causing pain. In this paper we explore how damage indication methods impact players emotional and cognitive experience of gameplay, rather than other metrics such as task efficiency (e.g., best score) – an approach termed "affective ludology" [8]. From this perspective, building player immersion and a sense of presence in the virtual world (i.e., total immersion [2]) is an integral part of a successful gaming experience. In this work, we compare three different damage indication methods in terms of how they impact gaming experience – this extended abstract is only a summary of the work [10].

Damage indicators are integral to many video games and have a long history, ranging from using abstract health-point systems (such as in ID Software's Doom franchise), toward more modern and more-realistic methods such as hindering character senses (vision and audio, as with Activision's Call of Duty) or movement (as in Ion Storm's Deus Ex). Some games add additional information including from which direction an injury came from (e.g., behind) using, for example, a simple arrow (as in 343 Industry's Halo 4). We found very little work in the research community on different first-person shooter damage indication methods.

Evaluation of a person's affective state, and correlating it with measures of immersion and enjoyment, are still active research problems with various facets ranging from qualitative analysis of written questionnaires and interviews [3], applying heuristics [4], administering subjective questionnaires [1], or using a whole range of biometric and psychometric assessment methods [9]. We draw from this work and apply some of these methods in our study.

D. Reidsma, H. Katayose, and A. Nijholt (Eds.): ACE 2013, LNCS 8253, pp. 660–664, 2013.
© Springer International Publishing Switzerland 2013

2   Damage Indicators

We investigated three damage indicators, a *red flash*, *paper doll*, and *X-ray*: the red flash indicator tints the player's screen red upon injury (Fig. 1, left); the paper doll indicator places a cut-out character silhouette at the top-left of the screen, flashing the screen background and associated body part red upon injury (Fig. 1, middle); the novel X-ray indicator overlays X-ray images of the injuries in semi-transparent red, indicating injury to either head, torso, an arm, or legs (Fig. 1, right, and Fig. 2). In all cases the opacity of the tint or flash is proportional to the severity of the injury. Thus, the three indicators form points on a range from less immersive design (red flash), more immersive intention due to providing first-person information (paper doll), and yet more immersive design due to the nature of presentation (X-ray).

Fig. 1. We compared the three indicators: a *red flash* (left) indicating an injury was incurred, a *paper doll* (middle) with red flash providing further information on where the character was injured (in the right arm), and an *X-ray* (right) showing that the character was hit in the left arm.

Fig. 2. The X-ray films used to show injury – left and right hands, head, torso, and foot

3   Study

We implemented a first-person shooting game using Epic Games' Unreal 3 first-person engine on a desktop PC. The game used a standard PC control scheme (WASD keys and a mouse), and a percentage-based health system.

We recruited 14 participants (explicitly with experience with PC first-person shooting games and the WASD+mouse scheme) from our local university population (age 18-32, M=25.0, 13 male, 1 female). After an informed consent and demographics questionnaire, participants played a sample level with no damage indicator to ensure that they were familiar with the controls and game scheme. Participants played three different levels using the three different damage indicators, with the order counterbalanced across participants. After each level the post-condition questionnaire was administered, and we ended the experiment with a post-test questionnaire.

The post-condition questionnaire asked the participant to rate "*how you felt* when your character took damage" and "how you think *your character felt* when taking damage," using the standard Self-Assessment Manikin [7] instrument. We administered the Game Experience Questionnaire [6] and further asked how "tough" they felt the character was and how "strong were the enemies," and finally asked them to rank how much they liked the particular damage indicator. This was followed by open-ended written questions regarding general comments and how each indicator impacted the perception of character damage, the enjoyability of the game, and the player-character relationship.

4   Results

We performed qualitative analysis on written feedback from the questionnaires, via cycles of open and axial coding, with our results presented in the themes below.

Injury Information was Appreciated. Most participants commented that the injury information was useful, and that it also added to the game experience. Such comments were evenly split between the X-ray and paper doll conditions.

Realism. There was an overall theme of participants talking about the indicators in terms of realism and how this made them feel. This was particularly common with the X-ray indicator. Discussion of realism was often observed when participants were asked to compare one indicator to the others. In particular, all participants who preferred the red flash discussed it in terms of realism, that the red flash was most realistic. Some noted that, rather than being a good thing, increased realism hindered their game play experience, and that their choice of damage indicator may depend on their relationship with the character as one participant preferred unrealistic damage indicators for not wanting to care about the main character.

Dialog with the Character. We analyzed participant response to the question of "what would your character have to say to you" in terms of comments that described injuries to the character, as an indication of how much the player was thinking of the character's health and wellbeing. We found that 3 participants discussed in such terms for red flash, 1 for paper doll, and 6 for X-ray. In all cases, participants only gave such feedback for one indicator, and said more generic things for others.

Lack of Paper Doll Salience. There was a great deal of complaint on the visibility of the paper doll. Some did not even use it. Many of those who used it reported that the location was too in the periphery, and this impacted game play and immersion. Some suggested to change the location of the paper doll or to have it blink when damaged.

X-Ray Occlusions. Even though the X-ray indicator was translucent, many people complained that it was visually obstructive, especially when the character was hit in several places at the same time and when the templates overlapped, and that this impacted how they can play the game. Many provided suggestions for how to improve the indicator such as making it less flashy and colorful, or making it smaller. Some participants recommended a hybrid indicator of the paper doll and the X-ray.

Quantitative Results We found no significant effects on affective response (SAM), or the Game Experience Questionnaire. We did find that the damage indicator had an effect on how strong participants perceived the enemies in the given trial (Friedman's ANOVA, $\chi^2(2)=6.067$, p=0.048, mean ranks: red flash=2.32, X-ray=2.04, and paper doll=1.64), although post-hoc tests did not reveal further effects, this suggests that enemies were perceived as being weaker for paper doll than for red flash, with the X-ray perhaps somewhere in the middle. Post-test preference responses were: 3.5 participants for paper doll, 4 for red flash, and 6.5 for the X-ray (0.5 for a tie).

5   Discussion and Recommendations

Participants reported the additional injury information provided by the X-ray and paper doll indicators was useful and caused them to think more about their characters, and their reports strongly suggest that this information, and how it was presented, contributed to their immersion. They also explicitly related the indicator to the "feeling" of receiving an injury, and for both indicators, talked a great deal more about character injuries than they did with the red flash. Finally, this finding correlates with how participants found enemies to be stronger with the red flash and weaker with the others, suggesting how the immersion can relate to quality of play or even perception of such. One surprising result was that immersion may actually hinder gaming experience, rather than improve enjoyability (as in [2]): some participants found the interaction to be too real in the X-ray case, which made them feel bad for their character and guilty, and some found the pain-type immersion to be demotivating.

The results of our new X-ray indicator were encouraging. There were many signs of immersion: participants used affective language, talked about feeling the pain, and talked more about their character's injuries in comparison to the red flash. In addition, a majority share rated the X-ray as their favorite, there was a great deal of positive feedback, and participants wrote more about the X-ray indicator than the others. Participants who did not like the indicator primarily cited the obstruction of vision, noting it made them? feel mechanically hindered instead of being injured. This is an important point to note, as the obstruction was a deliberate design decision intended to simulate the loss of senses when in pain. This tells us that designing the obstruction of senses has to be tactfully done to fit well within the game.

From our analysis and results we propose the following recommendations:

Damage indicators have a strong impact on gameplay and Immersion. Small damage indicator design changes can have a large impact on player experience and immersion, so consider this aspect of game design carefully.

Immersion has many dimensions. Increasing immersion in ways that clash with the game design may have negative experience effects, as X-ray may be too realistic.

Players can reasonably discuss aspects of immersion. Participants were clear and insightful about their experiences of immersion and gameplay, supporting self-report as a useful means for future studies.

References

1. Brockmyer, J.H., et al.: The development of the Game Engagement Questionnaire: A measure of engagement in video game-playing. J. Exper. Social Psych. 45(4), 624–634 (2009)
2. Brown, E., Cairns, P.: A grounded investigation of game immersion. In: Extended abst. of the 2004 Conf. on Human Factors and Computing Syst., CHI 2004, p. 1297. ACM Press, New York (2004)
3. Desurvire, H., et al.: Evaluating fun and entertainment: Developing a conceptual framework design of evaluation methods. In: Proceedings of CHI 2007. ACM (2007)
4. Desurvire, H., et al.: Using heuristics to evaluate the playability of games. In: Extended abst. of the 2004 Conf. on Human Factors and Computing Syst., CHI 2004, p. 1509. ACM Press, New York (2004)
5. Ermi, L., Mäyrä, F.: Fundamental components of the gameplay experience: Analysing immersion. Changing Views: Worlds in Play. Selected Papers of the 2005 Digital Games Res. Assoc.'s Internat. Conf., 15–27 (2005)
6. Ijsselsteijn, W.A., et al.: The game experience questionnaire: Devel. of a self-report measure to assess player experiences of digital games. FUGA techn. report, deliverable 3.3, TU Eindhoven (2008)
7. Morris, J.: Observations: SAM: the Self-Assessment Manikin; an efficient cross-cultural measurem. of emotional response. Jrnl. of Advertising Res. (December 1995)
8. Nacke, L., Lindley, C.A.: Affective ludology, flow and immersion in a first-person shooter: Measurem. of player experience. The Jrnl. of the Canadian Game Studies Assoc. 3(5) (2009)
9. Nacke, L.E.: Affective Ludology: Sci. Measurem. of User Experience in Interactive Entertainment. Blekinge Inst. of Technol. (2009)
10. Young, J.E., Shahin, I., Nakane, M.: Embodied damage indicators in first-person shooting games. University of Manitoba technical report HCI2013-03 (2013),
   http://mspace.lib.umanitoba.ca//handle/1993/22118

Author Index